Y0-BYB-643

Macroeconomics
Theory & Policy
in Canada
SECOND EDITION

DAVID A. WILTON
University of Waterloo

DAVID M. PRESCOTT
University of Guelph

Addison-Wesley Publishers

• Don Mills, Ontario • Reading, Massachusetts
• Menlo Park, California • Wokingham, England
• Amsterdam • Sydney • Singapore • Tokyo
• Madrid • Bogota • Santiago • San Juan

Text Design: Pronk and Associates
Cover Design: Brant Cowie/Artplus
Technical Art: Acorn Technical Art

Canadian Cataloguing in Publication Data

Wilton, David A.
   Macroeconomics: theory and policy in Canada

Includes bibliographical references and index.
ISBN 0-201-10708-2

1. Macroeconomics.   2. Canada — Economic policy —
1971–   . I. Prescott, David Martin, 1948–
II. Title.

HC115.W54 1986   339.5′0971   C86-095022-0

Copyright © 1987 Addison-Wesley Publishers Limited.

All rights reserved. No part of this publication may be
reproduced, stored in a retrieval system, or transmitted, in
any form or by any means, electronic, photocopying,
recording, or otherwise, without the prior written permission of the publisher.

Printed in Canada

   B   C   D   E   F — BP — 92   91   90   89   88

To Doreen and Jennifer

Table of Contents

PART II

PART III

PART IV

Preface

During the 1970s and 1980s macroeconomics once again became an exciting, controversial, and challenging subject. The 1960s myth that economists had solved the major macroeconomic problems and that government policymakers could "fine tune" the economy along a low inflation, low unemployment, high growth path was shattered by the harsh economic realities of the 1970s and 1980s. From 1974 through 1982 inflation averaged almost 10 per cent, the 1982–83 unemployment rate exceeded 12 per cent (the highest level since the Great Depression), the interest rates of the early 1980s exceeded 20 per cent and the Canadian government ran up record budgetary deficits (surpassing $30 billion per year in the mid 1980s). With deteriorating economic conditions, economists began to question the traditional Keynesian aggregate demand paradigm, the use of discretionary fiscal and monetary policies, and the possibility of an inflation-unemployment trade-off. New, more conservative, schools of macro-economic thought pushed Keynesian economics from centre stage.

Monetarism emerged as the most influential theory during the 1970s, followed by the New Classical macroeconomics in the 1980s. Unlike Keynesian economics, which emphasizes the demand-side of the economy and the use of discretionary monetary and fiscal policies, Monetarism and the New Classical economics shifted attention to supply-side factors, the natural rate of unemployment, rational inflation expectations and the ineffectiveness of Keynesian counter-cyclical monetary and fiscal policies. The macroeconomic tranquility of the 1960s has been replaced in the 1980s by a lively theoretical and policy debate between conflicting views of the macroeconomic system.

While the second edition of our textbook has been thoroughly up-dated and revised in response to reviews and letters from many instructors (and students), our major objectives remain the same as in the first edition. First, we want to provide second year students with a basic understanding of the current state of the art in macroeconomic theory. Second, we want to use this body of macroeconomic theory to tackle the important new issues, problems and challenges which have arisen during the 1970s and 1980s from a distinctly Canadian perspective. As in the first edition, much of this text is devoted to the development of a relatively simple theoretical model (the *IS-LM-PEP* model) which allows us to analyze the interrelated problems of inflation, unemployment, and interest rates. A common thread running throughout the text is an assessment of the various issues in the controversial and evolving public policy debate between Keynesian, Monetarist and New Classical economists. In developing our theoretical model of the Canadian economy, we pay particular attention to the key assumptions within the model that separate Keynesian policy *activists* from more conservative *non-interventionist* Monetarists and New Classical economists.

Improvements in the Second Edition

The revisions to the first edition consist of more than simply up-dating the statistical tables and relevant discussion to reflect economic events in the 1980s (which we, of course, have done). In response to suggestions from many instructors, we have included two new theoretical chapters and have re-organized some of the theoretical material on the *IS-LM-PEP* model. In addition, we have included new sections in many chapters to reflect the theoretical and policy developments of the 1980s.

While the structure of the first seven chapters remains intact, Chapter 8 is new to the second edition and provides a complete discussion of the aggregate demand/supply model and the determination of the aggregate price level. Given the controversy over the nature of the aggregate supply function, Chapter 8 derives three different aggregate supply functions based on three different sets of assumptions: (1) complete wage and price flexibility (the Classical case); (2) shortrun wage rigidity (the Keynesian case); and (3) the New Classical "price surprise" supply function. For each of these three different aggregate supply functions, the aggregate price level is determined diagrammatically and the implications of monetary and fiscal policy for the level of output and prices are analyzed (and contrasted). This new chapter closes with a discussion of the problem of unemployment in the context of these three different macroeconomic models.

Although the aggregate demand and supply diagram identifies equilibrium output and price levels, it is a very cumbersome technique for analyzing short-run (disequilibrium) adjustments, the problem of inflation and interest rate movements. In the first edition we developed the *IS-LM-PEP* model, first suggested by Richard Lipsey, to analyze the inter-related problems of inflation, output, unemployment and interest rates. In Chapter 9 the theory behind the Price Expectations augmented Phillips *(PEP)* curve is now directly linked to our analysis of the labour market (Chapter 8), with greater emphasis placed on the theoretical justification for including inflation expectations in the basic Phillips curve model. The *PEP* curve has been re-specified in terms of deviations of the unemployment rate from the equilibrium or natural rate of unemployment, which are directly linked to deviations of output from the equilibrium or natural level of output. Defining the equilibrium output level as the amount of output produced by the equilibrium quantity of labour, we have been able to dispense with the somewhat arbitrary concept of potential output and have more firmly grounded the concept of equilibrium output in the labour market and production sector of the economy.

As in the first edition, Chapters 10 through 15 analyze the theoretical and policy implications of the *IS-LM-PEP* model. Some re-organization in the second edition, however, has enabled us to shorten the overall length of this material. For example, the effect of a change in sales tax rates on price inflation has been moved from Chapter 9 to Chapter 15, thus removing one awkward element from the initial analysis of the *IS-LM-PEP* model and the natural rate of unemployment.

Chapter 17, the second new chapter, discusses alternative assumptions concerning the formulation of inflation expectations and explores in detail the New Classical model of macroeconomics. The opening section investigates the implications of adaptive expectations for a restrictive monetary policy in the context of the *IS-LM-PEP* model. However, most of Chapter 17 is devoted to an analysis of the implications of rational inflation expectations in the context of the New Classical model of macroeconomics. The basic assumptions of the New Classical model are presented and the necessary and sufficient conditions for the Policy Ineffectiveness Proposition (that anticipated government policy will have no effect on output or employment levels) are identified. This chapter closes with an evaluation of the New Classical Model of macroeconomics.

Besides these two new chapters and the necessary up-dating of statistical data, there are substantial revisions and improvements to other chapters. Much of Chapter 16, an overview of policy developments in the 1970s and 1980s, has been re-written to include a discussion of the severe recession of the early 1980s, the economic implications of large government deficits and the abandonment of monetary targets in 1982. In addition to up-dating our Case Study on Unemployment (for the year 1982) in Chapter 3, we have also added a new Case Study on the Canadian income tax system and inflation tax distortions.

Chapter 13 on Anti-Inflation Policy has been completely re-organized and up-dated: new theoretical material on the rationale for temporary wage and price controls has been added and an up-dated Case Study evaluating the Anti-Inflation Board has been included in this chapter. In Chapter 19, The Theory of Consumption, we have added a new section on the formulation of permanent income under both adaptive and rational expectations (including Hall's "random walk" hypothesis of consumer expenditures).

As in the first edition, the five major distinguishing features of the second edition are the following. First, we present a *balanced, integrated* model of inflation, unemployment, income and interest rates. Second, we provide an extensive discussion and assessment of the controversial and evolving debate between Keynesian policy *activists* and Monetarist and New Classical *non-interventionists*. Third, this text emphasizes policy, on both a theoretical and practical level. Policy decisions of the Canadian government are reviewed and assessed throughout the text, and a whole chapter (Chapter 16) is devoted to an analysis of Canadian government policy during the 1970s and 1980s. Fourth, throughout the text we repeatedly refer to Canadian data, often in the form of scatter diagrams, to illustrate the empirical validity of the key theoretical hypotheses of our model as well as the major policy implications of the complete model. Finally, we have provided numerous special *case studies* to explore and analyze interesting macroeconomic issues, such as the Canadian Anti-Inflation Board and the Monetarist proposition that "inflation is strictly a monetary phenomenon."

Prerequisites and Suggestions for One-Semester Courses

This text is designed for a second-year Canadian macroeconomics course, with the only prerequisite being an introductory economics course. Since we provide a review chapter on the *Keynesian cross* model and the multiplier process, even this prerequisite is not binding. While we develop our basic model in diagrammatic form, the algebraic counterpart for the *IS-LM* model is also provided in Chapters 5 and 6, for which only high school algebra is required. There is no calculus requirement to use this text, although students with calculus will find footnotes pointing out shortcuts in the analysis.

The length of this book reflects the fact that many Canadian universities offer macroeconomics courses which are a full year in length. For one-semester courses, a number of chapters will necessarily have to be omitted. If balance-of-payments adjustments are covered in a later course, Chapters 7 and 11 could be skipped (subsequent chapters have deliberately omitted the *BP* curve from the analysis to permit this flexibility). Similarly, if a later course covers the money, consumption and investment components of a macroeconomic model, then Chapters 18–20 could be omitted. For example, a one-semester course might include Chapters 1–16, excluding Chapters 7 and 11. Instructors who wish to emphasize the *IS-LM* model, aggregate demand and supply, along with the "components" might choose Chapters 1–8 along with Chapters 18–20 as the core of a one-semester course.

Acknowledgements

It is a pleasure to acknowledge our indebtedness to those who have contributed in various ways to the publication of this book. First, we must thank our own teachers who shaped our understanding of macroeconomics—E. Domar, A.G. Hines, E. Kuh, R.G. Lipsey, C. McIvor, F. Modigliani, P.A. Samuelson, R.M. Solow, G.R. Sparks, R.W. Thompson and J. Williamson. We suspect that each will find something in the text borrowed or distilled from one of his lectures. In particular, our intellectual debt to Richard Lipsey is enormous. It is Lipsey's integration of the Phillips curve into the *IS LM* framework that forms the basis of the model developed and used in the textbook.

We would also like to thank the following individuals and instructors for their comments on various chapters and drafts of the first and/or second editions of this text: Evy Adomait (University of Guelph), Isabel Anderson (University of Saskatchewan), Ron Bodkin (University of Ottawa), Louis Christofides (University of Guelph), Alan Crawford (University of Guelph), Paul Davenport (McGill University), Steve Ferris (Carleton University), David Foot (University of Toronto), Bruce Forster (University of Guelph), Derek Hum (University of Manitoba), David Laidler (University of Western Ontario), Ross Milbourne (Queen's University), Tony Myatt (University of New Brunswick), Ed Nosal (University of Waterloo), James Pesando (University of Toronto), Brian Scarfe (University of Alberta), Bill Scarth (McMaster University), John Smithin (York University), Robert Thompson (McMaster University), and Ron Wirick (University of Western Ontario). The comments and suggestions we have received have undoubtedly helped us to improve the clarity and content of the book, but none of the above individuals should be held responsible for any deficiencies in the second edition. Special thanks are due to Alastair Robertson (Sir Wilfred Laurier University) and

Stan Kardasz (University of Waterloo) for their careful reading of the entire manuscript and for many useful comments.

Finally, we would like to thank the following members (and former members) of the Addison-Wesley team for their friendly cooperation and assistance: Frank Burns, Allan Reynolds, Richard Kitowski, Andy Yull, Terry MacGorman, Steve O'Hearn, Craig Doyle, and, of course, George Bryson (for making it all happen).

Part 1

Introduction 1

Unemployment still tops list as our most important problem. [1]

During the 1970s inflation and unemployment clearly emerged as the major economic problems facing Canadian citizens. In a December 1984 Gallup poll (see Table 1-1), the majority of Canadians interviewed claimed that *unemployment* was the most important problem facing this country today, with *inflation* the second choice:

> Concern about jobs for Canadians continues to grow, with 56% today naming it our most important national problem. Unemployment has maintained its top position in the minds of Canadians since the beginning of 1983. . . .The economy, inflation and high prices remain in second place, with 25% feeling this is our most important problem. Governmental problems hold the attention of 6%, while nuclear war concerns 3%. [2]

While unemployment again became the dominant problem facing Canadians in the mid-1980s, from 1975 until the early 1980s *inflation* consistently ranked as the most important problem facing Canadians, typically attracting about one-half of the vote (see Table 1-1).

The reasons why "inflation, high prices and the economy" dominated public opinion surveys during the late 1970s and early 1980s are rather obvious. Double-

---

TABLE 1-1 What Do You Think Is the Most Important Problem Facing Canada Today?

	Inflation	Unemployment	Government	Other	Don't Know
December 1984	25%	56%	6%	11%	3%
February 1983	37%	40%	8%	13%	2%
July 1980	44%	15%	10%	26%	5%
July 1975	48%	13%	7%	29%	3%

Source: Compiled from *The Gallup Report* (Toronto: Canadian Institute of Public Opinion).

---

[1] Headline on press release for the Gallup Report (Toronto: Canadian Institute of Public Opinion), 28 January 1985.

[2] Ibid.

digit inflation hit the Canadian economy in 1974, and in the period from 1974 to 1982 the Canadian inflation rate averaged 9.9 per cent. In 1982, however, the unemployment rate jumped to 11.0 per cent (from an average of 7.1 per cent during the 1974-81 period) and remained in the 11-12 per cent range throughout 1983 and 1984, the highest levels of unemployment since the Great Depression. Not surprisingly, by early 1983 unemployment had overtaken inflation in public opinion polls as the most important problem facing Canadians.

Besides double-digit inflation and the worst unemployment rates since the Depression, the decade between 1975 and 1984 was also characterized by record high interest rates, record high government deficits, and a record low value for the Canadian dollar, in short an economic disaster. It is important to point out, however, that macroeconomic conditions have not always been this bad. Take Canada's Centennial year as an example. In 1967 the Canadian inflation rate was a modest 3.6 per cent and the unemployment rate was only 3.8 per cent. Interest rates were around 6 per cent and the government enjoyed a surplus of revenues over expenditures. No wonder the 1960s are called "the good old days." Even though most students of the 1980s cannot recall "the good old days," the Canadian economic record of the 1960s provides a startling contrast to the 1970s and 1980s, and raises a number of obvious questions.

1) What ever happened to a 4 per cent unemployment rate?
2) Why did persistent double-digit inflation occur in the mid-1970s?
3) Will interest rates ever return to 6 per cent?
4) What ails the Canadian dollar?
5) Why is it that the Canadian government cannot balance its budget?

As is obvious from this series of rhetorical questions (and the Gallup poll results cited above), macroeconomics deals with most of the important issues and questions of the 1980s.

Any subject that tackles such challenging questions is bound to generate a considerable amount of controversy. Contemporary macroeconomics is no exception. Although there are numerous skirmishes among academic macroeconomists over rather abstract theoretical issues (such as the role of inflation expectations, which is discussed in Chapter 17), the major battleground in contemporary macroeconomics is in the public policy arena. What role should the government play in attempting to navigate the economic system through troubled macroeconomic waters? Could some of the macroeconomic grief of the 1970s and 1980s have been avoided by a more "enlightened" government policy? If so, what were the major policy errors, both of omission and commission, during this period? If not, is the Canadian economy totally at the mercy of U.S. events, OPEC cartels and other uncontrollable external factors?

On one side of this public policy debate are economists who take their inspiration from Lord Keynes, the founder of macroeconomics (see Chapter 4). At heart, Keynesian economists believe that government intervention within the economic system can solve or at least alleviate the major macroeconomic problems of the day. By deliberately altering its fiscal and monetary policies, or perhaps by imposing an incomes policy, the government can improve the overall performance of the economy. On the other side of the arena are *monetarists* (see Chapter 6) and *new classical* economists (see Chapters 8 and 17), who advocate a *non-interventionist*, *laissez-faire* approach to macroeconomic policy. According to monetarist and new classical economists, government intervention along Keynesian lines, even if well-intentioned, will only make matters worse. The economic system runs best when left alone, and the "best" government is the "least" government. Much of the controversy in contemporary macroeconomics is of a political economy nature—"liberal" Keynesians and "conservative" monetarist and new classical economists debating the appropriate role for governments to play in the formulation of an "enlightened" macroeconomic policy.

The two major objectives of this textbook are:

1) to develop a simple theoretical macroeconomic model which will allow us to understand the interrelated problems of inflation, unemployment, and high interest rates, and

2) to assess this important public policy debate between the followers of Keynes and the proponents of a non-interventionist policy approach.

In developing a simple theoretical macroeconomic model of the Canadian economy, we pay particular attention to the key assumptions within the model which separate Keynesian economists from monetarist and new classical economists. As we shall see, many of these key differentiating assumptions between Keynesian and monetarist economists are of an empirical nature. Throughout this textbook we will repeatedly refer to Canadian data, often in the form of special case studies, to illustrate the empirical validity of the key theoretical components of our macroeconomical model. Theories or economic models which are contradicted by the "facts" are unlikely to improve our understanding of the macroeconomic system or lead to the formulation of an "enlightened" government policy. Before beginning our formal discussion of macroeconomics, it is useful to review briefly the Canadian macroeconomic record of the 1960s, 1970s, and early 1980s.

The Canadian "Stylized" Facts

Unlike microeconomics, which studies the individual components of the economic system (such as individual consumer behaviour and the demand for corn flakes), macroeconomics is concerned with the *overall* performance of the economy. The major economic aggregates that macroeconomics seeks to explain are the total level of output within the economy, the unemployment rate, the inflation rate and the interest rate. Charts 1-1 and 1-2 present annual data for gross national product (in constant 1971 dollars), the unemployment rate, the annual percentage change in the consumer price index, and interest rates for the 1960-84 period. Each will be discussed in turn.

Gross National Product

Gross national product (GNP) represents the value of all final goods and services produced in the economy during a given interval of time. Each individual item produced within the economy is multiplied by its price tag and added with all

CHART 1-1 Actual and potential output, and the unemployment rate

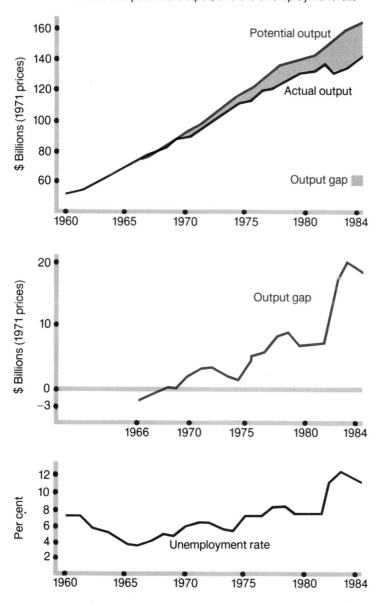

other final goods and services. In 1984 the value of goods and services produced in Canada totalled $421 billion, in comparison with only $94 billion in 1971.

Although Canadian GNP increased at a rapid pace during the 1970s and early 1980s, much of this increase can be simply attributed to inflation and rising price levels (see Chart 1-2). A much more meaningful measure of total output is obtained by removing the general effects of inflation and evaluating each year's total production in terms of a common set of prices. For example, if we measure the total value of goods and services produced in the year 1984 in terms of the price tags that existed in 1971, then 1984 GNP is only $141 billion (not $421 billion). This new calculated value, obtained by imposing 1971 price tags on the quantity of goods and services sold in 1984, measures 1984 GNP in *constant* 1971 dollars—that is, dollars which have a constant level of purchasing power equal to that which prevailed in 1971. Given a tripling of the price level during the 1971-84 period, two-thirds of the $421 billion 1984 GNP is pure price-tag inflation (compared with 1971). To avoid confusion, our original magnitude for 1984 GNP ($421 billion) measured in terms of the current 1984 set of prices will be referred to as *current* dollar or *nominal* output. By correcting for the general effects of inflation, the new constant dollar magnitude records the "real" value of goods and services produced, and can be used to determine the overall growth rate within the economy.[3]

In the upper panel of Chart 1-1 we have plotted annual GNP expressed in constant 1971 dollars for the period from 1960 through 1984. In these twenty-five years, real output in Canada has grown by an average annual rate of 4.1 per cent. However, this average annual 4.1 per cent growth rate conceals an important negative trend, a flattening out of the upward slope of GNP in Chart 1-1. In comparison with the 5.3 per cent annual growth rate from 1960 to 1974, the Canadian economy grew by only 2.4 per cent on average between 1975 and 1984. As discussed below, this period contains the very severe 1982 recession, when real GNP declined by 4.4 per cent, the largest decline since the Great Depression.

The major reasons for the secular growth, or growth trend, in real output are increasing supplies of factor inputs (labour and capital), as well as improved technology and greater productivity. Between 1960 and 1984 the Canadian labour force increased from 6.4 million to 12.4 million workers, an average annual increase of almost 2.7 per cent. With respect to improved technology and greater productivity, average real output per worker (measured in 1971 dollars) increased from $8,924 in 1960 to $12,783 in 1984, an average annual productivity increase of almost 1.5 per cent. Thus, the average annual 4.1 per cent growth rate of real output over the 1960-84 period can be explained in terms of increases in the size of the labour force and in labour productivity.

While the *long-run* aspects of real output growth are important, contemporary macroeconomics has focused primarily on *short-run* changes in output levels. For example, why did real output increase by 3.4 per cent in 1981, decline by 4.4 per cent in 1982, and then increase by 3.3 per cent in 1983? Changes in the labour force growth rate (2.5 per cent in 1981, 0.5 per cent in 1982, and 1.9 per cent in 1983) cannot account for such dramatic changes in real output growth. Why did we have a mini-recession in both 1970 and 1974-75? The answers to these important short-run questions are unlikely to be found in the growth rate of the labour force or the existing state of technology.

---

[3]For further discussion of the GNP concept and the methodology of the National Income Accounts, see Chapter 2.

CHART 1-2 Consumer Price Index and interest rates

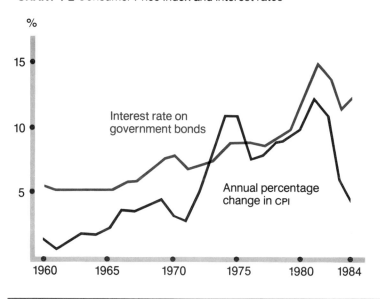

Given the existence of *long-run growth* factors, it is important to judge the year-by-year performance of the economy in terms of the *potential* level of output that the economy's resources of labour, capital, and technology are capable of producing. A 3 per cent annual increase in real GNP might be regarded as acceptable in an economy with a 1 per cent increase in the labour force, but as quite unacceptable in any economy with a labour force growing at four times that rate. The actual level of real output produced in any given year should be compared with the potential output level that could have been produced if all of the economy's resources were being fully utilized. James Brox of the University of Waterloo has recently provided estimates for potential output in Canada from 1966 to 1984.[4] In constructing these *hypothetical* estimates for Canadian potential output, a 95 per cent utilization rate was assumed to be the maximum sustainable production level at which the Canadian economy could consistently operate. By substracting the actual level of real GNP from this hypothetical potential output series, an estimate of the degree to which the economy was underperforming in any particular year can be obtained (see Chart 1-1). This difference between potential output (*YPOT*) and actual output (GNP), is typically referred to as the *output gap* (*YGAP*); that is:

(1-1) $YGAP = YPOT - \text{GNP}$

It provides a direct estimate of the *additional* amount of output which could have been produced if the economy's resources were being fully utilized.[5]

---

[4]James A. Brox, "A Note on Capacity Utilization, Productivity, and the Canadian Output Gap," *Empirical Economics*, Vol. 9 (1984), pp. 131-38.

[5]For further discussion of the potential output concept, see Chapter 2.

The second panel of Chart 1-1 presents the estimated real output gap in billions of 1971 dollars from 1966 to 1984. The movement in this time series graph is clearly cyclical: the strong Canadian expansion of the mid-1960s was followed by the recession in the early 1970s (increasing output gaps), the expansion in the 1972-74 period (declining output gaps), and the widening output gap in the late 1970s. At the depth of the severe recession of 1982-83, the output gap (measured in 1971 dollars) reached almost $20 billion. This cyclical motion in the Canadian economy also stands out when one reviews the track record of the Canadian unemployment rate.

The Unemployment Rate

Once a month Statistics Canada provides an estimate for the Canadian unemployment rate. Postponing a discussion of the methodological problems in measuring the unemployment rate until Chapter 3, the lower panel of Chart 1-1 presents the Canadian unemployment rate during the 1960-84 period . Following a recession in 1960-61 (with unemployment rates of 7 per cent), the vigorous economic expansion of the 1960s drove the unemployment rate down to 3.3 per cent in 1966, and at the end of the 1960s the unemployment rate still remained well under 5 per cent. In 1969-70 the Canadian government imposed a restrictive monetary and fiscal policy (see Chart 1-3 and discussion below), sending the Canadian economy into a recession and the unemployment rate back up to 6.2 per cent in 1971. However, a period of economic growth during the 1972-74 period, fostered by expansionary monetary and fiscal policies, brought the unemployment rate back down to 5.3 per cent in 1974. From 1975 through 1981 the unemployment rate drifted upwards but exhibited only minor variation, ranging from 6.9 per cent in 1975 to 8.3 per cent in 1978. However, during the severe recession of 1982-83—which was largely attributable to the Bank of Canada's very tight monetary policy (see discussion below)—the unemployment rate jumped to almost 12 per cent, the highest rate since the 1930s.

The Inflation Rate

By far and away the most commonly used measure of inflation is the *rate of change* in the Consumer Price Index (the CPI), which is plotted in Chart 1-2. In 1974 the Canadian government indexed the personal income tax system to the CPI,[6] and many of the government's transfer payments (such as old age pensions) are also indexed to the CPI. Again, a discussion of the methodology of the CPI is postponed until Chapter 3.

As depicted in Chart 1-2, the inflation rate was clearly moving upwards during the expansionary 1960s, from about 1 per cent in the early 1960s to almost 5 per cent by the end of the 1960s. From 1969 to 1970 the Canadian government pursued a restrictive anti-inflationary monetary policy (see Chart 1-3) and, in the words of former Prime Minister Pierre Trudeau, "inflation was wrestled to the

---

[6]See Case Study 1 in Chapter 3.

ground"—at the expense of a much higher unemployment rate (see Chart 1-1). In 1973, however, inflation "got off the mat" and began to escalate rapidly, reaching double-digit levels in 1974-75. Notwithstanding the imposition of temporary wage and price controls under the Anti-Inflation Board from October 1975 to April 1978 and the Bank of Canada's conversion to monetarism in 1975,[7] the Canadian inflation rate stabilized at approximately 8 to 10 per cent for the last half of the 1970s. With the inflation rate again on the rise in the early 1980s (touching 12.5 per cent in 1981), the Canadian government implemented an extremely tight monetary policy, which produced the worst recession since the 1930s. Given unemployment rates in the 11-12 per cent range, the inflation rate quickly moderated, dropping to 5.8 per cent in 1983 and 4.4 per cent in 1984, the lowest inflation rate since 1971.

Interest Rates

In Chart 1-2 we have also plotted the interest rate paid on long-term government bonds. Perhaps the most striking feature of long-term interest rate movements is their very close association with inflation rate movements. Over the 1960-83 period, long-term interest rates clearly followed the cyclical path of the inflation rate. As discussed in Chapter 3, there are very good economic reasons for a close association between interest rates and inflation rates. While the *spread* between market interest rates and the inflation rate—often referred to as the *real interest rate* (see Chapter 3)—generally remained at less than 4 per cent throughout the 1960-82 period, between 1983 and 1984 interest rates remained stubbornly high even though the inflation rate substantially declined. For example, in 1984 interest rates of almost 13 per cent were over 8 per cent higher than the inflation rate. These high real interest rates were a major contributing factor to the severe recession that occurred in the early 1980s.

Other Macroeconomic Indicators

To complete the Canadian macroeconomic facts, in Chart 1-3 we have plotted three other important macroeconomic indicators: the Canadian foreign exchange rate, the annual growth rate of the money supply, and the government budgetary surplus/deficit. As shown in the top panel in Chart 1-3, the government fixed the value of the Canadian dollar at $0.925 U.S. during the 1962-1970 period. When the Canadian dollar was allowed to float freely in value on world currency markets in June 1970, it remained close to $1.00 U.S. until 1976. (Note that the Canadian dollar actually traded for more than $1.00 U.S. in 1974 and again in 1976.) From 1976 to 1985, however, it has been all downhill. The value of the Canadian dollar fell to $0.88 U.S. in 1978, to $0.81 in 1982 and to $0.71 in early 1985.[8]

[7]The Anti-Inflation Board and the Bank of Canada's conversion to monetarism are fully discussed in Chapters 13 and 16, respectively.

[8]Chapter 7 provides an extensive discussion of foreign exchange rates and an analysis of the macroeconomic implications of fixed versus floating foreign exchange rates.

CHART 1-3 Other macroeconomic indicators

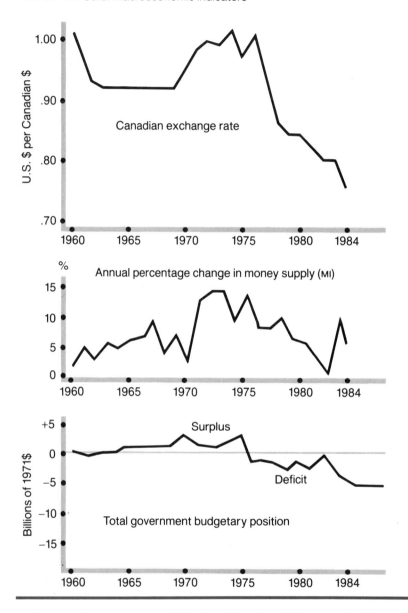

In regard to monetary and fiscal policy, the middle panel of Chart 1-3 presents the annual percentage change in the money supply during the period between 1960 and 1984. After a decade of expansionary monetary policy and gradually increasing inflation rates, the Bank of Canada sharply curtailed the growth rate of the money supply in 1970 as the Trudeau government tried to "wrestle inflation to the ground." Having pushed the Canadian economy into a mini-recession in 1970-

71 with its tight monetary and fiscal policies, the Canadian government adopted a very expansionary monetary policy during the 1971-75 period. (Indeed the money supply increased, on average, by 13 per cent each year over this four-year period). Not surprisingly, all this extra money created double-digit inflation. In 1975 the Bank of Canada converted to monetarism and committed itself to fighting inflation by *gradually* reducing the growth rate of the money supply (see Chapter 16). As the growth rate of the money supply declined sharply in 1981 and 1982, interest rates were pushed upwards (see Chart 1-2), and the economy was once again plunged into a serious recession.

In the bottom panel of Chart 1-3 we have plotted the surplus/deficit position for the composite government sector (federal, provincial and local governments) in constant 1971 dollars. As one can see from this chart, the government sector had a *surplus* of revenues over expenditures from 1964 to 1974, attaining a peak surplus of over $2 billion in 1969 and 1974. Since 1975, however, the government sector has continually been in a *deficit* position. The size of the deficits escalated during the severe recession of the early 1980s—reaching $9 billion 1971 dollars, or 27 billion current dollars, in 1984. These huge government deficits in the 1980s became a major public policy issue and a constraint on governments adopting stimulative fiscal policies. Chapter 16 provides a complete discussion of monetary and fiscal policy (including the size of the government deficit) during the 1960-84 period.

Outline of Textbook

In Part I of the textbook we discuss a number of important conceptual issues concerning the measurement of income, output, inflation and unemployment. After analyzing the costs of inflation and unemployment in Chapter 3, we review the origins of macroeconomics and the most elementary representation of Keynesian economics, the *Keynesian cross model*, in Chapter 4.

Building upon the Keynesian cross foundations of Chapter 4, Part II of the text explicitly incorporates interest rates, financial assets, foreign trade, and capital flows into the *IS—LM* macroeconomic model. (*IS* and *LM* refer to two curves in a macro diagram.) Throughout these three Keynesian-oriented chapters we assume *in*flexible price levels. A thorough understanding of Keynesian economics under stable price levels is a necessary prerequisite for our subsequent analysis of inflation and the monetarist critique of Keynesian economics. For expositional purposes we have organized our presentation of the *IS—LM* model into three chapters: (1) the Keynesian diagnosis of deficient aggregate demand and chronic unemployment (Chapter 5), (2) the Keynesian policy prescription (Chapter 6), and (3) balance of payments adjustments within the *IS—LM* model (Chapter 7).

Part III of the textbook permanently relaxes the restrictive Keynesian assumption of inflexible price levels. Chapter 8 introduces the concept of aggregate supply and solves the aggregate demand and supply model for the equilibrium price level (under Keynesian, monetarist and new classical assumptions). Chapter 9 analyzes the structural determinants of inflation, using the price-expectations-augmented Phillips (*PEP*) curve as the key integrating concept. In Chapter 10 we incorporate our theory of inflation—the *PEP* curve—into the basic Keynesian *IS—LM* model, thereby providing an integrated *IS—LM—PEP* model of inflation, output and unemployment. As will be demonstrated, once we throw our Keynesian *IS—LM* model into inflation *PEP* gear, many of our previous Keynesian conclusions are converted into monetarist conclusions. Chapter 11 is devoted to balance of payments adjustments for an open inflationary economy.

Part IV of the textbook investigates the major policy implications of the *IS—LM—PEP* theoretical model. Chapter 12 tackles the elusive issue of the trade-off between inflation and unemployment and completes our analysis of the *long-run* properties of the *IS—LM—PEP* model, particularly the long-run effects of monetary and fiscal policy on inflation, interest rates, output and unemployment. The next three chapters explore the *short-run* policy implications of the *IS—LM—PEP* model. Chapter 13 examines the painful short-run adjustment costs associated with the implementation of an anti-inflationary, restrictive monetary policy and the potential usefulness of temporary wage and price controls. Perhaps the central message of Keynesian economics is that a free enterprise system "*needs* to be stabilized, *can* be stabilized and therefore *should* be stabilized."[9] Chapters 14 and 15 analyze various stabilization policy options for demand shocks and supply-price shocks. As will be discussed in these two chapters, Keynesians and monetarist economists have quite different approaches to stabilization policy, neither approach being particularly well-suited for supply-price shocks such as OPEC. Finally, Chapter 16 attempts to explain economic events and government policy decisions during the 1970s and early 1980s, such as the Bank of Canada's conversion to monetarism, in terms of the theoretical models developed in Part III.

The final four chapters of the book give a more detailed discussion of the individual components of the *IS—LM—PEP* macroeconomic model. Chapter 17 investigates two alternative models of inflation expectations (the *adaptive* and *rational* expectations assumptions) and the macroeconomic implications of both models. Much of Chapter 17 is devoted to a presentation and evaluation of the new classical model of macroeconomics and its key *policy ineffectiveness proposition*, which states that anticipated government policy will have absolutely no effect on output or employment levels. Chapter 18 delves more deeply into the money market, providing a simple money supply model that illustrates how the Bank of Canada is able to control the stock of money. In addition, Chapter 18 analyzes the demand side of the money market and compares several theoretical approaches to the demand for money. The final two chapters return to the market for goods and services. Since the early 1950s, a number of theoretical and empirical contributions have improved our understanding of consumption and investment behaviour. Chapters 19 and 20 review the recent developments in consumption and investment theory, paying particular attention to the implications for interventionist and non-interventionist policy prescriptions.

---

[9]F. Modigliani, "The Monetarist Controversy or, Should We Forsake Stabilization Policies?" *American Economic Review*, March 1977, p. 1.

The National Income and Expenditure Accounts

Grown-ups love figures. When you tell them that you have made a new friend, they never ask you any questions about essential matters. They never say to you, "What does his voice sound like? What games does he love best? Does he collect butterflies?" Instead, they demand: "How old is he? How many brothers has he? How much does he weigh? How much money does his father make?" Only from these figures do they think they have learned anything about him.

Antoine de Saint-Exupéry[1]

In order to tackle the problems of unemployment, inflation and the balance of payments, the government must first of all gather reliable information. Without information on the economy's vital signs it is not possible to diagnose the disease properly, let alone prescribe the appropriate medicine and be reasonably confident about the prognosis.[2] Canada's system of National Income and Expenditure Accounts provides an enormous amount of information on the economic health of the country. While the system of national accounts does not in itself *explain* the country's economic performance, economists can use the information contained in the accounts to *describe* economic events. The data may show, for example, that a period of slow economic growth was accompanied by a drop in Canadian exports or a decline in business investment. We have already seen in Chapter 1 (Chart 1-1) that movements in the overall unemployment rate are closely linked to movements in the gap between actual and potential output. When this gap is large the unemployment rate tends to be high; conversely, when the gap is small the unemployment rate tends to be low. In addition to merely describing economic events, the data contained in the national accounts are necessary for establishing important *causal* relationships between economic variables. Knowledge of these underlying economic relationships is essential if appropriate policy prescriptions are to be made. Economists often disagree over the nature of these underlying

---

[1]A. de Saint-Exupéry, *The Little Prince* (New York: Harcourt Brace & World, 1943), pp. 16-17.

[2]During and just after the second world war, the deficiency in available economic information became obvious. In 1945 the White Paper on Employment and Income outlined the government's economic objectives for the reconstruction period and a group was established to develop a set of National Income and Expenditure Accounts for Canada. Estimates of GNP were published regularly in the second half of the 1940s but it was not until 1952 that annual estimates for the period 1926-50 were available.

relationships and consequently different policy recommendations are proposed. Such disagreements can be settled only by an appeal to the facts—many of which are recorded in the national accounts. In this chapter we will describe the structure of the Canadian National Income and Expenditure Accounts and discuss some of the conceptual issues involved in measuring such concepts as national income.

The bottom line of the National Income and Expenditure Accounts is **gross national product** (GNP) or **gross national expenditure** (GNE). These two concepts are alternative ways of describing exactly the same thing; namely, the market value of all final goods and services produced during a given period of time. One way to compute this number is to add up the expenditures that are made on currently produced final goods: this is the expenditure (GNE) approach. During the process of producing these final goods, incomes are generated: employees earn wages and salaries, owners of stocks and bonds earn interest and dividends, and landlords receive rents. The final price tag of any item can always be broken down into the income payments—wages, rent, interest and profits—that were paid out during the process of production.[3] Adding up all the income payments will always give the same total as adding up the total value of goods produced. If this were not so, part of the value of goods produced would mysteriously disappear from the economic system. The income approach to measuring economic activity yields gross national product (GNP). By their definitions, the income and expenditure approaches must give identical estimates of current economic activity.

Gross National Expenditure

We will distinguish more fully between these two conceptual approaches below, but first we should clarify an important point. GNE and GNP do not refer to the total value of *all* goods and services traded in the economy over a certain period of time, since this would greatly overestimate the level of economic activity. It is important to distinguish between *final* goods and *intermediate* goods.

Consider, for example, the manufacture of an automobile. A measure of the economic activity involved in producing this item is its market value. However, the production of the automobile involves many stages, some of which are separated by market transactions between different firms. Engine parts, tires, and cassette decks are all sold to the firm that finally assembles the car. If the value of these intermediate transactions were added together along with the value of the finished automobile we would obviously overestimate the value of economic activity involved. The value of the engine parts, tires, and cassette decks would all have been double-counted—once on their own account and again in the market value of the car itself.

To avoid this pitfall we distinguish between *final* goods, such as the automobile,

---

[3]This ignores the effect of government subsidies and sales taxes, which are also reflected in market prices. We return to this below.

which are primarily bought by households, and *intermediate* goods and services, which are purchased by firms and used up in the production process. Examples of intermediate goods and services are electricity and advertising purchased by the Ford Motor Company and the paper bought by Addison-Wesley Publishers. The important feature of intermediate goods and services is that their value is fully incorporated into the price of the final product. This argument suggests that we are certainly safe in adding up the value of goods and services bought by households, since these items do not become part of another product—they are final goods and services. On the other hand, we should not include in GNE the goods and services bought by firms, because these are all intermediate goods and services whose value will be included in the final goods that firms sell.

Unfortunately, there is an exception to this straightforward classification. Firms' purchases of capital goods are included in GNE. For example, the cars purchased by a firm for the use of its sales representatives, or a new building to store inventories are all included in GNE under the heading "Business Investment" in the national accounts. Since the lives of the car and the building are much greater than one year, the cost of the car and the building will not be fully reflected in the value of this year's output of final goods. (Firms do not charge very high prices in the first year of operation to recover the full cost of a new building.) But, bear in mind that national income accountants are interested in measuring current economic activity and regardless of whether the car (or new building) is used up entirely in the current year, economic activity took place to produce it. Consequently, purchases of capital goods are included in the current year's GNE. The reader might argue that, by classifying capital goods as final goods, double counting will exist, since costs associated with that part of the car and building that are used up during the current production period, which are referred to as depreciation costs, certainly will be reflected in the market price of the final goods and services. Over several years the full cost of the car and the building will have been fully incorporated into the value of the firm's output of final goods through the inclusion of depreciation costs in the total costs of production. At that time, both the car and the building will have been counted twice in GNE. It is precisely for this reason that the word "gross" is used. In order to measure *net* economic activity in any given year we must subtract total depreciation costs from GNE. We will meet this concept again when we consider the income approach to the national accounts.

To recapitulate, gross national expenditure measures the total value of market economic activity: the value of all *final* goods and services produced. The spending on these final goods can be categorized into a number of groups or expenditure components according to the nature of the item and the type of transaction involved. The four major categories are: personal expenditures; investment expenditures; goods and services purchased by the government; and net exports, which is the difference between Canada's exports and imports of currently produced goods and services. We will consider each of these separately. For reference, Table 2-1 shows some details of the GNE side of the National Income and Expenditure Accounts for 1984.

TABLE 2-1 Gross National Expenditure, 1984

		Billions of Dollars	Per cent of GNE
Personal expenditure		246.9	58.7%
Goods	136.0		
Services	110.9		
Business investment		69.3	16.5%
Residential construction	15.7		
Plant and equipment	51.9		
Value of physical change in			
inventories	1.7		
Government expenditure		102.8	24.4%
Current	90.8		
Capital	12.0		
Exports		131.9	31.3%
Imports		−130.7	31.3%
Residual error		0.6	
Gross national expenditure		420.8	

Source: Statistics Canada, *National Income and Expenditure Accounts*.

Personal Expenditure

By far the largest component of GNE is *personal expenditure* on goods and services. This spending amounted to $246.9 billion in 1984, which represented 59 per cent of the value of GNE ($420.8 billion). Included in this total are such things as households' purchases of food, beer, sports equipment, textbooks, automobiles and the services of hairdressers and dentists. Economists have found it useful to distinguish between total household *spending* on goods and services and total household *consumption* of goods and services. The former is recorded in the national accounts, while the latter refers to the quantity of consumer goods used up during the year. The difference between the two arises from the fact that some items that consumers purchased in the current year are not entirely consumed during the year. These items, such as automobiles and furniture, are called durable goods. A car that costs $10,000 and lasts ten years yields, on average, transportation services of $1,000 per year. A measure of actual household consumption, rather than spending, would include the amount households spend on services and non-durable goods plus that part of the stock of durable goods "used up" during the year. Obviously, from a practical point of view, the calculation of household consumption, which requires an evaluation of the flow of services from existing durable goods, is much more difficult than the calculation of household spending which simply requires information on current expenditure. However, the reason the national accounts include current expenditure is that GNE and GNP are measures of annual economic activity: the value of annual production of all goods and services. A car produced during the year should be included in this total regardless of the fact that it is fully consumed only after several years of use.

Business Investment

The second category of expenditure listed in Table 2-1 is *business investment*. It should be stressed that when we speak of "business investment" in this book, we mean the additions to the physical stock of capital goods. In general usage the word "investment" frequently refers to any action that is expected to give a return in the future. Thus, the purchase of gold bullion, Canada Savings Bonds and a Tom Thomson painting may be considered investments. However, none of these actions represents the purchase of a newly produced item and therefore they do not represent current economic activity. Purchases of this type simply involve the exchange of assets between individuals, and while one of the traders concerned may consider he has made an investment, no new physical capital goods have been produced, and the transaction is not recorded in the national accounts. It follows from this that the buying of stocks or bonds, or the takeover of one firm by another, is not investment as we mean it here.

Three items have been recorded separately under the heading of "Business Investment" in the national accounts: (1) residential construction, (2) spending on plant and equipment, and (3) the value of the physical change in inventories. The first represents the value of new additions to the stock of residential buildings such as single detached houses, duplexes and apartment buildings. It is a matter of convention that this item is recorded as business investment even though a good part is actually household expenditure. The second item, plant and equipment, refers to nonresidential construction such as office buildings, factories and warehouses as well as machinery of all types, such as lathes, typewriters and cars purchased by firms. The third item is the value of the physical change in inventories. This quantity can be either positive or negative. A positive number indicates that production during the year exceeded sales and inventories rose. If we measured total economic activity simply by adding up the various expenditure items, we would underestimate total annual production to the extent that inventories have accumulated. On the other hand, sales may exceed production, in which case inventory stocks would decline, and to measure current production we must subtract the change in inventories from the total value of sales.

The total of these three subcomponents is referred to as *gross* business investment. As pointed out above, the word "gross" indicates that no account has been taken of the fact that in producing the current year's output of goods and services, part of the capital stock wears out. *Net* business investment is equal to gross business investment less the investment required to replace the worn out capital stock. Since it is gross business investment that is added to the other expenditure components, this total is referred to as *gross national expenditure*. It is a gross measure of annual production because part of the national wealth, the stock of capital goods, is consumed during the process of production.

Government Expenditures

Since the services that the local, provincial and federal governments supply are not sold in the market place, there is no price that can be used to value the productive activities of government. National income accountants therefore equate the value of this production to the costs of providing it. That is to say, the value of government output is defined by the value of inputs purchased by government. The national accounts distinguish between current and capital expenditures. Capital spending by governments consists chiefly of construction activities such as building schools, hospitals, roads, airports, and other capital projects. All levels of government are included but the investment spending of government business enterprises such as the Canadian National Railway is recorded under business investment. Current spending includes purchases of goods and services by all levels of government. These goods and services are required by, for example, schools, hospitals, and the armed services. The major cost incurred by government in providing services is wages and salaries paid to civil servants, teachers, nurses, policemen, military personnel, and other public employees. This expense is included in the "at cost" measure of government production.

It should be emphasized that government expenditures relate to purchases of *goods and services* only. Government spending on transfer payments such as family allowances, unemployment insurance, interest on the public debt and the like are not included. Unlike the money spent on teachers' salaries, for example, none of these outlays is for the production of goods or services and consequently there is no corresponding government production. The family allowance program, for instance, is a vehicle for transferring income from one group to another. The act of transferring this income is one of the services that the government provides, and it is valued in the national accounts at the cost, in terms of the materials (paper for the cheques) and personnel (civil servants who prepare the cheques), of providing this service. The dollar value of family allowances actually transferred does not represent any equivalent productive activity and is not entered into the national accounts under government expenditure or anywhere else. It is important therefore to distinguish between two concepts of total government spending. The first is the national accounts concept, which measures the contribution of government to total economic activity, and the second is total government spending for all purposes, much of which involves transferring income from one set of citizens—taxpayers—to another set of citizens—for example, the recipients of interest on the public debt, unemployment insurance, subsidies and capital assistance. Certainly from a quantitative point of view the distinction is an important one. Table 2-1 shows that the contribution to total production of all levels of government was $102.8 billion in 1984, amounting to 24 per cent of GNE. Total government spending, on the other hand, including transfers to the private sector, amounted to $194.0 billion, or 46 per cent of GNE.

Imports and Exports

The Canadian economy is frequently referred to as being "open." By this it is meant that Canada has strong economic links to the rest of the world, the U.S. in particular. For example, in 1984 Canada exported 31 per cent of that year's total production of goods and services and imported a similar quantity of foreign goods and services. In addition to the international flow of goods and services, Canadians also make an enormous number of international transactions of a purely financial nature. Canadians place funds in U.S. banks, and buy foreign governments' bonds, to list just a couple of examples. In Chapter 7 we will discuss more fully the balance of payments accounts which summarize Canada's international transactions. For the moment we will concern ourselves only with the international flows of goods and services, since the estimate of Canada's annual production of final goods and services must obviously include those which are produced in Canada and exported to foreigners. Similarly, Canadian expenditure on goods and services brought into the country must be excluded from the calculation of Canadian GNE.

Consider again the case of a car assembled in Canada. If part of the car, say the engine, has been imported into Canada, then the value of the car in the market place overstates the value of Canadian economic activity. The import content of the car should be subtracted from its market price in order to properly estimate domestic economic activity. It is extremely difficult to do this on a product-by-product basis. It is much easier to add up the value of imports as they enter the country. Since all imports must ultimately become final goods or services one way or another, the import-content adjustment to GNE is made by simply subtracting the annual value of imports from the total value of expenditure on final goods and services.

Gross National Expenditure and Expenditure Shares

The final component of Table 2-1 is the *residual error*. This error arises because the two theoretically equivalent approaches to computing the value of annual production never agree in practice. Conceptually the income and expenditure methods should give identical numerical estimates but inevitably errors and omissions make this impossible. A simple resolution is adopted, namely to take the average of computed GNE and computed GNP. Tables 2-1 and 2-2 show that in 1984 the estimate of GNP exceeded that of GNE by $1.2 billion, so $0.6 billion was subtracted from the former and added to the latter.

It is convenient at this point to introduce a symbolic representation of the four major components of GNE. These are usually thought of as the sources of demand for the economy's output. Throughout the text the following symbols will apply: personal expenditure or consumption C, business investment I, government expenditures G, and net exports $X - M$, where X and M represent exports and imports respectively. Algebraically we can represent gross national expenditure as:

$$(2\text{-}1) \qquad Z = C + I + G + (X - M)$$

This identity will play an important role in the models that will be developed in later chapters.

Chart 2-1 shows how the ratios of these major expenditure components to GNE have varied over the 1950-84 time period. The vertical scales are identical for all of the graphs, which allows us to make comparisons between the variability of each series. *Business investment*, which has maintained a share of about 20 per cent of GNE, is the most volatile component. This variability is not fully apparent from the chart because investment spending and GNE are positively correlated; that is, investment booms are associated with high levels of output. Thus the

CHART 2-1 Percentage shares of expenditure components in GNE, 1950-84

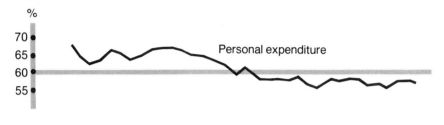

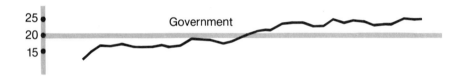

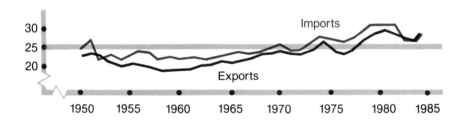

percentage share of investment shows more stability than does investment expenditure itself. *Personal expenditure,* on the other hand, is a fairly stable series, so the share of this component rises during recessions—for example, in 1975 and 1982. Over the last thirty-five years the share of personal expenditure has shown a slight downward trend.

The shares of *imports and exports* have been plotted together so that the trade balance is apparent. For most years since the Second World War imports have exceeded exports. Both imports and exports have grown rapidly since the mid-1960s, due in part to the signing of the 1965 Auto Pact between Canada and the United States (see Chapter 5). Finally, *government spending* on goods and services as a proportion of GNE has risen considerably since 1950.

As noted above, focusing on only government-produced goods and services seriously understates the increasing role of *total* government activity. In 1984, total government spending[4] was $194.0 billion, of which only $90.8 billion was spent on goods and services (the G component of GNE). Transfer payments to persons accounted for a further $53.8 billion. The fastest growing component of total government spending in recent years, however, has been the interest payments on government debt. High interest rates and the growing volume of government debt have combined to push interest payments up to $33.4 billion in 1984, up from $5.4 billion just ten years earlier. In turn, government revenues totalled $171.6 billion in 1984. Personal and corporate income taxes brought in $84.3 billion and a further $55.1 billion was collected through indirect taxes such as sales taxes. In 1984, total government revenues represented 41 per cent of GNE, as compared with only 25 per cent in 1950.

Gross National Product

As we pointed out earlier, the value of any final good can be decomposed into the payments that are made to the owners of the factors of production. The production costs that determine the factory gate price of a car, for example, are in fact the incomes received by the owners of the factors of production that make the car. These costs include wages and salaries paid to workers, interest income paid to individuals and firms that have made loans to the car manufacturer and the car manufacturer's profits, which go to the owners in the form of dividends or retained earnings. The cost of intermediate goods bought by the car manufacturer, such as tires, can be similarly broken down into the incomes paid to the owners of the factors of tire production. The sum of these costs or incomes would give us the value of the car "at factor cost." The corresponding figure for the economy as a whole is called **net national income** (NNI) at factor cost.

The first six lines of Table 2-2 show the breakdown of NNI into the various income components. The largest by far is *labour income*, which amounted to $235.0 billion, or 72.2 per cent of NNI, in 1984. Chart 2-2 shows the shares of the major income components over the past thirty-five years. Both labour's share and the share accounted for by *interest and dividend income* have risen over this period. The share of *profits*, however, has shown a slight downward trend.

An item so far unexplained is the *inventory valuation adjustment*, which appears on line seven of Table 2-2. Consider a year in which there is general inflation but the actual physical stock of inventories is unchanged. Let us consider a typical firm that has one unit of inventory at both the beginning and the end of the year. Suppose the initial price of this inventory is $100 but inflation during the year raises the price of the inventory to, say, $105. Since changes in the value of inventories are treated as income for the firm, the additional $5 will show up as part of profits (the second item of Table 2-2) and hence it will contribute to net

---

[4]Excluding transfers from one level of government to another, for example, federal government transfers to provincial governments.

CHART 2-2 Percentage shares of income components in
N.N.T. 1950-84

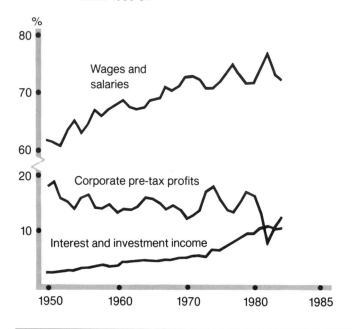

TABLE 2-2   Gross National Product, 1984

	Billions of Dollars
Add:	
Total labour income	235.0
Corporation pre-tax profits	39.7
Deduct:	
Dividends paid to nonresidents	−3.9
Add:	
Interest and investment income	32.8
Farm income	4.0
Nonfarm, unincorporated business income	20.4
Inventory valuation adjustment	−2.7
Equals:	
Net National Income at factor cost	325.3
Add:	
Indirect taxes less subsidies	44.3
Capital consumption allowances ·	51.8
Residual error	−0.6
Equals:	
Gross National Product at market prices*	420.8

*components do not sum to total due to rounding
Source: Statistics Canada, *National Income and Expenditure Accounts*.

national income. However, in the expenditure version of the national accounts, the corresponding item is the value of the physical change in inventories. Since in our example there has been no *physical* change in inventories this item would be zero. This is appropriate since an objective of the national accounts is to measure the value of current economic activity. If inventories rise in value simply because of inflation but remain unchanged in physical quantity, then their rise in value does not represent economic activity and should not be included in GNE or GNP. The upshot is that an adjustment is required if the income and expenditure methods are to agree. In the present example, profits would be adjusted downwards by $5; that is, the inventory valuation adjustment would be −$5. Table 2-2 shows that in 1984 the inventory valuation adjustment due to inflation amounted to $2.7 billion, which was subtracted from the total payment to factors of production to arrive at net national income.

To obtain GNP from NNI three adjustments have to be made. To explain this let us return to the example of the car. The incomes generated in producing the car sum to the "factor cost" of the car. This will differ from the market price on account of (1) depreciation costs, which cover the wear, tear, and obsolescence of the capital stock incurred during the car's production; (2) indirect taxes such as sales taxes levied on the car; and (3) any subsidies the manufacturer received from the government. We add the first two and subtract the third from the factor cost of the car to obtain its market price. At the aggregate level these three adjustments to net national income give us gross national product at market prices.

We argued earlier that GNE or GNP is a *gross* measure of current production and, over the long term, capital goods are double-counted—once on their own account when they are first produced, because capital goods are treated as final goods, and again in the value of the products that they help produce, because firms include the cost of capital depreciation in the price of the good or service produced. We now find that there is a second factor that causes GNP to exceed the value of current production (which is actually measured by net national income)—*indirect taxes*. Suppose, for example, that when the government raises an additional $1 billion in sales taxes the level of economic activity is unchanged. In this case GNP would rise by $1 billion because indirect taxes have increased, but total output would remain the same. The increased rate of sales tax drives up the market price of goods and services produced,[5] thus artificially raising measured GNE. To repeat, there are *no* physical goods and services on the other side of the national accounts to match indirect taxes—only higher prices—and indirect taxes do not represent a payment for a factor of production. The artificial contribution made to GNP by the inclusion of indirect taxes is substantial and amounted to over 10 per cent of GNP in 1984.

Personal Disposable Income

Personal disposable income is a very important concept in macroeconomics since the income people have at their disposal is the major determinant of how much

---

[5]See Chapter 15 for an analysis of tax changes and the rate of inflation.

they will spend on goods and services. We have already seen that personal spending accounts for a very large share of total spending in the economy as a whole. Later, we will see that the relation between personal disposable income and personal expenditure or consumption has played a major role in the development of modern macroeconomics.

In Table 2-3 the major sources of **personal income** are listed along with the deductions that the government takes out of this income. Personal income, net of these deductions, is equal to *personal disposable income*. The major sources of personal income are wages and salaries, which accounted for about 65 per cent of the total in 1984. Interest, dividends and other investment income is another important source, and one which has grown considerably in recent years because of historically high interest rates. In 1984, this component accounted for 12.9 per cent of personal income. Even more important that this, however, are the **transfers** from government to individuals. In 1984, over 15 per cent of personal income came in the form of government assistance cheques such as family allowances and unemployment insurance. The last two items that make up personal income are relatively small. Transfers from corporations to persons include charitable donations and bad debts that are written off. Transfers from nonresidents include gifts.

The observant reader will have noticed that personal income, at $360.7 billion, actually exceeded NNI in 1984, which was only $325.3 billion (see Table 2-2). How can it be that the incomes actually received by persons exceeded the total amount of income that was generated through the production of goods and services? The reason for this is that there is a considerable amount of double-counting in personal income. Suppose, for example, that the only source of personal income is the income that is generated through productive activity and that all of this income (NNI) is paid out to persons.[6] In this case personal income will be exactly equal to NNI. Now if the government steps in and taxes individual incomes and then channels this money back to the same people in the form of family allowance cheques, personal income will rise because personal income includes all government transfers to persons. Personal income will now exceed NNI by the value of all family allowance cheques.

From the point of view of individual purchasing power, after-tax or disposable income is more important than personal income. As Table 2-3 shows, income taxes are the most important part of total government deductions, although compulsory contributions to social insurance and government pensions are also significant.

Real, Nominal and Potential GNP

In previous sections we have considered in some detail how the value of current economic activity is measured. In 1984 the market value of goods and services produced was $420.8 billion. This figure is sometimes referred to as GNP measured in current dollars because the goods and services are valued at current year prices. The corresponding figure for 1983 GNP was $386.8 billion. Again, this

---

[6]In fact not all of NNI is paid out to persons. In 1984 over $15 billion was kept by corporations as retained earnings to finance future expansion.

TABLE 2-3   Sources of Personal Income and Personal Disposable
Income, 1984

	Billions of Dollars
Add:	
Wages and salaries*	235.0
Net farm income	3.3
Net income of non-farm unincorporated business including rent	20.4
Interest, dividends and miscellaneous investment income	46.4
Add Current Transfers:	
From government	54.4
From corporations	0.6
From nonresidents	0.6
Personal Income	360.7
Subtract:	
Income taxes	49.4
Contributions to social insurance and government pensions	19.2
Other transfers to government	3.7
Personal Disposable Income	288.4

*Includes military pay
Source: Statistics Canada, *National Income and Expenditure Accounts*.

value of goods and services produced was evaluated at current prices, that is, the prices prevailing in 1983. The change in the value of GNP between 1983 and 1984 was $34.0 billion, which represents 8.8 per cent growth. A natural question to ask is, how much of this increase represents an increase in the physical quantity of goods and services produced and how much simply reflects increases in the prices of these goods and services? This is an important question because it is increases in the physical quantity of goods and services which create job opportunities for those entering the labour force and for those currently unemployed.

In order to separate these two factors economists distinguish between **nominal GNP** (GNP measured in current prices) and **real GNP**, which measures the physical quantity of goods and services produced annually. Obviously these *real* goods and services have to be evaluated in dollars, since we cannot add together apples and oranges. Table 2-4 illustrates how this would be done for a simple economy that produces just two items, shirts and haircuts.

In this hypothetical economy the value of nominal GNP rose by $80 or 160 per cent over the period 1971-84. However, if the production of shirts and haircuts in 1984 is evaluated at 1971 prices we obtain a figure of $80, which represents real GNP in 1984 evaluated at 1971 prices. Real growth over this thirteen-year period would be measured by the difference between $80 and $50, equalling 60 per cent growth. Note that the actual output of shirts rose by 50 per cent while the quantity of haircuts doubled. We would expect real GNP to rise by an amount somewhere between these two. Our actual measure of 60 per cent lies closer to 50 per cent than 100 per cent because shirts have a higher price tag than haircuts and so the growth of shirt production is more heavily weighted than the growth in the number of haircuts.

Chart 2-3 shows how, in per capita terms, nominal and real GNP have changed over the years 1950-84. While the nominal per capita GNP series shows uninterrupted growth, the real GNP series identifies periods of strong physical growth, such as 1970-73, as well as years when the Canadian economy experienced recessions, such as 1975 and 1982. Without a correction for inflation, the change in nominal GNP can give a very misleading indication of the change in the production levels of goods and services.

Because it is changes in real GNP that have a major influence on unemployment rates, economists prefer to use information on real GNP rather than nominal GNP for judging the economy's performance. An obvious issue that arises in this context is the standard that we should use to judge the overall performance of the economy. Is 3 per cent real growth per annum a good performance or a poor performance? To answer this question, economists compare the volume of goods and services actually produced—real GNP—to the volume that could have been produced if all the economy's resources of labour and physical capital were fully employed—**potential** GNP. James Brox[7] has computed a potential output series for Canada. This is done by first finding the relationship between the factors of production, labour and capital equipment, and the economy's output of goods and services (real GNP). Such a relationship is called a production function and can be written as $Q = f(K, L)$, where Q, K, and L represent output, the capital stock in use and the quantity of labour employed, respectively. It is just a shorthand way of saying that output depends on, or is a function (f) of, the inputs used in the production process. Using information on the actual levels of inputs and outputs over the period 1960 to 1978, Brox estimates an actual functional relationship between the inputs, capital and labour, and the actual quantity of output (real GNP). This relationship can be used to calculate potential output by substituting into the estimated production function the quantities of capital and labour that were potentially available in each year (rather than the actual quantities). We have reproduced Brox's potential output series in Chart 1-1 of Chapter 1.

The Measurement of Inflation

In the next chapter many of the conceptual issues involved in the measurement of inflation and unemployment will be discussed. Since a comprehensive measure of the rate of inflation is implicit within the National Income and Expenditure Accounts, it is convenient to introduce this topic here.

If all of the thousands of individual prices in the economy changed by the *same* proportion over any given time interval, then we would have no difficulty at all in measuring the percentage change in the *general price level*; it would simply be identical to the individual price changes. In practice individual prices move by

---

[7]James A. Brox, "A Note on Capacity Utilization, Productivity, and the Canadian Output Gap" *Empirical Economics*, Vol. 9 (1984), pp. 131-38.

CHART 2-3 Real and nominal per capita GNP, 1950-84

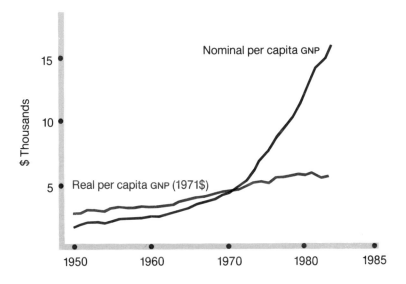

TABLE 2-4   An Illustration of Real and Nominal GNP

1971 Nominal GNP	1984 Nominal GNP	1984 Real GNP*
4 shirts at $10 = $40	6 shirts at $15 = $90	6 shirts at $10 = $60
5 haircuts at $2 = $10	10 haircuts at $4 = $40	10 haircuts at $2 = $20
$50	$130	$80

*evaluated at 1971 prices

different amounts and not necessarily in the same direction. The change in the general price level is an average of the individual price changes.

One comprehensive measure of inflation is the GNP *implicit price index*. It is comprehensive in that the prices of consumer goods and services, investment goods, imports and exports all enter the calculation. In the previous section the distinction was made between nominal GNP, the value of currently produced goods and services evaluated at their current prices, and real GNP, the value of those same goods and services evaluated at their prices in some base period. Implicit in these calculations is an overall measure of the average change in prices from the base period to the current period. The argument begins with the observation that the value of a group of items can be expressed in terms of the product of a quantity measure and a price measure. Consider, for example, $5.00 worth of apples which cost 50¢ each. Obviously the value of the apples can be expressed as the product of 10 (quantity of apples) times 50¢ (the unit price of

TABLE 2-5 An Illustration of the GNP Implicit Price Index

	Nominal GNP	Real GNP	GNP Price Index
1971	$ 50	$50	1.0
1984	$130	$80	1.625

apples). This idea can be extended to the measurement of GNP. By dividing nominal GNP (current value) by real GNP (a measure of quantity) we obtain the unit price of GNP implied by our measure of physical quantity. The *ratio* of nominal to real GNP is consequently referred to as the GNP implicit price index.

The shirt–haircut economy of Table 2-4 will again serve as an illustration. The relevant information is given in Table 2-5. The base year is 1971; that is to say, real GNP is calculated by evaluating production in any given year at 1971 prices. This means of course that nominal and real GNP have the same value in 1971, namely $50, so that their ratio is one. The unit price of real GNP is therefore unity in 1971. By 1984 nominal GNP reached $130. But measured in terms of 1971 prices, real GNP in 1984 was $80. The ratio of the value measure of GNP to the real or quantity measure of GNP gives the implicit unit price of GNP, which in 1977 was 1.625. Consequently, in this illustration, the unit price of GNP increased 62.5 per cent over the period 1971-84. Note that this overall measure of inflation is a weighted average of the increases in the price of shirts (50 per cent) and the price of haircuts (100 per cent) and that the price of shirts is more heavily weighted because shirt production contributes more to GNP than haircuts.

The GNP implicit price index is the most comprehensive measure of inflation in that the prices of all goods and services are included in the calculation. For many purposes the GNP implicit price index is too comprehensive. From the point of view of workers who are bargaining for increased wages to cover the higher cost of living, inflation means increases in the prices of the goods and services that they consume. A price index that includes the prices of capital equipment is not as useful as one that focuses on the items that a typical family purchases. The Consumer Price Index (CPI) is designed to measure the rate of inflation that faces the typical consumer. As such, it is much more widely used than the more comprehensive GNP implicit price index. In the next chapter, which examines some of the conceptual issues that arise in the measurement of inflation and unemployment, we will take a closer look at the CPI, pointing out some of the advantages and disadvantages of this measure of inflation.

Key Concepts

gross national expenditure (GNE)
gross national product (GNP)
net national income (NNI)
personal income
government expenditures and transfers
real, nominal and potential GNP
GNP implicit price index

Review Questions

1. Why is the distinction between intermediate goods and final goods important in the calculation of GNE?
2. How does the meaning of the word "investment" in the context of the National Income and Expenditure Accounts differ from its everyday meaning?
3. The value of goods and services produced by government cannot be measured by their market value because they are generally not sold in a market. How is the value of government production determined? What is the justification for this method?
4. In 1984 all levels of government in Canada spent a total of $194 billion, but the national accounts (Table 2-1) show current and capital government expenditures were only $103 billion. How do you reconcile these figures?
5. The value of GNE includes the value of final goods and services produced for consumption, investment, and exports as well as by government. Why is it necessary to subtract imports into Canada from this total?
6. What is the distinction between gross and net investment? How is this related to the concepts of GNP and NNI?
7. Why is it important to distinguish between real and nominal GNP? Construct an example to illustrate how this distinction is made in practice.

Inflation and Unemployment

Unemployment and inflation still preoccupy and perplex economists, statesmen, journalists, housewives and everyone else. The connection between them is the principal domestic economic burden of presidents and prime ministers, and the major area of controversy and ignorance in macroeconomics.

James Tobin[1]

In this chapter we examine the costs and consequences of inflation and unemployment, the two "most important problems facing this country today," according to recent Gallup poll surveys (see Chapter 1). The remaining chapters of this text analyze the causes and possible policy remedies for these two chronic macroeconomic diseases. While unemployment imposes unambiguous costs on individuals and society as a whole, the economic costs of inflation are more subtle and difficult to pin down. Before discussing the economic costs of inflation and unemployment, however, we will briefly consider various conceptual problems that arise in measuring each.

Inflation

Even though the GNP implicit price index (which was discussed in the last chapter) is the most comprehensive measure of prices, it is not the most widely used. By far and away the most frequently employed measure of inflation is the *rate of change* in the **Consumer Price Index** (the CPI), which is plotted in Chart 1-2 in Chapter 1. As its name suggests, the CPI is intended to measure price changes for the goods and services that are purchased by the typical consumer. When the Canadian government indexed the personal income tax system in 1974 to avoid the increasing tax burden that would otherwise result during periods of inflation (see Case Study 1 below), the CPI was chosen as the measuring rod for making the annual adjustments to the income tax structure. In addition, many government transfer payments are indexed to the CPI and over one million Canadian workers have their wages directly tied to the CPI through a cost-of-living allowance (COLA) clause.

The objective of the Consumer Price Index is to measure the change in the cost of purchasing a given "basket" of consumer goods and services. The given basket

[1]J. Tobin, "Inflation and Unemployment," *American Economic Review*, March 1972, p. 1.

of goods and services is intended to be representative of the typical consumer's purchases. Information collected on the expenditure patterns of Canadians is used to determine the *weight* attached to each item in the basket (for example, food products have a weight of 21.1 per cent, tobacco and alcohol a weight of 5.4 per cent and clothing a weight of 9.6 per cent). All told there are about 400 separate items that are priced each month in 64 urban centres (with populations of 30,000 or more). Statistics Canada personnel note the shelf prices of these items, as well as the relevant provincial sales tax which is applied to all taxable items. Consequently, an increase in provincial sales tax rates will increase the overall level of the CPI.[2] Because the weights attached to each item in the basket are fixed, changes in the CPI result only from changes in the prices of the items.

The use of *fixed* weights in the CPI avoids any potential problems arising from changes in the *mix* of goods which would affect the average price level. As real incomes rise over time, consumers likely shift their spending towards luxury items. For example, more meals may be eaten away from home. Since restaurant food costs more than home-prepared food, the average cost of food will rise over time simply as a result of changing spending patterns even if the prices of restaurant and home-prepared food do not change. The CPI avoids this difficulty by fixing the weight attached to the price of restaurant food at 5.6 per cent and the weight attached to the price of food for home consumption at 15.5 per cent. The CPI measures only price changes, and not changes in the mix of goods purchased. This does not mean, however, that the CPI is ideal for all purposes to which it is put.

As noted above, the CPI is often used to measure the rate of increase in the compensation that individuals receive to offset the effects of inflation on the purchasing power of their incomes. (COLA clauses are an example.) Two difficulties arise when the individual component prices within the CPI do not all change at the *same* rate. First, all individuals do not consume particular goods and services in exactly the same proportions. Low income households spend a larger part of their incomes on food and shelter than do high income households, so the CPI weights for these particular items are too low for the low income group. Thus, in times of rapidly increasing prices for food or shelter or both, the CPI will *under*state the rate of inflation for low income groups.

The second difficulty arises from the fact that households respond to relative price changes by switching their spending patterns. When the price of beef rises, consumers are likely to purchase close substitutes for beef, possibly pork or poultry. The full brunt of the rise in beef prices is therefore avoided. If consumers are compensated for the rise in beef prices to an extent determined by their original spending patterns, then they will have been *over*compensated to some degree. This argument depends on the assumption that the typical consumer spends his income in the best possible way. Given his income, there is no other bundle of goods that he can buy that gives greater satisfaction. Now if the price of beef rises and just enough additional income is given to the consumer so that he can buy his original choice of goods, he is certainly no worse off than before and

---

[2]The inflationary impact of increased sales tax rates is specifically considered in Chapter 15.

most probably better off. At minimum he can buy the same bundle of goods as before; he can be no worse off. In fact if he chooses to buy a different bundle of goods (a new bundle with less beef) on account of the increased relative price of beef, we know that he is now better off. Why? Because he freely chooses the second bundle in preference to the original bundle of goods. He is better off *after the income-compensated* rise in beef prices than before because he is consuming a preferred bundle of goods.

The implications of the above arguments are that the CPI is not the ideal measure of inflation encountered by particular groups in society, such as the poor and the old, and even if it were, it would tend to *over*state the monetary compensation that consumers need in order to be as well off as before the inflation occurred.[3] Nevertheless, the Consumer Price Index, with its infrequent updating of the fixed weights, provides a reasonably good measure of how much more consumers must pay to purchase a *given* basket of goods and is almost universally used to describe the inflation process.

The Economic Costs and Consequences of Inflation

Turning to an analysis of the economic costs and consequences of inflation, let us begin by considering a *pure* inflation in which all prices throughout the economy rise at the *same* rate. By abstracting from changes in relative prices (which occur regardless of whether there is general inflation or not), we are better able to understand the economic effects of inflation. Suppose that *all* prices throughout the economy rise by 10 per cent each year. What are the economic consequences of such a pure and steady inflation rate? Three propositions will be most useful in our analysis of the economic costs of inflation.

Proposition 1: Price Inflation Must Be Matched by (Nominal) Income Inflation

From our analysis of the national accounts in Chapter 2, we know that the value of all final goods produced within the economy must be distributed in the form of income payments to the various factors of production. If indirect taxes and depreciation are ignored, the sum of wages, interest, rent, and profits must be equal to the total value of goods produced. Thus if inflation increases the total value of all goods produced by 10 per cent, then this additional 10 per cent of total revenues must be distributed as increased income payments in the form of wages, interest, rent or profits. If one side of the national accounts goes up by 10 per cent, then the other side of the accounts must also go up by 10 per cent. The inflation-

---

[3]The importance of this point depends on the extent to which relative prices have changed during inflation.

induced increase in the value of all goods sold does not disappear from the economic system, but rather inflates total nominal income by 10 per cent. *Price inflation must be matched by nominal income inflation.*

If all factor prices increase at the *same* rate, then each individual's nominal

CHART 3-1 Price and income inflation

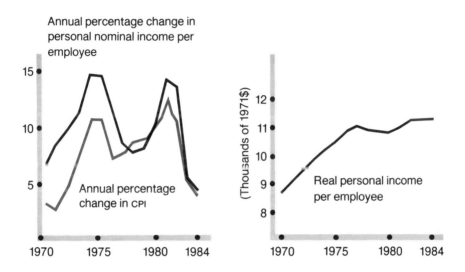

income level would rise by an amount exactly *equal* to the inflation rate. Such a pure inflation would appear to have little effect on each individual's economic welfare since each person would be able to purchase the *same quantity* of goods and services as before the inflation occurred. *Real* income or purchasing power would not be affected by pure inflation because all prices and (nominal) incomes would be rising at the same rate. Even if all individual incomes do not rise at the same rate, the National Income Accounts identity remains valid in aggregate or average terms. Total nominal income must rise by an amount equal to the inflation rate. If one particular individual receives an income increase that is *below* the inflation rate, some other individual must receive an income increase that is *above* the inflation rate.

Our preceding analysis suggests that the *average* Canadian income earner has *not* been hurt by inflation. Let us briefly review the evidence from the inflation-prone 1970s and early 1980s. In the left-hand panel of Chart 3-1 we have plotted the annual percentage change in the Consumer Price Index along with the annual percentage change in *average* personal (nominal) income per employee for the period 1970-84. Despite the record high inflation of the mid-1970s, average nominal income levels were rising at an even faster pace. Over this fifteen-year period, there are only *two* years (1978 and 1979) when the average increase in personal (nominal) income per employee failed to keep pace with the average inflation rate.[4]

As demonstrated in the right-hand panel of Chart 3-1, average *real* personal income per employee, measured in 1971 dollars, has increased from $8,660 in 1970 to $11,316 in 1984, an increase of almost 31 per cent over this fifteen-year period. However, it is obvious from Chart 3-1 that most of the gains in real income per employee were achieved in the early 1970s, when labour productivity growth rates were high and labour was heavily utilized (working more hours per year). Nevertheless, during the relatively stagnant 1975-84 decade (when the unemployment rate and the inflation rate both averaged 8.8 per cent), *real* personal income per employee did not decline but rather increased by over 10 per cent. While in any particular year *nominal* income increases may fall short of price increases (say because of a decline in hours worked per year), in general Canadian price inflation has been matched by nominal income inflation.

Proposition 2: Interest Rates Will Reflect the Expected Inflation Rate

Given that aggregate *real* income levels are unaffected by inflation, what influence will inflation have on real wealth? The real value of most components of personal wealth is also unaffected by inflation. The prevailing market prices of houses, summer cottages and automobiles will increase with the general inflation rate, and thus their *real* value should be unaffected by inflation. However, there is one category of wealth that appears to be eroded in value by the process of inflation, namely financial assets that are denoted in nominal dollar terms (such as bonds, savings accounts, and guaranteed investment certificates). Perhaps surprisingly, this assertion turns out to be incorrect. The interest rate paid on financial assets will reflect the inflation rate that is expected to prevail during the life of the financial asset, thus preserving the real value of the financial asset.

To illustrate this important point, suppose that I agree to loan you $1,000 for one year. Not being a particularly generous soul, I expect to receive an interest payment for giving up the use of my $1,000 for one year. Let us assume that we agree that 5 per cent would be a suitable interest payment for my giving up the use of my money for one year. Now, *if the inflation rate is zero*, at the end of the year the $1,000 repayment of the principal will allow me to purchase the *same* quantity of real goods that I might otherwise have purchased on the first day of the year. I take my $50 interest payment and everything is fine.

What happens if the inflation rate is not zero, but say 10 per cent? If I only charge you 5 per cent for the use of my money for one year, at the end of the year you will return to me $1,050 ($1,000 principal plus $50 interest) but my real purchasing power will be reduced because of the 10 per cent inflation rate. In fact,

---

[4]As will be discussed in Chapter 13, the overall inflation rate in these two years was substantially affected by unusually large increases in food prices (15.5 per cent and 13.2 per cent respectively). For the entire fifteen-year period, personal nominal income levels per employee increased by an average of 10.0 per cent each year, in comparison with an average CPI inflation rate of 7.8 per cent.

$1,050 one year later will only purchase $954 worth of real goods with inflated price tags (1050 ÷ 1.1). Obviously you would have come out ahead on this transaction, since you could have purchased $1,000 worth of real goods the day I lent you the money and I can purchase only $954 worth of real goods the day you pay me back. Not only do I not receive an interest payment, I end up with less purchasing power than I had on the day I loaned you the $1,000. Consequently, rather than charging you 5 per cent interest on the loan, I must increase the interest payment in order to maintain the real purchasing power of my $1,000 principal one year later. Given a 10 per cent inflation rate, I would charge you 15 per cent for the use of my money: 5 per cent interest plus 10 per cent to maintain the real purchasing power of my money.

Thus, the rate of interest charged by lenders and financial intermediaries will contain an **inflation premium** to reflect the *expected inflation rate* during the term of the loan. Defining the *real* interest rate RR as the interest rate which would prevail in a zero inflation world, the *nominal* or market interest rate R will equal the real interest rate plus the expected inflation rate $\dot{P}^e$:

(3-1) $R = RR + \dot{P}^e$

An increase in the *expected* inflation rate will cause an increase in the nominal interest rate. As Chart 1-2 in Chapter 1 illustrates, *nominal* interest rate movements have closely followed inflation rate movements during the 1960s, 1970s and early 1980s.

Commenting on high interest rates in late 1979, the Governor of the Bank of Canada noted:

> I would first like to remind you that "it takes two to tango." If there is a borrower there must be a lender, and one needs to look at the situation from his side as well. Lenders are usually thought of as banks or other financial institutions but it is more accurate to regard those institutions as intermediaries. The true lenders are the savers, the Canadians who hold deposits with banks, trust companies, credit unions and caisses populaires, who have life insurance policies, who contribute to pension funds and who own bonds. To lenders, interest rates do not look all that high because they know that the interest they receive is in effect reduced by the declining purchasing power of the money they have loaned and will eventually get back. Of course borrowers know this too; they know that the real cost of borrowing is nowhere near as high as the level of interest rates makes it look.[5]

This second proposition about inflation and interest rates also implies that the share of interest income in net national income (NNI) will rise when the expected inflation rate rises. Since total interest income is the product of the interest rate and the volume of loans outstanding, for a fixed volume of loans a jump in interest rates from 5 per cent to 15 per cent will cause a tripling of interest income. We

[5]Statement prepared for the appearance of G.K. Bouey, Governor of the Bank of Canada, before the House of Commons Standing Committee on Finance, Trade and Economic Affairs, 25 October 1979, reprinted in *Bank of Canada Review*, November 1979, pp. 3-4.

have already seen in the bottom panel of Chart 2-2 in Chapter 2 that the share of interest and investment income in NNI has continued to rise since the 1950s. There was a particularly steep rise in this share during the 1970s, which was due primarily to the upward drift in interest rates which reflected rising inflation expectations.

Proposition 3: The Foreign Exchange Rate Will Reflect the Relative Inflation Rate

A favourite argument of businessmen and bankers against inflation focuses on the *potential* adverse effects of inflation on exports and imports. It is frequently asserted that unless inflation is brought under control, Canadian exports will be "priced out" of foreign markets and cheap imports will supplant domestic production. According to this argument, inflation must be fought to maintain our "competitive edge" against international competition and to protect domestic jobs. Although this argument sounds convincing, for it to retain any validity it must be recast in terms of relative inflation, comparing the Canadian inflation rate to international inflation rates. If Canadian and world prices are rising at the same rate, Canadian industries will not lose their "competitive edge."

Even if the Canadian inflation rate exceeds international inflation rates, the "competitive edge" argument overlooks the fact that the foreign exchange rate will tend to adjust to offset differences between inflation rates in various countries. As discussed in Chapter 7, if the Canadian inflation rate exceeds the foreign inflation rate, the resulting reduction in high-priced Canadian exports and increase in low-priced foreign imports will exert downward pressure on the Canadian dollar in foreign exchange markets. A depreciating Canadian dollar will cause the price of imported goods to rise and the price of Canadian exports to decline. The "competitive edge" that is lost through a relatively higher inflation rate will, eventually, be restored by a depreciation of the Canadian dollar. The *purchasing power parity theorem*, which is presented in Chapter 7, states that long-run movements in international exchange rates are directly determined by differences in the inflation rates between trading countries. Thus, a freely fluctuating foreign exchange rate should maintain our "competitive edge" in those industries where Canada has a comparative advantage, irrespective of the Canadian inflation rate.

Anticipated and Unanticipated Inflation

Up to this point our analysis has been premised on the assumption that inflation is more or less correctly anticipated. However, during the early stages of a new outburst of inflation (or *dis*inflation as occurred in the early 1980s), the sudden change in the rate of inflation may take most people by surprise; that is to say, there may be *un*anticipated inflation. Plans will have been made, and contracts will have been signed, on the basis of an incorrect expectation of inflation. The major consequences of such inflation miscalculations are *shifts* of income and wealth between various groups in society.

The distributional effects of unanticipated inflation are most pronounced in financial asset markets. When inflation is unanticipated, the inflation premium included in the interest rate will be incorrect, and a transfer of purchasing power between the borrower and lender will occur. **Unexpected inflation** redistributes wealth from creditors to debtors. To illustrate the redistributional effects of incorrectly anticipated inflation, we return to our simple loan illustration. Assume that both the lender and the borrower anticipate a 10 per cent inflation rate. In return for the use of $1,000 for one year, the borrower agrees to pay an interest rate of 15 per cent, 5 per cent real interest plus a 10 per cent inflation premium. If inflation turns out to be exactly 10 per cent, at the end of the year the $1,150 proceeds from the loan will maintain the real purchasing power of the $1,000 principal and provide a $50 interest payment. If the actual inflation rate diverges from 10 per cent, however, the borrower must still return $1,150 to the lender at the end of the year. If the inflation rate turns out to be 20 per cent, the $1,150 repayment will not permit the lender to purchase $1,000 worth of real goods at 20 per cent inflated price tags. Given *unexpected inflation*, the *borrower* clearly wins: he or she was able to purchase $1,000 worth or real goods on the day the loan was made but would return less than $1,000 worth of real purchasing power to the lender at the end of the year. On the other hand, if actual inflation turns out to be *less* than anticipated, the *lender* would be the winner. For example, if inflation unexpectedly fell to zero, the borrower would still have to repay $1,150 to the lender, which would represent $1,150 worth of real purchasing power since prices have not risen.

To summarize, all financial assets such as bonds, mortgages, and savings accounts will bear an interest rate that offsets the effects of *anticipated* inflation. To the extent that inflation is correctly anticipated, the inflation premium contained in interest rates preserves the real value of financial assets. For example, as long as inflation is correctly anticipated, the interest earned on pension funds will preserve the real value of the principal invested and preserve the real value of the pension. However, *in*correctly anticipated inflation will generate a redistribution of purchasing power between borrowers and lenders. If *actual* inflation exceeds **expected inflation**, real purchasing power will be transferred from the lender to the borrower. Homeowners who negotiated 25-year mortgages fixed at 6 per cent during the tranquil 1960s (when inflation was expected to be 2 per cent) were the big winners from the unexpected inflation of the 1970s. The market value of houses and income levels of homeowners rose dramatically during the 1970s, whereas the 6 per cent interest payments on the 25-year mortgage never changed. In fact the interest payment did not even cover the annual inflation rate during the 1970s; that is, the real rate of interest was actually negative. On the other hand, individuals who had their savings tied up in long-term 5 per cent bonds suffered large financial losses from the unexpected inflation of the 1970s.[6] Unexpected

[6]See Chapter 18 for a discussion of the effects of changing interest rates on the market value of bonds.

inflation redistributes purchasing power from the lender to the borrower. Since the borrower's gain must be the lender's loss, the effects of unanticipated inflation are strictly distributional. There is *no aggregate loss* from unexpected inflation, only a redistribution of purchasing power between lenders and borrowers.

This is not to say that unanticipated inflation has no cost. On the contrary, the massive and arbitrary shifts in real income and wealth that result from unanticipated inflation tend to turn the economic system into a giant lottery in which economic gains are unrelated to effort, planning and foresight. Economic instability of this kind is not compatible with social harmony and the resulting feelings of resentment and sense of injustice are very divisive forces.

Other Aspects of Inflation

Besides the fortuitous and arbitrary redistributional aspects of unexpected inflation, economists have identified three other potential economic costs arising from inflation.

The "Shoe-Leather" Cost of Inflation

There is one component of wealth which is completely at the mercy of inflation. Money pays a zero interest rate and therefore cannot be protected against inflation by an interest rate inflation premium. In an economic sense, inflation is like a *tax* on holding money. To the extent that an individual holds wealth in the form of money, inflation will erode the real purchasing power of his or her money holdings.

As discussed in Chapter 5, individuals typically choose to hold part of their wealth in the form of money to facilitate day-to-day transactions. Rather than walking to the bank to withdraw funds from an interest-earning savings account every time a purchase is made, individuals find it more convenient to forgo the interest payments and hold cash balances. The time, trouble and "shoe-leather" associated with frequent trips to the bank outweigh the interest that could have been earned if one's cash balances were always invested.

Inflation will tip the balance towards more frequent trips to the bank. The higher the inflation rate, the larger the inflation premium in interest rates and the greater the opportunity cost of holding cash balances. Consequently, individuals will likely attempt to economize on their holdings of money as inflation rates rise, and they will make more frequent trips to the bank to withdraw smaller and smaller amounts of money. Idle cash will be kept in interest-earning accounts for as many days of the year as possible. Thus inflation diverts scarce resources to the task of cash management. Individuals will sacrifice time, energy and "shoe-leather" in an attempt to lessen the costs of holding money. Firms will hire more employees to work in the controller's office to manage and invest short-term funds. As such, inflation imposes an economic cost on society. Without inflation, some resources could be allocated to other, more socially productive uses.

While the above *theoretical* argument is undoubtedly correct, the *empirical* consequences of this inflation tax on the holdings of money are probably very slight.[7] As Robert Solow of M.I.T. concluded, "A perfectly anticipated pure inflation imposes a small deadweight loss on society, mostly through a waste of effort directed toward economizing on the holding of money. . . . Not good, one is tempted to say, but no worse than a bad cold."[8]

The "Menu" Costs of Inflation

Economists have identified another "small deadweight loss" imposed by inflation. The higher the inflation rate, the more frequently prices within the economic system must be altered. In an inflationary world, scarce resources must be diverted to the following types of activity: revising price tags, reprinting catalogues and restaurant menus, adjusting parking meters and vending machines, and devising smaller and smaller chocolate bars to fit into a 25 cent package. Inflation accelerates such "menu" price changes, and without inflation, some resources would be freed up for other more productive uses. However, one would not want to lose much sleep worrying about the extra output which might have been produced if workers did not have to spend some of their time revising price tags and reprinting menus.

Inflation-Induced Tax Distortions

Since virtually all taxes are based on nominal values, as inflation increases, the government will automatically collect more tax revenues. The key question is whether the percentage increase in nominal tax revenues *exceeds*, or just *equals*, the percentage increase in nominal incomes which is induced by inflation. Alternatively, does inflation cause the tax *rate* to rise? If tax revenues increase at *exactly* the same rate as inflation, the *average* tax rate will *not* change. For example, if a 50 per cent inflation increases an individual's income from $10,000 to $15,000 and income tax payments rise from $2,000 to $3,000 (exactly 50 per cent), then the individual's average income tax rate remains at 20 per cent. Since there has been no change in the rate of income tax or in the real after-tax income, there should be no change in economic behaviour. In this particular example, inflation interacting with the tax system has *not* changed real after-tax income levels or distorted economic decisions such as how many hours of labour an individual chooses to supply.

Suppose, however, that the inflation-induced percentage change in tax revenues *exceeds* the inflation-induced percentage change in nominal income. In terms of our previous example, suppose that tax payments rise by 100 per cent (to $4,000) when income inflation is only 50 per cent. In this case, the average tax rate will jump from 20 to 26.7 per cent ($4,000 ÷ $15,000), and the individual's real after-tax income will decline from $8,000 to $7,333 (an after-tax nominal income of $11,000 divided by an average price level of 1.5). Given an inflation-

---

[7]For example, in 1984 the total amount of money (M1) per capita was approximately $1,150. Even if the 1984 inflation rate 4.4 per cent increased to 10 per cent and interest rates rose by 5.6 per cent, there is only $64 extra forgone interest at stake for each person, or a little more than $1 per week.

[8]R.M. Solow, "The Intelligent Citizen's Guide to Inflation," *The Public Interest*, Winter 1975, p. 44.

induced higher tax rate and a lower after-tax real wage, an individual may decide to supply *fewer* hours of work (assuming a positively sloped labour supply curve).[9] Inflation interacting with the tax system has changed *real after-tax* wages, altering or distorting economic decisions concerning the allocation of resources.

Case Study 1: The Canadian Income Tax System and Inflation Distortions

Does inflation lead to a change in the average (and marginal) Canadian income tax rate? If inflation increases the *rate* of income tax, inflation will distort economic decisions throughout the economy, which will lead to a potentially serious misallocation of resources (a very *real* cost of inflation). In this case study we examine the effects of inflation on income tax rates for three different kinds of income: labour income, interest income, and capital gains. As we shall see, inflation can induce serious **tax distortion effects** in a progressive income tax system which has not been properly indexed for inflation.

Labour Income

Under a *progressive* income tax system, average and marginal tax rates *increase* as the level of income rises. Even though one's real income might not be changing, inflation increases nominal income levels, which leads to higher rates of taxation as individuals are pushed into higher and higher tax brackets. *Under a progressive income tax system that is not indexed for inflation, inflation will automatically lead to higher rates of taxation, lower real after-tax income levels, and distortions in labour supply decisions.*

To understand the distortionary effects of a progressive income tax system that is *not* indexed for inflation, consider the *average* Canadian employee in 1973 earning $11,167 per year in personal income. As is obvious from Table 3-1, the Canadian income tax system is *highly progressive*, with 1973 *marginal* tax rates ranging from 19.6 per cent (for taxable income less than $500) to 61.3 per cent (for taxable incomes in excess of $60,000). Assuming the standard set of income tax deductions for a spouse and two children, our average income-earner for 1973 would have had $7,317 in *taxable* income and would have paid $1,976 in total income taxes.[10] In 1973 our average income-earner pays an average income tax rate of 17.7 per cent (1,976 ÷ 11,167), but pays a 32.6 per cent tax rate on each *marginal* dollar of income (the seventh row or bracket in Table 3-1).

For illustrative purposes, let us assume that our average income-earner in 1973 receives income increases *exactly equal* to the inflation rate over the next eleven years. From 1973 to 1984 the consumer price index rose by 157 per cent, and thus our hypothetical average 1973 income-earner would be paid $28,699 in 1984

---

[9]For further discussion of the positively sloped labour supply curve, see Chapter 8.

[10]From the upper panel of Table 3-1: $1,873 on the first $7,000 of taxable income and $103 on the next $317 of taxable income (.326 × $317 = $103).

TABLE 3-1 Income Tax Schedule

Taxable Income	In 1973		
$ 500 or less		19.6% on first $	500
500	$	98 + 23.5 on next	500
1,000		215 + 24.8 on next	1,000
2,000		463 + 26.1 on next	1,000
3,000		724 + 27.4 on next	2,000
5,000		1,272 + 30.0 on next	2,000
7,000		1,873 + 32.6 on next	2,000
9,000		2,525 + 35.2 on next	2,000
11,000		3,230 + 40.5 on next	3,000
14,000		4,444 + 45.7 on next	10,000
24,000		9,011 + 50.9 on next	15,000
39,000		16,645 + 56.1 on next	21,000
60,000		28,429 + 61.3 on remainder	
	In 1984 after Indexation		
$ 1,238 or less		8.9% on first $	1,238
1,238		110 + 23.7 on next	1,238
2,476		403 + 25.2 on next	2,476
4,952		1,026 + 26.6 on next	2,476
7,428		1,686 + 28.1 on next	4,952
12,380		3,081 + 29.6 on next	4,952
17,332		4,544 + 34.0 on next	4,952
22,284		6,229 + 37.0 on next	12,380
34,664		10,810 + 44.4 on next	24,760
59,424		21,803 + 50.3 on remainder	

($11,167 multiplied by 2.57).[11] Assuming that the 1973 tax schedule has not been altered to correct for this 157 per cent inflation, our hypothetical individual would have to pay $9,443 in income taxes in 1984 (as computed from the eleventh row of the upper part of Table 3-1, for a 1984 *taxable* income of $24,849). Eleven years of double-digit inflation (totalling 157 per cent) would have pushed our average income-earner up four tax brackets to a marginal income tax rate of 50.9 per cent and an average income tax rate of 32.9 per cent (9,443 ÷ 28,699). *Even though our hypothetical individual has exactly the same gross real income in 1984 as in 1973, his or her after-tax real income has declined by 18.5 per cent.*[12] Without a change in statutory tax rates or a new income tax bill passed in Parliament, the 157 per cent inflation from 1973 to 1984 would have almost *doubled* the average income tax rate (from 17.7 per cent to 32.9 per cent) and would have resulted in marginal tax rates in excess of 50 per cent for the vast majority of Canadians. The *progressivity* of the income tax system automatically raises tax rates as inflation increases nominal income levels and pushes taxpayers into higher and higher tax brackets. Such inflation-induced increases in income tax rates (and corresponding

[11]Since we have given our hypothetical 1973 average income-earner wage increases only equal to the inflation rate (to hold his or her real income constant), the absence of any wage increases to reflect productivity growth will mean that our hypothetical 1973 average income-earner is considerably below average in 1984. (In fact, the average level of personal income per employee in 1984 is $32,795.)

[12]In 1973 dollars, a *net after-tax* 1984 income level of $19,256 ($28,699 − $9,443) is worth only $7,493 ($19,256 ÷ 2.57), compared with the original 1973 after-tax income level of $9,191.

reductions in after-tax real wage rates) would have had profound effects on labour market decisions, not to mention the size of the government sector.

Fortunately for our average 1973 income-earner, in 1974 the Canadian government *indexed* the personal income tax system to the inflation rate to prevent such inflation-induced increases in income tax rates. Since indexing the tax system is a fundamental fiscal reform that prevents the government from being a major beneficiary of inflation,.it is appropriate to let John Turner, then Minister of Finance, explain the rationale of the 1974 **inflation indexation** of the Canadian tax system:

> Mr. Speaker, I come now to an income tax measure of fundamental importance. I am deeply concerned about inflation and the effect that inflation has on a tax system which is based on a progressive rate schedule. I therefore propose to take steps now to provide a lasting solution to this problem should inflation continue.
>
> First let me explain more clearly how the problem arises....an increase in a person's income may be real or simply the result of inflation. Put another way, if a man gets a 5 per cent raise in salary, but the cost of living has also increased 5 per cent, he has the same real purchasing power he had before, and nothing more. Yet, the progressive tax system can leave him worse off than he was before because he has entered a higher tax bracket. What I want to do is eliminate that unfair and unintended result from our tax system.
>
> Beginning in 1974, I propose to introduce the following system. First, in each year an inflation factor would be determined based upon the increase in the Consumer Price Index in an immediately preceding period. Second, in each year the principal exemptions would be increased by this inflation factor.... Third, every year each of the brackets of taxable income would be adjusted upwards by the inflation factor.
>
> The indexing of rates and exemptions will produce a tax liability which will no longer erode a person's purchasing power as a result of inflation interacting with the progressive tax system. A person will no longer pay tax at a higher marginal rate simply because inflation swept him up into a higher tax bracket.... With the introduction of this change, Canada will join a very select group of countries which have eliminated the hidden revenues accruing to governments through the effect of inflation on a progressive tax system.[13]

In the lower panel of Table 3-1 the new indexed 1984 income tax schedule for an Ontario resident is given. As is obvious, the income brackets have dramatically changed. A marginal income tax rate of 30 per cent does not start until $12,380 of 1984 taxable income, compared with $5,000 of 1973 taxable income. Furthermore, the value of all exemptions were also indexed to the inflation rate (for example, the standard package of exemptions for a family of four increased to $9,350 in 1984 from $3,850 in 1973).

[13]*Hansard*, 19 February 1973, pp. 1434-35.

Now let us return to our example of the 1973 average income-earner with income increases exactly equal to the inflation rate. In 1984 a taxable income of $19,349 (that is, $28,699 less the standard package of exemptions equal to $9,350 in 1984) falls in the seventh tax bracket, with a marginal tax rate of 34 per cent, not much different from the 33 per cent marginal tax rate that our average income-earner faced in 1973. Since a special federal tax reduction existed in the early 1980s, we have simply looked up the total tax payable based on $19,349 taxable income in the *1984 General Tax Guide* (page 53) to determine that our hypothetical income-earner would have to pay $5,108 in total income taxes in 1984.[14] Thus the average rate of tax for our hypothetical 1973 income-earner in 1984 is 17.8 per cent, ($5,108 ÷ $28,699 earned income) virtually identical to the 17.7 per cent rate in 1973.

Even though there were a number of amendments to the Income Tax Act during the years 1974 through 1984 (for example, the marginal tax rates for the two highest income brackets were lowered, reducing the number of tax brackets from 12 to 10), *inflation indexation* of the income tax system eliminated the "unfair" and "hidden" income tax rate increases that would have occurred because of the interaction of inflation with a progressive income tax system. With the 1974 indexation of the income tax system, the average and marginal rates of income tax for a given level of real labour income remained virtually constant over the 1974-84 period. Without this inflation indexation of the income tax system, wage earners would have faced much higher average and marginal tax rates, which would have caused serious distortions within the labour market (perhaps forcing more individuals into the underground economy).

In May 1985, the newly elected Conservative government *modified* the inflation indexation of the income tax system. In an attempt to generate more tax revenues to reduce the size of the federal deficit, the government limited tax indexation to annual inflation in excess of 3 per cent: tax brackets and personal exemptions will not be adjusted for the *initial* 3 per cent inflation in each year. While wage earners are protected against "hidden" and "unfair" tax increases arising from annual inflation in excess of 3 per cent (assuming that the government does not again modify the inflation indexation factor in subsequent years), each year the government will be the beneficiary of a small "hidden" tax increase as the initial 3 per cent inflation slowly (but surely) pushes taxpayers into higher tax brackets.

Interest Income

While labour income is at least partially protected against inflation under the Canadian income tax system, *interest income* is *not* protected against inflation. As discussed earlier in this chapter, the nominal market rate of interest (R) will include an inflation premium $(\dot{P}^e)$ equal to the *expected* inflation rate. The real

---

[14]Computing 1984 income tax payable from the seventh row of the lower panel of Table 3-1 results in a calculation of $5,230, or $122 higher than the actual 1984 income tax payable after allowing for the federal tax reduction. The actual income tax payable on $19,349 taxable income is taken from the tax table in the *1984 General Tax Guide*.

rate of interest (RR) is obtained by subtracting the expected inflation rate from the nominal interest rate.

(3-1a) $RR = R - \dot{P}^e$

In a world of zero inflation, the real and nominal interest rates would be identical (as they were for the most part throughout the first half of this century). Inflation drives a wedge between the nominal interest rate and the real interest rate.

Given the presence of inflation, a *properly* indexed tax system would treat only real interest payments as taxable income. Unfortunately our current "indexed" tax system includes nominal interest payments in taxable income. As a result, the government taxes the inflation premium contained in nominal interest rates: an approach that can produce *negative* after-tax real returns.

To examine this inflation-induced tax problem, assume that an individual faces a marginal tax rate of t and receives nominal interest income equal to R (which includes an inflation premium of $\dot{P}^e$ to offset expected inflation). After paying income tax, our hypothetical individual will be left with $(1 - t) \times R$. However, to determine the *real after-tax rate of return*, one must subtract the expected inflation rate to allow for the loss in purchasing power (of the principal) associated with inflation:

$$\begin{aligned}
\text{Real after-tax rate of return} &= (1 - t)\,R - \dot{P}^e \\
&= (1 - t)\,(RR + \dot{P}^e) - \dot{P}^e \\
&= (1 - t)\,RR - t\dot{P}^e
\end{aligned}$$

For many (very realistic) values of t, RR and $\dot{P}^e$, this real after-tax rate of return will be *negative*.

To illustrate, let us assume that the marginal tax rate is 40 per cent and the real rate of interest is 4 per cent. Under such circumstances, the above formula suggests that the real after-tax rate of return will be negative for all (expected) inflation rates greater than 6 per cent (which was the case for every year from 1973 through 1982). Suppose the expected inflation rate was 10 per cent. Then the nominal interest rate (R) would be 14 per cent (the real rate of interest RR is assumed to be 4 per cent) and income tax payments account for 5.6 percentage points of the 14 per cent nominal interest rate. After income tax is paid, the net rate of return of 8.4 per cent is less than the 10 per cent inflation rate. Allowing for inflation and income taxes, there is a negative rate of return of 1.6 per cent. In contrast, the after-tax rate of return would be +2.4 per cent in a *zero* inflation world. *Inflation interacting with the income tax system has converted a net positive return into a net negative return.*

This incorrect tax treatment of interest income in an inflationary world causes a number of very serious distortions in financial markets and also creates resource misallocation problems. Since lenders will be reluctant to lend funds at negative real interest rates, they will demand much higher interest rates in order to pay the income tax on the inflation premium contained in nominal interest rates. To illustrate, suppose a lender demanded a 2.4 per cent after-tax real rate of return. Given a 10 per cent expected inflation rate and a 40 per cent marginal tax rate, our lender has to charge a nominal interest rate of *20.67 per cent* to *net a 2.4 per cent real after-tax rate of return* (the lender will get to keep 60 per cent of this 20.67

per cent nominal return after paying income tax, which is 12.4 per cent, and then must deduct 10 per cent for expected inflation).[15] The incorrect tax treatment of interest income substantially raises nominal interest rates, from 14 per cent to over 20 per cent. Besides raising interest rates, the incorrect tax treatment of interest income probably drives many lenders into the underground economy, where they then privately lend funds without declaring any taxable income (thus depriving the government of any interest-related income tax revenues.)

Correcting the income tax system to eliminate these inflation-induced tax distortion effects in financial markets is not nearly as straightforward as indexing the income tax system for the effects of inflation on labour income. Even though the appropriate taxable income concept is *real* interest income, individuals do not have financial records detailing the amount of real interest income received (as opposed to nominal interest received). The financial system would have to provide the taxpayer with two sets of computer records, detailing *both* nominal interest payment and real interest payments (which would be based on nominal interest rates less a suitable inflation adjustment). With the emergence of daily interest accounts, it would be most difficult for an individual with a fluctuating bank account to determine the exact inflation premium to deduct from nominal interest payments; that is, to claim only real interest payments for tax purposes. The Canadian income tax system partially gets around this inflation problem by exempting the first $1,000 of interest income from taxable income. Nevertheless, there are serious inflation-induced tax distortion effects associated with interest income, which cause higher interest rates and a misallocation of funds in financial markets.

Capital Gains

Before 1985, the Canadian income tax system required that one-half of any capital gain on the sale of financial securities and/or personal property (excluding one's principal residence) be included as taxable income. Unfortunately, the Canadian tax system did *not* distinguish between *real* and *nominal* capital gains. To the extent that capital gains simply represented the effects of inflation, investors would again be faced with *negative* after-tax real returns.

To illustrate this inflation-induced tax problem, let us assume that your father established a $1,000 stock portfolio for you in 1973, which you ask him to sell in 1984 to pay for your university expenses. Suppose that the value of this stock portfolio increased by exactly the inflation rate over the 1973-84 period (157 per cent appreciation).[16] When your father sells this *inflated* $2,570 portfolio of stocks he will have to declare a capital gain of $1,570, of which one-half ($785) will be taxable. If his marginal tax rate is 50 per cent, he will have to pay the

---

[15]To compute the appropriate interest rate to charge in order that the extra income tax associated with the inflation premium may be covered, one has to add the following additional factor to the nominal interest rate: $\dot{P}^e t/(1 - t)$

[16]In fact if your father received a 157 per cent inflation appreciation of his stock portfolio over the 1973-84 period, he would have done considerably better than the average performance of the market. Over this 11-year period the Toronto Stock Exchange index rose by only 92.4 per cent.

government additional income taxes of $392.50. His net after-tax return is only $1,177.50 (not $1,570) and in real terms (measured in 1973 dollars) the after-tax value of this original $1,000 portfolio is only $847.28 ($2,177.50 ÷ 2.57).

Given that the capital gains tax applied to inflation gains as well as real gains, in an inflationary world the after-tax real rate of return on stocks or real estate could easily turn out to be negative. Investors fearing a negative after-tax real rate of return might have channelled their funds away from securities markets, perhaps towards private loans and mortgages in the underground economy. Again, inflation interacting with the income tax system distorted real rates of return and caused a misallocation of resources.

In their first budget, the Conservative government granted individual Canadians a *lifetime* capital gains exemption of $500,000 (to be phased in over the 1985-90 period). In granting this large exemption for capital gains tax, no mention was made of any inflation distortion (indeed the annual inflation rate was less than 4 per cent in May 1985, when the exemption was introduced). The government simply argued that this exemption "will encourage more Canadians to invest in small and large businesses."

Summary of the Costs and Consequences of Inflation

In conclusion, the economic arguments against inflation are not as strong as one might think. As discussed above, price inflation must be matched by nominal income inflation. Increases in product price revenues from inflation do not disappear from the economic system, but rather reappear on the income side of the national accounts ledger. Second, most forms of wealth increase in value as prices rise. Even nominal dollar financial assets are protected against *expected* inflation. The interest rate paid on loans, bonds, savings accounts and pension funds include an inflation premium to offset the effects of expected inflation. In short, aggregate real wages, real personal income levels and real wealth have not been eroded by inflation during the 1970s and early 1980s.

When inflation is correctly anticipated there are few redistributional effects of inflation. Most people, such as wage earners, simply build the expected inflation rate into their economic decisions. By and large, the economic system adapts to a *stable* inflation rate, be it 3 per cent or 10 per cent. If inflation is *unexpected*, however, there may be large shifts in income and wealth between different groups in society, such as debtors and creditors. Unexpected inflation is like a large economic roulette wheel, with each spin creating a new set of winners and losers in a completely fortuitous manner. Undoubtedly the roulette-wheel aspects of unexpected inflation have created economic hardships and social tension. Even though for every loser there must be a winner, most people would rather not gamble their wage settlement or pension fund on a spin of the unexpected-inflation roulette wheel. However, the villain is not inflation per se, but rather inflation uncertainty. Uncertainty of any kind, whether over next year's price level or this year's final exam grades, will cause social tension. Again, if the future inflation rate were perfectly predictable, the economic system would adapt to this expected inflation rate and very few negative effects would likely arise.

Since 1973 the progressive income tax system has been (partially) indexed for inflation to prevent the government from being the beneficiary of inflation-swollen income tax revenues (in 1985 the government limited the indexation factor to annual inflation in excess of 3 per cent). While the *inflation indexation* of the income tax system has protected labour income against inflation-induced higher tax rates (arising from bracket creep), interest income and capital gains are *not* indexed against inflation. As discussed in Case Study 1, the inappropriate tax treatment of interest income and capital gains in an inflationary world can lead to serious distortions in financial markets and resource misallocation problems. However, the real problem may be an inappropriate tax system, and not inflation.

While economists are hard-pressed to make a strong case against inflation (other than to fall back on inflation-uncertainty arguments, the costs of holding money and tax distortions), there is probably a very powerful optical illusion at work with respect to the perception of the inflation process. Most people view price and income inflation in two very different ways. When prices rise for gasoline, beer, rent and tuition, that's inflation! But when prices rise for the things that one sells, that's not really inflation. Wage increases are the well-deserved rewards for hard work. Similarly, debtors view high interest rates with alarm, but lenders regard high interest rates as the legitimate reward for thrift. In short, most individuals perceive only one-half of the inflation process and are "blind" to the other side of inflation. Wage-earners and pensioners bemoan the eroding effects of inflation, but fail to realize that without inflation their wages and pensions (largely based on accrued interest) would be only a fraction of the size of their existing nominal values.

The Unemployment Rate

As discussed in Chapter 1, unemployment dominated the Gallup poll as the most important problem facing Canadians during the early 1980s. In this section we turn to methodological problems in measuring the unemployment rate. For example, who should be counted as an unemployed person? A spouse casually looking for a "good" job? A worker out on strike? A farmer during the winter months? A university student during the summer months? After briefly reviewing the conceptual problems in measuring the Canadian unemployment rate, this chapter concludes with a case study in which we investigate the economic costs of unemployment.

Once a month Statistics Canada personnel interview over 50,000 randomly selected Canadian households to determine the labour force status of all members within the household. On the basis of this sample, an *estimate* for the Canadian unemployment rate is obtained. The **unemployment rate** UR is defined as the number of unemployed persons (U) divided by the total size of the **labour force** (LF), where the labour force consists of all employed (E) and unemployed (U) individuals. In addition to this widely cited monthly unemployment rate, the labour force survey also provides information pertaining to the **participation rate** (PR), the proportion of the adult population ($APOP$) that is in the labour force.

(3-2)
$$LF = E + U$$

(3-3)
$$UR = \frac{U}{LF}$$

(3-4)
$$PR = \frac{LF}{APOP}$$

The task of the Statistics Canada interviewer is to determine, through a series of questions, whether the respondent and other members of the household are in the adult population, and, if so, whether they are employed, unemployed, or neither employed nor unemployed. Statistics Canada defines each of these three key concepts in the following manner:

1) *Adult Population*. All persons in the population 15 years of age and over residing in Canada with the exception of the following: persons living on Indian reserves, inmates of institutions and full-time members of the armed forces.

2) *Employed*. All persons (a) who did any work at all or (b) who had a job but were not at work because of illness, personal responsibilities, bad weather, labour disputes, vacation, or other such reasons.

3) *Unemployed*. All persons (a) who were without work and had actively looked for work during the past four weeks and were available for work,[17] or (b) who had not actively looked for work in the past four weeks but had been on layoff for 26 weeks or less and were available for work.

These *methodological* definitions raise a number of important conceptual questions pertaining to the measurement of unemployment.

1) What does it mean to have "actively looked for work"? How "active" does a person have to be to qualify as an "unemployed" member of the labour force rather than as a person who is "not participating" in the labour force? For example, is a spouse who reads the newspaper want-ads in the hope of finding an interesting, well-paying job an "unemployed" individual within the labour force? According to Statistics Canada, our hypothetical spouse is officially classified as an unemployed person if he or she responds to questions 56 and 57 of the labour force survey in the following manner: Question 56: In the past six months have you looked for work?
   Answer: Yes.

   Question 57: In the past four weeks what have you done to find work?
   Answer: Looked at job ads.

2) What about unemployed individuals who gave up actively looking for work because they knew that no jobs were available? Statistics Canada classifies such **discouraged** workers as being outside of the labour force and therefore not part of the unemployed. Every six months, however, Statistics Canada conducts a *special* labour force survey of such discouraged workers. For example, in its March 1984 survey, Statistics Canada found that there were 457,000 Canadians who wanted to work and were available for work but, who did not look for work (and were therefore classified as *not in the labour*

---

[17]The "available for work" condition disqualifies full-time students from the labour force.

force). Of these 457,000 individuals, 154,000 did not look for a job because they believed that no work was available, and 149,000 did not look for a job because they were waiting for replies or for recall. If Statistics Canada counted these 303,000 individuals who were not looking for work (but were obviously available and willing to work) with the 1,399,000 officially unemployed, then the March 1984 unemployment rate would have been almost 14 per cent, not the 11.4 per cent reported rate.

3) Is all of the employed labour force being fully utilized? For example, many employed individuals may be working only part-time because they cannot find a full-time job. In addition, firms tend to **hoard** labour when the unemployment rate is high, and much of the *employed* work force is underutilized when the economy is in a recession. Estimates by two economists with the Economic Council of Canada suggest that the amount of underutilized or hoarded labour is almost as great as the amount of unemployment during a recession.[18]

Although the official unemployment rate understates the degree of unemployment within the economy, Statistics Canada's labour force survey nevertheless provides a *consistent* cyclical measure of the state of the labour market. Even if one does not totally agree with Statistics Canada's exact definitions for "employed" and "unemployed," statistical consistency is an important virtue. By measuring labour force status in the same manner each month, movements in the unemployment rate provides a reasonably good indicator of changes in the state of the labour market and cyclical position of the economy.

Case Study 2: The Cost of Unemployment for the Year 1982

For both the individual and society as a whole, the costs of unemployment are both immediate and obvious. Each unemployed individual suffers a direct loss in personal income. On an aggregate basis, total factor incomes are substantially below what they might have been, and the economy's total production of goods and services will fall below its potential level to the extent that unemployment exists. In addition to the obvious economic costs of unemployment, "there is a substantial body of evidence which suggests that severe psychological stress is experienced by a significant proportion" of unemployed individuals.[19]

In this case study, we examine the economic costs of unemployment by focusing on the year 1982. The economic performance of the Canadian economy in 1982 was the worst since the Great Depression. Real output declined by 4.4 per cent in 1982 and the unemployment jumped from 7.5 per cent in 1981 to 11.0 per cent in

---

[18]T. Sidedule and K. Newton, "Another Labour Market Indicator; Some Estimates and Implications of Labour Hoarding in Canada," *Canadian Public Policy/Analyse de Politiques*, Winter 1980, pp. 101-5.

[19]F. Reid, "Conceptual Issues in the Evaluation of Worksharing in Canada" (mimeograph, Centre For Industrial Relations, University of Toronto, revised February 1983). For example, Reid cities a U.S. study in which the author found that an increase of one percentage point in the unemployment rate (sustained for five years) is associated with a 4.1 per cent increase in suicides, a 3.4 per cent increase in mental hospital admissions, a 4.0 per cent increase in prison admissions, a 1.9 per cent increase in cirrhosis of the liver and a 1.9 percent increase in deaths from cardiovascular disease.

1982, the highest level since the 1930s. More than 1.3 million Canadians were unemployed in the year 1982.

Although it is difficult to assess individual income losses arising from unemployment, an *estimate* of society's loss from the existence of cyclical unemployment can be computed by subtracting *actual* 1982 output from *potential* 1982 output. In 1982 the **output gap**, as plotted in Chart 1-1 in Chapter 1, was 16.6 billion (constant) 1971 dollars or 45.5 billion 1982 dollars (after multiplying the real output gap by the 1982 price index). In other words, if the Canadian economy had been operating at its potential level, which is assumed to be 95 per cent utilization of all resources, then an *extra* $45.5 billion worth of goods and services would have been produced in 1982. The 11 per cent unemployment rate in 1982 translates into a *$45.5 billion loss* in terms of aggregate output.

Before examining the distributional aspects associated with this output loss, we want to emphasize the magnitude of this loss in output arising from an 11 per cent unemployment rate. To put this eleven-digit number in perspective, $45,500,000,000 would have purchased the following in 1982:

- 700,000 new $65,000 homes (more than enough to re-house the entire Maritime provinces), or
- 6 million new cars (one for every fourth Canadian), or
- 3 billion cases of beer (125 cases of beer per capita).

Alternatively, the $45.5 billion output gap in 1982 was equal to the combined personal incomes of all of the residents of Newfoundland, Nova Scotia, Prince Edward Island, New Brunswick, Manitoba and Saskatchewan. No matter how you represent it, the aggregate loss associated with cyclical unemployment in 1982 was substantial.

While society as a whole suffers a substantial output loss from the existence of unemployment, on an *individual basis*, who actually "lost" this output? Put in a slightly different way, who would have received the additional output arising from a lower unemployment rate? For example, would any of this lost output have ended up on my kitchen table? To answer this important distributional question, we examine how this $45.5 billion worth of forgone 1982 output might have been distributed in income terms had the unemployment rate been 5 per cent rather than 11 per cent. By identifying the would-be recipients of the income payments associated with the lost output, we describe the distributional losses associated with unemployment.

First and most obvious, there are the previously unemployed individuals who will now be working and earning an income. By lowering the 1982 unemployment rate from 11 per cent to 5 per cent, approximately 720,000 formerly unemployed individuals would have had a job.[20] How much of this output gap would have gone to *now employed but formerly unemployed* individuals in the form of wage payments? In general, one would expect that the "potential" wage of an unem-

[20]This calculation is based on a 1982 labour force size of 12 million. We ignore any discouraged worker effects arising from a higher unemployment rate, and assume that the size of the labour force is unaffected by the level of the unemployment rate.

ployed individual would be somewhat less than the wage of the average worker (the unemployed may lack job specific skills and work experience). Given a 1982 average annual wage of $19,700, we arbitrarily assume that the unemployed might have earned $300 per week, or $15,600 per year. Collectively, the unemployed would have received $11.2 billion ($15,600 × 720,000) in wage income for the year 1982 if they were working.[21] Only about one quarter of the income associated with closing the output gap would have gone into the pockets of the unemployed workers who found a job.[22]

Who would have received the remaining three quarters of the income associated with closing the output gap? Perhaps surprisingly, most of this extra income would have gone to the factors of production that were already employed when the unemployment rate was 11 per cent. The two major recipients of this lost income would have been the *shareholders* of firms (through corporate profits) and the *existing work force*.

To understand where most of the lost income associated with unemployment occurs, we take a brief digression into the realm of managerial economics. For an individual firm, what are the implications of a decline in demand when the economy is in the midst of a recession? First, the firm must still recover its fixed costs such as property taxes, heating costs, and the president's salary, but out of a smaller total sales volume. Second, most firms will resist laying off experienced workers when sales decline. Not only are layoffs bad for morale, the firm runs the risk that its experienced workers will find jobs elsewhere. Since the firm has made a substantial investment in recruiting and training its work force, most firms try to hold on to or *hoard* their work force when sales decline. If possible, the firm may attempt to reduce the number of hours worked per week, rather than laying off part of its work force. But in many instances, the firm's work force is maintained (and paid) even though production is lower than it would have been if the economy were not in a recession.

As a result, changes in aggregate demand will have a dramatic effect on profit levels.[23] When unemployment rates are high and aggregate demand is low, fixed expenses and labour hoarding will substantially depress profit levels. Conversely, when the unemployment rate declines and aggregate demand increases, profit

---

[21]To the extent that the unemployed receive unemployment insurance (UI) or welfare payments, their *net* gain from being employed would be much lower. For example, if these 720,000 unemployed individuals had received 44 weeks of UI benefits (at two-thirds of our assumed $300 weekly salary), total UI payments would have been $6.3 billion. On a net basis the 720,000 formerly unemployed individuals would have been only $4.9 billion better off.

[22]Even if the unemployed earned the average annual wage in 1982, the total wagebill for the formerly unemployed of $14.2 billion (720,000 × $19,700) would still represent only 31 per cent of the output gap. Since this is a surprisingly low estimate, we performed the same set of calculations for the year 1971, when the unemployment rate was only 6.2 per cent, and found that the cyclically unemployed (had they been working at the average wage rate) would also have received only 31 per cent of the output gap.

[23]During the period from 1960 through 1984, corporate profits as a share of GNP ranged from a low of 5.9 per cent (in 1982) to a high of 13.6 per cent (in 1974). On a year-to-year basis, the percentage change in corporate profits ranged from +43 per cent to −36 per cent. Corporate profit movements are clearly much more volatile than changes in nominal GNP (which ranged from 4 to 19 per cent per year).

levels will increase at a very rapid pace, since overhead expenses would already be covered and the productivity of hoarded labour would increase. Thus, a reduction in the unemployment rate from 11 to 5 per cent would substantially increase corporate profits and greatly benefit the shareholders of corporations.

How much of this $45.5 billion output gap would have gone into corporate profits? To obtain a rough answer to this hypothetical question, suppose that when output levels are at their potential level, corporate profits are 10.5 per cent of total output. (This was the average share of corporate profits in GNP during the period 1960-84). In contrast, the depressed 1982 corporate profit share of GNP was only 5.9 per cent ($21.1 billion corporate profits divided by actual GNP of $357 billion). Thus, if a 10.5 per cent profit rate had been earned on a 1982 *potential* output level of $402 billion, corporate profits *would have been* $42.2 billion (0.105 × 402). Closing the $45.5 billion output gap in 1982 would have generated an additional $21 billion in corporate profits ($42.2 − $21.1).

If our "back of the envelope" calculations are reasonably accurate, we have yet to account for a large portion of the output gap. Persons now employed but formerly unemployed would earn about $11.2 billion in wages, and corporate profits would rise by perhaps $21 billion when the unemployment rate declines from 11 per cent to 5 per cent. Where is the remaining $13 billion of the $45.5 billion output gap going? Since very little of this additional income would likely end up as interest or rent payments (or in capital consumption allowances), most of the remaining income associated with closing the output gap would have ended up either in indirect (sales) taxes or in the pockets of those who were already employed in 1982. Recall from Chapter 2 that part of GNP is accounted for by indirect taxes (11.5 per cent in 1982). Applying this average 1982 indirect tax rate to the $45.5 billion of additional output, we estimate that the government's share from indirect taxation would have been $5.2 billion.[24] This leaves $8 billion to be shared by currently employed workers.

There are at least three different ways that the already employed work force might have had their 1982 labour income enlarged if the unemployment rate had been lowered to 5 per cent. First, more supervisors and managers are required to supervise the larger work force associated with a lower unemployment rate. Since it is unlikely that a firm would hire an unemployed person to be supervisor or manager, existing employees will reap the benefits of promotions and job reclassifications which accompany larger work forces. Second and more important, as discussed above, firms will also attempt to vary the number of hours worked per week as demand changes. As demand increases and unemployment declines, the existing work force will likely work more hours per week,[25] and many of these extra hours will command an overtime premium rate of pay. In addition to more paid hours of work, an increase in demand accompanying a reduction in the unemployment rate will also increase the productivity of hoarded workers. As a result, some firms will likely reward their employees with bonuses, incentive payments and additional wage adjustments.

---

[24]Of course the government would also find direct income tax revenues rising, but these revenues are not a component of GNP (see below).

In summary, the income associated with lowering the unemployment rate and closing the output gap will be widely dispersed throughout the entire economic system. The lion's share of the additional income would likely be distributed to corporate shareholders and to the existing work force in the form of more paid hours of work, overtime premium pay, promotions and bonuses. A smaller share (approximately one quarter) of this total additional income accrues to the formerly unemployed individuals who found jobs. Most of the additional output is produced by the factors of production which are already employed, but which are underutilized when the unemployment rate is high.

There is, of course, one other big winner in the distribution of the output gap— the government. Much of the additional income associated with closing the output gap would have flowed into government coffers in the form of income taxes. Since the extra income associated with closing the output gap is *at the margin*, the government's tax bite of this additional income is likely to be very substantial. Even if the government applied only its average 1982 tax rate (excluding indirect taxes) of approximately 28 per cent to the $40.3 billion additional income (net of indirect taxes), it would still have appropriated almost $11.3 billion of the output gap in the form of additional tax revenues (in addition to the $5.2 billion of indirect taxes). Considering that the government would have saved several billion dollars in the form of reduced unemployment insurance payments accompanying a lower unemployment rate, the government might well have ended up with an additional $19-20 billion in 1982. This would have been more than enough to pay off the total government deficit of $18 billion.

Although the income associated with the output gap would have been widely dispersed throughout the economic system, the *relative* costs of unemployment obviously fall most heavily on the unemployed. The unemployed lose their *entire* income, which might be partially offset by unemployment insurance, whereas the existing work force loses a relatively small, *marginal* proportion of their income. Not only is the relative cost of unemployment highest for the unemployed, the incidence of unemployment is neither randomly nor evenly shared. As shown in Table 3-2, the odds of being unemployed dramatically increase if you are either young or living in the Maritimes, Quebec or British Columbia. For a young person living in Newfoundland, the unemployment rate in 1982 was almost 30 per cent!

Following an analysis of the *burden* of Canadian unemployment in the years 1980 and 1982, R.P. Shaw offers the following seven labour market generalizations:[26]

[25]To illustrate the negative relationship between hours worked per week and the unemployment rate, in 1982 the unemployment rate was 11 per cent and the average number of hours worked per week in the manufacturing sector was 37.5 hours. In contrast, when the unemployment rate was much lower in 1980 and 1981 (7.5 per cent in both years), average hours worked per week were higher, 38.3 in both years. If the unemployment rate in 1982 were reduced to 5 per cent and all individuals worked 2 per cent *more* hours (that is, 38.3 rather than 37.5), total aggregate labour income would have increased by $4.2 billion (.02 × $19,700 × 10.6 million employees). In other words, approximately $4 billion of the *lost* output would have gone to workers who already had jobs in 1982, but who would have worked longer hours if the unemployment rate had been 5 per cent rather than 11 per cent.

[26]R. Paul Shaw, "The Burden of Unemployment in Canada," *Canadian Public Policy/Analyse de Politiques*, June 1985, pp. 143-60.

TABLE 3-2 1982 Unemployment Rates by Province and Age

	All ages	Ages 15-24	Ages 25 and over
Newfoundland	16.9%	28.5%	12.5%
Prince Edward Island	13.1	n.a.	10.0
Nova Scotia	13.2	23.0	9.7
New Brunswick	14.2	23.3	10.9
Quebec	13.8	23.2	10.9
Ontario	9.8	17.1	7.4
Manitoba	8.5	14.0	6.5
Saskatchewan	6.2	11.4	4.3
Alberta	7.5	12.6	5.6
British Columbia	12.1	21.2	9.2
Canada	11.0	18.8	8.4

Source: Statistics Canada, *The Labour Force Survey*, December 1982.

1) Workers in primary industries such as fishing, logging and construction experience more frequent spells (and longer durations) of unemployment than workers with managerial, professional, clerical, sales, or product-fabrications jobs.

2) Workers in the Atlantic provinces and Quebec experience the highest incidence of unemployment (and long-term unemployment).

3) Those susceptible to long-term unemployment usually possess skills that earn lower wage rates. Thus during a recession, unemployment is likely to exacerbate financial hardship among chronically unemployed individuals at the lower end of the income distribution.

4) Unemployment is particularly high among poorly educated youth.

5) Unemployed women who have dependent children suffer the greatest financial burden of unemployment.

6) The burden of unemployment is not distributed equally among ethnic groups.

7) Even though older workers have relatively low unemployment rates, when they lose their jobs they have much more difficulty finding another job and are more likely to leave the labour force in discouragement.

In conclusion, the relative costs of unemployment are disproportionately large for small, well-defined segments of the labour force. Most of the labour force never experiences unemployment, and only suffers small marginal income losses (in forgone overtime pay or bonuses) from higher unemployment rates. To put this key distributional aspect of unemployment into sharper perspective, consider a purely random unemployment-generating mechanism—an unemployment lottery. Suppose that once a month the government conducts a random draw of social insurance numbers to determine who will be the unemployed for the month. If the unemployment rate were 8.0 per cent, then approximately 1,000,000 Canadians would have their social insurance number selected each month. Each would receive the following prize: a month off from work without pay. On average, each member of the labour force would be selected once a year and thus experience one month of unemployment in each year. Unemployment would be equally shared by all. Obviously the real world is very different from this hypothetical unemployment lottery. Many workers never have their numbers drawn, while other individuals continually have their numbers pulled out. Even though the gains from closing the output gap are widely dispersed throughout the economic system, the relative costs of unemployment are disproportionately large for small, well-defined groups of Canadian citizens.

Key Concepts

Consumer Price Index
expected versus unexpected inflation
inflation premium in interest rates
indexation of the income tax system
inflation tax distortions on interest income and capital gains
labour force
unemployment rate
participation rate
discouraged workers versus hoarded workers
lost output from unemployment (the output gap)

Review Questions

1. What are the advantages and disadvantages of a *fixed* weight price index when individual prices change at different rates?
2. Explain why *price* inflation must be matched by *nominal* income inflation?
3. Explain why interest rates will incorporate a premium for the *expected inflation rate*?
4. Explain why foreign exchange rates will reflect differences in domestic versus foreign inflation rates?
5. Describe the debtor-creditor distributional effects arising from an *unexpected* inflation. Explain why there is a transfer of purchasing power from the borrower to the lender when the inflation rate turns out to be *lower* than expected.
6. What is meant by the "shoe-leather" and "menu" costs of inflation?
7. Carefully explain how the 1974 *indexation* of the Canadian income tax system protected labour income but not interest income from excessive taxation during inflationary periods.
8. Do you think that a steady 10 per cent inflation rate imposes serious economic hardships on society? Why?
9. Why does the unemployment rate likely *underestimate* the degree of unemployed and underutilized labour?
10. Why do corporate profits fluctuate cyclically to a greater degree than the unemployment rate?
11. How would you go about measuring the economic costs of unemployment?
12. Who bears the economic costs of unemployment? Discuss.

Introduction to Keynesian Economics and Macroeconomic Models

*To understand **my** state of mind, however, you have to know that I believe myself to be writing a book on economic theory which will largely revolutionise not, I suppose, at once but in the course of the next ten years—the way the world thinks about economic problems. When my new theory has been duly assimilated and mixed with politics and feelings and passions, I can't predict what the final upshot will be in its effect on action and affairs. But there will be a great change and, in particular, the Ricardian foundations of Marxism will be knocked away.*

I can't expect you, or anyone else, to believe this at the present stage. But for myself I don't merely hope what I say—in my own mind I'm quite sure.

John Maynard Keynes[1]

The origin of macroeconomics, as a separate field of study within the discipline of economics, dates back to 1936 and the publication of a book entitled *The General Theory of Employment, Interest and Money* by the British economist John Maynard Keynes (pronounced to rhyme with "brains"). In this "revolutionary" book, Keynes presented a set of theories which simultaneously explained (1) why an economy might sink into a serious recession or depression with persistent unemployment and (2) how the government could alleviate such depressed economic conditions. Keynes' penetrating new analysis of the problem of persistent unemployment, such as existed during the 1930s, provided both a *diagnosis* of the causes of the problem as well as a policy *prescription* for this recurring economic disease. Chapters 4, 5, and 6 of this textbook are devoted to an analysis of the basic ideas and theories of John Maynard Keynes, the father of modern day macroeconomics. For expositional purposes, we have organized our analysis of Keynesian economics into two *interrelated* parts: (1) the Keynesian diagnosis and (2) the Keynesian prescription. As good economic doctors we must first discover what is causing the disorder before we can prescribe appropriate economic medicine.

In this chapter we review the most elementary representation of Keynesian economics, (the *Keynesian cross*), the concept of a macroeconomic model,[2] the

---

[1]Keynes to George Bernard Shaw, 1 January 1935 in R.F. Harrod, *The Life of John Maynard Keynes* (London: Macmillan & Co., 1963), p. 462.

[2]We use the term *model* to describe a set of *interrelated* theories and assumptions pertaining to a particular economic phenomenon, such as chronic unemployment.

multiplier process, and the central message of the *General Theory*. The next two chapters incorporate additional theoretical components of the *General Theory* into this elementary Keynesian cross model. We pay particular attention to how the various individual components of Keynesian economics "fit together" and to the implications of the *set* of Keynesian theories when studied together. Subsequent chapters will incorporate additional theories and refinements into the basic Keynesian macroeconomic model to represent the development of macroeconomic thought from the 1950s to the 1980s. As we shall see, macroeconomics has come a long way since 1936. Before commencing our formal analysis of macroeconomics, several observations will help to place Keynesian economics into historical perspective.

Pre-Keynesian Economic Thought

Economics did not, of course, commence in 1936 with Keynes' publication of the *General Theory*. Most economists would at least date the start of their profession back to 1776 and the publication of another book, *The Wealth of Nations* by Adam Smith. Up until Keynes, however, most economists were preoccupied with what we now call *microeconomics*, the study of individual economic agents and the laws of supply and demand. Pre-Keynesian economics was largely devoted to an explanation of how changes in relative prices within a competitive market system will allocate resources between competing uses. If, for example, widgets are in short supply, then the excess demand for widgets would force up the price of widgets relative to the price of all other goods. This change in the relative price of widgets would increase the quantity of widgets supplied and decrease the quantity demanded. Relative prices would continue to adjust until the widget market was back in equilibrium with the initial shortage of widgets eradicated. Under competitive market conditions, the **invisible hand** of Adam Smith will see to it that there are just the right number of widgets, hamburgers, milkshakes, barbers, plumbers and textbook authors to satisfy society's demands.[3]

Prior to Keynes, economists and governments paid very little attention to aggregate output levels and unemployment rates.[4] While not denying the existence of periodic bouts of unemployment and a business cycle, pre-Keynesian or "classical" economists implicitly believed that the natural forces of supply and demand could be relied upon to restore full employment within a relatively short period of time. The labour market would function just like any other market. If there was an unemployment problem with a "glut" of workers, then the relative price of labour would be bid down to "clear" the labour market and eradicate the unemployment problem. Again, the "invisible hand" of Adam Smith should quickly work its magic and unemployment ought not to be a persistent problem. The competitive market system should maintain an aggregate output level which

---

[3]For a highly entertaining account of the "Wonderful World of Adam Smith," see R.L. Heilbroner, *The Worldly Philosophers* (New York: Simon and Shuster, 1980), Chapter 3.

[4]The Canadian government did not start to publish regular data on GNP and the unemployment rate until well after World War II.

is consistent with labour market equilibrium and full employment. Chapter 8 provides a formal analysis of the classical model of macroeconomics and its key assumption of flexible wage rates and a "competitive" labour market.

The Great Depression

Events of the 1930s completely shattered economists' mythical laws and complacent fatalistic attitudes towards the problem of unemployment. No industrialized country was spared from a decade of economic devastation. As Professor Safarian of the University of Toronto notes in the opening lines of his classic study of the Canadian Great Depression:

> The thirties were quite unlike any other period in the past sixty years. For almost every year of the decade the number of workers unemployed exceeded 10 per cent of the labour force, and in 1933 amounted to 20 per cent. The decline in activity to 1933 was severe, prolonged and uneven. The recovery after 1933 was also uneven, and it was far from complete when World War II began.[5]

As depicted in Chart 4-1, Canadian GNP declined by an incredible 43 per cent from 1929 to 1933. *For the entire 1930s*, the level of output in Canada was below the level attained in the late 1920s. The decline in aggregate labour income was just as staggering. Between 1929 and 1933, the total Canadian payroll of wages and salaries fell by 39 per cent! This tremendous decline in labour income reflects both a decline in the average wage rate and a decline in the number of workers who were employed. The average *annual* Canadian wage per employed worker fell from $764 in 1929 to $518 in 1933 (that works out to $9.96 per week!). Despite this 32 per cent reduction in wage rates (the "invisible hand" of Adam Smith), the level of unemployment reached epic proportions. Based on retrospective *estimates* for the Canadian unemployment rate during the 1930s,[6] the Canadian unemployment rate climbed from less than 3 per cent in the late 1920s to 24 per cent in 1933 and stayed above 10 per cent for the remainder of the 1930s (see Chart 4-1). It was not until Canada was well into World War II that the unemployment rate returned to more normal levels. One can only speculate how long the Great Depression would have lasted without the belligerence of Adolf Hitler.

As a final preliminary comment we would note that the 1930s were a very tough time to be an economist, somewhat akin to being a physician during the bubonic plague. In 1936, the year in which the *General Theory* was published, the unemployment rate continued to hover around 15 per cent. Despite the fact that wages had fallen by 25 per cent in the *seven* years since the Great Crash of 1929,

---

[5]A.E. Safarian, *The Canadian Economy in the Great Depression* (Toronto: University of Toronto Press, 1959), p. 1.

[6]These retrospective estimates of the Canadian unemployment rate during the 1930s are derived from extrapolations of Census data and other data sources. See Statistics Canada, *Canadian Labour Force Estimates, 1931-1945*, Reference Paper No. 23, 1951.

CHART 4-1 The Great Depression

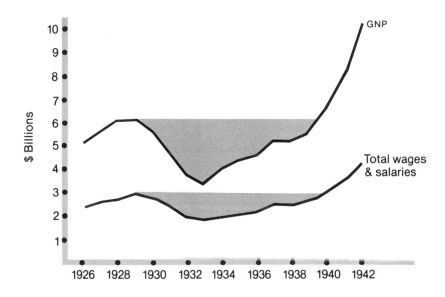

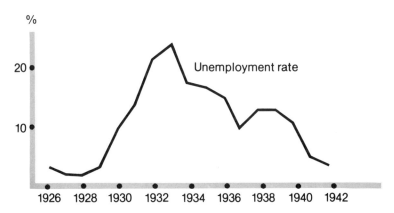

unemployment continued to be a fundamental problem. Other than advocating even further reductions in the wage rate, (perhaps by banning unions), a 1930s classical economist could offer no effective policy prescriptions for the problem of chronic unemployment, much like our unfortunate physician during the bubonic plague. According to the conventional economic wisdom, persistent depressions would not happen!

Into this intellectual and economic vacuum came John Maynard Keynes. While the *General Theory* did indeed revolutionize "the way the world thinks about economic problems," it is very much a product of its time. The *General Theory* was preoccupied with the overwhelming problem of the day—chronic unemployment. What causes a market economy to sink into a prolonged state of depression? What policies can the government implement to alleviate the problem of chronic unemployment? In seeking answers to these two important questions, the *General Theory* paid scant attention to the more contemporary problem of chronic inflation. During the 1930s price and wage levels were falling, not rising.[7]

A Simple Keynesian Macroeconomic Model

The major integrating theme of Keynes' new theoretical approach is the concept of **aggregate demand**. Aggregate demand is the *total* planned demand for final goods and services produced within the economy during a given period of time. Macroeconomists typically distinguish four different sectoral sources of aggregate demand:

1) consumer demand (food, beer, textbooks, cars)
2) investment demand (new machines, factories, houses)
3) net foreign demand (exports minus imports)
4) government demand (roads, hospitals, tanks, civil servants)

Even though we will draw fundamental *behavioural* distinctions between these four different sources of aggregate demand—we believe consumers "behave" differently than business investors—we do *not* distinguish between the myriad of different types of goods and services which are produced within the economy. As macroeconomists, we *assume* that all these different kinds of goods and services can be aggregated into one homogenous product called *output*. We leave it to the microeconomist to analyze how much of each particular type of good will be bought and sold, the role of relative prices, and the allocation of resources to different industries. In the macroeconomic arena, output is just output and we focus our attention on *aggregate* issues. What determines the demand for output within the consumer sector of the economy? How does consumer demand for output differ from business investment demand for output? Is there sufficient total aggregate demand for output to employ the economy's labour force?

As a starting point for our analysis, we *assume* that total aggregate demand Z consists of only two sectoral demand components: consumer demand C and business investment demand I, where both C and I are measured in real, constant dollar terms.

(4-1) $Z = C + I$

At a later stage in the analysis we will include the two remaining components of aggregate demand, namely net foreign demand and government demand for output. Having disaggregated aggregate demand into consumer and business investment components, we now turn to a brief analysis of each sectoral demand for output.

---

[7]The Consumer Price Index fell by 22 per cent from 1929 to 1933, and did not regain its 1929 level until 1946!

Consumer Demand—The Consumption Function

The cornerstone of Keynesian economics is the consumption function. Relying on his knowledge of psychology and human nature, Keynes hypothesized that the principal determinant of aggregate consumer expenditures is aggregate income. While increased income would lead to increased consumer expenditures, Keynes firmly believed that part of the increase in income would be saved. In the words of Keynes:

> The amount of aggregate consumption mainly depends on the amount of aggregate income. . . . The fundamental psychological law, upon which we are entitled to depend with great confidence both *a priori* from our knowledge of human nature and from the detailed facts of experience, is that men are disposed, as a rule and on the average, to increase their consumption as their income increases, but not by as much as the increase in their income.[8]

Both consumption and savings will be positively related to income levels.

The Keynesian consumption function is conventionally expressed as a simple linear relationship connecting consumer expenditures C to the level of disposable income. Since in our simplified model we have assumed away the government sector and taxes, disposable income and total income Y are equivalent.

$$(4\text{-}2) \qquad C = a + bY$$

In the upper panel of Chart 4-2 we have drawn this linear (straight line) consumption function (equation 4-2) with intercept a and slope b. The positive intercept of the consumption function reflects the fact that even if one's income falls to zero, some consumer spending on food, rent and other basics will still occur, presumably financed by drawing down past savings or borrowing against future savings. A one-unit or *marginal* increase in income will generate an increase in consumer spending equal to b, the slope of the straight line. As the above quotation indicates, Keynes thought that the slope of the consumption function would be less than unity ("not by as much as the increase in their income") as part of any increase in income would be saved. Given the strategic importance of the slope of the consumption function within his theory (see below), Keynes invented a special title for the slope of the consumption function, the **marginal propensity to consume**, often shortened to the MPC.

Since income must be either consumed or saved (the "taxman cometh" a little later in the analysis), saving is simply the difference between income and consumption:

$$S = Y - C$$

Substituting our consumption function (equation 4-2), we can algebraically derive a linear savings function (equation 4-3).

---

[8]J.M. Keynes, *The General Theory of Employment, Interest and Money* (London: Macmillan & Co., 1936), p. 96.

CHART 4-2 Consumption and savings functions

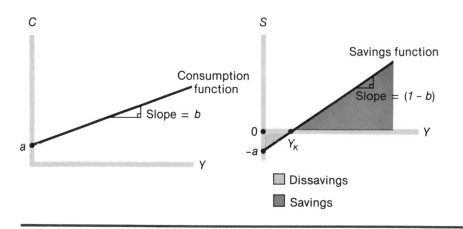

$$S = Y - a - bY$$
$$(4\text{-}3) \quad \text{or} \quad S = -a + (1 - b)Y$$

As long as the MPC b is less than unity, the savings function will be a rising function of income (see right-hand panel of Chart 4-2). There will be dissaving until income has reached a level of Y_K and positive savings for income levels in excess of Y_K.[9] To repeat, the Keynesian consumption function with a marginal propensity to consume of less than unity implies that *both* consumption and savings will rise as income levels increase.

Keynes' perception of the consumption/saving decision differed sharply from the prevailing economic thought of the 1930s. Most classical economists would likely have identified the *interest rate*, not income levels, as the prime determinant of savings. Interest payments are the economic rewards for abstaining from present consumption; the higher the interest rate, the greater the incentive to save. Keynes, on the other hand, thought that interest rates would have little effect on the consumption/saving decision:

> The usual type of short-period fluctuation in the rate of interest is not likely, however, to have much *direct* influence on spending either way. There are not many people who will alter their way of living because the rate of interest has fallen from 5 to 4 per cent, if their aggregate income is the same as before.[10]

[9]By setting savings equal to zero, we can algebraically determine the exact value of Y_K:
$$S = -a + (1 - b)Y = 0$$
$$Y_K = \frac{+a}{1 - b}$$

[10]Keynes, *General Theory*, pp. 93-94.

In Keynes' view, the propensity to consume is a "fairly stable function" and the level of consumption and savings will "mainly depend" on income levels.

The discussion of the preceding paragraph raises an obvious problem: we now have two alternative or competing theories of consumption/savings behaviour. Keynes hypothesized that consumption and savings will primarily depend on the level of income. Classical economic thought identified interest rates as the key determinant of savings and consumption. Which theory, if either, should we believe? How do we know when we have discovered the "true" theory? Throughout this textbook we will be presenting different economic theories to "explain" various types of macroeconomic behaviour, such as the aggregate consumption relationship. It is of paramount importance that we establish a general set of procedures and tests to evaluate whether a particular economic theory provides an "acceptable" explanation of macroeconomic behaviour. Consequently, before discussing the second component of our simple Keynesian model (investment demand), we explore the methods used by economists to evaluate competing theories.

Case Study 3:   How Economists Test Their Theories: The Consumption Function as an Illustrative Example

While there are many different criteria which might be used to evaluate the appropriateness of a particular economic theory (such as simplicity, generality, or mathematical elegance), economists typically judge their theories in terms of empirical accuracy. Is the theory supported by the *facts*? Does the theory generate accurate *predictions* of economic events? In short, the most important test of an economic theory is its ability to explain what is observed in reality and our confidence in a particular economic theory increases with each accurate prediction. Using the powerful techniques of mathematical statistics, economists "scientifically" test their theories for empirical accuracy.

To illustrate how economists test their theories, we return to our two alternative economic theories concerning consumption behaviour. While there are undoubtedly many different factors (economic, social, geographical, religious) which can influence consumer behaviour, each of these two competing theories abstracts one major or fundamental determinant of consumption expenditures from the maze of possible influences on consumer behaviour. Keynes hypothesized that aggregate consumption mainly depends on aggregate income. Classical economists contended that consumption varies inversely with interest rates; that is, an increase in interest rates will prompt more saving and less consuming. In each case, *all other* possible determinants of consumption behaviour are considered relatively unimportant and are ignored or omitted from the analysis.

Having advanced two different theories of aggregate consumer behaviour, we now must test whether either theory is empirically accurate. Each theory must be confronted with real-world data and subjected to statistical tests. Annual data for total consumer spending, disposable income and interest rates (on government bonds) have been collected for the period 1956 to 1984. To prevent any inflation distortions, we have expressed both consumption expenditures and disposable

CHART 4-3 Scatter diagrams for consumption expenditures

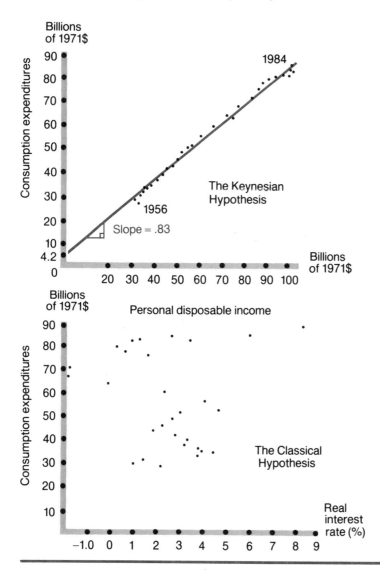

income in constant 1971 dollars and have subtracted the annual inflation rate from the nominal interest rate to obtain the real interest rate. As discussed in Chapter 3, borrowing and lending decisions in an inflationary world depend on the *real*, not the nominal, interest rate.

To facilitate our empirical analysis of these two alternative theories of consumption behavior, we have plotted each year's data in the form of a **scatter diagram** (a "scatter" of annual data points). In the upper panel of Chart 4-3, real consumption expenditures have been plotted against real personal disposable income, the

Keynesian consumption function hypothesis. For example, in 1956 real consumption expenditures were $28.4 billion and real personal disposable income in Canada was $31.1 billion (both measured in 1971 dollars). In the upper panel of Chart 4-3 we have located 28.4 on the vertical consumption axis and 31.1 on the horizontal income axis, and have plotted the observation for 1956. By 1984 real consumption expenditures had increased to $86.6 billion and real personal disposable income had risen to $99.5 billion (see the 1984 point in Chart 4-3). We have plotted the observations for the intervening years 1957-83 in Chart 4-3, but to keep the diagram as clean as possible, we have only labelled the 1956 and 1984 data points. For the time being, ignore the straight line in the upper panel of Chart 4-3.

The empirical evidence of Chart 4-3 unambiguously favours the Keynesian theory of consumption. As real income levels increased during the 1956-84 period, real consumption expenditures rose accordingly. There is a very systematic *upward-sloping* empirical relationship between consumer expenditures and personal disposable income. On the other hand, the classical hypothesis is clearly refuted by the data. The lower panel of Chart 4-3 is *all scatter*, with no evidence of any systematic empirical relationship between real interest rates and real consumer expenditures. In short, a quick visual inspection of these two scatter diagrams suggests that the Keynesian consumption function is consistent with the facts whereas the classical interest rate theory of consumer demand is contradicted by the facts.[11]

Rather than relying on visual inspections of scatter diagrams, although that is a useful first step, economists formally test their theories using modern statistical techniques and computers. The application of statistical techniques to economic problems is called *econometrics*, a growing field within the discipline of economics. Besides providing formal statistical tests of economic theories by using the laws of probability, econometrics also enables economists to quantify their theoretical relationships. By "fitting" the best straight line through a scatter diagram, an econometrician can provide statistical *estimates* for the intercept and slope of an economic relationship.

How does an econometrician decide what is *the* best straight line through a scatter diagram? As is evident from Chart 4-3, real-world data do not lie exactly along a straight line. Any particular straight line which one draws through a scatter diagram will miss most, if not all, of the actual data points.[12] Since there is an infinite number of possible straight lines which can be drawn through a scatter diagram, the econometrician is looking for the straight line which comes as close as possible to the scatter of data points. Statistical theory suggests that the vertical distances between the data points and the line be used as a measure of "closeness" or "goodness of fit," and that the best line is the line that minimizes the *sum of*

[11]If one plots real consumption expenditures against the nominal interest rate (rather than the real interest rate), there is a significant empirical relationship. However, the slope of this relationship is *positive* (i.e., consumer expenditures increase as nominal interest rates rise). Classical theory predicts a negative relationship between consumer spending and interest rates.

[12]The major reason that the points do not lie exactly along a straight line stems from the abstraction process in economic theorizing. All the minor influences on consumption behaviour have been ignored, thus causing our theory to make small errors in prediction.

squared vertical distances. This statistical technique of fitting a line through a scatter of data points by minimizing the sum of squared vertical distances is called *least squares*.[13]

Returning to the upper panel of Chart 4-3, the straight line drawn through this scatter diagram is obtained by the **least squares estimation technique**. Based on Canadian data from the 1956-84 period, the intercept of the Keynesian consumption function is estimated to be $4.2 billion and the slope (the MPC) is estimated to be .83, well under unity as Keynes hypothesized. Each additional dollar of Canadian disposable income would appear to generate an extra 83¢ of consumer spending and 17¢ of additional savings.

In conclusion, by using conventional statistical and econometric techniques we can test our economic theories as well as quantify or measure economic relationships. These numerical estimates for economic relationships will be of crucial importance when we discuss economic policy. A government must not only decide whether to increase (decrease) a particular policy instrument, it must also decide by exactly how much to increase (decrease) this policy instrument. To determine the particular *size* of policy action, the government must have reliable *quantitative* information on all economic relationships. One needs numerical information to generate numerical answers.

Investment Demand

Before discussing the determinants of investment, it is useful to review briefly what is meant by the term *investment*. As discussed in Chapter 2, investment does *not* mean the purchase of corporate shares, bonds, or guaranteed investment certificates. For the most part, such transactions simply reflect the swapping of one financial asset for another (money for bonds or stocks). In a macroeconomic context, investment refers to the process by which the economy's stock of *physical* capital is augmented. When a firm purchases new machinery and equipment or constructs a new factory, that's investment. Similarly, the construction of new homes or apartment buildings is considered to be investment expenditures.[14] In each case, the country's stock of physical capital has increased. Finally, an increase in the stock of inventories held by firms is also considered to be a form of investment. Since inventory investment or disinvestment is typically *not* "planned," we defer a discussion of inventory investment until a later point in this chapter and focus our attention on *planned* investment in machinery, factories, and housing.

Most investment decisions stem from the various dynamic elements within the economic system. To illustrate this point, consider a *static* economy where the *same* output level is produced each and every year. Under such static conditions, very little new investment would be required in any given year. Firms would

---

[13]For further details on least squares, the interested student is referred to any standard textbook on economic statistics or econometrics.

[14]In the national accounts, other consumer durables such as cars and yachts are classified as consumer expenditures, not investment.

already have the necessary factories and machines to produce the constant output level, and the work force would already be "housed." Other than replacing a few old machines and maintaining factory and housing facilities, little new investment would likely be required to produce the same output level in each year.[15] The real world, however, is not static and it is the dynamic elements within the economic system which give rise to most investment expenditures. New products and new technology invariably generate substantial increases in new investment.[16] In addition to technological developments, much investment can simply be attributed to a growing economy. As the labour force expands and the economy grows, a greater stock of physical capital will be required. In summary, relatively high rates of investment demand are likely to be found in dynamic, growing economies.

Since capital goods can last for decades, individual investment decisions depend critically upon the firm's *long-run* appraisal of future growth, profit and risks. Given the difficulty of predicting future economic events and formulating long-term expectations in a dynamic world, Keynes placed considerable emphasis on the "state of confidence" and "business psychology" as determinants of investment expenditures (what Keynes called the "animal spirits" of investors). If businessmen are not very confident of the future, they are not likely to invest in new plants and new machinery.

> The *state of confidence* . . . is a matter to which practical men always pay the closest and most anxious attention. . . . There is, however, not much to be said about the state of confidence *a priori*. Our conclusions must mainly depend upon the actual observation of markets and business psychology.[17]

Since Keynes thought that the state of business confidence was quite unpredictable and subject to "sudden and violent changes," he considered investment demand to be largely *autonomous*. Unlike consumer expenditures, which are a very stable, predictable function of income, Keynes felt that investment expenditures are much more unpredictable and volatile, with the source of this instability of investment demand lying outside the realm of macroeconomics.

While Keynes undoubtedly overstated the role of business psychology and "animal spirits" in the investment decision, investment expenditures are indeed more unstable and unpredictable than consumer expenditures.[18] Consider, for example, the Great Depression. From 1929 to 1933 real investment spending declined by a staggering 79 per cent! Compared to this unprecedented reduction in investment demand, real consumer expenditures declined by a much more modest 18 per cent over these four years corresponding to the worst downswing in

---

[15]In such a static world, investment would be a relatively small proportion of aggregate demand, roughly equal to the depreciation of the existing stock of capital.

[16]Some of the more dramatic innovations which stimulated enormous investment spending would include the following: the steam engine, hydro electricity, trains, cars, airplanes, rockets, computers, television, natural gas, tar sands technology.

[17]Keynes, *General Theory*, pp. 148-49.

[18]See Chart 14-1 in Chapter 14.

Canadian history—a 30 per cent decline in real output. To survive the Great Depression, consumers spent *more than* their current income by borrowing or drawing down past savings, with the *dis*saving rate reaching minus 9 per cent in 1933. The almost total collapse of business investment, which Keynes attributed to a collapse of business confidence, was a major cause of the Great Depression. This tremendous volatility in investment spending has characterized every decade and has been a recurring source of aggregate demand stimulus (as in 1964-66 and 1971-73) or contraction (as in 1959-62 and 1977-84). In general, consumer spending has tended to stabilize the Canadian economy,[19] whereas investment spending has exerted a destabilizing influence.

For purposes of this introductory analytical chapter we assume that all planned investment expenditures are autonomous. Investment demand is determined by factors outside the scope of our initial rudimentary macroeconomic model. The next chapter introduces interest rates as a negative economic determinant of investment demand and Chapter 20 provides an extensive review of the many different economic theories of investment, including dynamic theories such as the accelerator model of investment. Even though economists have made considerable progress in understanding the investment process, investment decisions are not always simple predictable functions of economic variables, and autonomous elements may still impart considerable instability to investment demand.

The Determination of Equilibrium Income

The Total Aggregate Demand Schedule

In developing a rudimentary model of Keynesian economics, we have imposed the following three key assumptions:

(A1) Aggregate demand consists of only two components: consumer and investment expenditures. (Exports, imports, and government spending have been temporarily ignored.)

(A2) Consumer expenditures are assumed to be a stable function of income (the Keynesian consumption function).

(A3) Investment expenditures are assumed to be autonomous (independent of current economic conditions such as income levels).

Making use of our previous linear consumption function (equation 4-2) and assuming that **planned autonomous investment** is equal to I_a (a given value), these three key assumptions can be combined to produce a linear total **aggregate demand schedule** (equation 4-4).

(4-1) $Z = C + I$

(4-2) $C = a + bY$

(4-4) $Z = a + bY + I_a = (a + I_a) + bY$

---

[19]The stability of consumer demand is examined in greater detail in Chapter 19 when the "permanent" income theory of consumption is presented.

CHART 4-4 Equilibrium in the Keynesian cross model

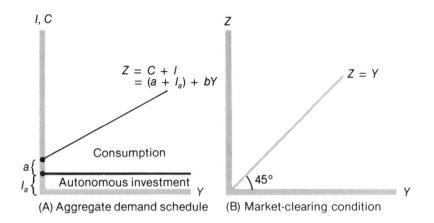

(A) Aggregate demand schedule   (B) Market-clearing condition

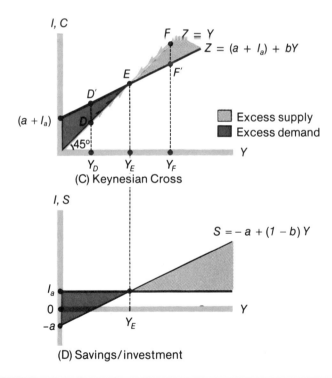

In panel A of Chart 4-4 we have plotted this total aggregate demand schedule by·placing the consumption function from Chart 4-2 on top of the *given* amount of autonomous investment. The slope of this new total aggregate demand schedule is obviously the same as the slope of the consumption function b, but the intercept will be equal to I_a, the given autonomous investment block, plus a, the intercept of the consumption function. Each point along the total aggregate demand schedule represents the total amount of planned consumption and investment spending which would occur at a given level of income.

Keynesian Aggregate Supply and the Aggregate Output Market-Clearing Condition

To determine which *particular* point along this aggregate demand schedule will represent the *equilibrium* point for our hypothetical economy, we must consider the concept of aggregate supply. At this stage in the analysis, Keynes introduced a crucial and highly controversial assumption:

(A4) Wage and price levels tend to be inflexible and unresponsive to changing economic conditions.

As a first-order approximation to reality, Keynes assumed that aggregate wage and price levels could be regarded as fixed. In Keynes' view, wages were primarily determined by institutional and historical factors, and were relatively immune from the rigours of the market place. Workers and unions strenuously resist any reductions in wage rates, even when there is widespread unemployment.[20] Given the unresponsiveness of wage rates to current labour market conditions, at least in the short run, Keynes argued that the flexible wage assumption implicit in Adam Smith's "invisible hand" should be replaced by an *in*flexible wage assumption.[21] In the words of Keynes, "the stability of prices rather than of employment" characterized a market economy.

Just as the Great Depression shattered classical economists' theories concerning the stability of output and employment, the 1970s and early 1980s have shattered Keynesian economists' theories on the stability of price levels. Most of this textbook is devoted to an analysis of the *joint* macroeconomic problems of unemployment and inflation. However, our analysis of these two interrelated macroeconomic problems must proceed in a slow, orderly fashion. Before we start to "run" with an *inflation–unemployment* macroeconomic model, we must learn to "walk" with a *fixed price level–output* macroeconomic model. Chapters 4 through 7 of this textbook present the basic elements of Keynesian economics, retaining Keynes' critical assumption of fixed price levels. In Chapter 8 we permanently relax this fixed price assumption, and Chapters 9 and 10 incorporate a theory of inflation into our macroeconomic model.

---

[20]Keynes thought that the collective bargaining practices of labour would maintain and preserve a stable pattern of wage differentials between various labour groups. In a decentralized bargaining system, any individual union would strongly resist a wage reduction when the unemployment rate increased, because it would have no guarantee that other unions bargaining at a later date would also accept a wage reduction. By accepting a wage cut, a particular union would be deliberately distorting the pattern of wage differentials against its own members. Consequently, nominal wages are likely to be inflexible, particularly in a downward direction.

[21]More on the responsiveness of wage rates to labour market conditions in Chapters 8 and 9.

Having assumed inflexible or **fixed wage and price levels**, the Keynesian concept of **aggregate supply** is rather artificial. Implicitly, Keynes assumed that as long as there was *any* unemployment, the aggregate supply curve would be horizontal in price–output space.[22] Given unemployed resources, firms could hire additional labour at the given wage and could therefore supply additional output without increasing the price level. Since wages are unresponsive to market conditions, a decrease in aggregate demand for output and employment would not generate a decline in wages, and the labour market would remain in disequilibrium with persistent unemployment until aggregate demand is restored. Under fixed price conditions, the level of output and employment is entirely demand-determined.

Even though the labour market may be in a state of disequilibrium because of inflexible wages, we invoke the usual market-clearing assumption for the aggregate output market. We *assume* that aggregate demand is equal to aggregate supply, with aggregate supply adjusting to equal aggregate demand. Whatever goods are demanded will be supplied at the given price level. As discussed in Chapter 2, the total value of final goods produced must be paid out in the form of income to the various factors of production. The sum of wages, interest, rent, and profits must be equivalent to the value of total aggregate supply. Making use of this national income accounting identity that aggregate supply must be totally paid out as aggregate income, aggregate demand Z is *assumed* to be equal to aggregate income Y. Equation 4-5 states that the aggregate output market is assumed to clear.

(4-5) $Z = Y$

In panel B of Chart 4-4 we have drawn this aggregate output, market-clearing condition in Z–Y space. Since both Z and Y are measured in the *same* units, this **aggregate output market-clearing condition is represented by a 45° ray through the origin**. Any point along the $Z = Y$ (45°) line is a possible equilibrium output position for our hypothetical economy.

Determining the Unique Equilibrium Income Position for the Economy

Having described all possible equilibrium positions for the economy (the $Z = Y$ line), we must now determine at which *particular* income level the economy will come to rest. In the parlance of a microeconomist, at what particular income level will the aggregate output market clear? To answer this important question, we must return to our aggregate demand schedule which describes total *planned* expenditures, $C + I$, in terms of income levels. In panel C of Chart 4-4 we have superimposed our aggregate demand schedule from panel A on top of our aggregate output market-clearing condition, $Z = Y$, producing the now famous

[22]Chapter 8 provides a complete analysis of the labour market and aggregate supply, for both Keynesian and classical macroeconomic models.

Keynesian cross diagram. Like all diagrams in economics, the intersection point E is of special significance. When income is at the level Y_E, planned aggregate demand expenditures Z are exactly equal to aggregate supply and income Y. Of all the possible equilibrium positions along the $Z = Y$ line, only point E coincides with the planned aggregate demand schedule. Given the aggregate demand schedule drawn in Chart 4-4, point E represents the unique **equilibrium income** point for this hypothetical economy.

To demonstrate that point E represents the unique equilibrium position, we briefly consider other possible income levels. Suppose that the economy were back at point D, another possible equilibrium point along the $Z = Y$ line, with a lower income level Y_D. At this lower income level, aggregate demand Z exceeds aggregate supply/income by the vertical distance DD'. Given a state of excess demand for output, firms can sell more goods than are currently being produced. As a consequence of this excess demand, the stock of inventories held by firms will be rapidly depleted and new factory orders will be initiated to supply the excess demand and replenish dwindling inventory stocks. With increased new orders, factories will increase the production of goods and generate increased income for the factors of production. The excess demand at Y_D has caused the level of income and output to increase.[23] As long as there is any excess demand, there will be further upward adjustments in income as firms continue to restock dwindling inventories and initiate new factory orders. Once income has reached Y_E there will be *no* excess demand and inventory stocks would remain at their normal levels. With no inventory adjustments required, factory production would remain constant and income would stabilize at Y_E, the unique income level where planned aggregate demand equals aggregate supply.

A similar set of downward adjustments would occur if the income level happened to exceed Y_E. At point F in panel C of Chart 4-4, a state of excess supply FF' will occur. Since there is insufficient aggregate demand to absorb aggregate supply, inventory stocks will start to rise. With inventories piling up, new factory orders will be cut back and factory production and income will decline. Given excess supply, there will be a continual series of downward adjustments in income and output levels until the economy has returned to Y_E.

In summary, the intersection point of the planned aggregate demand schedule and the aggregate output market-clearing condition ($45°$ line) represents a unique point of zero excess demand (or supply). It is the only point where planned expenditures are equal to aggregate supply/income and inventory stocks remain at their normal levels. For any income level other than Y_E, aggregate demand will not equal aggregate supply and inventory stocks will be either accumulating or declining. Changing inventory stocks will lead to changes in new factory orders and adjustments in aggregate production levels. Based on this inventory adjustment mechanism, aggregate income will increase when income levels are below this unique Y_E point and decrease when income levels are above Y_E. Thus, the economy is **stable** in the sense that it will always gravitate to this unique equilib-

---

[23]Keynes' critical assumption of an inflexible price level rules out any bidding up of prices under excess demand conditions.

rium position if it happens to find itself out of equilibrium. Once the economy reaches point E, where planned aggregate demand is equal to aggregate supply/income, there will be no further adjustment pressures. *Ceteris paribus*, the economy will perpetually remain at Y_E, the unique equilibrium point.

While we have defined equilibrium in terms of planned aggregate demand being equal to aggregate supply/income, for this simple Keynesian cross model it can be easily demonstrated that this equilibrium condition is equivalent to the equality of savings and investment. Since income must be either consumed or saved (we have ignored taxes),

$$Y = C + S$$

and aggregate demand consists of only consumption plus investment,

$$Z = C + I$$

equating Z to Y is equivalent to equating I to S (the C's can be cancelled out). The unique equilibrium position for our simple Keynesian cross macroeconomic model occurs when savings is equal to planned investment.[24] The final quadrant of Chart 4-4 displays the unique equilibrium income position Y_E for the economy using the Keynesian savings function (as drawn in Chart 4-2) and the given level of autonomous investment(I_a).

The Structural Determinants of Equilibrium Income

In the previous section we have defined the equilibrium income position for the economy in terms of planned expenditures being equal to aggregate supply/income and have demonstrated that this unique equilibrium income position is stable. In this section we wish to explore the fundamental structural determinants of equilibrium income. In a superficial sense, equilibrium income is simply determined by the intersection point of the aggregate demand schedule Z and the 45° line representing the aggregate output market-clearing condition. But what determines the exact intersection point in the Keynesian cross diagram? Since the 45° line is inviolate (the aggregate output market must clear in equilibrium), this intersection point depends exclusively on the intercept and slope of the aggregate demand schedule. Equilibrium income in a Keynesian macroeconomic model is exclusively demand-determined. In a fundamental **structural** sense, equilibrium income depends on (1) the behaviour of consumers as depicted by the consumption function and (2) the level of autonomous investment.

1) A Change in Consumer Behaviour

To illustrate the fundamental structural determinants of equilibrium income, we initially consider the behaviour of consumers. Suppose that consumers change their consumption behaviour. Rather than consuming 83¢ of every marginal

---

[24]Since the amount of income which is not consumed—savings—is exactly equal to planned investment, total planned spending is equal to aggregate supply/income and inventory stocks are neither accumulating nor declining.

CHART 4-5 Adjustment in the equilibrium level of income

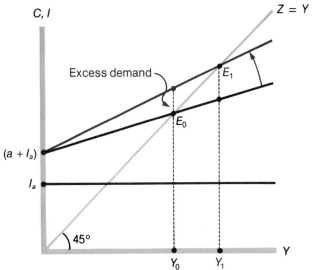

(A) An increase in the marginal propensity to consume

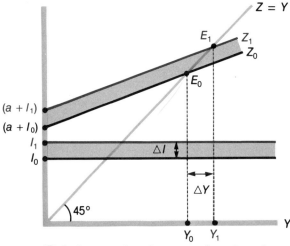

(B) An increase in autonomous investment

income dollar, suppose that consumers now consume 90¢ of every marginal income dollar. This change in consumer behaviour has increased the marginal propensity to consume from .83 to .90, causing both the consumption function and the aggregate demand schedule to be steeper. For simplicity we assume that the intercept is unaffected by this change in consumer behaviour. As shown in panel A of Chart 4-5, a steeper aggregate demand schedule will generate a higher intersection point in the Keynesian cross diagram (E_1 versus E_0) and a *higher equilibrium* income level (Y_1 versus Y_0).

The explanation for this *increase* in the equilibrium income level associated with a *higher* marginal propensity to consume is straightforward. At the *old* income level Y_0, the increase in the marginal propensity to consume has created excess demand conditions (see Chart 4-5) and a depletion of inventory stocks. As firms restock their inventories, aggregate production and income levels will rise. This upward adjustment in income will continue until income has reached the level of Y_1, where excess demand is zero and aggregate supply equals the *new* planned level of total expenditures, based on the *new* consumption function. Given the new lower marginal propensity to save, .10 rather than .17, a *higher* income level is required to generate a savings flow *exactly equal to the given level of planned investment* (the alternative formulation of the equilibrium condition). An increase (decrease) in the marginal propensity to consume will cause the equilibrium income level to increase (decrease).[25]

2) A Change in Autonomous Investment

Turning to the second fundamental structural determinant of equilibrium income, suppose that autonomous investment changes. For reasons inexplicable to economists, the state of business confidence abruptly changes and autonomous investment unexpectedly increases. Given an increase in autonomous investment from I_0 to I_1 in Chart 4-5, panel B, the entire aggregate demand schedule will shift upwards (from Z_0 to Z_1) by a vertical distance equal to the increase in autonomous investment. The equilibrium income level will rise from Y_0 to Y_1, again because of excess demand at Y_0, restocking inventories, and new factory orders. In terms of the diagram, the resulting increase in equilibrium income, represented by the horizontal distance between Y_1 and Y_0, appears to be much larger than the initial increase in autonomous investment, represented by the vertical distance between I_1 and I_0. Since the change in equilibrium income (represented by the symbol ΔY) may be a "multiple" of the change in autonomous investment ΔI, the ratio of ΔY to ΔI is usually referred to as a *multiplier*.

Before examining the multiplier effects on equilibrium income arising from an increase in autonomous investment, we briefly summarize the major conclusions of Chart 4-5. A change in consumer behaviour and/or a change in autonomous investment will lead to a change in the equilibrium income level. In a fundamental structural sense, the equilibrium income level in our rudimentary Keynesian model depends on two sets of factors: the underlying behaviour of consumers and the level of autonomous investment. Again, the equilibrium income is entirely demand-determined.

---

[25]This consumption/savings behavioural property of Keynesian equilibrium income levels is often called the "paradox of thrift." For a given level of autonomous investment, the more "thrifty" consumers are (the lower the MPC), the *lower* will be the equilibrium income level. If all Canadians decided to save a larger portion of their incomes, then the equilibrium income level in Canada would decline. In aggregate, "thrifty" consumer behaviour is no virtue.

The Multiplier Process

Returning to our analysis of the income effects arising from a change in autonomous investment, we now tackle one of the most crucial concepts in Keynesian economics: the **multiplier**. To illustrate this concept, consider the case of a hypothetical Keynesian-cross economy represented by the following equations:

$$C = 10 + 0.8Y$$

$$I = 9$$

$$Z = C + 1$$

In this hypothetical economy, the MPC is 0.8 and autonomous investment is $9 billion per year. Our hypothetical economy will be in equilibrium when aggregate demand Z is equal to aggregate supply/income. As computed below, the equilibrium income level is $95 billion per year:

$$Y = Z = 10 + 0.8Y + 9$$

$$Y = 19 + 0.8Y$$

$$0.2Y = 19$$

$$Y = 95$$

We can easily verify that $95 billion is indeed the equilibrium income level. First, the value of goods and services produced is equal to the income generated, namely $95 billion. At this level of income, consumers will spend $86 billion per year $(10 + 0.8 \times 95 = 86)$. Add to this $9 billion of autonomous investment and we obtain an aggregate demand of $95 billion—exactly equal to aggregate supply.

Now suppose that autonomous investment increases by $1 billion to a total of $10 billion per year. By how much will equilibrium income rise? At first glance, the answer would appear to be $1 billion per year since that is the value of the *additional investment* goods that will have to be produced each year. However, this figure seriously *understates* the potential income-generating effects of an increase in autonomous investment. A clue to the problem can be obtained from the equilibrium condition which states that $Y = Z = C + I$. Obviously if investment I increases one unit, income Y must also increase one unit. But this is not the end of the story. Since consumption depends on income, consumption will also increase, giving a further boost to income. The final change in equilibrium income will therefore be greater than the increase in investment spending that caused the initial increase in income.

The reason for this multiplier increase in income is straightforward. The construction workers who are engaged in the *new* investment projects are earning income that was not previously being earned. In fact, $1 billion of *extra* income is generated as a direct result of the expanded level of autonomous investment expenditure. Eight-tenths of this extra income will be spent on consumer goods and services, representing an increase in consumer spending of $0.8 billion per year. Additional factory workers, bartenders and clerks will have to be employed to produce the goods and services that the *newly* employed construction workers will demand. But as these extra goods and services are being produced, *additional* incomes of $0.8 billion per year will be paid to the factory workers, bartenders and clerks. Eight-tenths of *this new income* will be spent by the new factory workers, bartenders and clerks on consumer goods and services, resulting in $0.64 billion of *additional* consumer spending. The production of these additional consumer products generates an additional $0.64 billion income for a new group of workers. Even though our story is still not over, since 80 per cent of this $0.64 billion additional income will be spent on additional consumer goods (and so on), we spare readers further verses of the "multiplier house that Keynes built."

While the total income-generating effects of the initial $1 billion increase in autonomous investment will include the sum of all of these increases in consumer expenditures, we can take a shortcut to determine exactly how much additional income will be generated. At the end of all these additional rounds of spending, our hypothetical economy must be back in equilibrium with savings equal to investment. Given a $1 billion increase in autonomous investment, equilibrium income must rise by an amount that will cause total savings to rise by $1 billion per year. Since the marginal propensity to consume is .80, each $1 billion of additional income leads to $0.2 billion of additional savings. Consequently, it requires a $5 billion increase in income to raise savings by $1 billion. The income change is five times as large as the change in investment spending and the multiplier effect for this hypothetical economy is therefore 5.[26] As a final check on our calculations, we substitute the new $100 billion equilibrium level of income into the consumption function. Consumer expenditure will now be $90 billion per year (10 + .80 × 100). Adding on the new higher level of autonomous investment, $10 billion per year, aggregate demand will be $100 billion per year, which is exactly equal to the new equilibrium level of income and the supply of goods and services.

The above example, with all of its simplifying assumptions, illustrates several major macroeconomic propositions. First, a change in the level of autonomous investment will trigger a prolonged macroeconomic chain reaction as the economy moves to a new equilibrium position. Second, given the additional induced rounds of spending, equilibrium income changes will exceed the initial change in autonomous investment. Thus any instability in autonomous investment will have a magnified (multiplier) effect on income levels, a key Keynesian proposition. Third, the exact value of this multiplier effect depends crucially on consumer behaviour. If the marginal propensity to consume were to decline, then the successive rounds of induced consumer spending would be lower and the value of the multiplier would decline accordingly.

---

[26]In more general terms, the multiplier for this simple economy is $1/(1 - b)$, where b is the MPC and $(1 - b)$ is the additional saving per unit of additional income. One additional unit of saving will be generated by $1/(1 - b)$ additional units of income. Since the equilibrium condition for this simple economy is the equality of savings and investment, a one-unit increase in investment will result in an increase in equilibrium income of $1/(1 - b)$ units.

An Algebraic Representation of the *Keynesian Cross* Macroeconomic Model

Our initial analysis of a macroeconomic model has relied heavily on the use of graphical techniques, including the now famous Keynesian cross diagram. In this section of the chapter we retrace our first steps in macroeconomic model-building by recasting our graphical analysis into algebraic terms. While graphical analysis undoubtedly has intuitive appeal for many students, there are important advantages to be exploited in an algebraic analysis of macroeconomic models. Recall that a model is simply a set of interrelated theories and assumptions pertaining to a particular economic phenomenon. Since theories can be readily converted into equation form, analysis of macroeconomic models implicitly involves "solving" systems of interrelated equations. The use of a modest amount of high school algebra not only allows us to solve such macroeconomic models quickly, it also permits us to derive the key properties, characteristics and conclusions of our macroeconomic models in a very succinct, precise manner. The algebraic mode of analysis also has an important advantage in that *qualitative* propositions may be transformed into *quantitative* terms. By combining statistical and algebraic techniques, we can generate numerical answers for key macroeconomic questions, such as determining the actual size of the multiplier effect. Throughout this textbook we will rely on both graphical and algebraic techniques; a "good" student should be fluently bilingual in both analytical modes.

As a means of introducing some necessary "model jargon," we briefly review the basic components of the Keynesian cross macroeconomic model. As discussed above, the most rudimentary Keynesian macroeconomic model can be represented by the following three economic relationships:

(4-1)   The aggregate demand identity: $Z = C + I$

(4-2)   The consumption function: $C = a + bY$

(4-5)   The aggregate output market-clearing
equilibrium condition: $Z = Y$

Throughout this book, uppercase letters will be used to designate economic **variables** (examples: aggregate demand Z, consumption expenditures C, investment expenditures I and national income Y), and lowercase letters will be used to designate economic **parameters** (examples: a and b).

Economic Variables

Economic variables within a model can be generally classified into two distinct categories: exogenous and endogenous. An **exogenous** variable is a variable whose value is determined by forces *outside* the model. Its value does not depend on any of the other variables which are included in the model. An *exogenous* variable is regarded as a *given*, something which we do not explain. Variables which are explained and determined *within* the model are designated as **endogenous**. Z, C and Y in the Keynesian cross model are endogenous. In an algebraic sense, the *endogenous* variables are the *unknowns* in the model. The algebraic solution for the model will provide an explanation for each of the endogenous variables. Within the Keynesian cross model, investment expenditures are *assumed* to be *exogenous* (or autonomous), and the equilibrium level of income, the key endogenous variable, is "explained" in terms of a *given* level of autonomous investment.

Macroeconomic model-building is very much the art of variable classification. For a particular problem, can variable X, say investment, be considered exogenous—a given? If not, then variable X must be classified as an endogenous variable and explained within the model, and the overall model will increase in size by one equation. The more "realistic" the model, the greater the proliferation of endogenous variables and equations within the model. Unfortunately, as models get larger and more realistic, our basic understanding of the functioning of an economic model is quickly impaired. Only computers can sort out the complex interrelationships which exist in large scale macroeconomic models where everything depends on everything. For pedagogic reasons we start with very simple, small macroeconomic models in which key variables such as investment and inflation are *assumed* to be exogenous. As our understanding of macroeconomic phenomena increases, more and more variables will be "explained" and incorporated as *endogenous* variables within our macroeconomic model (for example investment becomes endogenous in Chapter 5 and inflation becomes endogenous in Chapter 9).

Parameters

Within an economic model, parameters are employed to describe the *stable* features of economic behaviour. For example, the Keynesian consumption function hypothesizes that consumer expenditure behaviour depends on income levels. Assuming that this hypothesized relationship is linear, the parameters a and b are used to represent the intercept and slope of the Keynesian consumption function. As discussed above, statistical and econometric techniques can be implemented to generate numerical *estimates* for these underlying behavioural parameters (see Chart 4-3). As a general rule we will assume that these underlying behavioural parameters are constant and will algebraically solve our macroeconomic models in terms of a stable set of *given* behavioural parameters. As discussed above, if economic behaviour were to change, then a new equilibrium solution to our model would emerge.

Model Solution

In summary, our simple Keynesian cross macroeconomic model consists of three equations including three endogenous variables Y, Z and C, one exogenous variable I, and behavioural parameters a and b. We now wish to solve this three-equation macroeconomic model for the equilibrium income level. Imposing our aggregate output market-clearing equilibrium condition,

$$Y = Z = C + I$$

and then substituting our Keynesian consumption function

$$Y = a + bY + I$$

produces the following *solution* equation for the equilibrium income level:

$$Y - bY = a + I$$

(4-6) or $$Y = \frac{a + I}{1 - b}$$

Equilibrium income, an endogenous variable, has been expressed strictly in terms of the *givens* within the model: the exogenous variable I and the behavioural parameters a and b. The feedback effects or interrelationships between C and Y have been allowed for in obtaining our Y solution equation. Note that C and Y jointly occur in both the consumption function and the market-clearing aggregate demand equation. In the parlance of a mathematician, we have "simultaneously" solved for Y. Our solution for Y "simultaneously" satisfies all appearances of Y within the three-equation model.

This solution equation for Y is conventionally known as the **reduced-form** equation for Y. Endogenous variables which appear on the right-hand side of the equation have been systematically eliminated by algebraic substitutions; the left-hand side *endogenous* variable Y has been "reduced" to an equation which consists entirely of the *givens* in the model. In fact one can obtain a reduced-form equation for *all* of the endogenous variables within the model. For example, substituting our reduced-form equation for Y into the consumption function we readily obtain a reduced-form equation for C:

$$C = a + bY = a + b \left(\frac{a + I}{1 - b} \right) = \frac{a(1 - b) + b(a + I)}{1 - b}$$

(4-7) $$C = \frac{a + bI}{1 - b}$$

The reduced-form equations of the model express each *endogenous* variable in terms of the *given exogenous* variables and *behavioural parameters*.

The Structural Determinants of Equilibrium Income Once Again

Returning to our reduced-form Y equation,

(4-6) $$Y = \frac{a + I}{1 - b}$$

the underlying structural determinants of equilibrium income within the Keynesian cross model are in full view. If either consumer behaviour or autonomous investment were to change, the equilibrium income level would be systematically altered. For example, if consumers became "thriftier" (a and/or b declined), equilibrium income would fall—the paradox of thrift once again. A decline in autonomous investment I will also cause a lower equilibrium income level. In a fundamental structural sense, the equilibrium income level depends on the value of the given exogenous variable(s) and the given behavioural parameters.

The Multiplier Once Again

Earlier we considered the multiplier effect on income that arose during the induced "rounds of spending" following an increase in autonomous investment expenditures. The reduced-form equation for income can be used to determine the precise value of this income multiplier effect.

To illustrate how one can compute the multiplier effect, suppose that the value of autonomous investment expenditures was equal to I_0. Given our reduced-form income equation (4-6), the equilibrium income level Y_0 corresponding to I_0 must be the following:

$$Y_0 = \frac{a + I_0}{1 - b}$$

If autonomous investment increases from I_0 to I_1, equilibrium income will rise to Y_1, where

$$Y_1 = \frac{a + I_1}{1 - b}$$

The increase in income ΔY arising from this increase in investment ΔI can be computed by subtracting Y_0 from Y_1:

$$Y_1 - Y_0 = \frac{a + I_1}{1 - b} - \frac{a + I_0}{1 - b}$$

or
$$\Delta Y = \frac{\cancel{a} + I_1 - \cancel{a} - I_0}{1 - b} = \frac{\Delta I}{1 - b}$$

or
$$\frac{\Delta Y}{\Delta I} = \frac{1}{1 - b}$$

A one-unit increase in autonomous investment causes a $1/(1 - b)$ unit increase in the equilibrium income level.[27] The multiplier effects on income from an increase in autonomous investment depend crucially on the underlying behaviour of consumers (b, the MPC). Since the marginal propensity to consume b is assumed to be less than one, this income "multiplier" effect must be greater than one. The closer the MPC is to unity, the larger is the multiplier effect.

Like the elasticity concept in microeconomics, the **multiplier concept** in macroeconomics is a very general or generic concept. The term *multiplier* is used to describe the change in the equilibrium level of *any endogenous* variable which

---

[27]Students with an elementary course in the calculus will immediately recognize that this multiplier effect is simply the derivative of the reduced-form income equation with respect to investment.

$$\frac{\Delta Y}{\Delta I} = \frac{dY}{dI} = \frac{1}{1 - b}$$

arises when *any exogenous* variable changes. Since most macroeconomic models consist of many endogenous and exogenous variables, by definition there are many different multiplier effects which can be computed. For example, within the Keynesian cross model we can compute the multiplier effect on equilibrium consumption expenditures from a one-unit change in autonomous investment directly from the reduced-form consumption equation (4-7),

$$\frac{\Delta C}{\Delta I} = \frac{b}{1-b}$$

To repeat, *a multiplier is simply the change in the equilibrium level of any specified endogenous variable given a one-unit change in a particular exogenous variable*. As we shall see in subsequent chapters, the numerical value of a particular multiplier effect, such as the effect of a change in autonomous investment on the equilibrium income level, depends crucially on the structure of the entire macroeconomic model.

The Central Message of the *General Theory*

The key integrating concept of Keynesian economics is *aggregate demand*. If aggregate demand declines (say, because autonomous investment declines), the equilibrium income level will decrease and the economy will slide into a recession. Given Keynes' critical assumption that wage and price levels are inflexible and unresponsive to current market conditions, the economy would be trapped in this recession until aggregate demand returned to its normal level. In the preface to his analysis of the Great Depression in Canada, Safarian boldly states the "failure in aggregate demand was at the root of the problem."

Keynes' diagnosis of the cause of persistent recessions immediately suggested a possible policy prescription. If the problem is insufficient aggregate demand, then the government should initiate policies to stimulate aggregate demand. The government has at its disposal a variety of different policies that are capable of stimulating aggregate demand and propelling the economy out of a recession. For example, the government could increase its own spending by building more post offices, buying more pencils and memo pads, or hiring more bureaucrats. Alternatively, the government could reduce taxes or increase welfare payments and other transfer payments to encourage spending in the private sector. In other words, any shortfall in aggregate demand could be offset by a government-induced increase in spending within another sector of the macroeconomy. Recessions could be cured by appropriate government fiscal policy!

The Role of Fiscal Policy in A Simple Keynesian Macroeconomic Model

To conclude this chapter we briefly consider the role of **fiscal policy** within the Keynesian cross model (Chapter 6 is devoted entirely to an analysis of Keynesian fiscal and monetary policy). As suggested above, the government can affect aggregate demand and equilibrium income in at least two different ways. First, government spending on goods and services represents an important additional component of aggregate demand. Second, the government can indirectly affect aggregate demand by changing taxes and/or transfer payments. To keep our model as simple as possible, we subtract transfer payments from taxes (transfers are like a "negative" tax) and *assume* that the amount of taxes net of transfers T is *independent* of income.[28] If *disposable* income is defined as total income less net taxes, a tax reduction will increase disposable income and thereby stimulate consumer expenditures and aggregate demand.

Adding government expenditures G to the aggregate demand identity and reformulating the consumption function in terms of disposable income, $Y - T$, our three-equation Keynesian cross model is amended in the following manner:

(4-1a) $Z = C + I + G$

(4-2a) $C = a + b(Y - T)$

(4-5) $Y = Z$

The inclusion of the government sector within the Keynesian cross model has added two new exogenous variables G and T to the model, which will have an important effect on the equilibrium level of income.

In Chart 4-6 we present the Keynesian cross diagram for this enlarged model. As before, the components of aggregate demand (I, G and C) are measured along the vertical axis. Both investment and government spending are assumed to be exogenous, and therefore do not depend on the level of income. Consequently, these two aggregate demand components are represented by rectangular blocks in Chart 4-6. Consumption does depend on the level of income, and it is the consumption function that gives the aggregate demand schedule its upward slope. The intercept of the aggregate demand schedule on the vertical axis indicates the level of aggregate demand when Y is zero. From the consumption function, when Y is zero C will be equal to $(a - bT)$. Thus, the vertical intercept of the aggregate demand schedule is $I + G + a - bT$. This is a very useful expression. It tells us that an *increase* in either investment or government spending will shift the aggregate demand schedule upwards by the amount of the increased spending. It also tells us that an increase in taxes of \$1 billion will shift the aggregate demand schedule *downwards* by b billion dollars, which is less than \$1 billion since b, the MPC, is less than unity. This tax-induced downward shift in the aggregate demand schedule arises because consumers will have \$1 billion less in after-tax disposable income, which will be reflected in a reduction in consumption of b billion dollars.

As discussed earlier in this chapter, the economy will be in equilibrium when total planned aggregate demand is equal to aggregate supply/income, point E_0 in Chart 4-6. Alternatively, equilibrium will occur when planned investment plus government spending is equal to savings plus taxes.[29] Given the aggregate demand

---

[28]In the next chapter, an income tax function is incorporated into the basic Keynesian model.

[29]Since all income must be either spent C, saved S or paid in taxes T, these two statements of equilibrium are algebraically equivalent:

$$Y = Z$$
$$\cancel{C} + S + T = \cancel{C} + I + G$$
$$S + T = I + G$$

CHART 4-6 Fiscal policy in the Keynesian cross macroeconomic model

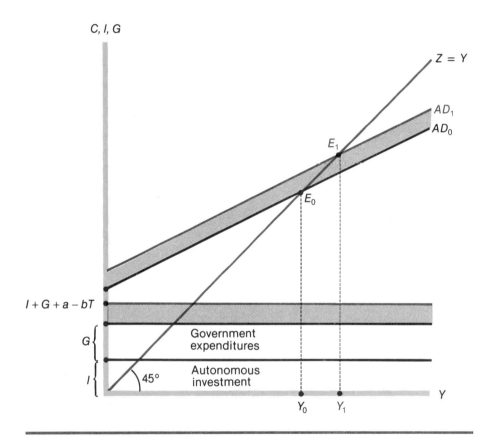

schedule AD_0 in Chart 4-6, for all levels of income other than Y_0 inventories will either be accumulating or declining. In the face of either excess supply or excess demand, income will gravitate towards Y_0, the unique, stable equilibrium income level.

Now assume that *either* autonomous investment *or* government spending increases by $1 billion. In either case, the total aggregate demand schedule will shift upwards by $1 billion (to AD_1) and the multiplier effect on equilibrium income will be the same ($Y_1 - Y_0$). Diagrammatically, it makes absolutely no difference whether the investment block or the government spending block increases by $1 billion. In each case, the shift in the aggregate demand schedule and the resulting multiplier effect are exactly the same. To illustrate this key proposition, consider the construction of a $1 billion new office building. Irrespective of whether the government or a private firm constructs this new office building, the subsequent rounds of spending will be exactly the same. It makes no difference to the construction or factory worker whether the government or the private sector initiated the building project. All paycheques are spent in the same manner. To repeat, *the income-generating effects of an increase in autonomous investment are exactly the same as those associated with an increase in government spending*. An important Keynesian proposition that follows from this is that *the macroeconomic effect of a decrease in autonomous investment can be exactly offset by an increase in government spending equal to the decrease in autonomous investment*.

Now let us turn to the macroeconomic effects of a change in taxes. Diagrammatically, a $1 billion *decrease* in taxes is represented by an *increase* in aggregate demand of b billion dollars. Not all of the tax cut will be spent, as consumers will save part of the increase in disposable income. Unlike the case where the government spends $1 billion, a $1 billion tax cut produces only b (the marginal propensity to consume) times $1 billion of "first round" consumer spending. Subsequent spending rounds in the multiplier process will be accordingly smaller and the overall tax cut multiplier effects will be smaller than the government spending multiplier effects. While the income multiplier effects from a tax change are only b times as large as the government expenditure multiplier effects, a tax cut can nonetheless provide an important stimulus to aggregate demand.

Suppose the government increases government spending by $1 billion and raises the required revenue to pay for this extra government spending through a $1 billion tax increase. The increase in government spending shifts the aggregate demand schedule *upwards* by $1 billion and the tax increase shifts the aggregate demand schedule *downwards* by b billion dollars. Since b (the MPC) is less than one, the net effect of the matched government spending and tax increase is to shift the aggregate demand schedule upwards by $(1 - b)$ billion dollars and therefore to raise income. Why does the economy get an income boost from an increase in the size of the government sector even when government spending is totally financed by taxes? When the government takes a dollar in taxes and spends it *all*, total spending is increased: consumers would have saved part of the dollar of disposable income that is now being spent by the government. In fact, the increase in aggregate demand is equal to what would otherwise have been saved, $(1 - b)$ of every dollar raised in taxes. (Note that this is the distance the aggregate demand curve shifts up as a result of the balanced increase in G and T.) This increase in aggregate demand arising from a balanced increase in government spending and taxes will have an effect on income, the **balanced-budget multiplier effect**.

All of the results that we have derived in this section can be demonstrated algebraically by examining the *new* reduced-form equation for equilibrium income. To obtain this *new* reduced-form income equation we follow exactly the same steps as before. First, substitute the consumption function into the aggregate demand identity.

$$Y = Z = C + I + G$$

$$Y = a + b(Y - T) + I + G$$

Now collect the Y terms,

$$Y(1 - b) = a - bT + I + G$$

(4-6a) $$Y = \frac{a}{1-b} - \frac{bT}{1-b} + \frac{I}{1-b} + \frac{G}{1-b}$$

This new reduced-form equation (4-6a) again lays bare the structural determinants of equilibrium income: the parameters of the consumption function (a, b) and the values of the three exogenous variables (T, I, G). In addition, the various multipliers can be determined directly from this *new* reduced-form equation. Consider, for example, a change in government spending from G_0 to G_1. The equilibrium income levels associated with G_0 and G_1 are Y_0 and Y_1 respectively.

$$Y_0 = \frac{a}{1-b} - \frac{bT}{1-b} + \frac{I}{1-b} + \frac{G_0}{1-b}$$

$$Y_1 = \frac{a}{1-b} - \frac{bT}{1-b} + \frac{I}{1-b} + \frac{G_1}{1-b}$$

Now subtract Y_0 from Y_1:

$$Y_1 - Y_0 = 0 + 0 + 0 + \frac{G_1}{1-b} - \frac{G_0}{1-b}$$

or $$\Delta Y = \frac{\Delta G}{1-b}$$

$$\frac{\Delta Y}{\Delta G} = \frac{1}{1-b}$$

Note that that income multiplier effect of a change in government spending is $1/(1-b)$, the coefficient of G in the reduced-form equation (4-6a). In general, the multiplier associated with a particular exogenous variable is its coefficient in the reduced-form equation. Thus, the investment multiplier effect on income is

$$\frac{\Delta Y}{\Delta I} = \frac{1}{1-b}$$

and the tax multiplier effect on income is

$$\frac{\Delta Y}{\Delta T} = \frac{-b}{1-b}$$

Finally, suppose an increase in government spending is fully financed by increased taxes. The associated change in income will be the sum of the multiplier effects from both ΔG and ΔT.

$$\Delta Y = \frac{\Delta G}{1-b} - \frac{b\Delta T}{1-b}$$

Since $\Delta G = \Delta T$, the new balanced-budget multiplier effect is the following:

$$\Delta Y = \frac{\Delta G}{1-b} - \frac{b\Delta G}{1-b} = \left(\frac{1-b}{1-b}\right)\Delta G = \Delta G$$

$$\frac{\Delta Y}{\Delta G} = 1$$

Under balanced-budget conditions in a Keynesian cross economy, equilibrium income will rise by the amount of the increase in government spending. As we shall see in Chapter 6 when our model is enlarged to include endogenous investment expenditures, imports and income taxes, the balanced-budget multiplier effect will fall substantially below unity.

Given a Keynesian cross economy, the key propositions of this section can be conveniently summarized:

> Proposition 1: The investment and government spending multipliers are identical and equal to $1/(1 - b)$.
>
> Proposition 2: The tax multiplier is $-b/(1 - b)$, and is smaller in size than the government spending multiplier because b, the MPC, is less than unity.
>
> Proposition 3: The balanced-budget multiplier is unity.

In conclusion, Keynesian economics provides both a diagnosis and a policy prescription for the problem of persistent recessions. Faced with insufficient aggregate demand, the diagnosed root cause of serious recessions, the government has a wide variety of fiscal policies available to stimulate aggregate demand and alleviate the unemployment problem. Any shortfall in aggregate demand, such as from a decline in autonomous investment, can be **offset** by an appropriate amount of fiscal stimulus. Recessions can be cured by appropriate fiscal policies. Keynesian economics rationalized a brand new "revolutionary" role for governments. According to Keynes, the government should manage or control aggregate demand and "the central controls necessary to ensure full employment will, of course, involve a large extension of the traditional functions of government."[30] The government should be an *active* player within the economic system, seeking to stabilize the economy by *changing* its spending and taxation policies. It is this Keynesian *activist* or *interventionist* policy approach to *stabilization* problems which has attracted a great deal of criticism from more conservative economists. As we shall see later, there are many difficulties in trying to implement an "appropriate" Keynesian stabilization policy, not to mention the inflation complications arising from pouring on too much Keynesian stimulus.

[30]Keynes, *General Theory*, p. 379.

Key Concepts

the "invisible hand" of Adam Smith
aggregate demand
the consumption (savings) function
the marginal propensity to consume (save)
scatter diagram
least squares estimation technique
autonomous investment expenditures
the aggregate demand schedule
Keynesian aggregate supply under inflexible wage and price levels
the aggregate output market-clearing condition and the
    45° line in the *Keynesian cross* diagram.
equilibrium income
the stability of equilibrium income
structural determinants of equilibrium income
the multiplier process
exogenous versus endogenous variables
structural parameters
the reduced form of a macroeconomic model
the multiplier concept (as derived from the reduced form)
fiscal policy
the balanced budget multiplier
fiscal offsets (for changes in autonomous investment)

Review Questions

1. Explain why a "classical" economist would have dismissed the notion that *persistent* unemployment could arise in a market economy.
2. With respect to the economic behaviour of consumers, how did Keynes' views differ from the views of "classical" economists?
3. Explain how a positively-sloped savings-income relationship can be derived from a Keynesian consumption function.
4. How do economists test their theories? Explain.
5. Why did Keynes think that most investment expenditures were autonomous?
6. What are the key assumptions behind the Keynesian cross representation of a simple macroeconomic model?
7. What determines the equilibrium income level in the Keynesian cross macroeconomic model? Explain.
8. Why is this unique equilibrium level of income stable? Explain.
9. In the Keynesian cross model, why must savings be equal to investment at the equilibrium income level?
10. Why will the equilibrium income level decline if consumers increase their marginal propensity to save?
11. What is the effect on equilibrium income when autonomous investment declines? Carefully explain why the income effect will exceed the decline in autonomous investment.

12. Explain why the multiplier effects on income from a change in autonomous investment depend on the marginal propensity to consume. (A numerical illustration might help.)

13. Explain how one can obtain the algebraic reduced form for a macroeconomic model. What are the key characteristics of the reduced-form equations? How many reduced-form equations are there in a macroeconomic model?

14. Explain the concept of a multiplier in terms of the reduced form of the model. How many different multipliers are there in a macroeconomic model?

15. How would you go about computing the actual value for the multiplier effects on income associated with a change in autonomous investment?

16. Given Keynes' diagnosis of the causes of chronic unemployment, what government policies did he recommend? Why?

17. In terms of a simple Keynesian cross model, what are the multiplier effects associated with (i) an increase in government spending and (ii) a decrease in taxes?

18. Why are the income effects associated with an increase in government spending identical to those associated with an increase in autonomous investment?

19. Why are the income-generating effects of a $1 billion tax cut less than those associated with a $1 billion increase in government spending?

20. What is the effect on equilibrium income if the government increases both government spending and taxes by the same amount? Explain carefully.

Part2

Keynesian Economics: I The Diagnosis

In particular it is an outstanding characteristic of the economic system in which we live that, whilst it is subject to severe fluctuations in respect of output and employment, it is not violently unstable. Indeed it seems capable of remaining in a chronic condition of sub-normal activity for a considerable period without any marked tendency towards recovery or towards complete collapse. Moreover, the evidence indicates that full, or even approximately full, employment is of rare and short-lived occurrence.

John Maynard Keynes [1]

As discussed in the previous chapter, the major integrating theme of Keynes' new theoretical approach is the concept of aggregate demand. While Keynes assumed that consumer expenditures were a relatively stable function of income levels (the Keynesian consumption function), business investment expenditures were considered to be much less stable and subject to important unpredictable autonomous shifts (the Keynesian "animal spirits"). A wave of pessimism in business confidence could cause a serious decline in investment spending which would reverberate throughout the economic system, producing a magnified reduction in output. The equilibrium equality between savings and investment might very well occur at a relatively low income level, and there are no guarantees that the "invisible hand" of Adam Smith will quickly work its magic. As quoted above, the economic system "seems capable of remaining in a chronic condition of sub-normal activity."

Fortunately, Keynes not only identified the cause of chronic recessions as insufficient aggregate demand, he also suggested a policy prescription for the problem. The government has, at its disposal, a variety of policies which are capable of stimulating aggregate demand and propelling the economy out of a recessionary state. In Keynes' view, governments had the ability, and therefore the responsibility, to "control" aggregate demand and to "stabilize" output and employment levels. Prolonged bouts of severe unemployment, such as occurred during the 1930s, can be avoided by government policy intervention. The management of aggregate demand, using various government policies, is the essence of Keynesian economics.

[1]J.M. Keynes, *The General Theory of Employment, Interest and Money* (London: Macmillan & Co., 1936), p. 249-50.

In this chapter we develop a more complete model of Keynesian economics, building upon the Keynesian cross foundations presented in Chapter 4. Two major additional features are incorporated into our Keynesian macroeconomic model. First we consider the role of interest rates and financial assets (money and bonds) in the macroeconomic system. As we shall see, interest rates play a pivotal role in our model, affecting both aggregate demand, particularly investment expenditures, and the demand for money. Second, we "open" up our macroeconomic model to include foreign trade. For a relatively small, industrialized country such as Canada, exports and imports represent important additional components of aggregate demand.[2] Following the practice adopted in the previous chapter, we divide our macroeconomic analysis into two interrelated parts: the Keynesian diagnosis and the Keynesian policy prescription. The next chapter provides a complete review of the policy implications of the basic Keynesian macroeconomic model, which is developed in this chapter. Throughout both of these chapters we continue to assume that price levels are fixed. Chapters 8 and 9 permanently relax this inflexible price level assumption and incorporate a theory of price level determination and inflation into our macroeconomic model. As we shall see, the supply of money, a new feature of this chapter, has a lot to do with the process of inflation.

The basic model which we present in this chapter, usually referred to as the *IS-LM* model (see below), represents the essential elements of Keynesian economics and is the core of modern day macroeconomics. The key to understanding this *IS-LM* model is the separation of the economy into two major aggregate markets: (1) the **product market** (the *IS* part of the model) and (2) the **financial assets market** (the *LM* part of the model). As discussed in the previous chapter, the myriad of different kinds of goods and services such as beer, hamburgers, books, and automobiles are aggregated into one giant product market in which there are no distinctions drawn between different kinds of goods and services. As macroeconomists we *assume* that there is only one homogenous product in the market place, and we leave it to the microeconomist to analyze the relative price of different kinds of goods and the allocation of resources to different industries. While there are many different forms of financial assets, such as money, savings accounts, guaranteed investment certificates, treasury bills, stocks and bonds, we *assume* that this set of financial assets can be represented by two assets: money and bonds. In our model, bonds are the representative financial instrument which allows individuals to earn interest on their accumulated savings, rather than having to hold savings in the form of money (which pays no interest).

In developing our basic Keynesian macroeconomic model, we will carefully examine economic behaviour within each of these two large aggregate markets, the product market and the financial asset market.[3] The various components of

---

[2]We postpone until Chapter 7 a discussion of balance of payment adjustment mechanisms and the role of the foreign exchange rate in a macroeconomic model.

[3]In Chapter 7 we consider balance of payments adjustment mechanisms and add a third market to our macroeconomic model, the foreign exchange market. In Chapter 8 we relax the inflexible price level assumption within the Keynesian model and add a fourth major market to our model, the labour market.

our model, such as a new investment function, will be kept as simple as possible in order that the key interactions between these two large aggregate markets can be fully understood. Equilibrium for the economy as a whole can only occur when both of these two separate but interrelated markets are individually in equilibrium. We begin our analysis by considering the role of interest rates in the investment decision, and then turn to the financial assets market. The last section of the chapter extends our analysis to include a government and a foreign trade sector.

Investment Expenditures and the Rate of Interest

Suppose that a firm is considering a new investment project, say the construction of a $1 million new factory. To determine whether this new factory will be profitable or not, the firm must carefully "estimate" the flow of all future revenues and costs associated with this new factory. After detailed study of the firm's future demand prospects, costs and risks, suppose that the controller's office of our hypothetical firm estimates that the annual net rate of return (profit) on this new factory would be 12 per cent.[4] Should our hypothetical firm go ahead with its $1 million new factory?

Since most firms do not have $1 million in idle cash, our hypothetical firm will probably have to borrow the funds to finance the construction of this new factory. Consequently, the decision to invest or not to invest depends crucially on the rate of interest which the firm must pay to borrow the required funds. If the rate of interest exceeds the expected 12 per cent rate of return on this investment project, then a profit-maximizing firm would not want to proceed with this new factory since the cost of borrowing funds would exceed the net return from the new factory. On the other hand, if the rate of interest is less than 12 per cent, the firm would "profit" by building this new factory. Even if the firm had $1 million in idle cash, the same principle would still apply. If the interest rate exceeds the net return on the new investment project, it would be more "profitable" for the firm to lend its $1 million at the market rate of interest than to undertake the new investment project at a lower rate of return.

Assuming that firms make investment decisions by comparing the prevailing interest rate to the expected rate of return on potential investment projects, when interest rates are high few investment projects will likely pass this profitability test. Conversely when interest rates are low, many investment projects will likely pass the profitability test. A similar argument applies with equal force to residential construction, another component of total investment. The higher the mortgage rate, the more reticent new home buyers become. The cost of borrowing funds is an important part of the investment decision and total investment expenditures should respond in a *negative* fashion to interest rate movements. Lower interest rates should lead to a greater investment demand.

---

[4]In Chapter 20 we discuss how the controller's office might calculate the rate of return for an investment project.

While Keynes accepted the proposition that investment expenditures will tend to vary inversely with the rate of interest, he emphasized the "precarious" process by which expectations concerning future prospective returns for an investment project are formulated. Given the difficulty in predicting future economic events and formulating long-term expectations of profit and risk, Keynes believed that the current state of business confidence was a more important factor in making investment decisions. If investors are not very confident about the future, they are unlikely to invest in new plant and equipment regardless of the prevailing interest rate. As discussed in Chapter 4, Keynes paid particular attention to the current state of business psychology, or as Keynes liked to refer to it—"the animal spirits" of investors: "If the animal spirits are dimmed and the spontaneous optimism falters, leaving us to depend on nothing but a mathematical expectation, enterprise will fade and die."[5] In Keynes' view, the level of investment depends much more on autonomous forces than on interest rates.

Was Keynes right? Are investment expenditures more dependent on autonomous elements than on interest rate movements? To examine this key question, Chart 5-1 provides a scatter diagram for Canadian investment expenditures and interest rates. As discussed in Chapter 3, in an *inflationary* world the market rate of interest will include an inflation premium to offset the loss in purchasing power attributable to inflation. In an inflationary setting, one must distinguish between the *nominal* market rate of interest and the *real* rate of interest (which is the market rate of interest less the expected inflation rate). In Chapter 20 we demonstrate that investment decisions will be based on the real rate of interest, not the nominal market rate of interest. Thus in Chart 5-1 we plot the real rate of interest on the horizontal axis, which we approximate by subtracting the annual percentage change in the Consumer Price Index from the interest rate paid on government long-term bonds.[6] Given the time lags in construction, we assume an average lag of one year from financing to completion of the investment project. Therefore last year's real interest rate is plotted against this year's investment expenditures. Finally, to remove the secular growth component from investment expenditures, we have divided this year's investment expenditures by last year's GNP (both measured in constant 1971 dollars) and have plotted the ratio of investment to total output on the vertical axis of our scatter diagram.

Unlike the statistical evidence presented for the Keynesian consumption function in Chapter 4, empirical evidence for the investment function is not nearly so clear cut. While the data points in Chart 5-1 are quite widely scattered, there is a discernable negative statistical relationship between investment expenditures (as a ratio to GNP) and real interest rates in Canada over the years from 1960 through 1984. The general drift of the scatter of data points is downwards to the right.[7] In fact, 19 of the 24 data points fall in a fairly narrow downward-sloping band. As a

[5]Keynes, *General Theory*, p. 162.
[6]Given the rapid acceleration in the inflation rate in the mid-1970s, our proxy for the real rate of interest turns out to be negative for the years 1973, 1974 and 1975.
[7]The least squares estimation technique produces an estimated intercept of .239 and an estimated slope of −0.0027, both estimates being significantly different from zero (at the 5 per cent error level).

CHART 5-1 Investment expenditures—interest rate scatter diagram, 1960-84

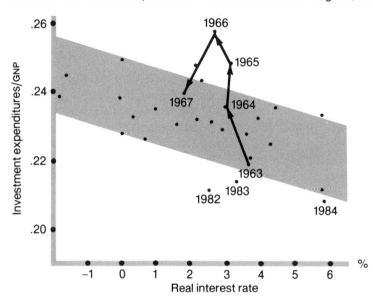

general rule, higher levels of investment appear to be associated with lower real interest rates.

Skeptics of the interest rate hypothesis of investment demand, including Keynes, would be very concerned with the wide scatter of points in Chart 5-1 and would zero in on the observations that do not fit the hypothesized interest rate pattern. For example, the data points for 1965 and 1966 lie well above the red band in Chart 5-1 while the 1982, 1983 and 1984 data points are below the red band. It should be noted that 1965-66 and 1982-84 represent two extreme states for the Canadian economy; compared to a 3.4 per cent record low unemployment rate in 1965, the unemployment rate in 1983 reached a post-1930s record high of 11.9 per cent. A follower of Keynes might well argue that a wave of business optimism swept the country in the mid-1960s and a wave of extreme pessimism prevailed in the 1982-83 recession.[8] In addition, large swings in investment spending can occur under very stable interest rate patterns. For example, the tremendous increase in investment expenditures from 1963 through 1966 occurred with only modest declines in the real interest rate. Even more damaging to the interest rate hypothesis, the large decline in investment spending in 1967 occurred as the real interest rate declined! Since large swings in investment spending can occur under very stable interest rate conditions, autonomous elements may exert an important influence on investment expenditures.

In summary, the statistical evidence on Canadian investment expenditures is somewhat inconclusive. While a negative relationship between investment expenditures and interest rates is discernable in the data, a number of observa-

---

[8]As discussed in Chapter 20, the accelator theory of investment might also be invoked to explain this highly cyclical pattern of investment.

tions clearly do not fit this negative pattern. The evidence presented in Chart 5-1 suggests that important shifts in investment demand have also taken place in Canada. Since these shifts are unrelated to interest rate movements and output levels (recall we normalized investment expenditures by dividing by GNP), autonomous elements in investment demand cannot be dismissed.

Postponing a more complete analysis of investment demand until Chapter 20, the following simple linear investment function captures the essential elements of Chart 5-1.

$$(5\text{-}1) \qquad I = I_a - eR$$

Henceforward we will refer to the intercept I_a of our investment function as the **autonomous** element in the investment process and the interest rate component eR as the **endogenous** element of investment spending, that is, the component of investment expenditures which is directly related to interest rate movements. Using Keynesian terminology, a sudden unpredictable change in business confidence causes the investment function to shift. As shown in Chart 5-2, a wave of business optimism (pessimism) increases (decreases) autonomous investment, causing an upward (downward) shift in the intercept of the investment function.[9] In Keynes' view, the intercept I_a of the investment function is subject to substantial and persistent shifts which will tend to swamp the influence of interest rate movements on investment spending. However, for a *given* state of business confidence, the intercept I_a of our investment function remains fixed and the level of investment expenditures depends negatively on the rate of interest. To summarize, *a change in autonomous investment* (or change in the state of business confidence) *will cause the investment function to shift, whereas a change in interest rates will cause a movement along a particular investment function* (based on a *given* state of business confidence).[10]

The *IS* Curve

Having postulated a new investment function in which investment expenditures respond negatively to interest rate movements for a given state of business confidence, we now must re-derive our aggregate demand schedule to reflect this important amendment to our macroeconomic model. To keep our initial analysis of this amended macroeconomic model as simple as possible, we return to a macroeconomic world in which, for the moment, there is no government sector and define aggregate demand as the sum of planned consumption and investment

---

[9]For example, the investment boom years of 1965-66 might lie on the high "optimism" curve whereas the stagnant years of 1982-84 might lie on the low "pessimism" curve. If the other years lie roughly along the "average" business confidence investment curve, Chart 5-2 would provide an explanation of the data scatter in Chart 5-1.

[10]Since Keynes thought that interest rates had a relatively minor influence on investment spending (the parameter e was quite low), Keynes would have drawn the investment function as a fairly flat line. Consequently, a change in interest rates would have a small quantitative effect on investment expenditures. The size of the intercept—autonomous investment—would be the key factor in determining investment demand.

CHART 5·2 Investment demand for different states of business confidence

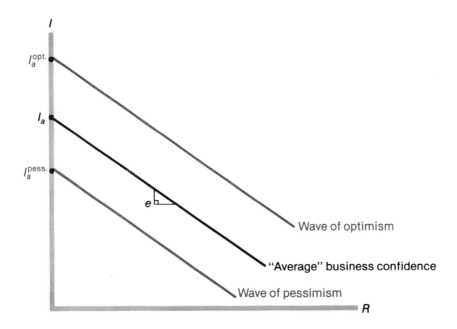

expenditures. Substituting our Keynesian consumption function from Chapter 4 (equation 4-2) and our new investment function (equation 5-1) into the aggregate demand identity (equation 4-1), we readily obtain the following amended version of our aggregate demand schedule (equation 5-2):

(4-1) $$Z = C + I$$

(4-2) $$C = a + bY$$

(5-1) $$I = I_a - eR$$

(5-2) $\therefore$ $$Z = a + bY + I_a - eR = (a + I_a - eR) + bY$$

Chart 5-3 illustrates our amended Keynesian macroeconomic model in diagrammatic terms. Panel A of Chart 5-3 reproduces the negative relationship between the level of investment and the rate of interest (equation 5-1) that was presented in Chart 5-2. (For the time being, disregard the red investment schedule.) The consumption function (equation 4-2) and our amended aggregate demand schedule (equation 5-2) are presented in panel B of Chart 5-3. Aggregate demand is the sum of consumption plus investment, but the level of investment now depends on the rate of interest. To illustrate how this amended aggregate demand schedule is constructed, suppose, for example, that the rate of interest is R_1. From panel A of Chart 5-3, an interest rate of R_1 generates investment spending equal to I_1. By adding this quantity of investment I_1 to the intercept of

CHART 5-3 Derivation of *IS* curve

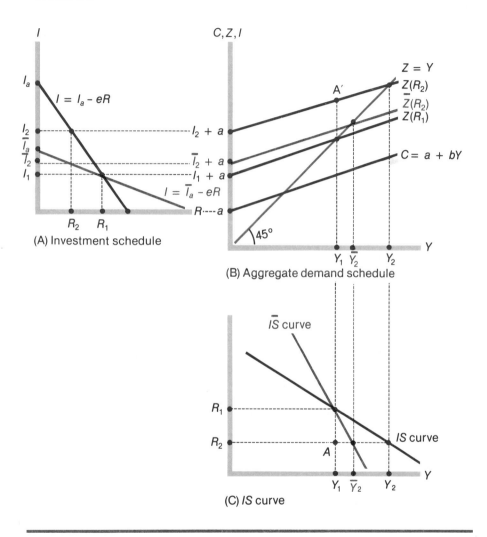

(A) Investment schedule

(B) Aggregate demand schedule

(C) *IS* curve

the consumption function, we obtain the aggregate demand schedule which corresponds to an interest rate of R_1, $Z(R_1)$ in panel **B**. If the interest rate were to decline to R_2, investment spending would increase to I_2 in panel **A** and the aggregate demand schedule in panel **B** would shift up to $Z(R_2)$, with an intercept of $I_2 + a$. Each interest rate will result in a different level of investment expenditures and a different aggregate demand schedule. As equation 5-2 indicates, the intercept of the aggregate demand schedule depends *negatively* on the interest rate. A decrease (increase) in the interest rate will cause this intercept to increase (decrease) and the aggregate demand schedule to shift upwards (downwards).

As we have seen in Chapter 4, the product market will be in equilibrium when planned aggregate demand Z is equal to aggregate supply, or total income Y. This equilibrium point is represented by the intersection of the aggregate demand schedule with the 45° ($Z = Y$) line. Given an interest rate R_1 and an aggregate demand schedule of $Z(R_1)$ in panel B of Chart 5-3, the equilibrium income level will be Y_1. For the lower interest rate R_2, the higher aggregate demand schedule $Z(R_2)$ will generate a higher equilibrium level of income, Y_2 in panel B. In our amended model, the equilibrium income level now depends crucially on the rate of interest. The lower is the rate of interest, the greater is the level of income that maintains equilibrium in the product market.

In the lower panel of Chart 5-3 (C), we have plotted our two potential equilibrium income levels Y_1 and Y_2 corresponding to interest rates R_1 and R_2. For *any* given interest rate and associated aggregate demand schedule we can determine the level of income which will maintain product market equilibrium, that is, the level of income which equates aggregate demand to aggregate supply. The collection of *(Y,R)* points that maintain product market equilibrium is called the **IS** *curve* (*I* for investment, *S* for saving).[11] The points *(Y₁,R₁)* and *(Y₂,R₂)* are just two of an infinite number of *(Y, R)* combinations which maintain product market equilibrium and lie along the *IS* curve.

> **Definition of the *IS* Curve: The *IS* curve is the collection of all possible combinations of income and interest rates which maintain equilibrium in the product market.**

Any point which is *not* on the *IS* curve would correspond to a state of disequilibrium in the product market. To demonstrate this, consider an income-interest rate combination which is *below* the *IS* curve, say point A *(Y₁,R₂)* in panel C of Chart 5-3. Based on the aggregate demand schedule $Z(R_2)$ corresponding to an interest rate of R_2, an income of Y_1 generates a level of aggregate demand equal to the vertical distance $A'Y_1$ in panel B of Chart 5-3. Point A' is above the 45° line, indicating that aggregate demand (measured along the vertical axis) *exceeds* aggregate supply (measured along the horizontal axis). All points such as A which lie below or to the left of the *IS* curve correspond to a state of excess demand in the product market. Similarly, all points above or to the right of the *IS* curve correspond to a state of excess supply in the product market. Only points along the *IS* curve represent equilibrium in the product market.

The Slope of the *IS* Curve

The *IS* curve has a downward slope because the *lower* is the rate of interest, the greater is the level of investment expenditure, the greater is aggregate demand, and therefore the larger is the equilibrium level of income. The actual steepness of the *IS* curve is determined by two key behavioural parameters: the slope of the

---

[11]As a historical footnote, Keynes did *not* invent the *IS* (or *LM*) curve. The *IS-LM* graphical apparatus was first suggested by Sir John Hicks in an article which reviewed and summarized the major features of the *General Theory* ("Mr. Keynes and the 'Classics'; A Suggested Interpretation," *Econometrica*, April 1937, pp. 147-59).

investment function e, and the marginal propensity to consume b. While there has been relatively little debate in macroeconomics about the size of the marginal propensity to consume b, the value of the parameter e has been much more controversial. The less sensitive investment expenditures are to the interest rate (the smaller is the parameter e), the smaller will be the upward shift in the aggregate demand schedule when the interest rate falls. This is illustrated by the red investment schedule in panel A of Chart 5-3, which is less interest-sensitive than the black investment schedule. For convenience, the investment schedule is rotated counterclockwise through the point (R_1, I_1). The level of investment now rises by a *smaller* amount (to $\bar{I}_2$) when the interest rate falls from R_1 to R_2. Consequently, the aggregate demand schedule shifts upwards by a *smaller* distance and the equilibrium income level $\bar{Y}_2$ is lower than the previous equilibrium income level Y_2 (which was based on the steeper, black investment schedule). This new equilibrium point $(\bar{Y}_2, R_2)$ is plotted in the lower panel and lies on the red $\overline{IS}$ curve, which is *steeper* than the black IS curve. The less sensitive (or less responsive) investment expenditures are to interest rate changes, the steeper the IS curve.[12]

Shifts of the *IS* Curve

The IS curve derived above was constructed by plotting the level of income which will maintain equilibrium in the product market for each interest rate. However, for any given interest rate the equilibrium income level also depends on the parameters of the consumption function and the level of autonomous investment. Consequently, the IS curve will shift if either one of these additional factors does change. To illustrate this point, Chart 5-4 demonstrates the effects of a *decrease* in autonomous investment on the position of the IS curve. First consider the black investment schedule corresponding to I_a units of autonomous investment. As in Chart 5-3, we select two arbitrary interest rates R_1 and R_2, add the corresponding investment levels I_1 and I_2 to the consumption function to produce the two black aggregate demand schedules $Z(R_1)$ and $Z(R_2)$, and then locate the two possible equilibrium income levels Y_1 and Y_2 corresponding to R_1 and R_2 respectively. In the lower panel of Chart 5-4 we plot these two possible equilibrium points (Y_1, R_1) and (Y_2, R_2), which are representative of the IS curve based on I_a units of autonomous investment.

Now suppose that a wave of business pessimism lowers autonomous investment by $\triangle I_a$ units, causing the intercept of the investment schedule to shift downwards (to $\bar{I}_a$ in panel A of Chart 5-4). Along this new red investment schedule, there will be less investment taking place at all interest rates, including R_1 and R_2. Thus, the

---

[12]Preoccupied with "animal spirits," Keynes thought that investment spending was very insensitive to interest rate movements. As a consequence, Keynes would have implicitly regarded the IS curve as being very steep and unstable because of the instability of autonomous investment. Modern-day critics of Keynes, usually referred to as monetarists, play down the role of autonomous elements in the investment decision and emphasize the sensitivity of investment expenditures to slight movements in the interest rate. Thus, a monetarist would implicitly think in terms of a very flat, stable IS curve. The policy implications of the slope of the IS curve are discussed in the next chapter.

two new red aggregate demand schedules $\overline{Z}(R_1)$ and $\overline{Z}(R_2)$ will lie below our previous two aggregate demand schedules $Z(R_1)$ and $Z(R_2)$ in panel B of Chart 5-4. Our two new equilibrium income levels $\overline{Y}_1$ and $\overline{Y}_2$ will both have declined relative to our original equilibrium income levels Y_1 and Y_2. In the lower quadrant of Chart 5-4 we have plotted these two new equilibrium points $(\overline{Y}_1,R_1)$ and $(\overline{Y}_2,R_2)$, representative of the new $\overline{IS}$ curve based on $\overline{I}_a$ units of autonomous investment. A decline in autonomous investment has caused the IS curve to shift downwards to the left.[13]

In general, any factor that shifts the aggregate demand schedule downwards (other than the interest rate) will shift the IS curve down to the left. Changes in the interest rate are, of course, reflected in movements *along* a given IS curve. Finally, factors (other than the interest rate) that shift the aggregate demand schedule upwards will cause the IS curve to shift upwards to the right.

The Financial Asset Market

The IS curve describes various *possible* combinations of income and interest rates which maintain equilibrium in the aggregate product market. To determine *the* equilibrium income level for the economic system as a whole, we now must turn our attention to the financial asset market. To simplify our analysis, we assume that the financial asset market is comprised of only two assets: money and bonds. In our model the bond is the financial asset which allows individuals to earn interest on their accumulated savings, rather than having to hold savings in the form of money. For purposes of this chapter we define money as the sum of currency (coins and dollar bills of various denominations) and demand deposits (chequing accounts) in banks.[14] The amount of money supplied at any particular time is determined by the Bank of Canada, a government agency. While we briefly discuss how the Bank of Canada "controls" the money supply a little later in this chapter, a full treatment of this topic is provided in Chapter 18. Just as the government must select particular values for tax rates and government spending (fiscal policy), the government must also select a particular value for the **money supply** (monetary policy). In model terminology, the money supply is an *exogenous* variable, a policy instrument under the direct control of the government.

Turning to the demand side of the market, from the individual's point of view money and bonds are two alternative financial assets. Given one's total amount of wealth, an individual must decide how much should be kept in the form of money and how much should be kept in the form of bonds. In making this portfolio decision, one must carefully weigh the relative costs and benefits of these two alternative financial assets. By identifying the functions of money, we can gain

---

[13]The exact distance that the IS curve shifts leftwards can be easily computed. For any given interest rate, aggregate demand initially declined by the amount ΔI_a. As computed in Chapter 4, *for a fixed interest rate* the multiplier effect of such a decline in autonomous investment on equilibrium income is $1/(1-b)$, where b is the marginal propensity to consume. Thus the leftward shift of the IS curve in panel C is equal to $\Delta I_a/(1-b)$.

[14]In Chapter 18 we consider other "broader" definitions of money which include savings accounts (M2) and other types of highly liquid financial assets.

CHART 5-4 Effects of a decrease in autonomous investment on the *IS* curve

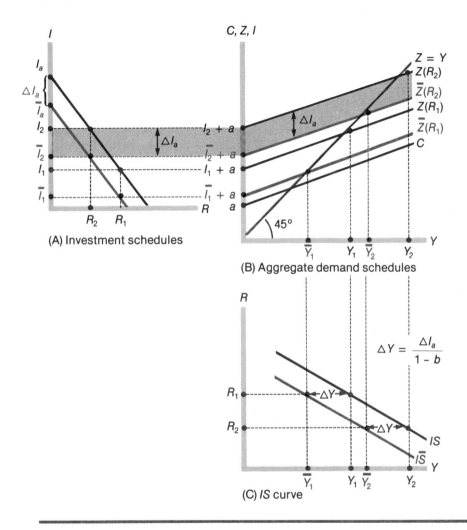

(A) Investment schedules

(B) Aggregate demand schedules

(C) *IS* curve

some insight into the advantages and disadvantages of holding financial wealth in the form of money.

First and foremost, money is the medium of exchange. Rather than having to barter good A for good B, people exchange money when they buy and sell goods, thereby avoiding the "double coincidence" of wants which is required under barter transactions.[15] Second, money can serve as a store of value or wealth. It

---

[15]In a barter transaction not only must I want to exchange good A for good B, someone else must want to exchange good B for good A. Without money as a medium of exchange, a considerable amount of time and effort would be necessary to find someone who has an opposite set of wants.

allows individuals to separate in time the two sides of a transaction. Using money as a medium of exchange, good A can be sold today and the proceeds can be used at some later date to purchase good B. However, since money earns no interest, the opportunity cost of storing one's wealth in the form of money is the rate of interest which one could have earned if one had purchased a bond.[16]

The Transactions Demand for Money and the Rate of Interest

Given these two major functions of money, we formulate a relatively simple economic theory concerning why individuals will choose to hold or demand money. First, the medium of exchange function of money suggests that individuals will hold money in order to facilitate economic transactions. While most individuals typically purchase goods and services such as food, cigarettes, magazines, and entertainment on a fairly regular basis, income payments are received relatively infrequently, perhaps once or twice a month. Given that the receipt of income is not perfectly synchronized with desired expenditure patterns, individuals find it convenient to hold money to bridge the interval between the receipt and disbursement of income. The greater the level of income and transactions, the greater the demand for money for transactions purposes.

However, to the extent that money is held to facilitate economic transactions, one forgoes the interest payments that could have been earned by purchasing a bond. The higher the rate of interest, the greater the opportunity cost of holding money for transactions purposes and therefore the greater the desire to economize on the holdings of idle cash balances by keeping funds invested in interest-earning assets. While each individual will likely differ with respect to the threshold interest rate which prompts him/her to transfer idle cash balances into interest-earning assets,[17] as the rate of interest rises more and more individuals (and corporations) will manage their holdings of money more carefully. Higher rates of interest, for a given level of transactions or income, will lead to a reduction in the demand for money as individuals switch idle cash balances into interest-earning assets. The higher the opportunity cost of holding cash balances, the less money will likely be held for transactions purposes.

As is our regular custom, in Chart 5-5 we present Canadian empirical evidence pertaining to our hypothesized theory of the **demand for money**. Since our theory suggests two determinants of the demand for money, income and interest rates, we have to resort to a "diagrammick" to depict three variables in two dimensions. Along the horizontal axis of Chart 5-5 we have plotted the stock of money divided by total income. Thus we have normalized each year's demand for money by the

---

[16]This point remains valid in an inflationary world. As discussed in Chapter 3, the expected rate of inflation will be incorporated into interest rates as an inflation premium. Thus, while a perfectly expected inflation will obviously erode the value of money as a store of wealth, the opportunity cost of holding money will rise accordingly.

[17]There are, of course, costs involved in transferring idle cash balances into interest-earning assets, such as brokerage charges and the time/inconvenience of engaging in financial transactions (see Chapter 18).

CHART 5-5 Demand for money scatter diagram, 1956-84

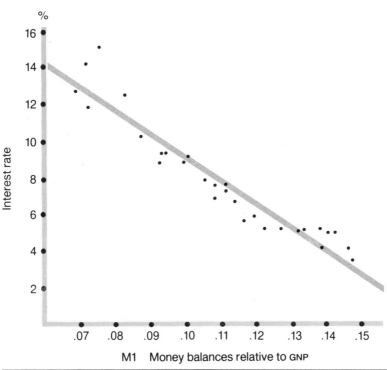

M1   Money balances relative to GNP

annual volume of GNP transactions. On the vertical axis we plot the interest rate, the opportunity cost of holding money. Our scatter diagram depicts the demand for money (relative to income levels) in conjunction with interest rate movements. The evidence presented in Chart 5-5 leaves little doubt that the demand for money varies *inversely* with the interest rate. All of the data points lie quite close to a downward-sloping straight line. As interest rates rise, the demand for money (relative to income levels) clearly decreases.

For the present analysis, we assume that the demand for money depends positively on income levels (the transactions demand)[18] and negatively on interest rates (the opportunity cost of holding money).[19] The empirical evidence presented in Chart 5-5 clearly supports the theoretical concept of a downward-sloping demand for money function. Collectively Canadians appear to have economized on their holdings of money (relative to income levels) as interest rates

[18]In an inflationary world, the demand for nominal money depends on nominal income levels. When we relax our assumption of fixed price levels in Chapter 8, the demand for real money will be assumed to depend on real income levels.

[19]As discussed in Chapter 18, Keynes included interest rates as a negative determinant in the demand for money function for quite different reasons. Rather than focusing on the opportunity cost of holding money when interest rates are high, Keynes suggested the possibility of making a *capital gain* by buying a bond when interest rates are high (the *speculative* motive for demanding more bonds and less money when interest rates are high).

have risen. Equation 5-3 provides a simple linear algebraic formulation of this demand for money ($\$^D$) function, where k and ℓ represent behavioural parameters.[20]

$$(5\text{-}3) \qquad \$^D = kY - \ell R$$

The parameter k in equation 5-3 describes the sensitivity of the demand for money to changes in the level of income, our proxy for the number of transactions taking place. Every extra dollar of income raises the demand for money by k dollars. Similarly the parameter ℓ describes the sensitivity of the demand for money to changes in the interest rate. Every extra percentage point increase in the interest rate causes a decline in the demand for money of ℓ dollars.[21] The size of the parameter ℓ is largely determined by the degree of substitutability between money and bonds. If, for example, money and bonds are highly substitutable, the parameter ℓ will be very large. A one percentage point increase in the interest rate will cause people to convert large amounts of money into interest-bearing bonds. To the extent that bonds and money are regarded as being rather poor substitutes, an increase in interest rates paid on bonds will have very little effect on reducing the demand for money balances. In that case, ℓ will be quite low.

Bond Prices and the Interest Rate— A Brief Digression

The most important way in which governments and corporations borrow funds is through the sale of bonds. The purchasers of *new* bonds lend money to the bond issuer for a given period of time at a *fixed* interest rate. However, once a bond is issued, it is unlikely to be shut away in a vault until the maturity (repayment) date of the bond. For a variety of reasons, the purchaser of a bond, (the lender) may want to convert the bond back into cash long before the bond matures. The bond market allows individuals to buy and sell existing bonds. Just as the stock exchange establishes a market price for existing corporate shares, the bond market establishes a market price for outstanding bonds. In this section we demonstrate that bond prices and interest rates move in *opposite* directions. *High* interest rates are associated with *low* market bond prices and vice versa.

Suppose that one year ago you purchased a new bond for $100 and that the bond pays $10 in interest each year for twenty years (at the end of twenty years the

---

[20]As drawn in Chart 5-5, there is an obvious linear relationship between ($\$^D/Y$) and R, say

$$\frac{\$^D}{Y} = \bar{k} - \bar{\ell}R$$

where $\bar{k}$ is the *horizontal* intercept in Chart 5-5. Multiplying both sides of this equation by Y produces the following equation:

$$\$^D = \bar{k}Y - \bar{\ell}RY$$

Except for the last term, this equation derived from the statistical evidence presented in Chart 5-5 is similar to equation 5-3 in the text.

[21]As presented in the case study in Chapter 6, estimated values for the parameters k and ℓ are 0.11 and 0.58 respectively.

bond matures and you will get your $100 back). This 10 per cent bond yield represented the prevailing market interest rate at the time the new bond was issued, at a par value of 100. Now suppose that one year later you need money and decide to sell the bond. What will you get for the bond on the bond market?

The market value of your bond depends crucially on what the current interest rate is. *If interest rates have remained at 10 per cent*, then you will receive $100 for your bond. A purchaser will be indifferent between paying you $100 for your one-year-old bond and buying a new bond which *also* yields 10 per cent. However, *if interest rates have risen since you purchased your bond*, say to 20 per cent, you will receive considerably *less* than $100 for your one-year-old bond. Why should a purchaser give you $100 for a financial asset which pays only $10 a year for 19 years when new bonds offer $20 per year, or a 20 per cent yield? The bond market would set a value for your old bond of slightly more than $50, because your old bond with its stream of $10 annual interest payments is worth only about one half as much as a new bond with its stream of $20 annual interest payments. On the other hand, *if interest rates have fallen since you purchased your bond*, say to 5 per cent, then the market price of your bond will have *risen* well above $100. Many people will want to purchase your old bond rather than new bonds which have much smaller interest payments. An excess demand for old bonds will push up their price relative to new bonds that were issued at $100 par value and pay only 5 per cent interest. As demonstrated in Chapter 18, there exists a precise mathematical relationship between bond prices and interest rates—they move in *opposite* directions.

Making use of this *negative* relationship between bond prices and interest rates, if bond prices are rising we know that interest rates must be falling. Conversely, if bond prices are falling, interest rates must be rising. For example, if the government wants to raise additional funds, the additional supply of bonds in the bond market will depress bond prices and raise interest rates. To entice purchasers to buy the new issue (supply) of bonds, the government must offer a higher interest rate. Demand and supply conditions in the bond market will be reflected in interest rate movements. In the following sections of this chapter we make considerable use of this inverse relationship between bond prices and current interest rates.

The *LM* Curve

Having provided a simple economic theory for the demand for money, we now derive a new curve that describes equilibrium in the money and financial asset market to go along with our *IS* curve, which depicts various possible equilibrium positions in the aggregate product market. Following the conventions of demand curve analysis in microeconomics, in the left-hand panel of Chart 5-6 we plot the quantity of money demanded on the horizontal axis and the interest rate cost (price) of holding money on the vertical axis. As demonstrated empirically in Chart 5-5, the demand for money curve, like the demand curve for all other products, slopes downwards to the right. A lower interest rate will cause a downward movement *along* the demand for money curve. However, an increase

CHART 5-6 Equilibrium in the money and financial asset market

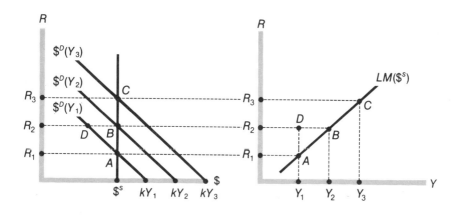

in the level of income will raise the total number of transactions within the economy, which will cause an upward shift in the demand for money curve.[22] In the left-hand panel of Chart 5-6 we have drawn three representative money demand curves corresponding to three different income levels, where $Y_3 > Y_2 > Y_1$. On the horizontal axis we locate the particular supply of money which the Bank of Canada has printed $\$^S$ and draw in the *given* vertical[23] money supply curve.

As in all other markets, the money market is in equilibrium when the demand for money is equal to the given supply of money.

$$(5\text{-}4) \qquad \$^D = \$^S$$

Based on these three hypothetical income levels Y_1, Y_2 and Y_3, points A, B and C represent three possible equilibrium points where the demand for money is equal to the given supply of money $\$^S$. These three potential money market equilibrium combinations of income and interest rates, (Y_1, R_1), (Y_2, R_2) and (Y_3, R_3), are plotted in the right-hand panel of Chart 5-6. Connecting these three representative points, we obtain a new curve which describes all possible combinations of income and interest rates that maintain equilibrium in the money market, for the given money supply $\$^S$. This new curve which describes all possible income and

---

[22]The *horizontal* intercept of the demand for money equation (5-3) is kY (set $R = 0$ and $\$^D = kY$). As income increases, this horizontal intercept shifts to the right and the demand for money curve will shift upwards to the right (see Chart 5-6).

[23]We assume that the quantity of money supplied by the Bank of Canada is *independent* of the prevailing interest rate—the money supply curve is vertical. As discussed in subsequent chapters, the government may choose to alter the supply of money depending on current economic conditions, such as the inflation rate, the unemployment rate, the interest rate and the foreign exchange rate.

interest rate combinations which maintain equilibrium in the money market is called the **LM curve**, L for liquidity[24] and M for money.

> **Definition of the LM Curve: The LM curve is the collection of all possible combinations of income and interest rates that equate the demand for money to the (given) supply of money and therefore maintain equilibrium in the financial asset market.**

Only points on the LM curve are compatible with equilibrium in the money and bond markets. Consider point D in Chart 5-6, which lies above and to the left of the LM curve. At point D, income and the interest rate are Y_1 and R_2 respectively. The left-hand panel of Chart 5-6 indicates that point D, with an interest rate of R_2, lies on the money demand curve $\$^D(Y_1)$ but to the left of the fixed money supply. For an income level of Y_1 and an interest rate of R_2, a state of excess supply will exist in the money market, equal to the distance DB. Given an excess supply of money, individuals will attempt to buy bonds (the alternative financial asset), and in the process will bid up the price of bonds and lower the interest rate. Assuming that the income level remains at Y_1, the interest rate will continue to fall until the excess supply of money has been eliminated. For a fixed supply of money $\$^S$ and a given income level Y_1, a lower interest rate R_1 is required to encourage individuals to hold larger money balances. The economy will slide down the money demand curve $\$^D(Y_1)$ from point D to point A and return to an equilibrium position in the money market.

To summarize, points which lie above and to the left of the LM curve represent positions of excess supply in the money market. Conversely, points which lie below and to the right of the LM curve represent positions of excess demand in the money market. In either *disequilibrium* situation, the economy will return to an *equilibrium* position in the money market, represented by a position on the LM curve.

The Slope of the LM Curve

The *upward* slope of the LM curve can be explained by considering the movement from point A to point B in Chart 5-6. At an income level of Y_1, the demand for money curve $\$^D(Y_1)$ intersects the vertical money supply curve $\$^S$ at an interest rate of R_1 (point A). Now suppose that the level of income rises to Y_2. Given this higher income level, the number of transactions increases and the demand for money curve shifts to the right to $\$^D(Y_2)$. Since the supply of money is *fixed* at $\$^S$, individuals attempt to obtain additional money balances to facilitate the increased transactions at the higher income level by offering to sell bonds. As bonds are offered for sale in the bond market, the price of bonds will be depressed and interest rates will rise. (Recall that bond prices and interest rates move in opposite directions.) With interest rates rising, individuals begin to economize on their holdings of money balances because the opportunity cost of holding money has

---

[24]In Keynes' original formulation of the demand for money, the interest rate effect was attributed to speculative motives and liquidity preferences (see note 19 above and Chapter 18).

increased. For financial asset equilibrium to be restored at this higher income level Y_2, the interest rate must rise sufficiently, to R_2, to equalize the demand for money and the fixed supply of money. The extra transactions demand for money resulting from an increase in income must be "rationed" by economizing on the holding of money balances as interest rates rise. Consequently the *LM* curve slopes *upwards to the right*. To maintain equilibrium in the money market with a fixed money supply, an *increase in income* must be accompanied by an *increase in interest rates* (the movement from point A to point B in Chart 5-6).[25]

Shifts in the *LM* Curve

Chart 5-7 illustrates how an increase in the money supply shifts the *LM* curve downwards to the right. The Bank of Canada, on behalf of the federal government, influences financial markets through its control of the money supply. To increase (decrease) the supply of money, the Bank of Canada must inject (withdraw) dollar bills into (from) the economic system. One way the Bank of Canada changes the supply of money is by engaging in the purchase and sale of bonds. These activities are called *open market operations*. When the Bank of Canada purchases bonds, new dollars enter the economic system. Conversely, when the Bank of Canada sells bonds, it receives money which will no longer be in circulation throughout the economy, and the money supply declines. The Bank of Canada's operations are fully discussed in Chapter 18.

Turning to Chart 5-7, suppose that initially the money supply is equal to $\$^S$. Our three representative combinations of income and interest rates which clear the money market are given by points A, B, and C, all of which lie along an *LM* curve corresponding to a money supply of $\$^S$. Now suppose that the Bank of Canada increases the money supply to $\overline{\$}^S$ by engaging in an open market purchase of bonds. Given this larger supply of money, our three representative combinations of income and interest rates which clear the money market will now be given by points $\overline{A}$, $\overline{B}$ and $\overline{C}$. In panel B of Chart 5-7 we have again plotted these three representative points and have drawn the new red *LM* curve associated with this larger money supply $\overline{\$}^S$. An increase in the supply of money has caused the *LM* curve to shift downwards to the right. For a given income level, say Y_1, the interest rate has declined (to $\overline{R}_1$). By purchasing bonds in the open market, the Bank of Canada has bid up the price of bonds and lowered the interest rate. To maintain equilibrium in the money market at an income level Y_1, the interest rate—the opportunity cost of holding money—must decline to $\overline{R}_1$ to persuade individuals to hold this larger money supply $\overline{\$}^S$.

Solution to the Basic Keynesian *IS-LM* Model

Graphical Approach

We now have in place the following major elements of a Keynesian model of income determination:

---

[25]The actual steepness of the *LM* curve depends on the relative size of the two behavioural parameters k and ℓ (see below).

CHART 5-7 Effects of an increase in the money supply on the *LM* curve

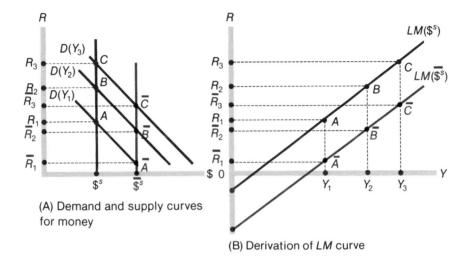

(A) Demand and supply curves for money

(B) Derivation of *LM* curve

1) Consumption/savings decisions depend on income levels.
2) While investment decisions depend to some extent on interest rate movements, investment expenditures are also influenced by autonomous forces.
3) The demand for money depends positively on income levels and negatively on interest rates.
4) Wage and price levels are inflexible and unresponsive to changes in aggregate demand

The first two elements have been combined to produce the *IS* curve. This downward-sloping *IS* curve describes all possible combinations of income and interest rate which maintain equilibrium in the product market. The third element has been used to derive the *LM* curve, given a fixed money supply. The upward-sloping *LM* curve describes all possible combinations of income and interest rates which maintain equilibrium in the money market.

There is only one combination of income and interest rates which will simultaneously maintain equilibrium in both the product market and the money market. As drawn in Chart 5-8, only Y_E and R_E will simultaneously clear *both* the product *and* money markets. By introducing the condition of money market equilibrium, we are now able to determine the unique income level at which the product market will clear.

For any income level other than that associated with the intersection point of the *IS* and *LM* curves, either the product market and/or the money market will be in a state of disequilibrium. Disequilibrium in either or both markets will cause a

CHART 5-8 Equilibrium in the *IS-LM* model

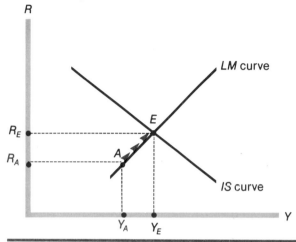

sequence of adjustments which will return the economy to its unique **equilibrium income** level Y_E. To illustrate this disequilibrium adjustment mechanism, suppose, for example, that the economy is at point A in Chart 5-8, with an income level Y_A that is less than the equilibrium income level Y_E (this point would correspond to point A in Chart 5-3). While the economy is in money market equilibrium (point A is on the *LM* curve), the product market is out of equilibrium (point A is off the *IS* curve). As discussed earlier, at point A there will be a state of *excess demand* in the product market. The interest rate R_A is too *low* to maintain product market equilibrium for an income level Y_A. At point A the combined demand of consumers and investors will exceed aggregate supply and inventories will be drawn down below normal levels. As we have seen, dwindling inventory stocks will trigger new factory orders and subsequent increases in income. Consequently the original income level Y_A will give way to a higher income level. This state of excess demand in the product market will continue to exist as long as the economy is below the *IS* curve. Assuming that the money market remains in equilibrium,[26] a series of inventory adjustments will carry the economy from point A back up the *LM* curve to point E (see arrows in Chart 5-8).[27] Income levels will continue to adjust until the economy has returned to its unique equilibrium level Y_E. Similarly, if income levels exceeded the equilibrium level, the economic system would undergo a series of downward income adjustments (as inventory stocks piled up) and would eventually return to its unique equilibrium income position. Only

[26]Through the purchase or sale of bonds, the money market likely adjusts very quickly to disequilibrium situations in the financial asset market. We have therefore assumed that the economy remains on the *LM* curve as equilibrium in the goods market is (slowly) achieved.

[27]We saw earlier that as the economy moves up a stationary *LM* curve, the increasing level of income raises the demand for money for transactions purposes. However, the simultaneous rise in the interest rate encourages people to economize on their holdings of money balances and maintains equality between the demand and *fixed* supply of money. Money balances are working harder at point E than at A because the same amount of money is supporting a greater volume of transactions.

when both the product and the money markets are simultaneously in equilibrium will the economic system remain at rest. The intersection point of the *IS* and *LM* curves is the unique **stable equilibrium position** for the macroeconomic system.

Algebraic Approach

As in Chapter 4, our graphical model can also be solved algebraically. For convenience, the equations which comprise the model are reproduced below:

(4-1) $Z = C + I$ $I = I_a - eR$ (5-1)

(4-2) $C = a + bY$ $\$^D = kY - \ell R$ (5-3)

(4-5) $Z = Y$ $\$^D = \$^S$ (5-4)

Equations 4-1, 4-2, 4-5 and 5-1 describe the aggregate product market, whereas equations 5-3 and 5-4 describe the money market.

As discussed above, the *IS* curve represents all combinations of income and interest rates which maintain equilibrium in the product market. Using the aggregate product market-clearing condition (equation 4-5) and the definition of aggregate demand (equation 4-1), we obtain:

$$Y = C + I$$

Now, substitute the structural equations for consumption and investment,

$$Y = a + bY + I_a - eR$$

and collect all *Y* terms on the left-hand side.

$$Y - bY = a + I_a - eR$$

(5-5) $$Y = \frac{a + I_a}{1 - b} - \left(\frac{e}{1 - b}\right)R$$

Equation 5-5 is the algebraic form of the *IS* curve for this model where income *Y* is expressed as a function of the interest rate *R*. Alternatively, *R* can be expressed as a function of *Y*:

(5-5a) $$R = \frac{a + I_a}{e} - \frac{(1 - b)}{e}Y$$

The *Y*-axis and *R*-axis intercepts for the *IS* curve can be found by setting *R* equal to zero in equation 5-5 and *Y* equal to zero in equation 5-5a.

Both vertical and horizontal intercepts for the *IS* curve are labelled in Chart 5-9. With *R* on the vertical axis (and on the left-hand side of equation 5-5a), the slope of the *IS* curve is $(1 - b)/e$. We know (from Chart 5-3) that the more sensitive investment spending is to interest rate movements (the larger the parameter *e*), the flatter will be the slope of the *IS* curve. As the parameter *e* increases, the *IS* curve will rotate counterclockwise about the *Y*-axis intercept.

CHART 5-9 Slopes and intercepts of the *IS* and *LM* curves

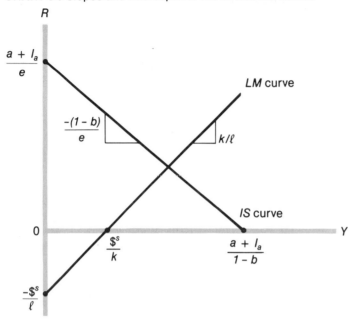

(Note that the Y-axis intercept for this *IS* curve does not depend on the parameter e.)[28] More important, an increase in autonomous investment causes the *IS* curve to shift upwards to the right. While the slope of the *IS* curve $(1 - b)/e$ is unaffected by autonomous investment, both the *vertical* intercept $(a + I_a)/e$ and the *horizontal* intercept $(a + I_a)/(1 - b)$ of the *IS* curve increase as autonomous investment rises. The *horizontal* rightward shift in the *IS* curve resulting from an increase in autonomous investment is equal to the simple Keynesian cross multiplier $1/(1 - b)$ times the increase in autonomous investment ΔI_a.

To derive the *LM* curve equation, we simply substitute the money market equilibrium condition (equation 5-4) into the demand for money equation (5-3),

$$\$^s = kY - \ell R$$

and rearrange terms to produce an upward-sloping $R = Y$ relationship:

$$(5\text{-}6) \qquad R = \frac{-\$^s}{\ell} + \left(\frac{k}{\ell}\right)Y$$

---

[28]By a similar argument, an increase in the marginal propensity to consume (the parameter b) will cause the *IS* curve to rotate upwards or counterclockwise about the R-axis intercept. The *IS* curve becomes flatter as the MPC rises—the paradox of thrift in reverse.

As shown in Chart 5-9, the slope of the *LM* curve is k/ℓ and the vertical and horizontal intercepts of the *LM* curve are $-\$^S/\ell$ and $\$^S/k$ respectively. Thus an increase in the exogenous money supply will not affect the slope of the *LM* curve, but will cause the *LM* curve to shift downwards to the right (the vertical intercept becomes a larger negative number and the horizontal intercept increases in value).

The *IS* and *LM* equations can be used to solve algebraically for the equilibrium income level. Since in equilibrium the *same* interest rate must prevail in both the money and product markets, to solve for *Y* we simply set the *LM* equation 5-6 equal to the *IS* equation 5-5a (which has *R* on the left-hand side):

$$ -\frac{\$^S}{\ell} + \left(\frac{k}{\ell}\right)Y = R = \frac{I_a + a}{e} - \left(\frac{1-b}{e}\right)Y $$

Collecting all *Y* terms on the left-hand side and moving the negative $\$^S$ term to the right-hand side produces the following equation:

$$ Y\left[\left(\frac{1-b}{e}\right) + \left(\frac{k}{\ell}\right)\right] = \left(\frac{I_a + a}{e}\right) + \frac{\$^S}{\ell} $$

To simplify this expression, we multiply both sides of the equation by e,

$$ Y\left[1 - b + \frac{ek}{\ell}\right] = (I_a + a) + \left(\frac{e}{\ell}\right)\$^S $$

and then divide both sides of the equation by $[1 - b + ek/\ell]$,

$$ (5\text{-}7) \qquad Y = \frac{I_a + a + \left(\dfrac{e}{\ell}\right)\$^S}{1 - b + \dfrac{ek}{\ell}} $$

By forcing the same rate of interest to prevail in both the product and money markets, the *IS* and *LM* equations can be used to generate an algebraic reduced-form equation for equilibrium income (equation 5-7).

As discussed in Chapter 4, the key characteristic of a reduced-form equation is that the *endogenous* variable *Y* is expressed solely in terms of the *given* behavioural parameters (a, b, e, k and ℓ) and *exogenous* variables (I_a and $\$^S$). None of the other endogenous variables in the model (such as *C*, *I* and *R*) appear in this reduced-form equation for equilibrium income. All of the interactions and feedback effects between the endogenous variables implicit in the structure of our macroeconomic model have been allowed for. By making use of this reduced-form income equation (5-7), one can readily obtain reduced-form equations for the remaining endogenous variables in the model.[29]

[29]For example, the reduced-form equation for consumption is equal to *a* plus *b* times the reduced-form equation for income. By substituting the given money supply and the reduced-form income equation into the demand for money function, a reduced-form equation for the interest rate can be derived.

The Structural Determinants of Equilibrium Income

What actually determines the equilibrium level of income in the Keynesian model? On a superficial level, equilibrium income is simply determined by the intersection point of the *IS* and *LM* curves. To pinpoint the precise **structural determinants of equilibrium income**, we must get behind these two "market-clearing" curves and return to the structural components of the *IS* and *LM* curves. In a fundamental structural sense, the equilibrium level of income is determined by the position (intercept and slope) of the *IS* and *LM* curves. The exact location of the *IS* curve is determined by the consumption and investment functions. Similarly, the exact location of the *LM* curve is determined by the demand for money function and the given money supply. Thus, the equilibrium level of income, in a fundamental structural sense, is determined by consumer behaviour, investment behaviour (including autonomous investment), money demand behaviour, and the given money supply.

The reduced-form equilibrium income equation (5-7) summarizes these structural factors in a very convenient, precise manner. A change in either a behavioural parameter or an exogenous variable causes the equilibrium income level to change. For example, if consumers become less thrifty and b (the MPC) increases, then the equilibrium income level will rise as the denominator of the reduced-form income equation (5-7) becomes smaller. Diagrammatically, the *IS* curve rotates upwards in a counterclockwise manner about the R-axis intercept, bringing about a new *IS-LM* intersection point at a higher income level. While most behavioural patterns in the economy are relatively stable and not subject to abrupt changes, the key exogenous variables I_a and $\$^S$ have not been nearly as stable. As discussed earlier, Canadian investment expenditures have been quite volatile and frequently subject to substantial swings that we have attributed to autonomous forces. Deferring a discussion of the effects of a change in the money supply until later, we now turn to an analysis of the multiplier effects of a change in autonomous investment I_a on equilibrium income levels.

A change in autonomous investment expenditures I_a will cause the *IS* curve to shift in a parallel manner. If autonomous investment declines, then the *IS* curve will shift downwards to the left, bringing about a new lower intersection point with the *LM* curve (see Chart 5-10). A decline in autonomous investment causes a reduction in the level of equilibrium income (from Y_0 to Y_1) as well as a decrease in the rate of interest (from R_0 to R_1). The downward slide along the *LM* curve is just the opposite to the case illustrated in Chart 5-8. In the present situation, a decline in autonomous investment reduces income levels and the volume of transactions. With a lower transactions demand for money and a *given* money supply, there will be a state of excess supply in the money market which will spill over into the bond market. The resulting increase in demand for bonds raises the price of bonds and lowers the interest rate. The interest rate must *decline* to encourage people to hold the given supply of money in the face of declining income and transactions, thereby restoring equilibrium in the money market.

To determine the exact magnitude of the effect on equilibrium income following a change in autonomous investment (the distance $Y_0 - Y_1$ in Chart 5-10), we

CHART 5-10 The effect of a decline in autonomous investment
        on equilibrium income

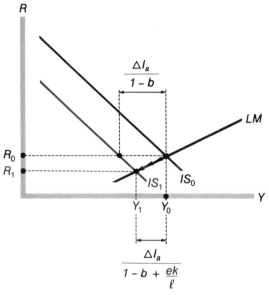

return to our algebraic reduced-form equation for equilibrium income (equation 5-7).

$$(5\text{-}7) \qquad Y = \frac{a + I_a + \left(\dfrac{e}{\ell}\right)\$^S}{1 - b + \dfrac{ek}{\ell}}$$

The effect of a one-unit change in I_a on Y is equal to the coefficient of I_a in this reduced-form Y equation:[30]

$$\frac{\Delta Y}{\Delta I_a} = \frac{1}{1 - b + \dfrac{ek}{\ell}}$$

[30]For students who have taken an elementary course in calculus, the above multiplier expression is simply the derivative of Y with respect to I_a, as computed from the reduced-form equation. For students who have not taken calculus, we can follow the steps outlined in Chapter 4 to obtain the change in Y associated with a change in I_a (from I_{a1} to I_{a2}).

$$Y_1 = \frac{a + I_{a1} + \left(\dfrac{e}{\ell}\right)\$^S}{1 - b + \dfrac{ek}{\ell}} \qquad Y_2 = \frac{a + I_{a2} + \left(\dfrac{e}{\ell}\right)\$^S}{1 - b + \dfrac{ek}{\ell}}$$

$$Y_2 - Y_1 = \frac{a + I_{a2} + \left(\dfrac{e}{\ell}\right)\$^S}{1 - b + \dfrac{ek}{\ell}} - \frac{a + I_{a1} + \left(\dfrac{e}{\ell}\right)\$^S}{1 - b + \dfrac{ek}{\ell}}$$

$$\Delta Y = \frac{\Delta I_a}{1 - b + \dfrac{ek}{\ell}} \quad \text{or} \quad \frac{\Delta Y}{\Delta I_a} = \frac{1}{1 - b + \dfrac{ek}{\ell}}$$

The precise numerical value for this income multiplier effect depends on the values of the four structural parameters b, e, k and ℓ.

Compared with our earlier Keynesian cross model, the above multiplier derived from the *IS-LM* macroeconomic model will be lower. Recall that the Keynesian cross multiplier effect on income from a change in autonomous investment is $1/(1 - b)$. Algebraically the difference between the Keynesian cross model multiplier and the corresponding *IS-LM* model multiplier is the presence of the positive ek/ℓ term in the denominator of the *IS-LM* multiplier expression (which will lower the size of the autonomous investment multiplier). Enlarging the Keynesian cross model to include a demand for money function and an interest-sensitive investment function has lowered the multiplier effect on income from a change in autonomous investment.[31]

The explanation for the *decrease* in the autonomous investment–income multiplier effect in the *IS-LM* model concerns the role of interest rates in the model. A decline in autonomous investment ΔI_a causes the *IS* curve to shift leftwards by $\Delta I_a/(1 - b)$ units, the simple Keynesian cross multiplier effect under *constant* interest rates. However, in the *IS-LM* model, a leftward shift in the *IS* curve also causes the *interest rates to decline*. With lower interest rates, firms will increase their *endogenous* investment spending since they can now borrow funds at a lower rate of interest.[32] A decline in *autonomous* investment creates a *secondary reaction via the interest rate* which will tend to offset part of the initial negative effects from the decline in autonomous investment. The extent to which this secondary reaction effect will decrease the Keynesian cross multiplier depends on the structural parameters in the investment and the demand for money functions, e, k and ℓ.[33] This secondary reaction effect on investment expenditures arising from induced changes in interest rates will be of considerable importance in future chapters.

The *IS-LM* Model Extended to Include a Government Sector and a Foreign Trade Sector

We now wish to enlarge the basic *IS-LM* model to include the government sector and a foreign trade sector. Federal, provincial and municipal levels of governments are consolidated into one giant government sector. Following the discussion of the national accounts in Chapter 2, our aggregate demand identity is expanded to include government spending G, exports X and imports M.

(4-1b) $Z = C + I + G + X - M$

---

[31]As we shall see, further elaboration and refinements to the Keynesian model, such as the inclusion of imports, will cause this key multiplier effect to decline even further.

[32]In addition, some consumers may also take advantage of this new lower interest rate to purchase a new house or a new car.

[33]For example, the greater the sensitivity of *endogenous* investment spending to interest rate movements, the greater the "offsetting" effect and the less the overall multiplier effect on equilibrium income from a change in *autonomous* investment.

Government spending and exports represent additional sources of demand for Canadian output, whereas imports from other countries represent an important diversion of Canadian aggregate demand to foreign production.

The Inclusion of a Government Sector Within the *IS-LM* Model

The addition of a government sector that collects taxes requires an amendment to the consumption function. Defining disposable income YD as total income Y less taxes T, we express our consumption function in disposable income terms:

(4-2a) $C = a + b(Y - T)$

Rather than assuming that taxes are a constant given level, we acknowledge the existence of an income tax system and assume that total government tax revenues vary directly with the level of income. Sales tax and income tax revenues obviously increase as total spending and income rise. Even though the progressivity of the income tax system would suggest a nonlinear relationship between income tax revenues and income levels,[34] to keep the algebra simple we adopt the following linear **tax function** (equation 5-8), where t represents the marginal tax rate for an additional dollar of income and T_0 can be thought of as "lump sum" tax which is levied irrespective of income levels, such as a licence fee.

(5-8) $T = T_0 + tY$

As demonstrated in Chart 5-11, this simple linear income tax function fits the data like a glove. A scatter diagram for total annual government tax revenues and annual income levels produces *very little* scatter. Based on the estimated slope t of the least squares fitted line in Chart 5-11, it would appear that the various levels of government in Canada collectively take about 42¢ in taxes out of every marginal dollar of income.

The Inclusion of a Foreign Trade Sector Within the *IS-LM* Model

The importance of international trade for the Canadian economy needs little elaboration. Throughout the history of our country, exports have played a vital role in developing the economy. Early exports of a few staple commodities, mainly cod, fur, timber and later wheat, have gradually evolved into a wide variety of export products. For example, in 1983 motor vehicle products accounted for 24 per cent of total exports and other manufactured goods (including fabricated metals) accounted for an additional 34 per cent of total exports. During the 1960-84 period, exports have ranged from 16 to 30 per cent of total Canadian output (see Chart 5-12), with about 70 per cent of all Canadian exports destined for the

---

[34]As income rises, tax payers are pushed into higher tax brackets and will pay higher rates of taxation. Therefore government revenues are likely to increase at an accelerating rate as income levels rise and tax payers move up into higher tax brackets. For further details on the "progressivity" of the Canadian income tax system, see the case study in Chapter 3.

CHART 5-11 Scatter diagram for tax function, 1960-83

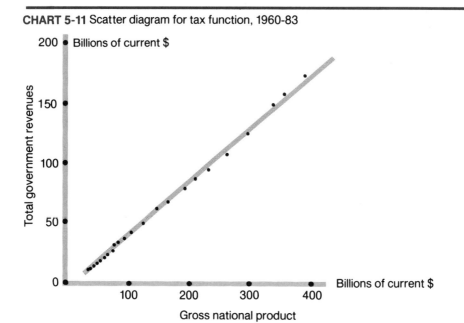

U.S. market. The rising relative importance of exports during the late 1960s is largely attributable to the signing of the Canada-United States Automotive Pact, a 1965 bilateral treaty which permitted "controlled" free trade in automotive products between the two countries.[35] Prior to the signing of this automotive pact, Canadian exports of motor vehicle products to the United States were virtually zero (5 to 15 *million* dollars per year). Following the North American rationalization of the automotive industry under the auto pact, motor vehicles quickly became Canada's leading export product.[36] By the mid-1970s annual exports of motor vehicle products to the U.S. had surpassed $10 *billion* and in 1983 total automotive exports exceeded $20 billion! More than ever before, Canadian production is inextricably linked to market conditions in the United States.

During the 1960-84 period, Canadian imports have typically exceeded exports (see Chart 5-12). Most Canadian imports are industrial and manufactured products purchased by consumers and business investors. Again, about 70 per cent of Canadian imports originate in the United States, and the signing of the auto pact accounts for much of the relative increase in imports in the late 1960s.

[35]As long as Canadian motor vehicle manufacturers met certain Canadian production requirements, existing automotive tariffs between Canada and the U.S. were abolished for the producers of automobiles.

[36]Under the provisions of the Auto Pact, Canadian (subsidiary) motor vehicle producers could specialize in the production of a few "makes and models" for domestic and export (U.S.) markets and the great variety of North American style cars could enter Canada duty-free from the U.S. (parent) industry. For an analysis of the Canadian macroeconomic effects during the first seven years of the Auto Pact, see D.A. Wilton, *An Econometric Analysis of the Canada-United States Automotive Agreement* (Ottawa: Economic Council of Canada, 1976).

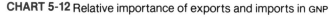

CHART 5-12 Relative importance of exports and imports in GNP

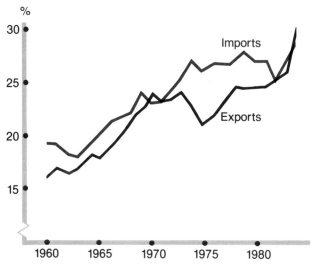

Having added exports and imports to our model, we must now either provide a structural explanation for these variables or declare them exogenous. Since imports are already included in the other components of aggregate demand, typically as consumer goods[37] or investment goods, the total level of imports obviously depends on the total level of aggregate demand. In short, Canadian imports will likely bear a very close relationship with total Canadian income or GNP. In Chart 5-13 we present a simple scatter diagram for Canadian imports M in terms of total Canadian GNP. As is clear from this scatter diagram, there is indeed a very close relationship between imports and income levels. As Canadian income levels have increased, so have imports. Given the slope of the least squares line through the scatter diagram, the marginal propensity to import out of income is about 33 per cent. Again keeping our macroeconomic model as simple as possible, the Canadian **import function** is represented by the following linear equation, where the parameter m represents the marginal propensity to import.

(5-9) $M = n + mY$

Following the same line of reasoning, if Canadian imports are directly related to Canadian income, then Canadian exports, which are imports to foreigners, will likely bear a close relationship to foreign income. To test this proposition, Chart 5-14 presents a simple scatter diagram for Canadian exports to the U.S. (our largest customer) and U.S. gross national product. Clearly Canadian exports have followed the general upward course of the U.S. economy during the 1960-84 period, although not in a perfectly linear relationship. When U.S output acceler-

[37]When Statistics Canada collects data on total consumer expenditures, it does *not exclude* foreign goods (Toyotas, Sonys, French wine) from total purchases by Canadian consumers.

CHART 5-13 Scatter diagram for imports and income, 1956-84

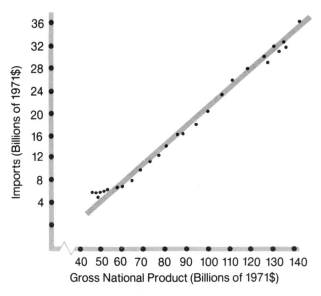

Imports (Billions of 1971$)

Gross National Product (Billions of 1971$)

CHART 5-14 Scatter diagram for Canadian exports to U.S. 1960-1984

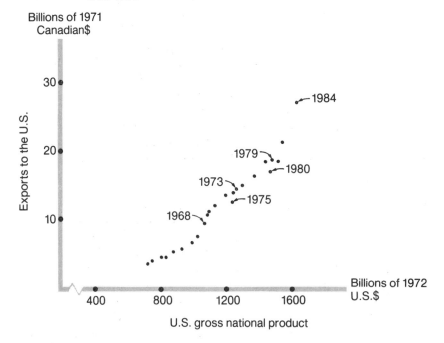

Billions of 1971
Canadian$

Exports to the U.S.

Billions of 1972
U.S.$

U.S. gross national product

ated upwards in the late 1960s and again in 1984, Canadian exports to the U.S. substantially increased. When the U.S. economy went into a serious recession in 1974-75 and again in 1980, Canadian exports to the U.S. declined (note that the 1975 and 1980 points lie downwards to the left of the 1973 and 1979 data points). This cyclical movement in Canadian exports to the U.S. is particulary acute in the motor vehicle industry. Having integrated our domestic motor vehicle industry into the total North American market in 1965, Canadian exports of motor vehicles are now highly dependent on U.S. economic conditions.

In summary, the economic performance of the U.S. (and world) economy is of vital concern to Canadian exporters and to the level of aggregate demand for Canadian output. Since Canadian exports depend crucially on income levels in foreign countries, we have classified **exports as an exogenous** (or external) **variable** within our *IS-LM* model of the Canadian economy. Just like other exogenous variables in our model, a change in exports arising from a change in U.S. and/or world economic conditions will have an important macroeconomic effect on the Canadian economy.

Before solving our enlarged *IS-LM* model and computing this income multiplier effect from a change in exports, we emphasize that our simplified treatment of foreign trade has omitted many other important factors. For example, the level of exports and imports can be affected by a wide range of government policies such as tariffs, quotas, licensing arrangements, and industry agreements such as the Canada-United States Automotive Agreement. In addition, movements in the Canadian exchange rate can exert a substantial influence on exports and imports. If the Canadian currency depreciates, then our exports become cheaper on world markets and imported goods become more expensive in the Canadian market place. As a result, currency depreciation will tend to increase exports and reduce imports as domestic production becomes more competitive with higher priced foreign goods. Chapter 7 is devoted to the macroeconomic ramifications of foreign exchange rate movements and balance of payments adjustment mechanisms.

Solution and Properties of an *IS-LM* Model Which Includes Both a Government Sector and a Foreign Trade Sector.

As a first step to deriving a solution for our enlarged and amended *IS-LM* macroeconomic model, we algebraically derive a new *IS* curve reflecting the addition of a government and foreign trade sector. Our amended consumption function now includes the effects of the income tax system:

$$C = a + b(Y - T) = a + bY - b(T_0 + tY) = a + bY - bT_0 - btY$$

Substituting the amended consumption function and the new import function (equation 5-9) into the expanded aggregate demand identity (equation 4-1b) produces the following equation:

$$Z = C + I + G + X - M$$
$$Z = (a + bY - bT_0 - btY) + (I_a - eR) + G + X - (n + mY)$$

Assuming that the product market is in equilibrium (equation 4-5), the above equation can be rearranged to produce a new *IS* curve that incorporates the effects of the government and foreign trade sectors:

$$Y = Z = a + bY - bT_o - btY + I_a - eR + G + X - n - mY$$

$$Y(1 - b + bt + m) = (a - bT_o + I_a + G + X - n) - eR$$

(5-10) $\qquad R = \frac{1}{e}(a - bT_o + I_a + G + X - n) - \frac{1}{e}(1 - b + bt + m)Y$

For all *R-Y* combinations which satisfy this *IS* equation (5-10), the aggregate product market will be in equilibrium.

The two new exogenous variables *G* and *X* represent important additional intercept components for the *IS* curve. Just as an increase in autonomous investment I_a will shift the *IS* curve upwards to the right, an increase in either government spending *G* or exports *X* will also shift the *IS* curve upwards to the right. Autonomous investment, government expenditures, and exports all enter the aggregate demand identity and the intercept of the *IS* curve in exactly the same way. A change in any one of these three key exogenous components of aggregate demand (I_a, *G*, or *X*) would produce exactly the same effect on the *IS* curve.

Turning to the slope of our enlarged *IS* curve, the inclusion of income taxes (as represented by the marginal income tax rate *t*) and a marginal propensity to import *m* have clearly increased the slope of the new *IS* curve. Without a government and foreign trade sector, the slope of the *IS* curve was $(1 - b)/e$. Now it is steeper, $(1 - b + bt + m)/e$. As income levels increase, both imports and taxes will increase, leading to a potential decline in aggregate demand for Canadian output. To maintain product market equilibrium under rising income levels, some other component of aggregate demand must increase to offset the effects of rising imports and income taxes. Since exports, government spending and the MPC are *given*, investment expenditures must now rise at a faster rate to offset the negative effects of increased taxes and imports. For a given *increase in income*, *larger interest rate reductions* will be required to generate enough new investment to offset the dampening effects of increased imports and income taxes that accompany higher income levels. The presence of income taxes and imports within the model produces a *steeper IS* curve.

In Chart 5-15 we have plotted this new, steeper *IS* curve reflecting the inclusion of both a government and a foreign trade sector. We *assume* that the *LM* curve is unaffected by the introduction of either a government sector or a foreign trade sector.[38] The equilibrium income level Y_E is again determined by the intersection point of the *IS* and *LM* curves. The economic system can only be at rest when both the product market and the money market are simultaneously in equilibrium.

By equating our new *IS* equation 5-10 to the original *LM* equation 5-6 and

---

[38]As discussed in the next chapter, the supply of money might be altered to finance a deficit in government spending (*G > T*). Monetary policy and balance of payments adjustment (when $X \neq M$) are discussed in Chapter 7.

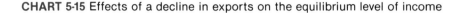

CHART 5-15 Effects of a decline in exports on the equilibrium level of income

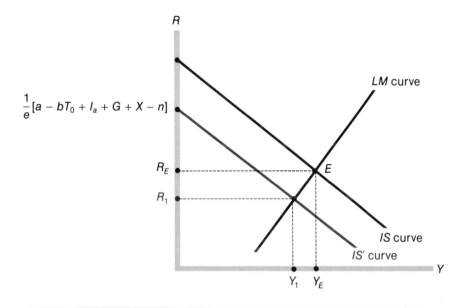

thereby forcing the same interest rate to prevail in both the product and money markets, we can again derive a reduced-form equation for equilibrium income based on our enlarged *IS-LM* model.

$$\frac{-\$^S}{\ell} + \left(\frac{k}{\ell}\right)Y = R = \frac{1}{e}(a - bT_0 + I_a + G + X - n) - \frac{1}{e}(1 - b + bt + m)Y$$

Multiplying both sides of the above equation by *e* and collecting all *Y* terms on the left-hand side produces the following equation:

$$\left(1 - b + bt + m + \frac{ek}{\ell}\right)Y = a - bT_0 + I_a + G + X - n + \left(\frac{e}{\ell}\right)\$^S$$

Dividing both sides of the above equation by $(1 - b + bt + m + ek/\ell)$, we obtain the following reduced-form income equation:

$$(5\text{-}11) \qquad Y = \frac{a - bT_0 + I_a + G + X - n + \left(\dfrac{e}{\ell}\right)\$^S}{1 - b + bt + m + \dfrac{ek}{\ell}}$$

Again, the equilibrium income level depends on all of the behavioural parameters in the model (a, b, e, n, m, k, ℓ) and all of the exogenous variables $(I_a, G, X, T_0, t, \$^S)$. If any of the behavioural parameters and/or exogenous variables were to change, a new level of equilibrium income would arise.

Since we fully analyze the effects of changes in government fiscal policy in the next chapter, we conclude our analysis in this chapter by briefly considering the macroeconomic effects associated with a decrease in Canadian exports, which typically occurs when the U.S. economy goes into a recession. A decrease in exports will lower the vertical intercept of the *IS* curve, resulting in a parallel inward shift of the *IS* curve (see Chart 5-15). Thus a decline in exports will cause equilibrium income and interest rates to decline (to Y_1 and R_1 in Chart 5-15). Using our reduced-form income equation 5-11, we can compute the downward multiplier effect on income arising from a decline in exports:

$$\frac{\Delta Y}{\Delta X} = \frac{1}{1 - b + bt + m + \frac{ek}{\ell}} = \frac{\Delta Y}{\Delta I_a} = \frac{\Delta Y}{\Delta G}$$

This export multiplier effect on income is exactly the same as the multiplier effect on income arising from a change in autonomous investment I_a or from a change in government spending G.[39] All three exogenous components of aggregate demand (I_a, G and X) have precisely the same effect on the intercept of the *IS* curve and the equilibrium level of income.

Summary of Keynes' Diagnosis in the *General Theory*

While the equilibrium level of income in the *IS-LM* model depends on the underlying behavioural parameters within the economy, the key structural determinants of equilibrium income are the exogenous components of aggregate demand. In Keynes' view, investment expenditures would be highly susceptible to changes in the state of business confidence and very unresponsive to movements in the rate of interest. The "delicate balance of spontaneous optimism" within the business community could easily be upset and a wave of business pessimism could generate a collapse in investment demand. Even though Keynes undoubtedly overstated the importance of "animal spirits" and "business psychology," Canadian investment expenditures have been highly volatile and are the most unstable component of aggregate demand. In addition to autonomous swings in investment expenditures, an economy as open as Canada's is subject to considerable export instability. The level of Canadian exports is highly dependent on U.S. and world economic conditions, and the international business cycle will be transmitted to Canada via changes in world demand for Canadian exports.

Given the instability of autonomous investment and exports, there is no reason to believe that the *IS* curve, which depends crucially on these unstable exogenous elements, will just happen to intersect the *LM* curve at an output level compatible with full employment. Autonomous investment and/or exports may be too low, and the *IS* curve may be located too far to the left. For any decline in autonomous investment and/or exports, the multiplier process will generate a magnified reduction in equilibrium income and the economy could come to rest in a serious

---

[39]In the next chapter, a special case study presents statistical estimates for the parameters in the model and estimates for the size of the various multipliers in the enlarged *IS-LM* model.

recession. In Keynes' view, the root cause of the problem of chronic unemployment was insufficient aggregate demand, principally arising from insufficient investment.

Keynes' "revolutionary" new macroeconomic theory of insufficient aggregate demand was completely at odds with the prevailing conventional economic wisdom. Classical economists firmly believed that the economic system, left alone and given sufficient time, would reach an equilibrium position in which full employment would prevail. Unemployment, in a free market system, simply could not persist as wages and prices would adjust to clear the aggregate labour market (see Chapter 8). With the Great Depression convincingly proving his case, Keynes argued that wage and price levels were relatively inflexible and the market system could not be counted upon to lift the economy out of a serious recession. Deliberate government actions must be undertaken to stimulate aggregate demand and propel the economy out of serious recessions. Having now outlined Keynes' "diagnosis" of the problem, in the next chapter we will examine the Keynesian policy "prescription."

Key Concepts

the product market
the financial asset market
the investment demand function
autonomous investment versus endogenous
    (interest-sensitive) investment
the *IS* curve
the money supply
the demand for money
the *LM* curve
equilibrium income
the stability of equilibrium income
the structural determinants of equilibrium income
the income tax function
the import function
exogenous exports

Review Questions

1. Why does the investment decision depend negatively on the market rate of interest?
2. Compare the effects of a change in interest rates versus a change in the state of business confidence on investment spending and the investment function. Given Canadian data since 1960, which factor do you believe to be more important in explaining aggregate investment expenditures?

3. Using the Keynesian cross diagram, derive a set of aggregate demand schedules corresponding to different interest rates. Does an increase in the interest rate cause the aggregate demand schedule to shift up or down? Explain.

4. Define and derive the *IS* curve. How would you categorize all points which lie below the *IS* curve? Why does the *IS* curve slope downwards to the right?

5. How would the *IS* curve be affected by each of the following events:
   a) an increase in autonomous investment?
   b) a decrease in the interest rate?
   c) an increase in the marginal propensity to consume?
   d) investment which is completely insensitive to interest rate movements?

6. Why do individuals hold (or demand) money? What are the economic determinants of the demand for money?

7. Define and derive the *LM* curve. How would you categorize all points which lie below the *LM* curve? Why does the *LM* curve slope upwards to the right? What effect does an increase in the money supply have on the *LM* curve?

8. What determines the equilibrium interest rate and equilibrium income level in a Keynesian (*IS-LM*) macroeconomic model? Carefully explain.

9. What would happen if the income level happened to exceed the equilibrium income level? Explain.

10. How would the equilibrium level of income and interest rates be affected by the following events:
    a) a decrease in autonomous investment?
    b) a decrease in the marginal propensity to consume?
    c) an increase in the money supply?

11. Carefully explain why the autonomous investment multiplier effect on income in the *IS-LM* model is smaller than that found in the simple Keynesian cross model.

12. How would the *IS* curve be affected by the inclusion of
    a) a government sector?
    b) a foreign trade sector?

13. If the United States goes into a serious recession, what will be the effect on the equilibrium income level and interest rates in Canada?

14. What is the effect on equilibrium income if the Canadian government restricts imports and effectively lowers the marginal propensity to import?

15. Compare the multiplier effects on income of the following events:
    a) a $1 billion increase in exports
    b) a $1 billion increase in autonomous investment
    c) a $1 billion increase in government spending.
    What explanation can you give for this comparative result?

16. In Keynes' view, what was the cause of chronic unemployment? Explain.

Keynesian Economics: II The Policy Prescription

The General Theory *was attacked at the time of its publication as a subversive, radical document, but Keynes was in fact a high-caste Establishment figure who condemned Marxists. . . . He saw himself as an economic saviour, providing a way of pulling the world out of the Great Depression without fatally damaging the free enterprise system.*

Peter Newman[1]

In the previous chapter we presented the basic elements of the Keynesian model of income determination. Given inflexible wage and price levels, a state of deficient aggregate demand may force the economy into an equilibrium position characterized by substantial unemployment. There is no guarantee that the *IS* and *LM* curves will necessarily intersect at an output level which coincides with the full employment of the economy's resources. In Keynes' view, the chief source of instability within the economy was autonomous investment. A wave of pessimism in business confidence could lead to a persistent decline in autonomous investment, and the economy could find itself trapped in the grips of a serious recession. Alternatively, an open economy such as Canada may be subject to domestic instability arising from changing external market conditions. For example, a serious recession in the United States may be transmitted to Canada via declining export sales. Again the Canadian economy would find itself with insufficient aggregate demand and a serious unemployment problem.

Fortunately the *General Theory* not only provided a diagnosis of the causes of persistent unemployment, it also provided a policy prescription. Rather than waiting for the painfully slow "invisible hand" of Adam Smith to restore equilibrium in the labour market via a series of *downward* adjustments in the wage rate (see Chapter 8), Keynes advocated that the government adopt an expansionary fiscal policy. A decline in autonomous investment or exports, and the resulting negative multiplier effects on income, could be offset by an increase in government spending. Given an enlightened fiscal policy, the economic disease of chronic unemployment could be cured.

---

[1]P.C. Newman, *The Canadian Establishment* (Toronto: McClelland and Stewart, 1975), p. 331.

The *General Theory* advocated a brand new role for government policy. Besides providing peace, order and security, Keynes argued that governments had the ability and therefore the responsibility to manage aggregate demand in such a way that serious recessions and depressions would be avoided. Discretionary changes in government spending and/or tax rates should be implemented to stabilize output and employment levels. A "responsible Keynesian government" would actively intervene within the economic system and deliberately run a deficit in its government budget during a recession in order to stimulate aggregate demand.

This chapter provides an analysis of Keynesian fiscal and monetary policy in the context of the enlarged *IS-LM* macroeconomic model developed in the last chapter. Our analysis of fiscal policy will pay particular attention to the various ways the government can finance an increase in expenditures. After reviewing the Keynesian policy prescription, we begin our analysis of the monetarist criticism of Keynesian economic policy. This important and highly controversial debate between Keynesian and monetarist economists will be a dominant theme throughout most of the remaining chapters of this textbook. In this chapter we introduce the monetarist opposition to Keynesian economics and review the early skirmishes between these two opposing camps. Most of the heavy artillery in the Keynesian–monetarist battle will not appear until later, when inflation is included in our macroeconomic model. Throughout this chapter we continue to assume that price levels are inflexible, an assumption which we permanently relax in Chapter 8. A thorough understanding of macroeconomics under inflexible price levels, the key assumption of the *General Theory*, is a necessary prerequisite for our subsequent analysis of monetary and fiscal policy and the Keynesian–monetarist controversy in the context of an *IS-LM* model with flexible prices.

Brief Restatement of the Keynesian *IS-LM* Model

Before analyzing the effects of monetary and fiscal policy on the economic system, we briefly summarize the Keynesian income determination model (see Table 6-1). As developed in the previous two chapters, our enlarged *IS-LM* macroeconomic model consists of the following four behavioural relationships: the consumption function, the investment function, an import function and the demand for money function. Each of these four key behavioural hypotheses is consistent with Canadian data, although the Canadian investment function does exhibit considerable instability reflecting autonomous elements. As listed in the top portion of Table 6-1, our macroeconomic model also includes an income tax function and an aggregate demand identity. By assuming that both the product and money markets are in a state of equilibrium, we are able to derive a downward-sloping R-Y product market equilibrium relationship, the IS curve, and an upward-sloping R-Y money market equilibrium relationship, the LM curve.

Overall our enlarged *IS-LM* macroeconomic model consists of eight equations, and eight endogenous variables: C, I, M, $\$^D$, Z, T, Y and R. Besides the underlying behavioural parameters a, b, e, n, m, k and ℓ, the key "givens" in the *IS-LM* model

TABLE 6-1   Summary of *IS-LM* Macroeconomic Model

Relationship	Equation Number	Equation	
Aggregate Demand Identity	4-1b	$Z = C + I + G + X - M$	
Consumption Function	4-2a	$C = a + b(Y - T)$	
Investment Function	5-1	$I = I_a - eR$	**IS**
Import Function	5-9	$M = n + mY$	**Curve**
Tax Function	5-8	$T = T_0 + tY$	
Product Market Equilibrium Condition	4-5	$Y = Z$	
Demand for Money Function	5-3	$\$^D = kY - \ell R$	**LM**
Money Market Equilibrium Condition	5-4	$\$^D = \$^S$	**Curve**

IS Curve (Equation 5-10): $R = \dfrac{1}{e}[a - bT_0 + I_a + G + X - n] - \dfrac{1}{e}(1 - b + bt + m)Y$

LM Curve (Equation 5-6): $R = \dfrac{-\$^S}{\ell} + \left(\dfrac{k}{\ell}\right)Y$

Reduced Form of the *IS-LM* model

(5-11) $Y = \dfrac{a - bT_0 + I_a + G + X - n + \dfrac{e}{\ell}\$^S}{1 - b + bt + m + \dfrac{ek}{\ell}}$

$R = \dfrac{-\$^S}{\ell} + \dfrac{k}{\ell}\left[\dfrac{a - bT_0 + I_a + G + X - n + \dfrac{e}{\ell}\$^S}{1 - b + bt + m + \dfrac{ek}{\ell}}\right]$

are the uncontrollable exogenous variables I_a and X and the government policy instruments $\$^S$, G, T_0 and t. By algebraically solving this eight-equation model, each endogenous variable can be expressed solely in terms of the givens in the model. In the lower portion of Table 6-1 we have reproduced the reduced-form equilibrium income equation (5-11) from Chapter 5,[2] along with the reduced-form equation for the interest rate, which is obtained by substituting the reduced-form income equation (5-11) into the *LM* equation (5-6).[3] As discussed in Chapters 4 and 5, the reduced-form equations summarize the fundamental structural determinants of equilibrium income and interest rates, and readily permit the calculation of the various multiplier effects within the economic system.

[2]Recall that this reduced-form income equation was obtained by forcing the same R to prevail in both the product and money markets. The right-hand sides of the *IS* and *LM* equations are equated, and all of the Y terms are collected together.

[3]A reduced-form equation for the endogenous variables C, I, M, T can be obtained by substituting the *reduced-form* equations for Y and R into the original *structural* equations (4-2a, 5-1, 5-9 and 5-8).

Fiscal and Monetary Policy: A Geometric Approach

As a starting point for our analysis of Keynesian policy, we return to our standard *IS-LM* diagram. Chart 6-1 reproduces our basic *IS-LM* diagram from the previous chapter, with intercepts and slopes labelled in the appropriate panels (also see Table 6-1). In each case, the impact of a change in government spending G, tax rates T_0 and t, and the money supply $\$^S$ can be easily determined by shifting the appropriate curve in the *IS-LM* diagram.

A Change in Government Spending

An increase in government expenditures G will cause the intercept of the *IS* curve to increase, thereby shifting the *IS* curve upwards to the right in a parallel fashion. Such an upward shift in the *IS* curve (from IS_0 to IS_1 in panel A of Chart 6-1) will generate a higher equilibrium income level (from Y_E to Y_1) as well as a higher interest rate (from R_E to R_1).

As discussed in Chapter 4, an increase in government expenditures creates an excess demand for goods within the economy, which will lead to a decline in inventory stocks and an increase in new factory orders. As production increases and inventories are restocked, additional incomes will be earned, generating further rounds of consumer spending (and further increases in production and income). This basic Keynesian income multiplier process will, however, be moderated by a rising interest rate, which will depress investment spending. Rising income levels, triggered by the increase in government spending, will raise the transactions demand for money balances. Given a fixed money supply, individuals will attempt to raise money balances for transactions purposes by selling bonds. Bond prices will be forced downwards and interest rates will be pushed upwards. The interest rate must rise to encourage individuals to economize on their holding of the *fixed* money supply.

As discussed in the previous chapter, an increase in G has exactly the same effect on the *IS* curve as an increase in autonomous investment I_a or exports X. All three are stimulants to aggregate demand and enter the *IS* curve in an identical manner. It should come as no surprise that Keynesian economists seized upon an increase in government spending as the cure for recessions. *When autonomous investment and/or exports decline*, the government could offset or counter the inward shift of the *IS* curve with a *corresponding increase in government spending*. As we shall see repeatedly throughout this text, **counter-cyclical fiscal policy** *is the essence of Keynesian economics*.

A Change in Tax Rates

In addition to altering its own expenditures, governments can also change tax rates. In our simple linear income tax function (Table 6-1), if the government were to *reduce* the tax parameter T_0, then the intercept of the *IS* curve would *increase* (a negative multiplied by a negative equals a positive) and the *IS* curve would again shift upwards to the right in a parallel fashion (from IS_0 to IS_1 in panel B of Chart 6-1). On the other hand, if the government were to *reduce* the marginal

CHART 6-1 Fiscal and monetary policy in the *IS-LM* model

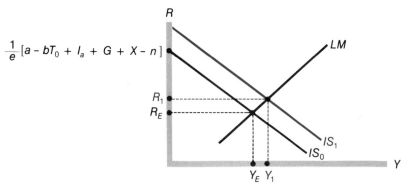

(A) An increase in government expenditures *G*

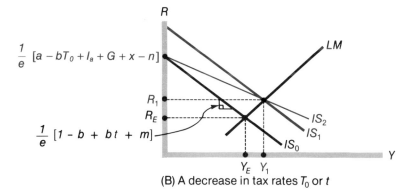

(B) A decrease in tax rates T_0 or t

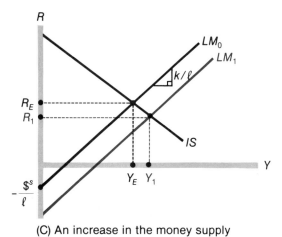

(C) An increase in the money supply

income tax parameter t, then the *IS* curve would become *less* steep and the *IS* curve would *rotate upwards* (from IS_0 to IS_2 in panel B of Chart 6-1).[4] As demonstrated in panel B of Chart 6-1, a reduction of tax rates (T_0 or t) produces either an upward shift or upward rotation of the *IS* curve leading to an increased level of output and a higher interest rate. In either case, an income tax cut increases disposable income and generates additional consumer spending.[5] Rather than the government increasing its own level of spending, tax cuts are an alternative Keynesian policy to stimulate aggregate demand and propel the economy out of a recessionary state.

A Change in the Money Supply

Recall from Chapter 5 that an open market purchase of bonds by the Bank of Canada increases the supply of money and causes the *LM* curve to shift downwards to the right. Comparing equilibrium positions in panel C of Chart 6-1, an increase in the money supply lowers the interest rate from R_E to R_1 and increases the equilibrium level of output from Y_E to Y_1. When the Bank of Canada buys bonds in the open market and injects money into the economic system, bond prices are bid up and interest rates decline. The lower interest rates associated with an expansionary monetary policy will spark new investment spending, which in turn will trigger the multiplier process with its additional rounds of spending. As we shall see below, Keynes was not very sanguine that *counter-cyclical monetary* policy would work. In particular he was concerned about whether investment would respond to lower interest rates in the middle of a recession when business confidence was at a low ebb.

Fiscal and Monetary Policy: An Algebraic Approach

To determine the *exact* magnitude of the multiplier effects on income and interest rates arising from a change in fiscal or monetary policy (the distances Y_1Y_E and R_1R_E in Chart 6-1), it is again useful to return to the reduced-form of our *IS-LM* model. From the reduced-form equations for income and interest rates given in Table 6-1, we can determine the multiplier effects on Y and R from a change in G, $\$^S$ and T_0.[6]

$$\frac{\Delta Y}{\Delta G} = \frac{1}{1 - b + bt + m + \dfrac{ek}{\ell}} = \frac{\Delta Y}{\Delta I_a} = \frac{\Delta Y}{\Delta X} \qquad \frac{\Delta R}{\Delta G} = \frac{\dfrac{k}{\ell}}{1 - b + bt + m + \dfrac{ek}{\ell}}$$

---

[4]The intercept of the *IS* curve is unaffected by the parameter t but the slope of the *IS* curve contains the term bt.

[5]As discussed in Chapter 20, tax incentives can also be used to increase investment spending.

$$\frac{\Delta Y}{\Delta T_0} = \frac{-b}{1 - b + bt + m + \dfrac{ek}{\ell}}$$

$$\frac{\Delta R}{\Delta T_0} = \frac{\dfrac{-bk}{\ell}}{1 - b + bt + m + \dfrac{ek}{\ell}}$$

$$\frac{\Delta Y}{\Delta \$^S} = \frac{\dfrac{e}{\ell}}{1 - b + bt + m + \dfrac{ek}{\ell}}$$

$$\frac{\Delta R}{\Delta \$^S} = \frac{-1}{\ell} + \frac{\dfrac{ek}{\ell^2}}{1 - b + bt + m + \dfrac{ek}{\ell}}$$

$$= \frac{-1\left(1 - b + bt + m + \dfrac{ek}{\ell}\right) + \dfrac{ek}{\ell}}{\ell\left(1 - b + bt + m + \dfrac{ek}{\ell}\right)}$$

$$= \frac{-(1 - b + bt + m)}{\ell\left(1 - b + bt + m + \dfrac{ek}{\ell}\right)}$$

An increase in G, a reduction in T_0, or an increase in $\$^S$ will each have a positive effect on equilibrium income, with the exact size of this multiplier effect depending on the values for the parameters b, e, m, k, ℓ and t.[7] We again note that the income effect arising from an increase in government expenditures is *exactly the same* as the income effect arising from an increase in autonomous investment or exports. As discussed above, G, I_a and X all enter aggregate demand and the *IS* curve in an identical manner. Consequently the effects of a decline in autonomous investment or exports can be offset or countered by a compensating increase in government spending. Alternatively, a tax cut or possibly an expansionary monetary policy could also be implemented to rescue the economy from a downturn in autonomous investment or exports.

[6]Since the marginal income tax parameter t appears in the denominator (not the numerator) of the reduced-form income equation, obtaining the multiplier effect of a change in t on Y is somewhat more complicated. Students with an elementary course in the calculus can easily verify that this multiplier effect is represented by the following expression.

$$\frac{\Delta Y}{\Delta t} = \frac{-b\left(a - bT_0 + G + I_a + X - n + \left(\dfrac{e}{\ell}\right)\$^S\right)}{\left(1 - b + bt + m + \dfrac{ek}{\ell}\right)^2}$$

or

$$\frac{\Delta Y}{\Delta t} = \frac{-bY}{1 - b + bt + m + \dfrac{ek}{\ell}}$$

Thus, the exact value of the income multiplier effects arising from a change in the marginal income tax rate depends on the level of income as well as the behavioural parameters.

[7]In a special case study later in this chapter we present numerical estimates for the key multiplier effects within our *IS-LM* model.

Keynesian Policy Formulation

By employing appropriate fiscal and/or monetary policies, output and employment levels can be stabilized and serious recessions should be a thing of the past. The Marxist prediction that the capitalist system would eventually collapse, a prediction that looked very good in the 1930s, need not become a reality. Rather than overthrowing the free enterprise system, as many socialist and communist parties were advocating throughout the world during the 1930s, Keynes argued that capitalism must be "managed." By direct government intervention, which was also a radical and revolutionary thought in the 1930s, aggregate demand could be controlled and chronic unemployment could be cured. As Peter Newman noted, Keynes saw himself as the "economic saviour of the free enterprise system."[8]

While direct government intervention to control aggregate demand is the essence of Keynesian economics, it is important to point out that there is *no unique* Keynesian policy prescription. A wide variety of alternative policy options are available to the government to stimulate or "manage" aggregate demand. In terms of our simple *IS-LM* model, the government could increase its own expenditures, cut taxes, increase the money supply, or combine these three basic elements. In diagrammatic terms, the *IS* curve and/or the *LM* curve can be shifted by the government to stimulate aggregate demand. As a consequence, Keynesian economics quickly became a popular rationalization for policy proposals from both ends of the political spectrum. "Liberal" policies of increased government services and improved transfer payments were frequently defended as necessary stimulants to revive a sagging economy. Similarly, "conservative" proposals for tax cuts and incentives for investment spending would also qualify as "good" Keynesian policies. As long as a policy affected aggregate demand, it could be defended in Keynesian terms.

Which particular policy option should the government choose to stimulate or control aggregate demand? Unfortunately there is no simple analytical answer to this important policy question, and "political economy" considerations may well dominate. The choice of which particular group of citizens will receive the direct benefits from a stimulative policy (such as a selective tax cut) is, at heart, a political decision. However, two basic economic principles apply to the selection of an "appropriate" Keynesian instrument for demand management policy.

First, a very important characteristic of Keynesian policy is that it is only a **temporary** policy, and therefore the policy option selected must be capable of being stopped or reversed at a later date. For example, if the U.S. enters a serious recession, thus depressing Canadian export sales, a Keynesian government would attempt to stimulate the Canadian economy by following an expansionary policy. However, once the U.S. recovers from its recession and Canadian exports return to their "normal" level, the stimulative policy is no longer needed. As we shall see in subsequent chapters, if the government continues with its stimulative policy when it is no longer required, the economy will experience serious inflationary prob-

---

[8]See quotation at the beginning of this chapter.

lems. Keynesian *counter-cyclical* policies are, by definition, *temporary* policies that must be stopped or reversed at a later stage in the business cycle. Thus, the government's choice of a particular stimulative policy ought not to include *permanent* changes in the fiscal system, such as hiring civil servants who cannot be released at a later date, raising old age pensions which cannot be lowered at a later date, or cutting taxes which cannot be raised at a later date. A "good" Keynesian policy instrument is one which can be quickly changed in either direction, without political or bureaucratic resistance. Unfortunately, the fiscal tap is much easier to turn on than to turn off. Governments are typically very reluctant to raise taxes or to cut back on services provided, and risk antagonizing particular political constituencies. On a political level, fiscal policy tends to be a "one way street" and is not easily reversed or made restrictive.

In addition to the **reversibility** criterion of Keynesian policy, the government must also carefully consider the effects of alternative policy options on a wide range of other key macroeconomic variables. Besides a stable level of output and employment, governments also seek to attain other desirable targets including stable price levels, a stable foreign exchange rate, low interest rates, economic growth and an equitable distribution of income. As the reduced form of the *IS-LM* model demonstrates, a change in a particular policy instrument (G, T_0 and $\$^S$) will affect to varying degrees the values of *all* endogenous variables within the model. For example, interest rates, often an additional target variable of government policy, will increase with a stimulative fiscal policy, but will decrease with a stimulative monetary policy. However, as we shall see in subsequent chapters, a stimulative monetary policy may lead to a higher inflation rate. It is exceedingly unlikely that any policy alternative will affect *all* target variables in a desirable manner. Consequently, government policy makers must carefully weigh the various costs and benefits of different Keynesian policy alternatives, and select the particular policy option that has the most desirable *net* effect on the set of target variables. Since each policy alternative will involve a different set of winners and losers, the choice of an appropriate Keynesian policy instrument is likely to be dominated by political economy considerations.[9]

Financing Fiscal Policy and the Government Budget Constraint

Leaving the government to make its own political choices about which government services will be increased or whose taxes will be lowered, we return to the world of macroeconomic theory. Earlier we demonstrated that an increase in government expenditures would have a multiplier effect on equilibrium income. A \$1 billion increase in G increases Y by $1/[1 - b + bt + m + (ek/\ell)]$ billion dollars. This raises an interesting and important question. Where does the government get that extra \$1 billion to increase G and stimulate aggregate demand? First of all, we

---

[9]In an opportunity cost sense, I am a "loser" every time the government chooses a stimulative policy which does not cut my taxes, increase my transfer payments or increase my consumption of government services.

know that the government (the Bank of Canada) does *not* print an extra billion dollars of money. If the government prints an extra billion dollars of money when *G* increases, then *both* the *IS* curve (from an increase in *G*) *and* the *LM* curve (from an increase in $\$^S$) would shift to the right. In our graphical analysis of government expenditure policy (see panel A of Chart 6-1), only the *IS* curve shifted. The above multiplier expression is calculated on the basis of a *constant* money supply.

If the government does not print extra money, how does the government finance an increase in its own expenditures? Besides printing money, there are two **alternative sources of funds** that the government can utilize to pay for an increase in government spending: tax revenues and funds borrowed from the bond market. Since an increase in government expenditures will increase income levels, the government will automatically collect more tax revenues via the income tax system. For example, if the marginal income tax rate is 40 per cent and the income multiplier effect from an increase in government expenditures is 1.5, then the government will automatically receive an extra $0.6 billion (.40 × 1.5) in tax revenues when it increases government spending by $1 billion. More than half of the funds required to finance the increase in government spending would be generated from the existing income tax structure (*without raising T_0 or t*). Consequently, an increase in government spending will increase the size of the government deficit, but not by the full amount of the increase in government spending (for example, the deficit would increase by only $1.0 − $0.6 = $0.4 billion in the above illustration).

"Bond-Financed" Government Expenditures

Suppose that the government chooses to finance the increase in the deficit associated with an increase in government expenditures by borrowing funds in the bond market. This case is illustrated in panel A of Chart 6-1. The increase in government spending shifts the *IS* curve from IS_0 to IS_1. The financing of the resulting government deficit through the sale of government bonds does not, in itself, cause additional shifts in either the *IS* or the *LM* curve.[10] As we shall see below, that is not the case when government spending is financed by either an increase in tax rates or by the printing of money.

Besides raising the equilibrium level of income, **bond-financed government expenditures** also alter the composition of aggregate demand. In particular the size of the government sector increases and the size of the private investment sector declines. In the parlance of a monetarist, expansionary fiscal policy financed in the bond market will "crowd out" new investment spending in the private sector. To illustrate the **"crowding out" effect** of bond-financed government expenditures, we return to panel A of Chart 6-1. The increase in govern-

[10]In more advanced treatments of the *IS-LM* model, the demand for money function (and the *IS* curve) would include a variable representing total wealth. Including the stock of bonds (part of total wealth) in the money demand curve, and therefore in the *LM* curve, would mean that bond-financed government expenditures would also shift the *LM* curve.

ment spending shifts the IS curve from IS_0 up to IS_1 and the economy moves up the given LM curve to an income level of Y_1. This rising level of income creates an additional demand for money for transaction purposes. Since the government has *not* supplied any additional money, individuals will attempt to sell bonds to increase their money holdings to facilitate the increased number of transactions. Bond prices will fall and interest rates will rise. Given a higher income level with *no* increase in the money supply, interest rates must rise to restore equilibrium in the money market. But rising interest rates will cause businessmen to reduce investment expenditures. While an increase in government spending increases income levels and consumption expenditures, the major casualty from an increase in bond-financed government expenditures is the investment goods sector.[11]

Assuming that the money supply and tax rates are held constant, an increase in government expenditures is jointly financed from increased income tax revenues and additional borrowing by the government. An expansionary bond-financed fiscal policy will increase the level of income (through the multiplier effect) as well as redistribute output *from* the business sector *to* the government sector. The crowding-out effect is the redistribution of output which accompanies the higher interest rates associated with expansionary fiscal policy. Rather than borrowing funds to finance the deficit arising from an increase in government expenditures, the government has two other options: print more money or raise tax rates. The multiplier effects on equilibrium income for each of these two alternative financing arrangements will be considered in turn.

"Money-Financed" Government Expenditures

Suppose that the government finances the budgetary deficit arising from an increase in government expenditures by simply printing the necessary dollar bills. From our previous analysis (see Chart 6-1) we know that when the government increases government expenditures the IS curve will shift upwards to the right, and when the government increases the money supply the LM curve will shift downwards to the right. Consequently an increase in government expenditures financed by an expansion of the money supply will give a *double boost* to income as both the IS and the LM curves shift to the right (see Chart 6-2). Since this double boost effect on income will also have a double boost effect on income tax revenues, *only a portion* of the funds necessary to finance an increase in government spending will actually have to be "printed." Again, most of the necessary funds to finance the increased government expenditures will be generated by the income tax system.

Clearly, financing government expenditures by printing money will have a much larger multiplier effect on equilibrium income than financing government

---

[11]We would point out that if exports (or any other autonomous aggregate demand component) were to rise by the same amount as government expenditures, the *same amount* of crowding-out in the investment goods sector would take place. This crowding-out effect arises because the IS curve has shifted, and interest rates have risen, irrespective of what caused the IS curve to shift.

CHART 6-2 An increase in government expenditures financed by an increase in the money supply

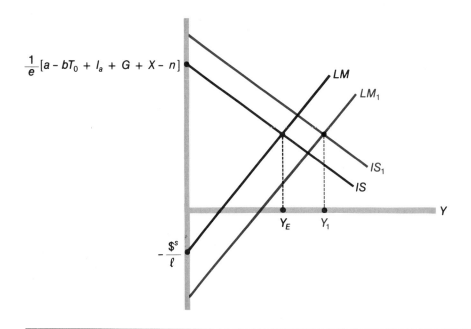

expenditures by bond sales. By supplying additional dollar bills, the increased transactions demand for money that accompanies rising income levels can be accommodated without pushing interest rates up (which would crowd out investment spending and limit the income-generating effects of the expansionary fiscal policy). Whether interest rates rise or fall under **money-financed government expenditures** is indeterminate in Chart 6-2. To determine whether interest rates rise or fall, we would have to know how much *additional* money was printed, that is, how far the *LM* curve shifted. As discussed above, the increase in the money supply required to finance additional government spending depends on the income tax system and on the size of the change in income.[12]

[12]The above analysis only considers the money financing of government expenditures in the *initial* time period. In the second and subsequent time periods, additional increases in the money supply will be required to finance any government deficit which still exists, leading to *further* shifts in the *LM* curve (not shown in Chart 6-2). These subsequent further increases in the money supply and rightward shifts in the *LM* curve will end only when income levels have sufficiently increased to generate *additional* income tax revenues $t \triangle Y$ that are *exactly* equal to the increase in government spending $\triangle G$, i.e., when there is no government deficit to be money-financed. For $\triangle G = t \triangle Y$, income levels must increase by $\triangle G / t$. A complete dynamic analysis of our *IS-LM* model suggests that the full income multiplier effects of money-financed government expenditures will be equal to the reciprocal of the marginal tax rate (t).

"Tax-Financed" Government Expenditures

The final option available to the government to finance an increase in government expenditures is to raise tax rates. In other words the government could increase its expenditures but at the same time increase tax rates by an appropriate amount to maintain a *balanced budget*. From our earlier analysis we know that an increase in tax rates will have a negative effect on income (an inward shift of the *IS* curve). Consequently a **tax increase financing arrangement** will tend to *offset* the positive stimulus on income from the increase in government expenditures (an outward shift of the *IS* curve). Will the negative income effect from an increase in tax rates totally offset the positive income effect from an increase in government expenditures? Alternatively, does an increase in government expenditures totally paid for by higher taxes have any effect on equilibrium income? To answer this important policy question we must return to the algebraic formulation of our model.

If the government maintains a *balanced* budget, then total tax revenues T must be equal to government expenditures G.

(5-8a) $T = G$

This new balanced-budget constraint (equation 5-8a) will now *override* our original income tax function (equation 5-8) in the model.

(5-8) $T = T_0 + tY$

The government must change either or both tax parameters T_0 and t to maintain a balanced budget. Which particular tax parameter the government chooses to vary (to keep $T = G$) has no effect on the analysis below.

Given a new amended macroeconomic model *with a balanced-government-budget constraint* (where equation 5-8a replaces equation 5-8), we must recompute the reduced form equilibrium income equation. Substituting our new balanced-budget equation directly into the consumption function,

$$C = a + b(Y - G)$$

we solve our *new amended IS-LM* equation system to produce a *new* reduced-form equilibrium income equation for a *balanced-budget* economy.

$$Y = Z = C + I + G + X - M$$

$$Y = a + b(Y - G) + I_a - eR + G + X - n - mY$$

$$Y = a + bY - bG + I_a - e\left(\frac{-\$^S}{\ell} + \frac{k}{\ell}Y\right) + G + X - n - mY$$

$$\left(1 - b + m + \frac{ek}{\ell}\right)Y = a + (1 - b)G + I_a + X - n + \frac{e}{\ell}\$^S$$

(5-11a) $$Y\Big|_{G = T} = \frac{a + (1 - b)G + I_a + X - n + \frac{e}{\ell}\$^S}{1 - b + m + \frac{ek}{\ell}}$$

The key distinguishing feature of this *new* reduced-form income equation (5-11a) is that it imposes the constraint that the government always maintains a balanced budget, hence our subscripting notation that $G = T$. Our *previous* reduced-form income equation (5-11 in Table 6-1) did not force the government to maintain equality between total tax revenues and expenditures.

From this new balanced-budget reduced-form income equation (5-11a), we can readily obtain the effect on equilibrium income of a *one-unit increase in government expenditures that is financed by raising tax rates*:

$$\frac{\Delta Y}{\Delta G}\bigg|_{G=T} = \frac{1-b}{1-b+m+\frac{ek}{\ell}}$$

As long as the marginal propensity to consume b is less than unity, the balanced-budget multiplier effect on equilibrium income must be positive (both the numerator and denominator will be positive). However, this **balanced-budget multiplier effect** will be *less than unity* since the denominator is larger than the numerator (by $m + ek/\ell$). The exact size of this *fractional* balanced-budget multiplier depends on the behavioural parameters b, m, e, k and ℓ. A special case study towards the end of this chapter suggests that the Canadian balanced-budget multiplier effect on income from an increase in government expenditures is less than one-half. Thus, a growing government sector which is financed totally by increased tax rates will exert a very modest expansionary effect on income levels.

In addition, the presence of a balanced-budget constraint will also alter the value of all other multiplier effects within the *IS-LM* model. For example, *under a balanced-budget constraint* a one-unit increase in autonomous investment or exports will have an income multiplier effect equal to the following expression:

$$\frac{\Delta Y}{\Delta I_a}\bigg|_{G=T} = \frac{1}{1-b+m+\frac{ek}{\ell}} = \frac{\Delta Y}{\Delta X}\bigg|_{G=T}$$

Compared with our *previously* computed multiplier effect, which did not constrain the government to maintain a balanced budget,

$$\frac{\Delta Y}{\Delta I_a} = \frac{1}{1-b+bt+m+\frac{ek}{\ell}} = \frac{\Delta Y}{\Delta X}$$

the *new* balanced-budget multiplier effect *must be larger*. The only difference between the two algebraic multiplier expressions is the *absence* of $+bt$ in the denominator of the balanced-budget multiplier expression (the smaller the denominator, the larger the multiplier).

The reason for the additional income-generating effect arising from an increase in autonomous investment or exports under balanced-budget conditions is straightforward. When I_a or X increases, income *and income tax revenues* will increase and the government budget is pushed towards a *surplus* position. Under a balanced-budget constraint, the government must cut taxes or increase government expenditures to restore balance within the budget. Such a tax cut or increased level of government expenditures will further stimulate income and *reinforce* the original output multiplier effects arising from the increase in I_a or X. Thus, an economy which maintains a balanced government budget will be subject to much larger swings in output arising from changes in exogenous components of aggregate demand.

Given that tax revenues are very closely tied to income levels via the income tax system, the *absence* of a balanced-budget constraint provides a very important "automatic" stabilizing influence on the macroeconomic system. If the economy starts to slide into a recession, say from a decline in exports, then income tax revenues will decline and the government budget will automatically move towards a deficit position.[13] The *stimulative* effects arising from an excess of government spending over taxation will somewhat offset the *negative* effects triggered by a decline in exports. If the government always balances its budget, then when exports decline (causing output and income tax levels to decline) the government would be forced to either cut government expenditures or raise taxes to maintain its balanced budget. Either balanced-budget policy option would further depress output levels and reinforce the original negative effects arising from the decline in exports.

In summary, the financing arrangements for government fiscal policy are of crucial importance. Depending on whether the government finances increased government expenditures by borrowing funds, printing money or raising taxes, the income multiplier effects will be very different. The most stimulative fiscal policy arises when government expenditures are financed by a new issue of dollar bills, in which case fiscal and monetary policy reinforce each other. The least expansionary effects of government spending occur when the government increases tax rates to pay for the extra government expenditures. The negative effect of the tax increase *almost* cancels out the positive effect from the increased government spending. In addition, the maintenance of a *balanced* government budget will increase the multiplier effects associated with a change in exports or autonomous investment; that is, economic system will be more unstable under balanced-budget conditions. An "unbalanced" government budget is the essence of Keynesian counter-cyclical fiscal policy.[14] When aggregate demand declines, a government following Keynesian policies would directly intervene within the economic system to stimulate aggregate demand, either by increasing government expenditures or cutting taxes. Either stimulative policy moves the government budget towards a negative position.

---

[13]In addition, rising transfer payments (such as unemployment insurance) will further reinforce the movement towards a deficit position.

[14]A Keynesian economist might well argue that the length of the business cycle is the appropriate time interval to maintain budgetary balance. Fiscal surpluses in the boom years would be used to pay for fiscal deficits in the recessionary years.

The Monetarist Attack
on Keynesian Economics

From the late 1940s through the early 1970s, this basic Keynesian *IS-LM* model dominated macroeconomic thought. The popularity of the *IS-LM* model was undoubtedly enhanced by the impressive economic track record of the 1960s. As discussed in Chapter 1, Canada, along with most of the Western World, enjoyed a decade of unprecedented economic prosperity and tranquility. Throughout most of the 1960s, the unemployment rate was well under 5 per cent and the inflation rate was 3 per cent or less. With the exception of the year 1967 when the growth rate dipped to 3.3 per cent, for eight successive years (1962-69) *real* output rose by *at least 5.2 per cent*. Given this remarkable economic performance, economists and policy makers came to believe that the *IS-LM* model must be correct. By carefully adjusting monetary and fiscal policies, the business cycle could indeed be tamed. At long last economics had finally shaken its reputation of being the "dismal science." Economists and policy makers appeared to be able to "fine tune" the economy for maximum performance. As the Anti-Inflation Board described the Canadian macroeconomic state of affairs in the early 1970s,

> There was a general and fundamental acceptance of the desirability and feasibility of "fine tuning". The government believed in the appropriateness of significant year-to-year changes in monetary and fiscal policies as a means of offsetting cyclical variations in the economy. This judgement reflected the implicit faith that if an error were made in the determination of policy, or if circumstances occurred which changed the desired policy setting, the adverse effects could be corrected by reversing the policy instruments to lean in the opposite direction. The public shared this belief and its corollary: if the economy is out of balance, this instability exists because the government has been unwilling or unable to implement the proper discretionary action.[15]

During these halcyon days of macroeconomics, critics of an interventionist Keynesian policy approach were decidedly out of favour. To question fiscal activism during the 1960s was to run the risk of being labelled an old-fashioned nineteenth century conservative. However, as economic conditions started to deteriorate in the 1970s, the critics of Keynesian economics began to make a comeback. Double-digit inflation in 1974-75 quickly rendered the Keynesian *IS-LM inflexible* price level model "old-fashioned." Coincident high rates of inflation *and* unemployment called into question the ability of the government to fine-tune the economy. In fact, many economists began to blame Keynesian economics and/or *in*appropriate Keynesian policy for the economic mess of the 1970s. Economics was once again the "dismal science," economists were again bickering amongst themselves and a non-interventionist conservative economic policy approach was back in fashion.

---

[15]Anti-Inflation Board, *Inflation and Public Policy* (Ottawa, 1979), p. 29.

Undoubtedly, the leading critic of Keynesian economics is Professor Milton Friedman, now retired from the University of Chicago. Much of Friedman's research has been in the general area of monetary economics, emphasizing the important influence of monetary policy on inflation and output levels (for which he received the 1976 Nobel prize in economics). In addition, Friedman is a leading exponent of the "Chicago school" of economics, which *opposes* almost all aspects of government intervention within the economic system including minimum wages, rent controls, wage and price controls, tariffs, fixed exchange rates, and compulsory health insurance.[16] Given Friedman's strong conservative inclinations, his academic expertise and his persuasive communication skills, the anti-Keynesian school of thought coalesced around Milton Friedman and the University of Chicago. Since it is always better to be in favour of something than against something else, this anti-Keynesian school of thought came to be known as monetarism (given its roots in monetary economics).

Labels tend to be confusing and uninformative, and the labels "Keynesian" and "monetarist" can mean many different things to different people. Just as Protestants come in many different colours and stripes from Southern Baptists to High Anglicans, there are many different brands of Keynesianism. The 384 pages of turgid prose[17] in the *General Theory* are open to many interpretations. Unfortunately Keynes died in 1946, well before his theory was popularized. Depending on one's interpretation of the "good book," Keynesians can range from perpetual fiscal and monetary stimulaters (haunted by memories of the Great Depression) to very cautious, conservative economists trying to *trade off* inflation for a lower unemployment rate (see Chapter 12). While the disciples of *IS-LM*ism differ widely in their religious fervour, at heart a Keynesian believes that government intervention within the economic system can alleviate economic problems such as unemployment. Monetarism is fundamentally a reaction to the deficiencies and excesses of Keynesian economics and government intervention within the economic system. The lack of a theory of inflation in Keynesian economics and the *presumption* that the government *can* manage aggregate demand are perhaps the two major themes of the monetarist attack on Keynesian economics. At the risk of misrepresenting and oversimplifying the differences between "Keynesians" and "monetarists," we briefly sketch out what we consider to be the major distinguishing features of each camp. Most macroeconomists tend to fall somewhere between a hard-core Keynesian and a hard-core monetarist, borrowing ideas from both sides.[18]

[16]For a highly readable and persuasive introduction to Friedman's basic philosophical position, see his now classic monograph, *Capitalism and Freedom* (Chicago: University of Chicago Press, 1962).

[17]As J.K. Galbraith has noted, Keynes' *General Theory* "is a work of profound obscurity, badly written and prematurely published.... Some of its influence derived from its being extensively incomprehensible" [*Money* (Boston: Houghton Mifflin Co., 1975) p. 218].

[18]As discussed in Chapter 17, a third macroeconomic camp has emerged in the 1980s—the *new* classicals (another confusing label). New classical economists, who are even more conservative than monetarists, believe that anticipated government policy will have absolutely no effect on output or employment levels (the Policy Ineffectiveness Proposition).

A Keynesian (circa 1965)

Taking the usual liberties of authorship, we define a 1960s **Keynesian** as an economist who believes that the *IS-LM* model described over the last two chapters is a reasonably good approximation to economic reality. Wage and price levels are reasonably stable,[19] whereas output and employment levels are subject to considerable instability. Frequent, persistent and sizeable shifts in autonomous investment and/or exports will have large multiplier effects on income and output. Given the assumed inflexibility of wage and price levels, prolonged periods of insufficient aggregate demand and chronic unemployment can easily arise. Fortunately, the fiscal multipliers are equally as large. Thus, an application of *stimulative* fiscal policy can *offset* the negative effects from a decline in autonomous investment and/or exports. By carefully deploying demand management policies, the government can smooth out the business cycle and stabilize output and employment levels. In short, the free enterprise system must be "managed" or "controlled" by an *interventionist* government. Without such government intervention, the economy would continue to be subject to violent swings in the business cycle, such as occurred in the 1930s.

A Monetarist

A hard-core **monetarist** would disagree with every sentence in the previous paragraph and would raise a number of new issues that have been omitted from the *IS-LM* model. Anticipating subsequent discussion of these new issues, we outline the main tenets of monetarism.

First and foremost, monetarists believe in the inherent stability of the free enterprise system, when the government leaves it alone. Exogenous changes in aggregate demand are relatively unimportant (rational businessmen have long ago tamed their "animal spirits"), and any such exogenous changes will have relatively small and short-lived multiplier effects on employment and output. The free enterprise system will quickly adjust to any exogenous changes in aggregate demand and will rapidly return to its *equilibrium* position (dubbed the "natural rate of unemployment" by monetarists). As a corollary to this first point, monetarists believe that fiscal policy (the Keynesian prescription) will also have very modest and short-lived multiplier effects on output and employment. Keynesian policies have *no permanent* effect on the equilibrium level of real output, and do not provide a permanent cure for the unemployment problem. At best, fiscal policies provide only a *modest* and *temporary* gain in output and employment.

Second, monetarists argue that attempts to implement this modest and temporary Keynesian fiscal policy stimulus are doomed to failure. Imperfect information, long and variable lags associated with policy changes, expectational considerations and political realities all militate against a successful Keynesian policy. More often than not, Keynesian policy will do more harm than good. For example, inappropriate timing of fiscal policy may aggravate the business cycle rather than

---

[19]As discussed in Chapter 12, a 1960s Keynesian also believed that modest amounts of inflation could be traded off for a lower unemployment rate.

smooth it out.[20] In fact, a hard-core monetarist would argue that the chief source of instability in the economic system is the government! Misguided attempts to stabilize or stimulate the economy by direct government intervention will lead to periods of recession or inflation, or both. Rather than run the risk of destabilizing the economic system by fiscal intervention, monetarists argue that the best stabilization policy is a "hands off" approach. Again, the free enterprise system is inherently stable and fully self-regulating. If an exogenous element of aggregate demand were to change unexpectedly, the free enterprise economic system would quickly return to its original equilibrium position. Consequently, there is no need to risk the negative consequences of Keynesian interventionism.

Third, as their name suggests, monetarists believe that monetary policy has very powerful effects on the economic system, something that Keynesian economists tended to overlook. However, the only lasting effects of monetary policy are confined to "nominal" economic variables, not "real" economic variables. An increase in the money supply will directly affect *nominal* aggregate demand. If the money supply and therefore nominal aggregate demand are increasing at a faster rate than the level of real output, then the average price level will be continually bid up. Inflation is strictly a monetary phenomenon. To control inflation all the government must do is control the growth rate of the money supply. Since expansionary monetary and fiscal policies *cannot* permanently decrease the unemployment rate,[21] and given the inherent difficulties in using monetary and fiscal policies for short-term stabilization purposes, monetarists advocate *no fiscal intervention* and a *low, constant* growth rate in the money supply. By controlling the rate of monetary expansion the government can control inflation, and the free enterprise system will solve any unemployment problems.

Round 1 of the Keynesian—Monetarist Debate: Early Skirmishing Over the Slopes of the *IS* and *LM* Curves.

As is evident from our thumbnail sketch of the monetarist position, monetarism represents a full frontal attack on Keynesian economics and the role of an interventionist government policy. In Chapters 9 through 15 we incorporate a theory of inflation into our macroeconomic model and carefully analyze each of these monetarist criticisms of Keynesian *IS-LM* economics. Much of the monetarist criticism turns out to be analytically correct. For example, when a theory of inflation is incorporated into the *IS-LM* model there are no *permanent* output effects associated with a change in the exogenous components of aggregate demand $(I_a, X, G$ or $T_0)$. However, there are important *short-run* multiplier effects associated with changes in exogenous variables and the debate between Keynesian and monetarist economists boils down to a question of *how long is the short run.* As discussed in Chapter 14, the length of this short-run adjustment period is a

---

[20]See the case study in Chapter 20.

[21]As discussed in Chapter 12, monetarists firmly believe that there is no permanent trade-off between inflation and unemployment. The government *cannot* achieve a permanently lower unemployment rate by accepting a higher *stable* inflation rate. Expansionary policies which attempt to achieve a permanently lower unemployment rate will generate an *accelerating* inflation rate.

key issue in the Keynesian–monetarist stabilization policy debate. If the self-regulating adjustment forces of the free enterprise system, on which monetarism relies, are quite *slow*, then one might well opt for a Keynesian interventionist policy. The *risks* of destabilizing the economy through Keynesian intervention might be less consequential than the *costs* of unemployment during a prolonged monetarist period of adjustment following a decline in exports or autonomous investment.

In this chapter we briefly look at the early skirmishing between monetarists and Keynesian economists over the size of the multipliers in the *IS-LM* model with inflexible price levels. As stated above, Keynesians implicitly believe that the output multipliers associated with a change in autonomous investment, exports and government spending are quite large, whereas the output effects of monetary policy are quite small. The economic system is prone to output instability that can be offset by fiscal policy. Monetarists disagree. Fiscal policy and exogenous aggregate demand components have little effect on output levels, but monetary policy is very powerful.

Depending upon how one draws the *IS-LM* diagram, one can obtain either Keynesian or monetarist conclusions. Keynesians quickly learn to draw steep *IS* curves and flattish *LM* curves (see panel A of Chart 6-3), thereby generating large output effects for a shift in the *IS* curve arising from a change in I_a, X, or G. A change in monetary policy $\Delta\$^S$ produces a very small output effect in the Keynesian *IS-LM* diagram (compare Y_2 to Y_1 in panel A of Chart 6-3). Monetarists, on the other hand, think that the *IS* curve is quite flat and the *LM* curve is very steep.[22] Consequently, a "monetarist" drawing of the *IS-LM* diagram (panel B of Chart 6-3) would lead to small output effects from an *IS* curve shift but large output effects from an *LM* curve shift. Not surprisingly, much of the early debate between monetarist and Keynesian economists focused on the slopes of the *IS* and *LM* curves.

We briefly consider the debate over the slope of the *IS* curve. As discussed in Chapter 5, the slope of the *IS* curve depends crucially on the sensitivity of investment expenditures to interest rate movements, the parameter *e*. Recall that the algebraic slope of the *IS* curve is equal to $(1 - b + bt + m)/e$. The greater the sensitivity of investment expenditures to interest rate movements (the larger the parameter *e*), the flatter the *IS* curve.

The battle lines were immediately drawn. Keynesians regarded autonomous elements ("animal spirits" and "business psychology") as the key factors in investment demand, with interest rate movements being of minor consequence (the parameter *e* is quite low). Therefore, the *IS* curve would be steep (due to the low value of *e*) and unstable (due to autonomous elements). Consequently, fiscal policy is the most powerful weapon to rescue the economy from a collapse in

---

[22]Many monetarists would be quite reluctant to concede the existence of an *IS-LM* diagram, the basic theoretical model of the Keynesian opposition. At the risk of antagonizing some monetarists, we translate the basic tenets of monetarism into Keynesian terms. As Milton Friedman once noted, "In one sense, we are all Keynesians now; in another, no one is a Keynesian any longer. We all use the Keynesian language and apparatus; none of us any longer accepts the initial Keynesian conclusions" [*Dollars & Deficits* (Englewood Cliffs, N.J.: Prentice-Hall, 1968), p. 15].

CHART 6-3 The Battle of the Slopes

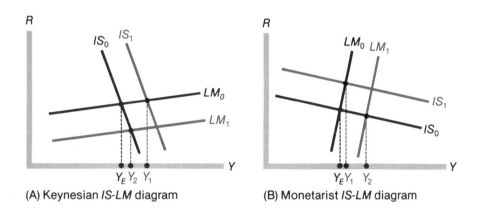

(A) Keynesian *IS-LM* diagram   (B) Monetarist *IS-LM* diagram

autonomous investment (or exports) and monetary policy will have very little effect on output levels.[23] In the words of Keynes,

> The collapse in the marginal efficiency of capital may be so complete that no practicable reduction in the rate of interest will be enough. If a reduction in the rate of interest was capable of proving an effective remedy by itself, it might be possible to achieve a recovery without the elapse of any considerable interval of time and by means more or less directly under the control of the monetary authority. But, in fact, this is not usually the case; and it is not so easy to revive the marginal efficiency of capital, determined, as it is, by the uncontrollable and disobedient psychology of the business world. It is the return of confidence, to speak in ordinary language, which is so insusceptible to control in an economy of individualistic capitalism. This is the aspect of the slump which bankers and business men have been right in emphasizing, and which the economists who have put their faith in a "purely monetary" remedy have underestimated.[24]

Monetarists would dismiss notions that the business world is ruled by an "uncontrollable and disobedient psychology" as highly fanciful. The "free enterprise" philosophy of a monetarist would lead to predictions that investment

---

[23]In fact by carefully drawing the *IS-LM* diagram, monetary policy *may* be incapable of offsetting an inward shift in the *IS* curve. The necessary downward shift in a flattish *LM* curve to offset a downward shift in a steep *IS* curve may generate a *negative* rate of interest; that is, the interest rate cannot be pushed down far enough to restore the original output level.

[24]Keynes, *General Theory*, pp. 316-17. For a discussion of the *marginal efficiency of capital*, see Chapter 20.

demand is highly sensitive to interest rate movements (the parameter e is very large). Investment decisions are made by rational businessmen who carefully weigh the expected future returns of an investment project against the cost of borrowing funds. A rise in the interest rate will exert a quick and substantial negative effect on investment expenditures. The profit motive rules out any capricious or "disobedient" investment behaviour. In *IS-LM* terms, a high value for the parameter e translates into a flattish *IS* curve and the usual monetarist predictions: low output multipliers for fiscal policy and strong effects for monetary policy. The potency of monetary policy arises from the sensitivity of investment spending to a change in interest rates which accompanies a change in the supply of money. The impotency of fiscal policy can be attributed to the monetarist "crowding out" effect. An increase in government expenditures forces up the interest rate, which produces a large, offsetting reduction in investment spending. Given an investment demand function that is highly responsive to interest rate changes, fiscal policy will have little effect on the level of output but will have a substantial effect on the distribution of output between government and business sectors.

Which side won the battle of the slopes? Probably the Keynesians, although for reasons that they might not appreciate. First, the Keynesians were playing softball on their own turf—an *inflexible* price level *IS-LM* model. Most of the monetarist attack is premised on a free market system where prices can adjust, and thus none of the monetarist power hitters have yet come to bat (hardball starts in Chapter 8). Second, the Keynesians really could not lose this opening game. As long as *either* fiscal *or* monetary policy has a *positive* multiplier effect, aggregate demand can be stimulated. Furthermore, even if the money multiplier effect exceeded the fiscal multiplier effect, a Keynesian could still use fiscal policy (although in larger doses than monetary policy). In short, the Keynesians really had nothing at stake in this opening round. Keynesian stabilization policy does not depend on the *relative size* of the fiscal and monetary multipliers. However, since both sides were guilty of confusing the "means" (choosing between fiscal and monetary policy) with the "ends" (affecting aggregate demand), perhaps neither side should be awarded this opening game.

One thing which this opening round reveals is that many of the important differences between Keynesians and monetarists reduce to *empirical*, not *theoretical*, propositions. The relative potency of fiscal versus monetary policy depends on the slopes of the *IS* and *LM* curves, which in turn depend on the underlying behavioural parameters within the model. As discussed above, both sides accepted the theoretical proposition that interest rates affect investment demand. The debate was over the *size* of this particular effect, the size of the parameter e. Monetarists claimed that e was very large whereas Keynesians regarded e as being quite low. As a general rule, empirical questions such as the size of the parameter e ought to be resolvable by empirical analysis. Econometric analysis can provide statistical estimates for the underlying parameters within the model, from which estimated numerical values for the various multipliers within the model can be readily computed. We close this chapter with a case study which provides econometric estimates for all of the parameters within our *IS-LM* model, based on

TABLE 6-2 Canadian Statistical Estimates of the Equations in the
IS–LM Model, 1956-84

The consumption function:	$C = 4.18 + .83(Y - T)$	$\overline{R}^2 = .996$
	$(.68)\ (.01)$	
The tax function: *	$T = T_0 + .31Y$	$\overline{R}^2 = .894$
	$(.01)$	
The investment function:**	$I = I_a + .21Y - .40R$	$\overline{R}^2 = .981$
	$(.01)\quad (.11)$	
The import function	$M = -7.87 + .33Y$	$\overline{R}^2 = .987$
	$(.69)\ (.01)$	
The demand for money function:†	$\$^D = 4.30 + .11Y - .58R$	$\overline{R}^2 = .894$
	$(.37)\ (.01)\quad (.10)$	

* To maintain consistency in the model, data for T was generated by subtracting real disposable income from real GNP. As such, T will have government transfers netted out of tax revenues, thus accounting for the lower value for the slope parameter than presented in Chart 5-11.

** As discussed in Chapters 5 and 20, real investment decisions depend on the *real* interest rate. To approximate the *real* interest rate we have subtracted the annual percentage change in the CPI from the *nominal* interest rate on long-term government bonds. The two variables in the investment function were lagged one year to reflect the construction lags in the investment process.

† To correct for the effects of inflation, the money supply (M1) was deflated by the CPI (see Chapters 5 and 8).

Canadian data. Besides finding out which side won this opening round (does monetary or fiscal policy have the larger multiplier effect?), this case study also provides a number of Keynesian *IS-LM* policy applications.

Case Study 4:   How Large are the Canadian Multipliers?

Throughout this book we present simple scatter diagrams for the various behavioural relationships within a macroeconomic model. By fitting a straight line through these scatter diagrams using the least squares technique (described in Chapter 4), we can obtain an "estimate" for the intercept and slope of each particular economic relationship.[25] In the estimated equations presented in Table 6-2, we have added an intercept to our demand for money equation and have included output as an additional explanatory variable in the investment equation (see Chapter 20). To facilitate the multiplier analysis below, we have retained the T_0 and I_a notation in our tax and investment equations. For those students with some background in statistics, we present the estimated standard errors in parentheses below each parameter estimate and the corrected $\overline{R}^2$ for the overall regression. The statistical estimates in Table 6-2 are based on annual Canadian data, measured in billions of 1971 dollars, covering the 1956-84 period.

As the first step in our quantitative analysis, in the upper portion of Table 6-3 we derive the empirical counterpart of our algebraic *IS* and *LM* curves, following the

[25]In cases where there are two righthand-side explanatory variables (such as in the demand for money), the least squares technique is used to estimate both slope parameters.

TABLE 6-3   Solving Our Estimated Canadian *IS–LM* Model

IS **Curve**

$Y = Z = C + I + G + X - M$

$Y = 4.18 + .83(Y - T_o - .31Y) + I_a + .21Y - .40R + G + X + 7.87 - .33Y$

$(1 - .83 + .26 - .21 + .33)Y = (12.05 - .83T_o + I_a + G + X) - .40R$

$.55Y = (12.05 - .83T_o + I_a + G + X) - .40R$

$$R = \frac{1}{.40}(12.05 - .83T_o + I_a + G + X) - \frac{.55}{.40}Y$$

$$R = (30.13 - 2.08T_o + 2.5I_a + 2.5G + 2.5X) - 1.38Y$$

LM **Curve**

$\$^S = \$^D = 4.30 + .11Y - .58R$

$$R = \frac{1}{.58}(-\$^S + 4.30 + .11Y)$$

$R = (-1.72\$^S + 7.41) + .19Y$

Derivation of Reduced Form Equations for Income and Interest Rates

$30.13 - 2.08T_o + 2.5I_a + 2.5G + 2.5X - 1.38Y = -1.72\$^S + 7.41 + .19Y$

$1.57Y = 22.72 - 2.08T_o + 2.5I_a + 2.5G + 2.5X + 1.72\$^S$

$Y = 14.47 - 1.32T_o + 1.59I_a + 1.59G + 1.59X + 1.10\$^S$

$R = (-1.72\$^S + 7.41) + .19(14.47 - 1.32T_0 + 1.59I_a + 1.59G + 1.59X + 1.10\$^S)$

$R = 10.16 - .25T_0 + .30I_a + .30G + .30X - 1.51\$^S$

---

same sequence of equation substitutions as outlined above. In Chart 6-4 we have plotted our estimates for the Canadian *IS* and *LM* curves. We have arbitrarily chosen the year 1984, when actual output was $140.6 billion and the interest rate was 12.75 percent, to establish the intersection point for our estimated *IS* and *LM* curves (to facilitate reading the graph, we have not depicted the first $140 billion in output). While any diagrammatic scaling is completely arbitrary, our estimated Canadian *IS* and *LM* curves look Keynesian (with a much steeper *IS* curve than *LM* curve).

Using our scale diagram we can determine the output and interest rate effects arising from a change in any one of the exogenous variables. For example, suppose that government expenditures were to increase by $1 billion, financed by borrowing the necessary funds in the bond market. Given our empirical estimates for the Canadian *IS* curve, a $1 billion increase in *G* will shift the *IS* curve upwards by 2.50 percentage points (the coefficient on *G* in the *IS* equation is 2.50). In Chart 6-4 we have drawn a higher parallel *IS* curve to reflect this $1 billion increase in government spending. According to our scale diagram, this extra $1 billion of government expenditures will increase the equilibrium income level to slightly more than $142 billion and raise the interest rate to just over 13 percent. A similar

CHART 6-4 Estimates of Canadian *IS* and *LM* curves

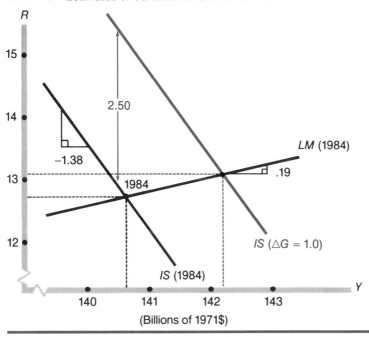

effect would occur for a $1 billion increase in exports or autonomous investment.

A more precise value for the multiplier effects associated with an increase in government expenditures can be obtained by deriving the reduced form of our estimated *IS-LM* model. Making use of our estimated parameter values in Table 6-2 in the lower portion of Table 6-3 we solve our complete macroeconomic model[26]. From these reduced form income and interest rate equations, we can readily determine the multiplier effects from a one-unit change in *any* of the exogenous variables. A $1 billion increase in government expenditures (or exports or autonomous investment) increases income by an estimated $1.59 billion and raises interest rates by an estimated 0.30 of a percentage point, both of which are rather modest multiplier effects. While Keynesians tend to think in terms of quite large output multiplier effects, Canadian reality would appear to be much closer to monetarist perceptions. However, it is not a complete victory for the monetarists. Expansionary fiscal policy has only a very modest upward effect on interest rates (there is very little crowding out) and the monetary multiplier effects on income levels (1.10, as calculated in Table 6-3) are even lower than the fiscal policy multiplier effects.

Next we compute the balanced-budget multiplier effects in our estimated Canadian *IS-LM* model. We assume that the government adjusts the tax parameter T_0 to maintain budgetary balance. Given our estimated tax function (Table 6-2),

---

[26]Because of the inclusion of the income variable in the investment function in Table 6-2, Table 6-3 includes an additional income term in the derivation of the reduced-form income equation.

the government's balanced-budget tax rule is as follows:

$$T_0 = G - .31Y$$

This tax-parameter constraint equation is then substituted into our previous estimated reduced-form equation.

$$Y = 14.47 - 1.32(G - .31Y) + 1.59I_a + 1.59G + 1.59X + 1.10\$^S$$

$$Y(1 - 1.32 \times .31) = 14.47 + (1.59 - 1.32)G + 1.59I_a + 1.59X + 1.10\$^S$$

$$Y = (1/.59)(14.47 + .27G + 1.59I_a + 1.59X + 1.10\$^S$$

$$Y\Big|_{G=T} = 24.53 + .46G + 2.69I_a + 2.69X + 1.86\$^S$$

Thus, a $1 billion increase in government expenditures which is totally financed by increasing the tax rate T_0 will raise income by only $0.46 billion. The balanced-budget government expenditure multiplier is less than one-third the size of the bond-financed government expenditure multiplier.

However, imposing the restriction that the government must always maintain a balanced-budget substantially increases the output multiplier effects arising from a change in exports, autonomous investment and the money supply. For example, the income multiplier effect from an increase in autonomous investment or exports rises from 1.59 (without a balanced-budget constraint) to 2.69 under the assumption that the government always maintains a balanced budget. As discussed earlier in the chapter, a *decrease* in autonomous investment or exports will lower income tax revenues and the government must either raise taxes or decrease government spending to balance its budget. Either option will further depress aggregate demand and reinforce the original downward multiplier effect associated with the decrease in autonomous investment or exports. Such a deliberate balanced-budget policy considerably strengthens the multiplier effects associated with changes in the exogenous components of aggregate demand, leading to a more *unstable* economic system. An economist of monetarist non-interventionist persuasions would be well-advised to stop short of advocating a policy which forces the government to balance its budget *each and every* year.

We briefly consider the multiplicity of Keynesian policy options available to the government. Suppose that the government wishes to increase output by $10 billion. Given the estimates of the multiplier effects computed in Table 6-3, the government would have at least the following three policy options available to generate an extra $10 billion in output:

1) increase government spending by $6.3 billion ($6.3 \times 1.59 = 10$),
2) cut taxes T_0 by $7.6 billion ($7.6 \times 1.32 = 10$),
3) increase the money supply by $9.1 billion ($9.1 \times 1.10 = 10$).

In addition, the government could *mix* the above policy alternatives. For example, a $4.0 billion increase in government spending coupled with a $3.3 billion increase in the money supply also generates an additional $10.0 billion in output. There are literally an infinite number of combinations of $\triangle G$, $\triangle T_0$ and $\triangle \$^S$ that can be used to generate a given amount of additional income.

In choosing which particular policy to implement, the government must carefully consider the effects of each policy option on other key macroeconomic (target) variables. For example, the three (single instrument) policy options outlined above to increase output by $10 billion have the following effects on the interest rate:

1) A $6.3 billion increase in government spending raises interest rates by 1.9 percent ($6.3 \times .30 = 1.9$).
2) A $7.6 billion tax cut also raises interest rates by 1.9 percent ($7.6 \times .25 = 1.9$).
3) A $9.1 billion increase in the money supply lowers interest rates by 13.7 percent ($9.1 \times 1.51 = 13.7$).

Government policy makers must carefully assess the impact of various policy alternatives on many different macroeconomic variables (including the inflation rate and foreign exchange rate, which are discussed in subsequent chapters) and choose that policy option which has the most desirable *net* effects on a range of important macroeconomic (target) variables.

Jan Tinbergen, a famous Dutch economist and contemporary of Keynes, forcefully argued that the multiplicity of policy instruments allows the government to achieve a number of desirable objectives. By making appropriate adjustments in the set of policy instruments, the government can simultaneously achieve a number of macroeconomic targets. To illustrate the Tinbergen policy approach, let us assume that the government wishes to achieve both a target level of output as well as a target interest rate. Suppose that the government wishes to *increase* output by $10 billion and *lower* interest rates by 2 per cent. To accomplish these two objectives, the government will have to shift the *IS* curve to the right (say with an increase in government expenditures) and shift the *LM* curve to the right, so that they now intersect at an output level that is $10 billion *higher* and an interest rate that is 2 percentage points *lower*. It requires at least two policy instruments (ΔG for the *IS* curve and $\Delta \$^S$ for the *LM* curve) to achieve two targets. A basic principle or rule of Tinbergen's policy analysis is that **the number of policy instruments must be at least equal to the number of targets** which the government is seeking to achieve. To hit two targets, one requires at least two bullets.

To determine the exact magnitude of the instrument adjustments required to achieve these two numerical targets ($\Delta Y = 10$ and $\Delta R = -2$), we must return one final time to the estimated reduced form for our Canadian *IS-LM* model (Table 6-3). Assuming that all other exogenous variables remain constant and that a change in government spending is used to shift the *IS* curve, the required instrument changes can be determined by solving the following two equations:

$$\Delta Y = 1.59\Delta G + 1.10\Delta \$^S = 10 \qquad \Delta R = 0.30\Delta G - 1.51\Delta \$^S = -2$$

To generate $\Delta Y = 10$ and $\Delta R = -2$, ΔG and $\Delta \$^S$ must be set at 4.7 and 2.3 respectively.[27]

---

[27]The Tinbergen rule that the number of instruments must be at least equal to the number of targets falls out of the algebra: two (target) equations in two (instrument) unknowns.

As a final postscript on the Tinbergen policy approach, it should be pointed out that Tinbergen actually put this policy model into practice in the Netherlands. Tinbergen was the first economist to estimate an econometric macroeconomic model (in 1936) and he used his estimated equations to formulate policy (instrument settings) for the Dutch economy. For his pioneering work in macroeconomic policy and econometrics, Tinbergen was selected as the *very first* recipient, along with Ragnar Frisch, of the Nobel prize in economics. To be selected "first" among all living economists is a singular honour indeed.

Concluding Comments and Qualifications

In this chapter we have illustrated the major policy implications of Keynesian *IS–LM* economics and have indicated the general points of criticism raised against Keynesian economics by monetarists (although our Keynesian–monetarist story is far from over). In doing so we have emphasized the "mechanics" of Keynesian policy formulation by resorting to diagrams, algebra and a special empirical case study. Unfortunately, the world in which the policy maker lives is not nearly as clean and clear cut as our exposition suggests. It is much easier to shift *IS-LM* curves on a blackboard than it is to turn "real-world" monetary and fiscal policy levers to stabilize the economy. The Keynesian policy analysis presented in this chapter is subject to at least three important sets of qualifications.

Theoretical Limitations of the *IS–LM* Model

Our analysis is based on a very simple and small theoretical macroeconomic model consisting of only four behavioural hypotheses: a consumption function, an investment function, an import function and a demand for money function. The real world is much more complicated than this and we have obviously omitted many important factors from our model, such as the foreign exchange rate and foreign capital flows. Most important, we have assumed inflexible price levels and have computed all multiplier effects on the assumption that a change in aggregate demand affects only real output levels and *not* price levels. As we shall see in Chapters 8 and 9, an increase in aggregate demand will cause price levels to rise, and the inclusion of inflation within the *IS-LM* model will dramatically affect the theoretical properties of the model and the size of the multiplier effects. The remainder of this text is devoted to refining this basic macroeconomic model and analyzing the theoretical and policy implications of various refinements to this model.

Empirical Limitations to the Implementation of Keynesian Policy

To determine *exact* policy instrument settings requires a substantial amount of quantitative information concerning economic behaviour (the parameters) and exogenous variables. Unfortunately, econometricians and forecasters are not infallible. First of all, there is the usual set of statistical problems inherent in obtaining *estimates* for the various behavioural parameters within the theoretical model. Even if our econometric equations appear to provide an extremely "good fit" of the data, there is always the possibility that one or more of the behavioural parameters might change. For some reason, perhaps inexplicable to economists, people might alter their marginal propensity to consume. While our theory continues to hold (people are still consuming on the basis of their disposable income), the estimated reduced form of our model would change and our policy instrument setting would have to be revised to reflect this structural change in economic behaviour. Finally, and most important, predicting the value of key exogenous variables is a mug's game at best. By their very nature, exogenous variables are often variables which economists cannot explain. As the Governor of the Bank of Canada once observed, "Economists are not good at predicting what ayatollahs will do."[28] Without a precise set of values for all of the behavioural parameters and exogenous variables within the model, one cannot determine the exact Keynesian instrument setting.

Dynamic Problems

The development and analysis of our simple *IS-LM* model has been completely static. No allowance has been made for the time lags, delayed reaction effects and dynamics which are an integral part of the economic system. For example, when the government changes its instrument settings, it will take a considerable length of time for the multiplier effects to work their way throughout the economic system. The Keynesian rounds of spending do not occur instantaneously. As Friedman has forcefully argued, consumers will not immediately adjust their spending to an unexpected change in their disposable income.[29] Given all of the lags in the economic system (which are discussed in subsequent chapters), a policy change may take two to three years to reach its peak impact effect.[30]

Thus a government must be able to make extremely accurate forecasts of future economic events in order to start the slow-working Keynesian policy antidote so that it affects aggregate demand when it is needed. Keynesian policy must be implemented well before it is needed, at a time when forecasts of a future recession are most uncertain. Keynesian policy is not for the faint of heart! If one waits until the economy is in the middle of a recession to apply the fiscal stimulus (when it is obvious that there is a recession), by the time the stimulus reaches its maximum effects (two or three years later) the economy may have recovered on its own. Under such circumstances, the ill-timed Keynesian policy would no longer be an offset, but rather would be an additional stimulant leading to the inflationary consequences of an overheated economy. Fiscal and monetary policies which are *not* synchronized with changes in exogenous variables may end up *destabilizing* the economy rather than stabilizing output levels.[31] Accurate forecasting and

---

[28]Reported in the *Globe and Mail*, 8 December 1979.

[29]Friedman's "permanent income" theory of consumption is fully discussed in Chapter 19.

[30]See, for example, L. De Bever and T. Maxwell, "An Analysis of Some of the Dynamic Properties of RDX2," *Canadian Journal of Economics*, May 1979, pp. 162-70.

[31]See the case study in Chapter 20.

precise timing are crucial for a successful counter-cyclical Keynesian policy. Unfortunately, what is good in theory may not work out in practice. As we shall see in subsequent chapters, some of the harshest criticism from the monetarist camp concerns the inherent difficulties in implementing Keynesian policies. Until economics develops a better track record in forecasting, even the best-intentioned Keynesian policies *may* end up doing more harm than good.[32]

Key Concepts

counter-cyclical fiscal policy (fiscal offsets)
temporary reversibility nature of Keynesian stabilization
    policy
the "crowding out" effect
alternative financing arrangements for fiscal policy
bond-financed government expenditures
money-financed government expenditures
tax-financed government expenditures
the balanced-budget multiplier effects
a Keynesian versus a monetarist
Tinbergen's instrument-target rule

Review Questions

1. Using either diagrammatic or algebraic techniques, determine the effects on equilibrium income levels and interest rates of the following economic events:
   a) a decrease in exports
   b) an increase in the marginal prospensity to import
   c) an increase in government spending
   d) an increase in the marginal tax rate.
2. Explain in words why the level of income rises when the money supply is increased. What are the various behavioural factors which determine the size of the multiplier effect on income arising from an increase in the money supply?
3. Assume that the government wants to increase income levels by $5 billion. What alternative Keynesian policies are available? What factors would you consider important in choosing a particular Keynesian policy from the set of alternative policy options?
4. Suppose that the government decides to increase government spending but refuses to raise tax rates or print money to pay for these extra government expenditures. How much funds will have to be borrowed in the bond market?

---

[32]There is an old forecasting adage which bears repeating: He who lives by the crystal ball may end up eating ground glass.

5. Other than bond-financed fiscal policy, how else might the government finance increased government spending? How will these different financing arrangements affect the fiscal policy multiplier effects on income and interest rates?

6. Why does a balanced-budget policy increase output instability in an economy?

7. What are the fundamental differences between Keynesians and monetarists? Explain.

8. Explain how the values for the interest rate parameters in the investment function and the money demand function affect the potency of fiscal and monetary policy. Do you think that the relative potency of fiscal versus monetary policy is a crucial issue in the debate between Keynesian and monetarist economists? Explain. How can an estimate for the actual size of a particular multiplier effect be determined?

9. If the government wishes to achieve both a target income level and a target interest rate, what are the implications for fiscal and monetary policy? Explain either diagrammatically or algebraically.

10. What are the major difficulties in implementing Keynesian stabilization policy?

The Balance of Payments and the Foreign Exchange Rate

The exchange rate is a very important price in a country that trades with the outside world on a scale that Canada does. . . . It is not therefore possible to ignore it, even when it floats.[1]

Every year Canadian residents make millions of financial transactions with Americans, Japanese and other nonresidents. A large number of these transactions are the result of Canada's trade with other countries, but others arise because Canadians travel abroad, send gifts abroad, buy property in foreign countries and invest in foreign assets such as U.S., German or Japanese stocks, bonds and bank accounts. And of course, nonresidents come to Canada for vacations and business trips and they invest in Canada by purchasing Canadian companies and property and by lending to Canadian institutions such as the federal and provincial governments, Hydro Quebec and Stelco.

These international transactions play an extremely important role in the Canadian economy. For example, in 1984 Canada exported goods and services worth about \$132 billion, representing about 31 per cent of GNP. But in addition to the flow of goods and services there are enormous flows of a purely financial nature, such as transactions involving stocks and bonds. In 1984 nonresidents purchased new issues of Canadian stocks and bonds amounting to \$9.7 billion. Economic linkages to the rest of the world (especially to the United States, which typically purchases over half of Canada's exports and about two-thirds of all Canadian stocks and bonds purchased by foreigners) make the Canadian economy particularly vulnerable to events in foreign countries.

Economies that are influenced by events that take place outside their borders are often described as "open." Frequently, the source of economic problems in open economies lies abroad and policy makers must deal with disequilibria in both their domestic goods and financial markets as well as in their balance of international payments. As the name suggests, **balance of payments** problems involve imbalances between the outflow of payments made by Canadian residents to nonresidents and the inflow of payments made by nonresidents to Canadians. The 1974-75 recession in the U.S. is an example of an external shock to the Canadian

[1]Bank of Canada, *Annual Report*, 1970, p. 9.

economy. U.S. recessions not only cause disequilibrium in the domestic goods market (export industries are depressed and unemployment increases) but also a disequilibrium in the balance of international payments because the immediate effect of a foreign recession is to reduce the value of Canadian sales to non-residents but not the value of purchases by Canadians from nonresidents. In short, a balance of payments deficit emerges.

As in all free markets, there are natural forces that tend to restore equilibrium to the balance of payments. From the Canadian point of view, a balance of payments deficit is reflected in a shortage of foreign exchange. Exports are not earning enough to pay for imports. The excess demand for foreign exchange tends to raise the value of foreign currencies in terms of the Canadian dollar, and the dollar falls in value or depreciates. As we shall see, this adjustment in the foreign exchange value of the Canadian dollar is part of the natural mechanism that restores equilibrium to the balance of payments. However, governments are not always prepared to accept equilibrium prices in important markets. The price of the Canadian dollar (the foreign exchange rate) is an example. In the early 1970s the Canadian government did not want to allow the exchange rate to appreciate to the extent that market forces dictated. Reflecting on monetary policy at the time, G.K. Bouey, then Senior Deputy Governor of the Bank of Canada, said:

> The primary objective of monetary policy over the past two years has been to encourage economic expansion; a related objective has been to moderate the upward pressure on the Canadian dollar in foreign exchange markets. An unduly strong Canadian dollar hampers both our export industries and those domestic industries that must compete with imports.[2]

But the story was quite different in the second half of the 1970s when market forces were pushing the dollar in the downward direction. Mr. Bouey, now Governor of the Bank of Canada, answered his own rhetorical question this way:

> How should a problem of this kind, basically a problem of confidence, be dealt with? Not, I believe, by standing completely aside and letting the Canadian dollar fall as far as it might on the basis of market forces....
>
> The trouble with standing aside was that the greater the fall in the exchange rate the greater the impact on our prices and costs.... We do not want to see a situation where exchange rate depreciation produces more inflation which, in turn, results in further depreciation—a vicious circle.[3]

Clearly one can list disadvantages to both a rise and fall in the exchange value of the Canadian dollar! The conclusion which most central bankers appear to draw is that the exchange rate should be stabilized at whatever the existing level happens

---

[2]Extract of remarks by G.K. Bouey at the annual meeting of the Canadian Mutual Funds Association, Toronto, 25 May 1972, reprinted in the *Bank of Canada Review*, June 1972, p. 8.

[3]Statement by G.K. Bouey before the House of Commons Standing Committee on Finance, Trade and Economic Affairs, 16 May 1978, reprinted in the *Bank of Canada Review*, June 1978, p. 4.

to be. The Governor of the Bank of Canada admitted as much in 1985, when he said:

> The Bank of Canada...is almost a daily participant in the exchange market, resisting sharp fluctuations in the exchange rate in either direction in as evenhanded a manner as the particular circumstances permit. Our objective is to have a steadying influence on the market forces, lending a measure of stability to the exchange rate and at the same time contributing to a sound and viable exchange market in Canada. We are very conscious, however, that strong and persistent moves in the exchange rate cannot be countered through intervention alone, and reinforcing domestic actions are typically required as well.[4]

For the greater part of the period after the Second World War, most countries have followed a fixed exchange rate policy. From time to time Canada has fixed the exchange value of the Canadian dollar in terms of the U.S. dollar. For example, from May 1962 to May 1970 the Canadian dollar was pegged at $0.925 in U.S. funds. Just as fixing the price of, say, bread will prevent the laws of supply and demand from restoring equilibrium in the market for bread, fixing the exchange value of the Canadian dollar suppresses an important mechanism through which equilibrium in the balance of international payments is restored following a disturbance. As we shall see, the effectiveness of monetary and fiscal policies is not independent of the government's exchange rate policy. Specifically, the multiplier effects within our macroeconomic model depend on whether the government intervenes to fix the foreign exchange rate or allows it to be determined by market forces.

The purpose of this chapter is to introduce the balance of payments into our macroeconomic model. Essentially we are adding one more market, the foreign exchange market, to our model to go along with the goods and money markets that have already been introduced. Full equilibrium in our expanded "open economy" model will be achieved only when all three markets are simultaneously in equilibrium. Throughout the analysis in this chapter we will continue to assume that the aggregate price level is fixed. In Chapter 9 and all subsequent chapters, this assumption is permanently dropped. In Chapter 11 we will examine the balance of payments adjustment process in an inflationary world.

Canada's Balance of International Payments

Four times a year Statistics Canada publishes details of Canada's international transactions.[5] Table 7-1 shows a summary of these accounts for 1986. As in all accounting systems, transactions are recorded as either current or capital items. The **current account** records all the payments that are made for current items, such as the importing of stereos or the exporting of wheat. The **capital account**

---

[4]Remarks by Gerald K. Bouey, Governor of the Bank of Canada, to the 27th Annual Congress of the Association Cambiste Internationale, Toronto, Ontario, 1 June 1985.

[5]See Statistics Canada, *Quarterly Estimates of the Canadian Balance of International Payments*.

TABLE 7-1   Canada's Balance of International Payments, 1986
(Millions of dollars)

Current Account

Merchandise Exports	120,630	Merchandise Imports	110,498
Service Receipts		Service Payments	
Travel	6,377	Travel	7,443
Transport	4,536	Transport	4,290
Business Services	5,464	Business Services	7,682
		Investment Income	23,918
Investment Income	7,100		
		Other Items	4,428
Transfers	4,289		
		Total Current Payments	158,259
Other Items	1,058		
Total Current Receipts	149,454		
NET CURRENT BALANCE			−8,805

Capital Account
(Net flows in millions of dollars)

Direct Investment	
Foreign investment in Canada	1,557
Canadian investment abroad	−4,812
Portfolio Investment	
Canadian holdings of foreign securities	−2,301
Nonresident holdings of Canadian securities	25,043
Other Capital Flows	−5,083
NET BALANCE ON CAPITAL ACCOUNT	14,404

Reconciliation

Net Balance on Current Account	−8,805
Net Balance on Capital Account	14,404
Statistical Discrepancy	−4,937
NET CHANGE IN OFFICIAL RESERVES	−662

records the transactions in financial assets, such as the sale of BC Tel bonds to a U.S. pension fund or the purchase of building land by the Cadillac Fairview Corporation.

The Current Account

Canadian residents sell both goods and services to nonresidents. The value of goods that are sold to nonresidents is recorded under the heading of Merchandise Exports, which amounted to just over $120 billion in 1986. Under the heading of Service Receipts are recorded such items as travel, transport and business services. Travel refers to the payments made by foreigners travelling in Canada for such things as hotel accommodation and restaurant meals. The next major item refers to the investment income received by Canadian residents on their holdings of foreign assets (interest on U.S. government or corporate bonds, dividends paid on U.S. stocks and rental income on Canadian-owned condominiums in Florida) which also enters as a positive item on the current account. One further item in the accounts, listed as Transfers, completes the total of current receipts. Included in this final item are gifts and inheritances received by Canadian residents from nonresidents and the funds that immigrants bring with them. Since all of these items generate receipts for Canadians they are entered as positive items in the balance of payments. Table 7-1 shows that total current receipts, which represent the value of all goods and services sold to nonresidents, amounted to almost $150 billion in 1986.

On the other side of the ledger there is a corresponding list of payments (negative items) that Canadians make to nonresidents for merchandise imports and services. Again services include such things as foreign travel by Canadians and the interest and dividend payments made by Canadians to nonresidents. Such interest payments are made by Canadian governments and corporations that have borrowed funds abroad sometime in the past. The dividend payments that flow out of Canada go to the foreign owners of Canadian firms.

Two frequently quoted indicators of the state of the balance of payments are the merchandise trade balance and the current account balance. The first is the difference between the value of merchandise exports and merchandise imports. As Chart 7-1 shows, Canada rarely experiences a payments deficit on the trade account. In 1986 the surplus amounted to $10.1 billion. The current account surplus or deficit is a broader measure since it includes services as well as merchandise trade. A deficit on the current account as a whole implies that the value of goods and services that Canadians are buying from abroad exceeds the value of goods and services that are being sold to nonresidents. Just as an individual must either sell some of his assets or borrow from someone else if he wishes to spend more in a year than he receives, so too must a country. Consequently, whenever a country runs a deficit on the current account of its balance of international payments the residents of that country are, in one way or another, reducing their assets or borrowing from nonresidents. This process can take many forms. Suppose, for example, that a Canadian firm that wants to expand its operations borrows from U.S. residents by selling bonds in the United States. The proceeds of this borrowing might be used to import capital equipment, steel and other supplies into the country. As long as the firm's investment projects yield a return which is greater than the cost of the borrowed funds, the foreign loan can be repaid out of the income generated by the new physical investment.

In other words, it can make good economic sense for a growing economy to run a current account deficit and borrow from abroad. However, if the borrowing is not used to finance new physical investment but is simply used to maintain a high level of consumption, then the country is in some sense living beyond its means. The foreign loans will eventually have to be paid back and, since the loans have not been used to create physical capital and therefore future income, the debt will be paid off at the expense of future consumption, and the country will be heading towards an inevitable period of "belt tightening".

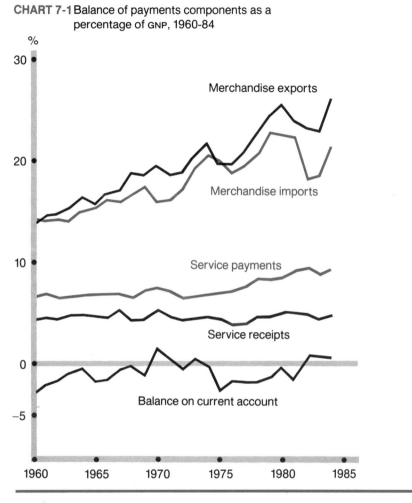

CHART 7-1 Balance of payments components as a percentage of GNP, 1960-84

The Capital Account

In our discussion of the current account we pointed out that any shortfall between total current receipts and total current payments must be reflected in either net foreign borrowing or an increase in foreign ownership of Canadian assets. That is to say, if Canadians pay out more than they receive in any given period, then Canadians must have financed this deficit by either borrowing abroad or selling off Canadian assets such as land, buildings, or stocks. It is the capital account that records the flow of assets between countries. Table 7-1 shows the net flow of the major items for the year 1986.

The capital account distinguishes between two kinds of capital flows, direct and portfolio investment.[6] The distinguishing feature is that *direct investment* implies

---

[6]In this context the term investment does not refer to the accumulation of physical capital goods but rather the wider concept of the acquisition of income-earning assets.

ownership whereas *portfolio investment* does not. When Canadian residents buy condominiums in Florida or when Canadian companies take over U.S. companies they become owners of U.S. assets. These transactions are recorded in the capital account as a negative item under the heading "Canadian Direct Investment Abroad." Recall that *imports* are included as *negative* items in the current account because these international transactions involve *payments* by Canadians. In the same way, the purchase of a condominium in Florida involves a *payment* by a Canadian resident; the ownership title to the property is imported. Conversely, direct investment that flows into Canada is entered as a *positive* item because by *exporting* the ownership title of Canadian land or stock, Canadian residents *receive* payment from nonresidents. An example of foreign direct investment in Canada would be the purchase of Stelco stock by a U.S. pension fund. This capital inflow is "direct" in the sense that foreign ownership of Canadian assets has increased.

The second type of capital flow is referred to as portfolio investment, which is further broken down into long-term and short-term flows. A large part of portfolio investment has no effect on the amount of foreign ownership in the Canadian economy or the amount of Canadian ownership of foreign assets. Consider the purchase of Stelco bonds by U.S. residents. In this case Stelco has simply borrowed funds from a foreign lender; the proportion of Stelco which is owned by nonresidents has not changed. Again, an *inflow* of portfolio investment is recorded as a *positive* item (Canada received payment for exporting Canadian bonds) and an *outflow* of portfolio investment is recorded as a *negative* item.

A large part of short-term capital flows involves bank deposits. Nonresidents' holdings of Canadian bank deposits may change simply as a result of other international transactions. If a U.S. exporter leaves the payment he received for his exported goods at a Canadian bank, then this transaction will appear as an import item on the current account (negative) and as an increase is nonresident holdings of Canadian bank deposits on the capital account (a short-term capital inflow, a positive item).

In the last few paragraphs we have made the point that any deficit (surplus) on the current account must be matched by a surplus (deficit) on the capital account. If Canadians import more than they export, then nonresidents must finance this by buying title to Canada's physical assets (an inflow of direct investment), by lending to Canadians (an inflow of portfolio investment) or by holding Canadian-dollar bank deposits (an inflow of short-term portfolio investment).

However, as Table 7-1 indicates, the deficit on the current account is not matched exactly by the surplus on capital account. Canadians can import more than they export to the extent that Canada's **official foreign exchange reserves** are run down. In 1986, for example, Canadian foreign exchange reserves were reduced by about 0.7 billion. In other words, the sum of the net balances on current and capital accounts equals the net change in Canada's official foreign exchange reserves (plus the inevitable accounting errors and omissions). The Bank of Canada manages Canada's foreign exchange reserves and it is through sales from (or additions to) this foreign exchange fund that the Bank of Canada is able to influence the exchange rate of the Canadian dollar. We turn now to consider the sources of the demand for and supply of foreign exchange, and how these demand and supply forces interact to determine the equilibrium value of the exchange rate.

The Foreign Exchange Market

In this section we will derive the supply and demand curves for foreign exchange from the Canadian perspective. Since each of the many countries in the world has its own currency, there are, of course, many exchange rates for the Canadian dollar (the *Globe and Mail* lists about 60 every day) but we will confine our analysis to a two-country world made up of Canada and the rest of the world, where the rest of the world will be represented by the United Kingdom for expositional convenience.

Table 7-2 illustrates three hypothetical balance of payments accounts for Canada. We will look at each in turn and discuss the supply and demand for Canadian dollars in the foreign exchange market which each set of transactions implies. In column **A**, Canada's international transactions consist of only current transactions. Exports of $100 are balanced by imports of $100. However, foreign trade is not typically barter, but involves the exchange of national currencies. Normally a British importer will need to obtain Canadian dollars in order to pay for the goods. If the British importer does pay in pounds stirling, then the Canadian exporter will have to exchange the pounds for Canadian dollars since he can pay his domestic expenses only in Canadian dollars. Either way, the *export of Canadian goods* to the U.K. ultimately gives rise to a *demand for Canadian dollars* in the foreign exchange market. Similarly, the Canadian importer of goods from the U.K. will need to pay the British exporter in British pounds. In order to get the required

TABLE 7-2   Three Illustrations of Canada's Balance of Payments

	A	B	C
Current Account			
Exports	+ $100	0	0
Imports	− $100	− $100	− $100
Current Balance	0	− $100	− $100
Capital Account			
Net Investment Flows into Canada:			
Direct	0	+ $ 50	0
Portfolio	0	+ $ 50	0
Capital Balance	0	+ $100	0
Reconciliation			
Current Balance	0	− $100	− $100
Capital Balance	0	+ $100	0
Net Change in Official Reserves	0	0	− $100

pounds, the Canadian importer will have to go to a bank and *offer Canadian dollars* in exchange for pounds stirling. Since we are focusing on the supply and demand for Canadian dollars in the foreign exchange market, this example illustrates that *imports into Canada* give rise to a *supply of Canadian dollars* in the foreign exchange market.

Our second example, illustrated in column B of Table 7-2, assumes that imports into Canada are valued at $100 but exports are zero. The net balance on current account is therefore –$100, which on its own implies a supply of $100 to the foreign exchange market. However, the capital account shows a net inflow of foreign investment totalling $100. This capital inflow is a receipt and therefore a positive item in the balance of payments. It may be that British residents have purchased $50 of Stelco stock and $50 of Quebec government bonds. In order to make these financial investments, British residents will need to obtain Canadian dollars. Again a positive item in the balance of payments corresponds to a demand for Canadian dollars in the foreign exchange market. In this example Canadian importers supply $100 to the foreign exchange market and British investors demand $100 in the foreign exchange market. Canadian and/or British banks reconcile the amount of currency demanded and supplied.

In the final column of Table 7-2 we illustrate the case where Canadian imports are financed not by exports, nor by net capital inflows but by a reduction in Canada's official foreign exchange reserves. Again the deficit of $100 on the current account implies a supply of Canadian dollars in the foreign exchange market. If British residents do not want Canadian exports (suppose there is a recession in the U.K.) and British investors do not want to invest in Canada (suppose high interest rates in the U.K. are more attractive), where will Canadians get the foreign exchange (British pounds) to pay for Canada's imports? We have a disequilibrium in the foreign exchange market that will set up forces which, left to themselves, would push the foreign exchange market towards equilibrium. However, in the present example this adjustment mechanism is short-circuited by government action. The Bank of Canada intervenes by selling foreign exchange (pounds) from its holdings of foreign exchange and buys up Canadian dollars. In other words, it is the Bank of Canada that supplies the needed pounds. Through the banking system the Canadian importer is therefore able to get the foreign exchange required to pay for the imports.

To summarize, the supply of Canadian dollars in the foreign exchange market derives from international payments that Canadian residents want to make, payments which typically cannot be made in Canadian dollars. These international payments consist of the negative items in Canada's balance of payments accounts and include such things as merchandise imports, foreign travel, outflows of interest and dividends and outflows of capital, both of the direct and portfolio type. All such payments give rise to a demand for foreign currencies and a supply of Canadian dollars in the foreign exchange market. Conversely, the demand for Canadian dollars in the foreign exchange market is derived from Canada's international receipts because Canadians need to receive payment in their own currency. These international receipts, which are entered in the balance of payments as positive items, are in turn the result of merchandise exports, inflows of interest

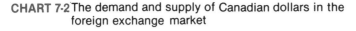

CHART 7-2 The demand and supply of Canadian dollars in the foreign exchange market

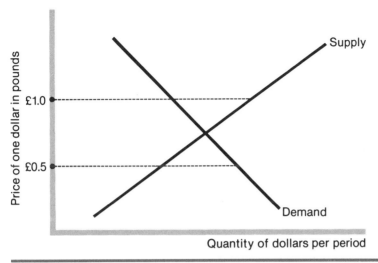

and dividends and inflows of foreign investment. In addition to these private supplies and demands there is the possibility that the Bank of Canada will supply (demand) Canadian dollars in the foreign exchange market by purchasing (selling) foreign exchange, thus adding to (reducing) Canada's official foreign exchange reserves.

In Chart 7-2 we have drawn supply and demand curves for the Canadian dollar in the foreign exchange market. As usual, along the horizontal axis we measure the quantity per time period—in this case the quantity of Canadian dollars offered or demanded per period of time. Along the vertical axis is measured the unit price of the Canadian dollar. In the foreign exchange market the price of the dollar is measured in terms of foreign currency (such as the pound) since it is foreign currency that must be given up in order to obtain dollars. Note that as the price of one dollar in terms of pounds rises (movement up the axis), the dollar is rising in value (one dollar buys more pounds), just as when the price of gold rises we can say the value of gold has risen. In other words, movement up the vertical axis implies that the Canadian dollar is rising in value or appreciating.

The Demand Curve

As with all demand curves, the demand curve for Canadian dollars slopes downward to the right. When the Canadian dollar depreciates, the dollar value of Canada's exports increases. Nonresidents require more dollars to purchase Canada's exports. Table 7-3 illustrates the case of Canadian cheese exports to Britain.

In the first row of the table we assume that the price of the dollar is £1 so that a package of cheese which sells for $2 in Canada will sell for £2 in Britain (we are ignoring transportation charges and any tariff that might apply). Suppose that at this price British demand for Canadian cheese is 10 packages per month. The

TABLE 7-3 Canadian Cheese Exports and the Quantity of
Canadian Dollars Demanded in
the Foreign Exchange Market

Exchange Rate	Price of Cheese/Package		Amount of Cheese Sold in Britain		
	In Canada	In Britain	No. of Pkgs	Value in £	Value in $
$1 = £1	$2	£2	10	£20	$20
$1 = £0.5	$2	£1	25	£25	$50

British value of this Canadian cheese is $10 \times £2 = £20$, which at the exchange rate of $1 = £1 amounts to $20. In order to import the 10 packages of Canadian cheese, a British importer must obtain $20 in the foreign exchange market. Now suppose the Canadian dollar depreciates to £0.5. We will assume that the Canadian dollar price of cheese is not affected by the value of the exchange rate so that the price in Britain falls to £1 per package.[7] As long as the British demand curve for Canadian cheese is downward-sloping, the fall in the price of cheese will lead to an increase in quantity demanded, say to 25 packages. The change in the British value of cheese sales when expressed in terms of pounds depends in general on the price elasticity of demand for Canadian cheese in Britain. In our example the value of cheese sales in Britain rises from £20 to £25 (the demand for Canadian cheese in Britain is price elastic). In terms of the foreign exchange market, the important point is that an increase in the quantity of cheese sold in Britain together with a fixed *Canadian* price of $2 per package means that the value of export sales in Canadian dollars must rise. Table 7-3 shows that the demand for Canadian dollars jumps from $20 to $50 per month. A depreciation of the Canadian dollar lowers the price in pounds of Canadian exports, which in turn makes Canadian goods more competitive. As a result both the *volume* and the *value* of exports in Canadian dollars increases, which implies an increase in the quantity of Canadian dollars demanded in the foreign exchange market. The demand curve for Canadian dollars in the foreign exchange market slopes downwards to the right, as shown in Chart 7-2.

The Supply Curve

We turn now to the slope of the supply curve for Canadian dollars. Table 7-4 illustrates the case of imports of British cars. The first row of the table shows the situation when the price of a Canadian dollar is £1. At this exchange rate a British car that costs £9,000 to produce in Britain will sell for $9,000 in Canada. At this price we assume that sales will be 10 cars per month. In the second row the Canadian dollar is assumed to have depreciated to £0.9, which implies that the

[7]An alternative assumption is that the price of Canadian cheese is determined by the world price of cheese so that changes in the exchange rate of the Canadian dollar have no effect on the world price of cheese but do affect the domestic price of cheese. This assumption also leads to the conclusion that the demand for Canadian dollars in the foreign exchange market increases as the Canadian dollar depreciates.

TABLE 7-4   Imports of British Cars and the Quantity of Canadian
Dollars Supplied in the Foreign Exchange Market

Exchange Rate	Price of British Car		Cars Sold in Canada		
	In Britain	In Canada	No. of Cars	Value in £	Value in $
$1 = £1	£ 9,000	$ 9,000	10	£ 90,000	$ 90,000
$1 = £0.9	£ 9,000	$10,000	8	£ 72,000	$ 80,000

£9,000 car now sells for $10,000 in Canada. A 10 per cent depreciation of the Canadian dollar raises the price of imports by 10 per cent. The higher price of British cars in Canada will mean that fewer are purchased. However, the change in the supply of dollars to the foreign exchange market depends on the change in expenditure in Canadian dollars on British cars. In general, the price elasticity of demand for a product determines whether total expenditure will rise or fall in response to an increase in price. A price-elastic demand curve implies total expenditure falls when price rises. The figures shown in Table 7-4 imply that the demand for British cars in Canada is elastic.[8] The increase in price leads to a fall in expenditure from $90,000 to $80,000. Note that if the demand for British cars had been perfectly inelastic at 10 cars per month, then the rise in British car prices would have implied an increase in total expenditure to $100,000. Clearly the slope of the supply curve of Canadian dollars in the foreign exchange market depends on the price elasticity of demand for imports. Since traded goods generally have close domestic substitutes (for example, domestic cars versus British cars) it seems reasonable to assume that the demand for imports as a whole is price-elastic. In conclusion, a depreciation of the Canadian dollar raises the price of imports, reduces the volume of imports and will reduce total expenditure on imports if the demand for imports is price-elastic. Given a price-elastic demand for imports, a depreciation leads to a reduction in the quantity of dollars supplied to the foreign exchange market. The supply curve slopes upwards to the right.

Equilibrium in the Foreign Exchange Market

The equilibrium point in the foreign exchange market, as shown in Chart 7-3, occurs where the supply and demand curves for Canadian dollars intersect. At the equilibrium price, the demand for Canadian dollars by nonresidents who want to buy Canadian goods and services or invest in Canada is exactly equal to the supply of Canadian dollars offered by Canadians who want to buy foreign goods and services or invest abroad. When the foreign exchange market is in equilibrium, Canada's balance of international payments must also be in equilibrium as the net balances on the current and capital accounts will sum to zero. There are no changes in official reserves when the balance of payments is in equilibrium.

To illustrate how the foreign exchange market adjusts to a disturbance, consider the effect of a recession in the U.K. This will have a direct effect in the foreign

[8]Note that the percentage change in quantity (20 per cent) is greater than the percentage change in price (10 per cent).

exchange market because Canada's exports to the U.K. will decline as part of the overall decline in aggregate demand in the U.K. economy. This initial fall in exports implies that the demand curve for Canadian dollars in the foreign exchange market will shift to the left. The left-hand panel of Chart 7-3 illustrates the situation. The excess supply of Canadian dollars causes the price of dollars to decline in terms of foreign exchange. The depreciation of the Canadian dollar makes Canada's exports cheaper from the point of view of foreign buyers and makes imports into Canada more expensive. As the Canadian dollar depreciates, Canada also becomes an inexpensive place to visit while at the same time foreign vacations become more expensive for Canadians. The effect of these relative price changes is to increase exports from their depressed level and to decrease imports. The effects of the depreciation of the Canadian dollar are reflected in *movements along* the supply and demand curves (S and D'). At the new equilibrium point the dollar has depreciated sufficiently to restore the balance between imports and exports that was disturbed by the recession in the U.K.

In the above illustration it is adjustments in the **foreign exchange rate** that restore equilibrium in the foreign exchange market and in the balances of payments. However, suppose the government is following a fixed exchange rate policy at the time of the decline in Canada's exports. As the right-hand panel of Chart 7-3 shows, the exchange rate P_e can be maintained only if the government, through the Bank of Canada, buys up the excess supply of dollars. The Canadian dollars are purchased by the Bank of Canada with foreign exchange reserves. In effect the Bank of Canada is supplying part of the foreign exchange that is needed to finance the current level of imports, which now exceed exports. By doing so the foreign exchange rate is maintained but the equilibrating mechanism is suppressed and the balance of payments will remain in disequilibrium.[9] In addition there is an important side effect to this policy. As the excess supply of dollars in the foreign exchange market is mopped up by the Bank of Canada, the stock of money in Canada is reduced. Again one can think of Canadian importers as buying their foreign exchange from the Bank of Canada. As they do so the quantity of Canadian dollars in the Canadian economy is reduced. Similarly, when there is an excess demand for dollars in the foreign exchange market, the Bank of Canada can prevent the exchange rate from rising by selling Canadian dollars for foreign exchange. In the process foreign exchange reserves are accumulated by the Bank of Canada and the stock of dollars—the Canadian money supply—is increased.

In summary, a **flexible exchange rate** ensures that imports and exports will always adjust so that the balance of payments is either in equilibrium or moving towards equilibrium. On the other hand, a **fixed exchange rate** regime that maintains the existing import and export levels requires that the government intervene in the foreign exchange market by either buying or selling Canadian dollars in exchange for foreign currencies depending on the state of the foreign

[9]Since foreign exchange reserves are finite, this balance of payments disequilibrium cannot be maintained indefinitely. Either the exchange rate must be allowed to fall or other policies aimed specifically at the balance of payments problem must be followed. One possibility is to engineer a recession so that the demand for imports will be reduced. Alternatively, import quotas or restrictions on capital outflows may be used to reduce the supply of dollars to the foreign exchange market.

CHART 7-3 Effect of a decline in Canadian exports in the foreign exchange market

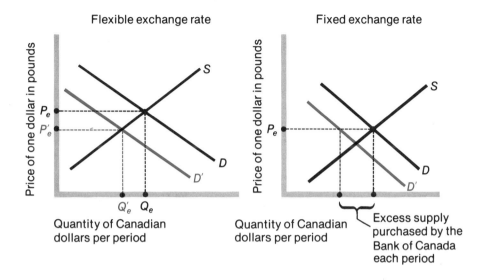

Flexible exchange rate

Fixed exchange rate

Quantity of Canadian dollars per period

Quantity of Canadian dollars per period

Excess supply purchased by the Bank of Canada each period

exchange market. An important corollary of a fixed exchange rate policy is that the domestic money supply responds to conditions in the foreign exchange market. Essentially, the government gives up control of the domestic money supply when it chooses to stabilize the exchange rate.

The analysis in this section has been partial in that we have looked at the foreign exchange market in isolation from the rest of the economy. In our illustration we ignored the effect of the drop in Canadian exports on the level of domestic income. The decline in income associated with the drop in exports will have repercussions on the demand for imports in Canada and on domestic interest rates, both of which have an impact on the balance of payments. In the next section we integrate the balance of payments into our *IS-LM* model so that we can discuss the full general equilibrium effects throughout the economy that result from both exogenous events and policy changes.

Balance of Payments Equilibrium: the *BP* Curve

In Chapter 5 we introduced the *IS* and *LM* curves. The *IS* curve describes all combinations of the interest rate and level of income that are consistent with equilibrium in the goods market. The *LM* curve describes all income–interest rate combinations which are consistent with equilibrium in the money market. Full equilibrium in our expanded open economy model also requires that the balance of payments be in equilibrium. In order that we can represent all three markets in one diagram it is useful to develop a new curve, the *BP* curve, which describes all the combinations of income and the interest rate that are consistent with balance of payments equilibrium.

As we discussed above, balance of payments *equilibrium* requires that:

$$\text{Exports + Capital Inflows = Imports + Capital Outflows}$$

This balance of payments equilibrium condition can be rearranged in the following way:

(7-1)   Net Capital Inflows + Net Exports = 0

The combinations of income and the interest rate that are consistent with equation 7-1, and therefore ensure **balance of payments equilibrium**, will define a curve that we will refer to as the **BP curve.**

> **Definition of the *BP* Curve: The *BP* curve is the collection of all interest rate and income combinations that are compatible with balance of payments equilibrium, given that all other factors which affect the balance of payments are held fixed.**

But how do the level of interest rates and the level of income affect the balance of payments? One of the major factors that influences where investors place their money is the rate of return that the funds will earn. If interest rates are high in Canada, then not only will Canadians find it attractive to invest in Canada but so too will Americans, Germans, and Japanese. Short-term funds are especially mobile across national boundaries because it is possible to make short-term investments that entirely avoid the risks of fluctuating exchange rates. For example, a U.S. corporation that wishes to invest funds for a three-month period can buy either U.S. or Canadian treasury bills. In order to buy Canadian treasury bills the U.S. corporation must first purchase Canadian dollars. In three months' time when the Canadian treasury bills mature, the U.S. corporation will receive Canadian dollars. To avoid the risk that the Canadian dollar might depreciate in terms of the U.S. dollar during the three months, the U.S. corporation can arrange *now* to sell the Canadian dollars that will be received in three months' time at a price that is agreed to now. This "future" exchange rate is called the three-month forward rate.[10] The rate of return that a U.S. corporation can earn from this strategy of investing in Canada and selling the proceeds at the *forward* exchange rate is called the *covered interest rate* because the investment is covered or protected from exchange rate risk. The difference between this "covered" rate and the U.S. treasury bill rate is called the *covered differential* on three-month treasury bills. If this covered differential is positive, then the U.S. corporation can invest in Canada with no exchange risk and earn a higher rate of return than if the U.S. corporation were to invest in U.S. treasury bills.

---

[10]In February 1981 the U.S. dollar price of a Canadian dollar was $0.8353. The three-month forward rate at that time was $0.8349. An American could therefore sign a contract in February 1981 to sell Canadian dollars in April 1981 at a rate of U.S. $0.8349 per Canadian dollar regardless of what the actual exchange rate would be in April 1981.

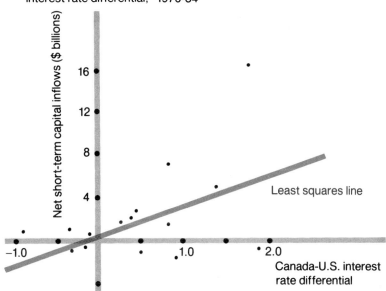

CHART 7-4 Net short-term capital inflows into Canada and the Canada-U.S. interest rate differential,* 1970-84

*The measure used here is the covered differential between Canadian and U.S. three-month treasury bill rates. See the text for a detailed explanation of this concept.

Do firms actually invest short-term funds in foreign countries on the basis of covered differentials? Chart 7-4 shows the scatter diagram for net short-term capital flows into Canada and the covered differential for three-month treasury bills. The least squares line has a positive slope,[11] which means that the data support the hypothesis that the greater is the covered differential the greater are net short-term capital inflows into Canada. In other words, higher Canadian interest rates, other things being equal, will generate greater net capital inflows into Canada because higher Canadian interest rates imply a larger covered differential. The linear relationship between net capital inflows, NCI, and the Canada–U.S. interest rate differential, $R - R^{US}$, that is shown in Chart 7-4 can be represented algebraically as:

$$(7\text{-}2) \qquad NCI = p + q(R - R^{US})$$

We turn now to the question of how the level of income affects the balance of payments. Chart 5-13 in Chapter 5 demonstrates clearly that imports depend directly on domestic income levels. We have represented this relationship in the form of a linear equation:

$$(5\text{-}9) \qquad M = n + mY$$

However, the level of income is not the only variable that determines the level of imports. The ratio of the Canadian price level to the foreign price level will

[11]The slope coefficient is statistically significantly different from zero.

influence the volume of imports into Canada and the volume of Canada's exports. The higher is the ratio of Canadian prices to foreign prices the larger will be the flow of imports into Canada and the smaller will be the level of exports from Canada. The ratio of Canadian to foreign prices can be represented by the quantity $\pi P / P^w$, where P is the Canadian price level (measured in dollars), P^w is the price level in the rest of the world (measured in, say, pounds sterling), and π is the Canadian foreign exchange rate (the price of one Canadian dollar in pounds sterling). The product πP is therefore the Canadian price level measured in terms of pounds sterling. For example, if the price of a car in the rest of the world is £5,000 and in Canada is $11,000, then with an exchange rate of £0.5 per Canadian dollar ($\pi = £0.5$ per $) the ratio of the Canadian price to the foreign price is:

$$(0.5 \times 11{,}000)/5{,}000 = 1.1$$

Since we will assume throughout the analysis that the world price level P^w expressed in foreign currency is fixed, it will be convenient to define the world price level to be unity ($P^w = 1$). Accordingly, the ratio of Canadian to foreign prices is simply πP.

The modified import function recognizes that the higher the ratio of Canadian to foreign prices, the larger will be the flow of imports:

(7-3) $\qquad M = n + s'(\pi P) + mY$

Similarly, the level of Canadian exports will decline as πP rises:

(7-4) $\qquad X = X_0 - s''(\pi P)$

By subtracting imports from exports we obtain an expression for net exports:

(7-5) $\qquad X - M = (X_0 - n) - s(\pi P) - mY$

where $s = s' + s''$.

The quantity $(X_0 - n) - s(\pi P)$ is the intercept in this equation. In order to find the combinations of the level of income and the rate of interest that are consistent with balance of payments equilibrium—the equation of the BP curve—we substitute equations 7-2 and 7-5 into the equilibrium condition (equation 7-1). This gives:

$$(X_0 - n) - s(\pi P) - mY + p + q(R - R^{US}) = 0$$

A more convenient form for this BP equation is obtained by expressing the Canadian interest rate R in terms of the other components of the model.

(7-6) $\qquad R = R^{US} + \dfrac{s\pi P + n - X_0 - p}{q} + \dfrac{m}{q}Y \qquad$ BP Curve

The Slope of the *BP* Curve

The left-hand panel of Chart 7-5 illustrates the BP Curve. The BP curve slopes upwards to the right because the slope coefficient m/q is the ratio of two positive parameters. To see why this must be so from a more intuitive point of view,

CHART 7-5 The Balance of Payments curve

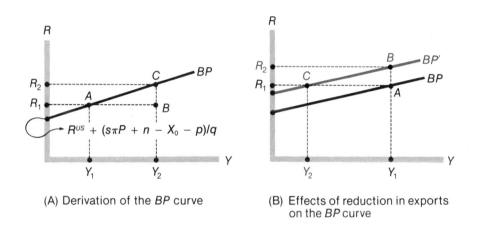

(A) Derivation of the *BP* curve

(B) Effects of reduction in exports
on the *BP* curve

suppose that the economy is initially in balance of payments equilibrium at point
A in the left-hand panel of Chart 7-5. Now suppose that the level of income rises
from Y_1 to Y_2 but that the Canadian interest rate remains at R_1. The economy will
move to point B. But because *net* exports decline as income rises, the balance of
payments will be in a *deficit* position at point B. Equilibrium can be restored to the
balance of payments at income level Y_2 only if net capital inflows increase
sufficiently to offset exactly the decline in net exports. This will require an
increase in domestic interest rates in order to attract foreign funds into Canada. In
Chart 7-5 this higher interest rate is labelled R_2. At point C the balance of
payments is back in equilibrium. It follows that the *BP* curve passes through the
points A and C and that the *BP* curve slopes upwards to the right. We have also
shown that all points *below* the *BP* curve, such as point B in Chart 7-5, correspond
to situations in which the balance of payments is in a *deficit* position. This is
because a movement to a point below the *BP* curve involves a drop in the domestic
interest rate at a given level of income and this in turn leads to a reduction in net
capital inflows. A similar argument shows that points *above* the *BP* curve correspond to situations in which the balance of payments is in a *surplus* position.

Equation 7-6 shows that the precise value of the slope of the *BP* curve is the
ratio m/q, where m is the marginal propensity to import and q is a measure of the
sensitivity of net capital inflows to changes in the level of Canadian interest rates.
Referring to the left-hand panel of Chart 7-5, we see that if the marginal propensity to import m is low, then the increase in income from Y_1 to Y_2 implies that only
a small current account deficit will emerge at point B and therefore only a small
increase in the interest rate is required to restore balance of payments equilib-

rium. A low marginal propensity to import implies a rather flat *BP* curve. In addition, the more sensitive capital flows are to interest rate differentials (the larger the parameter q), the smaller is the rise in the interest rate (to R_2 from R_1) that is needed to restore balance of payments equilibrium and therefore the flatter is the *BP* curve. The algebraic form of the *BP* curve confirms that the smaller is m and the larger is q, the smaller will be the slope of the *BP* curve, m/q.

In a world of perfect capital mobility between countries, Canada's interest rate could not deviate from the world interest rate, because any difference would result in massive capital flows. Higher interest rates in Canada would simply attract funds from other countries that would reduce the cost of borrowing in Canada. In terms of the net capital inflows equation, the slope coefficient q would tend to infinity. In this extreme case, the slope of the *BP* curve m/q will be zero, and the *BP* curve will be perfectly horizontal at the world interest rate. Chart 7-4 suggests that the short-term capital flows are sensitive to interest rate differentials and supports the view that the *BP* curve is fairly flat. However, long-term capital flows do not show the same responsiveness to interest rate differentials so that, overall, the responsiveness of the total of short- and long-term capital movements to interest rate changes is less than Chart 7-4 suggests. Empirical estimates indicate that the *BP* curve for Canada is about as steep as the *LM* curve.[12] Here we have drawn the *BP* curve flatter than the *LM* curve. However, it is important to note that in later analyses, some of the results will depend on which of the two curves is steeper. We indicate where this is so, but leave the details to the student.

Shifting the *BP* Curve

In general, any variable that affects the balance of payments, other than the rate of interest and the level of income, will shift the *BP* curve. In Chart 7-5, the intercept of the *BP* curve on the vertical axis is labelled:

$$R^{US} + \frac{s\pi P + n - X_0 - p}{q}$$

This expression is found by setting the level of income equal to zero in the *BP* curve (equation 7-6). By examining this intercept term we can see how different events affect the position of the *BP* curve. For example, a sudden *decline* in Canada's exports in the wake of a U.S. recession can be represented by a decline in the intercept X_0 in the export function (equation 7-4). The vertical intercept of the *BP* curve indicates that a decline in X_0, which has a negative sign attached to it, shifts the *BP* curve upwards through a distance $\triangle X_0/q$, where $\triangle X_0$ is the change in exports. This example is illustrated in the right-hand panel of Chart 7-5.

The initial position of the economy is at point A, but the decline in exports creates a balance of payments deficit at the initial income level Y_1 and the initial rate of interest R_1. To restore balance of payments equilibrium, either net capital

[12]J.F. Helliwell, "Trade, Capital Flows, and Migration as Channels for International Transmission of Stabilization Policies," in A. Ando, R. Herring and R. Marston, eds., *International Aspects of Stabilization Policies* (Boston: Federal Reserve Bank of Boston, 1974), pp. 241-78.

inflows must increase, which can be generated only by a rise in the rate of interest, say to R_2 (point B) or imports must decrease, which can be brought about only by a reduction in income, say to Y_2 (point C). The new BP curve corresponding to the lower level of exports passes through the points B and C, which are above and to the left of the original BP curve. Another way to look at this shift in the BP curve is to note that point A, which initially corresponded to a position of balance of payments equilibrium, represents a position of balance of payments deficit as soon as exports decline. It follows that after exports have dropped, A must be below and to the right of the *new* BP curve, and so the BP curve must have shifted upwards and to the left.

Indeed *any* event that creates an initial balance of payments deficit will shift the BP curve upwards and to the left. Examples of such events are a reduction in net capital inflows to Canada in response to fears of impending depreciation of the Canadian dollar which would reduce the value of Canadian assets and create capital losses (p of equation 7-2 falls and the vertical intercept of the BP curve rises); the threat of foreign exchange controls or government plans to nationalize some Canadian industries (again p falls); or an appreciation of the dollar (π rises) which reduces Canada's exports, increases imports and therefore reduces net capital exports. On the other hand, events which cause an initial balance of payments surplus will shift the BP curve downwards and to the right. Examples of such events are a depreciation of the dollar (π falls—this encourages exports and reduces imports) or a surge in net capital inflows due, perhaps, to the discovery of new natural resources (p rises).

General Macroeconomic Equilibrium: Fixed Exchange Rates

Full equilibrium in our open economy macromodel requires that the goods market, the money market and the balance of payments (the foreign exchange market) all be in equilibrium simultaneously. In diagrammatic terms, the equilibrium level of income and interest rate must lie on the IS curve, the LM curve and the BP curve. The immediate question is what are the forces that guarantee that these three curves will intersect at a single point; if they do not intersect at a single point, then the prevailing interest rate and income level will not correspond to equilibrium in all three markets. The answer to this question depends crucially on the government's exchange rate policy. In this section we deal with the case in which the exchange rate is fixed through government intervention in the foreign exchange market. The key proposition that emerges from the analysis is that the LM curve adjusts passively: wherever the IS and BP curves intersect, the LM curve will shift so that it too passes through this point.

The left-hand panel of Chart 7-6 illustrates this fixed exchange rate adjustment process. Suppose, for example, that the economy is initially at point B where the IS curve intersects LM_1. At this point both the goods and the money markets are in equilibrium, but the balance of payments is in disequilibrium. Because point B lies below the BP curve, the balance of payments is in a deficit position. This means that Canada's international receipts fall short of international payments and there

CHART 7-6 General macroeconomic equilibrium under fixed
exchange rates

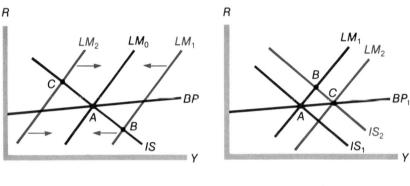

(A) Balance of payments adjustment   **(B)** Expansionary fiscal policy

is an *excess supply of Canadian dollars* in the foreign exchange market. Market
forces put downward pressure on the Canadian dollar, but because the government is maintaining a fixed exchange rate policy the Bank of Canada intervenes,
using existing foreign exchange reserves to buy up the excess Canadian dollars. As
noted earlier, the Bank of Canada's purchase of Canadian dollars in the foreign
exchange market causes a reduction in the stock of money as Canadians purchase
some of their required foreign exchange from the Bank of Canada. This reduction
in the money supply has the effect of shifting the *LM* curve to the left. One can
think of the economy sliding up the *IS* curve as the *LM* curve shifts left. However,
the balance of payments will remain in a deficit position as long as the economy is
below the *BP* curve. Consequently, as long as the *IS* and *LM* curves intersect at a
point that is below the *BP* curve, the Bank of Canada must continue to purchase
Canadian dollars in the foreign exchange market and therefore the *LM* curve will
continue to shift leftwards. This adjustment process will come to a halt when the
LM curve is at LM_0, where the *IS*, *LM* and *BP* curves all intersect at the single
point *A*. At this point, the balance of payments is in equilibrium, along with the
goods and money markets, and there is no need for further intervention in the
foreign exchange market.

A similar sequence of events will occur if the economy is initially at point *C*
where the money and goods markets are in equilibrium, but there is a balance of
payments surplus. In the foreign exchange market there is an excess demand for
Canadian dollars—foreigners need more Canadian dollars to buy Canada's exports
and to invest in Canada than Canadians are offering in the foreign exchange

market. To avoid the appreciation of the dollar that would otherwise result, the Bank of Canada supplies additional dollars to the foreign exchange market. Canada's official reserves are built up and the money supply increases. The increase in the stock of money pushes the LM curve to the right. The need for intervention by the Bank of Canada in the foreign exchange market will come to an end only when the LM curve has shifted down to LM_0. Again the economy is in full macroeconomic equilibrium at point A.

By following a fixed exchange rate policy, the government gives up its control of the domestic money supply. Monetary policy becomes a by-product of exchange rate policy, and the government cannot use monetary policy for domestic stabilization purposes as long as the government maintains a fixed exchange rate policy. For example, suppose that at point A in the left-hand panel of Chart 7-6 the level of income is well below the full-employment level. If the government attempts to stimulate investment spending by increasing the stock of money and lowering the rate of interest, the result is a balance of payments deficit and downward pressure on the dollar. This is because lower interest rates imply reduced net capital inflows and an increase in income leads to greater imports. Attempts to stabilize the foreign exchange rate by buying up the excess supply of Canadian dollars will simply reverse the original expansionary monetary policy. Expansionary monetary policy is incompatible with the fixed exchange rate policy; one or the other must be abandoned.

Fiscal Policy with Fixed Exchange Rates

Although monetary policy is tied down by events in the foreign exchange market when a fixed exchange rate policy is being followed, fiscal policy is not so encumbered. In the right-hand panel of Chart 7-6 the effect of an expansionary fiscal policy is illustrated. The initial less-than-full-employment position is assumed to be at point A, where IS_1, BP_1, and LM_1 all intersect. In order to stimulate demand in the economy, the government can either cut taxes or increase spending. The effect of each of these policy measures is to shift the IS curve to the right, say to IS_2. We know from our previous discussion that the result of the fixed exchange rate policy will be that the LM curve will passively adjust to the new intersection point of IS_2 and BP_1. The expansionary fiscal policy, which is financed in the bond market, will push up interest rates which in turn will cause an increase in net capital inflows so that at point B there is balance of payments surplus. To prevent the dollar from appreciating, the Bank of Canada must supply additional dollars to the foreign exchange market, buying up foreign exchange in the process. The effect of the increase in the stock of money is to shift the LM curve to the right. Ultimately balance of payments equilibrium will be restored when the LM curve comes to rest at LM_2 and the new equilibrium position for the economy will be at point C. Compared to our closed economy analysis of Chapter 6, fiscal policy has a much larger multiplier effect on income when the government is pursuing a fixed exchange rate policy.

What determines the size of the fiscal policy multiplier when the government is maintaining a fixed exchange rate? The answer essentially boils down to the flatness of the *BP* curve. A flat *BP* curve means that an increase in government spending, which shifts the *IS* curve to the right, has a relatively large impact on the level of income and only a small effect on the interest rate. The reason for this is that under a *fixed* exchange rate of policy the government expands the domestic money supply at the same time that the expansionary fiscal measures are put into effect. In our open economy model, any increase in the rate of interest attracts foreign funds into the country and causes the Canadian dollar to appreciate. In order to maintain the fixed exchange rate, the Bank of Canada has to sell Canadian dollars in the foreign exchange market, buying up foreign exchange in the process. But as more Canadian dollars are printed to buy up foreign exchange, the money supply is increased. This helps to keep down the interest rate and private investment in not crowded out by expansionary fiscal policy.[13]

While the fiscal policy multipliers are relatively large under a fixed exchange rate policy when the *BP* curve is relatively flat, there is an important side effect to expansionary fiscal policy. In the right-hand panel of Chart 7-6 the effect of the expansionary fiscal policy was to move the economy along the *BP* curve from point *A* to point *C*. By definition all points along the *BP* curve correspond to equilibrium points in the balance of international payments, but the composition of the balance of payments changes as the economy moves along the *BP* curve. At point *C* the interest rate is higher than at *A* so net capital inflows are greater at point *C* than at *A*. But the higher level of income at *C* implies that imports are greater than at *A*, and consequently the current account deficit is larger at *C* than at *A*. Note that exports will be the same at *A* and *C*. This structural change in the balance of payments—a larger capital account surplus coupled with a larger current account deficit—may cause some political concern because the larger current account deficit must be financed either through foreign borrowing (Canada's indebtedness to foreigners is increasing) or through foreign direct investment (foreign ownership in Canada is rising). The political ramifications of these shifts within the balance of payments may put constraints on the government's use of fiscal policy for internal stabilization purposes under a fixed exchange rate policy.

An External Shock Under Fixed Exchange Rates

Suppose the Federal Reserve Board (the U.S. central bank) decides to impose a tight monetary policy that raises interest rates and reduces aggregate demand in the U.S. economy. How does this external shock impinge on the Canadian economy and what will be its ramifications? There are two routes through which the "tight-money" policy in the U.S. will affect Canada. The most immediate effect will be seen in the capital account of Canada's balance of payments as funds

---

[13]If the *BP* curve is steeper than the *LM* curve, an expansionary fiscal policy will create a balance of payments deficit. The exchange rate will tend to depreciate. To avoid this, the Bank of Canada must buy up Canadian dollars thereby reducing the Canadian money supply and causing the *LM* curve to shift leftwards. In this case the *"openness"* of the economy reduces the effect of fiscal policy on the level of income because the maintenance of the fixed exchange rate requires a reduction in the money supply.

CHART 7-7 The effect on the Canadian economy of monetary restraint in the United States*

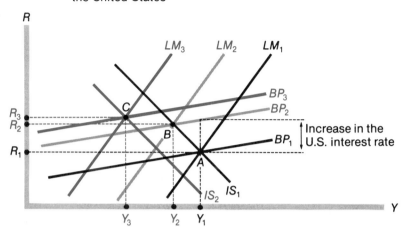

*Canada is assumed to be following a fixed exchange rate policy

of Canadian and U.S. investors will be drawn from Canada to the United States by the higher U.S. interest rates. The second effect will be felt somewhat later. As the level of aggregate demand in the United States declines in response to higher interest rates, the demand for Canada's exports will also decline. An early casualty is typically the Canadian lumber industry because it is tied to the U.S. housing market, which is particularly sensitive to swings in interest rates.

These two effects are analyzed in Chart 7-7. The initial position is described by IS_1, LM_1, and BP_1, which intersect at point A. The immediate effect of the higher interest rates in the United States is to reduce Canada's net capital inflows as funds are attracted to the U.S. capital market. The BP curve therefore shifts upwards through a vertical distance equal to the size of the increase in the U.S. interest rate. Note that in equation 7-6 (the equation of the BP curve) the intercept of the BP curve on the vertical axis is:

$$R^{US} + \frac{s\pi P + n - X_0 - p}{q}$$

Consequently, the vertical intercept increases point for point with the U.S. interest rate, R^{US}.[14] The original equilibrium position, point A, will now lie below the new BP curve and therefore the balance of payments is in a deficit position

[14]Note that at any given level of Canadian income, Canada's imports and exports are also given. But because the interest rate rises in the U.S., a difference emerges between Canadian and U.S. interest rates that causes Canada's net capital inflow to decline. The interest rate differential can be restored to its previous level only if the Canadian interest rate rises by the same amount as the U.S. interest rate. This would also restore Canada's net capital inflow to its previous level and so the balance of payments would again be in equilibrium. In other words, the BP curve shifts upwards through a vertical distance equal to the rise in the U.S. interest rate.

since net capital inflows have declined. Market forces would normally cause the Canadian dollar to depreciate, *but* because the government is following a fixed exchange rate policy the Bank of Canada uses foreign exchange reserves to buy up the excess supply of Canadian dollars in the foreign exchange market. By taking Canadian dollars out of circulation the Bank of Canada reduces the Canadian money supply and the *LM* curve shifts to the left. The economy moves up the *IS* curve until it finally reaches point *B* where the balance of payments is again in equilibrium and no further Bank of Canada intervention is required in the foreign exchange market.

This analysis has demonstrated how a *fixed* exchange rate policy forces Canadian monetary policy to be in lock step with U.S. monetary policy. As we have seen, a tight-money policy in the U.S. will inevitably lead to a tight-money policy in Canada if the exchange rate is to be maintained at its original level. The consequences of an increase in U.S. interest rates under a fixed foreign exchange rate policy are that the Canadian interest rate rises and the level of Canadian income falls (compare points *A* and *B*). Of course, the drop in the level of Canadian income can be linked to the higher Canadian interest rate that discourages investment in plant and equipment. But the original cause was a restrictive U.S. monetary policy coupled with a Canadian fixed exchange rate policy. One final point is that the rise in the interest rate in Canada is not as large as in the U.S. The reason is that by the time the economy reaches point *B* the balance of payments deficit that emerged at point *A* is partially offset by a decline in imports into Canada—the level of Canadian income has fallen. Consequently, net capital inflows at *B* do not have to be restored to their original level at point *A*, and the required rise in the Canadian interest rate is not as large as the vertical shift in the *BP* curve.[15]

We turn now to the second-round effects of the U.S. tight-money policy which are also illustrated in Chart 7-7. Higher interest rates in the U.S. will eventually cause a drop in U.S. aggregate demand that will ultimately be felt by Canada's export industries. A drop in exports shifts the *IS* curve downwards and to the left, but it also causes a further deterioriation in the balance of payments deficit. The *BP* curve will again shift upwards because of the fall in exports. Point *B* will lie below the new *BP* curve BP_3 and above the new *IS* curve IS_2. In the domestic goods market there is an excess supply of goods—inventories build up when export markets are depressed—and the balance of payments is again in a deficit position. The result is that the level of income declines and there is downward pressure on the dollar. In order to maintain the exchange value of the dollar the Bank of Canada intervenes, buying up more Canadian dollars and causing the *LM* curve to shift further to the left. As we have argued above, the final equilibrium position is at the point where the *IS* and *BP* curves intersect, point *C*. The *LM* curve responds passively; the fixed exchange rate policy ensures that the domestic money supply will change and the *LM* curve will also pass through the point *C*. By comparing point *C* with point *B* we can see that the decline in exports has had a relatively large effect on the level of income. Again monetary policy has been

---

[15]None of these conclusions is altered if the *BP* curve is assumed to be steeper than the *LM* curve.

handcuffed to the fixed exchange rate policy. Had the money supply been kept constant, the domestic recession would have caused the Canadian interest rate to drop, which would have stimulated physical investment and partly offset the effects of declining exports. In addition, without the support of the Bank of Canada, our dollar would depreciate, which would improve the competitive position of Canadian industry and soften the impact of the U.S. recession. Consequently, the maintenance of the fixed exchange rate increases the vulnerability of the Canadian economy to external shocks, such as a decline in exports. This conclusion is not contingent on the *BP* curve being flatter than the *LM* curve.[16]

The major conclusions of our analysis of an open economy under a fixed exchange rate policy regime can be summarized as follows. First, by choosing to maintain a fixed exchange rate the government effectively ties monetary policy to the foreign exchange market. It is impossible for Canada to follow a monetary policy that is independent of U.S. monetary policy. We have illustrated this proposition with an example in which the U.S. follows a tight-money policy. However, it is equally true that if the Federal Reserve Board decides to increase the money supply, then Canada will have to follow suit with an ultimately inflationary expansionary monetary policy if the exchange value of the dollar is to be maintained. In short, the Canadian economy is more vulnerable to external disturbances when the Canadian government follows a fixed exchange rate policy. A second example was provided by the case of a drop in exports from Canada, which has a greater impact on Canadian income under a fixed exchange rate policy than under a flexible exchange rate policy. These conclusions do not depend on the relative slopes of the *BP* and *LM* curves. Turning to fiscal policy, given that the *BP* curve is flatter than the *LM* curve, the multiplier effect of fiscal policy on income is greater in the open economy under a fixed exchange rate than in a closed economy. This larger fiscal multiplier effect under a fixed exchange rate is due to the fact that the money supply increases passively as the Bank of Canada maintains the fixed exchange rate and this reinforces the rightward shift of the *IS* curve. However, when the *BP* curve is steeper than the *LM* curve, an expansionary fiscal policy causes the Canadian dollar to depreciate. A by-product of the Bank of Canada's support of the Canadian dollar in the foreign exchange market is a reduction in the Canadian money supply. This in turn causes a leftward shift of the *LM* curve and limits the multiplier effect of fiscal policy.

General Macroeconomic Equilibrium: Flexible Exchange Rates

When the exchange rate is allowed to find its own level according to the supply and demand conditions in the foreign exchange market, the achievement of balance of payments equilibrium ceases to be a policy concern. Monetary policy is

---

[16]A decline in exports will tend to cause a depreciation of the Canadian dollar, whichever of the *LM* and *BP* curves is steeper. This is because a drop in exports causes a leftward shift of the *BP* curve ($\Delta X/m$) that is larger than the leftward shift of the *IS* curve [$\Delta X/(1 - b + bt + m)$]. This implies that the intersection point of the new *IS* curve and the original *LM* curve will be below the new *BP* curve. Thus, after the decline in exports, the point where the goods and money markets are in equilibrium corresponds to a balance of payments deficit.

no longer preoccupied with exchange rate considerations, and the *LM* curve no longer moves passively to the point where the *IS* and *BP* curves intersect. On the contrary, now that the exchange rate is flexible, it is the *IS* and *BP* curves that shift as conditions in the foreign exchange market change. Consider, for example, the effect of a depreciation of the Canadian dollar on the position of the *IS* and *BP* curves. Since a depreciation of the Canadian dollar tends to make imports more expensive for Canadians and exports from Canada less expensive for foreigners, the effect of a depreciation is to give a boost to exports but to reduce the flow of imports. As we saw in Chapter 5, an increase in exports will shift the *IS* curve to the right. This effect is compounded by the reduced flow of imports. Not only are export industries given a boost by the depreciation of the dollar, but so too are import-competing industries.

The effect of a depreciation of the Canadian dollar on the *BP* curve is to shift the *BP* curve downwards and to the right. At any given level of income and the interest rate, a depreciation results in an increase in *net* exports, and a movement towards a balance of payments surplus. As discussed above, any event which causes a balance of payments surplus to arise shifts the *BP* curve down and to the right. From an algebraic point of view, a decline in the value of π, which appears in the vertical intercept term of the *BP* curve (equation 7-6) with a *positive* sign, causes the vertical intercept of the *BP* curve to decline.

The process of adjustment to a point of overall macroeconomic equilibrium is illustrated in Chart 7-8. The initial disequilibrium state is described by the curves IS_1, LM_1 and BP_1. These curves do not intersect at a single point and so there is no interest rate–income combination that is consistent with simultaneous equilibrium in all three markets. Suppose the economy is initially at point A, which lies on IS_1 and LM_1 but is below BP_1. Points below the BP_1 are characterized by an excess supply of Canadian dollars in the foreign exchange market. In the absence of Bank of Canada intervention, the Canadian dollar will depreciate. As the Canadian dollar depreciates (and exports rise and imports fall), the *IS* curve shifts up and to the right and the *BP* curve shifts down and to the right. It is useful to think of the economy as sliding up the *LM* curve as the *IS* curve shifts up. At the same time, the downward-moving *BP* curve will also be sliding down LM_1. This process continues as long as the balance of payments deficit persists and the Canadian dollar continues to depreciate. Eventually the *IS* and *BP* curves cross the stationary LM_1 at the same point (point B in Chart 7-8). Once the economy is at point B, all three markets are simultaneously in equilibrium and the exchange rate stabilizes at its new equilibrium level.

Monetary Policy Under Flexible Exchange Rates

The left-hand panel of Chart 7-9 illustrates the effect of an increase in the supply of money under a flexible exchange rate policy. Initially, the economy is at point A, where IS_1, LM_1, and BP_1 intersect. When the Bank of Canada increases the stock of money, the *LM* curve shifts rightwards to LM_2. The immediate effect of the expansion of the stock of money is to reduce the interest rate. This encourages business investment in plant and equipment and gives the economy a boost. In the

CHART 7-8 Balance of payments adjustment under flexible exchange rates

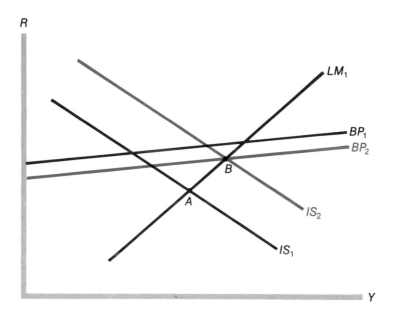

CHART 7-9 Monetary and fiscal policy under flexible exchange rates

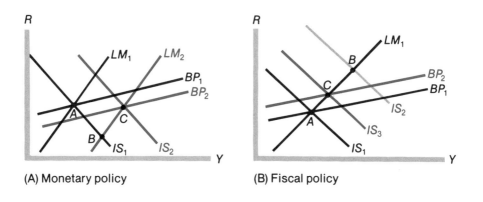

(A) Monetary policy   (B) Fiscal policy

absence of balance of payments considerations the new equilibrium would be at point B where LM_2 cuts IS_1. But point B lies below the BP curve BP_1, meaning that the balance of payments is in a deficit position. This is due to the fact that the lower interest rate discourages capital inflows into Canada and the higher income raises imports. There is an excess supply of Canadian dollars in the foreign exchange market and the dollar depreciates. It is this depreciation of the Canadian dollar that restores overall macroeconomic equilibrium. The analysis is exactly as we described in the last section. As the Canadian dollar depreciates, exports increase and imports decrease in response to the relative price changes of Canadian and foreign goods and services. In the diagram the *IS* curve shifts up and to the right while the *BP* curve shifts down and to the right until eventually they both intersect LM_2 at the same point, *C*. At this point all three markets are again back in equilibrium.

By comparing point *C* with point *A* we can see that the effect of the increase in the money supply is to increase the level of income. Furthermore, since point *C* is to the right of point *B*, the effect on income is greater than it would have been in a closed economy. The reason for this larger multiplier effect on income is that the drop in the interest rate associated with an expansionary monetary policy causes a depreciation of the dollar because net capital inflows decline, and this in turn gives the economy a boost by making both export and import-competing industries more competitive. In other words the foreign-exchange-rate effects of the monetary expansion reinforce the direct interest-rate effects and make monetary policy a potentially more potent policy tool when the exchange rate is flexible.[17]

Fiscal Policy Under Flexible Exchange Rates

The right-hand panel of Chart 7-9 illustrates the effect of fiscal policy. Again at the initial point *A*, IS_1, LM_1, and BP_1 intersect. An increase in government spending (or a tax cut) shifts the *IS* curve rightwards to IS_2. In a closed economy the effect would be to increase income and drive up the interest rate, giving rise to the new equilibrium point *B* where IS_2 cuts LM_1. But point *B* is above BP_1, which means the balance of payments is running a surplus. This is due to the increase in net capital inflows following from the rise in the interest rate that is associated with an expansionary fiscal policy. In the foreign exchange market there is an excess demand for Canadian dollars which causes the dollar to appreciate. This appreciation makes imports less expensive in Canadian funds but raises the price of Canadian exports in terms of foreign currencies so that Canada's export- and import-competing industries become less competitive. As the Canadian dollar appreciates, the *IS* curve shifts down and to the left while the *BP* curve shifts up and to the left. This process continues until both curves intersect LM_1 at the same point. This occurs at the intersection point of IS_3, BP_2 and LM_1, which is labelled *C*.

Note that point *C* lies between *A* and *B* on LM_2. An expansionary fiscal policy has a smaller effect on income in a flexible exchange rate, open economy than in a closed economy. In an open economy, the higher interest rates associated with an expansionary fiscal policy cause the exchange rate to appreciate, which puts export and import-competing industries at a disadvantage compared to their foreign competitors. In other words, the indirect balance of payments effects of

[17]The conclusions of this section are not altered when the *BP* curve is assumed to be steeper than the *LM* curve.

TABLE 7-5 Comparison of Money and Fiscal Policy Multipliers in Closed and Open Economy Models*

Endogenous Variable	Fiscal Multipliers†	Money Multipliers
	Fixed Exchange Rate Regime	
Income Y	$\left\|\dfrac{\Delta Y}{\Delta G}\right\|_O > \left\|\dfrac{\Delta Y}{\Delta G}\right\|_C$	$\left\|\dfrac{\Delta Y}{\Delta \$^S}\right\|_O = 0 < \left\|\dfrac{\Delta Y}{\Delta \$^S}\right\|_C$
Rate of Interest R	$\left\|\dfrac{\Delta R}{\Delta G}\right\|_O < \left\|\dfrac{\Delta R}{\Delta G}\right\|_C$	$\left\|\dfrac{\Delta R}{\Delta \$^S}\right\|_O = 0 < \left\|\dfrac{\Delta R}{\Delta \$^S}\right\|_C$
	Flexible Exchange Rate Regime	
Income Y	$\left\|\dfrac{\Delta Y}{\Delta G}\right\|_O < \left\|\dfrac{\Delta Y}{\Delta G}\right\|_C$	$\left\|\dfrac{\Delta Y}{\Delta \$^S}\right\|_O > \left\|\dfrac{\Delta Y}{\Delta \$^S}\right\|_C$
Rate of Interest R	$\left\|\dfrac{\Delta R}{\Delta G}\right\|_O < \left\|\dfrac{\Delta R}{\Delta G}\right\|_C$	$\left\|\dfrac{\Delta R}{\Delta \$^S}\right\|_O < \left\|\dfrac{\Delta R}{\Delta \$}\right\|_C$

*The open economy multipliers are subscripted with an o and the closed economy multipliers are subscripted with a c. The absolute values of the multipliers are compared.
†These inequalities, which are based on the assumption that the BP curve is flatter than the LM curve, are reversed when the BP curve is steeper than the LM curve.

fiscal policy work against the direct expansionary effect.[18] This is quite the opposite to the fixed exchange rate case where fiscal policy multipliers were found to be relatively large because the monetary adjustments prevent domestic interest rates from rising and the Canadian dollar from appreciating.

Money and Fiscal Multipliers: A Summary

Table 7-5 summarizes the comparisons we have made between the money and fiscal policy multiplier effects on income in an open economy framework and the closed economy multipliers that were obtained in Chapter 5. Clearly, in an open economy the size of money and fiscal policy multipliers depends crucially on the nature of the government's foreign exchange rate policy. For example, under a fixed exchange rate regime the money supply is endogenous within the model; it simply adjusts to the prevailing conditions in the foreign exchange market. Consequently, unlike the closed economy model, in the open economy model

[18]The conclusions are reversed when the BP curve is steeper than the LM curve, in which case the multiplier effects of the fiscal policy are enhanced by the balance of payments effects because the exchange rate depreciates.

with a fixed exchange rate there is no possibility of an independent monetary policy and the money multipliers do not exist. The effectiveness of fiscal policy under a fixed exchange rate policy depends on the slope of the *BP* and *LM* curves. If the *BP* curve is flatter than the *LM* curve, fiscal policy has a large multiplier effect because the money supply expands as the Bank of Canada intervenes in the foreign exchange market to prevent the exchange rate from appreciating. On the other hand, if the *BP* curve is steeper than the *LM* curve, then the fiscal multipliers are relatively small. An expansionary fiscal policy is accompanied by a decrease in the money supply as the Bank of Canada intervenes to support the foreign exchange value of the Canadian dollar, which would otherwise depreciate.

Under a flexible exchange rate policy the government is able to follow an independent monetary policy. Compared to the closed economy model, the money multiplier effect on income is relatively large because as the economy expands imports increase and a merchandise trade deficit emerges. Moreover, as domestic interest rates fall, net capital inflows also decline. The effect of the deficits on both the current and capital accounts is to cause a depreciation of the Canadian dollar. It is this depreciation that gives monetary policy its extra punch in the flexible-exchange-rate open-economy case because exports increase and imports decline in response to the changes in relative international prices. Unlike the case of fiscal multipliers, these conclusions do not depend on the relative slopes of the *BP* and the *LM* curves.

Finally, the effectiveness of fiscal policy in the open economy model with flexible exchange rates depends on the relative slopes of the *BP* and *LM* curves. If the *BP* curve is flatter than the *LM* curve, then an expansionary fiscal policy has a limited multiplier effect on income because the expansion leads to an appreciation of the Canadian dollar—due to large capital inflows—and this hampers Canada's import-competing and export industries. On the other hand, if the *BP* curve is steeper than the *LM* curve the expansionary fiscal policy leads to a depreciation of the Canadian dollar because the large import flows that accompany the rise in income levels create a balance of payments deficit. The depreciation gives a competitive advantage to Canada's importing-competing and export industries, which consequently expand production. This effect reinforces the initial effect of the expansionary fiscal policy.

Flexible Prices and the Foreign Exchange Rate

Throughout our discussion we have assumed that the price level is fixed. In Chapter 9 this assumption will be dropped so that the problems of inflation and unemployment can be dealt with in one consistent model. In this section we briefly consider how the flexibility of prices affects the analysis of the foreign exchange market. While most countries have experienced chronic inflation since the end of the Second World War, rates of inflation have differed greatly across countries. Such differences in national rates of inflation initially tend to give a competitive advantage to the country that has a relatively low rate of inflation. If the inflation rate in country *A* is *lower* than the inflation rate of country *B*, the relatively inexpensive exports from country *A* will expand while at the same time high-priced imports into country A will be squeezed out of domestic markets by country A's low-cost producers. Consequently, country A will find that its balance of payments will move towards a surplus position. In the foreign exchange market there will be an excess demand for country A's currency. But country B, which has a relatively high rate of inflation, will experience a decline in export sales and a rise in imports. Country B will move towards a balance of payments deficit position and in the foreign exchange market there will be an excess supply of country B's currency. Market forces will cause an appreciation of country A's currency vis-à-vis country B's currency. Over the long term the required adjustment in exchange rates due to differences in national inflation rates may be so large that the adjustment cannot be prevented by central bank intervention or by other kinds of intervention such as restrictions on trade and capital flows. Indeed, *over the long term the major determinant of exchange rate movements is the difference in the rates of inflation between trading countries*. This proposition is referred to as the **purchasing power parity (PPP) theorem.**

The central idea of the PPP theorem is that foreign exchange rates must be at levels which ensure that the prices of traded goods are identical in all markets throughout the trading world (apart from transportation costs and customs duties). Take, for example, the case of Canada and Britain. Let the prices of traded goods in these two countries be P^C and P^B, respectively. These prices are expressed in terms of the appropriate *domestic* currency—P^C in dollars and P^B in pounds sterling. The PPP theorem states that the exchange rate π between dollars and pounds sterling—the price of one dollar in pounds—must be such that the prices of traded goods are the same in Canada and Britain whether these prices are quoted either in dollars or pounds sterling. Converting Canadian dollar prices to pounds sterling, the following relationship must hold for traded goods:

$$\pi P^C = P^B$$

The accuracy with which differences in national rates of inflation predict exchange rate movements has recently been examined by Professor L.H. Officer.[19] Using data from 14 countries over periods as long as 125 years, Officer finds that there is substantial support for the PPP theorem. For example, Officer calculates that from Canada's perspective, the ratio of the foreign price level to the Canadian price level rose by 18.1 per cent over the period 1910 to 1975. The PPP theorem predicts that the Canadian dollar would appreciate against a suitable average of other currencies by 18.1 per cent. In fact, the Canadian dollar appreciated by 22 per cent over this 65-year period, implying that the forecast error of the PPP theorem was less than 4 per cent over a 65-year period. The PPP forecast error can be interpreted as meaning that on the basis of price-level movements alone, the Canadian dollar was overvalued in 1975 by 4 per cent.[20] Given the subsequent behaviour of the Canadian dollar, few will disagree with that assessment.

---

[19]L.H. Officer, "Effective exchange rates and price ratios over the long run: A test of the purchasing-power-parity theory," *Canadian Journal of Economics*, May 1980, pp. 206-230.

[20]This presumes the Canadian balance of payments was in equilibrium in 1910 and ignores the fact that factors other than relative rates of inflation affect exchange rates. The discovery of new resources, for example, could raise the exchange value of a nation's currency.

Canada's Recent Exchange Rate Policy

From May 1962 to May 1970, Canada followed a fixed exchange rate policy which pegged the Canadian dollar at the value of $0.925 U.S. Since May 1970, the value of the Canadian dollar has been determined largely by market forces, although the Bank of Canada has intervened regularly to moderate the dollar's movement. This is illustrated in Chart 7-10, where the value of the Canadian dollar in U.S. funds is plotted, along with the quantity of Canada's international reserves. The fact that these two series have such similar paths is evidence that the Bank of Canada has attempted to offset market forces. During periods when the Canadian dollar was falling in value, the quantity of foreign exchange reserves has also fallen, indicating that reserves have been used to buy up Canadian dollars, thereby slowing the depreciation. Conversely, when the dollar has appreciated, foreign exchange reserves have been accumulated. For example, immediately after the freeing of the Canadian dollar in May 1970, strong upward pressure on the exchange rate was resisted by the Bank of Canada. Purchases of foreign exchange (sales of Canadian dollars which were in strong demand) throughout 1970-72 period are reflected in the rising quantity of international reserves. Despite the Bank of Canada's interventions, the dollar continued to rise towards par with the American dollar, and even exceeded it at times.

The reasoning behind this exchange rate policy was a belief that the Canadian economy needed stimulation as it recovered from the 1969-70 recession. A rising Canadian dollar could have hindered that recovery by making imports more competitive and raising the price of Canadian exports in foreign currencies. The Bank of Canada therefore resisted the appreciation of the dollar to protect the economic expansion. As it turned out, the expansion continued in very strong fashion both here and abroad. By the mid-1970s the world-wide growth of economic activity lead to the highest peace-time rates of inflation in living memory in many Western countries. Because Canada's inflation had been generally higher than in the United States, by 1976 the Canadian dollar was overvalued (the purchasing power parity theorem). In the late 1976 the Canadian dollar began a slide that, as of mid-1985, has not been reversed.

Over the nine years between 1976 and 1984, the Canadian dollar depreciated approximately 30 per cent. Throughout the decline the Bank of Canada has defended the dollar whenever it has come under severe pressure. The second quotation on page 161 makes it very clear that the Governor of the Bank of Canada feared speculative overshooting in the downward direction at a time when inflation was the primary policy issue. Since a depreciating dollar raises import prices, it aggravates the inflation problem. Moreover, inflation itself leads to downward pressure on the exchange rate. The Bank of Canada wanted to avoid this "vicious circle" of inflation and depreciation.

The unusually deep recession of 1982 saw the inflation problem diminish, yet the downward pressure on the Canadian dollar continued. The major reason was the high level of U.S. interest rates, which attracted heavy flows of foreign capital, including Canadian capital, into the United States. Although high domestic interest rates inhibit economic expansion at a time when unemployment is high,

CHART 7-10 Canada's international foreign reserves and
foreign exchange rate (Quarterly, 1970-84)

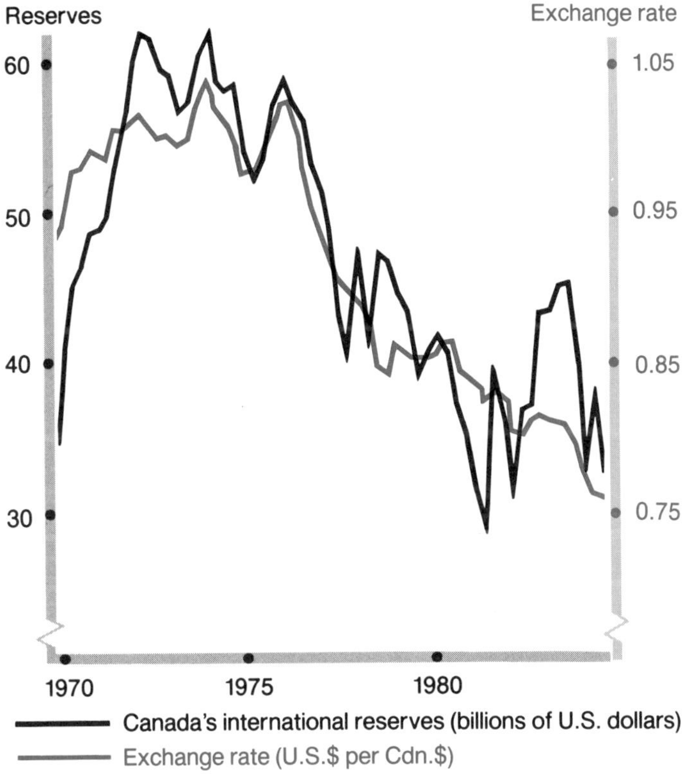

Reserves   Exchange rate

60   1.05

50   0.95

40   0.85

30   0.75

        1970   1975   1980

━━━━━━ Canada's international reserves (billions of U.S. dollars)
━━━━━━ Exchange rate (U.S.$ per Cdn.$)

unfortunately Canada's interest rates cannot be set independently of world levels given the integration of Canada's financial market with the world market. Only to a very limited extent can Canadian interest rates take an independent course when world interest rates rise and then only to the degree that we accept a depreciating dollar. In his *Annual Report* of 1984, The Governor of the Bank of Canada noted that Canada's response to high U.S. interest rates has been to "allow some of the resulting impact to be taken on Canadian interest rates and some of it on our exchange rate."[21] That is, Canadian interest rates have gone up with U.S. rates, but not enough to avoid a declining exchange rate. However, the Governor warns that we should not attempt to keep domestic interest rates low by allowing the dollar to depreciate substantially because this "carries the risk of disrupting the progress we have made on inflation."[22] Again, exchange rate policy has focused primarily on maintaining "an orderly market" rather than fixing the exchange rate at a particular level.

We can summarize the Bank of Canada's exchange rate policy since 1970 as one of leaning against the wind. The Bank has attempted to moderate exchange rate

[21]Bank of Canada, Annual Report, p. 8.
[22]Ibid., at p. 10.

movements to avoid speculative overshooting, but has not tried to maintain a fixed exchange rate. Such a policy of stabilizing a floating exchange rate is sometimes rather ungraciously referred to as a "dirty float."

Apart from this last section where we have discussed how flexible prices affect the analysis of the foreign exchange market, we have assumed that the aggregate price level is fixed; our analysis has been confined to a non-inflationary world. In the following chapter we will discuss how the aggregate price level is determined and then we will be concerned with the causes of inflation and the role of monetary and fiscal policies in economies that face the two major problems of unemployment and inflation. In order to keep the analysis of this expanded model manageable, the balance of payments repercussions are deferred until Chapter 11. In Chapter 11 the *BP* curve will be integrated into the expanded model to demonstrate how an inflationary open economy responds to shocks under fixed or inflexible exchange rates. It will also be shown that the expanded model is consistent with the purchasing power parity theorem.

Key Concepts

the current and capital accounts of the balance of
    payments
official foreign exchange reserves
the foreign exchange rate
fixed and flexible exchange rates
balance of payments equilibrium and the *BP* curve
the purchasing power parity (PPP) theorem

Review Questions

1. What is meant by balance of payments equilibrium?
2. Which international transactions give rise to a demand for (supply of) Canadian dollars in the foreign exchange market?
3. How does a depreciation of the dollar affect Canada's export and import-competing industries?
4. Explain the concept of the "covered interest rate differential" and its importance for short-term capital flows.
5. Distinguish between portfolio and direct investment.
6. What is meant by the *BP* curve? Explain why it slopes upwards to the right.
7. How does the structure of the balance of payments change as the economy moves up a stationary *BP* curve?
8. In general, what kind of events cause the *BP* curve to shift down and to the right (up and to the left)?
9. Do points above the *BP* curve correspond to balance of payments deficits or surpluses? Explain.

10. Full equilibrium requires that equilibrium be attained in the goods market, the money market and the balance of payments, that is, that the *IS*, *LM* and *BP* curves all intersect at a single point. If these curves do not intersect at a single point, which curve(s) adjust(s) when the exchange rate is a) fixed and b) flexible? Explain the adjustment mechanism in each case.

11. If the government is following a fixed exchange rate policy at a time when foreigners suddenly find Canada a very attractive place to invest their funds, what will happen to Canada's foreign exchange reserves and money supply?

12. To what extent is the Canadian economy insulated from events in the rest of the world when the foreign exchange rate if flexible?

13. What is meant by the term "perfect capital mobility"? What does the *BP* curve look like in such a case? Examine the effects of fiscal and monetary policy when the exchange rate is flexible and capital is perfectly mobile.

Part 3

Aggregate Demand, Aggregate Supply, and the Determination of the Aggregate Price Level

If I were writing again, I should feel disposed to define full employment as being reached at the same moment at which the supply of output in general becomes [price] inelastic.

John Maynard Keynes[1]

Throughout the last four chapters we have assumed that wage and price levels are fixed and do not respond to changing economic conditions. Although the assumption of stable wages and prices was perhaps a valid approximation to economic reality during the first half of this century, inflation has plagued the Canadian economy since the early 1960s. For the ten years from 1973 through 1982, the Canadian inflation rate averaged almost 10 per cent. In this chapter we finally drop the assumption of inflexible price levels and analyze the determinants of the equilibrium price level. In the next chapter we turn our attention to an analysis of the process of inflation.

To determine the equilibrium price level, we must first identify the aggregate demand curve and the aggregate supply curve. As in microeconomics, the equilibrium price level is determined by the intersection point of the aggregate demand and supply curves. While the aggregate demand curve is reasonably straightforward and noncontroversial, the aggregate supply curve has been the subject of considerable macroeconomic debate and controversy. In this chapter we present three different aggregate supply curves based on three different assumptions about supply behaviour. These supply curves are usually associated with three different macroeconomic models: the **classical model**, the **Keynesian inflexible-wage model** and the **new classical model**, which have very different perspectives on the nature of unemployment and the implications of macroeconomic stabilization policies. In this chapter we will explore these differences in some detail.

The Aggregate Demand Curve

The aggregate demand curve represents the quantity of goods and services demanded at various price levels. To derive the aggregate demand curve, we must return to the *IS-LM* model, which contains the key demand relationships within

[1]J. M. Keynes, *The General Theory and After: A Supplement*. Volume 29 of *The Collected Writings* (edited by D. Moggridge), Cambridge University Press, 1979, page 235.

the goods and financial asset markets. Our development of the *IS-LM* model in Chapters 5 and 6 was premised on *inflexible* price levels and *real* quantities of output, consumption, and investment. Any change in output reflected a change in the *real* volume of output and not just a change in the *nominal* value of output (since price levels were assumed to be fixed). If we can identify how the *IS* and *LM* curves will be affected by a change in price levels, we can plot the aggregate demand for goods and services (based on the intersection of the *IS* and *LM* curves) against the changing price level, and we will have uncovered the aggregate demand curve.

Effects of a Change in Price Levels on the *IS* and *LM* Curves

The derivation of the *IS* curve (as presented in Chapter 5) will continue to hold as long as all variables are measured in real or constant dollar terms. The underlying theories behind the IS curve describe real macroeconomic behaviour. For example, the consumption function describes the real quantity of goods and services consumed in terms of real disposable-income levels. While a change in price levels will increase the nominal level of both consumption expenditures and income levels, the underlying consumption function continues to hold in real terms (after nominal consumption expenditures and income levels have been deflated by the price level).[2] Subject to a minor qualification discussed in Chapter 19, a change in price levels will have *no* effect on *real* consumption. *We assume that the position of the* IS *curve is unaffected by a change in the level of prices*.[3]

As in the preceding chapters, the aggregate demand components implicit in the *IS* curve (C, I, G, X, M) and income Y on the horizontal axis of our *IS-LM* diagram will continue to be measured in real or constant dollar terms. If we wish to write the nominal value of a variable, such as income, it will be expressed as the real variable multiplied by the price level—that is, PY.

A change in price levels will, however, have a direct impact on the money market and the position of the *LM* curve. Since the supply of money is obviously a nominal concept, changing price levels will directly affect the real purchasing power of the nominal money supply and will result in a shift of the *LM* curve. The position of the *LM* curve depends crucially on both the supply of nominal money and the existing price level.

To illustrate the effect of changing price levels on the *LM* curve, we return to a discussion of the demand for money. As discussed in Chapter 5, there two major determinants of the demand for money: income and interest rates. The inclusion of income in the demand for money function reflects a transactions demand for

---

[2]See Chapter 2 and Chart 4-3 in Chapter 4.

[3]As discussed in Chapter 7, a change in relative price levels between countries will affect export and import flows. Canadian price increases that are not matched by world price increases or a depreciation in the Canadian exchange rate will lead to a deterioration in the Canadian balance of international trade and inward shift in the *IS* curve. Chapter 11 incorporates the balance of payments (and the *BP* curve) into an inflation macroeconomic model and discusses the effects of domestic inflation on trade flows and the *IS* curve.

cash balances. Transactions balances are needed because the receipt of income and the purchase of goods and services are not perfectly synchronized. Obviously the transactions demand for money balances depends on the *nominal* value of expenditures, that is, the real quantity of purchases multiplied by the prevailing price level. If, for example, the price level were to double, one would expect that the transactions demand for cash balances would also double, since the same real quantity of goods would now cost twice as much as before.[4]

Since the rest of our macroeconomic model is cast in *real* terms, this *nominal* dollar demand for money relationship is converted into real or constant dollar terms. Both the nominal stock of money and nominal income, our proxy for the transactions demand for money, are deflated by the existing price level. Recognizing that the price level is flexible, we must modify the demand for money equation (5-3) by writing the demand for *real* money balances in terms of real income Y and the interest rate R.

$$(8\text{-}1) \qquad (\$/P)^D = kY - \ell R$$

We assume that the demand for real money balances, like most other commodities, depends positively on the level of real income and negatively on its implicit price. Since the interest rate reflects the opportunity cost of holding money balances, it is the implicit price paid for the use of money.

In panel A of Chart 8-1 we present two representative demand curves for real cash balances $(\$/P)^D$, which are labelled $D(Y_1)$ and $D(Y_2)$. Higher real income levels generate larger demands for real cash balances, and at a given level of real income, each money demand curve is a declining function of the nominal interest rate. The *supply* of real cash balances will be equal to the *nominal* stock of money $\$$, which is directly controlled by the Bank of Canada, deflated by the prevailing price level P. For illustrative purposes, we initially assume that the price level is P_0 and thus the vertical real money supply curve S_0 will intersect the horizontal axis at the point $\$/P_0$.

Points A and B depict two different combinations of real income and interest rates which equate this given real money supply $\$/P_0$ to the demand for real cash balances. These two potential money market equilibrium combinations of real income and interest rates (Y_1, R_1) and (Y_2, R_2) are plotted in panel B of Chart 8-1. As discussed in Chapter 5, these two representative points can be connected to obtain an *LM* curve for this given supply of real money $\$/P_0$. This new *LM* curve describes all combinations of real income and interest rates which equate the demand for real cash balances to the real money supply (that is, the nominal money supply $\$$ divided by the price level P_0.

What effect will changing price levels have on this new *LM* curve derived from the concept of real money? Clearly if the price level increases from P_0 to P_1, then the real purchasing power of the given *nominal* money supply $\$$ will decline and the vertical *real* money supply curve in panel A of Chart 8-1 will shift to the left, say to S_1. For this new, lower supply of real money $\$/P_1$, our two representative combinations of real income and interest rates which equate the demand and

---

[4]See Chapter 18.

CHART 8-1 The derivation of the aggregate demand curve

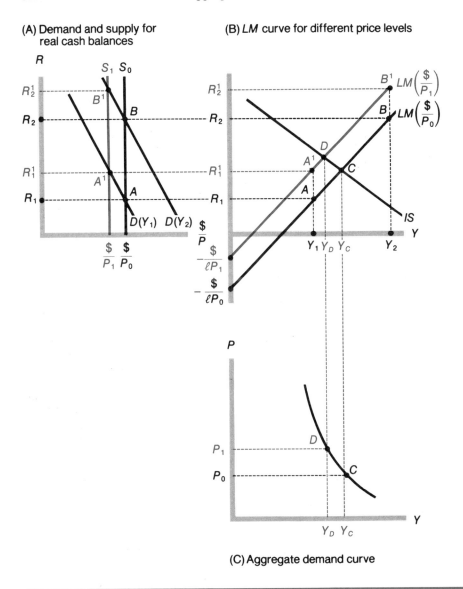

(A) Demand and supply for
    real cash balances

(B) *LM* curve for different price levels

(C) Aggregate demand curve

supply of real money balances will now be given by points A^1 and B^1 in panel A of Chart 8-1. In panel B of Chart 8-1 we have again plotted these two new representative points, A^1 and B^1, and have drawn the new LM curve associated with this lower real money supply $\$/P_1$, where P_1 exceeds P_0. This new *LM* curve for a *reduced* real money supply $\$/P_1$ has the same slope as our previous LM curve but has shifted *upwards*.

The effects of price-level changes on the *LM* curve operate in exactly the *opposite* direction to changes in the supply of nominal money. A *decrease* in the nominal money supply given a fixed price level or an *increase* in the price level given a fixed nominal money supply both cause the *LM* curve to shift upwards. In either case, the real supply of money has declined. This proposition can most easily be verified by examining the algebraic representation for the *LM* curve. Assuming a given supply of real money $/P and our previous equation (8-1) describing the demand for real cash balances, the *LM* curve for a flexible price level macroeconomic model has the following algebraic form:

$$(8\text{-}2) \qquad LM: \quad R = \frac{-\$}{\ell P} + \left(\frac{k}{\ell} \right) Y$$

The negative intercept of the *LM* curve will approach the origin when either the nominal stock of money *declines* or the price level *rises*. Such a reduction of the negative intercept will cause an upward parallel shift in the *LM* curve. Note that the slope of the LM curve is unaffected by either $ or *P*.

An increase in price levels, or inflation, will reduce the real purchasing power of the given nominal money supply and lead to an upward shift in the *LM* curve. While we have assumed that the *IS* curve is unaffected by the level of prices, for each different price level there will be a different *LM* curve (given a fixed nominal money supply).

The Derivation of the Aggregate Demand Curve

In panel B of Chart 8-1 we have included an *IS* curve, which we assume is unaffected by the level of prices. Suppose that the price level is P_0. Corresponding to this P_0 price level, there will be a unique *LM* curve, based on a real money supply of $/$P_0$. Thus for a P_0 price level, the *IS* and *LM* curves will intersect at the level of output Y_C. In Panel C of Chart 8-1, we have plotted this output (aggregate demand) level Y_C associated with a price level of P_0.

Now consider the implications of a higher price level P_1. For a given nominal money supply, a *higher* price level will produce a *lower* real money supply and cause an upward shift in the *LM* curve (see red curves associated with the higher price level P_1 in panels A and B of Chart 8-1). This higher price level P_1 and associated higher *LM* curve has produced a lower output level Y_D and a higher interest rate (intersection point *D* in panel B). The increase in price levels lowers the real value of the money supply, causing excess demand conditions to prevail in the money market (at the previous output level Y_C). Excess demand conditions in the money market will push up interest rates, which in turn will lead to a reduction in investment expenditures. Excess supply conditions in the goods market (triggered by declining investment expenditures) will lead to a downward adjustment in output levels. The lower output (aggregate demand) level Y_D associated with the higher price level P_1 is also plotted in the lower quadrant of Chart 8-1.

While we have only considered two different price levels, P_0 and P_1, we could repeat this exercise for all other price levels.(Each different price level would be associated with a different *LM* curve, a different *IS-LM* intersection point and a different output level.) The locus of output levels and different price levels can be plotted in panel C of Chart 8-1. Points *C* and *D* represent two such combinations of output and price level. This downward-sloping *price–output* relationship represents the economy's **aggregate demand curve**.

Several important characteristics of the aggregate demand curve should be noted. First, all points along the aggregate demand curve represent equilibrium in both the goods and financial asset markets. Second, as one moves along the aggregate demand curve, the interest rate is changing; the interest rate declines as one moves down the aggregate demand curve (in panel B of Chart 8-1, point *C* has a lower interest rate than point *D*). Finally, and most important, the aggregate demand curve slopes downwards to the right. As the price level declines, the real value of the given nominal money supply increases causing a downward shift in the *LM* curve and lower interest rates. This decline in interest rates triggers an increase in investment expenditures and aggregate demand. A declining price level will lead to an increase in aggregate demand and output levels.

Shifts in the Aggregate Demand Curve

In Chart 8-1 we derived the aggregate demand curve and demonstrated that the quantity of goods demanded varies inversely with the price level. If either the *IS* curve shifts or the nominal money supply changes, the derived aggregate demand curve will also shift. In Chart 8-2 we illustrate the effects of a shift of the *IS* curve and a change in the nominal money supply on the aggregate demand curve. First we derive the aggregate demand curve (AD_0) based on the original IS_0 curve and the nominal money supply $\$_0$, again using two different price levels P_0 and P_1 (the solid black curve in the lower panel Chart 8-2). Now suppose that the *IS* curve shifts upwards to the new red curve IS_1, because government spending, autonomous investment or exports have increased. The new (solid red) aggregate demand curve corresponding to this new higher *IS* curve will lie upwards to the right in the lower quadrant. An outward shift in the *IS* curve causes an outward shift in the aggregate demand curve.

Next consider the effects of a decline in the nominal money supply (from $\$_0$ to $\$_1$). For each price level, the (broken red line) LM curves associated with the lower nominal money supply will lie upwards to the left (that is, a decrease in the nominal money supply shifts the *LM* curve upwards to the left). Deriving the new aggregate demand curve based on this lower nominal money supply, we find that this new (broken red line) aggregate demand curve lies downward to the left of the original AD_0 curve. A decline in the nominal money supply pushes up interest rates, lowers investment expenditures and lowers aggregate demand, producing a downward shift in the aggregate demand curve.

In summary, a shift in the *IS* curve or a change in the nominal money supply will produce a shift in the aggregate demand curve. A change in any exogenous variable which stimulates aggregate demand, such as an increase in government spending, the nominal money supply or exports, will cause the aggregate demand curve to shift outward to the right.

CHART 8-2 Shifts in the aggregate demand curve

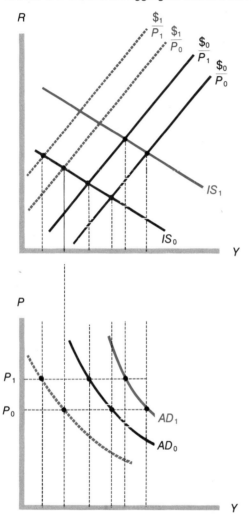

Aggregate Supply

In this part of the chapter we will be concerned with the aggregate supply of goods. In particular, we need to establish the relationship between the price level P and the quantity of goods supplied, that is, the aggregate supply curve. We will then be able to combine the demand and supply components of our model to determine the equilibrium price and output levels for the economy as a whole in much the same way that the supply and demand curves for bread determine the equilibrium price and quantity of bread.

CHART 8-3 Derivation of the demand for labour

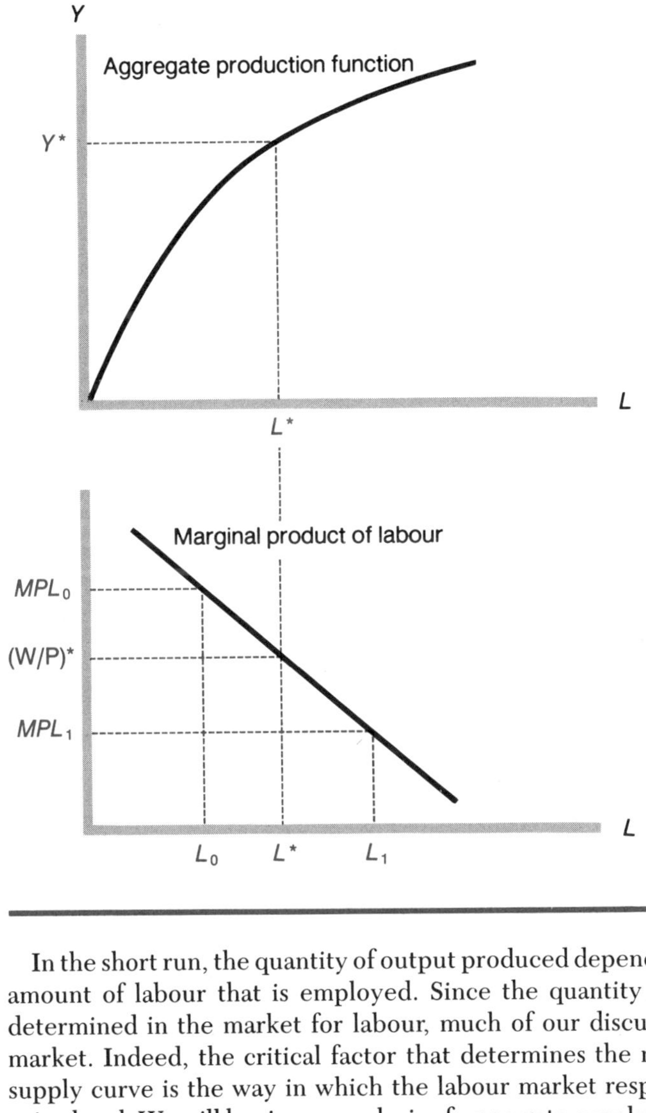

In the short run, the quantity of output produced depends fundamentally on the amount of labour that is employed. Since the quantity of labour employed is determined in the market for labour, much of our discussion will focus on this market. Indeed, the critical factor that determines the nature of the aggregate supply curve is the way in which the labour market responds to changes in the price level. We will begin our analysis of aggregate supply with a discussion of the aggregate production function and its relationship to the demand for labour.

The Aggregate Production Function

The upper panel of Chart 8-3 shows the relationship between the amount of labour employed and the quantity of output produced, under the assumption that the quantity of capital is fixed. This is a reasonable assumption, because we are concerned with the relatively short period of time that is required to complete a business cycle. Clearly, the level of employment does vary during the business cycle. However, the amount of net investment that takes place is relatively small compared to the huge size of the capital stock. For simplicity, we take the stock of capital to be fixed in the short run.

The declining slope of the aggregate production function indicates that additional units of labour add less and less to total output as more labour is added. The increase in total output when one extra unit of labour is hired is called the **marginal product of labour.** The declining slope of the aggregate production function implies that the marginal product of labour, or MPL, declines as the amount of labour employed increases. This inverse relationship between the MPL and employment is illustrated in the lower panel of Chart 8-3. Given a level of labour input, say L_0, the MPL schedule indicates that the amount of extra output produced by one more unit of labour is MPL_0. At a greater level of labour input, such as L_1, one extra unit of labour will still raise output, but by only MPL_1 units.

Profit-maximizing firms are prepared to hire one extra unit of labour provided the extra revenue exceeds the increase in costs. As long as revenue increases more than costs, total profits rise. Let us consider the effect on profits of hiring one more unit of labour. Taking the price of output to be fixed at P, and noting that an extra unit of labour produces MPL units of output, we find that the increase in revenue is $P \times$ MPL. At the same time, costs rise by W (the wage rate) when one extra unit of labour is hired. The change in profits is $P \times$ MPL $- W$. Clearly, profits rise if $P \times$ MPL is greater than W. However, as more labour is hired, MPL declines and at some level of labour input, the point is reached where

$$P \times \text{MPL} = W.$$

This is the point where profits are maximized, because if more labour is hired, MPL will continue to decline and contributions to revenue will fall short of the rise in costs—that is, $P \times$ MPL will be less than W.

An alternative but equivalent way of writing the profit-maximizing condition is

$$\text{MPL} = (W/P).$$

That is, the marginal product of labour equals the *real* wage, W/P.

Firms that operate in competitive output and input markets take the price of output, P, and the wage rate, W, as given. Hence, such firms take the real wage, W/P, as given to them by the market place. Firms must decide how much labour to hire given the real wage, W/P. In fact, the demand for labour is precisely the amount of labour that ensures profits are maximized—that is, the level of labour input that equates the marginal product of labour to the real wage.

Chart 8-3 illustrates this point. Suppose the real wage is $(W/P)^*$. Firms would like to hire more labour than L_0 because at this level of labour input $MPL_0 > (W/P)^*$. Profits rise as more labour is hired. Conversely, at L_1 too much labour has been hired, and with $MPL_1 < (W/P)^*$ profits rise as less labour is hired. At L^*, MPL $= (W/P)^*$ and profits are maximized. We conclude that given the real wage $(W/P)^*$, profit-maximizing firms will hire L^*.

We could repeat this argument for any real wage. We would find that the (profit-maximizing) demand for labour is given by the MPL schedule. In other words, in a diagram with the real wage on the vertical axis and the quantity of labour on the horizontal axis, the MPL curve is the demand for labour schedule.

The Supply of Labour

The theory of labour supply is based on the utility-maximizing behaviour of individuals. It is supposed that individuals enjoy both their leisure or spare time, S, and their level of goods consumption, C. Utility is therefore a function of these two enjoyable items:

$$U = f(S,C)$$

In order to pay for consumption, individuals need to work for wages. However, the more time that is spent working, the less spare time the individual has. The utility maximization problem therefore becomes a problem of how to allocate time between work and spare time.

Let us consider the opportunity cost to a worker of giving up one more hour of spare time. This opportunity cost must be measured in terms of the quantity of consumption goods forgone, since spare time S and consumption C are the two variables in the utility function. A one-hour increase in spare time requires a one-hour reduction in work time. This entails a drop in earnings of W, the hourly wage rate. The price of the consumption good is P, so the drop in earnings of W implies that consumption falls by (W/P). For example, if W is \$10 per hour and P is \$2 per unit, then the cost of taking one more hour of spare time is a drop in consumption of $10 \div 2 = 5$ units. This argument demonstrates that the opportunity cost of an hour of spare time is the real wage, W/P. This means that the demand for spare time is a function of the real wage. An increase in the real wage is likely to reduce the amount of spare time an individual chooses to take because spare time has become more costly in terms of the consumption good. But choosing to take less spare time is the same thing as choosing to work more hours. Hence this argument suggests the supply of labour is an increasing function of the real wage.[5]

Equilibrium in the Labour Market

The equilibrium position in the labour market is illustrated in Chart 8-4. The intersection of the supply and demand curves for labour is at the equilibrium real wage, $(W/P)^*$, and the equilibrium employment level, L^*. At this real wage,

---

[5]It is theoretically possible for an increase in the real wage to lead to a reduction in the hours of labour supplied. This occurs if the income effect of an increase in the real wage outweighs the substitution effect, resulting in an increase in the demand for spare time. A good deal of empirical evidence has been reviewed by Mark Killingsworth in *Labour Supply*, Cambridge Surveys of Economic Literature (the University Press, 1983). The results are certainly not unambiguous, but on balance suggest that labour supply is an upward-sloping function of the real wage.

CHART 8-4 The equilibrium levels of employment and output

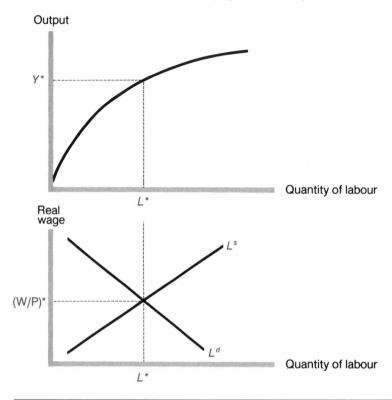

competitive firms maximize profits by hiring the amount of labour L^*. At the same time, individuals, who treat the real wage $(W/P)^*$ as given by the labour market, maximize their utility by supplying the amount of labour L^*. The aggregate production function determines the quantity of output, Y^*, that this level of employment produces.

It is important to note that while the equilibrium real wage is determined in the labour market, the nominal wage and the price level can be determined only when the complete macroeconomic model is specified, and this we have not yet done. The equilibrium wage $(W/P)^*$ can be achieved by an infinite set of nominal wage rate and price level pairs, subject only to the condition that their ratio is equal to $(W/P)^*$. For example, suppose that the nominal wage is W_0 and the price level is P_0 and that $(W_0/P_0) = (W/P)^*$. Clearly, the labour market is in equilibrium. Now suppose that both the nominal wage and the price level rise by, say, 5 per cent to W_1 and P_1. Since both P and W rise by the same proportion, their ratio remains unchanged, that is, $(W_1/P_1) = (W/P)^*$. The labour market is in equilibrium at the new nominal wage and price level because the real wage is unchanged. This point is important in the development of the classical model, to which we turn in the next section.

CHART 8-5 The classical aggregate supply curve

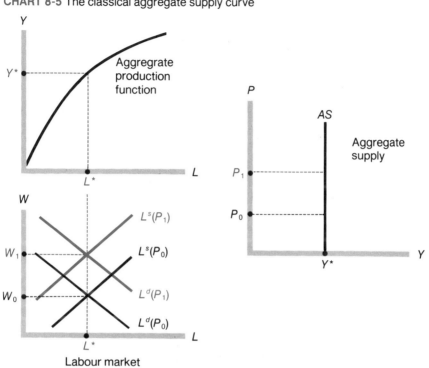

Labour market

The Classical Model

In this section we will show that the classical aggregate supply curve is vertical at the output level Y^* (derived in Chart 8-4). The critical assumption behind this conclusion is that nominal wages are completely flexible and adjust fast enough for the labour market to be considered in equilibrium at all times. The role of this assumption is illustrated in Chart 8-5. Note that the nominal wage rate appears on the vertical axis in the diagram of the labour market. The supply and demand for labour are shown to be functions of the wage rate and the price level (the real wage in fact). In Chart 8-5, the price level is taken as given by firms and workers. Given an initial price level, P_0, a lower nominal wage means a lower real wage. Hence, the demand for labour slopes down to the right (a higher demand at low real wages). The supply curve slopes upwards, because at a higher nominal wage, the real wage is also higher (given the price level P_0), and individuals are willing to supply more labour at the higher real wage.

Given the price level P_0, the supply and demand curves for labour intersect at the equilibrium nominal wage rate W_0 and equilibrium employment L^*. This is precisely the same point as in Chart 8-4. The key difference is that in Chart 8-4 only the equilibrium real wage $(W/P)^*$ is determined. In Chart 8-5 we have assumed the price level is given, and this extra information allows us to determine the equilibrium nominal wage rate W_0 as well. The real wage implied by Chart 8-5 is (W_0/P_0) and this is equal to the equilibrium real wage $(W/P)^*$. The equilibrium employment level is L^*, and given the current capital stock and state of technology, the supply of output is Y^*.

Now suppose that the price level rises by 5 per cent from P_0 to P_1. At the nominal wage rate W_0, the real wage is now lower. A lower real wage means firms would like to hire more labour while workers would like to supply less labour. In Chart 8-5 the effect of raising P from P_0 to P_1 is to shift the demand for labour to the right and the supply of labour to the left. At the nominal wage rate W_0 and the new price level P_1, there is an excess demand for labour. Market forces push up the nominal wage rate to its new equilibrium level of W_1, where $L^S(P_1)$ and $L^D(P_1)$ intersect. Since we have already determined in Chart 8-4 that the equilibrium real wage is $(W/P)^*$, it will follow that nominal wages must rise by 5 per cent to restore the real wage to its equilibrium level; that is,

$$(W_0/P_0) = (W_1/P_1) = (W/P)^*$$

It also follows that the level of employment in equilibrium is again L^*.

In the classical model, the price level has no effect whatsoever on the equilibrium level of employment and output. As we have seen, the *demand* for labour depends on the marginal product of labour (the state of technology), and the *supply* of labour depends on the tastes of individuals (their utility functions). Thus, fundamentally, the equilibrium employment level, the equilibrium real wage, and the equilibrium level of output depend on technology and tastes. There is a complete separation between these real variables and nominal variables such as the price level and the nominal wage. As long as nominal wages are perfectly flexible, any change in the price level will be matched by an equal percentage change in the nominal wage rate that will maintain the equilibrium real wage at $(W/P)^*$ and the equilibrium employment and output levels of L^* and Y^* respectively. The independence of the level of output Y^* and the price level P means that **in the classical model the aggregate supply curve is entirely price-inelastic**, that is, vertical. This is illustrated in the right-hand panel of Chart 8-5.

Macroeconomic Equilibrium in the Classical Model

Having developed the price-inelastic classical aggregate supply curve in the previous section, we can now complete the classical model by adding the aggregate demand curve. This is done diagrammatically in Chart 8-6.

The initial equilibrium point is labelled A. We begin the story in the product market, which is illustrated in panel B of Chart 8-6. As we have seen, the position of the aggregate demand curve is determined by all exogenous components of demand and the nominal stock of money. The initial aggregate demand curve is labelled $AD(G_0)$. The only shift-variable shown explicitly is the level of government spending G_0, because in a moment we will analyze the effect of an increase in government spending in the classical model. The inelastic classical supply curve intersects $AD(G_0)$ at P_0. Thus, in the product market the equilibrium price level is P_0, and the equilibrium output level is Y^*.

CHART 8-6 An increase in government expenditures and equilibrium in the classical model

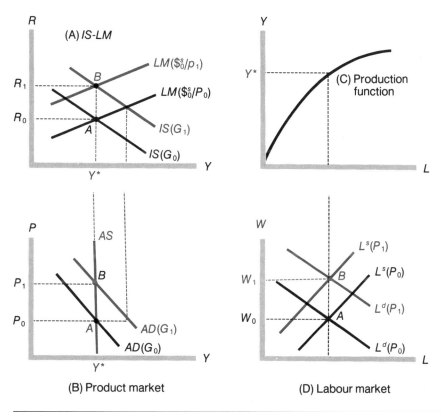

Moving to panel A, we see that the $IS(G_0)$ curve and the $LM(\$_0^S/P_0)$ curve intersect at the equilibrium interest rate R_0. The labour market is shown in panel D. The equilibrium price level P_0 determines the positions of the supply and demand curves $L^S(P_0)$ and $L^D(P_0)$, respectively. These curves intersect at the equilibrium nominal wage, W_0. The equilibrium real wage is of course $(W_0/P_0) = (W/P)^*$, which is precisely the equilibrium real wage that we described in the previous section. The labour market also determines the equilibrium employment level L^*, which, through the production function, produces the equilibrium output level Y^*.

An Increase in Government Expenditures

We turn now to the question of how an increase in a component of aggregate demand, such as government spending, affects the equilibrium position in the classical model. In so doing, we will also be illustrating the basis of the important "crowding out" effect. A bond-financed increase in government spending to G_1

shifts the *IS* curve rightwards to $IS(G_1)$ (panel B of Chart 8-6), and the aggregate demand curve also shifts rightwards to $AD(G_1)$. At the original price level P_0 there is clearly a state of excess demand in the goods market and there will be upward pressure on the price level. The new equilibrium price level is at P_1, where the new aggregate demand curve $AD(G_1)$ intersects the aggregate supply curve (point *B*) in panel B. Because the price level is higher in the new equilibrium position, the real stock of money will be lower and, in the top left-hand panel, the *LM* curve will shift leftwards to $LM(\$_0^S/P_1)$. The reduction in the real stock of money means that the equilibrium interest rate will be higher and the level of private sector investment will be lower. At point *B*, the interest rate has risen precisely the right amount to reduce aggregate demand back to equality with the equilibrium output level Y^*. An important implication of the classical model is that total aggregate demand must always equal the supply-determined equilibrium level of output Y^*. A permanent increase in one component of demand must crowd out other components. In this case, the increase in government spending has caused an equal decline in private investment. The mechanism that guarantees this complete crowding out is a rising price level that reduces the real stock of money, which in turn drives up the rate of interest.

The increase in government spending also has an effect in the labour market, which is illustrated in panel D. The excess demand for goods causes the price level to rise. As we saw in the previous section, this results in a leftward shift in the supply of labour and a rightward shift of the demand for labour schedules, because at the original nominal wage W_0 the real wage is reduced by the rising price level. The resulting excess demand for labour forces up the nominal wage rate to W_1. However, the real wage at point *B* is precisely the same as the real wage at *A*. Both firms and households are satisfied with the equilibrium level of employment L^* at this unique equilibrium real wage. The total volume of output remains unchanged between points *A* and *B*, although the *product mix* does shift in favour of government goods and services at the expense of private investment expenditures (more public and less private housing for example).

An Increase in the Money Supply

The classical model provides a very precise prediction concerning the effect of changes in the nominal stock of money. An increase of, say, 10 per cent in the nominal stock of money will raise both the price level and the nominal wage by 10 per cent, but the equilibrium levels of employment and output will be unaffected. And, unlike the case of an increase in government spending, the composition of aggregate demand will be unchanged by movements in the stock of money. Because changes in the stock of money affect no real variables (only nominal ones), the stock of money is said to be neutral in the classical model. The **neutrality of money** is illustrated in Chart 8-7.

The initial equilibrium is again described by point *A* in all panels. Let us disturb this equilibrium by raising the nominal stock of money by 10 per cent from $\$_0^S$ to $\$_1^S$. The immediate effect is that the *LM* and *AD* curves (panels A and B) shift rightwards to $LM(\$_1^S/P_0)$ and $AD(\$_1^S)$, respectively. Note that at the initial price

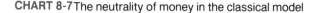

CHART 8-7 The neutrality of money in the classical model

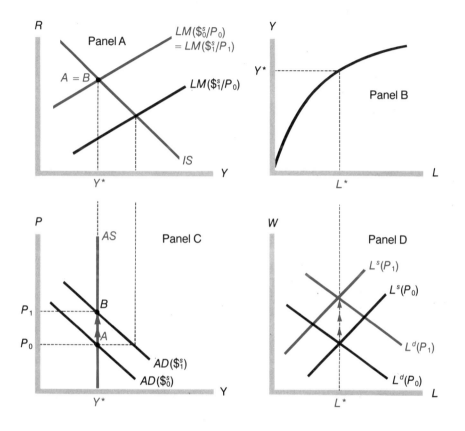

level P_0, there is now a state of excess demand in the product market. The price level will rise to its new equilibrium level, P_1, where the new aggregate demand curve $AD(\$_1^s)$ intersects the aggregate supply curve. This higher price level causes a reduction in the real stock of money to $\$_1^S/P_1$ which will shift the LM curve leftwards. Since the equilibrium output level Y^* is supply-determined, the demand for output must equal Y^*. This means the LM curve must return to its original position, where it once again intersects the IS curve at the equilibrium level of output Y^*.

The fact that the LM curve returns exactly to its original position has an important implication. We have already seen that the position of the LM curve depends on the real stock of money $\$^S/P$. Since the LM curve returns to its original position, the real stock of money must also be restored to its original level, that is,

$$\$_0^S/P_0 = \$_1^S/P_1$$

But this means that the percentage change in the price level from P_0 to P_1 must be exactly the same as the increase in the nominal money stock that started the whole process. The classical model predicts that a 10 per cent rise in the nominal stock of money will raise the equilibrium price level by exactly 10 per cent.

Of course, the inelastic supply curve of the classical model means that the equilibrium output level in panel C remains an Y^*. In the labour market (panel D) the higher price level shifts the supply and demand curves for labour, creating a state of excess demand for labour. This is removed as nominal wages rise and the real wage is restored to its original level. In our example, a 10 per cent increase in the nominal stock of money raises both the price level and the nominal wage by 10 per cent, leaving the equilibrium real wage unchanged.

Now let's turn to the question of the composition of demand. In fact, the components of aggregate demand are no *different* in the new equilibrium from what they were originally. The *IS* and *LM* curves are exactly where they were, so that the interest rate and the level of investment are also unchanged. The increase in the stock of money affects only the *nominal* variables P and W. All *real* variables, such as the level of employment, output and the components of aggregate demand are *unaffected*. In this sense, money is *neutral* in the classical model.

While the neutrality of money proposition is the most important single feature of the classical model, it also has very definite implications for fiscal policy. As we have seen, the level of government expenditure has no role in determining the equilibrium level of output. Fiscal multipliers are zero. This is because output in the flexible-price and flexible-wage classical model is determined exclusively by *supply-side* factors, namely the state of technology, the size of the capital stock and the supply of labour. This is quite the opposite to the *fixed*-price *IS-LM* model of chapters 4 to 7, where equilibrium output is demand-determined. In that Keynesian fixed-price model, equilibrium output can fall short of the economy's potential capacity to produce goods and services. But in the Keynesian model, fiscal and monetary policies do have real effects. In the next section we will return to the Keynesian view that wages are not perfectly flexible in the short run because of institutional rigidities in the labour market. We will derive the Keynesian short-run supply curve and examine the role of fiscal and monetary policy in this alternative model.

The Keynesian Inflexible-Wage Model

Aggregate Supply With Wage Inflexibility

The modern interpretation of the Keynesian inflexible-wage model focuses on the role played by labour contracts. It is a matter of fact that nominal wage rates are not determined on a daily basis according to the forces of supply and demand. For a large part of the work force, wage rates are negotiated and then fixed for a period of time. The explicit terms of **wage contracts** detail the wage rates to be paid during the life of the contract. It has been argued that wage contracts also have an unwritten or implicit component. For example, firms may implicitly agree not to treat employees as casual labour that can be hired or fired according to daily needs. Rather, there is an implicit agreement that minor variations in demand will not lead to changes in employment. This does not rule out the possibility of layoffs when demand declines substantially and for sustained periods of time, but it does imply a degree of employment stability in normal times. For their part, employees agree to work additional hours in the event that demand is temporarily high, without demanding a new wage contract.

Until the double-digit inflation of the 1970s, wage contracts were often in force for up to three years. In these circumstances, wages are fixed in nominal terms for long periods of time. Only for that small part of the labour force currently renegotiating its contract is the wage rate flexible; over the economy as a whole, wages are essentially contractually fixed in the short run. As inflation accelerated during the 1970s, the average length of wage contracts declined and cost-of-living clauses became somewhat more common. Both of these innovations tend to make wages more flexible in the short-run, at least in the upward direction (cost-of-living clauses do not typically allow for the possibility of wage reductions). For example, if all wage contracts last three years, then in any given year only one-third of workers will be renegotiating their wages. In this case, wage levels in the economy as a whole are only partially flexible in the short-run period of one year. But if wage contracts last only two years on average, then in any given year one-half of contracts will be renegotiated, making the economy-wide average wage somewhat more flexible in the short run.

While average contract length is the major determinant of wage flexibility in the upward direction, other factors limit the degree of downward flexibility of wages. Industry-wide unions often take the view that hard-won wage levels and benefit packages should not be given up lightly. In some cases this pits local workers against their own union. For example, during the very deep recession of 1982, the International Woodworkers Union resisted wage cuts at sawmills in British Columbia. The union took the view that if the weakest firms succeeded in getting wage concessions in order to maintain employment, then all firms would demand the same concessions and all workers would suffer. Moreover, the union would have to fight battles already won in order to restore wage and benefit levels once market conditions improved. Despite attempts by some local groups to decertify their union status, wage cuts were resisted and many sawmills were closed.

In this section we will develop an aggregate supply curve that recognizes the short-run inflexibility of wages. As we will see, this leads to a **positively sloped short-run aggregate supply curve**. Over a period of time long enough for the renegotiation of wage contracts, wages are flexible in the upward direction and the long-run aggregate supply curve is vertical, as it is in the classical model. However, in the downward direction the supply curve is vertical only after a much longer period of time, because even when contracts come up for renewal, employees often stoically resist wage cuts. Chart 8-8 illustrates the Keynesian inflexible-wage model.

In the labour market diagram (panel B) the initial position is at point A, where the labour supply, L^S (P_0^e), and the labour demand L^D (P_0^e), schedules intersect.

CHART 8-8 Aggregate supply with inflexible wages

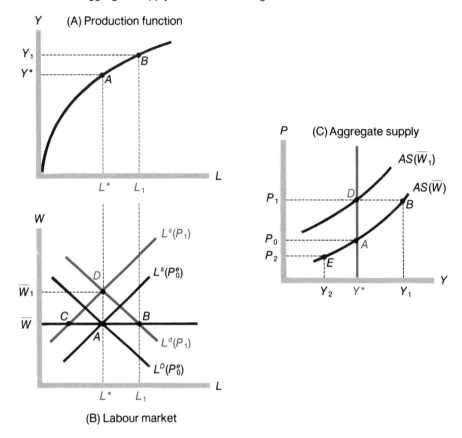

(A) Production function

(B) Labour market

(C) Aggregate supply

The nominal wage rate W represents the negotiated wage rate that will be in force during the life of the contract. The symbol P_0^e stands for the price level that is expected to hold, on average, during the life of the contract. At the time of wage negotiations, firms and employees do not know what the actual price level will be. That is, the *real* wage during the contract is unknown. But it is the real wage that determines the demand for and supply of labour. Consequently, firms and employees must make an estimate of what the price level will be. The supply and demand curves are drawn on the basis of the price expectations that are held at the time of negotiations. Given the negotiated equilibrium nominal wage $\overline{W}$, the expected real wage is $\overline{W}/P_0^e$ and the anticipated level of employment is L^*.

Now suppose that during the contract period the actual price level turns out to be P_1, which is above the expected price level P_0^e. The actual demand for labour schedule shifts rightwards to $L^D(P_1)$. Unlike the classical model, in which wages are perfectly flexible, this model assumes that the nominal wage $\overline{W}$ is contractually fixed in the short run. However, the fact that the price level is higher than expected means that the real wage is lower than expected. Profit-maximizing firms would like to hire more labour. We will assume that under the implicit terms of the contract, employees will work all the hours demanded at the negotiated wage $\overline{W}$. In other words, the short-run supply curve of labour in panel B is perfectly horizontal (infinitely elastic) at the nominal wage $\overline{W}$. Consequently, the actual price level P_1 leads to an actual employment level of L_1 in the short run. This level of employment produces the output level Y_1. The aggregate supply diagram (panel C) shows that the actual price level P_1 results in an actual output level of Y_1. The short-run positive relationship between prices and output is labelled $AS(\overline{W})$ to indicate that this supply curve is based on the contractually fixed nominal wage $\overline{W}$, which in turn depends on the expected price level P_0^e. Recall that the movement along $AS(\overline{W})$ from A to B is due to a decline in the real wage below the equilibrium level. It is this decline in the real wage that makes it profitable for firms to raise employment and output.

Returning to the labour market (panel B), we see that the higher than expected price level, P_1, shifts the long-run supply curve of labour to $L^S(P_1)$. Employees are not in long-run equilibrium at point B. At the real wage $\overline{W}/P_1$ the desired supply of labour is at point C on $L^S(P_1)$. Evidently, the higher price level P_1 and the negotiated wage of $\overline{W}$ leaves employees supplying more labour in the short run than they would ultimately like to supply at the real wage $(\overline{W}/P_1)$. Over time, the renegotiation of nominal wages to a new level $\overline{W}_1$ will restore equilibrium to the labour market. Based on the price level P_1, the new equilibrium is at point D where the real wage is once again at its equilibrium level and employment is L^*. Consequently, over the long run, as contracts expire, wages are flexible upwards and the aggregate supply curve is vertical above the output level Y^*.

Just as there is a short-run aggregate supply curve passing through point A in panel C (based on the contractually fixed wage $(\overline{W})$, there is also a short-run aggregate supply curve passing through point D. This second short-run curve is labelled $AS(\overline{W}_1)$ in panel C. Provided the price level stays at P_1 (and is expected to stay at P_1 for the duration of labour contracts), the negotiated wage will remain at $\overline{W}_1$. In these unchanging circumstances the economy will remain at point D in panels B and C and the level of output will continue to equal Y^*. However, if price expectations are not fulfilled, the economy will move away from point D along the short-run supply function $AS(\overline{W}_1)$. For example, if the actual price level unexpectedly rises above P_1, the real wage will be lower than expected. In this case, employment and output will rise in the short run. Although only two short-run aggregate supply curves are illustrated in Chart 8-8, there is an entire family of positively sloped short-run supply curves. Every single point on the vertical long-run supply curve has a positively sloped short-run supply curve passing through it.

In the last few paragraphs we have considered the effect of an unexpected *rise* in the price level and shown how a fixed money wage results in an *increase* in employment and output. A similar argument shows that a *decline* in the price level together with a fixed money wage results in a higher real wage and a *reduction* in the demand for labour. Employment declines and so does output. In the aggregate supply diagram (panel C of Chart 8-8), a decline in the price level to P_2 is associated with a decline in output to Y_2, point E on $AS(\overline{W})$.

We have seen that short-run nominal wage inflexibility implies an upward sloping short-run supply curve. The supply curve $AS(\overline{W})$ is essentially a mirror image of the demand for labour schedule, $L^D(P)$, projected through the production function. Given a fixed nominal wage, variations in the price level create variations in the real wage. Since employment is *demand-determined* in the short run, employment and output rise with a rising price level (a falling real wage). An important feature of the short-run aggregate supply curve is that it is based on short-run disequilibrium in the labour market. At point B on $AS(\overline{W})$, employees would like to supply less labour. At point E there is an excess supply of labour. Only in the long run are nominal wages flexible and hence only in the long run is the labour market in equilibrium and the aggregate supply curve vertical.

Demand Shocks With Inflexible Wages

Panel A of Chart 8-9 shows the effect of an *increase* in demand in our model of aggregate supply with inflexible wages. The initial position is point A, where AD_0 intersects the short-run aggregate supply curve $AS(\overline{W}_0)$. The notation makes it clear that this short-run supply curve is based on the fixed (in the short term) nominal wage rate $\overline{W}_0$. Now suppose that some unexpected event shifts the demand curve rightwards to AD_1. The event could be an increase in any exogenous component of aggregate demand, or an increase in the stock of money. Immediately following this unexpected event, there is a state of excess demand in the product market, and market forces cause the price level to rise. With nominal wages fixed at $\overline{W}_0$ in the short term, the rise in prices causes the real wage to fall. Profit-maximizing firms hire more labour and output rises. During this process the economy moves from point A to point B along the short-run aggregate supply curve. Comparing point B with point A we see that the increase in aggregate demand raises both output and the price level.

However, in our earlier discussion we noted that workers are supplying more labour than they would like at points such as B. As wage contracts come up for renegotiation the excess demand for labour will put upward pressure on the nominal wage. That is, nominal wages are flexible in the long run. As soon as labour market equilibrium is restored, the economy finds itself on the vertical supply curve at point C, where the short run supply curve $AS(\overline{W}_1)$ intersects the aggregate demand curve, AD_1.

The implications of short-run wage inflexibility are that increases in aggregate demand lead to both price and output increases in the short run. During this expansion of economic activity the real wage is lower than its equilibrium level; that is, the real wage follows a counter-cyclical path. Over a longer time the nominal wage adjusts, and output, employment and the real wage return to their long-run equilibrium values.

The analysis of a *decrease* in aggregate demand, which is shown in the panel B of Chart 8-9, is essentially the opposite of what we have just done. A decline in demand that shifts AD_0 to AD_1 results in a fall in both the price level and the level of output. Prices fall because of the decline in the demand for goods. With a fixed

CHART 8-9 Demand shocks with wage rigidity

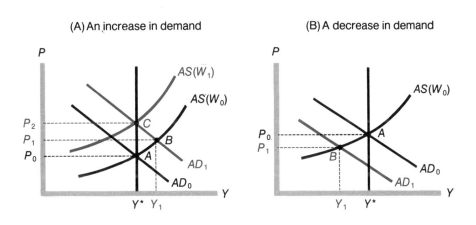

(A) An increase in demand   (B) A decrease in demand

nominal wage, the real wage rises. Profit-maximizing firms reduce employment and output levels. The difference between this case and the one in which demand increased is that, as experience shows, the nominal wage will not necessarily fall even when contracts expire if unions are prepared to see some of their members laid off rather than accept industry-wide wage cuts. If this is the case, the economy could spend a great deal of time in the depressed state described by point B. A government may not wish to wait for the long-run equilibrium position to be restored. Instead it may choose to stimulate the economy through monetary or fiscal policies, or both, thereby shifting AD_1 back to AD_0. The important implication of employee resistance to wage cuts is that a decline in demand leads to a prolonged recession and therefore provides a rationale for stabilization policies—something for which the classical model had no role whatsoever. Indeed, in the classical model, equilibrium is always assured and output never deviates from the long-run equilibrium value. While the classical model does provide several long-run predictions, such as the neutrality of money proposition, it does not provide an explanation of the business cycle. The inflexible-wage model is capable of providing an explanation of why output deviates, in the short run, from its long-run value. It is an explanation that relies on a short-term state of disequilibrium in the labour market brought about by short-term institutional rigidities such as wage contracts and resistance to cuts in nominal wage rates. In the next section we will turn to the new classical model, which provides an alternative explanation of the business cycle. True to its classical tradition this explanation is based on continuous market clearing, that is, continuous equilibrium in both labour and product markets.

The Aggregate Supply Function in the New Classical Model

According to the new classical economists, the explanation of why output and employment vary around normal levels (the business cycle) should not be based on persistent market disequilibrium. The new classical school believes that the only fruitful line of enquiry into the nature of business cycles is through models of equilibrium in which the behaviour of rational economic agents is at all time consistent with profit and utility maximization.[6] Further, it is argued that once this principle of rational behaviour is abandoned, it becomes impossible to predict the behaviour of economic agents. Consequently, models of the macro economy that are not consistent with microeconomic equilibrium will necessarily lead to mean-ingless predictions. This controversial view of macroeconomics embodies a very clear vision of the role of governments in macroeconomic policy. According to the new classical school, business cycles are principally caused by capricious and unpredictable movements in the money supply, which are, of course, the result of government actions. In short, unpredictable government policies cause business cycles. Moreover, since the economy is always said to be in equilibrium, even at the trough of a business cycle, there is no need for government intervention. More than that, any systematic (and hence predictable) policy rule that calls for counter-cyclical policies will have no effect at all on output and employment. In short, discretionary fiscal and monetary stabilization policies are both unnecessary and entirely ineffective.

A complete discussion and appraisal of this "policy ineffectiveness proposition" appears in Chapter 17. In this chapter we will confine our discussion to the new classical school's analysis of the short-run aggregate supply function. This entails an "equilibrium" explanation of why the short-run supply curve has a positive slope.

There are several steps we must follow before we reach this result. First, we will consider the factors that influence the supply and demand curves for labour in *local* markets. Then, we will introduce the key assumption that individuals and firms base their decisions on incomplete information. Finally, we will argue that an increase in the general price level may be interpreted as simply an increase in *local* prices. If this is the case, there will be an increase in output in all local markets, and hence in aggregate output.

Panel A of Chart 8-10 shows the supply and demand for labour in a local market such as the city of Guelph, Ontario. The nominal wage received by workers in the local market of Guelph is denoted by w. Since workers in Guelph purchase goods from all markets throughout the country, it is the *general* economy-wide price level that is relevant to the calculation of their real wages. However, the **new**

---

[6]A clear description of the new classical theory of business cycles is contained in "Understanding Business Cycles" by R.E. Lucas in Karl Brunner and Alan H. Meltzer, eds., *Stabilization of the Domestic and International Economy*, Carnegie-Rochester Conference Series on Public Policy, Vol. 5 (Amsterdam: North Holland, 1977). A balanced critique of the new classical economics has been provided by Stephen Sheffrin, *Rational Expectations* (Cambridge University Press, 1983).

CHART 8-10 The new classical short-run supply curve

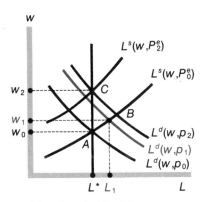

A local market for labour

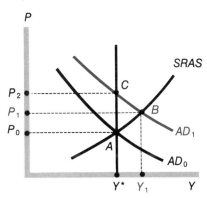

The economy-wide product market

classical model assumes that individuals and firms do not have complete information on all current prices in the economy. While the local wage in Guelph, w, and the price of goods produced in Guelph, p, are both known at the local level, the general economy-wide price level can only be estimated on the basis of available information. This incomplete set of known information includes the prices of locally produced goods, but this is only a small part of the general price level. Consequently, the local labour supply schedule is labelled $L^S(w,P^e)$, where P^e is the best available *estimate* of the general price level. Employees estimate that the real wage in the local market is w/P^e.

We turn now to the demand curve for labour in the *local* market. The information that is vital to local firms is, first, the price of their own output—that is, the price of locally produced goods (local output prices)—and second, the wage rate in the local labour market. For example, the demand for labour by the fibreglass plant in Guelph depends on the wage rate paid to workers in that plant (the local wage rate) and the price of fibreglass products (local output prices). From the point of view of local firms, the real wage is the ratio of the local nominal wage, w, to the price of locally purchased goods, which is initially p_0. Consequently, the demand for local labour is written $L^D(w,p_0)$. It is important to note that the economy-wide general price level does not affect the demand for labour in the local market.

Now suppose that there is an *unanticipated* increase in the money supply that disturbs the initial equilibrium position (point A in both panels of Chart 8-10), and shifts the aggregate demand curve (panel B) rightwards to AD_1. We will assume that the change in the money supply is both *unanticipated* and *unobserved* by workers and firms; that is, information that is available to economic agents *does not* include the fact that the money supply has risen nor that the aggregate price level has risen to P_1. At the local level, all that is observed in the short run is that the price of locally produced goods has risen to p_1. Let us consider what this means for the local market (panel A of Chart 8-10).

The increase in local output prices shifts the demand for labour schedule rightwards to $L^D(w,p_1)$. The effect on the supply of labour depends on how the rise in local prices is interpreted by local workers. If experience shows that local output prices tend to move up and down primarily as a result of factors *specific* to the market for local output and only infrequently as a result of *general* increases in demand, then there is no strong reason for local workers to believe that a particular rise in local output prices is due to a rise in the general price level. Indeed, in these circumstances, assuming local output price rises are associated with general price rises would more often be wrong than right. The new classical model makes the assumption that there is a sufficiently weak connection between local output prices and the general price level that workers who see only a rise in local prices *do not* revise their estimate of the general price level. Under this critical assumption, the rise in local prices from p_0 to p_1 has no effect on the estimated general price level P^e, and consequently the labour supply schedule remains stationary.

In panel A of Chart 8-10 the effect of a general price increase, which is interpreted to be merely a rise in local output prices, is to raise the local wage to w_1 and local employment to L_1. It is important to note that point B is an equilibrium position. Workers supply more labour at B because the real wage is incorrectly perceived to be higher than at A. Firms find it profitable to hire more workers because local wages have risen less than the price of locally produced goods, that is $(w_1/p_1) < (w_0/p_0)$. To local firms, the real wage is lower at B than at A. Thus, we see that the assumption of incomplete information means that a general price increase can lead, for a short period of time, to greater employment and output in all local markets. At the level of the macro economy, the price level and aggregate output are both raised. This is illustrated in panel B of Chart 8-10, where the rightward shift of the aggregate demand curve causes a movement up the short-run aggregate supply (*SRAS*) curve. At the aggregate level, the price level has risen to P_1 and output to Y_1. The rise in the price of locally produced output from p_0 to p_1 is part of the increase in the general price level, although this is not yet known at the local level.

However, as soon as everyone becomes aware that the rise in the price of local output is due to an increase in the stock of money that must eventually raise the general price level to P_2, the economy immediately moves to the new equilibrium position described by point C in both panels of Chart 8-10. In the local labour market the labour supply schedule shifts upwards to $L^S(w,P_2^e)$ as workers revise their estimate of the general price level. This new labour supply curve intersects the demand for labour schedule, $L^D(w,p_2)$, at the nominal wage w_2. Note that the local output price of p_2 is consistent with the new equilibrium general price level, P_2. At point C in panel A, the equilibrium real wage is w_2/p_2, which is identical to the real wage at point A. Equilibrium employment is once again at the level L^* and the aggregate output is Y^*. Thus, in the long run when full information is available,

CHART 8-11 An unanticipated decline in demand in the new classical model

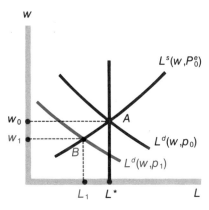

A local market for labour

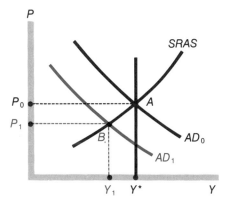

The economy-wide product market

the aggregate supply curve is vertical. The short-run supply curve has a positive slope only to the extent that individuals are surprised by actual price levels that differ from their expectations. If there are no price surprises, output does not deviate from Y^*.

The treatment of an unanticipated decline in demand follows the same line of argument. The aggregate price level will fall and output will decline below Y^* (see point B in panel B of Chart 8-11). However, an important feature of this reduced level of output and employment is that the labour market is in equilibrium. Workers choose to supply less labour because they perceive the real wage to be lower than it actually turns out to be. Given their incomplete information, workers are optimizing. There is no involuntary unemployment at point B. This interpretation of the labour market during a recession is very different from the one implied by the inflexible-wage model. We will return to this issue in the final section of this chapter, where the nature of unemployment is discussed more fully.

Finally, we should point out that this interpretation of the new classical economics suggests that workers rather than firms are the victims of incomplete information. In our discussion, it is workers who miscalculate their real wages. Firms are also assumed to have incomplete information, but our story has not indicated how this might hurt them. New classical economists, such as Robert Lucas, point out that when firms interpret general price increases to be relative price increases, they may respond by allocating investment expenditures towards the production of the higher priced goods. This, of course, will be a mistake if relative prices have not changed. This will generate less than expected (possibly negative) returns. Thus, decisions based on partial information can be costly to both firms and workers.

Unemployment

In this chapter we have discussed three models of aggregate supply: the classical model, the inflexible-wage model and the new classical model. In each case we have examined the effect of a change in aggregate demand on prices and output. We saw that the classical model always maintains equilibrium at a supply-determined level of output while the two more modern theories provide alternative explanations for the cyclical behaviour of prices and output. In this last section we turn to the vitally important question of unemployment. In the context of the classical model we will introduce the concept of the equilibrium unemployment rate. Then we will look at the very different interpretations that the inflexible-wage and new classical models put on cyclical variations in the unemployment rate around its equilibrium value.

In the classical model, output is always equal to its supply-determined equilibrium level and the labour market is always in equilibrium. Yet the unemployment rate is not zero in this model. For a variety of reasons there will be unemployed people and unfilled job vacancies existing simultaneously even when the labour market is, in some sense, in equilibrium. For our purposes we can define labour market equilibrium to mean equality between the number of unemployed persons and the number of job vacancies. Unemployment exists because the unemployed are not yet matched with the vacancies. This **equilibrium unemployment** has two components: frictional and structural.

Frictional unemployment exists because the Canadian labour market is always in a state of flux: former students join the labour force and retirees leave, employed people quit to take jobs elsewhere or to leave the labour force altogether, while others who have previously dropped out re-enter the labour force. Since it takes time for job seekers to find suitable jobs and for employers to fill vacancies with suitable employees, it follows that even in equilibrium there will always be frictional unemployment.

The second component of equilibrium unemployment is due to *structural* factors: a mismatching of the characteristics of the unemployed and the job vacancies. For example, at any given point in time some industries are in a state of relative decline while others are experiencing rapid growth. This may lead to a mismatch between the skills of the unemployed and the skills demanded by the growing industries. Alternatively, the declining and expanding sectors may be in different locations and, given the cost of moving, unemployment and job vacancies my well exist simultaneously.

From this brief discussion of the nature of the equilibrium unemployment rate it is clear that the equilibrium unemployment rate is not necessarily fixed through time. Frictional unemployment will be low if job seekers find jobs after brief searches. For example, in a hypothetical case, job search may take no time at all, which would imply a zero rate of frictional unemployment. In practice, the time people spend searching for a job depends on such factors as the generosity of the unemployment insurance program. Liberal benefits encourage long searches and hence raise the equilibrium unemployment rate. Structural unemployment can also vary over time. During periods of rapidly changing patterns of demand or rapid technological change the structural unemployment rate could well rise. In Chapter 11 we will present estimates of the Canadian equilibrium unemployment rate and discuss two important features that have caused it to change over time.

We turn now to the nature of *cyclical unemployment*. The inflexible-wage and the new classical models have profoundly different interpretations of cyclical unemployment. Panel B of Chart 8-9 shows the effect on output and prices of a decline in aggregate demand in the inflexible-wage model. The movement down the short-run aggregate supply curve $AS(\overline{W}_0)$ to point B leads to both a lower price level and lower output. Because the nominal wage rate is contractually fixed in the short run, the lower-than-expected price level raises the real wage above its equilibrium level and profit-maximizing firms lay off workers. Employment is reduced to a level that is consistent with the lower output level Y_1. However, because the real wage is higher at point B than at point A, labour supply is also greater. Clearly there is involuntary unemployment at point B. There are people willing to work at the current real wage but there are no jobs available. If the excess supply of labour results in lower nominal wages over time, then the short-run aggregate supply curve will shift down, and output and employment gradually rise. But, if the Keynesian view that nominal wage rates are very, very slow to shift down is correct, then the involuntary unemployment at B will persist until aggregate demand is increased either in the natural course of events or as a result of government policies. The important point is that the inflexible-wage model is consistent with the view that **cyclical unemployment is involuntary** and that it may well persist for long periods of time.

The effect of a decline in demand in the new classical model is illustrated in Chart 8-11. Again, in panel B, there is a movement down the short-run aggregate supply curve to point B. The aggregate price level declines to P_1 and aggregate output declines to Y_1. In local markets, workers and firms are assumed not to have current economy-wide information. All they know is that the price of locally produced output has fallen. In panel A, the demand for labour, which depends on local product prices and local wages, shifts leftwards. However, since the new classical model assumes the general price decline is misperceived as just a fall in local prices, the labour supply schedule does *not* shift (its position depends on the expected overall price level and this is assumed not to change). As a result, there is a movement down the labour supply schedule as local nominal wages and employment decline. The important point to this approach is that point B in the local market is a temporary equilibrium position. Based on the limited information that is available, workers and firms are in equilibrium. Firms have reduced employment because the real wage that is relevant to them has risen; that is, $(w_1/p_1) > (w_0/p_0)$. Their product prices have fallen more than local nominal wages. But to workers, the decline in the nominal wage is also as decline in the real wage because the relevant price level is the aggregate price level. This is not observed in the current period, but is estimated to be P^e. Workers supply less labour because they estimate their real wage has fallen.

Individuals who were working at A and are not working at B are, in fact, indifferent between holding a job and not holding a job at the lower estimated real wage, w_1/P^e. That is to say, they are on their individual supply curves. If these people are considered unemployed, they are not involuntarily unemployed. On the contrary, their lack of employment is the result of a choice not to work at the available wage. The new classical school argues that markets are always in equilibrium; supply equals demand even during recessions. Measured unemployment may well rise during a recession, but this is not due to involuntary unemployment.

It is important to note that the new classical school's analysis of cyclical unemployment does *not* argue that individuals are just as well off during a recession as they are at normal levels of output and employment. On the contrary, individuals are much worse off at B than they are at A because the value of their labour is so much lower. What is being argued is that the labour market is in equilibrium at all points. During the recession, jobs are available at wage rates below normal, but the "unemployed" choose not to take them. There is only **voluntary unemployment** in the new classical economics.

In this last section we have discussed the nature of the equilibrium unemployment rate that exists when the economy is producing at its long-run equilibrium output level. We have also shown how the inflexible-wage model is consistent with the view that cyclical unemployment is largely involuntary; that is, many individuals would like to work at the going wage but there are no jobs available. This model is also consistent with the view that recessions can be long-lived and that there can be a role for fiscal and monetary policies in controlling the level of aggregate demand, output and employment. The new classical model offers a very different interpretation. In this view, cyclical increases in the measured unemployment rate do not reflect increasing involuntary unemployment but rather the free choices of individuals who react to a perceived decline in the real wage by supplying less labour. We have also seen in this chapter that the new classical model sees no role whatsoever for effective counter-cyclical policy measures. Only unanticipated changes in demand result in changes in output. Repeatedly used counter-cyclical policies cannot be unanticipated and therefore cannot affect output. This policy ineffectiveness proposition is discussed in greater detail in Chapter 17.

Key Concepts

the aggregate demand curve
marginal product of labour
real wage
the price-inelastic classical supply curve
the neutrality of money
the positively sloped short-run aggregate supply curve
wage contracts
Keynesian inflexible-wage model
the new classical model
equilibrium unemployment
involuntary cyclical unemployment (inflexible-wage model)
voluntary cyclical unemployment (new classical model)

Review Questions

1. Suppose points A and B lie on a particular aggregate demand curve and that point B corresponds to a lower price level and higher output than point A. Compare the levels of consumption, investment and the rates of interest at points A and B. Explain the differences.

2. Explain the factors that determine the size of the horizontal shift in the aggregate demand curve when the level of government spending rises by $1 billion.

3. What is meant by the 'neutrality of money' in the classical model?

4. In the classical model, analyze the effects of an autonomous decline in investment expenditure on the price level, the interest rate and the level of consumption.

5. Explain how the existence of wage contracts leads to a positively sloped short-run aggregate supply curve.

6. What factors influence the size of the equilibrium unemployment rate?

7. How do the inflexible-wage and new classical theories differ in their interpretation of the nature of cyclical unemployment?

The Phillips Curve and the Structural Determinants of Inflation

On the usual time scale of the dissemination of ideas in economics, the Phillips curve and the associated "Dilemma" problem achieved a prominent place in undergraduate textbooks almost instantly. . . .[T]he déjà vu reaction was so strong that the Phillips curve immediately achieved a life of its own in professional discussion.

Axel Leijonhufvud[1]

As discussed in Chapter 5, the central disturbing conclusion of Keynesian economics is that a free enterprise economy left to its own devices will likely experience sustained periods of unemployment. To generate such a conclusion, Keynes replaced the classical assumption of flexible wage rates and labour market equilibrium with the assumption of (downward) inflexible wage rates and persistent labour market disequilibrium (see Chapter 8). In Keynes' view, wage rates respond very *slowly*, if at all, to excess supply conditions in the labour market. Thus if the economy were to slip into a serious recession, say because of a decline in exports, the downward inflexibility of wage rates would result in a prolonged period of unemployment. Rather than wait for the slow-working "invisible hand" of Adam Smith to clear the labour market (the classical assumption of wage flexibility), Keynes advocated a stimulative fiscal policy to boost aggregate demand and create additional employment opportunities (see Chapters 6 and 8). Given Keynes' belief that wage and price levels are unresponsive to changing demand conditions (particularly during periods of chronic unemployment), such an expansionary demand-management policy undertaken in a recession would generate minimal inflation pressures. Expansionary policies would only lead to persistent inflation when the economy reached a state of full employment. Whatever the merits of the *General Theory*, a new theory of inflation it is not.

In the previous chapter we derived the aggregate demand curve and aggregate supply curve (under both Keynesian and classical assumptions), with the equilibrium price level being determined by the intersection of the aggregate demand and supply curves. Under classical *wage flexibility* assumptions, this equilibrium price level also corresponds to equilibrium in the labour market and a state of *full* employment. If the aggregate demand schedule shifts downwards, the wage rate

[1]Axel Leijonhufvud, "Comment: Is there a Meaningful Trade-Off Between Inflation and Unemployment," *Journal of Political Economy*, July 1968, p. 738.

is (quickly) bid downwards to maintain output and employment levels at their equilibrium, full employment levels. In contrast, under the Keynesian assumption of *downward inflexibility* in the wage rate, a decline in aggregate demand leads to lower output and employment levels. Given reduced demand conditions and downward inflexibility of wage rates, the equilibrium price level in the goods market (determined by the intersection of the aggregate demand curve and the Keynesian aggregate supply curve) is accompanied by persistent disequilibrium (unemployment) in the labour market.

In effect, Chapter 8 analyzes two polar cases. The classical (and new classical) model assumes that wage adjustments are virtually instantaneous and the labour market is generally in a state of equilibrium, whereas the Keynesian model assumes that wage rates are inflexible and the labour market can experience prolonged periods of disequilibrium (chronic unemployment). In this chapter we examine a more realistic, intermediate case in which the wage rate is assumed to respond to both excess demand and supply conditions, but does not move instantaneously to its new equilibrium level. Following a change in demand, the labour market will undergo a period of *short-run* disequilibrium adjustment as the wage rate adjusts to its new equilibrium value. If, as classical economists believe, wages are very flexible and responsive to labour market conditions, then this short-run adjustment period will be very short and the labour market will typically be in a state of equilibrium. On the other hand, if wages are very slow to adjust to changing demand conditions (say because of the existence of long-term contracts), then the labour market would be subject to a lengthy short-run disequilibrium adjustment period.

A major objective of this chapter is to analyze the process by which wages and prices adjust to their new equilibrium levels. We begin the chapter with a discussion of the now famous Phillips curve. After outlining the essence of Phillips' hypothesis, that wage adjustments are negatively related to unemployment rates, we then analyze the important subsequent contributions of Lipsey and Friedman. In particular, we examine the role of price expectations as a determinant of wage adjustments, which leads to the formulation of the price-expectations-augmented Phillips curve. Following an evaluation of the empirical evidence of whether Canadian wage adjustments and unemployment are in fact inversely related, we conclude the chapter with an analysis of the determinants of the rate of price inflation.

The Rise of the Phillips Curve

In 1958 A. W. Phillips of the London School of Economics published a paper demonstrating that the rate of British wage inflation was systematically related to the level of unemployment. As the opening lines of this now famous study reveal, Phillips was simply applying a basic economic principle to wage rates within the labour market:

> When the demand for a commodity or service is high relatively to the supply of it we expect the price to rise, the rate of rise being greater the greater the excess demand. Conversely when the demand is low rela-

tively to the supply we expect the price to fall, the rate of fall being greater the greater the deficiency of demand. It seems plausible that this principle should operate as one of the factors determining the rate of change of money wage rates, which are the price of labour services. When the demand for labour is high and there are very few unemployed we should expect employers to bid wage rates up quite rapidly, each firm and each industry being continually tempted to offer a little above the prevailing rates to attract the most suitable labour from other firms and industries.[2]

When unemployment rates were low, Phillips found that the rate of British wage inflation was relatively high; and conversely when unemployment rates were high, the rate of British wage inflation was low (or negative).

Phillips' scminal paper provided economists and policy makers with an important "new" relationship connecting wage changes, and implicitly inflation, to the level of unemployment—the now famous **Phillips curve**. Even though a great deal of controversy has subsequently engulfed the Phillips curve, it is important to re-emphasize the simple and straightforward economic principle behind the Phillips curve. The wage rate, the price of labour, will respond to demand and supply conditions within the labour market.

Given the simplicity of the essential idea behind the Phillips curve, it should come as no surprise that other economists before Phillips had considered the possibility of a "Phillips curve" effect. While Keynes recognized the possibility that wages might be affected by labour market conditions, he dismissed this *theoretical* possibility as being of minor *empirical* consequence:

> When there is a change in employment, money-wages tend to change in the same direction as, but not in great disproportion to, the change in employment; i.e. moderate changes in employment are not associated with very great changes in money-wages. This is a condition of the stability of prices rather than of employment.[3]

In less convoluted language, the "Phillips curve" effect of unemployment on wage inflation is likely to be so slight that it can be safely ignored. About the same time that Keynes was dismissing the relationship between wage inflation and unemployment, Tinbergen explicitly recognized its importance. In the Dutch economist's pioneering effort at macroeconometric model building, the very *first* equation in his 1936 econometric model of the Dutch economy is a Phillips curve:

> It is assumed that the change in the wage level from year to year is influenced by the changes in the cost of living and by the state of employment. . . .[W]hen employment exceeds the value which is consid-

---

[2]A.W. Phillips, "The Relation Between Unemployment and the Rate of Change of Money Wage Rates in the United Kingdom, 1861-1957,"*Economica*, November 1958, p. 283.

[3]J.M. Keynes, *The General Theory of Employment, Interest and Money*, Macmillan and Company, London, 1936, p. 251. As discussed in Chapter 4, in Keynes' view wage rates are primarily determined by institutional and historical forces, and, as a consequence, are unresponsive to labour market conditions (particularly in a *downward* direction).

ered normal wages will rise, while a subnormal level of employment leads to wage decreases.[4]

As is obvious from the preceding discussion, the basic idea that wage inflation might be systematically related to the level of unemployment goes back much further than Phillips' 1958 paper. The importance of Phillips' study was not so much the discovery of a new theoretical relationship but rather the discovery of an *apparently* stable empirical relationship between wage changes and unemployment rates. Relying repeatedly on visual displays of the data, Phillips skillfully explains almost one hundred years of British wage inflation in terms of one major causal factor—the unemployment rate.

Lipsey's Reformulation of the Phillips Curve Model

Phillips' 1958 paper was quickly followed by a study by Lipsey. The contribution of Lipsey's follow-up paper was twofold. First Lipsey used more conventional econometric techniques in his analysis of the same one hundred years of British data and reconfirmed Phillips' basic empirical findings:

> The data are shown to support Phillips' main contention that there is a significant relation between the rate of change of money wage rates and the level...of unemployment.[5]

Second, and perhaps more important, Lipsey recast Phillips' verbal rationale for a relationship between wage changes and unemployment into an explicit wage adjustment function based on the existence of disequilibrium in a (competitive) labour market. A brief review of Lipsey's reformulation of the Phillips curve is useful to highlight the key assumptions implicit in the Phillips curve model.

To illustrate the mechanics of Lipsey's disequilibrium model, panel A of Chart 9-1 depicts a conventional set of demand and supply curves for labour services, with the nominal (money) wage rate plotted on the vertical axis. The market-clearing wage rate is W^* and L^* represents the equilibrium *full* employment level of employment (see Chapter 8). A wage rate of W_A would give rise to a state of excess labour demand (XLD), while a wage rate of W_B would result in a state of excess labour supply (XLS). In each case, the excess labour demand or supply is represented by the horizontal distance between the labour demand and supply curves for the particular disequilibrium wage rate, W_A and W_B, respectively. Elementary economics argues that the wage rate will be bid up in the event of excess labour demand and will be bid down in the event of excess labour supply. In either case, competitive labour market pressures will force the wage rate to return, eventually, to its equilibrium wage level, W^*.

---

[4]Jan Tinbergen, "An Economic Policy for 1936," in L.H. Klassen et al., eds., *Jan Tinbergen: Selected Papers*, North-Holland, Amsterdam, 1959, pp. 51-52.

[5]R.G. Lipsey, "The Relation Between Unemployment and the Rate of Change of Money Wage Rates in the United Kingdom, 1862-1957: A Further Analysis," *Economica*, February 1960, p. 2.

CHART 9-1 Derivation of Phillips Curve

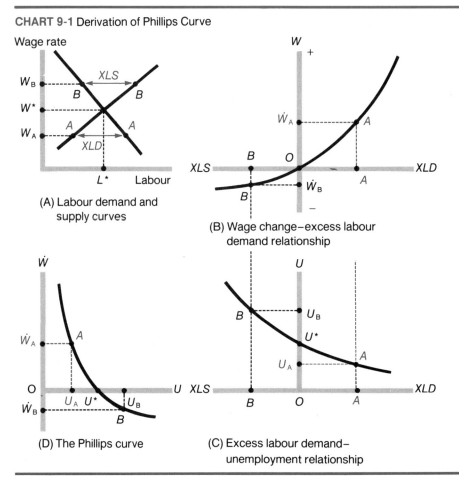

(A) Labour demand and
    supply curves

(B) Wage change–excess labour
    demand relationship

(D) The Phillips curve

(C) Excess labour demand–
    unemployment relationship

While nearly all economists would accept the labour-market-clearing hypo-thesis,[6] Lipsey's reformulation of the Phillips curve model goes one step further. Lipsey hypothesized that the speed of the wage adjustment is directly related to the *amount* of excess demand (disequilibrium pressure) in the labour market. The greater the amount of excess labour demand (supply), the larger the upward (downward) adjustment in wage rates in a given interval of time. In panel B of Chart 9-1 amounts of excess labour demand (positive values) and excess labour supply (negative values) are plotted on the horizontal axis and the wage adjust-ment per unit of time is plotted on the vertical axis. When the labour market is in equilibrium (zero excess labour demand), there will be no change in the wage rate. Thus, point *O* (for origin) in panel B of Chart 9-1 corresponds to labour market equilibrium. Lipsey's key new assumption is represented in panel B of Chart 9-1 by the upward-sloping line, which goes through the origin. Larger

[6]For a dissenting view, see J. Cornwall, "Do We Need Separate Theories of Inflation and Unemploy-ment," *Canadian Public Policy—Analyse de politiques*, Supplement, April 1981, pp. 165-78.

amounts of excess labour demand (supply) are assumed to generate larger wage increases (decreases) during a given interval of time.

The line representing wage adjustments as a function of excess labour demand probably is curved. Wages are much less likely to be flexible in a downward direction than in an upward direction as workers (and their unions) strongly resist any decrease in the wage rate. For example, in 1984 workers (with an average annual salary in excess of $20,000) at a Burns meat-packing firm in Kitchener, Ontario refused to accept a 10 per cent wage reduction, knowing full well that by rejecting the company's final wage offer the plant would be permanently closed (which it was). A given amount of excess labour demand (distance OA in panel B of Chart 9-1) will likely generate a larger wage increase than the wage decrease associated with a corresponding amount of excess labour supply (distance OB in panel B). The Phillips curve does indeed curve.

The classical and Keynesian models presented in Chapter 8 can be identified as polar opposites in terms of this wage change–excess demand diagram. The classical model assumes that wages adjust very quickly to any change in demand or supply. Any excess labour demand or supply would generate a sufficiently large wage adjustment to immediately restore labour market equilibrium. Under strict classical assumptions the labour market would be in a state of equilibrium (zero excess demand), with appropriate instantaneous wage adjustments to maintain labour market equilibrium. Thus the *classical* wage change–excess labour demand relationship can be represented by the *vertical* axis of panel B of Chart 9-1. The Keynesian assumption of *downward inflexibility* in wage rates implies a zero wage change whenever there is any amount of excess labour supply. Thus, the *Keynesian* wage change–excess labour supply relationship corresponds to the *horizontal* axis to the left of the origin.

Lipsey's reformulation of the Phillips curve represents an intermediate position between the classical and Keynesian assumptions. When excess supply conditions prevail, the wage rate is assumed to decline through time, but not instantaneously to its new equilibrium level. The more workers resist wage reductions, the flatter the wage adjustment–excess demand relationship to the left of the origin. When excess demand conditions prevail, wages are assumed to rise, but not instantaneously, to their new equilibrium level. The greater the amount of excess labour demand, the larger the hypothesized wage adjustment.

To make the Phillips curve model operational, *excess labour demand*, an unobservable theoretical concept, must be approximated by an existing data series. Like Phillips and Tinbergen before him, Lipsey chose the *unemployment rate* to approximate demand and supply conditions in the labour market. As the amount of excess demand in the labour market *increases*, Lipsey assumed that the level of unemployment systematically *decreases*—workers are more in demand and it is therefore easier for the unemployed to find a job. Since the unemployment rate cannot fall below zero, this hypothesized relationship between the unemployment rate and excess labour demand is not likely to be linear. As excess labour demand increases, the level of unemployment will decline at a decreasing rate as the economy approaches some minimum level of unemployment (see panel C of Chart 9-1).

As discussed in Chapter 8, some unemployment will always exist, even when the labour market is in a state of equilibrium. *Frictional* unemployment occurs because an unemployed worker typically requires time to locate a job that matches his or her set of skills, education and work experience. Furthermore, the existence of a "generous" unemployment insurance program may lengthen the period of time in which an unemployed individual keeps searching for that ideal job. *Structural* unemployment occurs when there is a mismatching of unemployed persons and available jobs; that is, the unemployed do not have the necessary skills to fill the vacant jobs. The pronounced seasonal weather patterns and the vast expanse of Canada, not to mention the fluctuating demands for Canada's basic resource products (which are typically located in remote regions), heighten the amount of equilibrium unemployment in Canada. Since equilibrium unemployment occurs, by definition, when excess labour demand is zero, we can easily locate the equilibrium unemployment rate (U^*) in panel C of Chart 9-1. U^* must be the point at which the unemployment–excess labour demand relationship crosses the vertical unemployment axis (where excess labour demand is zero).

Given a wage change–excess labour demand relationship (panel B of Chart 9-1) and an unemployment–excess labour demand relationship (panel C of Chart 9-1), the Phillips curve can be easily derived. For a given level of excess labour demand (say distance *AA* in panel A of Chart 9-1, we can plot the corresponding change in the wage rate (from panel B) along with the corresponding unemployment rate (from panel C) over in the lower left-hand panel D of Chart 9-1 (note that the distance *OA* in panels B and C is equal to the distance *AA* in panel A). This new point *A* represents one point on the derived Phillips curve. Similarly *B* represents a second point on the derived Phillips curve, depicting a level of excess labour supply equal to *BB* in panel A. Taking all possible levels of excess labour demand and supply, we can trace out a smooth Phillips curve that relates *wage changes* to *unemployment rates*. Again we can easily locate the *equilibrium* unemployment rate in panel D of Chart 9-1. U^* occurs when excess labour demand is zero and there is a zero wage change. Thus the point at which the Phillips curve crosses the horizontal axis must be U^*.

In Chart 9-1 we have graphically derived a negative *curved* relationship between the size of wage adjustments and the unemployment rate, a proxy for excess labour demand. To facilitate subsequent algebraic derivations, we can use the following equation to convert the Phillips *curve* into a *linear* expression:

$$\dot{W} = j(U^* - U)$$

(9-1)   or $$\dot{W} = jU^* - jU$$

where $\dot{W}$ (read W dot) denotes the percentage change in the wage rate and U^* is the equilibrium unemployment rate. If the actual unemployment rate is equal to the equilibrium unemployment rate, then the rate of wage inflation will be zero. For unemployment rates below (above) the equilibrium unemployment rate, wage inflation will be positive (negative). The greater the **gap** between the actual unemployment rate and the equilibrium unemployment rate, the larger the wage change (be it positive or negative). The parameter j indicates the effect on the size of wage changes for each one percentage point movement in the unemployment rate (for a given U^*). The greater the responsiveness of wages to labour market (disequilibrium) conditions, the larger will be the parameter j and the steeper the Phillips curve. Finally, if the equilibrium unemployment rate were to increase for any reason, the Phillips curve would shift upwards to the right (the vertical intercept jU^* would increase).

Friedman and the Role of Inflation Expectations

As Milton Friedman noted in his presidential address to the American Economics Association in December 1967,

> Phillips' analysis of the relation between unemployment and wage change is deservedly celebrated as an important and original contribution. But, unfortunately, it contains a basic defect—the failure to distinguish between *nominal* wages and *real* wages.[7]

Friedman argued that the Phillips curve must be restated in terms of the **real wage**, not the **nominal wage**:

> A lower level of unemployment is an indication that there is an excess demand for labor that will produce upward pressure on real wage rates. A higher level of unemployment is an indication that there is an excess supply of labour that will produce downward pressure on real wage rates.[8]

Even though wage rates (or wage contracts) are typically set in nominal terms, Friedman argued that both firms and workers make labour market decisions in terms of the real wage rate. Labour is obviously interested in the real value of its nominal wage; that is, the nominal wage adjusted to reflect its real purchasing power. Labour will demand wage increases to offset increases in retail prices and will strongly resist any wage settlement that does not keep pace with the cost of living. As discussed in Chapter 8, an increase in the price level (from P_0 to P_1) will shift the nominal wage–labour supply schedule to the left (from $S(P_0)$ to $S(P_1)$ in Chart 9-2). Without any compensating increase in the nominal wage, workers will reduce their supply of labour when the price level increases. Labour supply decisions are based on the real wage rate, not the nominal wage rate.

The firm's demand for labour also depends on the nominal wage adjusted for price level movements. In Chart 9-2 we have drawn a conventional downward-sloping labour demand curve in terms of the *nominal* wage rate. Now if all prices throughout the economy increase, including the price of the firm's output, this nominal wage–labour demand schedule will shift to the right. Given that the firm can now sell its products at a higher price level (P_1), the firm will want to expand production and hire more labour at the given nominal wage rate. An increase in

---

[7]Milton Friedman, "The Role of Monetary Policy," *American Economic Review*, March 1968, page 8.
[8]Ibid.

CHART 9-2 Demand and supply of labour under different price levels

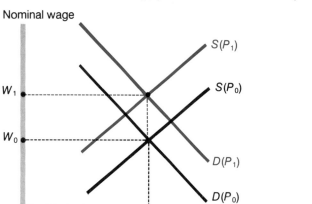

the price level produces an increase in the firm's demand for labour (from $D(P_0)$ to $D(P_1)$ in Chart 9-2).

Thus if all prices throughout the economy were to rise from P_0 to P_1, as drawn in Chart 9-2, the labour supply schedule would shift to the left and the labour demand schedule would shift to the right. At the existing wage rate W_0, a state of excess labour demand would arise and the nominal wage rate would eventually be bid up to its new *equilibrium* value, W_1. However, once the labour market has returned to equilibrium, the quantity of labour demanded and supplied (L^*) will be exactly the same as before prices increased. The nominal wage rate will have increased in direct proportion to the increase in price levels. As discussed in Chapter 8, *an increase in the price level has no effect on the real wage or the equilibrium quantity of labour*. Labour demand and supply decisions depend on the *real* wage, not the *nominal* wage.

It is important to recognize that the labour market differs from many other markets in one very important respect. Unlike auction markets, such as the stock exchange or commodity markets, the price of labour services does not typically change hourly, or daily, or even monthly. Approximately 40 per cent of the work force belongs to unions or employee associations, which typically sign wage contracts fixing the wage schedule for one, two or three years. Non-unionized employees usually have their wages reviewed once a year (an annual performance review), with an appropriate annual adjustment made to the wage rate. Explicit or implicit contracts in the labour market severely limit the short-run flexibility of the wage rate. Unlike auction markets, where prices are always changing, wage rates tend to be contractually fixed for considerable periods of time (one to three years).

Given such contractual rigidities in the labour market, Friedman argued that the relevant price consideration in formulating the *real* wage rate is the *expected* value of *future* prices. In bargaining for a new contract, workers judge a prospective wage rate for the *next* contract period vis-à-vis the *expected* price level of goods that will be purchased during this future contract period. If workers expect price levels to rise in the future, they will demand higher *current* wage settlements to compensate them for this *expected future* inflation. Firms will be willing to pay higher wage rates because they also expect their product prices, and therefore their total revenues, to rise.

Returning to Chart 9-2, suppose that a firm and a union are about to negotiate a new one-year contract. Let us assume that at the time of the negotiations the labour market is exactly in equilibrium, with a nominal wage rate of W_0 and a price level of P_0. Now if the labour demand and supply schedules are *expected* to remain stable over the next year, no wage adjustment will be required; the labour market is expected to remain in *equilibrium* throughout the year at the current *nominal* wage rate, W_0.

However, if price levels are expected to rise from P_0 to P_1 during the upcoming year, the labour demand and supply schedules will not be expected to remain stable, but rather will be expected to shift upwards during the course of the year. If *no* nominal wage adjustment is included in the new contract, these expected price increases (to the extent that they materialize) will create a disequilibrium state of excess labour demand for the entire contractual period (as the nominal wage remains at W_0). Such labour market disequilibrium imposes costs on both workers and the firm. Workers obviously suffer a real wage loss during the year if prices increase but nominal wage rates do not increase. If the real wage rate is below its competitive equilibrium level (because the nominal wage rate has not been increased), the firm will find it difficult to hire new workers to satisfy its additional demand for labour and to replace disgruntled workers who have quit because of the decline in the real wage rate during the course of the year.

If the nominal wage rate is not increased to offset the effects of this (expected) increase in the price level, a substantial amount of excess labour demand will build up over the course of the year. While this build-up of excess labour demand will trigger a "Phillips curve" wage adjustment at the time of the next contract negotiation (one year later), during the up-coming year both labour and the firm will experience disequilibrium costs arising from a decline in the *real* wage. To avoid these disequilibrium costs, the *nominal* wage rate should be increased to offset the effects of *expected* inflation. If the nominal wage rate increases in direct proportion to any price increase, the real wage rate will remain constant and the labour market will remain in a state of equilibrium (at L^* in Chart 9-2) throughout the contractual period.

Thus, the basic Phillips curve, as reformulated by Lipsey, must be augmented to include the expected inflation rate (over the next contractual period). Denoting the expected inflation rate by $\dot{P^e}$, equation 9-2 presents a *linear* version of the **price-expectations**-augmented **Phillips** curve, the *PEP* curve for short:

(9-2) $\dot{W} = \dot{P^e} + j\,(U^* - U)$

The rate of wage inflation now depends on two factors: excess demand in the labour market (which we represent by the difference between the equilibrium unemployment rate U^* and the actual unemployment rate U) and the expected inflation rate ($\dot{P^e}$). Either a decrease in the unemployment rate (for a given U*) or an increase in the expected inflation rate will lead to the larger wage increases.

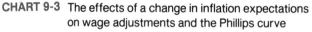

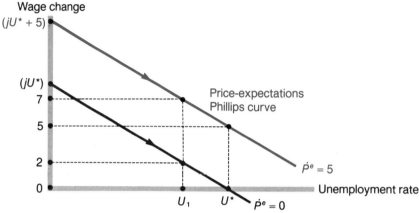

CHART 9-3   The effects of a change in inflation expectations on wage adjustments and the Phillips curve

Note in equation 9-2 we have assumed that the *nominal* wage rate will increase by the percentage increase in the *expected price level*; that is, the coefficient on $\dot{P}^e$ is implicitly unity. Each extra point of *expected* inflation increases the intercept of the (linear) Phillips curve by exactly one point. As depicted in Chart 9-3, an increase in the expected inflation rate from zero to 5 per cent will cause a 5 percentage point upward shift in the underlying Phillips curve and result in wage increases that are 5 per cent higher, irrespective of the level of the unemployment rate.

While earlier studies of the Phillips curve, such as those by Lipsey and Tinbergen, include a price inflation variable in their equations, Friedman's contribution to the Phillips curve literature is twofold. First, Friedman stressed that it is the *expected* inflation rate that is relevant in the wage determination process, as labour market participants are *forward-looking* (not *backward-looking*) in their wage behaviour. Second, on the basis of labour market theory, Friedman argued that the coefficient on inflation expectations in the price-expectations Phillips curve should be exactly equal to *one*, to preserve the *real* wage rate. Earlier studies of the Phillips curve frequently reported estimated inflation coefficients that were substantially less than unity. For *theoretical* reasons Friedman rejected the *empirical* possibility that the inflation coefficient could be less than unity. As we shall see in Chapter 12, a unity coefficient on expected inflation within the price-expectations Phillips curve has very important implications for the existence of a trade-off between inflation and unemployment.

Wage Adjustments and the Role of Productivity Growth

Conventional microeconomic theory suggests that workers will be paid their marginal product. Thus an increase in labour productivity ought to be reflected in an increase in the wage rate. For example, if workers increase their labour productivity by 2 per cent annually, then wages should increase by 2 per cent, *ceteris paribus*. In terms of our standard labour demand and supply diagram, an increase in labour productivity will shift the demand for labour schedule to the right as profit-maximizing firms will want to hire additional "more productive" workers, whatever the prevailing wage rate. For a given labour supply curve, such an increase in labour demand will cause an increase in the equilibrium wage rate.

Using the same argument as outlined above, if workers are expected to increase their productivity during the next contract period, a new wage contract signed by the firm will likely include an additional wage adjustment to reflect this expected increase in labour productivity. Without such a wage adjustment, the firm would be faced with the disequilibrium costs of excess labour demand during the contract period (because the demand for labour curve shifts to the right but the wage rate has not been adjusted). To avoid these disequilibrium costs, the new wage contract should include a provision for the *expected* growth in labour productivity. We assume that firms base their expectations of labour productivity growth on the average productivity growth rate over the recent past, which we represent by $P\dot{R}ODAV$.

Expanding our price-expectations augmented Phillips curve to include the effects of **labour productivity growth**, our linear *PEP* equation can be represented in the following manner:

$$(9\text{-}3) \qquad \dot{W} = P\dot{R}ODAV + \dot{P^e} + j(U^* - U)$$

Each extra point of labour productivity growth is assumed to increase the rate of wage inflation by one point. Even when the labour market is in equilibrium, the *real* wage rate increases one-for-one with labour productivity growth. However, the presence of the unemployment rate variable $(U^* - U)$ in equation 9-3 continues to give the Phillips curve its essential disequilibrium characteristics. Whenever the labour market is in disequilibrium, *nominal* wage rates will be changing and the labour market will be heading back towards a state of equilibrium. A non-zero value for labour productivity growth and/or expected inflation represents additional determinants of the rate of wage inflation, and affects nominal wage rates whether the labour market is in equilibrium or not.

The Empirical Evidence for a Canadian Phillips Curve

The Phillips, Lipsey and Friedman papers provided the stimulus for a great outpouring of empirical research on the wage determination process, and wage movements were no longer considered exogenous in macroeconomic models. While a number of early Canadian studies played a prominent role in the international acceptance of the Phillips curve concept,[9] the 1966 Economic

---

[9]Most notably the papers by S.F. Kaliski, "The Relation Between Unemployment and the Rate of Change of Money Wages in Canada," *International Economic Review*, January 1964, pp. 1-33; and John Vanderkamp, "Wage and Price Level Determination: An Empirical Model for Canada," *Economica*, May 1966. pp. 194-218.

Council of Canada special study entitled *Price Stability and High Employment: The Options for Canadian Economic Policy* has been described as the "definitive study of the 'trade-off' between price changes and unemployment in Canada up to the mid-1960's."[10] The central chapters of this 300-page study are devoted to an empirical analysis of wage and price relationships for Canada and five other countries. The authors summarize their lengthy econometric investigation of Canadian wages in the following manner: "With regard to the determinants of wage changes, we have found that the traditional explanatory variables, the level of unemployment and the rate of change of consumer prices, have a statistically significant influence."[11] Over the years 1953-65 the rate of Canadian wage inflation was found to vary *inversely* with the Canadian unemployment rate but *directly* with the rate of price inflation (although the estimated price coefficients were always less than unity).

In the upper panel of Chart 9-4 we present a scatter diagram for average annual wage settlements, based on new wage contracts (without a COLA clause) signed each year, and the unemployment rate. Since Labour Canada did not publish data on the size of new wage settlements until 1967, our scatter diagram is based on the years 1967 through 1984. In two dimensions this scatter diagram is somewhat discouraging, since the points appear to be almost randomly scattered throughout the diagram. However, our theoretical *PEP* curve model asserts that nominal wage settlements depend on three factors:

1) the gap between the equilibrium unemployment rate and the actual unemployment rate,
2) the expected inflation rate, and
3) the average labour productivity growth rate.

Assuming that the average productivity growth rate and the equilibrium unemployment rate remained relatively constant over this time period, the *PEP* curve model predicts that the size of wage settlements will depend on the unemployment rate and the expected inflation rate. A two-dimensional diagram ($\dot{W}$ and U) may easily produce a wide scatter of points if the missing factor ($\dot{P}^e$) is not constant over the time period.

The Canadian inflation rate and the expected inflation rate clearly were not constant over the 1967-84 period. For the years 1967 through 1972, the Canadian inflation rate fluctuated in the narrow interval between 2.9 and 4.8 per cent, averaging less than 4 per cent. For the next ten years the Canadian inflation rate ranged from 7.5 to 12.5 per cent, with an average value of 9.6 per cent. Finally, in 1983 and 1984 the inflation rate receded to 5.8 and 4.4 per cent.

To bring a little order to this scatter diagram, we have plotted the first six years, 1967-72, of relatively low inflation in red. These six *low* inflation observations tend to be scattered around a *low PEP* curve. The remaining observations for the

[10]S.F. Kaliski, *The Trade-Off Between Inflation and Unemployment: Some Explorations of the Recent Evidence for Canada*, Economic Council of Canada, Ottawa, 1972, p. v.

[11]R.G. Bodkin et al., *Price Stability and High Employment: The Options for Canadian Economic Policy*, Economic Council of Canada, Ottawa, 1966, p. 155.

CHART 9-4 Wage settlements–unemployment scatter
diagram, 1967-84

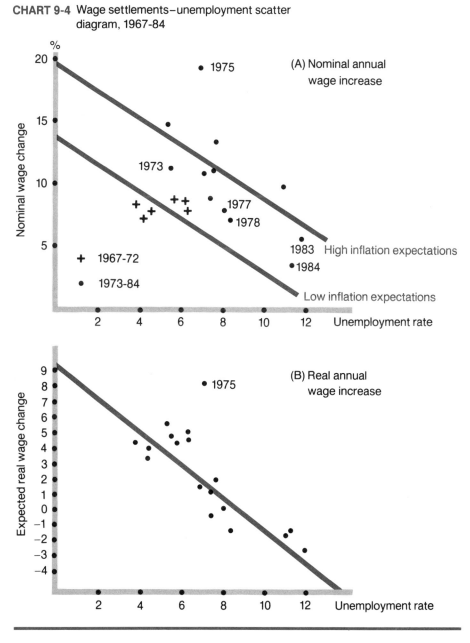

years 1973-84, plotted in black, tend to be scattered about a *high PEP* curve. The 1973 observation clearly straddles the low and high *PEP* curves, as do the 1983 and 1984 observations. The most obvious *outlier* is the 1975 observation. The extremely high average wage settlement of 19.2 per cent in 1975 reflected a substantial amount of wage *catch-up* for the unexpected double-digit inflation of

1974 and 1975.[12] The scatter of data points in the upper panel of Chart 9-4 is consistent with a *price-expectations Phillips* curve. As the (expected) inflation rate increased during the 1970s, the rate of wage inflation rose accordingly.

A more direct test of the Friedman price-expectations Phillips curve hypothesis would be to plot the change in the *expected real* wage against the unemployment rate. However before we can perform such a test, we must first quantify *inflation expectations*, another unobservable theoretical construct, to go along with excess labour demand. By their very nature, price expectations are highly subjective and difficult to quantify. There is a world of difference between obtaining a measure of today's price of beef and providing an estimate of what people *think* next year's price of beef will be. While attitudinal survey data on expected future price movements are available in some countries, no continuous survey data exist for Canada. This data deficiency has forced Canadian wage analysts to create their own synthetic inflation-expectations data. Postponing a discussion of the various ways people might form expectations of the future inflation rate until Chapter 17, we simply assume that labour market participants average the current and past annual inflation rate to produce an estimate for the expected future inflation rate (that is, future rates of inflation can be predicted from past inflation rates). To compute a proxy for the *expected real* wage change, we subtract this average inflation rate over the past two years (our estimate for $\dot{P}^e$) from the average size of current wage settlements.

The lower panel of Chart 9-4 presents a scatter diagram relating our proxy for the *expected real* wage change to the Canadian unemployment rate. Unlike the wide scatter of points in the upper panel, once the effects of inflation expectations have been taken into account, the Phillips curve provides a remarkably good explanation of changes in the *expected real* wage rate. Most of the points lie within one percentage point of the least squares line.[13] The estimated slope of the least squares regression line is −1.04, suggesting that each additional point of unemployment lowers the *expected real* wage increase by approximately 1 per cent. The empirical evidence presented in Chart 9-4 clearly demonstrates that nominal wage increases in Canada are strongly influenced by the unemployment rate and the expected inflation rate.

Price Movements

Domestic Costs

Having identified the factors that determine the size of wage changes throughout the economy (equation 9-3), we now turn our attention to an explanation of the factors that determine the rate of change of price levels. Unlike our static price

---

[12]Multi-year wage contracts signed before the unexpected outbreak of double-digit inflation were based on inflation expectations estimates that were far too low, and large "catch-up" wage increases were required to restore the *real* wage rate. For example, if a three-year wage contract signed in late 1972 was based on an expected inflation rate of 4 per cent, the cumulative 1973-75 inflation rate of over 29 per cent would have produced an unexpected real wage decline of over 17 per cent.

[13]Since the 1975 catch-up observation is an obvious outlier, we have omitted it from the calculation of the least squares line.

level analysis in Chapter 8, in this chapter we focus on the dynamics of inflation. Rather than specifying an aggregate supply function, we provide a direct explanation for the price determination process and the rate of price inflation. Given a downward-sloping aggregate demand curve, it is immaterial whether one completes the macroeconomic model with an aggregate supply function or a price determination equation. They represent opposite sides of the same coin. For example, if a firm knows its demand curve and sets a profit-maximizing price, this price decision determines exactly how much the firm will supply to the market place. The firm's pricing decision also represents the firm's supply function.

As a starting point for our analysis of the inflation rate, we assume that firms set individual prices by *marking up* the average cost of producing one unit of output. For example, if it costs $1.00 to produce one unit of output, a firm might sell its product at a price of $1.10, with the additional 10 per cent markup representing the firm's profit margin. In the following simple pricing equation, average unit costs (UC) are multiplied by the markup factor k, which exceeds unity in value ($k = 1.1$ in the above illustration).

$$P = k \times UC$$

As demonstrated in the appendix to this chapter, this simple **price markup model** is not incompatible with profit-maximization behaviour.

Before we can test this very simple hypothesis about firm pricing behaviour, we must define average (unit) costs. In total, wages account for almost three-quarters of net national income at factor cost. Postponing a discussion of other input costs until later, we begin by restricting our attention to average **unit labour costs** (ULC), the largest component of the economy's cost structure. *Average unit labour costs are the wage payments to labour for producing one unit of output.* Since most workers are paid on an hourly or weekly basis (not on a "piece rate" basis), wage rates must be converted into average unit labour costs. Obviously unit labour costs depend not only on the wage rate (W) but also on the productivity ($PROD$) of workers. If a worker can produce two widgets per hour and the wage rate is $5 per hour, then the ULC of one widget is $2.50.

$$ULC = W/PROD$$

Either an increase in the wage rate (say to $10 per hour) *or* a decrease in labour productivity (say to one widget produced per hour) would increase unit labour costs (to $5 per widget) and result in a higher "marked up" price for widgets. It is important to note that if wages and productivity levels *both* increase by the *same* percentage, then unit labour costs will *not* change. Only wage increases in excess of productivity increases result in higher unit labour costs and higher "marked up" prices.

To test this simple price markup model at the aggregate level, the upper panel of Chart 9-5 presents a scatter diagram in which the level of the Consumer Price Index (CPI) is plotted against the average unit labour cost (ULC) for all commercial non-agricultural industries in Canada (as published by Statistics Canada). As is obvious from the upper panel of Chart 9-5, the level of the Consumer Price Index is quite closely related to average unit labour costs in Canada. Most of the data points lie very close to an upward-sloping straight line.

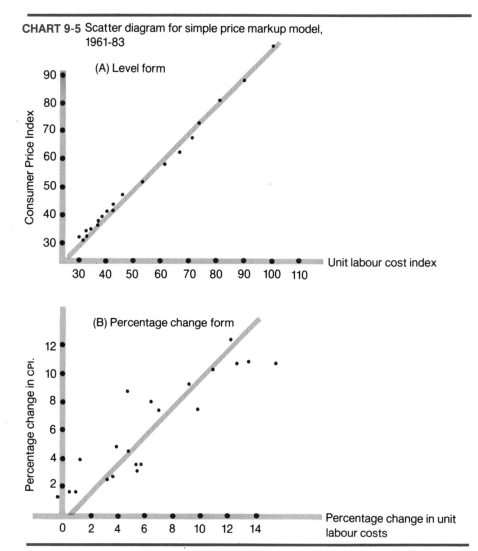

CHART 9-5 Scatter diagram for simple price markup model, 1961-83

(A) Level form

(B) Percentage change form

Throughout the remainder of this textbook we are primarily interested in the *rate* of price increase (the process of inflation), rather than the *level* of prices. Assuming a constant markup factor (k), the percentage change in price levels will be equal to the percentage change in average unit labour costs, which can be approximated by the percentage change in wage rates $(\dot{W})$ minus the percentage change in labour productivity growth $(P\dot{R}OD)$.[14]

$$(9\text{-}4) \qquad \dot{P} = U\dot{L}C = \dot{W} - P\dot{R}OD$$

[14]For example, if wage rates rise from \$5.00 to \$5.50 per hour (a 10 per cent increase) and productivity levels rise from 5.0 to 5.15 widgets per hour (a 3 per cent increase), unit labour costs will rise from \$1.00 to \$1.068 per widget(\$5.50/5.15). The percentage change in unit labour costs (6.8 per cent) is approximately equal to the percentage change in wage rates (10 per cent) minus the percentage change in labour productivity (3 per cent).

In terms of our previous widget example, when *ULC* increases by 100 per cent (from \$2.50 to \$5.00), the price of widgets also increases by 100 per cent (if *k* equals 1.1, the price of widgets increases from \$2.75 to \$5.50).

While the upper panel of Chart 9-5 provides strong statistical support for the proposition that the *level* of the Consumer Price Index is systematically related to average unit labour costs, this statistical relationship is not nearly as precise when the price markup model is transformed into percentage change form (see the lower panel of Chart 9-5). The *rate of change* in the Consumer Price Index (inflation) is positively related to the rate of change in average unit labour costs, but there is much more scatter to the diagram. By converting our price markup model into percentage change form, we have magnified the underlying errors in the model and have raised the possibility that perhaps our simple model is too simple. Other factors besides changes in average unit labour costs may influence the rate of price inflation in Canada. In the next section of the chapter we examine the influence of *changes* in the price of intermediate inputs, raw materials, and internationally traded goods on the domestic Canadian inflation rate. But before exploring the role of raw material and international price movements, we offer one minor amendment to the price markup model, an amendment that eliminates some of the statistical variation in the lower quadrant of Chart 9-5.

Most price analysts express the markup model in terms of *normal* unit labour costs, where the wage rate is divided by the average labour productivity growth rate. Given the strong cyclical elements in labour productivity growth (because of the use of overtime labour in booms and the hoarding of labour in recessions), expressing unit labour costs in terms of the current year's actual productivity growth imparts considerable variation to the percentage change in unit labour costs (see column 6 of Table 9-1). Since most firms wish to minimize transitory movements in price levels, they typically price their products in terms of *normal* unit labour costs, costs that would occur under *normal cyclical* conditions. Substituting average labour productivity growth rate ($P\dot{R}ODAV$) for the actual labour productivity growth rate ($P\dot{R}OD$) produces the following equation:

(9-4a) $\dot{P} = \dot{W} - PR\dot{O}DAV$

The rate of price inflation depends on the rate of wage inflation minus the average growth rate of labour productivity.

The Role of International Price Movements

At the individual firm level, the cost of producing a particular good depends not only on average labour costs but also on the price of material inputs that are necessary to produce the good. For example, General Motors must not only hire labour to produce an automobile, it must also purchase large quantities of steel, glass, rubber and other materials. In establishing a price for an automobile, General Motors must recover all production costs and will mark up material costs as well as labour costs. While this argument is undoubtedly important at the level of the individual firm, it loses much of its relevance for the economy as a whole. To produce the necessary material inputs for an automobile, other firms producing "intermediate" goods must hire labour. In other words, intermediate goods (such as steel and glass) can be traced back to an original source firm in which labour is the principal factor input (if one goes back far enough, one will find a worker). Consequently for the economy as a whole, average labour costs should also reflect the price level of most intermediate goods that are used in the production process.

For a self-contained *closed* economy one might safely dismiss raw-material price movements as a determinant of *aggregate* price levels and simply focus on labour costs. However, for an economy as *open* as Canada's, world price movements have a direct influence on the Canadian inflation rate. Obviously, Canadians must pay the world price for imported goods (which account for approximately 30 per cent of GNP). In addition, prices for foreign goods affect the prices of domestically produced goods that compete directly with imported goods. The price of a Toyota has a considerable influence on the price of a Ford or Chevrolet.

The influence of world prices on the Canadian inflation rate extends beyond the obvious effects from imported foreign goods. Consider the general case of internationally traded commodities and raw materials, such as grains, minerals and lumber. A large proportion of Canadian production is in the form of such raw materials, with much of this production being exported. Clearly world market conditions, not Canadian labour costs, are the prime determinant of the international price of such traded goods. In most instances, the Canadian supply of the traded good is a relatively small part of the world supply and has a minor impact on the international price for that particular good. Consequently, the price of many intermediate or raw material inputs into the Canadian production process will largely depend on world demand and supply conditions. If the raw material is imported, the Canadian importing firm must obviously pay the international price. Even if the intermediate input is domestically produced, the Canadian intermediate goods producing firm will charge the international price. Why should Stelco or Dofasco charge Canadian steel buyers a lower price than can be realized on world markets? To the extent that world prices are moving at a different rate than domestic unit labour costs, the Canadian rate of price inflation will be affected.

To allow for the influence of exogenous changes in the relative price of internationally traded goods, we expand our percentage change price-markup model to include the variable $\dot{FP}$,

(9-4b) $\dot{P} = \dot{W} - \dot{PRODAV} + f\dot{FP}$

where $\dot{FP}$ is defined as the percentage change in the price of internationally traded goods in excess of the percentage change in domestic unit labour costs (based on average labour productivity growth). If international prices are moving at the same rate as domestic labour costs, then $\dot{FP}$ is zero and has no additional impact on the domestic inflation rate. The parameter f indicates the extent to which $\dot{FP}$ affects the domestic rate of price inflation. Open economies that rely extensively on international trade will have a larger value for the parameter f than economies that are closed and self-sufficient.[15]

Changes in the relative prices of internationally traded goods, including food products, have had a major impact on the rate of Canadian price inflation. In

TABLE 9-1 Annual Percentage Changes in Key Price and Cost Indexes

	(1) Consumer Price Index	(2) Food Price Index	(3) CPI Excluding Food Prices	(4) World Commodity Prices	(5) Industry Selling Price Index	(6) Unit Labour Costs
1961	0.9	1.5	—	−2.8	0.3	—
1962	1.2	1.9	1.0	−2.4	1.0	−0.5
1963	1.7	3.2	1.2	13.7	1.3	0.8
1964	1.8	1.6	1.9	7.7	0.8	0.1
1965	2.5	2.6	2.3	1.1	1.3	3.0
1966	3.7	6.4	2.9	5.0	2.9	5.3
1967	3.6	1.3	4.4	−5.3	1.9	5.1
1968	4.0	3.3	4.4	−1.6	2.1	1.0
1969	4.5	4.3	4.6	8.8	3.7	4.5
1970	3.4	2.3	3.8	5.2	2.4	5.1
1971	2.8	1.1	3.5	−6.7	2.0	3.3
1972	4.8	7.6	3.7	29.3	4.4	3.8
1973	7.6	14.6	5.1	63.0	11.2	6.9
1974	10.9	16.3	8.8	23.0	19.0	13.3
1975	10.8	12.9	10.0	−13.3	11.2	15.3
1976	7.5	2.7	9.4	17.1	5.1	9.4
1977	8.0	8.3	7.9	21.4	7.9	6.4
1978	8.9	15.5	6.4	5.1	9.2	4.6
1979	9.2	13.2	7.9	22.0	14.5	7.5
1980	10.2	10.7	10.0	17.8	13.5	11.3
1981	12.5	11.4	12.8	−13.5	10.2	12.6
1982	10.8	7.2	11.8	−13.6	6.0	11.2
1983	5.8	3.7	6.4	12.7	3.5	2.0
1984	4.3	5.5	4.0	−1.0	4.1	—

Source: Canada, Department of Finance, *Economic Review*, April 1985. Column (4) is the *Economist* index of world commodity prices.

Table 9-1 we present annual percentage changes during the 1960s, 1970s and very early 1980s for a number of key price and cost variables. Columns two and three of Table 9-1 split the Consumer Price Index into two parts: the food component and all other components of the CPI. During the 1960s Canadian food prices fluctuated within a fairly narrow interval, but then rapidly accelerated during the 1970s.

---

[15]As discussed in Chapter 7, the effects of foreign price movements on domestic price levels depend on the foreign exchange rate policy adopted by the government. Under a *fixed* exchange rate policy, any change in foreign prices will be fully reflected in the variable *FP* in equation 9-4b. However, under a *flexible* exchange rate policy, the foreign exchange rate will tend to adjust to offset differences between domestic and international price movements (the *purchasing power parity* theory). Provided that we measure foreign price movements and the variable *FP* in Canadian dollars, equation 9-4b remains valid for a *flexible* exchange rate policy. Compared with a *fixed* exchange rate policy, a *flexible* exchange rate will tend to mute part of the effects of foreign price increases that are in excess of domestic price increases and thus reduce the value of the variable *FP*.

Compared with an average increase of 3 per cent a year during the 1960s, the average annual increase in food prices during the 1970s was 9.5 per cent and exceeded 12 per cent in five different years (1973, 1974, 1975, 1978 and 1979). Such an escalation in food prices can largely be attributed to weather conditions in Canada and other agricultural producing countries. Given the 21.5 per cent weight attached to food prices within the CPI, exogenous changes in international food prices can exert a significant impact on the overall rate of increase in consumer prices. For example, the two very large increases in food prices in 1973 and 1974, 14.6 per cent and 16.3 per cent respectively, pushed the total CPI up by an *extra 2.3 per cent per annum*. On the other hand, the very modest increase in food prices in 1976 (2.7 per cent) substantially moderated the overall inflation rate (from 9.4 per cent down to 7.5 per cent). Erratic movements in food prices, which are largely determined by weather and international market conditions, can cause the overall inflation rate to deviate from the path of domestic labour costs.

The rapid escalation of food price increases during the early 1970s is but one example of the unprecedented explosion of raw material and commodity prices on world markets. Even setting aside crude oil price increases and the OPEC cartel (which are discussed in Chapter 15), commodity price increases during 1973 and 1974 were simply astounding. The British *Economist* index of world commodity prices, column 4 in Table 9-1, more than doubled (when compounded) during these two years. For the more than 100 years for which the *Economist* commodity price index has been compiled, there has never been a one-, two-, or three-year change that can match the commodity price movements of the early 1970s. Compared with an average annual increase of over 16 per cent for the 1970s, the average annual increase in world commodity prices was only 2.4 per cent during the 1960s.

Given this very sharp rise in raw material and commodity prices during the early 1970s, the prices of most manufactured products rose accordingly. For example, the Canadian wholesale industry selling price index, column 5 in Table 9-1, increased by almost 33 per cent (when compounded) during 1973-74 whereas domestic unit labour costs, column 6 in Table 9-1, rose by only 21 per cent during these two years. This rapid escalation in the prices of internationally traded goods, relative to domestic labour costs, was a key factor in the emergence of double-digit inflation in 1974. The Canadian inflation rate can easily diverge from the path of average labour costs when the prices of food, raw materials and other internationally traded commodities suddenly increase or decrease.

Summary and Concluding Comments

Our structural explanation of the inflation process is based on two interrelated theories of wage and price behaviour. Invoking a *markup* theory of firm pricing behaviour, the rate of increase in price levels is assumed to vary directly with the percentage change in *normal* unit labour costs and with the rate of increase in foreign prices in excess of domestic labour costs. Approximating the percentage change in normal unit labour costs by the percentage change in wage rates ($\dot{W}$) minus the percentage change in average labour productivity growth ($\dot{PRODAV}$), we obtain the following markup equation for the rate of price inflation.

(9-4b) $\dot{P} = \dot{W} - \dot{PRODAV} + f\dot{FP}$

While we assume that the average labour productivity growth rate and foreign price changes are *exogenously* determined, the rate of wage inflation is a key *endogenous* variable within our model.

Following the important research of Phillips, Lipsey and Friedman, we assume that the rate of wage inflation depends on three factors: (1) the *expected* rate of price inflation $(\dot{P}^e)$, (2) the average labour productivity growth rate $(\dot{PRODAV})$, and (3) excess labour demand, which we represent by the gap between the equilibrium unemployment rate U^* and the actual unemployment rate (U). A decrease in the unemployment rate (for a given U^*) will cause an increase in the rate of wage inflation. Our basic *price-expectations Phillips* curve is represented by equation 9-3.

(9-3) $\dot{W} = \dot{P}^e + \dot{PRODAV} + j(U^* - U)$

Substituting this *disequilibrium* Phillips wage-change relationship into the above *markup* price change equation produces the following combined inflation relationship:

(9-5) $\dot{P} = f\dot{FP} + \dot{P}^e + j(U^* - U)$

Since the two $\dot{PRODAV}$ terms cancel each other out, the rate of price inflation depends on foreign price movements $(f\dot{FP})$, inflation expectations $(\dot{P}^e)$, and the gap between the equilibrium unemployment rate (U^*) and the actual unemployment rate (U). To keep the subsequent analysis as simple as possible, we ignore the effects of foreign price changes $(\dot{FP})$ until Chapter 15, at which time we undertake a complete macroeconomic analysis of price shocks such as the OPEC quadrupling of oil prices in the early 1970s. Temporarily assuming that $\dot{FP}$ is zero, equation 9-5 further simplifies to the following equation:

(9-5a) $\dot{P} = \dot{P}^e + j(U^* - U)$

The rate of price inflation depends on the *expected* inflation rate and the unemployment rate (for a given equilibrium unemployment rate), the *price-expectations Phillips* curve.

The Phillips curve can be thought of as a bridge between the *classical* assumption of instantly flexible wage rates with labour market equilibrium and the *Keynesian* assumption of downward wage rigidity with persistent unemployment. Under the Phillips curve hypothesis, wage and price inflation (deflation) will occur whenever the unemployment rate is below (above) the equilibrium unemployment rate. By expanding the Phillips curve to include the role of inflation expectations, the simultaneous occurrence of both high inflation (because of high inflation expectations) and high unemployment can also be explained. Thus the Phillips curve provides an explanation, absent from both classical and Keynesian models, of how an economic system can simultaneously experience *both* inflation *and* unemployment.

Before leaving this chapter, we briefly consider the meteoric rise of the Phillips curve concept during the 1960s. Simple variants of the Phillips curve (without price expectations) were quickly assimilated into the conventional economic wisdom and almost immediately the Phillips curve took on "a life of its own."[16] This rapid acceptance of the Phillips curve concept by both economists and policy makers can largely be attributed to two basic factors. First, from a macroeconomic perspective the Phillips curve describes an economic system in which *both* inflation *and* unemployment can simultaneously exist. Macroeconomics was no longer confined to the straight jacket of either *zero* inflation or *full* employment.

Second, the policy ramifications of a negative relationship between inflation and unemployment were ominous and could not be overlooked. The Phillips curve introduced an important new constraint into macroeconomic policy formulation. If the government pursues an expansionary demand-management policy to reduce unemployment, wages and prices will start to rise at faster and faster rates. The desirable goals of low employment and low inflation are not mutually obtainable, and the Phillips curve suggests that low rates of unemployment may have to be *traded off* against higher rates of inflation, or vice versa. Conducting macroeconomic policy was now thought to be akin to riding a teeter-totter. The more one tries to get one end down, say inflation, the higher up the other end, unemployment, will go. In this context, the rapid conversion of policy makers to the Phillips curve concept is perhaps understandable. A government should not be expected to lower *both* inflation *and* unemployment *simultaneously*: the best that policy makers can do is to *trade off* one problem for the other. The notion of a trade-off between unemployment and inflation was quickly incorporated into the politician's lexicon, and the Phillips curve became a popular explanation or rationalization for the existence of either unemployment or inflation.

As we shall see in subsequent chapters, our explanation of the inflationary process runs much deeper than the Phillips curve. To determine the rate of price inflation we must know the unemployment rate and the expected inflation rate, both of which are *endogenous* in a full macroeconomic model. As discussed in Chapters 5 and 6, the level of output and employment is determined within the *IS-LM* model by another set of exogenous variables including the government's choice of monetary and fiscal policy. If the government pursues a more expansionary monetary or fiscal policy, the unemployment rate would decline and the inflation rate would rise (via the Phillips curve). However, when the inflation rate increases, people might adjust their inflation expectations upwards, thus causing the price-expectations Phillips curve to shift upwards. Under such circumstances, an expansionary policy produces both a movement along and a shift in the Phillips curve. The Phillips curve would *not* represent a *stable* inflation–unemployment *trade-off* curve that policy makers could exploit.

The next six chapters sort out the complex interactions that are likely to take place in a macroeconomic model in which both the inflation rate and the unem-

---

[16]To illustrate the speed with which the Phillips curve was assimilated into economic theory, the 1961 revision of Samuelson's widely used introductory economics textbook included a section on Phillips' 1958 paper.

ployment rate can vary. The next chapter begins this process by incorporating the *price-expectations Phillips* curve into the *IS-LM* framework, and the following chapters are devoted to a systematic analytical review of the major policy implications of this integrated output–unemployment–inflation macroeconomic model. As we shall see in Chapter 12, the policy implications of the Phillips curve are much more subtle than they appeared to be in the 1960s. The inclusion of inflation expectations within the Phillips curve eliminates the possibility of a permanent or lasting *trade-off* between inflation and unemployment. Attempts by Keynesian policy makers to lower the unemployment rate below the equilibrium unemployment rate will lead to repeated upward shifts in the Phillips curve as inflation expectations are continually adjusted upwards. Keynesian policy cannot permanently reduce the unemployment rate (below the equilibrium unemployment rate) by accepting a higher *stable* inflation rate. Any attempts to do so will trigger a wage-price spiral and an accelerating inflation rate. Even though the possibility of a permanent trade-off between inflation and unemployment has been discredited, the *trade-off* dogma continued to live on. One cannot help but recall Lord Keynes' closing remarks in the *General Theory*:

> The ideas of economists and political philosophers, both when they are right and when they are wrong, are more powerful than is commonly understood. Indeed the world is ruled by little else. Practical men, who believe themselves to be quite exempt from any intellectual influences, are usually the slave of some defunct economist. Madmen in authority, who hear voices in the air, are distilling their frenzy from some academic scribbler of a few years back.[17]

Appendix: Marginal-Cost Pricing Behaviour

A central tenet of microeconomic theory is the assertion that a profit-maximizing firm will attempt to equate the marginal cost of producing one extra unit of output to the marginal revenue obtained from selling one extra unit of output. Since marginal revenue can be directly linked to the firm's product price by making use of the price elasticity of the firm's demand curve, and marginal cost depends on the price and productivity of the factors of production, a marginal cost-marginal revenue pricing rule is not incompatable with a simple markup model of firm pricing. Before illustrating how one might translate the marginal cost–marginal revenue rule into a price markup model, we briefly review several concepts from microeconomics.

Marginal Revenue

Given a downward-sloping demand curve, a firm must lower its price level to sell additional units of output. The change in total revenues ΔTR associated with a

---

[17]Keynes, *General Theory*, p. 383..

downward movement along the demand curve can be approximated by the following expression:

(9A-1) $\Delta TR = (P \bullet \Delta Q) + (Q \bullet \Delta P)$

The first component of equation 9A-1 measures the extra revenues associated with selling more units of output while the second component reflects the loss in revenues from selling all previous units of output at the new lower price level, where ΔP is negative and ΔQ is positive. The marginal revenue MR from selling one more unit of output can be obtained by dividing equation 9A-1 by ΔQ.

$$MR = \frac{\Delta TR}{\Delta Q} = \left(P \bullet \frac{\Delta Q}{\Delta Q}\right) + \left(Q \bullet \frac{\Delta P}{\Delta Q}\right)$$

(9A-2)   or $MR = P + \left(Q \bullet \dfrac{\Delta P}{\Delta Q}\right)$

By factoring P out of the MR expression and rearranging terms, the following relationship between MR, P and the price elasticity of the firm's demand curve ρ can be obtained:

$$MR = P\left[1 + \left(\frac{Q}{P} \cdot \frac{\Delta P}{\Delta Q}\right)\right]$$

$$MR = P\left[1 + \left(\frac{1}{\dfrac{P}{Q} \cdot \dfrac{\Delta Q}{\Delta P}}\right)\right]$$

(9A-3) $MR = P\left[1 + \dfrac{1}{\rho}\right]$

Marginal Cost

To determine the marginal cost of producing an additional unit of output, we assume that labour L is the only variable factor of production. Marginal cost can then be represented by the wage rate W that must be paid to additional workers divided by the marginal productivity of labour MPL.

(9A-4) $MC = \dfrac{W}{MPL}$

The marginal productivity of labour will depend on the precise nature of the production function (or process). If we assume that the production function has the following Cobb-Douglas form,

(9A-5) $Q = L^\alpha K^\beta$

then, with a little help from calculus, the MPL can be shown to be directly proportional to the *average* level of labour productivity $PROD$.

(9A-6) $$MPL = \frac{dQ}{dL} = \alpha L^{a-1}K^{\beta} = \alpha\left(\frac{L^{\alpha}K^{\beta}}{L}\right) = \alpha\left(\frac{Q}{L}\right) = \alpha PROD$$

Thus, the marginal cost of producing an extra unit of output under Cobb-Douglas production conditions is directly proportional to the ratio of the wage rate divided by the average level of labour productivity.

(9A-7) $$MC = \frac{W}{MPL} = \left(\frac{W}{\alpha PROD}\right)$$

If the profit-maximizing firm has achieved equality between MC and MR, we can then equate equations 9A-3 and 9A-7 to describe the firm's pricing decision.

$$MR = MC$$

$$P\left(1 + \frac{1}{\rho}\right) = \frac{W}{\alpha PROD}$$

(9A-8) $$P = \frac{W}{\left(1 + \frac{1}{\rho}\right)\alpha PROD} = \lambda\left(\frac{W}{PROD}\right) = \lambda(ULC)$$

Assuming Cobb-Douglas production conditions and a *constant* price elasticity of demand ρ, marginal-cost pricing suggests that the price level will be directly proportional to the wage rate divided by average labour productivity, where the proportionality factor λ depends on the parameters α and ρ. Provided that the price elasticity of the demand curve ρ and the underlying production technology α do not change, the profit-maximizing firm would mark up unit labour costs $W/PROD$ by the constant factor λ. A markup theory of pricing behaviour is not incompatible with profit-maximizing behaviour.

Key Concepts

Phillips curve
the gap between the equilibrium and actual unemployment rate
nominal versus real wage rates
price expectations as a determinant of wages
labour productivity
markup model of firm pricing behaviour
unit labour costs

Review Questions

1. Contrast the views of Keynes, Tinbergen and Phillips with respect to the causes of wage inflation.
2. Outline and explain the key assumptions in Lipsey's theoretical derivation of a wage adjustment function.
3. Explain why an increase in the equilibrium unemployment rate will cause the Phillips curve to shift upwards to the right.

4. Why does Friedman argue that 100 per cent of inflation expectations will be incorporated into wage settlements? Do Canadian data support Friedman's inflation expectations–wage inflation hypothesis?
5. Explain why wage settlements and the wage Phillips curve will reflect an increase in labour productivity.
6. What are the major factors that determine the price that a firm will charge for its products? How can these pricing factors be translated into a theory of aggregate price inflation?
7. Explain why foreign price movements affect the Canadian inflation rate.
8. How does declining productivity growth affect the rate of price inflation and the Phillips curve?

A Macroeconomic Model of Inflation, Interest Rates, Unemployment and Output: *IS-LM*ism with *PEP*

10

The following sketchy account of the "prospecting"–ceremony among the Macro brings out several of the riddles that currently perplex Econologists.... The elder grasps the LM with his left hand and the IS with his right and, holding the totem out in front of himself with elbows slightly bent, proceeds in a straight line—"gazing neither left nor right" in the words of their ritual—out over the chosen terrain. The grads of the village skip gaily around him at first, falling silent as the trek grows longer and more wearisome. On this occasion, it was long indeed and the terrain difficult... the grads were strung out in a long, morose and bedraggled chain behind their leader who, sweat pearling his brow, face cast in grim determination, stumbled onward over the obstacles in his path.... At long last, the totem vibrates, then oscillates more and more; finally, it points, quivering, straight down. The elder waits for the grads to gather round and then pronounces with great solemnity: "Behold, the Truth, and Power of the Macro."[2]

Axel Leijonhufvud[1]

The objective of this chapter is to combine the theories of the last five chapters into an integrated macroeconomic model of inflation, interest rates, output, and unemployment. The *IS-LM* apparatus, the essence of Keynesian economics, will continue to form a key part of our macroeconomic model. However, the inclusion of a price-expectations-augmented Phillips (*PEP*) curve within the model allows us to consider the determination of output and interest rates in an inflationary world. In the course of analyzing the properties of the *IS-LM* model with a *PEP* curve, we will be able to shed considerable light on some of the key differences between the monetarist camp and economists of a more Keynesian persuasion. Perhaps surprisingly, the *IS-LM-PEP* model is consistent with both Keynesian and monetarist beliefs about the effects of fiscal and monetary policy on output and unemployment rates. Even though fiscal and monetary policy can have very important *short-run* effects on output (a Keynesian proposition), the *long-run* multiplier effects may very well turn out to be zero (a monetarist proposition).

As in Part II of this textbook, we begin our analysis of the basic properties of the *IS-LM-PEP* macroeconomic model by abstracting from balance of payments considerations. The next chapter incorporates the *BP* curve analysis of Chapter 7

[1]A. Leijonhufvud, "Life Among the Econ," *Economic Inquiry*, September 1973, pp. 331-32.

into the *IS-LM-PEP* model and analyzes the effects of fiscal and monetary policy in an open, inflationary economy under both flexible and fixed foreign-exchange rates. Before providing a more formal analysis of the macroeconomic effects of monetary and fiscal policy in the context of inflation, we must first demonstrate that our *IS-LM-PEP* model has a unique, stable equilibrium solution. Only one missing link must be discussed before solving the complete *IS-LM-PEP* model. First, we must directly link up the unemployment rate from the *PEP* diagram with the level of real output in the *IS-LM* diagram.

The *PEP* Curve Expressed in Output Terms

We have frequently referred to an increase in the level of output as being synonymous with a lower unemployment rate. If output increases, then more labour will be required to produce this additional output and, *ceteris paribus*, the unemployment rate should fall. In this section of the chapter we review and formalize this negative relationship between movements in the unemployment rate and movements in output levels.

The upper panel of Chart 10-1 presents a conventional set of labour demand and supply curves. When the labour market is in equilibrium at the real wage $(W/P)^*$, the quantity of labour employed will be L^*. Given the economy's aggregate production function (see the middle panel of Chart 10-1), this equilibrium quantity of labour L^* will produce the equilibrium output level Y^*. As discussed in Chapters 8 and 9, even when the labour market is in equilibrium, some frictional and structural unemployment (which we denote by U^*, the equilibrium unemployment rate) will still exist. In the lower panel of Chart 10-1, which plots the relationship between the unemployment rate and the level of output, point A represents this equilibrium combination of output Y^* and unemployment U^*.

Now suppose that the real wage rate rises to $(W/P)_1$. Given this higher real wage, firms will decrease their demand for labour services from L^* to L_1, and a number of previously employed individuals will find themselves out of work. As employment and output levels decline below their equilibrium levels, the unemployment rate increases above the equilibrium unemployment rate U^*. In the bottom panel of Chart 10-1 we have also plotted this higher unemployment rate, labelled U_1, against the lower level of output Y_1 (point B).

As the amount of labour employed declines below the equilibrium employment level L^*, say to L_1, the unemployment rate rises from U^* to U_1 and the output level falls from Y^* to Y_1. Connecting points A and B in the lower panel of Chart 10-1 produces a downward-sloping line; a decrease in output is accompanied by an increase in the unemployment rate. This downward-sloping U-Y line can be represented by the following equation, which links deviations in U from U^* to deviations in Y from Y^*:

(10-1) $(U^* - U) = -v(Y^* - Y)$

or $U = U^* + v(Y^* - Y) = U^* + vY^* - vY$

Whenever Y is equal to Y^*, U will be equal to U^*. However, as Y declines below Y^*, U rises above U^*. A decrease in output Y will be accompanied by an increase

CHART 10-1 The relationship between unemployment and output

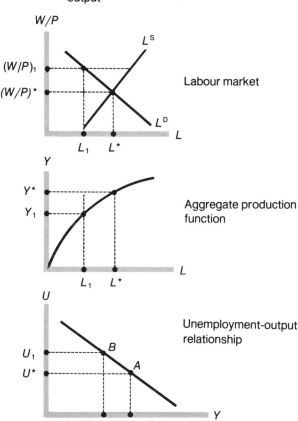

Labour market

Aggregate production function

Unemployment-output relationship

in the unemployment rate U, assuming U^* and Y^* remain constant.

Since the *IS-LM* diagram is expressed in output terms, there are obvious advantages in converting our inflation–*unemployment PEP* curve relationship into an inflation–*output* relationship. If all major macroeconomic curves (*IS*, *LM* and *PEP*) are expressed in output terms, we can then employ a common horizontal output axis for both the *IS-LM* diagram and the *PEP* curve diagram. The unemployment axis in the *PEP* curve diagram can be readily converted to an output axis by substituting equation 10-1 into our price-expectations-augmented Phillips curve equation (9-5).

(9-5) $\quad \dot{P} = \dot{P}^e + f\dot{F}P + j(U^* - U)$

(10-2) $\quad \dot{P} = \dot{P}^e + f\dot{F}P - jv(Y^* - Y)$

$\quad$ or $\quad \dot{P} = \dot{P}^e + f\dot{F}P - jvY^* + jvY$

A higher level of output corresponds to a lower unemployment rate, and therefore a higher rate of wage and price inflation. In output terms, the *price-expectations-augmented Phillips* curve slopes upwards.

In Chart 10-2 we have plotted this upward-sloping inflation–output *PEP* curve. In fact, this *upward*-sloping inflation–*output PEP* curve is simply a mirror image of the *downward*-sloping inflation–*unemployment PEP* curve of Chapter 9 (see, for example, Chart 9-3).[2] If one views the inflation–output diagram from right to left—that is, backwards—then the inflation–output *PEP* curve slopes downwards. Lower rates of wage and price inflation are associated with lower output levels and higher unemployment rates. Since it will frequently be useful to switch back to an inflation–unemployment context, in Chart 10-2 we have included a lower horizontal axis running from right to left. This backward-facing axis denotes the implicit unemployment rate associated with a particular income level. As described by equation 10-1, unemployment is a *negative* function of the level of real output (for a given U^* and Y^*). Throughout the remainder of the text, we will frequently include this unemployment axis to allow us to translate output levels into unemployment rates.

The *IS-LM-PEP* Model

Brief Summary of Major Components

Having analyzed the relationship between the level of output and the rate of unemployment, we can now bring together the various economic relationships developed in earlier chapters to form an integrated macroeconomic model that will determine the inflation rate, the level of output, the interest rate, and the unemployment rate. Postponing a discussion of balance of payments (*BP* curve) repercussions and the foreign exchange rate until the next chapter, our macroeconomic model now consists of the following three major composite relationships:

(5-10)   *IS* Curve: $R = \dfrac{1}{e}(a - bT_0 + I_a + G + X - n) - \dfrac{1}{e}(1 - b + bt + m)\,Y$

(8-2)   *LM* Curve: $R = -\$/\ell P + (k/\ell)Y$

(10-2)   *PEP* Curve: $\dot{P} = \dot{P}^e + f\dot{F}P - jvY^* + jvY$

Recall from Chapter 8 that in an inflationary world one's demand for *nominal* money depends on the price level, as well as on real income levels and market interest rates. Consequently, the intercept of the *LM* curve depends on the *real* money supply, the *nominal* money supply deflated by the existing price level. As also discussed in Chapter 8 (and portrayed in Chart 10-1), Y^* represents the amount of output that can be produced, according to the economy's aggregate production function, when the labour market is in equilibrium.

The *IS*, *LM*, and *PEP* curves are the major building blocks of our inflation–output macroeconomic model and will be used extensively throughout the

---

[2] As a historical footnote, we note that Phillips first suggested such an upward-sloping inflation–output relationship in 1954, four years prior to his now famous 1958 paper (see A.W. Phillips, "Stabilisation Policy in a Closed Economy," *Economic Journal*, June 1954, pp. 290-323). In a sense, this upward-sloping inflation–output curve is a 1954-vintage Phillips curve.

CHART 10-2 The PEP curve

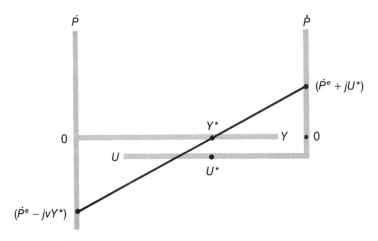

remaining chapters of this text. The key exogenous variables in our model can be divided into two categories: (1) policy instruments that are under the direct control of the government (G, T_0, t, $\$^S$) and (2) uncontrollable autonomous factors (I_a, X, $\dot{F}P$). If any of these exogenous variables change, either the *IS*, *LM*, or *PEP* curve will shift and a state of macroeconomic disequilibrium will arise. Much of this chapter is devoted to an analysis of the macroeconomic disequilibrium that follows a change in the value of various exogenous variables and to an analysis of the characteristics of macroeconomic equilibrium.

Before "solving" our macroeconomic model, we must clarify the status of one particular variable, the expected inflation rate $\dot{P}^e$. In the previous paragraph we have not classified $\dot{P}^e$ as an exogenous variable, nor have we provided a structural equation to "explain" inflation expectations. It would be very hard to argue that the expected inflation rate is exogenous and independent of macroeconomic phenomena. One's expectations concerning future inflation rates are undoubtedly shaped by recent inflation experience and government policies adopted (or not adopted) to "fight inflation". The precise process by which people form their expectations concerning the future inflation rate is not obvious, however, and the process of inflation expectations formation has become the subject of intense debate in macroeconomics. Given the inherent problems in measuring the expected inflation rate, most of this macroeconomic debate has been highly theoretical and speculative.

Instead of adopting a particular theoretical hypothesis about the manner in which people *might* form their inflation expectations, we have chosen to introduce the concept of inflation expectations into our macroeconomic model in stages. We begin our analysis by assuming that the expected inflation rate is fixed at zero ($\dot{P}^e = 0$). Having solved our complete macroeconomic model under this admittedly unrealistic assumption, we then allow inflation expectations to adjust (in a single step) to past inflation rates. Finally, a complete analysis of different inflation-expectations models, and their macroeconomic implications, is presented in Chapter 17. By staging the entry of inflation expectations into our macroeconomic story, we not only simplify the early analysis of our *IS-LM-PEP* model, we also highlight the key role that inflation expectations have played in the development of macroeconomic thought and in the debate between Keynesian, monetarist and new classical economists.

Equilibrium in the *IS-LM-PEP* Macroeconomic Model

As summarized above, our integrated output–inflation model consists of three composite relationships or equations (the *IS*, *LM* and *PEP* equations), plus the amount of output Y^* produced when the labour market is in equilibrium. Chart 10-3 presents our basic two-panel diagram, which will be used extensively throughout the remainder of this text. The upper panel depicts the *IS-LM* curves while the lower panel presents our derived inflation–output *PEP* curve.[3] Both panels share a common horizontal axis, the level of real output. We have identified the level of output Y^* associated with labour market equilibrium and have added a backward-facing unemployment axis in the lower panel. For our initial analysis of the *IS-LM-PEP* model, we assume that the expected inflation rate is zero, and have labelled the *PEP* curve accordingly. Unlike the aggregate demand and supply model presented in Chapter 8, the *IS-LM-PEP* model permits us to determine the inflation rate and the interest rate directly from the diagram, as well as providing a convenient analytical tool to describe disequilibrium adjustments in the economy.

Suppose that the labour market is in equilibrium and the economy is producing an aggregate output level of Y^*. Given the existing positions of the *IS* and *LM* curves in Chart 10-3, Y^* represents the only real income level that is consistent with both product market and money market equilibrium (Y^* is the intersection point of the *IS* and *LM* curves). As long as the *IS* and *LM* curves do not shift, Y^* and R^* represent the equilibrium position for this economy, as all three major macroeconomic markets (goods, money, and labour) are simultaneously in a state of equilibrium. Assuming a *given* set of *exogenous* variables (G, T_0, $\$^S$, X and I_a), the only variable that could prevent Y^* and R^* from being the equilibrium solution to our model is the *endogenous* price level, a variable that can shift the intercept of the *LM* curve. As discussed in Chapter 8, if the price level changes, the *real* money supply $\$^S/P$ will change, and the *LM* curve will shift. If the *LM* curve shifts, Y^* and R^* no longer correspond to the intersection point of the *IS* and (new) *LM* curves. Under such circumstances, the goods market or money market (or both) are no longer in a state of equilibrium at an income level of Y^*. For Y^* and R^* to be the equilibrium position for the economy, it must be demonstrated that the *LM* curve will not shift (that is, the price level will not change).

---

[3]To our knowledge, this two-panel diagram of the *IS-LM*-Phillips curve was first suggested by Richard Lipsey. While Professor Lipsey used this two-panel diagram extensively in classroom presentations at Queen's University during the early 1970s, we believe that it first appeared in print in 1978. See R. G. Lipsey, "The Place of the Phillips Curve in Macroeconomic Models," in *Stability and Inflation*, A. R. Bergstrom et al., ed., (Chichester, England: John Wiley & Sons, 1978), pp. 49-75.

CHART 10-3 Equilibrium in the basic *IS-LM-PEP* model

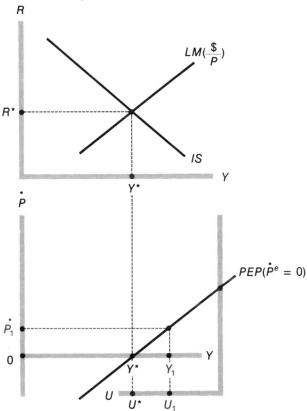

As drawn in the lower panel of Chart 10-3, a real income level of Y^* generates a zero inflation rate along the *PEP* curve. Provided that the *PEP* curve does not shift (Y^*, U^* and $\dot{P}^e$ do not change), when income is equal to Y^* price levels will remain constant and the *LM* curve will remain stationary. For the given set of exogenous variables, the economic system will remain at Y^* and R^*, the equilibrium solution to our *IS-LM-PEP* model. Note that in equilibrium the inflation rate is zero, and people's inflation expectations (which we assume to be zero) are correct.

It can easily be demonstrated that this equilibrium income level (Y^*) is *unique*. For all income levels other than Y^*, the inflation rate generated by the *PEP* curve will *not* be zero and price levels will be changing. For example, when income is at the level Y_1 in Chart 10-3, price levels will rise by $\dot{P}_1$ during each interval of time. As discussed in Chapter 8, a change in price levels will affect the real supply of money, causing the *LM* curve to shift. For all income levels other than Y^*, price levels will be changing and the *LM* curve will be shifting. Each time the *LM* curve shifts, a new *IS-LM* intersection point will emerge and a new level of income will arise. The economy clearly cannot be at rest in an equilibrium position if income levels are constantly changing. Since Y^* represents the unique income level for which price levels are constant and therefore the *LM* curve remains stationary, it is the only income level which will sustain itself. All other income levels will lead to inflation or deflation, shifts in the *LM* curve, and a changing output level.

Although we have demonstrated that Y^* represents the unique income level in our model for which the goods, money, and labour markets are all simultaneously in equilibrium, we have not yet proved that this is a *stable* equilibrium position. What will happen if the economic system experiences a level of income different from the equilibrium value of Y^*? Will the economic system remain out of equilibrium or will it tend to gravitate back towards the equilibrium income level Y^*? With all economic models it is important to demonstrate that the equilibrium position is stable, that the economic system will move from any disequilibrium state back to the equilibrium position. In demonstrating the **stability of the Y^* equilibrium income position** in our macroeconomic model, we also obtain a preview of the key dynamic features of the *IS LM PEP* model.

Chart 10-4 replicates the basic two-panel diagram presented in Chart 10-3, with one crucial difference: the red *LM* curve associated with a real money stock of $\$/P_1$ does not intersect the *IS* curve at the equilibrium income level Y^*. As displayed in Chart 10-4, the economic system is experiencing an income level Y_1 that is considerably larger than our equilibrium income level Y^*. The key question is whether the economic system can sustain this higher income level Y_1, or will the economic system gravitate back to the equilibrium income level Y^*?

Tracing this higher Y_1 income level down to the lower panel, we observe that the economy is experiencing a considerable amount of inflation $\dot{P}_1$ per time period. Because the unemployment rate U_1 is substantially below the equilibrium unemployment rate U^*, wage rates are bid up and firms increase prices as they "markup" higher unit labour costs. By the end of the first interval of time, the price level rises from P_1 to P_2. However this rising price level will trigger the key feedback effect within the money market. For a given nominal stock of money, a rise in the price level will diminish the real money supply and cause the *LM* curve to shift upwards (from $LM(\$/P_1)$ to $LM(\$/P_2)$ in Chart 10-4. This upward shift in the *LM* curve will raise the interest rate from R_1 to R_2, which in turn will bring about a reduction in investment expenditures and a downward (multiplier) adjustment in real income, to Y_2.

Having shown that an income level of Y_1 will trigger an inflationary chain reaction leading to a lower income level Y_2, we must now consider the viability of Y_2. Will the income level Y_2 sustain itself, or will Y_2 (like Y_1) give way to a further downward adjustment in the level of income? Using the same argument as above, it can be demonstrated that Y_2 will set off a similar inflationary chain reaction that will produce a new lower income level Y_3. Along the *PEP* curve Y_2 also generates a *positive* inflation rate $\dot{P}_2$, although slightly lower than the previous inflation rate of $\dot{P}_1$ at Y_1. Again the price level will rise to P_3, eroding the real money supply $\$/P_3$ and causing the *LM* curve to shift upwards again. The interest rate is forced up another notch, to R_3, "crowding out" more investment spending and leading to a further decline in real income, to Y_3.

In a similar fashion, Y_3 will give way to a subsequent lower level of income Y_4, which will give way to Y_5, and so on. This disequilibrium adjustment process will

CHART 10-4 The stability of the *IS-LM-PEP* model

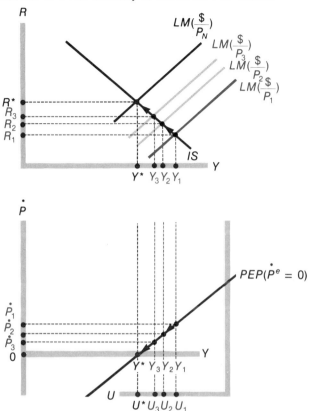

continue to lower the level of income as long as the inflation rate is greater than zero. For any positive inflation rate, the real money supply will decline and the *LM* curve will shift upwards. Only when the inflation rate reaches zero will this adjustment process come to a halt. This, of course, corresponds to our equilibrium income position Y^*. A salient characteristic of equilibrium within the *IS-LM-PEP* model is a *stationary LM* curve. Given a constant nominal money supply, the *LM* curve will only be stationary under conditions of zero price inflation. In the Phillips curve panel, Y^* must occur at the point where the *PEP* curve crosses the output axis, that is, where the inflation rate is zero.[4]

In summary, any income level greater than Y^* will generate a sufficient amount of inflation to return the economy to the equilibrium income level Y^*, the amount of output which can be produced by the equilibrium quantity of labour. In a diagrammatic sense, the economic system is simultaneously sliding down the *PEP*

---

[4]As will be demonstrated in Chapter 12, if we allow the exogenously determined *nominal* money supply to change each period, then the equilibrium solution to our *IS-LM-PEP* model will no longer exhibit this unrealistic property of zero inflation.

curve and climbing up the *IS* curve (see arrows in Chart 10-4). Each step down the *PEP* curve produces a further increase in the price level, thereby causing the *LM* curve to climb one step further up the *IS* curve. The economic system will eventually return to the equilibrium income level Y^*, the unique income level that is consistent with labour market equilibrium. A similar argument can be advanced to explain how the economic system will converge to Y^* from an income level below the equilibrium income level (see the next section of this chapter). In short, no matter what level of income happens to exist, the economic system will automatically gravitate back towards Y^*, the unique equilibrium income solution to our *IS-LM-PEP* macroeconomic model. Once the economic system is at Y^*, the labour, goods, and money markets will all be simultaneously in equilibrium and the economy will be at rest (no pressure will exist to cause the *LM*, *IS* or *PEP* curves to shift).

Our emphasis on the stability of the equilibrium level of income within the *IS-LM-PEP* model is not meant to imply that the economy must necessarily return *quickly* to its equilibrium position. While the structure and logic of our *IS-LM-PEP* model ensures that the economy will always gravitate towards its equilibrium position, we have not yet discussed how long it will take the economy to get back to Y^*. The length of the disequilibrium adjustment process is one of the most controversial issues in macroeconomics. Monetarists argue that the economy will quickly return to its natural equilibrium position (with the labour market in equilibrium); whereas Keynesian economists emphasize the slowness of the macroeconomic adjustment process (and the likelihood of prolonged cyclical unemployment). Before formally analyzing the length of the adjustment period in our model, we first reconsider the **determinants of the equilibrium income level** Y^* and then re-examine the nature of the multiplier process within a flexible price macroeconomic model.

The Determinants of Y^*

In a fundamental structural sense, the equilibrium level of income Y^* is determined in the labour market and supply sector of the economy. Y^* *is simply the amount of output that can be produced when the labour market is in equilibrium*. If the aggregate production function, the demand for labour, or the supply of labour were to shift, then the equilibrium quantities of labour and output would change. In this section of the chapter we demonstrate how (and why) the equilibrium output level will be affected by an increase in labour supply.

In panels A and D of Chart 10-5 we have reproduced our standard diagrams of the labour market and the aggregate production function. Given the black demand and supply curves for labour, the equilibrium quantity of labour L_0^* produces the equilibrium quantity of output Y_0^*. In panels B and C of Chart 10-5, this equilibrium level of output Y_0^* corresponds to a zero inflation rate, the point at which the black *PEP* curve crosses the output axis in the lower panel, and is characterized by a stationary *LM* curve in the upper panel.

Now suppose that the economy's labour supply increases from L_0^S to L_1^S, say because of a greater number of graduates than retirees. At the *previous* equilib-

CHART 10-5 The effect of an increase in labour supply on the equilibrium output level

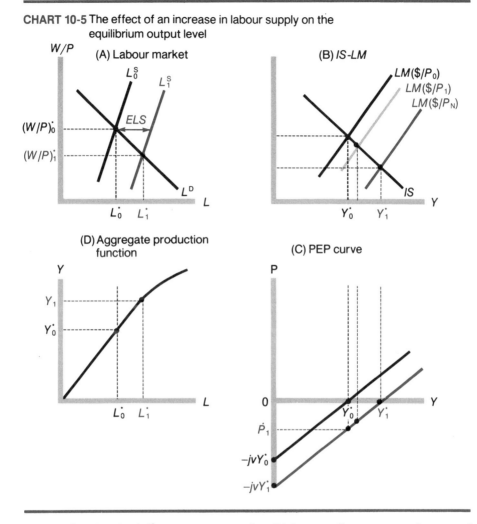

rium real wage $(W/P)_0^*$ an excess supply of labour will now exert downward pressure on wages within the labour market. Given sufficient time, this excess supply of labour will force the real wage down to its new equilibrium level $(W/P)_1^*$. At this new lower equilibrium wage rate, a larger number of individuals will now be employed $(L_1^* > L_0^*)$ and the economy's aggregate production will increase from Y_0^* to Y_1^*.

In panel C of Chart 10-5, this increase in the equilibrium level of output from Y_0^* to Y_1^*, an increase that arises from an increase in the supply of labour, will cause the *PEP* curve to shift downward to the right (recall that the intercept of the *PEP* curve contains the term $-jvY^*$). At the *original* equilibrium income position Y_0^*, this downward shift in the *PEP* curve will cause the inflation rate to decline from zero to the negative number $\dot{P}_1$. The increased supply of labour puts downward pressure on nominal wages in the labour market. As nominal wages decline (because of the excess supply of labour), firms face lower unit-labour costs and are thus able to lower prices.[5]

With a *negative* inflation rate, the price level will *decline* from P_0 to P_1 and the real money supply will *increase* from $\$/P_0$ to $\$/P_1$. This increase in the real money supply will cause the *LM* curve to shift downwards and the interest rate to decline. Lower interest rates will lead to an increase in investment and a consequent (multiplier) increase in output levels. The additional labour force participants will begin to find jobs as Y and L begin to rise from their original levels.

As long as excess supply conditions prevail in the labour market, wages and prices will continue to decline. Declining prices (a negative inflation rate) will generate further increases in the real money supply and the *LM* curve will continue to shift downwards, pushing the interest rate even lower. Falling interest rates will continue to spark new investment spending, which will lead to further increases in output and employment. This disequilibrium adjustment process will continue until the excess supply conditions in the labour market have been eliminated, at which point wages and prices will stop falling and the *LM* curve will no longer shift downwards. Once labour market equilibrium has been restored, output will have increased to Y_1^*, the inflation rate will once again be zero and the *LM* curve will be stationary. The economy is once again back in macroeconomic equilibrium, but at a higher output level Y_1^*, a lower price level P_N and a lower interest rate R_1^*. In fact, it is the lower interest rate (attributable to falling prices and an increasing real money supply) that triggers new investment expenditures, increased output, and greater employment.

In summary, the *equilibrium* levels of income and employment are fundamentally determined by the aggregate production function, the demand for labour, and the supply of labour. As demonstrated above, an increase in labour supply increases the equilibrium output and employment level. Even though the *IS* and *LM* curves are very important in establishing the *stability* of this equilibrium income position, the *IS-LM* part of the model plays no role in establishing the equilibrium levels of output and employment. As we shall see below, aggregate demand management policies which act on the *IS* and *LM* curves do not affect the equilibrium income level, only the equilibrium price level. To repeat, *the equilibrium income level is determined exclusively in the labour market and production sector of the economy*.

A Reappraisal of the Keynesian Multiplier Process

In Chapters 5 and 6 the multiplier effects on income which arise from a shift in the *IS* and *LM* curves were analyzed under the assumption of inflexible price levels. In this section, we repeat the diagrammatic analysis of the multiplier process for an economy with flexible price levels (as depicted by a Phillips curve). To keep our analysis as simple as possible, we again defer balance of payments considerations until the next chapter and we retain our assumption that inflation expectations are fixed at zero. We first examine the output and inflation effects of a shift in the *IS*

---

[5]Since the real wage rate is falling in the labour market, the decline in prices will not be as large as the decline in nominal wages.

curve and then similarly analyze the effects associated with an increase in the nominal money supply. As we shall see below, relaxing our inflexible-price-level assumption and including a Phillips curve within our macroeconomic model substantially alters our earlier conclusions concerning the nature of the multiplier process. Perhaps surprisingly, our *IS-LM-PEP* macroeconomic model is consistent with *both* Keynesian *and* monetarist conclusions, depending upon one's perception of the length of the inflationary disequilibrium adjustment period.

The Inflation and Output Effects Associated with a Shift in the *IS* Curve

In Chart 10-6 we have reproduced our standard two-panel *IS-LM-PEP* diagram. Our hypothetical economy is assumed to be initially in equilibrium at Y^*, with a zero inflation rate and a price level of P_0. Now suppose that the IS_0 curve shifts upwards to IS_1, say from an increase in exports, autonomous investment, or government expenditures. Since the *nominal* money supply has *not* changed, this increase in aggregate demand and upward shift in the *IS* curve will initially push the economy up the given *LM* ($\$/P_0$) curve to a new higher income level Y_1 and a higher interest rate R_1. However, down in the Phillips curve panel of Chart 10-6, this higher income level Y_1 and lower unemployment rate U_1 will generate a substantial amount of wage and price inflation $\dot{P}_1$. As price levels increase, the real stock of money will decrease and the *LM* curve will start to drift upwards. The upward drift in the *LM* curve will force interest rates up even further and lead to a decline in investment expenditures. As investment is crowded out by higher interest rates, this initially higher level of income will begin to decline. In the time period following the outward shift in the IS_0 curve, the inflation rate $\dot{P}_1$ will have increased the price level to P_1, shifted the *LM* curve up to *LM* ($\$/P_1$), raised the interest rate to R_2 and lowered the income level from Y_1 down to Y_2.

However our story is by no means over. An income level of Y_2 will still generate inflation down in the Phillips curve panel. Even though the inflation rate $\dot{P}_2$ in the second time interval is less than the inflation rate $\dot{P}_1$ in the initial period of disequilibrium, price levels are still rising. During this second time period after the outward shift in IS_0, the price level will again rise (to P_2), the real money supply will decline accordingly, the *LM* curve will again shift up (to *LM* $\$/(P_2)$), the interest rate will be pushed up further (to R_3), more investment expenditures will be crowded out, and the income level will further decline (to Y_3). But an income level of Y_3 still generates a positive rate of inflation $\dot{P}_3$ down in the Phillips curve panel. Again the real stock of money will decline, the *LM* curve will shift upwards, interest rates will again rise, investment expenditures will be further crowded out and income levels will further decline. As discussed earlier in this chapter, this inflation-induced erosion in the real stock of money, and consequent reductions in investment expenditures and output, will only come to a halt when the economy has moved all the way back to Y^*, where the inflation rate is zero and the *LM* curve remains stationary. The economic system will climb up the *new* higher IS_1 curve and slide down the *PEP* curve until it returns to its *original* equilibrium position Y^*.

CHART 10-6 Effects of a shift in the *IS* curve

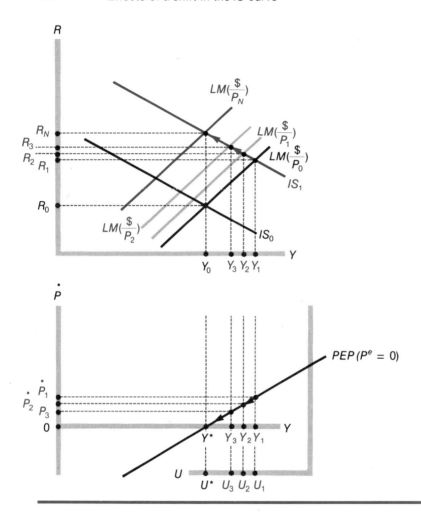

In summary, an increase in government expenditures, or an increase in exports or autonomous investment, has *no lasting* income and employment effects. An outward shift in the *IS* curve will *initially* produce a Keynesian multiplier effect on income. However, down in the Phillips curve panel, the inflation resulting from the initially higher income level will erode the real money supply, push up interest rates, reduce investment expenditures and eventually return the economy to its *original equilibrium* income position. The only permanent effects from an increase in government expenditures are a higher price level, a higher interest rate and a redistribution of output from the business sector to the government sector. To repeat, *an outward shift of the IS curve in the flexible-price IS-LM-PEP macroeconomic model does not produce a higher equilibrium income level or a lower equilibrium unemployment rate.*

CHART 10-7 Effects of an increase in the nominal money supply

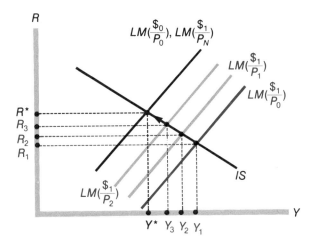

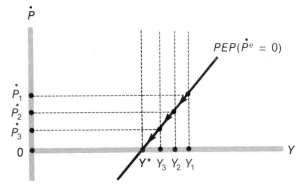

The Inflation and Output Effects Arising from a
Change in the Nominal Money Supply

The macroeconomic effects associated with an increase in the *nominal* money supply are very similar to the macroeconomic effects arising from a shift in the *IS* curve. As demonstrated in Chart 10-7, an increase in the nominal money supply from $\$_0$ to $\$_1$ will initially cause the *LM* curve to shift downwards, bringing about a lower interest rate R_1, an increase in investment spending, and a higher income level Y_1. However, this increase in income following an increase in the nominal money supply will trigger the same inflationary chain-reaction process described above. The inflation rate $\dot{P}_1$ associated with the increased income level Y_1 will erode the *real* value of the increased *nominal* money supply and the *LM* curve will begin to drift back up. Each round of inflation ($\dot{P}_1$, $\dot{P}_2$, $\dot{P}_3$ in Chart 10-7) will erode the real stock of money (to $\$_1/P_1$, $\$_1/P_2$, $\$_1/P_3$) and continually push the *LM* curve back upwards. These upward shifts in the *LM* curve lead to higher and higher interest rates and lower and lower income levels. As in the previous case of an outward shift in the *IS* curve, this disequilibrium adjustment process following an increase in the *nominal* stock of money will only come to a halt when the *inflation rate is back to zero* and the economy has returned to its original equilibrium income level, Y^*. The *LM* curve will have shifted back up to its original position, with $\$_1/P_N$ equal to $\$_0/P_0$. The only difference from the case where the *IS* curve shifted, discussed above, concerns the interest rate. An increase in the nominal money supply will *temporarily* depress the interest rate below its equilibrium level, but once the adjustment process has concluded the rate of interest will have returned to its original equilibrium level R^*. The only permanent effect from an increase in the *nominal* stock of money is a higher price level P_N, but not lasting inflation. The inflation rate is back to zero.

Round 2 of the Keynesian-Monetarist Debate: The Multiplier Effects Associated with Shifts in the *IS* and *LM* Curves

As described above, a shift in the *IS* curve or a shift in the *LM* curve will initially produce a Keynesian multiplier effect on income, but in the end the economy will return to its original equilibrium income position. The output and employment gains associated with an outward shift in the *IS* curve or *LM* curve are strictly temporary. Inflation generated from an outward shift in the *IS* curve will erode the *real* money supply, raise interest rates and crowd out investment expenditures. The decline in investment will be equivalent to the initial stimulus in aggregate demand which caused the *IS* curve to shift outwards. An increase in the *nominal* money supply will generate a sufficient amount of inflation to erode the *real* money supply back to its original level. *There are no permanent employment or output effects from a shift in the IS curve or from an increase in the nominal money supply.*

Thus, the major conclusions from our *IS-LM-PEP* macroeconomic model would appear to be very monetarist in tone.[6] An exogenous shift in exports or autonomous investment will have *no* lasting effects on income or employment levels. In the parlance of a monetarist economist, the free enterprise system is inherently stable. Second, monetary and fiscal policy will also have *no* lasting effects on employment or output levels. Keynesian demand-management policies do *not* provide a *permanent* cure for the unemployment problem. Again in the parlance of a monetarist economist, expansionary fiscal policy will simply crowd out investment expenditures and divert output from the private sector to the public sector. The equilibrium output level is determined in the labour market and production sector of the economy and is unaffected by fiscal policy.

While the basic conclusions from our flexible-price *IS-LM-PEP* macroeconomic model appear to be very damning for Keynesian economists, one should not lose sight of the fact that during the disequilibrium adjustment period following a shift in the *IS* or *LM* curve, the economy experiences income levels which differ from the equilibrium income level. There are *temporary* increases or decreases in

---

[6]A review of the basic tenets of monetarism, which were discussed in Chapter 6, might be in order.

CHART 10-8 Temporal effects following a shift in the *IS* curve

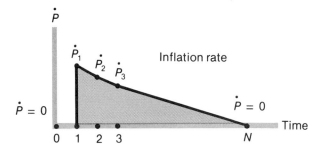

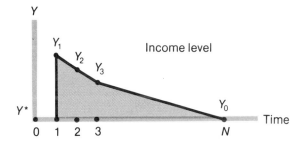

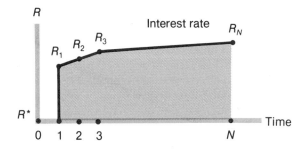

output and employment during the adjustment period following a shift in the *IS* or *LM* curve. In Chart 10-8 we have plotted the time profiles for the inflation rate, income level and the interest rate following an outward shift in the *IS* curve (as analyzed in Chart 10-6). The *initial impact* effects of this outward shift in the *IS* curve are to raise both the inflation rate (to $\dot{P}_1$) and the level of income (to Y_1). These inflationary-expansionary effects will diminish through time as inflation erodes the real money supply, pushes the *LM* curve upwards, forces the interest rate up, crowds out investment expenditures, and reduces output levels. While the economy will eventually slide down the *PEP* curve and return to its original equilibrium income level Y^* with a zero inflation rate, *during the disequilibrium adjustment period* there may be considerable *temporary* gains in output and employment accompanied by inflation (see the shaded areas in Chart 10-8).

Consequently, an assessment of the output, employment, and inflation effects associated with a shift in the *IS* or *LM* curve depends critically on the time period considered. If one adopts a **long-run** equilibrium perspective and focuses on the multiplier effects *after* all of the inflation feedback effects have worked their way throughout the economic system, then the income and employment multiplier effects are indeed zero. Under such a *long-run* perspective, a change in government expenditures has *no permanent* effect on the level of output or on the unemployment rate (only the price level, the interest rate and the distribution of output between the investment and government sectors are affected). On the other hand, if one focuses on the **short-run disequilibrium-adjustment** phase following a shift in the *IS* curve or following an increase in the nominal money supply, then clearly a change in government expenditures (or exports or the nominal money supply) does affect output and inflation, although these effects will diminish through time.

In a temporal sense our *IS-LM-PEP* macroeconomic model is consistent with both monetarist and Keynesian conclusions. Monetarists would look to the *long-run* equilibrium properties of our *IS-LM-PEP* macroeconomic model, whereas Keynesian economists would be much more interested in the *short-run* disequilibrium properties of the model. A key area of dispute between Keynesian and monetarist economists concerns the length of the short-run adjustment period. How long does it take the economy to get through the (Keynesian) short-run disequilibrium-adjustment period before it reaches the (monetarist) long-run equilibrium position? Monetarists tend to think that long-run equilibrium is "just around the corner," while Keynesian economists are more apt to respond with Keynes' now famous dictum, "In the long run we're all dead!" *If* the short-run adjustment period is in fact quite long, a Keynesian policy maker might be tempted to stimulate aggregate demand and "enjoy the slide down the Phillips curve." During the "quite long" short-run adjustment period, the economy would experience a *temporarily* low unemployment rate, albeit at the expense of inflation. In the next section of this chapter we examine the major determinants of the length of the short-run disequilibrium-adjustment phase in the *IS-LM-PEP* macroeconomic model. In doing so, we enter the arena in which monetarist and Keynesian economists are most frequently pitted. The wise reader will be well-armed. A quick review of the last several sections of the chapter and the intricacies of the *IS-LM-PEP* diagram might be in order.

Determinants of the Length of the Short-Run Adjustment Period

As described above, the adjustment mechanism that returns the economy to its equilibrium income level Y^* is a sequence of inflation-induced shifts in the *LM* curve arising from repeated changes in the *real* stock of money. For any level of output greater than Y^*, a positive inflation rate erodes the real money supply and causes the *LM* curve to drift upwards. This upward drift in the *LM* curve will only come to a halt when the inflation rate is back to zero and the economy has returned to Y^*. The adjustment process must increase the price level sufficiently so that the *LM* curve intersects the *IS* curve at the equilibrium income level *Y**. The short-run adjustment period can be defined as the length of time required to move the existing disequilibrium price level to the new equilibrium price level. In terms of Chart 10-6, how long does it take to increase the price level from P_0 to P_N? Alternatively, how long does it take for the *LM ($/P_0)* curve to shift up to the new equilibrium position *LM($/P_N)*?

Within the *IS-LM-PEP* macroeconomic model, the price expectations Phillips curve determines the speed with which prices adjust during this short-run disequilibrium-adjustment process. Both (1) the slope of the underlying Phillips curve and (2) the manner in which inflation expectations are formed will affect the duration of the short-run adjustment period. Not surprisingly, much of the macroeconomic controversy between monetarist and Keynesian economists has concerned the properties of the Phillips curve. We briefly consider how the slope and the inflation-expectations component of the Phillips curve will affect the length of the short-run adjustment period.

The Slope of the Underlying Phillips Curve

To illustrate the key role that the slope of the underlying Phillips curve plays in the macroeconomic adjustment process, Chart 10-9 presents our standard *IS-LM-PEP* diagram with two very differently sloped *PEP* curves passing through the equilibrium income point *Y**. Following a shift in the *IS* curve from IS_0 is IS_1, the *steep* (black) *PEP* curve generates very high rates of inflation and consequently very sizeable shifts in the *LM* curve. After three rounds of substantial inflation associated with the steep *PEP* curve, the level of output is almost back to its equilibrium level. For the same *IS* curve shift, the relatively *flat* (red) *PEP* curve generates very modest amounts of inflation. The (red) *LM* curve shifts generated by this relatively flat *PEP* curve will be much smaller since the real money supply will be only slightly diminished by the very modest rates of inflation. Unlike the "quick slide" down the steep *PEP* curve, the economy will "slowly inch" down the relatively flat *PEP* curve. After three rounds of very modest inflation generated by the relatively flat *PEP* curve, the economy still has a very long way to go before it will be back to the equilibrium output level. *The steeper the underlying Phillips curve*, the larger the price adjustments, the greater the change in the real money supply, the larger the shifts in the *LM* curve, the faster the level of output will return to its equilibrium level, and *the shorter the length of the adjustment period*.

The Formulation of Inflation Expectations

If we relax our restrictive assumption that inflation expectations are fixed at zero, the adjustment process may also be speeded up. Suppose, for example, that people adjust their inflation expectations to past rates of price inflation. Then the inflation generated from an outward shift in the *IS* curve ($\dot{P}_1$ in Chart 10-6) would cause inflation expectations $\dot{P}^e$ to be revised upwards from zero (our initial assumption) and the *PEP* curve will shift upwards (recall that $\dot{P}^e$ is an intercept component of the *PEP* curve). Labour would demand larger wage settlements to

CHART 10-9 The slope of the Phillips Curve and the length of the short-run adjustment process

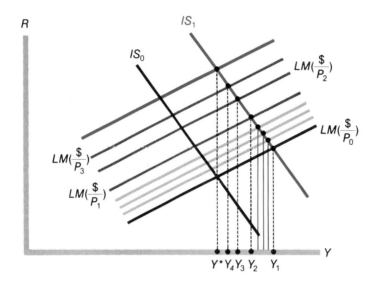

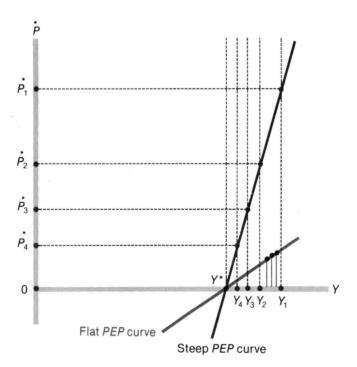

compensate for the expected rate of inflation (which is no longer zero) and firms would mark up these higher unit labour costs into higher price levels. Under such adjustable (or adaptive) inflation expectations, a rightward shift in the *IS* curve will now generate a *double* inflation effect: (1) a movement up the *PEP* curve from an increase in output and (2) an upward shift in the *PEP* curve as inflation expectations are revised upwards to reflect the higher actual inflation rate. Thus if inflation expectations are adjusted to prevailing inflation rates, a rightward shift in the *IS* curve will generate a larger inflation impact, a greater erosion of the real money supply, a larger upward shift in the *LM* curve, a more rapid decline in output levels, and a "shorter" short-run adjustment period. Having established the proposition that the length of the short-run adjustment period depends on the nature of the inflation-expectations assumption, we defer further analysis of the process by which inflation expectations are formed until the Chapters 12 and 17.

To summarize, inflation (or deflation) generated during the short-run disequilibrium-adjustment period is the self-correcting mechanism that returns the economy to its equilibrium income level. For an outward shift in the *IS* or *LM* curve, the higher the inflation rate during the adjustment period, the faster the return trip to the equilibrium income level and the shorter the short-run adjustment period. Since the magnitude of the inflation rate during the adjustment period depends on the slope of the underlying Phillips curve and the inflation-expectations assumption, it does not take much imagination to guess how monetarist and Keynesian economists will line up on the Phillips curve issue.

By emphasizing the natural flexibility of the free enterprise price system, monetarists implicitly believe that the underlying Phillips curve must be very steep. If the government would only leave the economic system alone, wages and prices would quickly adjust to changing market conditions. Furthermore, "rational" economic agents will quickly adjust their inflation expectations in light of current economic circumstances.[7] Given competitive market conditions—the "invisible hand" of Adam Smith—and rapidly adjusting inflation expectations, the free market system will be inherently stable in output and unemployment terms. Thus any shift in the *IS* curve, say from a change in fiscal policy or exports, would immediately produce a substantial disequilibrium price effect that would quickly move the economy back to its equilibrium income and employment position. The *LM* curve rapidly shifts to offset any shift in the *IS* curve. From a monetarist perspective, there is a great deal of *PEP* in the *IS-LM-PEP* macroeconomic model. The *long-run* equilibrium properties of the *IS-LM-PEP* quickly materialize, and, for all intents and purposes, the Keynesian short-run income multiplier effects are zero.

As discussed in previous chapters, Keynes emphasized the very slow response of wages and prices to changing economic conditions. The yet-to-be invented Phillips curve was sufficiently flat that it could be ignored. Given a *very* flat underlying Phillips curve, the short-run adjustment period would persist indefinitely and in the long run we would likely be *dead*. Modern day followers of Keynes do not deny the existence of a Phillips curve, but rather argue (1) that "wages, and

[7]See Chapter 17.

perhaps prices, do not adjust quickly to eliminate excess supplies and demands, especially excess supplies"[8] (the underlying Phillips curve is relatively flat) and (2) that inflation expectations tend to be adjusted quite slowly. In addition, the existence of multi-year wage contracts in the labour market impedes the adjustment of wages to changing labour market conditions and inflation expectations. From a Keynesian perspective, there is very little *PEP* in the *IS-LM-PEP* model as wages and prices respond very sluggishly to changing economic conditions. Consequently, the short-run output effects associated with a shift in the *IS* curve are likely to persist for a number of years.

While Keynesian and monetarist arguments are frequently stated in the polar terms of a model with either no *PEP* or an infinite amount of *PEP*, reality undoubtedly lies somewhere between these two extremes. Unlike Keynes' crucial "inflexibility" assumption, *wages and prices do respond to changing economic conditions*—but not nearly as fast as monetarists would like to think. Inflation expectations are adjusted to reflect changing economic circumstances, but not instantaneously. Thus, the length of the short-run adjustment phase lies somewhere between the "ephemeral" short run of a hard core monetarist and the "permanent" short run of Keynes. Consequently we cannot dismiss important short-run output effects (as many monetarists tend to do), nor can we dismiss long-run inflationary considerations (as Keynes did). Both the short-run disequilibrium-adjustment phase and the long-run equilibrium properties of our *IS-LM-PEP* model must be carefully studied, and, as we shall see repeatedly throughout this text, the nature of the Phillips curve is often the crucial factor in our analysis.

Key Concepts

inflation-output *PEP* curve
stability of equilibrium income level in the *IS-LM-PEP* model
the determinants of equilibrium income in the *IS-LM-PEP* model
the short-run disequilibrium-adjustment period
the short run versus the long run

Review Questions

1. What is the relationship between the unemployment rate and the level of output? How can this relationship be used to translate a downward-sloping inflation-unemployment Phillips curve into an upward-sloping inflation-output Phillips curve?

2. How does the level of prices affect the demand for money and the position of the *LM* curve? For a given supply of nominal money, what effect does inflation have on the *LM* curve?

---

[8]R.M. Solow, "Alternative approaches to macroeconomic theory: a partial view," *Canadian Journal of Economics*, August 1979, p. 343. In this nontechnical article, Professor Solow of M.I.T. outlines a number of reasons why money wage rates tend to be "sticky."

3. What determines the equilibrium level of output, the unemployment rate and interest rates? Demonstrate that this equilibrium income level is both unique and stable.

4. In determining the equilibrium level of output and interest rates, what role does the *IS-LM* part of the model play?

5. Carefully examine the *short-run adjustment* and *long-run equilibrium* effects on output, unemployment, interest rates and inflation of the following events:

   a) a decrease in labour supply

   b) a decrease in exports

   c) an increase in government spending

   d) an increase in the nominal money supply

   e) an increase in labour demand.

6. Explain in a "temporal" sense how the *IS-LM-PEP* model is consistent with both Keynesian and monetarist conclusions.

7. What factors determine the length of the short-run adjustment period?

8. How do you assess the debate between Keynesian and monetarist economists over the length of the short-run adjustment period?

Inflation, Unemployment and Output in an Open Economy

11

The recent gyrations of the dollars have looked more to me like a gold standard on the booze than the ideal managed currency which I hope for.

John Maynard Keynes[1]

Half a century has passed since Keynes made the above comment and we have yet to see the "ideal managed currency" that Keynes hoped for. In recent years the international economy has been buffeted by a number of disturbances (oil price shocks and large differences between national rates of inflation to name two significant ones) which have caused large swings in exchange rates. The Canadian dollar declined approximately 30 per cent against the U.S. dollar over the period from 1976 to 1986. Now that we have introduced inflation and the *PEP* curve into our *IS-LM* model, we can consider the balance of payments adjustment process in an inflationary economy by incorporating into the *IS-LM-PEP* model the *BP* curve that was introduced in Chapter 7. First we will examine the effects of disturbances in **domestic demand** (consumption, investment and government spending) under both **fixed and flexible exchange rate** regimes and then we will consider the effects of an increase in the Canadian money supply on the price level and the exchange rate. In a case study we tackle the question of whether Canada should follow a fixed or flexible exchange rate policy in the face of a tight U.S. monetary policy that maintains U.S. interest rates at very high levels. In the final section we examine the adjustment that follows a decline in Canadian exports. This is an example of an *external* shock that disturbs both the Canadian balance of payments and the domestic goods market.

Domestic Disturbances under Flexible Exchange Rates

Chart 11-1 shows our standard two-panel diagram with the economy initially described by IS_0, LM_0 and BP_0.[2] The initial equilibrium income level and interest rate are Y^* and R^* respectively (point A). In the upper panel, R^* and Y^* lie on all three of the curves IS_0, LM_0 and BP_0, so that at this income level and interest rate the goods market, the money market and the balance of payments are all in

---

[1]J.M. Keynes in 1933, quoted in "Sayings of our Times," *Observer*, 31 May 1953.

CHART 11-1 The effects of an increase in domestic demand under flexible exchange rates

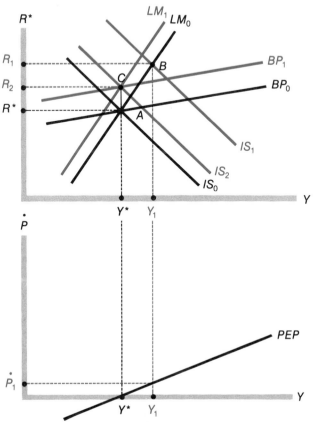

equilibrium. The economy is simultaneously in both internal and external balance. Recall that at all points along the *BP* curve, any surplus or deficit on the current account of the balance of payments is exactly matched by a deficit or surplus on the capital account. Consequently, in the absence of any intervention by the Bank of Canada, the demand for and supply of Canadian dollars in the foreign exchange market are equal at the initial equilibrium exchange rate.

As the lower panel of Chart 11-1 shows, at the income level Y^* the rate of inflation is zero. Indeed, as long as the government maintains a fixed *nominal* money supply, a zero rate of inflation is necessarily a characteristic of the

[2]The charts in this section show the *BP* curve to be flatter than the *LM* curve. However, unlike the fixed-price model of Chapter 7, none of the conclusions discussed here is *necessarily* changed when the *LM* curve is assumed to be flatter than the *BP* curve. While the exchange rate may tend to appreciate or depreciate in response to an increase in domestic demand depending on the sizes of certain parameters in the model, the relevant parameters include more than the slopes of the *BP* and *LM* curves. This point is developed later in this section and is treated formally in the appendix to this chapter.

equilibrium position. If the rate of inflation is not zero, then with a fixed *nominal* stock of money the *real* stock of money will be changing. For example, a positive rate of inflation will cause the real stock of money to decline and the *LM* curve will shift leftwards. Since in equilibrium all curves must be stable, it follows that the rate of inflation must be zero in equilibrium. The lower panel of Chart 11-1 shows that the *only* income level that is consistent with zero inflation is Y^*, where *PEP* cuts the horizontal axis. In all of the exercises that we do in this chapter, both the initial and final equilibrium output levels will be at Y^*. To a considerable extent our attention will be focused on the behaviour of the economy during the disequilibrium period as the economy moves from one equilibrium position to another.

Returning to Chart 11-1, suppose that there is an increase in one component of domestic demand, such as business investment or government spending, which causes the *IS* curve to shift rightwards from IS_0 to IS_1.[3] The curves IS_1, and LM_0 intersect at point B, which lies *above* BP_0. At the income level Y_1 and the interest rate R_1, while the goods and money markets are in equilibrium, there is a balance of payments surplus. (Recall from Chapter 7 that all points above the *BP* curve are characterized by balance of payments surpluses.) This surplus arises despite the fact that the current account of the balance of payments deteriorates as the level of income rises from Y^* to Y_1. While the level of imports increases with the level of income, the higher rate of interest stimulates additional net capital inflows. The net effect is that the overall balance of payments is in a surplus position. Consequently, at the point (Y_1, R_1) there is an excess demand for Canadian dollars in the foreign exchange market which results in an appreciation of the Canadian dollar. The lower panel of Chart 11-1 shows that at the new income level Y_1 the rate of inflation has risen to $\dot{P}_1$ from the initial position of zero inflation at Y^*. In summary, the effect of the increase in domestic demand is to shift the *IS* curve from IS_0 to IS_1. At the intersection point of IS_1 and LM_0 the exchange rate is appreciating and the price level is rising at the rate $\dot{P}_1$.

Let us now determine how the appreciation of the Canadian dollar and the positive rate of inflation $\dot{P}_1$ affect the positions of the *IS*, *LM* and *BP* curves which are presently at IS_1, LM_0, and BP_0. Since the price level is rising and the *nominal* money supply is given, the *real* stock of money is falling. As a result, the LM_0 curve will shift leftwards. The fact that the Canadian dollar is appreciating in value does not affect the position of the *LM* curve. However, as the dollar appreciates, the price of Canadian goods rises *relative* to the price of foreign goods, causing imports into Canada to become cheaper and Canadian exports to become more expensive for foreigners. The effect of the appreciation of the Canadian dollar on relative international prices is reinforced by the higher Canadian inflation rate. Both the appreciation of the Canadian dollar and the higher rate of inflation cause the price of Canadian goods and services to rise *relative* to prices in the rest of the world, assuming as we do throughout that the rate of inflation in the rest of the world remains at zero. As a result, Canadian exports decline and imports into

[3]If the disturbance in aggregate demand involves either imports or exports, both the *IS* and *BP* curves will shift. We will consider an example of such an *external* shock at the end of the chapter.

Canada rise. This decrease in exports and increase in imports will cause the *IS* curve to shift to the left. In addition, because the trade balance deteriorates as a result of the change in relative international prices, the *BP* curve also shifts to the left (see Chapter 7). Consequently, at point *B*, where IS_1 intersects LM_0, the disequilibria in the labour market and the balance of payments set up the forces of price inflation and currency appreciation which push all three curves (*IS*, *LM* and *BP*) to the left.[4]

To establish where the new equilibrium will be following a permanent increase in domestic demand, consider the properties of macroeconomic equilibrium. As we discussed earlier, when the government maintains a fixed nominal money supply the *LM* curve will be stationary only when the price level is stable. Consequently, in the final equilibrium position the rate of inflation must be zero. The lower panel of Chart 11-1 shows that the only income level that is consistent with a zero rate of inflation is Y^*. Given that the economy will converge back to Y^*, the intersection point of the leftward shifting *IS*, *LM* and *BP* curves must be at Y^*. In Chart 11-1 the new equilibrium is at point *C* where the three curves IS_2, LM_1 and BP_1 intersect. The level of income is Y^* and the interest rate R_2. At this point the rate of inflation is once again zero and, because the balance of payments is in equilibrium, the foreign exchange rate is again stable.

It is instructive to compare this new equilibrium position with the original equilibrium position that existed prior to the increase in domestic demand. First, note that a shift in the *IS* curve has no lasting effect on the level of real income. During the adjustment phase the level of income rises above Y^*, but ultimately returns to this level once again. During the disequilibrium period the rate of inflation is positive so that the domestic price level is higher in the new equilibrium position than initially. It is this rise in the price level that causes the real stock of money to decline and the *LM* curve to shift to the left. And, because the real money supply is lower in the final equilibrium compared to the initial position, the rate of interest must be higher. During the adjustment phase the exchange rate appreciates so that in the new equilibrium the foreign exchange value of the Canadian dollar is greater than initially. This, together with the fact that the Canadian price level rises during the adjustment phase, means that the price of Canadian goods rises relative to foreign prices. Thus, in the new equilibrium the merchandise trade surplus (deficit) is smaller (larger) compared to the initial position. However, the overall balance of payments is once again in equilibrium because the higher Canadian interest rate results in larger net capital inflows—the deterioration on the current account is exactly matched by an improvement on the capital account.

The introduction of the balance of payments into the analysis does not change the conclusion that a shift in the *IS* curve has no lasting effect on the equilibrium

---

[4]Strictly speaking, the *PEP* curve shifts downwards to the right when the Canadian dollar appreciates because import prices are falling. However, in the new equilibrium the foreign exchange rate will be stable, *FP* will be zero and *PEP* will return to its original position. Thus, this effect does not change the final equilibrium position although it does affect the dynamic path that the economy follows to get to the new equilibrium. To simplify the diagrammatic analysis we suppress this temporary shift in the *PEP* curve which accompanies the changing foreign exchange rate.

level of income. The equilibrium income level is Y^* both before and after the IS curve shift. However, the adjustment mechanism for an open economy with a flexible exchange rate is more complex. In our previous analysis (Chart 10-6) the adjustment to a rightward shift of the IS curve comes about because the price level rises, the real stock of money falls and the rate of interest rises. It is the rise in the rate of interest that crowds out private investment expenditures. This adjustment mechanism is reinforced by the balance of payments effects in the open economy model. Both the rise in the domestic price level and the appreciation of the Canadian dollar depress Canada's export and import-competing industries. Excess aggregate demand in the Canadian economy is reduced both because investment expenditures fall in response to higher interest rates and because exports fall and imports rise as Canadian prices rise relative to foreign prices. An open economy with a flexible exchange rate should adjust more quickly to a shift in domestic demand than a closed economy, because the balance of payments repercussions push the economy back towards the equilibrium income level.

Domestic Disturbances Under a Fixed Exchange Rate

Chart 11-2 illustrates the adjustment of an open economy to a rightward shift in the IS curve when the government has a fixed exchange rate policy. The initial situation is described by the three curves IS_0, LM_0 and BP_0, which intersect at point A. Initially the economy is in equilibrium with a zero rate of inflation. Now suppose the IS curve shifts to the right to IS_1 because of an increase in government expenditures. The effect of the increase in demand is to raise income and domestic interest rates (compare point B with point A in Chart 11-2). As we saw in the previous section, the rise in domestic interest rates puts upward pressure on the value of the Canadian dollar in the foreign exchange market because higher Canadian interest rates attract larger inflows of foreign capital. In order to maintain a fixed exchange rate, the Bank of Canada must purchase foreign currency and supply Canadian dollars. The expansion of the domestic money supply will moderate the rise in domestic interest rates. As discussed in Chapter 7, under a fixed exchange rate policy, monetary policy is concerned exclusively with maintaining a fixed exchange rate. Consequently, under a fixed exchange rate policy the *rightward* shift of the IS curve is accompanied by a *rightward* shift of the LM curve to LM_1 as the Bank of Canada increases the money supply to prevent the exchange rate from appreciating. The comparison of points B and C in Chart 11-2 shows that the rightward shift of the LM curve accentuates the effect on income of the rightward shift of the IS curve. At point C in Chart 11-2, where IS_1, LM_1 and BP_0 intersect, the balance of payments is in equilibrium, but the rightward shifts of the IS and LM curves have caused a positive rate of inflation $\dot{P}_1$ to emerge. It is the positive rate of domestic inflation that pushes the economy back to its final equilibrium position.

Since the Canadian rate of inflation $\dot{P}_1$ exceeds the rate of inflation in the rest of the world, which we assume throughout to be zero, the prices of Canadian goods will rise relative to prices in the rest of the world. This will put Canadian industries

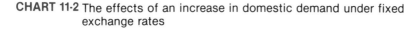

CHART 11-2 The effects of an increase in domestic demand under fixed
exchange rates

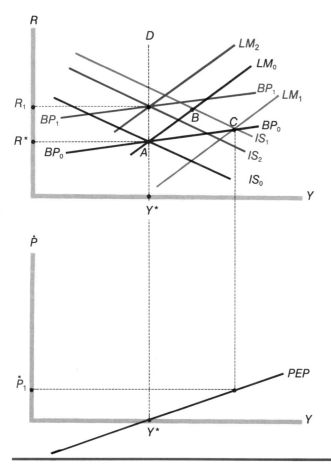

at a steadily worsening disadvantage that will eventually cause exports to drop and
imports to rise. Both of these factors cause the *IS* and *BP* curves to shift to the left.
The intersection point of the *IS* and *BP* curves will therefore shift leftwards.
Because monetary policy is devoted to the task of maintaining balance of payments equilibrium at the original exchange rate, the *LM* curve will adjust passively so that it too passes through the intersection point of the *BP* and *IS* curves.
As the intersection point of the *BP* and *IS* curves drifts leftwards, the level of
income and the rate of inflation both decline until ultimately the level of income
returns to Y^* and the rate of inflation returns to zero. Once again, only at the
income level Y^* is the rate of inflation zero. The final equilibrium position is at
point *D*, where IS_2, LM_2 and BP_1 intersect. At point *D* the nominal money supply,
the price level and the foreign exchange rate are all stable.

Nothing we have said so far tells us whether the new equilibrium interest rate
will be equal to, below or above the initial interest rate R^*. In fact, the final

equilibrium interest rate R_1 must be above R^*. The reason is that throughout the inflationary adjustment phase the current account of the balance of payments steadily deteriorates as exports decline and imports increase. In order for the balance of payments to return to equilibrium, the worsening current account must be matched by an equal improvement on the capital account; net capital inflows must increase. This can be achieved only if domestic interest rates rise to attract additional capital inflows. Consequently, in the new equilibrium the current account of the balance of payments has a smaller surplus (larger deficit) than initially while the capital account has a larger surplus (smaller deficit) than initially.

Again we find that a shift in the *IS* curve has no permanent effect on the level of income. An autonomous boom in one sector of the economy, whether due to an increase in government spending or some other component of domestic demand, leads to higher interest rates and a positive rate of inflation. The higher interest rates cause a decline in investment expenditures on plant and equipment while the rate of inflation causes a reduction in exports and an increase in imports. In the final equilibrium these two negative effects exactly offset the positive effect of the initial increase in spending so that ultimately the overall level of aggregate demand and the level of income are unchanged. This can be represented conveniently in symbols. The equation that represents the initial equilibrium position is:

(11-1) $Y^* = C_0 + I_0 + G_0 + (X - M)_0$

If, for example, government expenditures are increased to G_1, the equilibrium income level is once again equal to Y^*. While the level of investment expenditure I and net exports $X - M$ will change as a result of the increase in government spending, the level of consumption will not. This is because consumption depends only on the level of income, which is once again equal to Y^*. The equation that describes the *new* equilibrium position is:

(11-2) $Y^* = C_0 + I_1 + G_1 + (X - M)_1$

Subtracting equation 11-1 from equation 11-2 gives:

$$0 = 0 + (I_1 - I_0) + (G_1 - G_0) + (X - M)_1 - (X - M)_0$$

or $0 = \triangle I + \triangle G + \triangle(X - M)$

To reveal more clearly the fact that the increase in government spending crowds out an equal amount of investment spending and net exports, this last equation can be rewritten:

$$\triangle G = -\triangle I - \triangle(X - M)$$

An interesting conclusion (which is demonstrated in the appendix) is that the final equilibrium interest rate, level of income and the ratio of domestic prices to foreign prices are all independent of which exchange rate policy the government adopts. Given the size of the initial increase in government spending $\triangle G$, the same quantity of investment I and net exports $X-M$ has to be crowded out. The rise in the interest rate R crowds out investment and the rise in the ratio of the domestic price level to the foreign price level crowds out net exports. Whether the government follows a fixed exchange rate policy or a flexible exchange rate policy does not change this fact; nor does it change the share of the crowding-out burden that is borne by the two expenditure components (investment and net exports). Consequently, the increase in the interest rate, which crowds out investment, and the increase in the ratio of domestic to foreign prices, which crowds out net exports, following a rightward shift of the IS curve is exactly the same whether the government adopts either a floating or a fixed exchange rate policy. What is different between the two exchange rate policy regimes is the way in which the increase in the ratio of domestic to foreign prices is achieved.

The ratio of Canadian to foreign prices can be written as:

$$\frac{\pi P}{P^W}$$

where P is the Canadian price level in Canadian dollars and π is the exchange rate. The product πP is therefore the Canadian price of Canadian goods expressed, for example, in pounds sterling. The price of foreign goods in the rest of the world in pounds sterling is P^W. Suppose the price ratio $\pi P/P^W$ rises 10 per cent from one equilibrium position to another. Under the fixed exchange rate regime π is fixed so that the domestic price level must rise by the full 10 per cent. In the flexible exchange rate case, the total change in the ratio of domestic to foreign prices is broken down into an exchange rate movement and a domestic price level movement. For example, the 10 per cent rise in the overall ratio may be achieved by a 5 per cent appreciation of the Canadian dollar and a 5 per cent rise in the Canadian price level P. It would appear that in the flexible exchange rate case the domestic price level rises less than under a fixed exchange rate policy when the economy is subject to an increase in exogenous spending. This is because the flexible exchange rate policy allows the exchange rate to appreciate. This rise in the value of the Canadian dollar contributes to the increase in the ratio of domestic to foreign prices, which is necessary for the crowding out of net exports. In the fixed exchange rate case the upward pressure on the exchange rate is removed by an expansion of the nominal money supply. It is this expansion in the nominal money supply that fuels the extra inflation when a fixed exchange rate policy is followed.

This argument suggests that when a domestic demand shock hits the economy, a flexible exchange rate regime will allow the economy to recover more quickly than if a fixed exchange rate is maintained. Following an increase in demand, the period of excess demand will be shorter under a flexible exchange rate policy than under a fixed exchange rate policy because the amount by which domestic prices must rise to restore equilibrium is less in the former case. This argument is put into sharper focus when we consider a decline in autonomous domestic demand. For example, if autonomous investment is reduced, the price level must fall for equilibrium to be restored. If the exchange rate is flexible and if a depreciation follows the decline in demand, then the required reduction in the domestic price level is less than if the exchange rate is fixed because the depreciation stimulates net exports, which bolsters aggregate demand. Under a fixed exchange rate policy the only force pushing the economy back to Y^* is the declining price level. With a fixed exchange rate, the economy will languish for a longer period of time in a state of high unemployment. Output will be below Y^* until the domestic price level has fallen sufficiently.

The above argument is based on the assumption that an *appreciation* of the Canadian dollar accompanies an *increase in domestic demand* and a *depreciation* accompanies a *decrease in domestic demand*. Unfortunately, we cannot say that this will always be the case. In the flexible exchange rate case the actual breakdown of the total change in the ratio of domestic to foreign prices between an exchange rate movement and an increase in domestic prices depends on a number of parameters in the model. It is demonstrated in the appendix to this chapter that it is possible that a rightward shift of the *IS* curve will actually cause a depreciation of the foreign exchange rate.[5] In terms of our previous numerical example it may be, for example, that the 10 per cent rise in the ratio of domestic to foreign prices is achieved by a 15 per cent rise in domestic prices and a 5 per cent *depreciation* of the Canadian dollar. In this situation an increase in exogenous domestic spending leads to a more severe inflation under a flexible exchange rate regime than under a fixed exchange rate regime. This situation will occur if, for example, net exports are very sensitive to changes in the ratio of domestic to foreign prices. As the domestic price level rises following the increase in domestic spending, net exports are crowded out to such a large degree that a depreciation is necessary in order to limit the crowding out of net exports. A second factor is the sensitivity of net capital inflows to interest rate differentials. If net capital inflows are unresponsive to interest rate differentials between Canada and the rest of the world—the *BP* curve is very steep—then the rising interest rate that follows an increase in domestic demand draws in only a small amount of additional net capital inflows. Consequently, only a small decline in net exports is required to restore balance of payments equilibrium. In this case the rise in the domestic price level that is needed to raise the interest rate and displace investment spending may cause too large a decline in net exports. A depreciation will be required so that there is only a modest rise in the ratio of domestic to foreign prices.

If the structure of the economy is such that an *increase* in autonomous domestic demand leads to a *depreciation* under a flexible exchange rate policy, then such a policy leads to a prolonged period of disequilibrium compared with a fixed exchange rate policy. In the case of an increase in domestic demand the maintenance of a fixed exchange rate will force the Bank of Canada to buy Canadian dollars and sell foreign exchange. The reduction in the money supply exerts a dampening influence on the excess demand and equilibrium is restored more quickly with less inflation than if the exchange rate were flexible. Similarly, in the case of a decline in domestic demand the maintenance of a fixed exchange rate policy will require the Bank of Canada to sell Canadian dollars in the foreign exchange market, thereby expanding the domestic money supply. This stimulus helps to push the economy back to the equilibrium level of output Y^*. The amount by which the domestic price level must fall is less than if the exchange rate were

---

[5]Whether the exchange rate appreciates or depreciates following a rightward shift of the *IS* curve does not depend uniquely on the slopes of the *LM* and *BP* curves. The exchange rate may appreciate (depreciate) even if the *BP* curve is steeper (flatter) than the *LM* curve.

flexible and so the economy languishes in an underemployed state for a shorter period of time.

In summary, *in an open economy a permanent change in one component of domestic demand will have no lasting effect on the level of real income*. For example, in the case of an increase in domestic demand, during the adjustment phase the price level rises, the real stock of money declines and the interest rate rises. It is the increases in the rate of interest and the ratio of domestic to foreign prices that crowd out investment and net exports respectively. The sum of the declines in investment and net exports is exactly equal to the size of the stimulus that shifted the *IS* curve and disturbed the initial equilibrium. The effect of the exogenous stimulus on the exchange rate is ambiguous—it may appreciate or it may depreciate depending on the size of certain parameters in the model. If net capital flows are very sensitive to interest rate differentials between Canada and the rest of the world and net exports are insensitive to changes in the ratio of Canadian to foreign price levels, then an increase in domestic demand will tend to cause an appreciation of the Canadian dollar while a decrease in domestic demand will tend to cause a depreciation of the Canadian dollar. In these circumstances a flexible exchange rate policy allows the economy to adjust quickly to the disturbance with a relatively small change in the domestic price level compared with the situation in which a fixed exchange rate is maintained. This means that a decline in domestic demand leads to less unemployment for a shorter period of time if the exchange rate is flexible.

However, if net capital inflows are unresponsive to interest rate differentials and net exports are very sensitive to the ratio of the Canadian price level to the foreign price level, then the government may follow a fixed exchange rate policy in the face of a decline in domestic demand. Such a policy will minimize the unemployment problem during the recession. In the case of an increase in domestic demand the government can shorten the period of excess demand and inflation by following a fixed exchange rate policy. Of course the government may prefer to bathe in the euphoria of excess demand and have few concerns about a prolonged bout of inflation, in which case it might allow the exchange rate to depreciate. Output will be above Y^* for a longer period of time, but the resulting inflation will be greater.

An Increase in the Stock of Money under Flexible Exchange Rates

In this section we analyze the effects of an increase in the nominal stock of money within the *IS-LM-BP-PEP* model under the assumption of a flexible foreign exchange rate. The major conclusion is that an increase in the nominal money supply of, say, 10 per cent will lead to a period of inflation that will raise the price level 10 per cent and cause the currency to depreciate 10 per cent in the foreign exchange market. The model is therefore consistent with the purchasing power parity theorem, which was discussed in Chapter 7.

Chart 11-3 illustrates the analysis. The economy is initially in equilibrium at the point where IS_0, LM_0 and BP_0 intersect. The inflation rate is initially equal to zero.

CHART 11-3 The effect of an increase in the nominal stock of money in an open economy

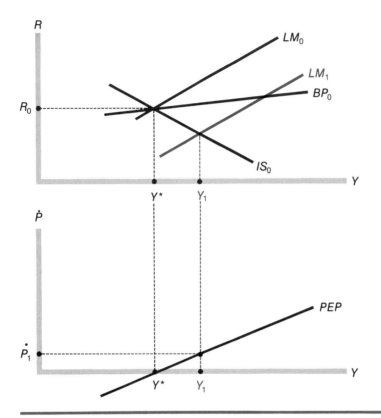

Now suppose the monetary authority increases the nominal stock of money so that the *LM* curve shifts rightwards to *LM₁*. The increase in the nominal stock of money lowers domestic interest rates, stimulates investment expenditures, and raises the level of income to Y_1. Both the drop in the rate of interest and the increase in the level of income tend to cause a balance of payments deficit to emerge; lower interest rates discourage net capital inflows while a higher level of income reduces net exports. Consequently, at the point where *LM₁* cuts *IS₀* there is a positive rate of inflation equal to $\dot{P}_1$ and the exchange rate is depreciating in the foreign exchange market.

One effect of this domestic inflation is to raise domestic prices relative to foreign prices (which are assumed to be fixed in foreign currency). This would tend to reduce net exports and cause both the *BP* and *IS* curves to shift *leftwards*. However, the Canadian dollar is depreciating and this reduces domestic prices relative to foreign prices. For example, Canadian exports become cheaper in terms of British pounds. The effect of the depreciation is therefore to push both the *IS* and *BP* curves *rightwards*. In other words, the domestic inflation and the depreciation of the exchange rate shift the *IS* and *BP* curves in opposite directions.

Let us assume that these countervailing forces exactly balance one another so that the *IS* and *BP* curves remain stationary.

The *LM* curve, however, cannot remain stationary. The new inflation rate of $\dot{P}_I$ reduces the real stock of money and shifts the *LM* curve back to the left. It is convenient to think of the economy sliding up the stationary *IS* curve as the *LM* curve shifts leftwards. As the economy moves up the *IS* curve, the level of income falls towards Y^* and the rate of inflation diminishes towards zero. At the same time the economy moves closer to the *BP* curve so that the balance of payments deficit is gradually removed.

Ultimately, the *LM* curve will return to LM_0, the interest rate will again be R^* and the level of income will once more be at Y^*. Since the *LM* curve has returned to its original position, the *real* stock of money in the final equilibrium position must be exactly equal to the initial *real* stock of money. That is, the percentage increase in the price level during the adjustment period is exactly equal to the percentage increase in the nominal stock of money so that the real stock of money remains unchanged. Since the *IS* and *BP* curves have not shifted during the adjustment period, the ratio of domestic to foreign prices is exactly the same in the final equilibrium as it was initially. In other words, the foreign exchange value of the Canadian dollar depreciates by exactly the same percentage as the Canadian price level rises. This leaves the foreign price of Canadian goods and services unchanged. This result is exactly what the purchasing power parity theorem predicts (see Chapter 7).

The results we have obtained do not depend on the fact that the *IS* and *BP* curves were assumed to be stationary throughout the analysis. Even if these curves do shift during the disequilibrium period, they must eventually return to their original positions. Moreover, the fact that the *BP* curve is drawn flatter than the *LM* curve does not in any way influence the conclusions that the percentage changes in the price level and the exchange rate are equal (in absolute value) to the percentage change in the nominal stock of money that disturbs the initial equilibrium. These points are developed formally in the appendix to this chapter.

Case Study 5:   Should the Canadian Dollar Float When the U.S. Adopts a Restrictive Monetary Policy?

We have already seen that the government's exchange rate policy has an important bearing on the path that the economy follows as it moves from one equilibrium position to another. Choosing the wrong exchange rate policy can lead to more unemployment than necessary when there is a decline in domestic demand, or more inflation than necessary when there is an increase in domestic demand. However, we found that choosing the correct exchange rate policy in the face of disturbances in domestic demand requires knowledge of key structural parameters within the model. Economists who disagree about the size of these parameters will disagree about which exchange rate policy is appropriate. However, we will see in this case study and in the following section that when the disturbances that rock the Canadian economy are external in source, the predictions of our model are unambiguous. This conclusion will be illustrated in this case study by considering the effect of a tight U.S. monetary policy on the Canadian economy under alternative exchange rate regimes. As we saw in Chapter 7, a tight U.S. monetary policy affects Canada through the capital account of the balance of payments. High U.S. interest rates change the Canada–U.S. interest rate differential and therefore the flow of capital.

High U.S. Interest Rates: Flexible Exchange Rate

Chart 11-4 illustrates the effect of an increase in U.S. interest rates when the Canadian government is following a flexible exchange rate policy. The initial position is described by the curves IS_0, LM_0 and BP_0, which intersect at point A. Note that in the initial equilibrium the level of output is at Y^* where the PEP curve cuts the horizontal axis, indicating that the price level is stable.

In Chapter 7 we developed the equation of the BP curve, which we reproduce here for convenience:

$$(7\text{-}6) \qquad R = R^{US} + \frac{s\pi P + n - X_0 - p}{q} + \left(\frac{m}{q}\right)Y$$

It is clear from equation 7-6 that an increase in the U.S. interest rate R^{US} will shift the BP curve upwards through a distance that is exactly equal to the increase in the U.S. interest rate. In Chart 11-4 the new "high U.S. interest rate" BP curve is labelled BP_1. At the initial equilibrium position (point A), which is below BP_1, the balance of payments is in deficit because the increase in the U.S. interest rate reduces the net flow of capital into Canada. In the foreign exchange market there is an excess supply of Canadian dollars, and the Canadian dollar begins to depreciate. This depreciation reduces the ratio of the Canadian price level to the foreign price level $\pi P/P^W$ and net exports increase. The economy is given a boost and output increases beyond the non-inflationary output level Y^*.

During the disequilibrium phase, the economy will pass through a point such as B. Let us consider what is happening to each of the three curves in the upper panel while the economy is temporarily at point B. First, the output level is above the non-inflationary output level Y^* and, as the lower panel shows, there is a positive rate of inflation equal to $\dot{P}_B$. Because the price level is rising, the real stock of money is falling and the LM curve is shifting upwards and to the left. We turn now to the IS and BP curves. At point B, which is below BP_1, the balance of payments is in deficit because of the reduction in net capital inflows that was caused by the increase in R^{US}. To restore balance of payments equilibrium, net exports must rise. This can happen only if the ratio of the Canadian price level to the foreign price level falls. The balance of payments deficit implies there is an excess supply of Canadian dollars in the foreign exchange market. The excess supply precipitates a rapid deterioration of the Canadian dollar, which ensures that the international price ratio $\pi P/P^W$ falls despite the fact that the Canadian price level P is rising at the rate $\dot{P}^B$. This is no accident: the higher the Canadian inflation rate, the more expensive will be Canadian exports, the larger will be the balance of payments deficit and the faster will be the depreciation of the Canadian dollar. Because the ratio of Canadian to foreign price levels $\pi P/P^W$ is declining, the IS curve is shifting

CHART 11-4 The effects of an increase in U.S. interest rates on the Canadian
economy

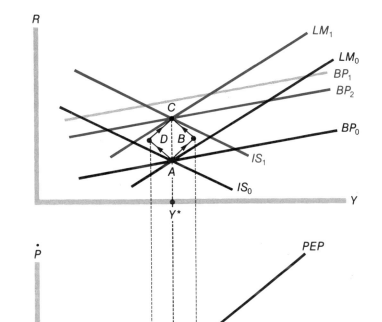

upwards and to the right as net exports expand. At the same time the *BP* curve is
shifting from *BP₁* downwards and to the right.[6]

To summarize, at point *B* output is above the equilibrium level *Y**, and there is a
positive rate of inflation that is pushing the *LM₀* curve upwards and to the left. The
balance of payments is in deficit and the resulting depreciation pushes the *IS₀*
curve upwards and to the right while the *BP₁* curve is shifting downwards and to
the right.

The new equilibrium point is labelled *C*, where *IS₁*, *LM₁* and *BP₂* intersect at the
non-inflationary output level *Y**. It is useful to compare this new equilibrium
position with the original equilibrium position (point *A*). Note that the Canadian
interest rate has risen by an amount that is equal to the vertical distance between

---

[6]As we pointed out earlier in this chapter, while the Canadian dollar is depreciating, the *PEP* curve
will be in a higher position because a depreciating dollar raises the price of imports and therefore the
overall rate of inflation at every given level of output. In equilibrium the exchange rate is stable and the
PEP curve will return to its original position. In the text we ignore this temporary effect, which does not
alter the final equilibrium position, in order to keep the analysis as straightforward as possible.

points A and C. Recall that the U.S. interest rate rose by a larger amount, which is represented by the vertical distance between the curves BP_0 and BP_1. Consequently, overall, the U.S. interest rate has risen relative to the Canadian rate, which means that net capital inflows are lower at point C than at point A. Nevertheless, the balance of payments is once again in equilibrium, because the ratio of Canadian to foreign price levels $\pi P/P^W$ has fallen (the percentage decline in the exchange rate is greater than the percentage increase in the price level) and net exports are greater at point C than at point A. However, investment expenditures decline throughout the disequilibrium phase as the Canadian interest rate rises. Indeed the decline in investment that takes place as the economy moves from point A to point C is exactly equal to the increase in net exports. This must be so because in equilibrium aggregate demand must again be equal to the output level Y^*. An increase in one or more components of aggregate demand must be offset by an equal decline in other components. In this case only two components change: net exports increase and business investment declines, leaving total aggregate demand unchanged.

An important prediction of our *IS-LM-PEP-BP* model is that the adoption of a flexible exchange rate policy in the face of a tight U.S. monetary policy that raises U.S. interest rates will result in a period of excess demand during which output will be above its long-run level and there will be a positive rate of inflation. At the same time, the *Canadian dollar will depreciate* and Canadian interest rates will rise, but by less than U.S. interest rates.

High U.S. Interest Rates: Fixed Exchange Rate

Chart 11-4 can also be used to illustrate the effects of an increase in the U.S. interest rate when the Canadian government adopts a fixed exchange rate policy. Initially, the economy is at point A, where the curves IS_0, LM_0 and BP_0 intersect. The immediate effect of the increase in the U.S. interest rate is to shift the BP curve upwards to BP_1 and to create a balance of payments deficit as net capital imports decline. The excess supply of Canadian dollars in the foreign exchange market puts downward pressure on the Canadian dollar. Under a fixed exchange rate regime the government does not allow the dollar to depreciate. The Bank of Canada's response to the "balance of payments crisis" is to enter the foreign exchange market and buy up Canadian dollars with Canada's foreign exchange reserves. This supports the value of the dollar, but also reduces the domestic money supply. At the current level of income Y^* the transactions demand for money exceeds the diminishing supply of money and interest rates are bid up. As Canadian interest rates rise, the volume of investment spending declines and the Canadian economy is dragged into a recession. The level of output declines below Y^* and during the disequilibrium phase the economy passes through a point such as D in Chart 11-3. Unlike the flexible exchange rate case there is no offsetting stimulus to net exports from a depreciating Canadian dollar.

Consider now the forces that are acting on the curves IS_0, LM_0 and BP_1 while the economy is at point D. From the lower panel it is clear that the Canadian price level is falling at the rate $\dot{P}_D$. With a fixed exchange rate, the decline in the Canadian price level reduces the ratio of Canadian to foreign prices. This gives an increasing advantage to Canadian import-competing and export industries, which expand their output. The effect on the *IS* curve is a shift up and to the right, while the *BP* curve shifts down and to the right. While the economy is at a point such as *D*, there are two opposing forces influencing the position of the *LM* curve. First, because the economy is in a depressed state the price level is falling at the rate $\dot{P}_D$. The effect of the falling price level is to raise the real stock of money which, by itself, would push the *LM* curve down and to the right. However, the second and more powerful influence on the real stock of money is due to the Bank of Canada's purchases of Canadian dollars in the foreign exchange market which reduce the nominal stock of money. How do we know that the nominal money stock is falling faster than the price level so that the real money stock is falling? As long as the economy is below the BP_1 curve, the balance of payments crisis persists and the Canadian dollar will be subject to downward pressure. The only way to restore equilibrium to the balance of payments is to create a domestic recession by reducing the *real* stock of money. A reduction in the real stock of money will do two things: the domestic price level will fall, allowing net exports to increase; and second, domestic interest rates will rise, which will raise net capital inflows from their depressed level. The cost of maintaining a fixed exchange rate when U.S. interest rates are increased is that the government must engineer a domestic recession in order to restore equilibrium to the balance of payments. This is done by reducing the real stock of money and shifting the *LM* curve upwards and to the left.

The final equilibrium point is labelled *C*, where the curves IS_1, LM_1 and BP_2 intersect. This is exactly the same position that the economy would reach if the government had allowed the exchange rate to depreciate. As we discussed earlier, the final values of the real endogenous variables in the model following any disturbance are independent of the particular exchange rate policy that the government follows. In the present case the disturbance is a sudden increase in the U.S. interest rate. Regardless of the Canadian government's exchange rate policy, the economy will move from its initial position at point *A* to a new equilibrium position at point *C*. However, the paths that the economy takes under the alternative exchange rate regimes are entirely different. Under a flexible exchange rate policy the economy experiences an inflationary boom with output temporarily rising above its equilibrium level. Under the fixed exchange rate policy the level of output declines and the unemployment rate rises during the disequilibrium period.

The following example illustrates how these two very different paths can lead to the same final equilibrium position, at least as far as the real variables are concerned. Consider the flexible exchange rate case first. Suppose that during the disequilibrium period the Canadian price level rises 10 per cent. This means that the real stock of money declines 10 per cent and it is this decline that pushes the *LM* curve from LM_0 to LM_1. In addition, suppose that the Canadian dollar depreciates by 15 per cent. This means that the ratio of the Canadian price level to the foreign price level $\pi P/P^W$ declines by 5 per cent. It is this reduction in relative prices that allows Canadian net exports to increase and to help restore equilibrium to the balance of payments. In the fixed exchange rate case, the ratio of the

Canadian price level to foreign price level must also decline by 5 per cent. This is achieved by a 5 per cent decline in the Canadian price level itself. Since the real stock of money must decline by 10 per cent in order to shift the LM curve from LM_0 to LM_1, it follows that the Bank of Canada must reduce the *nominal* stock of money by 15 per cent.

The options that face the Canadian government at the time that the U.S. interest rate rises are therefore twofold. First, to continue with our numerical example, the government can allow the exchange rate to depreciate by 15 per cent and experience a temporary inflationary boom that will raise the price level by 10 per cent. Alternatively, the government can maintain a fixed exchange rate by reducing the nominal stock of money by 15 per cent and drag the economy through a recession that will cut the price level by 5 per cent.[7] In 1981, when U.S. interest rates soared above 20 per cent, the federal government came much closer to following the second alternative than the first. It would appear that the government's fears of inflation were much greater at that time than its fears of unemployment and recession. As we will see in later chapters, from the middle of the 1970s the main preoccupation of macroeconomic policy was to reduce the rate of inflation. When the U.S. adopted an extremely tight monetary policy in 1981, the Canadian government was faced with the choice of either supporting the Canadian dollar and maintaining its tight-money, anti-inflationary stance, or allowing the dollar to depreciate and suffering additional inflationary pressures. The fact that the Canadian inflation rate had been accelerating upwards during the previous several years was no doubt an important factor in the government's decision to support the value of the Canadian dollar by reducing the growth rate of the money supply and living with the recessionary effects. However, it is doubtful that the government anticipated the severity of the 1982 recession, which turned out to be the most severe economic decline since the Great Depression of the 1930s.

An External Disturbance: A Decline in Exports

In this final section we examine the effects of an *external* shock that disturbs both the Canadian balance of payments and the Canadian goods market. In particular, we will look at the adjustment that follows a decline in exports. Throughout the analysis we will assume that the government takes no *internal* policy initiatives, such as changes in tax rates or changes in government spending. However, at the end of the section we will briefly comment on what fiscal policies might be adopted to speed up the adjustment towards the new equilibrium position. Rather than trying to describe the dynamic path that the economy embarks on when exports decline, we will first establish some properties of the new equilibrium position. We will then go back and consider the paths the economy might follow as it moves between the initial and final equilibrium positions. As we shall see, the

---

[7]Of course the government could choose any number of intermediate courses. For example, the government could reduce the nominal money supply by 10 per cent and watch the exchange rate depreciate by 5 per cent. In this case the price level would not change between one equilibrium and another. The rate of inflation would average out to zero and the level of output would be, on average, equal to Y^*.

government's exchange rate policy has an important bearing on this question.

A decline in net exports immediately disturbs two markets: the balance of payments will be in deficit and there will be excess supply in the domestic goods market as unsold exports accumulate. The size of the balance of payments deficit and the amount by which aggregate demand is deficient are identical, and in the following discussion we will use the symbol D to denote this quantity. To restore equilibrium to the balance of payments, net exports and/or net capital inflows must increase. To restore equilibrium to the domestic goods market, aggregate demand must increase. This could be achieved by an increase in net exports and/or an increase in investment expenditures. Note that an increase in net exports helps to restore equilibrium to both markets. Suppose, for example, that net exports increase by D so that net exports return to their original level. Clearly, both markets will be back in equilibrium and neither net capital inflows nor investment expenditures will have changed between the original and final equilibrium positions. In fact this is precisely what must happen. Suppose, for example, that net exports increase during the adjustment period but by less than D. Balance of payments equilibrium will be restored only if there is an increase in the Canadian interest rate that stimulates additional capital inflows. While this will restore balance of payments equilibrium, it is not consistent with equilibrium in the goods market. Because net exports increase by less than D, aggregate demand is still deficient. The gap can be removed only if the interest rate falls and investment is stimulated. If net exports increase by less than D, the rate of interest must rise to restore equilibrium to the balance of payments, but the rate of interest must fall to restore equilibrium to the domestic goods market! The inescapable conclusion is that net exports will, in fact, increase by D, and net exports will return to the original level.

Whether the government follows a fixed or flexible exchange rate policy, the fact remains that a sudden decline in net exports that creates a balance of payments deficit and an excess supply in the domestic goods market must be followed by a process of adjustment that restores net exports to their former level. In comparing the original and final equilibrium position no other *real* variables will change—the interest rate, the level of investment expenditures, net capital inflows and the *real* money supply will all show no net change. The increase in net exports is realized through a decline in the ratio of the Canadian price level to the foreign price level. Under a flexible exchange rate policy, the exchange rate will depreciate sufficiently to restore net exports to their former level. In the fixed exchange rate case, it is through a decline in the domestic price level itself that the required drop in the ratio of the Canadian price level to the foreign price level is achieved. Let us now look at the dynamic adjustment process under alternative exchange-rate policies.

Flexible Exchange Rate

Chart 11-5 illustrates the adjustment process that follows a decline in Canadian exports. The initial position is at point A, where the curves IS_0, LM_0 and BP_0 intersect. The immediate effect of the drop in export sales is that the IS curve

CHART 11-5 An example of an external shock: a decline in exports

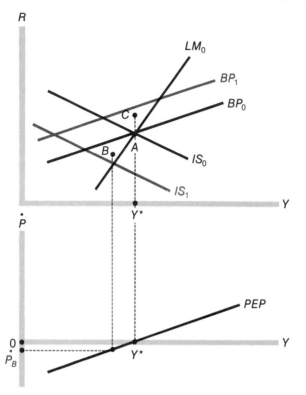

shifts downwards and to the left to IS_1, and the BP curve shifts upwards and to the left to BP_1. At the initial position two markets are out of equilibrium. Because of the drop in exports the balance of payments is in deficit (point A is below BP_1) so that there is an excess supply of Canadian dollars in the foreign exchange market which puts downward pressure on the value of the Canadian dollar. Also, in the domestic goods market there is an excess supply of goods (point A is above IS_1) because export sales have declined. As we have seen, the final equilibrium position is also at point A.

In the flexible exchange rate case, one version of the dynamic story is that the economy never leaves point A. The exchange rate adjusts so quickly that as one component of exports declines with the falling U.S. income, the exchange rate depreciates and another component of Canadian exports increases because of the relative price advantage that is created by the depreciation of the Canadian dollar. In this version, the IS and BP curves, strictly speaking, never deviate from the original positions IS_0 and BP_0. They remain quite stationary as the simultaneous declines in U.S. real income and the value of the Canadian dollar have instantaneously offsetting effects that leave net exports at a constant level. The balance of payments never experiences a deficit and the Canadian economy suffers no excess supply of goods even for a moment. Left to itself, the free enterprise price system works its marvellous magic: the flexible exchange rate so perfectly insulates the Canadian economy from the external shock that it is not even noticed, even for a moment.

A somewhat more realistic possibility is that when the level of U.S. income declines, Canadian exports to the U.S. will also decline, and that there will indeed be a balance of payments deficit and a state of excess supply in the Canadian goods market. The economy will soon find itself at a position such as B in Chart 11-5, where output is below Y^*. The lower panel shows that in this depressed state the price level is declining at a rate $\dot{P}_B$. Interestingly, this implies that the dynamic adjustment path back to point A involves a cyclical approach during which the level of output will exceed Y^* and the economy will experience a positive rate of inflation. As we have seen, the final equilibrium position is at point A. The LM curve must come back to LM_0 and the *real* money supply must be the same at the end of the adjustment process as it is in the initial equilibrium position. However, under a flexible exchange rate policy, the *nominal* money supply is fixed so that the price level must also remain unchanged after the adjustment process has worked itself out. If the decline in exports pushes the economy to point B in Chart 11-5, where the price level is falling, the *real* money supply will temporarily increase, which will eventually stimulate the economy and push the level of output beyond Y^*. The resulting inflation will then reduce the *real* money supply back to its original level.

In conclusion, the probable response of the Canadian economy to a drop in exports under a flexible exchange rate regime is that the level of output will oscillate around Y^*, first declining as the drop in exports creates unemployment and a falling price level and then rising beyond Y^* to create a period of high employment and a positive rate of inflation. Since the price level must remain unchanged overall, the price inflation must exactly offset the initial price defla-tion. For example, if the price level initially falls by 10 per cent when output is below Y^*, the level of output will rebound above Y^* until the price level has risen by 10 per cent.

Fixed Exchange Rate

When the government maintains a fixed exchange rate policy there is no doubt that in the absence of fiscal policies the economy will go through a recession that will not be offset by a period of high employment. Indeed, it is through the effects of the recession on the Canadian price level that net exports are stimulated and the disequilibria in the balance of payments and the goods market are removed. Chart 11-5 illustrates the story.

Again the initial equilibrium position is at point A. As we have seen, the drop in exports shifts the IS and BP curves to IS_1 and BP_1 respectively. The decline in exports creates an excess supply of goods which leads to a decline in output below the equilibrium level Y^*. The economy therefore moves to a position such as B, which is above IS_1—there is an excess supply of goods—and below BP_1—there is a balance of payments deficit and an excess supply of Canadian dollars in the foreign exchange market. The lower panel of Chart 11-5 shows that the price level is falling at a rate equal to $\dot{P}_B$. This tends to increase the real stock of money. However, since there is an excess supply of Canadian dollars in the foreign exchange market, the Bank of Canada must use foreign exchange reserves to buy up Canadian dollars. These purchases of Canadian dollars reduce the nominal stock of money. For simplicity, let us assume that the rate of decline of the price level $\dot{P}_B$ is exactly equal to rate of decline of the nominal money stock at point B. Given this assumption, the real money stock remains constant and the LM curve remains stationary at LM_0.

However, the IS and BP curves will not remain at IS_1 and BP_1. As the Canadian price level declines, the ratio of the Canadian price level to the foreign price level also declines. This stimulates net exports and shifts the IS curve upwards and to the right while the BP curve shifts downwards and to the right. This process will continue until net exports have been restored to their original level. At this point the IS and BP curves will be back at IS_0 and BP_0 respectively. The level of output will once more be at Y^* and the price level will be constant.

It is interesting to compare the adjustment paths following a drop in Canadian exports under alternative exchange-rate policies. Whether the exchange rate is flexible or fixed, the adjustment involves a reduction in the ratio of the Canadian price level to the foreign price level which is just sufficient to restore exports to their original level. In the *flexible exchange rate case* this is achieved through a depreciation of the Canadian dollar. As we have seen, it is likely that during the depreciation the level of output will oscillate around the equilibrium value. An initial and relatively mild recession will later give way to a period of higher employment and inflation. However, when the dust finally settles and the level of output returns to its unique equilibrium level, the recession and boom cycle will have cancelled each other out in the sense that the Canadian price level will end up at exactly the point where it started. The decline in the price level during the recession is exactly offset by an equal rise in the price level during the boom phase.

The adjustment under a *fixed exchange rate* is quite different. Since the exchange rate is prevented from falling, the price level itself must decline. If the adjustment requires a 10 per cent decline in the value of the Canadian dollar under a flexible exchange rate policy, then a fixed exchange rate policy will drag the economy into a recession and hold it there until the domestic price level has fallen by 10 per cent. This is an example of how an external shock can create a "balance of payments crisis" under a fixed exchange rate policy and force the government to take harsh restrictive domestic policies to correct the situation. Advocates of flexible exchange rates argue that such harsh policies are unnecessary since a flexible exchange rate will insulate the domestic economy from external shocks.

Our analysis of the adjustment process under a fixed exchange rate regime following a decline in Canadian exports has assumed that the government simply allows the adjustment process to work itself out and that the government does not intervene with offsetting fiscal policies. As we have seen, the decline in exports immediately disturbs two markets. The balance of payments is in a deficit position and there is an excess supply of goods in the domestic goods market. One way to remove this state of excess supply is to increase government spending by an amount exactly equal to the decline in exports. In Chart 11-5 the leftward shift of IS_0 to IS_1 due to the decline in exports is immediately offset by the increase in government spending, and the IS curve returns to IS_0. The state of the economy is now described by IS_0, LM_0 and BP_1. Assuming that the expansionary fiscal policy occurs simultaneously with the decline in exports so that the economy remains at the initial position at point A, only the balance of payments will be in disequilibrium on account of the decline in exports.

The arrangement of the IS, LM and BP curves is now exactly the same as in Chart 11-4, when the increase in U.S. interest rates shifted the BP curve upwards to BP_1. Consequently, the adjustment process that the economy follows after the simultaneous drop in exports and the exactly offsetting increase in government spending is exactly as we described in the case study. Balance of payments equilibrium will be restored through a combination of an increase in the Canadian interest rate, which will raise net capital inflows, and a decline in the Canadian price level, which will raise Canadian exports. In Chart 11-5 the final equilibrium position with fiscal policy will be at a point such as C rather than at A. Because the Canadian price level must decline under a fixed exchange rate policy, the Canadian economy will not be spared from a recession as it moves from point A to point C. However, the interesting point is that since capital inflows will be higher at point C than at point A, net exports do not have to be restored to the original level for balance of payments equilibrium. The expansionary fiscal policy that immediately restores equilibrium in the domestic goods market leaves the economy with a *smaller* price level adjustment and consequently a less severe recession. In other words, the fixed exchange rate adjustment process in the absence of any offsetting fiscal policy takes the economy from point A through a recession and back to point A. This recession is deeper than the one that the economy suffers if an expansionary fiscal policy is adopted and the economy moves from point A to point C.

Summary

In this chapter we have introduced the balance of payments into our flexible price model. We have considered the adjustment process following a number of disturbances. In this regard, we have found that there is a distinction to be made between *internal* and *external* disturbances. The effect of internal disturbances on the equilibrium value of a flexible exchange rate is ambiguous in the sense that different results obtain depending on the size of key structural parameters. However, in the case of external disturbances the effect on the exchange rate is clear. In a case study into the effects of an increase in U.S. interest rates we were able to obtain unambiguous predictions concerning the consequences of adopting fixed or flexible exchange rate policies. Finally, in the last section we established that a flexible exchange rate policy offers more protection to the Canadian economy in the face of a decline in Canadian exports than a fixed exchange rate policy. However, given that a fixed exchange rate policy is adopted, we showed that fiscal policy can be used to mitigate the recessionary effects of a decline in exports.

Appendix: An Algebraic Approach

In this appendix an algebraic approach is used to derive some of the key propositions that have been developed in this and the previous chapter. First we examine the effects of (1) an exogenous demand stimulus and (2) an increase in the nominal money supply within the *IS-LM-PEP* model. Then the analysis is extended to the *IS-LM-BP-PEP* model.

The *IS-LM-PEP* Model

An important proposition that was developed in Chapter 10 is that given the monetary authority maintains a constant nominal money supply, the equilibrium position of the economy must be characterized by zero inflation. The equilibrium level of income must be at the point where the *PEP* curve intersects the output axis. We designate this level of output Y^*. The product-market clearing condition requires that the level of output be equal to the sum of the expenditure components. The following equations describe two possible equilibrium positions.

$$C_0 + I_0 + G_0 + (X - M)_0 = Y^*$$
$$C_0 + I_1 + G_1 + (X - M)_1 = Y^*$$

Note that the levels of output and consumption are equal to Y^* and C_0 in both cases (we assume that consumption depends only on the level of income). Now subtract the first equation from the second:

(11A-1) $\Delta I + \Delta G + \Delta(X-M) = 0$

Equation 11A-1 says that in comparing one equilibrium with another, following a disturbance in any component of autonomous demand or a change in the money supply, the sum of the changes in investment spending, government spending and net exports must be zero. Another useful result can be obtained from the *LM* curve (equation 8-2):

$$\ell P_0 R_0 = -\$_0^S + k P_0 Y^*$$
or $$\ell P_1 R_1 = -\$_1^S + k P_1 Y^*$$

Again, these two equations represent two alternative equilibrium positions; in both cases the equilibrium level of income is Y^*. Note that the change in a product such as PR can be approximated by

$$\Delta PR = P_0 \Delta R + R_0 \Delta P.$$

Consequently, subtracting the first *LM* equation from the second gives

$$\ell (P_0 \Delta R + R_0 \Delta P) = -\Delta \$^S + k Y^* \Delta P.$$

Now collect together the ΔP terms:

$$\Delta P(k Y^* - \ell R_0) = \Delta \$^S + \ell P_0 \Delta R$$

The term in parentheses is simply the demand for real money balances which in equilibrium must equal the supply of real money

(11A-2) $\left(\dfrac{\$_0^S}{P_0}\right)\Delta P = \Delta \$^S + \ell P_0 \Delta R.$

Equation 11A-2 shows how the changes in the price level, the nominal money supply and the interest rate are related between one equilibrium position and another, regardless of the type of exogenous shock that caused the economy to move from one equilibrium position to another.

A Fiscal Stimulus

Suppose the government increases its expenditures by an amount ΔG. Net exports will not change from one equilibrium to another since we initially assume that exports X are exogenous and that imports M depend only on the level of income which remains unchanged at Y^*, where the *PEP* curve cuts the horizontal axis. The role of relative international prices in determining net export flows is incorporated later in this appendix. Under these assumptions, $\Delta(X-M)$ of equation 11A-1 is zero following an increase in government spending. Equation 11A-1 reduces to

$$\Delta G = -\Delta I.$$

This demonstrates the proposition that an increase in government spending will eventually crowd out an equal amount of investment spending. This is achieved through an increase in the interest rate. From the investment equation 5-1 we have

$$\Delta I = -e\Delta R.$$

Given the increase in government spending ΔG we can use the last two equations to determine by how much the interest rate must rise in order to crowd out an equal amount of investment spending:

$$\Delta R = -\frac{1}{e}\Delta I$$

or $\Delta R = \dfrac{1}{e}\Delta G$

As we have seen, the interest rate rises because the excess demand created by the increase in government spending causes a bout of inflation which in turn reduces the real stock of money. Using equation 11A-2 we can determine exactly how much prices will increase following a permanent increase in government spending. Note that the nominal money supply is unchanged so 11A-2 reduces to

$$\left(\frac{\$_0^S}{P_0}\right)\Delta P = \ell P_0 \Delta R.$$

We have just seen that the change in the interest rate given the demand stimulus ΔG is $\Delta G/e$. Consequently:

$$\left(\frac{\$_0^S}{P_0}\right)\Delta P = P_0\left(\frac{\ell}{e}\right)\Delta G$$

This can be rearranged to show the effect of the demand stimulus on price levels:

$$\frac{\Delta P}{P_0} = \frac{\ell\,\Delta G}{e(\$_0^S/P_0)}$$

where $\Delta P/P_0$ represents the proportionate change in the price level. Note that, given the size of the demand stimulus ΔG, the percentage change in the price level depends directly on ℓ and inversely on e. Recall that in the new equilibrium, investment expenditures will be reduced by exactly the same amount as the increase in government spending. The more sensitive investment is to changes in the interest rate (the larger e is), the "easier" it is to displace investment expenditures. The larger is e, the smaller is the required increase in the price level and decline in the real stock of money. On the other hand, if the demand for money is very interest-elastic (ℓ is large) it will take a very large decline in the real stock of money, and therefore a large increase in the price level, to raise the interest rate by the required amount.

An Increase in the Nominal Money Supply

Now suppose the government increases the nominal money supply by an amount $\Delta\$^S$. Consider first equation 11A-1. Since neither net exports, which depends only on the level of income, nor government spending, which is exogenous, will change in response to an increase in the nominal money supply (again the price effects on net exports are ignored temporarily) it follows that

$$\Delta I = 0.$$

In other words, an increase in the nominal money supply has no effect whatsoever on the real variables in the model. Since investment depends on the rate of interest (see equation 5-1) it must be that the rate of interest is unchanged following an increase in the nominal money supply,

$$\Delta R = 0.$$

Using equation 11A-2 we can establish the effect on prices of an increase in the nominal money supply of $\Delta\$^S$:

$$\left(\frac{\$_0^S}{P_0}\right)\Delta P = \Delta\$^S + 0$$

or
$$\frac{\Delta P}{P_0} = \frac{\Delta\$^S}{\$_0^S}$$

This demonstrates that the proportionate rise in the price level is identical to the proportionate rise in the nominal money supply. The real money supply does not change.

The *IS-LM-BP-PEP* Model

The extension of the model to include the balance of payments constraint that net capital inflows plus net exports must sum to zero in equilibrium and the effect of relative international prices on net exports does not invalidate equations 11A-1 and 11A-2, but it does provide an additional equation representing the *BP* curve.

$$(7\text{-}6) \qquad R = R^{US} + \frac{s\pi P + n - X_0 - p}{q} + \left(\frac{m}{q}\right)Y \qquad\qquad BP \text{ curve}$$

It will be convenient to rearrange this equation as follows:

$$qR_0 - qR_0^{US} - s(\pi_0 P_0) - n + X_0 + p - mY^* = 0$$

where the subscript $_0$ refers to the initial equilibrium position and Y^* is the long-run equilibrium level of output. A new equilibrium will be established if an exogenous shock disturbs the economy. The new equilibrium is:

$$qR_1 - qR_1^{US} - s(\pi_1 P_1) - n + X_0 + p - mY^* = 0$$

Note that the level of income remains unchanged at Y^*, where the *PEP* curve cuts the horizontal axis. We have also assumed that the parameters n, X_0 and p remain unchanged. This is simply because the exogenous disturbances that we consider below do not involve these parameters.[1] Subtracting the first equation from the second, we obtain the relationship between the change in the ratio of the Canadian price level to the foreign price level $\triangle \pi P$ and the change in the interest rate $\triangle R$ when comparing one equilibrium with another.

$$q\triangle R - q\triangle R^{US} - s\triangle(\pi P) = 0$$

$$(11A\text{-}3) \text{ or } q\triangle R - s\triangle(\pi P) = q\triangle R^{US}$$

An Increase in Domestic Demand: A Fiscal Stimulus

In this section we consider the effects of an increase in government spending on the important endogenous variables within the model. Before we even introduce the issue of what exchange rate policy the government is following, equations 11A-1 and 11A-3 can be used to solve for $\triangle R$ and $\triangle(\pi P)$, given the increase in government spending $\triangle G$. It is convenient to reproduce these equations here:

$$(11A\text{-}1) \qquad \triangle I + \triangle G + \triangle(X - M) = 0$$

---

[1]If, however, we wanted to consider the effect of a sudden increase in imports that is unrelated to the level of income and to the ratio of domestic prices to foreign prices we would allow the parameter n to rise.

(11A-3) $\qquad q\triangle R - s\triangle\pi P = q\triangle R^{US}$

First, recall that the change in investment expenditures is always determined by the change in the interest rate, $\triangle I = -e\triangle R$. In addition, the equation for net exports (see equation 7-5 in Chapter 7) shows that the change in net exports is determined by the change in the ratio of Canadian to foreign prices, $\triangle(X - M) = -s\triangle(\pi P)$. Using this information, equation 11A-1 can be rewritten:

$$-e\triangle R + \triangle G - s\triangle(\pi P) = 0$$

(11A-1a) $\quad$ or $\ e\triangle R + s\triangle(\pi P) = \triangle G$

Equation 11A-3 can also be modified, since in the present case there is no reason to expect the U.S. interest rate to change, $\triangle R^{US} = 0$:

(11A-3a) $\qquad q\triangle R - s\triangle(\pi P) = 0$

Equations 11A-1a and 11A-3a form a two-equation system in $\triangle R$ and $\triangle(\pi P)$. The solutions are:

(11A-4) $\qquad \triangle R = \dfrac{\triangle G}{q + e} > 0$

(11A-5) $\qquad \triangle(\pi P) = \dfrac{q\triangle G}{s(q + e)} > 0$

These equations show that a permanent increase in government expenditures, or any component of autonomous expenditure, will raise both the interest rate and the ratio of Canadian to foreign prices. The increase in the interest rate crowds out private investment expenditures. The increase in the ratio of Canadian to foreign prices crowds out net exports. The actual increases in the rate of interest and the ratio of Canadian to foreign prices are independent of the government's exchange rate policy. However, the ratio of Canadian to foreign prices has two components: the Canadian price level P and the exchange rate π. How the total change in πP is broken down between a change in π and a change in P does depend on the nature of the government's exchange rate policy. We will examine the flexible and fixed exchange rate cases in turn.

1) Flexible Exchange Rate

In this case the money supply is exogenously determined by the government. When government expenditure is increased, the money supply is assumed to remain fixed, $\triangle\$^s = 0$. From equation 11A-2 we have

$$\left(\frac{\$_0^S}{P_0}\right)\triangle P = \ell P_0\triangle R,$$

so, using equation 11A-4,

$$\left(\frac{\$_0^S}{P_0}\right)\triangle P = \frac{\ell P_0\triangle G}{q + e}$$

(11A-6) $$\frac{\triangle P}{P_0} = \frac{\ell \triangle G}{(q+e)(\$_0^S/P_0)} > 0.$$

Equation 11A-6 shows that under a flexible exchange rate policy an increase in government spending will lead to an increase in the domestic price level. We now determine the effect on the foreign exchange rate. The total change in the ratio of Canadian to foreign prices πP has two components:

(11A-7) $\triangle(\pi P) = P_0\triangle\pi + \pi_0\triangle P$

Substituting 11A-5 and 11A-6 into 11A-7 we have:

$$\frac{q\triangle G}{s(q+e)} = P_0\triangle\pi + \frac{\pi_0\ell P_0\triangle G}{(q+e)(\$_0^S/P_0)}$$

This can be solved for $\triangle\pi$:

(11A-8) $$\triangle\pi = \frac{\triangle G}{(q+e)}\left[\frac{q}{sP_0} - \frac{\pi_0\ell}{(\$_0^S/P_0)}\right]$$

Since all the parameters and initial values in this expression are positive, the sign of $\triangle\pi$ depends on the specific parameter values. For example, if q is large, meaning that capital flows are very sensitive to the interest rate, and s is very small, meaning that net exports are insensitive to the ratio of Canadian to foreign prices, then the exchange rate will appreciate following an increase in government expenditure. However, if s is sufficiently large, or if q is zero, $\triangle\pi$ will be negative. Note that the slopes of the *BP* and *LM* curves, m/q and k/ℓ respectively, are independent of s so that the slopes of these two schedules alone do *not* determine whether the exchange rate will appreciate or depreciate following an expansionary fiscal policy. The parameter s determines the sensitivity of net exports to changes in the ratio of Canadian to foreign prices and therefore the speed with which the *IS* and *BP* curves shift leftwards when the ratio of Canadian to foreign prices rises.

2) Fixed Exchange Rate

Under a fixed exchange rate policy $\triangle\pi = 0$, but the money supply becomes endogenous. From equation 11A-7 we have

$$\triangle(\pi P) = \pi_0\triangle P,$$

and from 11A-5

$$\pi_0\triangle P = \frac{q\triangle G}{s(q+e)},$$

(11A-9)   or $$\triangle P = \frac{q\triangle G}{s\pi_0(q+e)} > 0.$$

Comparing 11A-9 and 11A-6 we have

$$\Delta P(\pi \text{ fixed}) - \Delta P(\pi \text{ flexible}) = \frac{\Delta G}{(q+e)}\left[\frac{q}{s\pi_0} - \frac{\ell P_0}{(\$_0^S/P_0)}\right]$$

$$= \frac{\Delta G\, P_0}{(q+e)\,\pi_0}\left[\frac{q}{sP_0} - \frac{\ell\,\pi_0}{(\$_0^S/P_0)}\right]$$

so, using 11A-8
$$= \Delta\pi\left(\frac{P_0}{\pi_0}\right),$$

or $\quad \dfrac{\Delta P}{P_0}(\pi \text{ fixed}) - \dfrac{\Delta P}{P_0}(\pi \text{ flexible}) = \dfrac{\Delta\pi}{\pi_0}.$

This demonstrates that if the exchange rate appreciates (depreciates) following an increase in government spending, then domestic inflation will be greater (less) under a fixed exchange rate policy than under a flexible exchange rate policy.

An Increase in the Nominal Money Supply

Equations 11A-3a (derived from the *BP* curve) and 11A-1a (derived from the crowding-out equation 11A-1) apply as equally to an increase in the nominal money supply as to an increase in exogenous spending. However, since there is no increase in government spending, equation 11A-1a reduces to 11A-1b,

(11A-1b) $e\Delta R + s\Delta(\pi P) = 0$

(11A-3a) $q\Delta R - s\Delta(\pi P) = 0$

Adding one equation to another reveals that $\Delta R = 0$ provided that $q \neq -e$, which we assume to be the case. This in turn implies $\Delta(\pi P) = 0$.

Since $\Delta R = 0$ it follows that $\Delta I = 0$ because investment depends only on the interest rate. Equation 11A-1 shows that with $\Delta I = \Delta G = 0$, it follows that $\Delta(X - M) = 0$. Hence, an increase in the nominal money supply has no effect on real variables $Y, I, C, (X - M)$.

Finally, combining $\Delta R = 0$ with equation 11A-2 and $\Delta(\pi P) = 0$ with equation 11A-7 gives

$$\frac{\Delta\$^S}{\$_0^S} = \frac{\Delta P}{P_0} = -\frac{\Delta\pi}{\pi_0},$$

which demonstrates that a given proportionate increase in the nominal money stock leads to an equal proportion *rise* in the price level and *decline* in the value of the Canadian dollar in the foreign exchange market.

An Increase in U.S. Interest Rates

In this section we examine the effects of an increase in U.S. interest rates on the Canadian economy. As we saw in the last section, some headway can be made even before we consider what exchange rate policy the government is following. Again, equations 11A-1 and 11A-3 form the basis of the preliminary analysis. In the present case, there is no increase in government spending and so equation 11A-1a, which was derived from 11A-1, reduces to

(11A-1b) $e\triangle R + s\triangle(\pi P) = 0.$

For ease of reference we reproduce equation 11A-3.

(11A-3) $q\triangle R - s\triangle(\pi P) = q\triangle R^{US}$

Equations 11A-1b and 11A-3 form a two-equation system that can be solved for $\triangle R$ and $\triangle(\pi P)$:

(11A-10) $$\triangle R = \frac{q}{(q+e)}\triangle R^{US} > 0$$

(11A-11) $$\triangle(\pi P) = \frac{-eq}{s(q+e)}\triangle R^{US} < 0.$$

Equation 11A-10 shows that the increase in the U.S. interest rate will lead to a rise in the Canadian interest rate *regardless of the exchange rate policy*. However, the Canadian interest rate rises by less than the U.S. interest rate because $q/(q+e)$ is less than unity. The more sensitive net capital inflows are to the Canadian-U.S. interest rate differential (the larger q is), the closer the ratio $q/(q+e)$ will be to unity. In the limiting case that q tends to infinity, capital is perfectly mobile and the Canadian interest rate is equal to the U.S. interest rate. In this limiting case the *BP* curve is horizontal and cuts the vertical axis at R^{US}. Note that $q/(q+e)$ also tends to unity in this limiting case so that $\triangle R = \triangle R^{US}$.

The second factor that determines how the Canadian interest rate responds to changes in the U.S. interest rate is the sensitivity of investment spending to changes in the interest rate, measured by the parameter e. As we have seen, the Canadian interest rate rises by a smaller amount than the U.S. interest rate. Consequently, net capital inflows will be smaller in the final equilibrium position compared with the initial equilibrium position. This means that net exports must rise to maintain balance-of-payments equilibrium. However, an increase in net exports must be exactly offset by a decline in investment spending since total aggregate demand must be equal to Y^* in all equilibrium positions.[2] It is the rise in the interest rate that reduces investment spending. If investment is highly interest elastic (e is large), only a small increase in the Canadian interest rate is required to induce the necessary decline in investment.

Equation 11A-11 shows that regardless of the government's exchange rate policy, an increase in the U.S. interest rate will reduce the ratio of Canadian to foreign prices. As we pointed out in the previous paragraph, this is necessary because in the new equilibrium net exports will be greater.

Now we turn to examine how exchange rate policy determines the breakdown of the decline in the ratio of Canadian to foreign prices into a Canadian price level adjustment and an exchange rate adjustment.

---

[2]Note that equation 11A-1 implies $\triangle(X - M) = -\triangle I$.

1) Flexible Exchange Rate

In this case the money supply is exogenously determined by the government, $\triangle\$^S = 0$. Equation 11A-2 reduces to

$$\left(\frac{\$_0^S}{P_0}\right)\triangle P = \ell P_0 \triangle R.$$

We can use 11A-10 to substitute for the change in the interest rate:

$$\left(\frac{\$_0^S}{P_0}\right)\triangle P = \frac{q\ell}{(q+e)}P_0\triangle R^{US}$$

(11A-12) $\qquad \dfrac{\triangle P}{P_0} = \dfrac{q\ell}{(q+e)}\dfrac{\triangle R^{US}}{(\$_0^S/P_0)} > 0$

In order to find the change in the exchange rate we use equations 11A-7, 11A-11 and 11A-12:

$$\frac{-eq\triangle R^{US}}{s(q+e)} = P_0\triangle\pi + \pi_0\left[\frac{q\ell P_0\triangle R^{US}}{(q+e)(\$_0^S/P_0)}\right]$$

Solving for $\triangle\pi$, we have

$$\triangle\pi = \frac{-q\triangle R^{US}}{(q+e)P_0}\left[\frac{e}{s} + \frac{\pi_0\ell P_0}{(\$_0^S/P_0)}\right] < 0.$$

Here we can state unambiguously that a rise in the U.S. interest rate will cause a depreciation of the Canadian dollar. We have already seen that the Canadian price level rises under a flexible exchange rate policy and that the ratio of Canadian to foreign prices must *fall*. The depreciation must be sufficiently large to offset the rise in the Canadian price level.

2) Fixed Exchange Rate

Under a fixed exchange rate policy, all the adjustment in the ratio of Canadian to foreign prices is achieved through a decline in the Canadian price level. From equation 11A-7 we have:

$$\triangle(\pi P) = \pi_0\triangle P$$

Using equation 11A-11:

$$\triangle P = \frac{-eq}{\pi_0 s(q+e)}\triangle R^{US} < 0$$

Unlike the flexible exchange rate case, in which the Canadian price level rose, when the exchange rate is fixed, higher U.S. interest rates cause the Canadian price level to fall. The level of output will be *below* Y* throughout the adjustment phase. In order to maintain the fixed exchange rate, monetary policy must be very restrictive to force down the Canadian price level. The Canadian economy therefore approaches the new equilibrium via a recession rather than a period of excess demand.

In this section we have looked at the effects of both internal and external shocks on the Canadian economy. The case of a decline in Canadian exports was considered in the main body of the chapter. We leave it to the interested student to develop the algebraic details of this and other disturbances.

Key Concepts

domestic demand
internal and external disturbances
fixed and flexible exchange rates
the relationship between exchange rate policy and the
   breakdown of a change in the ratio of the Canadian
   price level to the foreign price level into an exchange
   rate adjustment and a price level adjustment.

Review Questions

1. Use the *IS-LM-BP-PEP* model to analyze the effects of a decline in autonomous investment under both fixed and flexible exchange rate regimes.
   a) Does the particular exchange rate policy that the government adopts influence the final equilibrium values of net exports, net capital inflows, the interest rate, the real money supply, the nominal money supply, the price level and the ratio of the Canadian price level to the foreign price level?
   b) What factors determine whether the exchange rate will appreciate or depreciate when the exchange rate is floating?
   c) If the exchange rate is subject to upward pressure, which exchange rate policy will minimize the unemployment problem during the adjustment period?
2. Suppose the federal government adopts long-term policies that encourage Canadian ownership of resource industries. If this reduces net capital inflows over the long term, what will be the effects of these policies on the economy as a whole? What exchange rate policy would you recommend the government adopt as it pursues its "Canadianization" program?
3. One effect of an increase in U.S. interest rates is to cause Canadian interest rates to rise. What factors determine by how much Canadian rates will rise, *given* the size of the increase in U.S. rates?

Part4

The Unemployment–
Inflation Trade-Off
Reconsidered

It is easy to beat inflation, we could just put the money supply increase down to zero and we won't have inflation... so what happens is you slow down the economy so darn much that you have massive unemployment...

Pierre Elliot Trudeau[1]

In the previous two chapters it was demonstrated that the equilibrium income level in our *IS-LM-PEP* macroeconomic model is determined in the labour market and production sector of the economy. If the government attempts to increase the level of income and employment by a good dose of fiscal policy, the economy will automatically gravitate back to its original equilibrium income position. The only permanent effect of an increase in government expenditures is a higher price level and a higher rate of interest, which will crowd out an equivalent amount of new investment to offset the increase in government expenditures. The best that the government can hope for is a *short-run* stimulative effect on output. As discussed in Chapter 10, the duration of this short-run stimulative effect following an expansionary fiscal policy depends on the characteristics of the Phillips curve. The steeper the Phillips curve and/or the faster the adjustment in inflation expectations, the shorter the short-run adjustment period and the less the potential for even a temporary gain in output from an expansionary fiscal policy.

In this chapter and the next three chapters, we wish to probe further the policy implications of the *IS-LM-PEP* macroeconomic model. During the 1960s and early 1970s, Keynesian policy makers thought that they could "beat the Phillips curve at its own game." By continually expanding the money supply, the government *might* be able to *perpetuate* the short-run adjustment period and therefore bring about a *permanent* increase in the level of output and employment. The price the government would have to pay for such a *permanent* increase in output and employment would be an *enduring* inflation rate. This possibility brings us face-to-face with the now famous inflation–unemployment trade-off. In this chapter we analyze the nature of this elusive inflation–unemployment trade-off within our *IS-LM-PEP* macroeconomic model, from both Keynesian and monetarist perspectives. Since the trade-off issue is basically a *long-run* issue (*perpetuate* the short run, a *permanent* increase in output, an *enduring* inflation rate), it should come as no surprise that the monetarists, denizens of the long run, hold the upper

[1]*Toronto Star*, 24 February 1979.

hand in this chapter. *In the long run*, there is *no* trade-off between inflation and unemployment, and the government *cannot* permanently decrease the level of unemployment by implementing Keynesian demand-management policies. However, the government can permanently lower the inflation rate. In the now famous words of Milton Friedman, "Inflation is always and everywhere a monetary phenomenon. It is always and everywhere produced by a more rapid rise in the quantity of money than in output."[2] By restricting the growth rate of the money supply, the government can control the long-run (equilibrium) inflation rate.

While there is *no long-run* trade-off between inflation and unemployment, there is an important *short-run* relationship between inflation and unemployment when the macroeconomic system is in disequilibrium. In Chapter 13 we explore the *short-run* inflation–unemployment path that the economy travels during the *disequilibrium adjustment* period accompanying the implementation of an anti-inflationary, restrictive monetary policy. As we shall see, the *short-run* adjustment costs of a *long-run* anti-inflationary restrictive monetary policy may be very severe. Even though the *long-run* inflation–unemployment trade-off curve is dead, the *short-run* Phillips curve relationship between inflation and unemployment is very much alive.

A Keynesian Gimmick: Trying to Beat the Phillips Curve at Its Own Game

In Chart 12-1 we have replicated our basic *IS-LM-PEP* two-panel diagram from Chapter 10.[3] We assume that the labour, goods and money markets are all in equilibrium and that the economy is initially at Y^*, R^* and U^*, with a zero inflation rate and zero inflation expectations. Now assume that the IS_0 curve shifts rightwards to IS_1, say from an expansionary fiscal policy. As discussed in Chapter 10, the inflation generated at Y_1 will erode the *real* money supply, causing the *LM* curve to drift upwards to the left (see the red *LM* curves in Chart 12-1). The economy will slide down the *PEP* curve as the *LM* curve climbs up the new IS_1 curve (see arrows in Chart 12-1), with the economic system eventually returning to its original equilibrium position at Y^* and U^*, but with a higher interest rate R_N. An expansionary fiscal policy cannot permanently increase the level of income, nor can it permanently lower the unemployment rate.

While the mechanics of the adjustment process described above are undeniable, our analysis has overlooked one important question. Is the government necessarily a captive of this adjustment process? In other words, must the government sit idly by and watch the real value of money decline and the economy return to Y^*? Obviously not. The government controls the nominal stock of money and in each period the Bank of Canada can change the nominal money supply by any amount it chooses. If a 10 per cent inflation rate erodes the *real* value of money by 10 per cent, the Bank of Canada can increase the *nominal* money stock by 10 per cent, or by any other amount it wishes.

---

[2]*Hamilton Spectator*, 15 July 1980.
[3]To simplify the analysis, we ignore balance of payments considerations and the *BP* curve.

CHART 12-1 Monetary validation

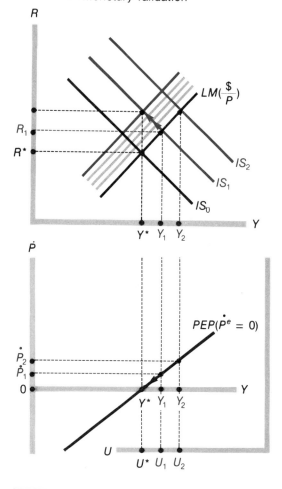

What would happen if the Bank of Canada were to adopt a policy whereby the nominal money supply was allowed to increase by an amount exactly equal to the inflation rate? Under such circumstances, the real stock of money $\$/P$ would not change, since both the numerator $\$$ and the denominator P would be rising at the same rate. If the *real* money supply does not change, the *LM* curve will not shift. The adjustment process will be thwarted.

Returning to Chart 12-1, we now assume that the government couples its expansionary fiscal policy with such a "clever" expansion of the nominal money supply. The *IS* curve is again shifted outwards to IS_1, but the nominal money supply is also increased by an amount exactly equal to the inflation rate $\dot{P}_1$ generated at Y_1. As long as the rate of increase in the nominal money supply is exactly equal to the rate of increase in the price level, namely $\dot{P}_1$, the real stock of money remains constant and the *LM* curve is prevented from shifting backwards. The economy will stay at Y_1 with an inflation rate of $\dot{P}_1$.

It is important to note that in each subsequent period of time the Bank of Canada must further increase the *nominal* money supply by $\dot{P}_1$ to match the inflation rate that will be generated by this higher output level Y_1. To keep the *LM* curve permanently anchored under such inflationary circumstances, a continual expansion of the *nominal* money supply is required. To prevent any inflation-erosion of the existing *real* money supply, each round of inflation must be matched or validated with a new issue of dollar bills. Henceforward we will refer to a monetary policy which increases the nominal money supply by an amount exactly equal to the prevailing inflation rate as a **monetary validation policy**. The existing inflation rate is *validated* by a new issue of dollar bills, thus preserving the *real* value of the economy's money supply. By following a monetary validation policy, it would *appear* that a *Keynesian* government could override the *monetarist* self-correcting adjustment mechanism (shifts in the *LM* curve) and achieve a permanent increase in output and employment levels.

The possibility of such a permanent increase in output from an expansionary fiscal policy *coupled with a monetary validation policy* suggested the concept of a policy trade-off between inflation and unemployment. Each point along the *PEP* curve conceivably represented a potential inflation–unemployment rate combination that could be achieved and sustained by an appropriate expansionary fiscal and monetary validation policy. For example, in Chart 12-1 the government could just as easily shift the IS_0 curve to IS_2 by using a larger dose of fiscal policy and increase the rate of monetary expansion to $\dot{P}_2$. Such a policy would sustain an income level of Y_2 and validate an inflation rate of $\dot{P}_2$. Again the *LM* curve remains anchored against the economic system's self-correcting adjustment mechanism. Given an entire range of unemployment–inflation rate possibilities along the Phillips curve, government policy makers *thought* that they could choose any particular unemployment rate, such as U_2, and live with the implied inflation rate $\dot{P}_2$. Since the slope of the underlying Phillips curve appeared to be relatively flat, policy makers assumed that they could permanently trade off a modest amount of inflation for a permanently lower unemployment rate. Subject to the Phillips curve constraint and the adoption of a monetary validation policy, Keynesian fiscal policy still appeared to offer a permanent cure for the unemployment problem.

The Monetarist Rebuttal: There Is No Lasting Trade-off Between Inflation and Unemployment

In his 1967 American Economics Association presidential address, Milton Friedman pointed out a "basic defect" in attempting to beat the Phillips curve by using expansionary fiscal and monetary validation policies: "Implicitly, Phillips wrote his article for a world in which everyone anticipated that nominal prices would be stable and in which that anticipation remains unshaken and immutable whatever happened to actual prices and wages."[4]

Returning to Chart 12-1, suppose that the government attempts to move up the *PEP* curve to Y_1 by continually validating the inflation rate $\dot{P}_1$. If this policy were successful, the economy would experience a permanent increase in output and a permanent inflation rate $\dot{P}_1$. However, the *PEP* curve in Chart 12-1 only holds for

[4]M. Friedman, "The Role of Monetary Policy," *The American Economic Review*, March 1968, p. 8.

an expected inflation rate of zero—that is, "stable prices." For Y_1 and $\dot{P}_1$ to be a long-run equilibrium position, people must continually expect zero inflation even though the actual inflation rate is always $\dot{P}_1$! As Abraham Lincoln once noted, while the government may be able to fool *all* of the people *some* of the time, it cannot fool *all* of the people *all* of the time. Sooner or later, people will realize that the prevailing inflation rate $\dot{P}_1$ is *not* what they expected and will revise their inflation expectations upwards (from $\dot{P}^e = 0$ to $\dot{P}^e = \dot{P}_1$). But as soon as people revise their inflation expectations upwards, the *PEP* curve will shift upwards, creating a new disequilibrium adjustment period. The position Y_1 and $\dot{P}_1$ is *not* a final equilibrium position for the economy.

As Friedman pointed out, the "basic defect" in attempting to use the Phillips curve as a trade-off curve is the assumption that inflation expectations are "unshaken and immutable" regardless of the inflation rate which the government chooses to validate. Any attempt by policy makers to increase output permanently by moving along the *PEP* curve will cause the *PEP* curve to shift upwards as inflation expectations will be adjusted upwards. In short, the Phillips curve does *not* provide policy makers with a *stable* trade-off curve that can be exploited to lower the unemployment rate permanently.

To illustrate this key monetarist proposition that Keynesian aggregate demand policy *cannot* beat the Phillips curve in the long run, we reconsider the expansionary Keynesian policy depicted in Chart 12-1. Initially, our economy is in equilibrium at Y^* and U^* with *both* $\dot{P}$ and $\dot{P}^e$ equal to zero. The government then employs an expansionary fiscal policy to shift the *IS* curve outwards to IS_1 and validates the resulting inflation rate $\dot{P}_1$ by increasing the nominal money supply by $\dot{P}_1$ in each period of time. With price levels and the *nominal* money supply increasing at the same rate $\dot{P}_1$, the *real* money supply is constant and the *LM* curve is stationary. The self-correcting inflation adjustment forces of *LM* curve shifts are neatly thwarted.

However, there is a second set of inflation-adjustment forces at work in the labour market. Recall from Chapter 9 that the rate of wage inflation depends on both the level of unemployment *and the expected inflation rate*. In Chart 12-2 we have reproduced our basic inflation-expectations-augmented Phillips wage adjustment curve. A decrease in the unemployment rate causes an upward movement *along* the Phillips wage curve, whereas an increase in inflation expectations causes an upward *shift* in the Phillips wage curve. Both factors lead to a higher rate of wage inflation. Given an unemployment rate of U^* (from Chart 12-1) and zero inflation expectations, wage inflation will initially be running at $\dot{W}_0$ (point A in Chart 12-2). Now when the government stimulates output by implementing an expansionary fiscal policy (see Chart 12-1), the new lower unemployment rate U_1 will cause the rate of wage inflation to increase to $\dot{W}_1$. Initially, the economy moves from point A to point B in Chart 12-2. However, this higher rate of wage inflation will be "marked up" by firms and the rate of price inflation will rise to $\dot{P}_1$. Rather than letting this new inflation rate erode the *real* stock of money, the government then steps in and validates the $\dot{P}_1$ inflation rate by continually expanding the nominal money supply by $\dot{P}_1$ per time period.

While the "Keynesian" story ends at this point, the "monetarist" story is just beginning. With the inflation rate now running at $\dot{P}_1$, sooner or later workers will

CHART 12-2 The effects of unemployment changes and revised inflation expectations on wage adjustments

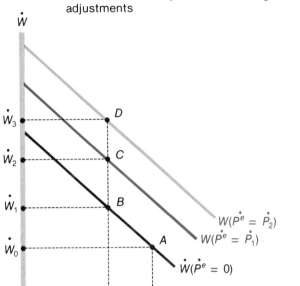

revise their inflation expectations upwards from zero to $\dot{P}_1$. It would be a very strange world if workers continued to expect a zero inflation rate when the prevailing inflation rate was perpetually $\dot{P}_1$! When workers adjust their inflation expectations upwards, the original wage inflation curve ($\dot{P}^e = 0$) in Chart 12-2 will shift upwards (to the $\dot{P}^e = \dot{P}_1$ wage inflation curve) and the wage inflation point B will give way to point C. Both the lower unemployment rate U_1, due to the expansionary fiscal policy, and the higher expected inflation rate $\dot{P}_1$, due to monetary validation, will cause the rate of wage inflation in the labour market to increase (to $\dot{W}_2$ in Chart 12-2). Again, firms will mark up this second set of wage adjustments from $\dot{W}_1$ to $\dot{W}_2$ and the rate of price inflation will rise beyond $\dot{P}_1$. The composite *PEP* curve will shift upwards reflecting this higher rate of expected inflation.

In Chart 12-3 we have replicated our diagram from Chart 12-1, and have added this new higher PEP_1 curve corresponding to an expected inflation rate of $\dot{P}_1$. Based on an unemployment rate of U_1, corresponding to the IS_1-LM intersection point of Y_1, and an expected inflation rate of $\dot{P}_1$, the new inflation rate will now be $\dot{P}_2$ (point C in Chart 12-3). The upward revision of inflation expectations from zero to $\dot{P}_1$ in wage contracts has pushed the rate of price inflation up from $\dot{P}_1$ to $\dot{P}_2$ (from point B to point C in Chart 12-3).

However, our "monetarist" story is by no means over. Point C in Chart 12-3 is clearly *not* a final equilibrium point either. The expected inflation rate $\dot{P}_1$ is again less than the actual inflation rate $\dot{P}_2$. Equally as important, the actual inflation rate $\dot{P}_2$ exceeds the growth rate of the nominal money supply (recall $\dot{\$} = \dot{P}_1$). Thus, the

CHART 12-3 Expansionary fiscal policy with a constant increase in the nominal money supply

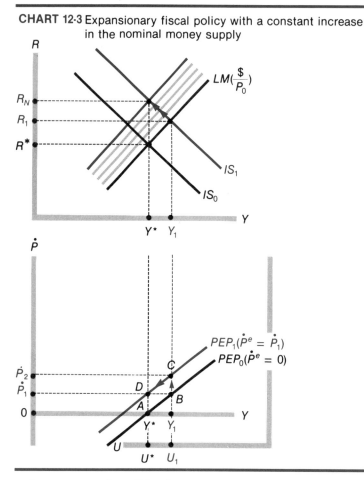

real money supply will be decreasing and the *LM* curve will again start to drift upwards. We consider *two possible* disequilibrium adjustment paths premised on two very different assumptions about monetary policy. First, we assume that the government continues to increase the *nominal* money supply by a *constant* $\dot{P}_1$ per time period, even though the actual inflation rate exceeds $\dot{P}_1$. Secondly, we assume that the government *validates* whatever inflation rate materializes, for example the government expands the nominal money supply by $\dot{P}_2$ in the second period. As we shall see, these two different monetary policies give radically different macroeconomic results.

A *Constant* Increase in the Nominal Money Supply

Returning to Chart 12-3, if the government maintains a *constant* increase in the *nominal* money supply of $\dot{P}_1$ per time period, then at point *C* the *real* money supply $\$/P$ must start to decline. The numerator $\$$ is rising by $\dot{P}_1$ whereas the denominator P is rising by $\dot{P}_2$, where $\dot{P}_2 > \dot{P}_1$. With the *real* money supply being eroded by this new higher inflation rate, the *LM* curve will start to drift upwards (see red *LM* curves in Chart 12-3) and our standard inflation-adjustment mechanism will start to lower real output levels. As the real money supply declines, interest rates are pushed further upwards (beyond R_1), investment spending declines and real income levels decrease. The economy will begin to slide down the PEP_1 curve and climb up the IS_1 curve (see diagonal arrows in Chart 12-3). The output and employment gains from an expansionary fiscal policy coupled with a *constant* increase in the nominal money supply ($\dot{\$} = \dot{P}_1$) begin to disappear.

How far will the economy slide down the PEP_1 curve? As long as the *real* stock of money is declining, the *LM* curve will continue to drift upwards, interest rates will continue to rise and the level of income will continue to decline. The *LM* curve will continue to drift upwards until the inflation rate generated along the PEP_1 curve is brought down to $\dot{P}_1$, the rate at which the *nominal* money supply is increasing. Eventually the economy will reach point D in Chart 12-3, where both the price level and the nominal money supply will be growing at the rate $\dot{P}_1$ per time period. At point D the real stock of money $\$/P$ will be constant, because both the numerator and denominator are increasing by the same $\dot{P}_1$ rate, and the *LM* curve will be stationary. Note that point D in Chart 12-3 lies exactly above point A. The economy has returned to its original equilibrium income level Y^*.[5] Finally, we note that at point D the expected rate of inflation $\dot{P}_1$ is equal to the actual rate of inflation $\dot{P}_1$. Therefore, point D represents a final resting point for the economic system on the assumption that the monetary authorities continue to increase the *nominal* money supply by $\dot{P}_1$ each period. The *real* stock of money is constant, the *LM* curve is stationary, and the actual inflation rate corresponds exactly to the expected inflation rate.

In summary, if the government attempts to increase the level of output from Y^* to Y_1 by shifting the *IS* curve outwards to IS_1 and increasing the nominal money supply by $\dot{P}_1$ in each time period, inflation expectations will be adjusted upwards to $\dot{P}_1$ and the economic system will eventually return to its original equilibrium income level Y^*, but will have a higher interest rate R_N. In the words of Milton Friedman, "There is always a temporary trade-off between inflation and unemployment; there is no permanent trade-off."[6] Keynesian policy makers *cannot* permanently increase the level of output by implementing an expansionary fiscal policy coupled with a constant increase in the nominal money supply.

A Monetary *Validation* Policy

The problem with the expansionary policy described above is an eroding *real* money supply. After inflation expectations are adjusted upwards to $\dot{P}_1$, the actual inflation rate $\dot{P}_2$ exceeds the growth rate in the *nominal* money supply ($\dot{\$} = \dot{P}_1$), the real stock of money $\$/P$ declines, the *LM* curve drifts upwards, interest rates are pushed up, investment and output levels decrease, and the economy slides down the new higher PEP_1 curve (with $\dot{P}^e = \dot{P}_1$)to the point D, where the actual inflation rate equals the increase in the nominal money supply. Given that the problem is an erosion of the *real* money supply and an upward-drifting *LM* curve, what would

---

[5]The proposition is proved algebraically in a later section of this chapter.
[6]Friedman, "Monetary Policy," p. 11.

happen if the government decided to anchor the *LM* curve by *validating* whatever inflation rate materialized? Replicating the basic features of Chart 12-3 in Chart 12-4, suppose that the government steps up the growth rate of the *nominal* money supply to $\dot{P}_2$ per period when inflation expectations are adjusted upwards to $\dot{P}_1$ and the economy moves from point *B* to point *C*. With both the price level and the *nominal* money supply now increasing by $\dot{P}_2$ per period, the *real* stock of money will remain constant and the *LM* curve will be stationary.

Even though the government *can* anchor the *LM* curve by validating the new $\dot{P}_2$ inflation rate (with $\dot{\$} = \dot{P}_2$), this new position *C cannot* be a final equilibrium resting point for the economic system. The problem this time is *incorrect* inflation expectations. Point *C* is on the *PEP$_1$* curve, which assumes that the *expected* inflation rate is $\dot{P}_1$. For point *C* to be a final equilibrium resting point for the economic system, people must continually expect an inflation rate of $\dot{P}_1$ even though the actual validated inflation rate is $\dot{P}_2$! Sooner or later people will "catch on" to the fact that the actual inflation rate validated by the government is $\dot{P}_2$ and *will again revise upwards* their inflation expectations. Of course, when inflation expectations are adjusted upwards from $\dot{P}_1$ to $\dot{P}_2$, the wage inflation curve will shift up in Chart 12-2 and the *PEP* curve in Chart 12-4 will shift up to *PEP$_2$* (with $\dot{P}^e = \dot{P}_2$). On the basis of increased inflation expectations, labour will bargain for larger wage settlements ($\dot{W}_3$ in Chart 12-2) and firms will pass on these higher labour costs in the form of a higher rate of price inflation ($\dot{P}_3$ in Chart 12-4). In terms of Chart 12-4, a monetary validation policy will cause the economy to move from point *C* to point *E* after inflation expectations are revised upwards from $\dot{P}_1$ to $\dot{P}_2$.

Having adopted a monetary *validation* policy, the government must further *increase the rate of expansion* of the *nominal* money supply to $\dot{P}_3$, to validate the new higher inflation rate at point *E*. But again point *E cannot* be a final equilibrium resting point for the economic system. At point *E* on the *PEP$_2$* curve, people are expecting an inflation rate of $\dot{P}_2$ but the actual inflation rate, validated by the government, is $\dot{P}_3$! Again inflation expectations will be adjusted upwards, the *PEP$_2$* curve will shift up to *PEP$_3$* (with $\dot{P}^e = \dot{P}_3$) and a new higher inflation rate $\dot{P}_4$ will materialize (point *F* in Chart 12-4). As long as the government continues to validate each new inflation rate with a further increase in the rate of expansion of the *nominal* money supply, inflation expectations will continue to rise and the rate of wage and price inflation will continue to spiral upwards (see vertical arrows in Chart 12-4).[7]

In summary, the only way that the government can permanently increase the level of output beyond *Y** is to *continually increase the growth rate* of the *nominal* money supply. Under such conditions, the economic system will experience an *ever-accelerating rate of inflation,* $\dot{P}_1$, $\dot{P}_2$, $\dot{P}_3$, $\dot{P}_4$, and so on. Again, there is *no permanent* trade-off between unemployment and a *stable* inflation rate. The cost of a permanent reduction in the unemployment rate is an *ever-accelerating* **wage-price inflation spiral.**

---

[7]As discussed later in this chapter, the nominal interest rate will also spiral upwards as inflation expectations continue to rise.

CHART 12-4 Expansionary fiscal policy with a monetary
validation policy

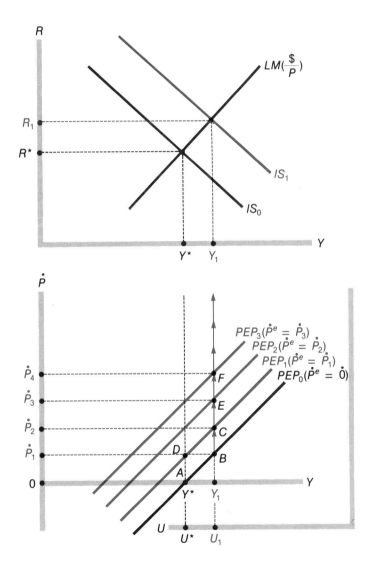

Short-Run Versus Long-Run Phillips Curves

As our analysis clearly demonstrates, it is very important to distinguish between
short-run disequilibrium positions (such as points B, C, and E in Chart 12-4) and
long-run equilibrium positions (such as A and D in Chart 12-3). For the

macroeconomic system to be in *long-run equilibrium*, the following conditions must hold:

1) the labour market must be in equilibrium
2) the goods market must be in equilibrium
3) the money market must be in equilibrium
4) the actual inflation rate must equal the expected inflation rate (that is, there is no unexpected inflation)

In terms of the *IS-LM* diagram, the first three conditions require that the equilibrium income level Y^* (the amount of output produced by the equilibrium quantity of labour) coincide with the intersection point of a *stable IS* curve and a *stationary LM* curve. Provided that the government *validates* the actual inflation rate with a corresponding increase in the *nominal* money supply, the *LM* curve will be stationary. However, there is no unique inflation rate associated with a stationary *LM* curve, because any particular inflation rate can be validated. The final equilibrium condition asserts that whatever inflation rate the government chooses to validate (say $\dot{P}_1$ in Chart 12-3), it must be fully expected. In the long run, people can not be permanently fooled by a validated inflation rate that is different from what they expected. There can be no unexpected inflation in long-run equilibrium.

Even though inflation expectations must be brought into line with the actual *validated* inflation rate in the long run, inflation expectations may not be adjusted immediately. For a short-run period, inflation expectations may diverge from the actual or validated inflation rate. Labour market participants may not be sure whether a new unexpected inflation rate (perhaps caused by a new government policy) will be permanent and may prefer to wait a while to see if the new inflation rate (and new government policy) persists before revising their inflation expectations. During the time prior to any revision in inflation expectations, the economy will move along a particular *PEP* curve. *For a given rate of expected inflation*, there is a *short-run* positive relationship between the actual inflation rate and the level of output. Our original *PEP* curve (equation 10-2) describes this *short-run* relationship between inflation and output levels under the assumption of *constant* inflation expectations:[8]

(10-2) $\qquad \dot{P} = \dot{P}^e - jvY^* + jvY$

As long as inflation expectations (and Y^*) remain unchanged, the economy will simply move along a given **short-run PEP curve**, depending on movements in the *IS* and *LM* curves.

In the long run however, inflation expectations must be brought into line with the actual validated inflation rate. Again, people cannot be permanently fooled by an inflation rate that is consistently different from what they expected. If we substitute this final equilibrium condition (that $\dot{P}^e$ must equal $\dot{P}$) into equation 10-2, we can derive the *long-run equilibrium* relationship between inflation and output levels:

---

[8]We continue to ignore the effects of foreign price changes (*fFP*) on the rate of inflation until Chapter 15.

$$\dot{P} = \dot{P} - jvY^* + jvY$$

$$0 = -jvY^* + jvY$$

(12-1) or $\qquad\qquad Y\Big|_{\dot{P} = \dot{P}^e} \;\;= Y^*$

After substituting $\dot{P}$ for $\dot{P}^e$ in equation 10-2, the two $\dot{P}$ terms cancel each other out and we are left with equation 12-1. In the long run, when the expected inflation rate must be equal to the actual inflation rate, the level of output Y will equal Y^*, the amount of output produced by the equilibrium quantity of labour. Similarly, in the long run (when $\dot{P} = \dot{P}^e$), the unemployment rate U will equal U^*.

$$\dot{P} = \dot{P}^e + j(U^* - U)$$

$$\dot{P} = \dot{P} + j(U^* - U)$$

$$0 = j(U^* - U)$$

(12-2) or $\qquad U\Big|_{\dot{P} = \dot{P}^e} \;\;= U^*$

In long-run equilibrium, when the expected inflation rate must be equal to the actual inflation rate, there is no *relationship between the level of output (or unemployment rate) and the inflation rate.* From a monetarist perspective, there is *no lasting trade-off* between inflation and unemployment which a (Keynesian) policy maker can exploit. The long-run equilibrium level of output Y^* is determined in the labour market and the production sector of the economy; Y^* is independent of the validated inflation rate and the rate of monetary expansion.

The absence of a *long-run equilibrium* relationship between inflation and output levels was the major conclusion of Chart 12-3. If the government tried to *validate* the inflation rate $\dot{P}_1$ in the hope of permanently increasing output levels to Y_1, once this new *validated* inflation rate became anticipated the economic system would return to its original income level Y^*, but with a higher inflation rate $\dot{P}_1$ (point D in Chart 12-3). *Validating* a higher inflation rate does *not* increase the output level after inflation expectations have been brought into line with the new higher validated inflation rate. In the long run, the Phillips curve is a *vertical* straight line at Y^* (points A and D in Chart 12-3). The *long-run equilibrium* output level Y^* and unemployment rate U^* are independent of the *validated* inflation rate and are determined in the labour market and production sector of the economy. An appendix to this chapter examines the necessary conditions for this **long-run vertical Phillips curve** and the absence of a permanent trade-off between inflation and output levels (or unemployment rates).

In his 1967 presidential address, Milton Friedman referred to the *equilibrium* unemployment rate U^* as the **natural rate of unemployment.** Friedman's choice of words is regrettable, as U^* is obviously not an immutable act of nature. Economists who do not like the connotations of the word *"natural"* frequently refer to U^* by the mnemonic NAIRU (non-accelerating inflation rate of unemployment). A key property of U^* and Y^* is a *constant* inflation rate. As discussed above, any attempt by the government to permanently increase output beyond Y^* will lead to an *accelerating* inflation rate (the wage–price spiral of Chart 12-4). Thus

U^* represents the *unique* unemployment rate that in the long run will have a *non-accelerating* inflation rate; U^* is the non-accelerating inflation rate of unemployment, the NAIRU.

Case Study 6: The Canadian *Natural* Rate of Unemployment (NAIRU)

The purpose of this case study is to provide an estimate for the *natural* rate of unemployment (or NAIRU) in Canada during the 1970s and early 1980s, based on econometric estimates for the *PEP* equation (9-3).

$$(9\text{-}3) \qquad \dot{W} = \dot{P}^e + P\dot{R}ODAV + j(U^* - U)$$

$$\text{or} \qquad \dot{W} - \dot{P}^e = (P\dot{R}ODAV + jU^*) - jU$$

In Chart 9-4 we presented a scatter diagram for the relationship between the expected real wage change and the unemployment rate. The least squares estimates for the line drawn through this scatter diagram are given below (with standard errors for the two coefficients given in parentheses below the respective coefficients):

$$\dot{W} - \dot{P}^e = 9.48 - 1.04\ U \qquad R^2 = 0.79$$
$$\qquad\quad (1.01)\ \ (0.13)$$

Comparing the parameters in the theoretical *PEP* equation (9-3) with the above statistical estimates, the sum $[P\dot{R}ODAV + jU^*]$ is estimated to be 9.48 and the parameter j is estimated to be 1.04. To determine the value of jU^* we must subtract the average productivity growth rate $P\dot{R}ODAV$ from 9.48. From 1967 through 1984, the average growth rate of labour productivity, as measured by real output per employee in commercial non-agricultural industries, was 1.5 per cent per annum. Subtracting a value of 1.5 (for $P\dot{R}ODAV$) from 9.48, the estimated value of jU^* is 7.98. Dividing 7.98 (jU^*) by 1.04 (j), the natural rate of unemployment in Canada is estimated to be approximately 7.7 per cent.

Our econometric results for the price-expectations-augmented Phillips curve suggest that during the 1970s and early 1980s the *equilibrium* unemployment rate in Canada was likely on the order of 7 to 8 per cent. In calculating this estimate for U^* we have made a number of important assumptions, which we briefly enumerate. First, we have linearized the Phillips curve. Second, we have approximated inflation expectations by a simple two-year average of past inflation rates and have assumed that the coefficient on inflation expectations in the Phillips curve equation is exactly one. Third, we have assumed a constant labour productivity growth rate of 1.5 per cent over the entire period from 1967 to 1984 even though there has been a substantial decline in productivity growth since 1973. Fourth, we have ignored all other factors which might have influenced wage settlements, such as the Anti-Inflation Board (1975-78). Finally, we have assumed that the equilibrium unemployment rate has remained constant over this entire 17-year period.

As discussed in Chapter 8, the equilibrium or natural rate of unemployment depends on specific features of the labour market which determine the amount of frictional and structural unemployment. A general consensus exists that the

Canadian equilibrium or natural rate of unemployment increased around 1970. In retrospect, most economists now believe that the Canadian economy was very buoyant in the early 1970s, and that the 1971 and 1972 unemployment rates of 6.2 per cent (the highest unemployment rate since 1961) represented a very misleading picture of the state of the Canadian labour market. The Economic Council of Canada concluded in its 1976 study of the Canadian labour market that "basic changes in the labour market have rendered the message of the unemployment rate today rather different from that of a decade ago."[9] In other words, unemployment rates for the 1970s and 1980s cannot be directly compared with unemployment rates for the 1950s and 1960s. A 6 per cent unemployment rate is *high* in the 1960s but *low* in the 1980s, because the *equilibrium* unemployment rate increased from about 5 per cent to around 7 per cent during the early 1970s.

Two possible explanations have been suggested to account for this increase in the *equilibrium* unemployment rate. The first explanation focuses on demographic changes in the Canadian labour force. During the 1960s and 1970s the age, sex and family status characteristics of the Canadian labour force dramatically changed. The participation rate of females aged 25 to 54 doubled, rising from 28.9 per cent in 1960 to 57.8 per cent in 1979. In addition, the under-25 age component of the labour force substantially increased during this same time period. The composition of the labour force and the unemployed clearly shifted towards younger individuals and secondary earners in the family. The traditional stereotype of the unemployed worker as a prime-age male with a family to support became less and less typical. This trend towards multiple-earner family units may have alleviated some of the economic hardship associated with unemployment and may have reduced the urgency for some secondary workers to obtain a job (that is, secondary earners may be able to spend longer periods of time searching for a "suitable" job). In addition, the changing demographic composition of the labour force likely heightened structural unemployment problems, as the skills and experience levels of the large number of new entrants into the labour force may not have matched the existing set of job vacancies. For a variety of reasons, the changing demographic structure of the Canadian labour force during the 1960s and early 1970s may have resulted in a higher equilibrium unemployment rate.

An alternative explanation for an increase in the *natural* rate of unemployment focuses directly upon revisions to the Unemployment Insurance Act in 1971, revisions which may have exacerbated demographic effects. The 1971 Unemployment Insurance Act revisions increased unemployment insurance benefits, extended benefit periods and decreased qualification time periods. After reviewing unemployment insurance programs in the United States and Europe, the Economic Council of Canada concluded that "Canada's unemployment program is among the most generous."[10] The improvements in the unemployment insurance program in 1971 significantly altered the incentive structure within the labour

[9]Economic Council of Canada, *People and Jobs: A Study of the Canadian Labour Market*, Ottawa, 1976, p. 211.

[10]*Ibid.*, p. 271.

market, particularly for secondary workers. It would be very surprising if some workers did not respond to this new, enriched unemployment insurance *dis*incentive structure and change their labour supply behaviour. As the Department of Finance has acknowledged:

> Other things being equal, such changes [in unemployment insurance] would be expected to increase the attractiveness of labour force participation, increase the rate at which people tend to quit existing jobs and lengthen the duration of time unemployed people tend to spend unemployed. Each of these effects would tend to increase the measured unemployment rate associated with each rate of inflation. The available evidence suggests that in varying degrees all three effects could very well have been operating after 1971.[11]

To the extent that individuals responded to the 1971 improvements in the unemployment insurance program and exercised more discretion over the choice of jobs which they would accept, the equilibrium or natural rate of unemployment would have increased. A number of studies have examined the impact of the 1971 unemployment revisions and have concluded that the level of unemployment in Canada was significantly higher than it would have been in the absence of any changes to the act.[12]

Inflation, Interest Rates and Monetary Policy

In the first half of this chapter, the possibility of a permanent trade-off between inflation and unemployment was dismissed. The long-run equilibrium output and employment levels were shown to be independent of monetary and fiscal policy, as well as independent of the validated inflation rate. As demonstrated in the last half of this chapter, however, the long-run inflation rate and nominal interest rate depend crucially on monetary policy. By continually increasing the nominal money supply, the government dictates that inflation (and high nominal interest rates) will prevail. Before we analyze this crucial link between changes in the nominal money supply and inflation, we briefly reconsider the important distinction between nominal and real interest rates.

Nominal Versus Real Interest Rates: A Brief Digression

As discussed in Chapter 3, the interest rate paid on financial assets (bonds, mortgages, savings accounts) will incorporate an additional premium to cover the inflation rate that is expected to prevail during the term of the financial asset. Returning to our earlier illustration in Chapter 3, if I am willing to lend you $1,000 at a 5 per cent interest rate when there is zero inflation, then I would want to

---

[11]Department of Finance, *Canada's Recent Inflation Experience*, Ottawa, November 1978, p. 36.

[12]See, for example, C. Green and J.-M. Cousineau, *Unemployment in Canada: The Impact of the Unemployment Insurance Act* (Ottawa: Economic Council of Canada, 1976).

charge you 15 per cent interest when the inflation rate is expected to be 10 per cent. To the extent that inflation is correctly anticipated, the 10 per cent inflation premium contained in the interest rate will preserve the real purchasing power of my $1,000 loan. You will be willing to pay the 15 per cent interest rate because you also expect inflation to be 10 per cent and realize that you will be able to repay the $1,000 principal in dollar bills that have been eroded by inflation to 90¢.

Given this inflation distortion, economists distinguish between the market, or *nominal* rate of interest, 15 per cent in the above illustration, and the *real* rate of interest, 5 per cent. The real interest rate RR, is simply the market interest rate R *less* the inflation premium $\dot{P}^e$, the 10 per cent expected inflation rate in the above illustration.

$$(3\text{-}1) \quad RR = R - \dot{P}^e$$

Alternatively, the market, or nominal interest rate, will equal the underlying real interest rate plus the inflation premium. The higher inflation is expected to be, the higher the nominal interest rate will be. The evidence presented earlier in Chart 1-2 clearly supports the proposition that Canadian interest rates systematically move with expected inflation rates.

To incorporate this key distinction between **nominal and real interest rates** into our *IS-LM-PEP* macroeconomic model, one additional refinement must be introduced. As we will see in Chapter 20, business investment decisions concerning new factories and machines (*real* goods) depend on the *real* interest rate RR, and not on the *nominal* interest rate R. Businessmen know that product prices and sales revenues will tend to rise with the general inflation rate, thus allowing the firm to pay the inflation premium contained in nominal interest rates. The profit- maximizing firm will make investment decisions by comparing *real* rates of return with the *real* cost of borrowing. Thus, our simple investment function of Chapter 5,

$$(5\text{-}1a) \quad I = I_a - eR$$

must be recast in terms of the real interest rate RR:

$$(12\text{-}3) \quad I = I_a - eRR$$

Recasting our investment function into *real* interest rate terms implies that our *IS* curve should be reconstructed in terms of the real interest rate. To do so would raise an obvious problem in our *IS-LM* diagram, as the vertical axis of the *IS-LM* diagram is based on the nominal interest rate. Furthermore, the demand for money balances depends on the nominal interest rate—the opportunity cost of holding money in an inflationary world—and thus the *LM* curve remains a function of the nominal interest rate. In short, the *IS* curve depends on the *real* interest rate, whereas the *LM* curve depends on the *nominal* interest rate. How can we fit a *real* interest rate *IS* curve and a *nominal* interest rate *LM* curve into one diagram? Fortunately, equation 3-1 can be used to solve our problem. By making use of our new relationship that connects nominal and real interest rates to the expected inflation rate, we can convert our new *real* interest rate investment function (equation 12-3) back into *nominal* interest rate terms:

(3-1) $$RR = R - \dot{P}^e$$

(12-3) $$I = I_a - eRR$$

(12-3a) $$I = I_a - e(R - \dot{P}^e) = (I_a + e\dot{P}^e) - eR$$

In an inflationary world, *real* investment expenditures depend negatively on the *nominal* market rate of interest corrected for the *expected rate of inflation*.[13]

Substituting this *new* inflation-expectations-augmented investment function (equation 12-3a) into our standard Keynesian macroeconomic model produces the following inflation-expectations-augmented *IS* curve:

$$Y = Z = a + bY - bT_0 - btY + I_a + e\dot{P}^e - eR + G + X - n - mY$$

or $$Y(1 - b + bt + m) = (a - bT_0 + I_a + e\dot{P}^e + G + X - n) - eR$$

or $$R = \frac{1}{e}(a - bT_0 + I_a + e\dot{P}^e + G + X - n) - \frac{1}{e}(1 - b + bt + m)Y$$

(12-4) or $$R = \frac{1}{e}(a - bT_0 + I_a + G + X - n) + \dot{P}^e - \frac{1}{e}(1 - b + bt + m)Y$$

After the algebraic dust has settled, recasting the investment function into *real* interest rate terms produces only one change in our *original nominal* interest rate *IS* curve. As shown in equation 12-4, the expected inflation rate $\dot{P}^e$ enters the intercept of the nominal interest rate *IS* curve equation with a coefficient of unity. For a given level of real income, a one percentage point increase in the expected inflation rate will cause the *IS* curve to shift upwards by exactly one percentage point on the nominal interest rate axis.[14] Alternatively, for a given level of *nominal* interest rates, an increase in the expected inflation rate will cause the *IS* curve to shift to the right. For a given *nominal* interest rate a higher expected inflation rate implies a lower *real* interest rate (lower real borrowing costs) which would prompt more investment spending and higher income levels. In the next section of the chapter we illustrate the mechanics of the *IS-LM-PEP* model with this new inflation-expectations-augmented *IS* curve.

A Famous Proposition: Inflation is always and everywhere a monetary phenomenon.

While the long-run *equilibrium* unemployment rate U^* and output level Y^* are independent of monetary and fiscal policy, the long-run inflation rate and interest rate are *not* independent of government policy. The long-run equilibrium solution to our *IS-LM-PEP* macroeconomic model accords with a fundamental monetarist proposition. In the long run, inflation is strictly a **monetary phenomenon**. There can be no lasting inflation unless the nominal money supply is growing, and continual increases in the money supply will guarantee that there is enduring inflation.

---

[13]For further analysis, see Chapter 20.

[14]This exact one-to-one upward shift in the *IS* curve for an increase in the expected inflation rate follows from our *assumed* one-to-one relationship between nominal interest rates, real interest rates and the expected inflation rate (equation 3-1).

CHART 12-5 Inflation and interest rates in long-run equilibrium

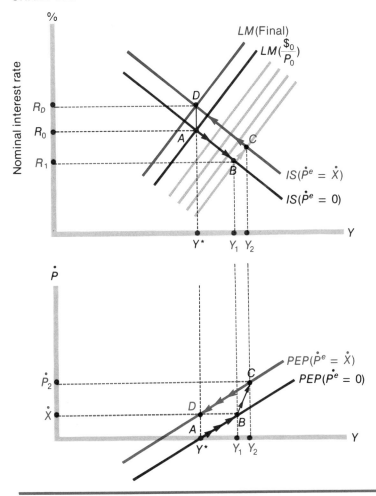

To illustrate this famous monetarist proposition, in Chart 12-5 we have reproduced our basic *IS-LM-PEP* macroeconomic model and have assumed that our
hypothetical economy is initially in *equilibrium* at an output level of Y^* (position
A in both panels of Chart 12-5), with a price level of P_0, a zero inflation rate, zero
inflation expectations and a *zero* growth rate in the *nominal* money supply. Note
that both the original black *PEP* and *IS* curves depend on this zero expected
inflation rate, and have been labelled accordingly. In this non-inflationary world,
the equilibrium *nominal* interest rate R_0 would also be the *real* interest rate since
inflation expectations are zero.

Now suppose that the government decides to increase the growth rate of the
nominal money supply from 0 to $\dot{X}$ per cent. To simplify the macroeconomic story,
we discuss the various adjustments that will take place in a sequential fashion. In
the real world, many of these adjustments will be taking place simultaneously.

Given an *initial zero* inflation rate and a *zero* expected inflation rate, an increase in the *nominal* money supply will cause an increase in the *real* money supply, a rightward shift in the *LM* curve, a decline in both the nominal and real interest rates (which are identical when $\dot{P}^e$ is zero) and an increase in investment and output levels. *Assuming inflation expectations temporarily remain at zero*, during the first phase of the adjustment process following an increase in the growth rate of the nominal money supply to $\dot{X}$, a sequence of *LM* curve shifts will take the economy from point *A* to point *B* in both panels of Chart 12-5. The real money supply keeps rising until the inflation rate is pushed up to $\dot{X}$, the new growth rate of the nominal money supply. At point *B* the inflation rate is equal to the growth rate of the nominal money supply ($\dot{X}$), *but* inflation expectations are still zero.

In the second phase of our sequential adjustment process, we assume that everyone throughout the economy realizes that the government's monetary policy is now validating an inflation rate of $\dot{X}$. Workers demand wage increases to cover this new expected inflation rate and firms incorporate an expected inflation rate of $\dot{X}$ into both their labour market and investment decisions. *Both* the inflation expectations Phillips *PEP* curve *and* the inflation-expectations-augmented *IS* curve will now shift upwards by exactly $\dot{X}$ per cent.[15] Given this new higher *IS* curve, the economy will move from point *B* to *C* in the upper panel of Chart 12-5 as businessmen realize that the *real* cost of borrowing is much lower than the market interest rate R_1 and increase their investment spending accordingly. In the Phillips curve panel, the rate of inflation will jump to $\dot{P}_2$ (point *C*). Workers are demanding larger wage increases for two reasons: (1) inflation expectations have been adjusted upwards from 0 to $\dot{X}$ (a higher *PEP* curve) and (2) given increased investment expenditures, the level of output has risen to Y_2 and the level of unemployment has fallen.

At point *C* in Chart 12-5 the inflation rate $\dot{P}_2$ now exceeds the growth rate of the *nominal* money supply $\dot{X}$ and the *real* supply of money will start to decline. Assuming that inflation expectations remain at $\dot{X}$, the eroding real money supply and upward-shifting *LM* curve will carry the economy back down the *PEP* ($\dot{P}^e = \dot{X}$) curve from point *C* to point *D*. At point *D* the actual inflation rate has been lowered to the growth rate of the *nominal* money supply $\dot{X}$ and the *real* supply of money is once again constant. Furthermore the actual inflation rate $\dot{X}$ is correctly anticipated by workers and businessmen. Thus the *LM, IS* and *PEP* curves will all remain stationary and the economy is once again back in long-run equilibrium, at the natural rate of output Y^*. In the *IS-LM* panel of Chart 12-5, the upward-shifting *LM* curve has carried the economy up to point *D* with a nominal interest rate of R_D. Since the *IS* curve has shifted upwards by exactly $\dot{X}$ (the intercept of the *IS* curve rose by $\dot{P}^e = \dot{X}$), the distance *AD* must be equal to $\dot{X}$. The final equilibrium interest rate R_D must be $\dot{X}$ higher than the *initial* interest rate of R_0. The *long-run equilibrium nominal* interest rate will fully reflect the validated, expected inflation rate $\dot{X}$.

To summarize, both the long-run inflation rate and the long-run equilibrium nominal interest rate in our *IS-LM-PEP* macroeconomic model are monetary

---

[15]Both the *PEP* curve and the *new* inflation-expectations-augmented *IS* curve have intercepts that include the term $\dot{P}^e$ with a coefficient of unity.

phenomena. Whatever growth rate $\dot{X}$ the government chooses for the nominal money supply, it will eventually be reflected in the inflation rate and the market rate of interest. The greater the growth rate of the nominal money supply, the greater the long-run inflation rate and interest rate will be. By controlling the growth rate of the nominal money supply, the government can control the long-run inflation rate, as well as the interest rate. It is continual increases in the nominal money supply that fuel inflation, reinforce inflation expectations and drive up interest rates.

As the Governor of the Bank of Canada has acknowledged, the short-run interest rate effects from monetary policy must be clearly distinguished from the long-run interest rate effects:

> In a market-oriented economy there is a direct interaction between monetary expansion and interest rates. A reduction in the rate of monetary expansion will, other things being unchanged, push up short-term interest rates, and vice versa. In the longer term the relationship is different. A reduction in the rate of monetary expansion will over time lead to a lower rate of inflation than would otherwise have existed and interest rates will be lower than they would otherwise have been. But the first effect on interest rates is in the other direction.[16]

If the government *permanently* increases the rate of monetary expansion, we can confidently predict that *in the long run* both inflation and market interest rates will rise. However, the short-run movement of interest rates following a change in monetary policy is more difficult to predict. Given the inherent lags in the economic system and slowly adjusting inflation expectations, a permanent increase in the rate of monetary expansion may *initially* produce a *decline* in nominal interest rates (from A to B in the *IS-LM* panel of Chart 12-5), as well as an initial increase in output. But one should not be lulled into believing that an increase in the rate of monetary expansion will generate permanent interest rate reductions or permanent gains in output. Once inflation expectations are adjusted, nominal interest rates will start to rise. In terms of the upper panel in Chart 12-5, once inflation expectations are revised upwards the economy will begin to loop up and around (B to C to D), heading back to the equilibrium output level Y^* and to a higher nominal interest rate R_D. The shorter the lags in the economic system and the faster the adjustment in inflation expectations, the faster the economy will move to its new long-run equilibrium position (point D in Chart 12-5) and the less likely that an expansionary monetary policy will generate temporary interest rate reductions and temporary output (employment) gains.

Case Study 7:   Is Inflation Really a Monetary Phenomenon?

Our theoretical *IS-LM-PEP* macroeconomic model leads us to predict that in the long run the rate of price inflation will be directly related to the growth rate of the nominal money supply. Since this is an extremely important policy implication of our *IS-LM-PEP* macroeconomic model, the empirical validity of this famous

[16]Bank of Canada, *Annual Report*, 1980, p. 6.

monetarist prediction must be verified. Do data from the real world support the theoretical conclusion that the long-run inflation rate is directly related to the growth rate of the nominal money supply?

In the upper panel of Chart 12-6 we have plotted the annual rate of inflation (CPI) against the annual increase in the Canadian money supply (M1) for the 1960s and 1970s. While there is a tendency for higher rates of price inflation to be associated with larger increases in the money supply, that is, the points tend to drift upwards to the right in the upper panel of Chart 12-6, this statistical relationship is by no means precise. The points are widely scattered and for any given money supply increase there are quite divergent inflation rates. For example, in the three years 1967, 1974, and 1978 the Canadian money supply increased by approximately 10 per cent, but the inflation rate ranged from 3.6 per cent in 1967 to 10.9 per cent in 1974.

However, much of the breadth of the scatter of points in the upper panel of Chart 12-6 can be explained when one allows for the *variability* of the rate of monetary expansion and the *lags* in the economic system. Unlike our *theoretical model*, where the money supply is growing at a *constant* rate of $\dot{X}$ causing a *constant* rate of inflation, monetary increases in the *real world* have been quite *variable*—erratic, to use a less polite adjective. For example, the successive annual percentage increases in the Canadian money supply during the six years from 1966 to 1971 were like a bouncing ball: 6.9, 9.7, 4.3, 7.5, 2.3, and 12.8 per cent. Given a *variable* rate of growth in the nominal money supply, the *speed* with which the economic system adjusts to a new rate of monetary expansion (that is, the length of the short run) becomes a very important question. If the monetary authorities change the rate of expansion of the nominal money supply, how quickly does the inflation rate adjust to this new monetary policy? How quickly does the economic system move from point A to point D in Chart 12-5? If the economic system adjusts very quickly to changes in monetary policy (that is, the short run is very short), then each year the inflation rate should mirror that particular year's growth rate in the nominal money supply. On the other hand, if the economic system adjusts more slowly to a change in monetary policy, then it may take several years before the long-run inflation rate reflects the *new* rate of growth of the nominal money supply. If the short run is prolonged, the *actual* inflation rate in any particular year will not correspond exactly to the *current* rate of monetary expansion (for example, point C in Chart 12-5).

There are many reasons to believe that the economy adjusts quite slowly to changes in monetary policy and that it may take a number of years before the full inflationary effects of an increase in the rate of monetary expansion are present. In the words of Milton Friedman, the lags in monetary policy are likely to be "long and variable." We briefly consider two of the key lags between a change in monetary policy and the generation of a new inflation rate. After an increase in the rate of monetary expansion has lowered the interest rate, a considerable amount of time may pass before new investment projects actually start and real output begins to rise. Before the first worker sets foot on a new construction site, the following sequence of events must transpire: the board of directors must meet to approve the project, architects must be hired, construction firms must prepare

CHART 12-6 Inflation and the growth of the nominal money supply, 1960-79

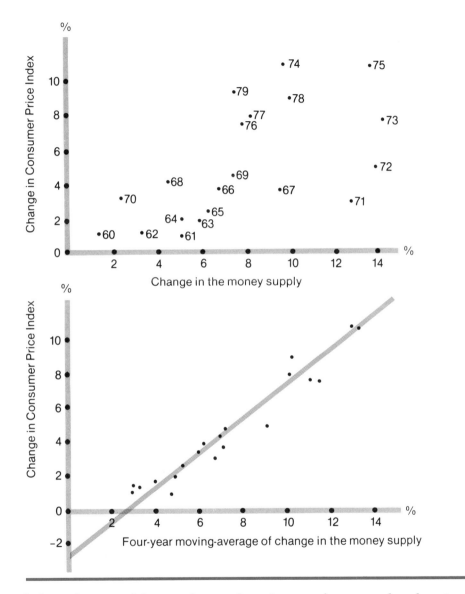

bids on the cost of the new factory, financing must be arranged, and contracts awarded. Once construction actually starts, the completion of the new factory may easily take one or two years. Overall, the total time lag from the decrease in the interest rate to the completion of the new investment project may be on the order of two to three years.

Given the basic lags in the investment process, output will slowly start to increase following an increase in the rate of monetary expansion and unemployment will slowly start to decline. This lower unemployment rate will theoretically trigger a "Phillips curve" increase in the rate of wage inflation, which will feed through to a higher rate of price inflation. However, much of the Phillips curve effect on the rate of wage inflation will not take place for several years. Union workers typically sign multi-year wage contracts that dictate the wage schedule for a number of years. Thus, many workers (perhaps including the above construction workers) may not be able to adjust their wages immediately upwards and must wait until their wage contract expires before a new contract can be negotiated. In the non-union sector, most employees have their wages adjusted only periodically (normally annually) and would not likely receive an instantaneous wage adjustment just because the monthly unemployment rate has declined. As discussed in Chapter 13, the wage-price feedback effects following a change in monetary policy may permeate their way throughout the economic system very slowly.

The full inflationary effects following an increase in the rate of monetary expansion will *not* occur in the initial year of the policy change, but rather will be spread out over a number of years. Thus, the inflation rate in any particular year will depend not only on the rate of monetary expansion of that particular year, but will also depend on the rates of monetary expansion in previous years—a delayed reaction effect. The *long lags* in the monetary transmission mechanism must be explicitly recognized.

To incorporate these important monetary policy lags into our empirical analysis, we *arbitrarily* assume that the inflationary effects following an increase in the growth rate of the nominal money supply are *equally* spread out over a period of *four* years. In other words, one quarter of the total inflationary impact from an increase in the rate of monetary expansion is assumed to occur in the initial year, and one quarter in each of the following three years. Under such an assumption, the inflation rate in any particular year would depend equally upon the rate of monetary expansion in that particular year and in the three previous years.

$$\dot{P}_t = 1.0[.25 \ \dot{\$}_t + .25 \ \dot{\$}_{t-1} + .25 \ \dot{\$}_{t-2} + .25 \ \dot{\$}_{t-3}]$$

While this *four-year equal weight* assumption is a completely arbitrary, though defensible, approximation for the lags in monetary policy, it does permit us to reassess our inflation rate–monetary expansion scatter diagram in Chart 12-6 allowing for a lagged reaction effect.

In the lower panel of Chart 12-6 we have again plotted the current inflation rate on the vertical axis, but this time we have plotted a four-year equally weighted moving average of the current and the past three annual increases in the nominal money supply on the horizontal axis.[17] The statistical improvement in the price

[17]Given the six successive annual percentage increases in the money supply between 1966 and 1971 (6.9, 9.7, 4.3, 7.5, 2.3 and 12.8 per cent), the four-year moving averages for the years 1969, 1970 and 1971 are computed as follows:

$$1969 = \tfrac{1}{4}(6.9) + \tfrac{1}{4}(9.7) + \tfrac{1}{4}(4.3) + \tfrac{1}{4} \ (7.5) = 7.1$$
$$1970 = \tfrac{1}{4}(9.7) + \tfrac{1}{4}(4.3) + \tfrac{1}{4}(7.5) + \tfrac{1}{4} \ (2.3) = 6.0$$
$$1971 = \tfrac{1}{4}(4.3) + \tfrac{1}{4}(7.5) + \tfrac{1}{4}(2.3) + \tfrac{1}{4} \ (12.8) = 6.7$$

These four-year moving averages are obviously much *smoother* than the individual annual percentage changes in the nominal money supply.

inflation–monetary expansion empirical relationship is quite remarkable. Nearly all of the points in the lower panel of Chart 12-6 lie very close to the least squares fitted line. Despite the arbitrariness of the four-year equal weight lag assumption and the presence of other exogenous factors that have undoubtedly influenced average price levels (such as OPEC),[18] there is a very close systematic relationship between the current Canadian inflation rate and a weighted average of current and past changes in the nominal money supply.

As our *IS-LM-PEP* macroeconomic model predicts, the slope of the least squares fitted line in the lower panel of Chart 12-6 is 1. In the long run, each extra percentage point of nominal money supply growth leads to an extra percentage point of price inflation. The intercept for the least squares fitted line on the *horizontal* axis is almost 3 per cent. In other words, a 3 per cent rate of monetary expansion appears to be consistent with stable Canadian price levels. This empirical result can be attributed to the fact that in the real world the equilibrium income level grows each year with the growth of the labour force, increased labour productivity and new capital goods. As the economy grows in real terms, the quantity of money required to facilitate economic transactions without rising interest rates must also expand. According to Canadian data from the 1960s and 1970s, on average the money supply should increase by about 3 per cent each year simply to keep pace with the growing transactions demand for money balances. Only monetary expansion in excess of the underlying growth in the economy will be inflationary.

One final comment about the empirical relationship between inflation and the rate of monetary expansion. During the three years 1971-73, the Bank of Canada increased the money supply by 12.8, 14.0 and 14.4 per cent respectively. Our *IS-LM-PEP* macroeconomic model and empirical relationship presented in Chart 12-6 predict that if the nominal money supply is increased by about 14 per cent per year for three successive years, then in the fourth year, 1974, the inflation rate would very likely be in the 10 to 11 per cent range. Any government that decides to increase the money supply by 42 per cent over three years ought not to be surprised by an ensuing bout of double-digit inflation. While there were other aggravating events (such as OPEC) and extenuating circumstances, this excessive expansion of the money supply in the early 1970s was the root cause of much of our inflationary problems during the mid 1970s and early 1980s. As discussed in Chapter 13, it is a very slow, painful process to bring the inflation rate back down once it gets firmly entrenched.

Summary

Assuming that wage rates fully reflect the expected inflation rate, there is no enduring long-run inflation–unemployment trade-off that policy makers can exploit. The long-run equilibrium unemployment rate (the NAIRU or the natural rate of unemployment) is determined in the labour market and is independent of Keynesian demand-management policies. If the government attempts to use

---

[18]More on oil prices and other supply-price shocks in Chapter 15.

expansionary monetary and fiscal policies to lower the long-run unemployment rate, an accelerating wage–price inflation spiral will be triggered. While the *long-run equilibrium* output level and unemployment rate are independent of monetary and fiscal policies, the *long-run equilibrium* interest rate and inflation rate depend crucially on monetary policy. In the long run, the interest rate and the inflation rate will mirror the growth rate of the nominal money supply. By restricting the growth rate of the nominal money supply, the government can control the long-run inflation rate and interest rate. As discussed in the next chapter, however, getting a high inflation rate down to a relatively low inflation rate will likely entail a prolonged, painful short-run adjustment period of high unemployment and high interest rates.

Appendix: Is the Long-Run Inflation–Output Relationship Necessarily Vertical?

The absence of a *long-run equilibrium* relationship between inflation and output levels—a vertical long-run Phillips curve—can be traced back to the cancellation of the two inflation terms $\dot{P}$ and $\dot{P}^e$ in equation 12-1. These two inflation terms will cancel out if, and only if, the coefficient on the expected inflation rate variable $\dot{P}^e$ in the original *PEP* equation 10-2 is unity. The coefficient on $\dot{P}^e$ will be unity if, and only if, the expected inflation rate is fully incorporated into wage settlements (see Chapter 9). Thus, the crucial assumption behind a *vertical long-run* relationship between inflation and output levels is the assumption that labour can negotiate wage increases to match the expected inflation rate.

Suppose that workers do *not* receive wage increases to match the expected inflation rate. What would happen to the long-run equilibrium inflation–output relationship if workers received only a fraction g of the expected inflation rate in the form of increased wage rates? Our original *PEP* equation 10-2 would now contain the term $g\dot{P}^e$ rather than $\dot{P}^e$ and our new *long-run equilibrium* inflation–output relationship (after we substitute $g\dot{P}$ for $g\dot{P}^e$) would have $(1 - g)\dot{P}$ on the left-hand side, not zero. If g is less than unity, the two $\dot{P}$ terms no longer cancel each other out in equation 12-1. In the *long run*, after inflation expectations are adjusted to the actual inflation rate, there would still remain a persistent *equilibrium* relationship between (validated) inflation and output:

$$\dot{P} - g\dot{P} = -jvY^* + jvY$$

$$\dot{P} = \left(\frac{-jv}{1-g}\right)Y^* + \left(\frac{jv}{1-g}\right)Y$$

If workers do *not* receive wage increases to match the expected inflation rate, meaning that g is less than unity, the *long-run* inflation–output relationship has a positive slope $jv/(1-g)$, and policy makers can increase the level of output permanently by *validating* a higher inflation rate.

Before discussing whether the wage inflation parameter g might be less than unity, a possibility that opens the door to a *long-run* trade-off between inflation and unemployment, we offer several brief observations about the slope of this long-run equilibrium inflation–output relationship. If g were zero, indicating that workers receive *no* wage compensation for expected inflation, then the slope of the *long-run* inflation–output curve $jv/(1 - 0)$ would be the same as the slope of the *short-run PEP* curve, jv. Price inflation would not affect wage behaviour and there would be no wage-price spiral effects in the macroeconomic system. As the parameter g increases towards unity, the denominator of the long-run slope coefficient $jv/(1 - g)$ gets smaller and smaller, and the long-run inflation–output curve gets steeper and steeper. Once g reaches *unity*, meaning that workers are fully compensated for expected inflation, the slope of the long-run inflation–output curve becomes infinitely large (the denominator of the slope is zero) and there is *no long-run equilibrium* relationship or trade-off between inflation and output. A positively sloped *long-run* inflation–output curve requires a value for the wage inflation parameter g which is less than unity. For there to be a persistent long-run trade-off between inflation and unemployment, workers must be willing to accept wage increases that do *not* fully match the expected inflation rate.[1]

In his presidential address to the American Economic Association, Milton Friedman dismissed the possibility that the wage parameter g might be less than unity on purely theoretical grounds. As discussed in Chapter 9, what matters in the labour market is the *real* wage rate, not the *nominal* wage rate. Workers will bargain for wage settlements that maintain their *real* wage regardless of the expected inflation rate *and* firms will be willing to pay such "inflationary" wage increases because they expect their product prices to rise accordingly. If workers do *not* receive full wage compensation for expected inflation, then higher rates of expected inflation will erode the *real* wage rate. Why should workers voluntarily accept a lower real wage rate simply because the expected inflation rate is 10 per cent rather than 5 per cent? Labour market theory forcefully argues that the nominal wage rate should *fully* reflect the expected inflation rate.

Even though economic theory predicts that this critical price expectations coefficient g in the wage inflation equation should be unity, early empirical evidence suggested that this critical wage inflation parameter g might be less than unity. For example, the influential 1966 special study for the Economic Council of Canada reported price coefficients in the wage inflation equation that ranged from .44 to .60,[2] well under unity. On the basis of those estimates for g, the Economic Council of Canada strongly promulgated the view that a *long-run* inflation–unemployment trade-off curve existed in Canada:

> For all the intricacies in the technical derivation of such "trade-off" curves, this analysis conveys a simple message: price increases tend to be relatively high when unemployment is low and the economy is buoyant; and conversely, price increases tend to be much lower when unemployment is high and the economy is slack. . . .Chart [12A-1], however, indicates a "trade-off zone" which, apart from illustrating the nature of

---

[1]In diagrammatic terms, the wage inflation curves in Chart 12-2 and the *PEP* curves in Chart 12-3 shift upwards by *less* than 1 per cent when expected inflation increases by 1 per cent.

[2]R.G. Bodkin et al., *Price Stability and High Employment: The Options for Canadian Economic Policy* (Ottawa: Economic Council of Canada, 1966), p. 124.

CHART 12A-1 "Trade-off zone"
unemployment and price change, 1953-65

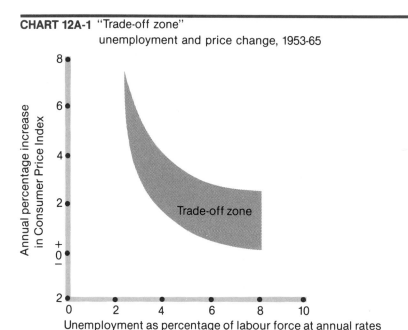

Trade-off zone

Annual percentage increase in Consumer Price Index

Unemployment as percentage of labour force at annual rates

this relationship, would generally reflect and accommodate actual experience in Canada since 1953. . . .

Even after full allowance for qualifications, the central analysis of this special study strongly confirms the existence of an inherent reconciliation or trade-off problem between the goals of high employment and reasonable price stability in Canada in the post-war period. Moreover, careful evaluations of the results, together with some probing of pre-war experience in Canada and post-war experience of other countries, reinforces the view that the reconciliation problem is a persistent and pervasive phenomenon and has nowhere lent itself to easy solution, even under widely differing economic conditions and developments. The result is that this problem. . . poses hard tasks for economic policy. . . . When actual output in the economy is falling persistently and substantially below potential output, with accompanying heavy unemployment and generally stable prices, it is clear that expansionary fiscal and monetary policies would be appropriate—and that it should be feasible to achieve a significant reduction in unemployment without encountering any significant degree of inflation. Conversely, when actual output is tending to press strongly and persistently against potential output (even though potential output is expanding), the general economic situation will almost invariably be one of very low unemployment and relatively strong general price advances. In these circumstances, it would be appropriate to deploy restraining fiscal and monetary policies—and it should be feasible to achieve a significant moderation of price and cost pressures without precipitating a substantial rise in unemployment. In short, the essential task of these so-called "big levers" of policy should be to try to keep the economy away from the upper and lower extremities of the trade-off zone.[3]

Most economists in the 1960s and 1970s shared similar views concerning the possibility of an inflation–unemployment trade-off. Since nearly all of the initial pioneering wage inflation studies reported price coefficients well under unity, it appeared possible for the government to decrease the level of unemployment permanently by accepting a higher validated inflation rate. In fact, much of the policy debate in economics during the 1960s revolved around the trade-off concept. How much inflation should be traded off to lower the unemployment rate? For example, the special study for the Economic Council of Canada discussed earlier concluded that "when the unemployment rate is 3 per cent, the Consumer Price Index can be expected to rise at 4.0 per cent per year."[4] Should Canada accept a 4 per cent inflation rate in order to lower the unemployment rate down to 3 per cent?

In retrospect the 1960s trade-off debate reads like a chapter from *Alice in Wonderland*. By the mid-1970s the Canadian inflation rate was into the double-digit range and the unemployment rate was hovering around 7 per cent. Nowhere in the 290 pages of analysis in this special study for the Economic Council of Canada is there any suggestion of such numbers.[5] The inflation–unemployment trade-off curve had vanished, and embarrassed economists were scrambling for an explanation.

As it turns out, the mystery of "whatever happened to the trade-off curve" has an interesting and relatively straightforward solution. The econometricians did it. Those *low* initial estimates for the critical price expectations coefficient g in the wage inflation equation (which went against theoretical priors) were unreliable. Subsequent wage studies which incorporate data from the late 1960s and 1970s report price expectations coefficients in the wage equation which are *not less than unity*. For example, Professor Reid at the University of Toronto found that over the 1967 to 1978 period "the coefficient of $\dot{P}^e$ exceeds 1 but is not significantly different from its theoretical expected value of unity."[6] Based on empirical evidence drawn from the 1960s, 1970s and 1980s, this critical price expectations parameter in the wage inflation equation is *not less than unity*, which in turn leads us to conclude that there is *no long-run trade-off* between inflation and unemployment. The possibility of a permanent inflation–unemployment trade-off was an econometric hoax, based on unreliable statistical estimates for the wage inflation parameter g.

Having solved the mystery by declaring that the alleged victim—the trade-off curve—never existed, we briefly consider those unreliable *initial* econometric

[3]Reproduced with permission from Economic Council of Canada, *Third Annual Review: Prices, Productivity and Employment* (Ottawa, 1966), pp. 143-45.

[4]Bodkin et al., *Price Stability*, p. 217.

[5]Under the "worst" scenario, the study predicted a 3½ per cent inflation rate at 7 per cent unemployment (Bodkin et al., *Price Stability*, p. 176).

[6]F. Reid, "The Effect of Controls on the Rate of Wage Change in Canada," *Canadian Journal of Economics*, May 1979, p. 218.

estimates for the parameter g. While there are many possible explanations for the "low" initial estimates for the price expectations coefficient in the wage inflation equation,[7] it must be remembered that this "early" time period was characterized by relative price stability. From 1953 to 1965 (the time period of the special study for the Economic Council of Canada), the average inflation rate in Canada was only 1.5 per cent per annum. In fact, in 9 of these 13 years the inflation rate was below 1.5 per cent! Given this period of unusual price stability, these initial estimated coefficients for $\dot{P}^e$ may give a very misleading indication of wage behaviour during periods of high and/or unstable inflation. For example, when price inflation is typically less than 1.5 per cent per annum, wage bargaining may be relatively insensitive to expected inflation since the inflation rate is barely perceptible. In any event, econometric estimates should only be used to predict economic behaviour under similar economic conditions. Using estimated wage coefficients derived from a period of low inflation to predict wage behaviour under double-digit inflation may be as unreliable as using 1930s data to predict 1960s investment behaviour. As "high" inflation observations from the late 1960s and 1970s were added to econometric wage equations, estimates for the critical price expectations parameter g quickly rose to unity. Most economists now accept the fact that the inflation expectations parameter in the Phillips wage equation is in the neighbourhood of unity; and, parenthetically, regret the fact that they let "poor" econometric estimates override "good" economic theory.

On the basis of labour market theory and Canadian empirical evidence drawn from the late 1960s, 1970s and 1980s, we assume that the price expectations parameter within the wage inflation equation is unity—workers bargain in terms of the real wage. We therefore conclude that in the *long run*, after inflation expectations have been brought into line with the *validated* inflation rate, there is *no* trade-off between inflation and the level of output or unemployment. The long-run equilibrium output level is independent of the inflation rate.

Key Concepts

monetary validation policy
wage-price inflation spiral
short-run versus long-run Phillips curve
natural rate of unemployment
NAIRU
inflation as a monetary phenomenon
real versus nominal interest rates

---

[7] See D.A. Wilton, *Wage Inflation in Canada, 1955-75* (Ottawa: Economic Council of Canada, 1980).

Review Questions

1. How does a monetary validation policy affect labour market behaviour? Under a monetary validation policy, explain why an attempt by policy makers to move along the Phillips curve will cause a shift in the Phillips curve.

2. Assuming that the monetary authorities continually validate whatever inflation materializes, carefully explain why an expansionary fiscal policy will lead to an accelerating inflation rate. How can this wage-price inflation spiral be halted? What are the output and unemployment ramifications of halting this inflation spiral?

3. Do you think there is a sustainable inflation–unemployment trade-off available to policy makers? Explain.

4. Why did the Canadian equilibrium unemployment rate rise during the 1970s? Explain.

5. What role can Keynesian demand-management policy play in lowering the unemployment rate?

6. Using the *IS-LM-PEP* model, analyze the short-run and long-run inflation, interest rate and output effects if a *fixed* nominal money supply is allowed to increase by X per cent each year.

7. In the long run, what determines the inflation rate? Explain.

8. Using an *IS-LM-PEP* macroeconomic model, under what conditions will nominal interest rates reflect the rate of increase in the nominal money supply?

9. Suppose that the government decreases the rate of expansion of the nominal money supply. Explain why interest rates might initially rise, but will eventually decline.

10. If inflation is theoretically a monetary phenomenon, why is the current inflation rate often unrelated to current monetary policy? How do you explain the fact that a 3 per cent growth rate of the money supply might produce a zero inflation rate in the real world?

Anti-Inflationary Policy

. . .short-term pain for long-term gain. . .

John Crosbie, former Finance Minister

As discussed in Chapter 12, to lower the *long-run* equilibrium inflation rate the government must restrict the growth rate of the nominal money supply. Unfortunately the *short-run* adjustment costs of such an anti-inflationary, restrictive monetary policy may be very painful. Gearing the economy down from a high inflation rate to a low inflation rate may entail a prolonged period of high unemployment and high interest rates. Even though the *long-run* inflation–unemployment trade-off curve may be dead, the *short-run* Phillips curve relationship between inflation and unemployment is "dangerously" alive. In the words of our colleague, John Vanderkamp,

> Ultimately the rate of monetary expansion determines the rate of inflation in this model, but the Phillips curve plays a very important role in the adjustment process. . .in the downward direction the path of *adjustment* is likely to be tortuous. . . . If price change expectations are slow to adjust, then the unemployment experience along the adjustment path is likely to be very prolonged and severe. . . an incomes policy may well be a useful tool when it is employed together with a restrictive monetary policy to aid in the downward adjustment from an established inflation rate. The incomes policy would then reduce the unemployment burden resulting from the transition to a lower inflation rate. . . . this model suggests that the Phillips curve is not dead, but that it is in fact a more dangerous device than the simple trade-off approach implies. The danger lies in the costs of reducing inflation, which may not be realized when the economy is moving to higher inflation rates.[1]

In this chapter we return to an analysis of the *short-run* properties of the *IS-LM-PEP* model. The initial section of this chapter explores the "tortuous" *short-run* inflation–unemployment–interest rate path which the economy travels during the disequilibrium *adjustment* period accompanying an anti-inflationary, restrictive monetary policy. Given the likelihood of a "very prolonged and severe"

---

[1]John Vanderkamp, "Inflation: A Simple Friedman Theory with a Phillips Twist," *Journal of Monetary Economics*, January 1975, pp. 120-22.

recession accompanying a restrictive monetary policy, a number of economists (including Vanderkamp) have advocated the use of *temporary* wage and price controls to "reduce the unemployment burden" associated with a restrictive monetary policy. As discussed in the middle section of this chapter, temporary wage and price controls might be implemented in conjunction with a restrictive monetary policy (a necessary requirement to sustain a lower long-run inflation rate) to minimize the "short-term pain" associated with an anti-inflationary monetary policy. The chapter concludes with a case study evaluation of the Anti-Inflation Board (1975-78), Canada's first peacetime experiment with wage and price controls.

The Costs of An Anti-Inflationary, Restrictive Monetary Policy: "Short-term Pain"

In Chart 13-1 we have reproduced our standard *IS-LM-PEP* macroeconomic model and have assumed that our hypothetical economy is originally in long-run equilibrium at position A with an income level of Y^* and a "high" inflation rate of $\dot{P}_H$, say 10 per cent.[2] For whatever reason, the government has allowed the money supply to increase by 10 per cent each year and people have come to expect an inflation rate of 10 per cent. Both the *PEP* curve and the *IS* curve reflect an *expected* inflation rate of 10 per cent.[3] Now suppose that the government decides that it wants to reduce this high 10 per cent inflation rate to a lower rate $\dot{P}_L$, say 5 per cent. From our analysis of Chapter 12 the policy prescription is obvious: the government must restrict the growth rate of the nominal money supply to 5 per cent each year. The arrows in Chart 13-1 depict the *short-run* adjustment path that our hypothetical economy may follow once the growth rate of the nominal money supply is lowered to 5 per cent.

In the first phase of the adjustment period, inflation expectations will likely remain high. People may be unsure whether the government is serious about lowering the inflation rate and may wait for evidence that the actual inflation rate does indeed decline (and remains permanently lower) before they lower their inflation expectations.[4] With inflation expectations and the actual inflation rate remaining high, the new lower (5 per cent) growth rate in the nominal money supply will cause the *real* money supply to decline and the *LM* curve to drift upwards to the left. The restrictive monetary policy will initially push interest rates upwards, leading to a reduction in investment expenditures and a decline in income levels. The economy will begin to slide down the PEP_H curve and will continue to slide down the PEP_H curve until the inflation rate has been brought down to 5 per cent, the new lower growth rate of the nominal money supply (point

[2]To simplify the analysis we have again ignored balance of payments considerations.

[3]As discussed in the previous chapter, investment decisions will depend on the *real* interest rate and the *IS* curve will shift if the expected inflation rate were to change.

[4]Chapter 17 provides an extended discussion of the formation of inflation expectations. The anti-inflationary monetary policy option discussed in this chapter is re-examined in Chapter 17 under the assumption of *adaptive* inflation expectations, and the implications of *rational* expectations are fully explored.

CHART 13-1 Effects of an anti-inflationary, restrictive monetary policy

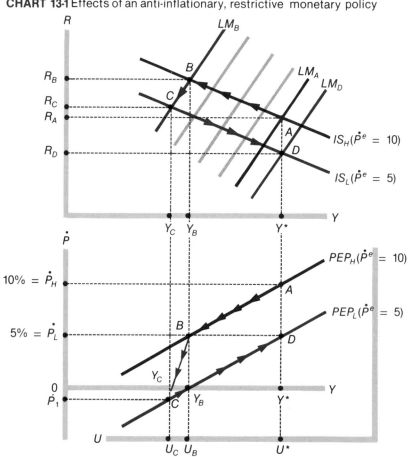

B in Chart 13-1).[5] Note that during this early phase of the adjustment period following the implementation of a restrictive, anti-inflationary monetary policy, both the unemployment rate and the interest rate are continually rising. The economy is unmistakably in the midst of a serious and growing recession, all because the government decided to "wrestle inflation to the ground" with a tight monetary policy.[6]

The economy will remain stuck in this depressed state (at Y_B, R_B and U_B) until people lower their inflation expectations from 10 per cent down to 5 per cent (the new validated inflation rate). Once inflation expectations are lowered, *both* the PEP_H curve *and* the IS_H curve will shift downwards to PEP_L and IS_L respectively in

---

[5]For expositional convenience we assume that inflation expectations remain at 10 per cent as the economy slides down to point *B* in Chart 13-1.

[6]As discussed at the end of this chapter (and in Chapter 16), the Canadian government implemented such an anti-inflationary, restrictive monetary policy in 1980-82, thereby precipitating the severe 1982-83 recession.

Chart 13-1. Given a *nominal* interest rate of R_B and a *lower* expected inflation rate, the *real* interest rate will have further increased, leading to a *further reduction* in investment expenditures and output levels (the downward shift of the *IS* curve). The economy is pushed even further into a recession (point C in Chart 13-1) and the unemployment rate has risen to U_C. However, the lowering of inflation expectations and the consequent downward shift in the *PEP* curve (coupled with the higher unemployment rate U_C) will considerably lower the inflation rate (to $\dot{P}_C$, a negative number, in Chart 13-1). With the inflation rate $\dot{P}_C$ now *below* the 5 per cent growth rate of the *nominal* money supply, the *real* money supply will start to increase and the *LM* curve will drift back downwards to the right. Interest rates will begin to recede from their high levels, investment expenditures will start to pick up and income levels will begin to increase. The economy will gradually lift itself out of this government-induced "tight money" recession. The economic system will climb up the new lower PEP_L curve, eventually returning to the long-run equilibrium point D in Chart 13-1 (where $\dot{\$} = \dot{P} = \dot{P}^e = 5$ per cent). At point D, the level of output and the unemployment rate have returned to their *original* long-run equilibrium values, Y^* and U^*, and the prevailing inflation rate has been permanently lowered from 10 per cent to 5 per cent (which is fully expected and validated). As discussed in the previous chapter, the *nominal* interest rate will be 5 per cent lower at position D than A (since the distance AD is equal to the difference in inflation expectations along the two *IS* curves), and the *real* interest rate will be back to its *original* long-run equilibrium level.

Behind this *IS-LM-PEP* "tortuous" adjustment path is the economist's ubiquitous assumption of a free enterprise market system. In particular, investment expenditures are assumed to respond to changing real interest rates and wage inflation is assumed to vary with the level of unemployment. Assuming competitive labour market conditions, a decrease in the inflation rate requires excess supply conditions in the goods market, which can be generated *either* by increasing supply relative to demand *or* by reducing demand relative to supply. Since aggregate supply is the product of a demographically determined labour force, a capital stock accumulated over many decades, and technology, it is not easy for the government to affect aggregate supply, at least in the short run. Any government-induced increase in aggregate supply designed to dampen the inflation rate is likely to be "too little, too late":

> An extreme, and currently very popular, version of supply-side economics is that the way to tackle the inflation problem is from the supply side, especially by cutting taxes. The argument is simply that inflation results from an excess demand over supply, and there is no sense in correcting that by the painful method of restricting demand when it could be done by the pleasant way of raising supply. The answer is of course equally simple. What we can do on the supply side is not big enough to solve the problem. We have demand growing by about 12 percent a year and supply growing by about 2 percent a year, which yields a 10 percent inflation (in 1980-81). To increase the rate of growth of supply by 50 percent from 2 percent a year to 3 percent a year, which is a difficult task, would still leave an enormous inflation, especially if the increase of

supply is accomplished by means like cutting taxes which at the same time increase demand.[7]

As a consequence, to generate excess supply conditions the government restricts aggregate demand by raising short-term interest rates.

Thus, the term *anti-inflationary* monetary policy should be understood as a euphemism for reduced aggregate demand, higher interest rates, and higher unemployment.[8] The cutting edge of an anti-inflationary, restrictive monetary policy is a larger pool of unemployed workers that will increase the competition for jobs and thereby restrain wage (and price) increases. The economic cost of lowering the *long-run* inflation rate is a *short-run* increase in the interest rate and the unemployment rate. Both Keynesians and monetarists agree on this fundamental if discouraging point:

Richard Lipsey: I don't believe our policy of so-called monetary gradualism will bring down the inflation rate without a major recession.[9]

Milton Friedman: I know of no example of a country that has cured substantial inflation without going through a transitional period of slow growth and unemployment.[10]

In the immortal words of former Finance Minister Crosbie, Canadians must endure "short-term pain for long-term gain."

The magnitude and duration of the "short-term pain" depend crucially on how quickly the market system adjusts to changing economic circumstances. As discussed in Chapter 10, the length of the short-run adjustment period depends on the nature of the underlying price-expectations-augmented Phillips (*PEP*) curve. If wages and prices are relatively *in*sensitive to changing aggregate demand conditions, then the short-run adjustment period will be prolonged. Under such circumstances, increases in unemployment will generate only very slight short-run reductions in wage and price increases. After reviewing the existing empirical literature, the Department of Finance concluded that the Canadian Phillips curve is indeed "very flat."

> The general conclusion is that the short-term curve is very flat at current rates of unemployment. If the unemployment rate increases from 8.5 per cent to 11.5 per cent, the estimated reduction in wage inflation is in the range of .22 to .89 percentage points, or an average of .47 points. In other words, 3 extra points on the unemployment rate (or a reduction in real GNE of 7 to 8 per cent) buy a reduction in wage inflation in the order of one half of one percentage point.[11]

---

[7]H. Stein, "Some 'Supply-Side' Propositions," *Wall Street Journal*, 19 March 1980.

[8]Finance Minister Macdonald, in introducing his 1975 Anti-Inflation Program, euphemistically described his fiscal and monetary policies as being "aimed at increasing total demand and production at a rate consistent with declining inflation" ("Attack on Inflation: A Program of National Action," Policy Statement tabled in the House of Commons, 14 October 1975, p. 3). Cutting through the political rhetoric, the word "increasing" really means "restricting."

[9]*Financial Post*, 6 December 1980.

[10]*Newsweek*, 12 November 1979.

[11]Department of Finance, *Canada's Recent Inflation Experience*, November 1978, p. 44.

Given a "very flat" short-run Phillips curve and a "high degree" of wage inflexibility, increases in unemployment accompanying a restrictive monetary policy will have "relatively little effect" in moderating the rate of wage inflation. If the rate of wage inflation does not decline very quickly, then it will take a considerable length of time and a substantial amount of unemployment to bring the inflation rate down to the new lower validated rate and move the economy from position A to position B in the lower panel of Chart 13-1.

Even though the underlying Canadian Phillips curve may be quite flat, it is *theoretically* possible that labour market participants might quickly lower their inflation expectations and reduce the size of wage settlements when the government implements a restrictive, anti-inflationary monetary policy. However, as Professor Lipsey has pointed out, this theoretical possibility is unlikely to occur as labour market participants may be very reluctant to lower their inflation expectations.

> This theory depends on firms realizing that, because the government will no longer validate by monetary expansion any rate of inflation that emerges from the bargaining table, wage settlements that do not make sense at current prices will lead to losses and in extreme cases, to business failure. Before firms become convinced of this once again, as they no doubt were in previous non-inflationary periods, some firms will have to be punished by losses and/or failure. No one knows how many firms must go to the wall and how many workers must lose their jobs before management and labour are finally convinced.[12]

Since the government's *previous* expansionary monetary policy validated and perpetuated "high" inflation rates, people may not believe that the government's new monetary policy will work or that the government is now serious about lowering the inflation rate and willing to tolerate a recession to lower the long-run inflation rate. Several painful years of recession may be necessary to convince people that the policy is indeed working and that the government is seriously committed to lowering the inflation rate. Chapter 17 provides an extended discussion of the formation of inflation expectations and the macroeconomic implications of different inflation-expectations assumptions for an anti-inflationary monetary policy.

In addition to the *short-run* costs of a restrictive, anti-inflationary monetary policy, there are *long-run* costs as well. During the *entire short-run* adjustment period, the *real* rate of interest will be above its initial level (at position A in Chart 13-1). Consequently, investment expenditures will be *lower* throughout the *entire* short-run adjustment period accompanying a restrictive monetary policy. Thus the capital stock will be lower at position D in Chart 13-1 than it would have been if the economy had remained at position A. Since aggregate output depends on both the amount of capital and labour employed in the production process, a smaller and perhaps less technologically up-to-date capital stock will reduce aggregate supply and lower the long-run equilibrium level of output (not shown in

[12]R.G. Lipsey, "World Inflation," *The Economic Record*, December 1979, p. 295.

Chart 13-1). The supply-side aspects of a tight monetary policy—lower invest-ment and a smaller capital stock—should *not* be ignored and may represent a substantial *long-run cost* for society. As Professor Lipsey has noted,

> If the monetarists' inflation cure of a major recession were tried and it took anything between twice as long as many monetarists think and half as long as many Keynesians think, the cumulative effect on investment could be very serious indeed. When the inflation had finally been stopped, or slowed sufficiently, after a prolonged bout of unemployment in the range of 10 to 15 per cent and the economy allowed to expand its output, capital-capacity bottlenecks might be reached at, say, an 8 to 9 per cent unemployment rate. After such a long period of suffering no democratic government could admit that the "natural rate of unemploy-ment" was now 9 per cent and they would surely go on expanding demand to try for 6 to 7 per cent. This would be inflationary and within a couple of years we could be back to an underlying inflation rate of 5 to 10 per cent.[13]

To summarize, a *restrictive* monetary policy will lower the inflation rate in the long run. However, there are both short-run and long-run costs to such an anti-inflationary policy. During the entire short-run adjustment period accompanying a restrictive monetary policy, the unemployment rate and the real interest rate are higher than they would have been. The lags for a restrictive monetary policy are likely quite long and the "short-term pain" may last for a number of years—perhaps lasting longer than the government which initiated the anti-inflationary policy for "long-term gain." During this prolonged and severe short-run adjust-ment period, the increase in the real interest rate will lead to reduced investment expenditures. Thus, the short-run recessionary effects of an anti-inflationary monetary policy are likely to leave the economy with a relatively smaller and less technologically up-to-date capital stock. As a result, the new long-run *equilibrium* position following a restrictive monetary policy may have a *lower* level of output, albeit with a *lower* inflation rate.

Temporary Wage and Price Controls

Rather than waiting for the economy to slowly and painfully gear down to a new lower inflation rate, the government could impose *temporary* **wage and price controls** to expedite its anti-inflationary monetary policy. The government could directly intervene in the economy to control the size of wage and/or price increases, and thereby *force* the rate of inflation down to the government's new target inflation rate. Under such a program, it would be illegal to accept or grant a wage increase, or establish a price increase, that exceeded the government's prescribed legal norm or guideline. Anyone who violated the legal norm would be prosecuted and "excessive" wage and price increases would be "rolled back" by the government. In October 1975 the Government of Canada resorted to a three-

---

[13]R.G. Lipsey, "Supply-Side Economics: A Survey," in *Policies for Stagflation: Focus on Supply* (Toronto: Ontario Economic Council, 1981), vol. 1, p. 22.

CHART 13-2 Temporary wage and price controls

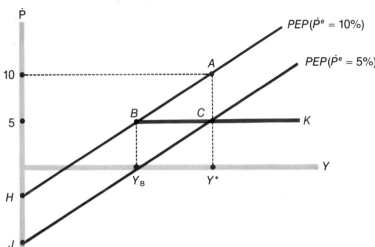

year program of wage and price controls "to halt and reverse the spiral of costs and prices that jeopardizes the whole fabric of our economy and our society."[14] The case study at the end of the chapter provides a lengthy discussion of the mechanics of the Anti-Inflation Board, as well as a post-mortem of Canada's first peacetime attempt to control the inflation rate legally.

To illustrate the *theoretical* case for imposing *temporary* wage and price controls along with a *restrictive* monetary policy, we assume that the economy is initially in *long-run* equilibrium (at Y^*) with a *validated and expected* inflation rate of 10 per cent (position A in Chart 13-2). Again the government decides to lower the inflation rate from 10 per cent to 5 per cent, and therefore restricts the growth rate of the nominal money supply to 5 per cent. In addition to a restrictive monetary policy, suppose that the government also imposes temporary wage and price controls to limit *immediately* the inflation rate to 5 per cent.[15] Given the imposition of wage and price controls, our *PEP* curve (for $\dot{P}^e$ = 10 per cent) will now be *kinked* at point B in Chart 13-2. Wage and price controls have *no* effect if the inflation rate is *below* 5 per cent and the original *PEP* curve ($\dot{P}^e$ = 10 per cent) remains valid for all output levels below Y_B. However, inflation rates *above* 5 per cent (associated with output levels greater than Y_B) are now *illegal* under the new controls program. The original *PEP* curve ($\dot{P}^e$ = 10 per cent) rotates downwards at point B to a *horizontal* line, since the government has imposed a 5 per cent ceiling on the inflation rate. The new *controlled PEP* curve ($\dot{P}^e$ = 10 per cent) is represented in Chart 13-2 by the *kinked* line *HBK*.

With wage and price controls effectively limiting the inflation rate to 5 per cent, the economy will move from point A to point C in Chart 13-2. Since the *nominal*

---

[14]"Attack on Inflation," p. 25.

[15]In our earlier analysis of an *anti-inflationary*, restrictive monetary policy, it took a considerable length of time for the inflation rate to fall to 5 per cent (point B in Chart 13-1).

money supply has been restricted to a 5 per cent growth rate (equal to the 5 per cent legal ceiling on the inflation rate), the *real* money supply will be constant, the *LM* curve will be stationary and output levels will remain at Y^*. The economy has at least temporarily achieved a new lower 5 per cent inflation rate without a recession.

However, the economy is not yet in *long-run* equilibrium. While the new legally enforced 5 per cent inflation rate is validated by a 5 per cent growth rate in the nominal money supply, inflation expectations remain at 10 per cent. To achieve a *permanently* lower inflation rate, wage and price controls must remain in force until people lower their inflation expectations to 5 per cent. Once inflation expectations have been reduced to 5 per cent, the *PEP* curve shifts down to *PEP* ($\dot{P}^e = 5$ per cent) and the *kink* in the *controlled PEP* curve (*JCK*) now appears at point C. Again wage and price controls prevent inflation rates from exceeding the 5 per cent legal ceiling, but have no effect on inflation rates below 5 per cent. With inflation expectations now lowered to 5 per cent, point C represents the long-run equilibrium position for the economy. The 5 per cent inflation rate is fully expected and validated, and the economy is at the *natural* rate of output Y^*.[16]

More important, once inflation expectations have been lowered to 5 per cent, wage and price controls are no longer required. Given the lower *PEP* curve corresponding to $\dot{P}^e = 5$ per cent, the inflation rate would be 5 per cent at Y^* *without wage and price controls*. Wage and price controls are required only until inflation expectations have been lowered to 5 per cent. If wage and price controls are removed *before* inflation expectations are lowered (as was the case in Canada in 1978), then the economy will revert back to its original 10 per cent inflation rate (point A in Chart 13-2), and will have to rely on the recession generated by the restrictive monetary policy to bring the inflation rate down to 5 per cent. Thus the success of a temporary wage and price control program depends on whether inflation expectations are lowered to the new target inflation rate (which the government's restrictive monetary policy is validating).

Wage and price controls represent one potential government policy instrument that might be implemented to ease the economy back down to a lower long-run inflation rate. The sole purpose of wage and price controls would be to lessen the "short-term pain" associated with a restrictive, anti-inflationary monetary policy. In the words of the Governor of the Bank of Canada: "It is useful to supplement financial discipline by direct action to restrain increases in incomes and prices. . . . This approach can bring about the needed adjustment at less cost in terms of unemployment and lost output, and with less serious inequities, than would result from sole reliance on monetary and fiscal policies."[17] The imposition of wage and price controls would be a *temporary short-run* policy implemented *in conjunction*

---

[16]There is one additional complication. When inflation expectations are lowered to 5 per cent, the *IS* curve will also shift downwards (see Chart 13-1), which will produce an output level below Y^* and an inflation rate below 5 per cent (a mini-recession). Given a 5 per cent increase in the nominal money supply, the real money supply will increase, the *LM* curve will shift downwards to the right and the economy will return to Y^* with a 5 per cent inflation rate.

[17]Bank of Canada, *Annual Report*, 1975, p. 11.

with a permanent, restrictive monetary policy. Wage and price controls do not remove the necessity for a restrictive monetary policy, nor do they lower the long-run equilibrium inflation rate. At best, wage and price controls alleviate some of the hardships caused by unemployment and high interest rates that accompany an anti-inflationary, restrictive monetary policy. As such, temporary wage and price controls should be thought of as a "recession analgesic" and not as an "inflation cure." To the extent that wage and price controls reduce the need for *high* (real) interest rates, the long-run costs associated with lower investment expenditures during the short-run adjustment period may also be avoided.

Whether a government should implement temporary wage and price controls is a highly controversial issue. Citizens generally favour wage and price controls[18] and economists oppose them.[19] Much of economists' opposition to wage and price controls stems from their ideological belief in the market system. In general, economists are opposed to any government attempt to legislate a price for a market commodity, be it minimum wages, doctors' fees, oil prices, rent controls or wage and price controls. When the Canadian government introduced wage and price controls in October 1975, most economists opposed the policy.[20] Leading the charge against Canadian wage and price controls was Professor Richard Lipsey, perhaps Canada's leading and most influential economist.[21] We quote from Lipsey's address to the Canadian Economics Association in June 1976.

> The themes of this paper are that both theoretical reasoning and historical experience teach three important lessons concerning wage-price controls. First, the benefits they yield are entirely of a temporary nature; and even these benefits are almost negligibly small. Second, the policy of attempting to contain inflation by wage-price controls is unlikely, when it has been tried once, to be confined to situations of extraordinary economic crises. It is more likely to be resorted to frequently, increasing in its degree of severity with each subsequent application, until it threatens to become a permanent and serious feature of the economy. Third, the indirect and long-term effects of wage-price controls are almost totally on the cost rather than on the benefit side. The effects on the economy are almost always harmful, and the political consequences on the organization of society are potentially disastrous. This leads me to the general conclusion that wage-price controls should be opposed

[18]A 1980 Gallup poll asked the question: "Would you favour or oppose the imposition of wage and price controls by the Federal government?" Of the 1,051 Canadians interviewed, 51 per cent were in favour and 34 per cent were opposed (15 per cent did not know). Reported in the *Toronto Star*, 6 December 1980.

[19]In a 1979 survey of American economists, 72 per cent were generally opposed to wage and price controls and only 6 per cent were generally in favour of wage and price controls to control inflation (see J.R. Kearl et al., "A Confusion of Economists," *American Economic Review, Papers and Proceedings*, May 1979, p. 30).

[20]The front-page headline in the *Globe and Mail* of 3 December 1975 proclaimed "17 economists say controls won't work."

[21]Among other activities, Professor Lipsey authored an Economic Appendix to the Legal Factum submitted by the Canadian Labour Congress to the Supreme Court of Canada in support of the CLC's contention that wage and price controls were *ultra vires*.

under virtually all peacetime circumstances since they produce at best small and transitory short-term benefits in return for large and persistent long-run costs. . . .

The obvious costs are the administrative costs, and they are borne both by the public and the private sectors. The less obvious costs concern the distortions that are introduced into the economy by any centrally administered set of prices and wages. These costs, of course, get larger the longer the controls are in place because the controlled prices at least start by bearing some close relation to market conditions. There is also a further set of hidden costs that concern the quality changes that occur when prices are effectively controlled. These short-term costs clearly exist and are not negligible. . . .

My main message then is as follows. Wage-price controls are shown by economic theory, and demonstrated by an enormous wealth of factual evidence, to have no permanent effect on the price level. If these controls are never repeated in Canada, the long-term effects of this one attempt are not likely to be too serious. There are forces, however, that will be at work to cause the experiment to be repeated. . . .

I say, therefore, that *now* is the time to stand up and be counted. Now is the time to say loudly and clearly that wage-price controls are ineffective in their main objective and extremely harmful in all of their other effects. Now is the time to do everything that we can do to influence public opinion. In doing this economists will be fighting for the integrity of their own subject, since economic analysis clearly shows that the price level cannot be permanently determined by legislation. It is my considered opinion that, not only will we be fighting for the integrity of economics, we will also be doing battle at the barricades in a not insubstantial fight in the defence of human freedom.[22]

As time passed and inflation expectations became more firmly entrenched, however, economists became more willing to consider the idea of temporary wage-price controls to ease the painful adjustment down to a lower long-run inflation rate. Three years after rousing Canadian economists to "stand up and be counted" against wage and price controls, Professor Lipsey conceded to a group of Australian economists that "wage and price controls might be used to force the rate of inflation down" and that if he were Prime Minister he would "slap on a six month wage-price freeze followed by a flat modest percentage increase for a further transitional period."

Breaking inflationary expectations is thus crucial to reducing inflation. But this is easier said than done. . . . Breaking these expectations by restricting demand probably requires enough business failures and unemployment for management and labour to become convinced that governments will no longer bail them out with expansionary demand

[22]R.G. Lipsey, "Wage-Price Controls: How to do a lot of harm by trying to do a little good," *Canadian Public Policy—Analyse de Politiques*, Winter 1977, pp. 1-13.

policies. . . . It is doubtful if any government would be willing to induce the mass unemployment and the wave of business failures that might result from [a sharp restrictive monetary policy]. In an effort to eliminate these undesirable side effects, wage and price controls might be used to force the rate of inflation down to its new expected level (consistent with OPEC etc.) and hold it there long enough to create low-inflationary expectations. . . .

What would I do were I in Mrs. Thatcher's shoes in the UK or better in Joe Clark's shoes in Canada? . . .[I would] cut the rate of monetary expansion to 3-5 per cent within months; slap on a six months wage-price freeze followed by a flat modest percentage increase for a further transitional period; use fiscal policy to mop up any remaining excess demand; cut unemployment benefits to establish a significant differential between such benefits and wages; try to attack restrictive practices and manning agreements; and wear a bullet proof vest every time I showed myself in public.[23]

In his 1981 presidential address to the Canadian Economics Association, Professor Lipsey (sans vest) outlined a six-point anti-inflation program which included wage-price controls:

We should not wait forever for the monetarists' longrun which may come, according to neo-Keynesian theory, when we are all dead. . . .

To a neo-Keynesian the preferred alternative may be to try some form of incomes policy. . . . I have been a longterm opponent of wage-price controls. I opposed them in 1975 because the government had not yet tried traditional monetary and fiscal policies. . . and because I thought it would be an excuse, as it was for two decades in the United Kingdom, for doing little else by way of anti-inflationary policy. . . . Alone they are clearly not sufficient, and since they do involve major costs, they should not be used as *the* anti-inflationary instrument.

But if present policies do not work, I would be prepared to try controls as a part of a full policy package. . . . What, then, is my package?

First, and as its centerpiece, there is a tight monetary policy directed at a monetary magnitude more comprehensive than M1. The rate of monetary expansion would be reduced rapidly over two to three years to levels consistent with a very low rate of inflation.

Second, there is increased fiscal restraint. . . .

Third, wage-price controls can then be used in an attempt to cut through the inflationary inertias and accomplish what the Keynesian view says the free market cannot easily do—get wage inflation down *rapidly* in line with the much lower inflation rate, which is all that is being validated by monetary and fiscal policy. . . .

Fourth, once-for-all measures such as cutting indirect taxes which give downward supply-side shocks can also be employed. . . .

[23]Lipsey, "World Inflation," pp. 294-95.

Fifth, some supply-side incentive measures should also be a part of the package. . . .

Sixth and finally, the package should include some post-controls policy. Post-controls, wage-price guidelines should be used. . . . These measures are designed to attack any upward-bounding of inflationary expectations.[24]

Even conservative monetarist economists have conceded that wage controls can have a role to play in complementing monetary restraint. As the following quotation from Professor Thomas Courchene, one of Canada's most vocal and influential monetarists, makes clear, wage and price controls can reduce the "economic pain" associated with "defusing inflationary expectations":

In order for economic agents to be willing to revise their expectations downward, they must first and foremost be convinced that the Bank of Canada intends to stand firm in its commitment to a gradual reduction in the rate of money supply growth and, hence, to an unwinding of inflation. . . . It is precisely in this context that controls acquire an economic rationale, and probably their only rationale. Controls, in themselves, will not provide a lasting solution to the inflation problem. . . . However, they can have a role to play in complementing monetary restraint in order to minimize the real (employment and output) cost of defusing inflationary expectations.[25]

Both professors Lipsey, a Keynesian, and Courchene, a monetarist, now concede that wage-price controls coupled with monetary restraint "may/can" reduce the short-run unemployment costs associated with lowering the long-run inflation rate. Both economists would undoubtedly point out that wage-price controls also entail administrative and resource misallocation costs, which must be balanced against the potential benefits (less unemployment and lower interest rates) of controls. When Prime Minister Trudeau imposed a three-year program of wage and price controls in October 1975, it was one of the most dramatic and breathtaking policy reversals of all time.[26] The following case study analyzes whether the Anti-Inflation Board, Canada's first peacetime experiment with wage and price controls, was successful. As we shall see, what may be good in theory does not always work out well in practice.

---

[24]Quoted with the permission of R.G. Lipsey. The entire presidential address, entitled "The Understanding and Control of Inflation: Is There a Crisis in Macro-Economics?", was published in the *Canadian Journal of Economics*, November 1981.

[25]T.J. Courchene, *The Strategy of Gradualism: An Analysis of Bank of Canada Policy from Mid-1975 to Mid-1977* (Montreal: C.D. Howe Research Institute, 1977), p. 65.

[26]During the 1974 federal election campaign, Prime Minister Trudeau had vigorously campaigned *against* the Progressive Conservative's key election promise that if elected the PC's would bring in wage and price controls. On 25 May 1974 Prime Minister Trudeau is reported to have said that controls are "a proven disaster looking for a new place to happen." On 13 October 1975 Prime Minister Trudeau went on national television to announce that wage and price controls "will take effect at midnight tonight," but failed to add his famous 1974 election campaign one-liner: "Zap, you're frozen!"

Case Study 8:   The Canadian Anti-Inflation Board—An Evaluation

On October 14, 1975, the Honourable Donald S. Macdonald, then Minister of Finance, tabled in the House of Commons a policy statement entitled *Attack on Inflation, a Program of National Action*. The government's "program of national action" was to consist of four major elements:

1) fiscal and monetary policies aimed at increasing total demand and production at a rate consistent with declining inflation
2) government expenditure policies aimed at limiting the growth of public expenditure and the rate of increase in public service employment
3) structural policies to deal with the special problems of energy, food and housing, to ensure a more efficient and competitive economy and to improve labour-management relations
4) a prices and incomes policy establishing guidelines for responsible social behaviour in determining prices and incomes of groups, together with machinery for administering these guidelines and ensuring compliance where necessary.[27]

Undoubtedly the most visible and important component of the "attack on inflation" was the prices and incomes policy. For the first time in Canadian peacetime history, mandatory wage and price controls were imposed. The "guidelines for responsible social behaviour" established *ceilings* for wage compensation increases with the value of the wage compensation guideline determined by the sum of the following three elements:

1) a basic protection factor which was set at 8 per cent in the first [Anti-Inflation Board] program year, 6 per cent in the second and 4 per cent in the third;
2) a national productivity factor of 2 per cent; and
3) an experience adjustment factor which varied between plus and minus 2 per cent per year depending on a group's experience relative to the rise in the Consumer Price Index (CPI) over the past two or three years.[28]

While all Canadians were expected to comply with these wage compensation guidelines, major employer/employee groups[29] were legally bound by these guidelines and had to submit to the Anti-Inflation Board (AIB) details of their negotiated wage settlements (more on AIB administrative and compliance procedures below).

In addition to restraining wages, the AIB's terms of reference also included the monitoring and "policing" of prices and profits. With respect to price and profit

---

[27]"Attack on Inflation: a Program of National Action," p. 3.

[28]*AIB Third Year Report* (Ottawa, 1978), p. 24.

[29]These groups included firms with more than 500 employees, firms in the construction industry with 20 or more employees, firms thought to be of strategic importance, professionals, as well as the employees of the federal, provincial and municipal governments and their agencies.

guidelines, "the general principle is that increases in prices should be limited to amounts no more than required to cover net increases in costs":[30]

> The guidelines stipulate that a firm's pricing policy include only allowable costs plus a predetermined percentage profit margin (i.e. the target margin). If the profit margin attained in a given compliance period exceeds a company's target margin, the company is said to have generated excess revenue....
>
> As of August 18, 1978, a cumulative total of 882 excess revenue cases had been examined by the Board. These involved 719 companies and a total of $224.51 million in excess revenue....
>
> In all cases, compliance plans were filed with the Board detailing the manner in which companies would divest themselves of their excess revenues. The usual methods adopted included price reductions on specific products and product lines, price freezes, discounts, customer refunds, and company absorption of rising costs over some future period.[31]

If wage increases could be brought down to more reasonable levels and if firms were prevented from either increasing discretionary expenditures (such as landscaping and advertising expenditures) or increasing profit margins, then price inflation would also be restrained. By monitoring and controlling wage increases and profit margins, the AIB would indirectly control the level of prices and the rate of price inflation.[32]

The Anti-Inflation Board was given a three-year mandate "to halt and reverse the spiral of costs and prices that jeopardizes the whole fabric of our economy and our society."[33] Three years later, in explaining the economic reasons for the imposition of wage and price controls, the government invoked an argument very similar to that presented earlier in the chapter:

> The purpose of incomes policies is to reduce inflation by shifting the short-term inflation–unemployment trade-off curve towards the origin, so that at any given unemployment rate the rate of inflation will be reduced. If incomes policies succeed in this aim and if they are in place for a sufficient length of time, then it is likely that expectations of inflation will also be reduced. If this happens, then the short-term trade-off curve will not shift outwards again once the incomes policies are removed. Temporary incomes policies will have succeeded in reducing price expectations and shifting the trade-off curve directly, so that less unemployment is required to achieve a given reduction in inflation.... sole reliance upon demand management policies in combating inflation was rejected, because of the extent of the output losses and the higher

[30]"Attack on Inflation: a Program of National Action," p. 16.
[31]*AIB Third Year Report*, p. 14.
[32]However, the Anti-Inflation Act did empower the AIB to request companies to give the Board advance notification of "significant" price increases. This right was exercised and, by the end of the third program year, 342 companies were "subject to pre-notification." See *AIB Third Year Report*, p. 13.
[33]"Attack on Inflation: a Program of National Action," p. 24.

unemployment rates which would likely have resulted. Instead, the A[nti-] I[nflation] P[rogram], which was designed to directly reduce the rates of growth of wages and prices, and through this to reduce inflationary expectations, was introduced. Consistent monetary and fiscal policies were regarded, however, as an essential part of the AIB.[34]

As is clear from the above quotation, the AIB was intended as a "temporary" policy used in conjunction with "consistent monetary and fiscal policies." The AIB was never intended as the permanent solution to the inflation problem. On October 20, 1977 the Minister of Finance announced that the AIB would be phased out during 1978, slightly ahead of schedule.

The restraint of wages was crucial to the potential success of the government's Anti-Inflation Program. While all elements of this program merit careful scrutiny, a necessary *but not sufficient* condition for the success of this program rested with its ability to restrain wage inflation. If the Anti-Inflation Board had no effect on wage increases, then it would be difficult to argue that the AIB had any effects on "reducing price expectations" or "halting the inflation spiral."

Before measuring the quantitative effect of the AIB on the rate of Canadian wage inflation, a brief review of AIB administrative and compliance procedures is useful. First labour and the firm had to negotiate and agree on a proposed wage contract, which was then submitted to the AIB for approval. Table 13-1 indicates the number of employees for whom wage compensation plans (proposed contracts) were submitted to the AIB for each program year. Wage settlements that provided wage increases at or below the government guidelines required no formal AIB decision. Approximately two-thirds of all employees covered by wage compensation plans submitted to the AIB settled for wage increases that did *not* exceed the guidelines!

Turning to the minority of cases that required an AIB decision (that is, cases where *proposed* wage compensation increases exceeded the guidelines), the AIB would typically recommend a wage "rollback" to the parties involved. Through consultation and negotiation the AIB would then endeavour to persuade the company and union to amend the wage contract to reflect this recommended rollback. If the AIB's persuasive efforts failed to elicit a voluntary amendment to the wage contract reflecting the AIB-recommended rollback, the matter would be referred to the government Administrator who had full legal powers to *enforce* a wage rollback.

Early on the AIB and the Administrator (the "enforcer") adopted a "soft cop–tough cop" stance. The AIB was often prepared to be somewhat lenient in interpreting the wage guidelines (particularly the third component of the formula) whereas the Administrator enforced the letter of the law. In its first private sector case, the "tough cop" Administrator fined the Irving Paper Company $125,000 for defying the AIB's recommended wage rollback. In many instances, the Administrator further rolled back lenient AIB recommendations. For example, consider the plight of the employees of the Cyprus Anvil Mining Corporation (in the Yukon). After they had signed a two-year wage contract calling for wage increases of 36.5 per cent in the first year and 10.4 per cent in the second year, the

[34]Department of Finance, *Canada's Recent Inflation Experience*, p. 51.

TABLE 13-1 Compensation Increases Submitted To The AIB
And AIB Decisions

	Program Year 1 October 14/75 to October 13/76	Program Year 2 October 14/76 to October 13/77	Program Year 3 October 14/77 to October 13/78
Total Number of Employees Submitting Plans	3,256,604	3,983,999	1,682,790
Percentage of Employees for Whom Compensation Increases Were At or Below Guidelines	59.1	69.6	65.7
Number of Employees for Whom AIB Decisions Were Taken	1,463,929	1,343,398	538,080
AIB Decisions:			
i) Average % Increase Submitted	12.1	8.6	6.3
ii) Average % Arithmetic Guideline	9.1	7.1	5.5
iii) Average % Increase Allowed	10.1	7.5	5.7
iv) Average % Rollback Recommended	2.0	1.1	0.6
Estimate of Average Size of AIB Recommended Rollback in Terms of All Employees Submitting Compensation Plans	0.8	0.3	0.2

Source: AIB *Third Year Report*, p. 8-9.

AIB recommended rollbacks which reduced the wage settlement to 14 per cent plus 10 per cent. The United Steelworkers Union appealed this AIB decision to the Administrator, who promptly enforced a settlement of 8 per cent plus 10 per cent! As the AIB has noted, the "evidence showed that the Administrator very often made a tougher decision than the Board,"[35] and it soon became apparent that any appeal to the Administrator ran the risk that the (tough cop) enforcer might very well impose a wage rollback even more severe than the rollback recommended by the (soft cop) AIB. As of September 1978, *only 277* compensation plans had actually been referred to the Administrator, representing *only 1 per cent* of all AIB decisions. In other words, the AIB's persuasive efforts (backed, if necessary, by the legal powers of the "tough cop enforcer") were about 99 per cent effective in obtaining the "voluntary" consent of the firm and union to amend their wage contract to reflect the AIB recommended rollback.

Table 13-1 also summarizes AIB wage compensation decisions, providing information on (1) the average wage compensation increase submitted to the AIB, (2)

[35]*Chronicles of the Anti-Inflation Board*, (Ottawa, 1979), p. 60.

the average wage guideline, (3) the average wage increase allowed by the AIB[36] and (4) the implicit average size of the AIB-recommended wage rollback for each program year. Perhaps the most surprising features of Table 13-1 are the relatively low *average* percentage wage increase submitted to the AIB (for example, 12 per cent in the first program year compared with 20 per cent settlements in the pre-AIB period; see Chart 13-3) and the very modest size of the *average* AIB recommended wage rollback (2 per cent in the first program year). While 20 per cent wage settlements and large AIB wage rollbacks received great publicity, *most* wage settlements submitted to the AIB were relatively close to the guidelines and/or necessitated fairly modest AIB-recommended wage rollbacks.

If the average AIB-recommended wage rollback is weighted with the majority of cases which did *not* involve AIB wage rollbacks (wage compensation plans that did not exceed the guidelines), an estimate can be obtained for the *average* size of the wage rollback in terms of *all* employees submitting wage compensation plans to the AIB. As presented in Table 13-1, the *average* size of the wage rollback in terms of *all* employees is very small, *totalling only 1.3 per cent over the life of the entire AIB program*. This is not meant to imply that particular bargaining groups may not have suffered a very large wage rollback (recall our Cyprus Anvil Mining Company employees), but rather suggests that *in aggregate* the *direct* AIB rollback effect on wage inflation was not very large.

However, the *direct* impact of AIB rollbacks on wage settlements constitutes only one possible channel through which wage settlements may have been moderated by the AIB. Even though wage rollbacks were by far the most visible aspect of the Anti-Inflation Program, a less obvious and more *indirect* AIB effect on negotiated wage settlements may have also occurred. The existence of formal government wage guidelines and the presence of the AIB, coupled with the enforcement powers of the Administrator, may have altered the size of negotiated wage settlements *before* they were submitted to the AIB for formal approval. Firms and unions may have been coerced into negotiating lower wage settlements by the *threat of a wage rollback*, much the same way that radar traps, marked police cruisers and the threat of a speeding ticket slow down the traffic flow along a highway. The possibility of being caught by the AIB for breaking the law (the wage guidelines) may have caused a *change* in wage behaviour—a slowdown in wage settlements along the inflation highway. *If* such a *change* in wage behaviour did occur, the actual size of the AIB-recommended rollback would give a very misleading indication of the "AIB-induced" reduction in wage inflation. The success, or failure, of an *anti-speeding* highway patrol program is *not* measured by the number of speeding tickets issued but rather by the average *speed* of the traffic flow, compared with what it would have been in the absence of a highway patrol program. One would not want to conclude that a highway (inflation) patrol program was totally ineffective simply because no speeding (rollback) tickets were issued when the flow of traffic (wage settlements) was proceeding at the speed limit (the guidelines).

---

[36]Given special circumstances, such as a "historical relationship" between particular bargaining groups, the AIB frequently permitted larger wage settlements than the arithmetic guidelines dictated (as the lenient "soft cop" referred to above).

While the *direct* AIB rollback effects can easily be tabulated, an entirely different methodology must be used to quantify the *indirect* (threat) effects on wage behaviour attributable to the presence of the AIB and the Administrator. To measure this indirect effect, one must first forecast what wage settlements *would have been in the absence of the AIB*.[37] In essence the empirical analysis must be counter-factual. Having produced a (hypothetical) *forecast* for the likely rate of wage inflation *if* the AIB had never been implemented, one can then compare the *actual* (AIB) rate of wage inflation with these hypothetical (no AIB) wage inflation *forecasts*. Substantial differences between the *actual* (AIB) wage inflation rate and the hypothetical (no AIB) wage inflation *forecast* could be attributed to this indirect (threat) effect of the AIB on wage behaviour.

A number of empirical studies have examined the size of this indirect AIB (threat) effect on the rate of wage inflation.[38] All of these studies conclude that the AIB exerted a significant effect on wage inflation, depressing wage changes below the level which likely would have prevailed (in the absence of the AIB). In quantitative terms, results from these studies suggest that wage settlements in Canada were about 3 per cent per annum lower than they would have been in the absence of the AIB. Given the existence of long-term wage contracts, the impact of the AIB on the aggregate wage inflation rate would, however, accumulate very slowly, as many workers were locked into (inflationary) *pre*-AIB wage contracts for much of the early life of the AIB. It was only as these *pre*-AIB long-term wage contracts expired that the AIB program could be brought to bear on reducing the rate of wage inflation. On the basis of the existing bargaining cycle, Christofides and Wilton estimated that:

> the cumulative impact of the AIB on private sector wage rates was only about 0.8 per cent after one year and 3.2 per cent after two years, but rose quite dramatically to 6.1 per cent after three years and 7.2 per cent after four years. . . . In short, the existence of the AIB (with specific wage guidelines) and the Administrator (with rollback powers) appears to have substantially moderated wage inflation over levels which might have prevailed assuming that the wage structure in the decade prior to the imposition of the AIB would have continued to exist throughout the remainder of the 1970's.[39]

The moderating effects of the AIB on Canadian wage inflation are obvious when one reviews the pattern of wage changes during the 1970s. In Chart 13-3 we have

[37]In terms of our highway patrol illustration, one would have to forecast the average highway speed in the absence of speed limits, radar traps, marked police cruisers, and tough judges.

[38]D.A.L. Auld, L.N. Christofides, R. Swidinsky and D.A. Wilton, "The Impact of the Anti-Inflation Board on Negotiated Wage Settlements," *Canadian Journal of Economics*, May 1979, p. 195-213; L.N. Christofides and D.A. Wilton, *Wage Controls in Canada (1975:3-1978:2): A Study of Their Impact on Negotiated Base Wage Rates* (Ottawa: Anti-Inflation Board, 1979); J.-M. Cousineau and R. Lacroix, "L'Impact de la Politique Canadienne de controle des Prix et des Revenus sur les Ententes Salariales," *Canadian Public Policy—Analyse de Politiques*, Winter 1978, p. 88-100; F. Reid, "The Effect of Controls on the Rate of Wage Changes in Canada," *Canadian Journal of Economics*, May 1979, pp. 214-27; and P. Fortin and K. Newton, "Labour Market Tightness and Wage Inflation in Canada," in M.N. Baily, ed., *Workers, Jobs and Inflation* (Washington: The Brookings Institution, 1982).

[39]Christofides and Wilton, *Wage Controls*, pp. 88-89.

CHART 13-3 Wage and price inflation in the 1970s

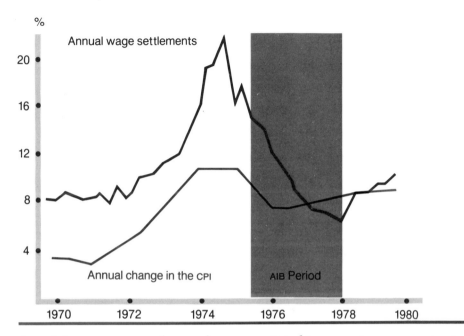

plotted the average *annual* wage change negotiated in *new* union wage contracts, as collected by Labour Canada.[40] For comparison purposes, we have also plotted the annual percentage change in the consumer price index. There is a clear deceleration in the rate of wage inflation during the life of the AIB, with actual wage settlements falling *below* the rate of change in the CPI during 1977 and 1978. As the Department of Finance noted,

> During the controls period both money supply growth and real growth declined, and the unemployment rate rose. These factors would have exerted some downward pressure on wage and salary increases even in the absence of controls. Inflationary expectations may also have been declining prior to the imposition of controls. However... these forces by themselves would not have been adequate to reduce the rate of increase of base wage rates from over 20 per cent in 1975 to a little over 12 per cent in 1976 and to 8 per cent in 1977.[41]

In summary, all empirical evidence points to the fact that the AIB exerted a moderating influence on the rate of wage inflation, with a total *cumulative* controls wage effect of 6 per cent to 8 per cent. Despite predictions of a post-controls wage rebound effect (to recapture "lost" wage increases during the period of controls), there were no obvious signs of such a wage rebound. As shown in Chart 13-3, new wage settlements negotiated during the first two years after

[40]Given the lack of reliable data on cost-of-living allowance (COLA) clauses, we have excluded all wage contracts which included a COLA clause.

[41]Department of Finance, *Canada's Recent Inflation Experience*, pp. 51-52.

the AIB was terminated barely kept pace with the inflation rate, compared with very large *real* wage gains in the early 1970s. In this initial two-year period after controls were lifted, 80 per cent of all wage settlements were less than 10 per cent per annum and only 4 per cent of all settlements exceeded 13 per cent per annum. Not only were there no obvious signs of a post-controls wage rebound effect (to offset or recapture the 6-8 per cent controls effect), post-AIB wage settlements were extremely moderate in comparison with wage settlements in the pre-AIB period.[42] Since there is no evidence that aggregate profit margins rose during the AIB period,[43] one would surmise that this AIB-induced moderation in wage inflation must have produced a lower rate of price inflation than would have prevailed in the absence of the AIB. In Table 13-2 we have presented annual percentage change data for consumer prices and labour compensation, along with the government's inflation targets. Since food prices at the farm gate were specifically excluded from AIB control and energy prices were allowed to continue to rise towards world levels, we have also presented CPI changes *excluding* these two key "uncontrolled" components. Table 13-2 clearly demonstrates the influence of food and energy price increases on the overall CPI during the AIB period. As the Department of Finance noted,

> In the first program year, the 8-per-cent target was easily achieved because of an unexpected decline in food prices. In 1977 the re-emergence of double-digit increases in food prices was in large part responsible for the CPI growth rate's exceeding the target rate. In both years, the policy of letting energy prices continue to rise towards world levels put further pressure on the all-items CPI.[44]

If we judge the AIB in terms of prices it was trying to control—the CPI excluding food and energy—the underlying inflation rate was significantly lowered during the life of the AIB, from 10 per cent to about 6 per cent. Even though controlled wages and domestic costs were more or less on target during the AIB period, exogenous food price increases and the government's energy policy (of allowing oil prices to move towards world prices) shocked this *underlying* inflation by almost 3 per cent. Given that most people form their inflation expectations in terms of the expected price increase for *all* goods (even the heartiest Canadian must "eat and heat"), the AIB probably had very little impact on *reducing inflation expectations*. Entering the 1980s, the actual and *expected* inflation rate remained stubbornly at about 10 per cent (what it was in 1975). Perhaps if we had had a better break on food price increases in 1978-80 (an average per annum increase of 13 per cent), or if we had absorbed higher energy prices in the mid-1970s (like most other countries), or if we had maintained wage and price controls in place for a couple more years, the *actual* and *expected* inflation rates might have been reduced. Since the *raison d'etre* of the AIB was to lower the actual inflation rate

---

[42]See L.N. Christofides and D.A. Wilton, "Wage Determination in the Aftermath of Controls," *Economica*, 1985.

[43]In fact, the ratio of total corporation profits to GNP fell slightly from 0.119 in 1975 to 0.110 in 1978.

[44]Department of Finance, *Canada's Recent Inflation Experience*, p. 53.

TABLE 13-2   Annual Percentage Changes in Inflation Indicators

	Labour Compensation*	Total CPI	CPI Excluding Food	CPI Excluding Food & Energy	AIP Targets
1971	7.5	2.9	3.4	n.a.	
1972	7.1	4.8	3.7	n.a.	
1973	10.1	7.6	5.1	n.a.	
1974	13.6	10.9	8.8	n.a.	
1975	14.1	10.8	10.1	9.6	
1976	12.7	7.5	9.4	8.8	8
1977	6.7	8.0	7.9	7.4	6
1978	5.4	8.9	6.4	6.1	4
1979	7.0	9.1	7.9	7.6	

*Labour Compensation per person employed in all commercial non-agricultural industries.
Source: Department of Finance, *Economic Review*.

and to reduce inflation expectations, the AIB obviously failed to achieve its major objective. Even though the AIB may have won the battle on the wage front, it lost the war against inflation expectations.

Nevertheless, the AIB should not be deemed a total failure. Without wage and price controls in place, these unexpected price shocks would have pushed the Canadian inflation rate to approximately 11 per cent in 1978, despite the existence of a restrictive monetary policy. Under the AIB, the 1978 inflation rate was just under 9 per cent, about 2 per cent lower than it would have been in the absence of controls. Furthermore, in the absence of any price shocks (including energy price increases) the AIB would likely have lowered the actual inflation rate to about 5 per cent.[45] While the AIB failed to achieve its inflation targets (and was consequently considered by many to be a failure), it at least halted and prevented any further acceleration of the inflation rate that would have occurred because of rising energy prices and the food-import price shocks of 1977-78. In the words of Wilson and Jump, "we could have done far worse" without the AIB.[46]

In conclusion, all empirical studies agree that the AIB significantly reduced the rate of wage inflation in Canada (by about 3 per cent per annum) and there is no evidence of an outburst of additional wage inflation when controls were lifted in 1978. The major benefits of a *temporary* controls program are measured in real opportunity-cost terms. Wage inflation deceleration can be accomplished without having to endure a severe painful recession with very high unemployment rates, high real interest rates and a substantial loss in output. Assuming that the slope of the Canadian Phillips curve is 0.5,[47] to accomplish the same degree of wage restraint achieved by the AIB *without controls* would have required an additional 6

[45]See D.A. Wilton, "An Evaluation of Wage and Price Controls in Canada," *Canadian Public Policy—Analyse de Politiques*, 1984, pp. 167-76.

[46]T.A. Wilson and G. Jump, *The Influence of the Anti-Inflation Program of Aggregate Wages and Prices* (Ottawa: Anti-Inflation Board, 1979).

[47]A Phillips curve estimate of 0.5 exceeds that reported in any of the seven studies reviewed by the Department of Finance in 1978 (see footnote 11).

per cent unemployment (that is, unemployment rates of approximately 13 per cent for 1976-78). Alternatively, the economic benefits of imposing temporary wage and price controls translated into approximately 600,000 more jobs. While the AIB imposed some administrative and resource distortion costs on the Canadian economy, these undocumented costs undoubtedly fall far short of the substantial economic costs associated with a major recession engineered to generate the same degree of wage restraint as produced by the AIB.

As a final postscript to our case study on the AIB, we note that the Trudeau government rejected the use of temporary wage and price controls in 1981-82 when it again decided to fight inflation with a restrictive monetary policy. During this two-year period, the Bank of Canada *reduced* the *real* money supply (as measured by M1 deflated by the CPI) by over 16 per cent, as the *nominal* money supply grew by only 3.9 per cent and 0.6 per cent in 1981 and 1982. Given this highly restrictive monetary policy, our analysis suggests that both interest rates and unemployment rates will rise substantially above their equilibrium values as the economy slowly gears down to a lower inflation rate. This is precisely what happened. During 1981-82 the prime lending rate of chartered banks averaged over 17 per cent and the unemployment rate jumped from 7.5 per cent in 1981 to 11.0 per cent in 1982. In output terms, real GNP fell by 4.4 per cent in 1982. This severe recession, in large part induced by a very restrictive monetary policy, had the predicted effects on the inflation rate. The 12.5 per cent inflation rate of 1981 was driven down to 5.8 per cent in 1983 and 4.4 per cent in 1984. A restrictive monetary policy will indeed lower the long-run inflation rate, but at a very high short-run cost.

Review Questions

1. Carefully analyze the short-run and long-run costs of a restrictive, anti-inflationary monetary policy.
2. Are the benefits of a lower inflation rate worth the costs of a restrictive monetary policy?
3. What is the economic rationale for wage and price controls?
4. Do you think that the potential economic benefits of wage and price controls outweigh the costs? Do you think that the AIB was a success or failure?
5. Suppose that the government implements a *tough* program of wage and price controls but *fails to restrict* the rate of monetary expansion. What do you predict will happen? Explain using an *IS-LM-PEP* diagram.

Stabilization Policy: Demand Shocks

Nonmonetarists accept what I regard to be the fundamental practical message of the **General Theory** *that a private enterprise economy using an intangible money needs to be stabilized,* **can** *be stabilized, and therefore* **should** *be stabilized by appropriate monetary and fiscal policies. Monetarists by contrast take the view that there is no serious need to stabilize the economy. . . .*

Franco Modigliani[1]

In Chapter 12 we analyzed the long-run properties of the *IS-LM-PEP* macroeconomic model. *In the long run*, demand-management policies will have *no* effect on the level of output and employment, but the inflation rate can be controlled by appropriate monetary policy. *In the long run* the economy will come to rest at the natural rate of unemployment (or the NAIRU), with an inflation rate corresponding to the rate at which the government chooses to increase the nominal money supply. Unfortunately, we live in a *short-run unstable* world and the economic system rarely ever comes to rest at its *long-run equilibrium* position. Our economy is continually buffeted by various kinds of unexpected events, disturbances and shocks. To cite but two examples, when the United States went into a serious recession in 1974-75, the level of Canadian exports declined accordingly, exerting a negative demand shock on the Canadian economic system. The quadrupling of oil prices in early 1974 by the OPEC cartel inflicted a serious supply-price shock on the world economic system, Canada included. In reality, the economic system is rarely ever at its long-run equilibrium position. Most of the time the economy is reacting to one or more shocks or disturbances which have displaced the economic system from its long-run equilibrium position.

While there are natural self-correcting adjustment forces that will bring the economic system back to its long-run equilibrium position, the short-run adjustment period following a shock may be quite long and painful in terms of higher unemployment rates, higher interest rates and/or higher inflation rates. Given an unexpected shock or disturbance to the economic system, what if anything should the government do? There is undoubtedly a strong temptation for the government to intervene and attempt to stabilize the economic system, thereby minimizing the short-run unemployment and/or inflation costs associated with the shock or

---

[1]Franco Modigliani, "The Monetarist Controversy or, Should We Forsake Stabilization Policies?" *American Economic Review*, March 1977, p. 1 (Presidential address to the American Economic Association).

disturbance. In this chapter and the next we analyze various stabilization policy options that are available to the government to combat shocks and disturbances to the economic system. Given the *long-run equilibrium* position for the economic system, we now focus on the important *short-run* macroeconomic issue: how should the government go about managing the economy on a year-by-year basis?

We begin this chapter with a brief discussion of the nature of instability within the economic system. Having identified and classified shocks or disturbances to the economic system by their source of origin—demand versus supply-price shocks—we then examine the *disequilibrium* path which the economy might travel during the short-run adjustment period accompanying and immediately following a *demand* shock. The economic costs associated with a demand shock are analyzed under both a Keynesian interventionist stabilization policy and a monetarist non-interventionist policy. As we shall see in the next chapter, *supply-price* shocks, the economic disease of the 1970s, are very troublesome for both Keynesian and monetarist economists. Throughout these two chapters we assume that inflation expectations are constant and unaffected by the occurrence of shocks or policy actions. We postpone a discussion of adaptive and rational inflation expectations until Chapter 17, at which point the new classical macroeconomic model and the policy ineffectiveness proposition will be formally presented.[2]

Sources of Instability Within the Economic System

In the context of a macroeconomic model, there are two different ways in which a shock to the economic system might arise. First, the value of one or more of the *exogenous variables* within the model might change. For example, if the level of exports or autonomous investment were to change, there would be obvious Keynesian multiplier repercussions throughout the economy. Second, the value of one or more of the *behavioural parameters* within the model might change. For example, consumers might become more thrifty, thus causing the marginal propensity to consume to decline. Any change in behaviour will alter some of the behavioural parameters within the model and cause a shock or disturbance to the entire economic system.

In this chapter and the next we focus our analysis on *temporary* changes in exogenous variables and/or behavioral parameters within the context of our *IS-LM-PEP* model.[3] For analytical purposes it will prove useful to classify such shocks into the following two categories in terms of their point of origin within the *IS-LM-PEP* diagrammatic representation of the economic system:

---

[2]The policy ineffectiveness proposition states that anticipated government policy, such as Keynesian stabilization policy, will have absolutely no effect on output and employment levels (see Chapter 17).

[3]Previous chapters (particularly 10 and 12) have analyzed the macroeconomic effects of a *permanent* change in an exogenous variable.

Demand Shocks

Shocks or disturbances which arise within the *IS-LM* quadrant of our macro-economic model are classified as demand shocks. This quadrant depicts the key demand relationships within the economic system and *changes* in autonomous investment, exports, government expenditures or the nominal money supply are good illustrations of **demand shocks**.

Supply-Price Shocks

Disturbances which originate within the Phillips curve-inflation quadrant of our model are classified as **supply-price shocks**. The Phillips curve describes pricing decisions of firms and labour market behaviour, the supply side of our macroeconomic model. The key exogenous variable within the Phillips curve quadrant of the model is the change in the relative price of internationally traded commodities. For example, the dramatic increase in oil prices clearly exerted a substantial supply-price shock to the economic system during the mid-1970s.

Although an analysis of demand shocks is the essence of Keynesian economics, supply-price shocks have become increasingly more important since the 1970s and are the most difficult type of shock for governments to counteract. Before tackling these troublesome supply-price shocks (in the next chapter), however, we analyze demand shocks and the various stabilization policy approaches which are available to counteract demand shocks to the economic system.

Illustrations of Demand Shocks

Perhaps more than any other issue, the choice of an appropriate stabilization policy for demand shocks goes to the heart of the debate between Keynesian and monetarist economists. The instability of aggregate demand (the *IS* curve) is the *raison d'être* of Keynesian economics. Keynes clearly identified the instability of investment expenditures as the major cause of the business cycle (see Chapters 5 and 20). Since capital formation depends crucially on the long-run appraisal (expectation) of profits and risk, Keynes regarded the "state of confidence" and "animal spirits" as important determinants of investment expenditures. In Keynes' view, if the "delicate balance of spontaneous optimism" was upset, investment spending would be curtailed and the economy would be plunged into a serious recession.

Before analyzing Keynesian and monetarist policy approaches for demand shocks and *IS* curve instability, we briefly examine the extent to which demand shocks have impinged on the Canadian economic system over the 1960-84 period. In Chart 14-1 we display the five major components of aggregate demand along with the Canadian money supply (in both nominal and real terms), each plotted in annual percentage change form (to the same scale). Summary statistics for the annual percentage changes in these key demand variables are presented in Table 14-1. The key column of Table 14-1 is the last one, which provides a statistical measure of the variation in the year-to-year percentage changes for each

CHART 14-1   Annual percentage change in demand variables

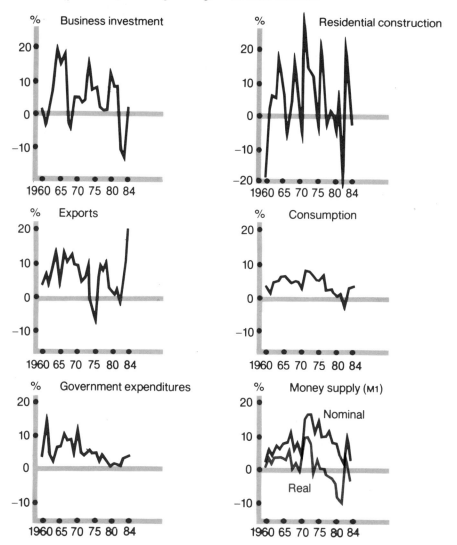

TABLE 14-1   Summary Statistics for Key Demand Variables (1960-84)

	Percentage Change			
	Average	Minimum	Maximum	Variance
Business investment	4.2	−12.3	17.2	56.5
Investment in residential construction	2.9	−21.0	29.5	155.0
Exports	6.8	−6.4	19.7	31.5
Consumer expenditures	4.1	−2.1	7.9	5.4
Government expenditures	4.1	0.5	13.8	11.2
Nominal money supply	7.2	0.7	14.5	16.1
Real money supply	1.5	−9.1	9.7	19.8

demand variable over this 25-year period.[4] The larger the variation (or variance) of the demand variable, the greater its instability.

As is obvious from Chart 14-1 and Table 14-1, the two investment components exhibit by far and away the greatest variability or instability. For example, during 1964-65, total business investment increased by over 30 per cent and residential construction increased by more than 20 per cent, clearly exerting a substantial, positive demand shock on the economic system during these two years. In Table 14-1, the variance of the two investment components substantially exceeds the variance of the other demand variables. For example, the variance of business investment is ten times larger than the variance of consumption expenditures and the variance of residential construction is twenty-nine times larger than that of consumption. Given this very pronounced volatility in Canadian investment expenditures, it would be difficult to dismiss changes in investment expenditures as a prime source of demand shocks and instability to the Canadian economic system.[5]

Turning to the other components of aggregate demand, consumption expenditures are clearly the most stable component of aggregate demand. In general consumption expenditures tend to stabilize total GNP, smoothing out the peaks and troughs of the income cycle.[6] Exports, on the other hand, exhibit considerably more variation. The level of Canadian exports depends crucially on the level of economic activity (or business cycle) in the United States and the rest of the world. For example, the serious U.S. recession in 1974-75 resulted in an 8½ per cent decline in total Canadian exports.[7] On the other hand, Canadian exports received a substantial stimulus during the mid-1960s from the Vietnam war-induced "boom" in the U.S. Since exports represent approximately one-quarter of total Canadian production, the Canadian economy is very susceptible to world market conditions. A sharp recession or boom within the U.S. will directly affect Canadian exports, exerting a substantial demand shock on the Canadian economic system.

Of the two government-controlled demand variables, government expenditures on goods and services have been quite stable during the 1970s and 1980s. The two largest increases in government expenditures occurred in 1961 and 1970, two of the worst years for income growth in the Canadian economy over these twenty-five years. Since 1973 there has been a gradually declining trend in the *growth rate* of government expenditures, but it too has proceeded in a relatively stable manner. On the other hand, monetary policy has not been nearly so stable. As discussed in Chapter 12 (and displayed in Chart 14-1), the Bank of Canada rapidly expanded the *nominal* money supply in the early 1970s, leading to double-digit inflation in the mid-1970s. To purge inflation out of the economy, in the early 1980s the Bank of Canada deliberately restrained the growth rate of the nominal money supply. During 1981-82 the *real* money supply *declined* by over 16 per cent, driving up interest rates, depressing investment levels, and pushing the

---

[4]The statistical variance is computed by summing the squared deviations of each element in the series from the average of all elements in the series, and then dividing by the total number of elements.

[5]See also the discussion of the accelerator theory of investment in Chapter 20.

[6]See Chapter 19 for a discussion of the permanent income hypothesis of consumption.

[7]See also Chart 5-14 and accompanying discussion in Chapter 5.

economy into the worst recession since the 1930s. The macroeconomic effects of these major *government-engineered* monetary policy demand-shocks (that is, the "excessive" monetary expansion of the early 1970s and the severe contraction of the early 1980s) are discussed at length in Chapter 16.

In summary, Canada has experienced considerable instability in aggregate demand and the Canadian *IS* and *LM* curves have been buffeted about by substantial, persistent demand shocks. From the Great Depression (see Chapter 4) to the boom and bust of the 1960s, 1970s and 1980s (see Chapter 16), the Canadian economy has been subjected to strong negative and positive demand shocks. Since the adverse unemployment effects accompanying a *negative* demand shock are much more obvious than the inflationary effects accompanying a *positive* demand shock, we maintain the Keynesian tradition of initially focusing our policy analysis on *negative* demand shocks. After analyzing Keynesian and monetarist policy approaches for negative demand shocks, we then briefly consider positive demand shocks and an inconsistent "flip-flop" stabilization policy that encompasses a monetarist policy for positive demand shocks and a Keynesian policy for negative demand shocks.

Stabilization Policy Options for a Negative Demand Shock

Let us assume that a hypothetical economy is initially in long-run equilibrium at Y^* (see Chart 14-2) with a fully anticipated *validated* inflation rate of $\dot{P}_0$. The government can maintain the inflation rate $\dot{P}_0$ indefinitely without there being any pressure for the inflation rate to increase (or decrease) simply by ensuring that the nominal money supply grows at the rate $\dot{\$} = \dot{P}_0$. As discussed in the previous chapter, a lower rate of monetary expansion will ultimately lead to a lower inflation rate at the same level of real income Y^*, but this cannot be achieved without severe short-run economic costs. We assume that the government has decided to live with an inflation rate of $\dot{P}_0$, which is validated by appropriate monetary expansion ($\dot{\$} = \dot{P}_0$ in Chart 14-2).

Now assume that a strong *negative* demand shock hits this hypothetical economy, shifting the IS_0 curve inward to IS_1 in Chart 14-2. Our hypothetical economy is abruptly displaced from its long-run equilibrium position: the level of income has substantially declined (to Y_1) and the inflation rate has moderated slightly (down to $\dot{P}_1$). The inward shift of the *IS* curve has thrown our hypothetical economy into a recession. Given the obvious economic costs of rising unemployment, what if anything should the government do to counteract this negative demand shock? We first analyze the Keynesian prescription for a negative demand shock and then turn to the monetarist approach. To simplify the following analysis, we continue to ignore balance of payments repercussions (the *BP* curve)[8] *and* assume that inflation expectations are *not* affected by temporary demand shocks

---

[8]We leave it to a senior course in either macroeconomics and/or international finance to incorporate explicit balance of payments adjustment mechanisms into the *IS-LM-PEP* model, as we concentrate our attention on the key underlying stabilization issues which exist irrespective of balance of payments and foreign exchange rate considerations.

CHART 14-2 Keynesian policy for a negative demand shock

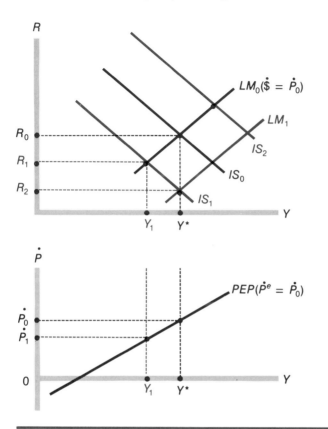

to the economic system. By assuming *constant* inflation expectations in the short run, we avoid a shifting *IS* curve (the real versus nominal interest rate distinction discussed in Chapter 12) and a shifting *PEP* curve. As a consequence of this latter assumption, we do not enter the expectations arena in which adaptive expectations models are pitted against rational expectations models (see Chapter 7).

Keynesian Intervention: Counter-cyclical Demand-Management Policy

The problem of severe, persistent negative demand shocks during the 1930s prompted Keynes to formulate the *General Theory*. Rather than endure the unemployment costs associated with a negative demand shock, Keynes argued that the government should stimulate aggregate demand to offset the adverse effects of the negative demand shock. Similarly, when an (inflationary) positive demand shock occurs, aggregate demand should be restricted. According to Keynes, the government should pursue a policy of actively intervening within the economic system to stabilize aggregate demand. The free enterprise system must be "managed" to maintain output and employment stability. In terms of our diagrammatic representation of the economic system, the government should undertake *discretionary* fiscal and/or monetary policies to maintain Y^*, the long-run equilibrium position, as the intersection point of the IS and LM curves. If successful, such an interventionist **demand-management policy** would smooth out the business cycle, hence the title counter-cyclical demand-management policy.

Returning to Chart 14-2, the government has at least three different Keynesian policy options to restore Y^* after a *negative* demand shock has pushed the IS_0 curve back to IS_1 and lowered the income level to Y_1. First, the government could increase its own expenditures on goods and services G, thereby shifting the IS_1 curve back to IS_0. The government could purchase more tanks, mail boxes, flags, pencils and memo pads; or it could hire more civil servants to drive the tanks, deliver the mail, hoist the flags and write memos. Second, the government can shift the IS_1 curve back to IS_0 by cutting taxes and/or increasing transfer payments. In this case, the offsetting expenditures would be made by consumers who would experience an increase in their disposable income. Third, the government could shift the LM_0 curve rightwards to LM_1 by a "one-shot" increase in the nominal stock of money (over and above the regular increases of $\dot{\$} = \dot{P}_0$ each year). Such a policy would lower the interest rate (to R_2), causing an increase in investment expenditures and aggregate demand. While all three Keynesian demand-management policy options would *offset* the negative demand shock and return the economy to its long-run equilibrium income level Y^* and original inflation rate $\dot{P}_0$,[9] the key differences between the three Keynesian policy options concern (1) the resulting interest rate and (2) which sector will be the direct beneficiary of the additional spending (the government sector, the consumer sector or the investment/business sector).

Given these three possible policy options to offset negative demand shocks, Keynes clearly leaned towards fiscal policy and discretionary changes in government expenditures[10] as the most potent counter-cyclical weapon in the government's arsenal. As discussed in Chapter 6, Keynes believed that investment expenditures were only mildly sensitive to interest rate movements—the IS curve in our model is likely to be very steep. Consequently, it would likely require a very large increase in the money supply and a very large decline in interest rates to generate a sufficient increase in investment expenditures to offset the negative demand shock. Such a monetary policy offset would have a very destabilizing effect on the interest rate. Whereas a fiscal policy offset for a demand shock to the IS curve returns the interest rate to its original equilibrium value R_0, a monetary policy offset necessarily pushes the interest rate further away from its equilibrium value (to R_2 in Chart 14-2). Since a widely fluctuating interest rate will have other adverse economic consequences (including redistributing wealth between bond holders and debtors, disrupting the balance of payments, and destabilizing the construction industry), one can make a strong stability argument for using fiscal policy offsets for demand shocks. Intuitively, it makes sense to offset a shift in the

[9]Note that our assumption of *constant* inflation expectations (of $\dot{P}_0$) would be "correct."

[10]During the 1930s taxes were very low, providing the government with little scope to use tax cuts to stimulate consumer spending.

IS curve with a policy which operates on the same curve; that is, use fiscal policy to shift the *IS* curve back. In addition, the use of *fiscal* policy offsets for negative demand shocks avoids any inflationary consequences of getting trapped in an expansionary monetary policy which might lead to an increase in inflationary expectations and a wage-price spiral.[11] Most Keynesian economists argue that demand-management policy offsets should be of a fiscal nature, rather than discretionary changes in monetary policy.

There is a most important corollary of Keynesian counter-cyclical demand-management policy that is frequently overlooked. *When the demand shock is over,*[12] *the demand-management (fiscal) policy offset must be removed.* Returning to Chart 14-2, let us assume that the government does *not* remove its discretionary fiscal policy offset when the negative demand shock ends. The termination of the negative demand shock will cause the IS_1 curve to shift back to the original IS_0 position. However, the *continuing* presence of the *positive* fiscal policy offset *which is no longer needed* will now push the IS_0 curve out to IS_2. The *old* and *now inappropriate* fiscal policy offset (the increase in government spending or tax cut) will function as a *new* positive demand shock to the economic system. As discussed below, a government which deliberately generates positive demand shocks will sooner or later get into trouble with a wage-price spiral (from rising inflationary expectations). To avoid future inflationary complications, the government *must* remove its positive fiscal policy offset when the negative demand shock terminates.

In summary, Keynesian stabilization policy calls for *temporary* demand-management policies to offset demand shocks and to propel the economy quickly back to its long-run equilibrium position. When the negative demand shock is over, the stimulative fiscal policy offset must be removed; otherwise a new positive demand shock to the economic system will occur. Consequently, a vital characteristic of Keynesian stabilization policy is that it *must be temporary and reversible*. Unfortunately, the fiscal tap is much easier to turn on than to turn off and governments are typically reluctant to cut back on services provided, fire civil servants and/or raise taxes. Nevertheless, Keynesian stabilization policy calls for *temporary* counter-cyclical measures and Keynesian economics ought *not* to be used to rationalize new government programs and/or permanent changes in the fiscal structure of the economy.

Monetarist Non-Intervention: A Laissez-Faire Approach

The monetarist approach to stabilization policy is diametrically opposed to Keynesian intervention within the economic system. Rather than undertaking discretionary counter-cyclical changes in fiscal and/or monetary policy, monetarists rely on the natural, self-correcting adjustment forces within the economic

[11]A large increase in the money supply could be misinterpreted as a new validation policy rather than a stabilization policy.

[12]For example, if the negative demand shock arose because of a decline in exports, the demand shock will end when the U.S. economy recovers from its recession and Canadian exports return to "normal" levels.

system to counteract demand shocks. According to monetarists, the economic system, when left alone, will display strong recuperative tendencies that will quickly offset any demand shocks that may arise and government intervention along Keynesian lines may further disrupt the economic system, leading to a more unstable situation.[13] The best stabilization policy is for the government not to interfere, simply to let the natural, self-correcting tendencies of the economic system counteract any shocks or disturbances that might arise.

The two key planks in the monetarist approach to stabilization policy are the following: (1) the *nominal* money supply should grow at a *constant* rate, and (2) *no discretionary* (or counter-cyclical) fiscal policies should be implemented.[14] For expositional purposes we assume that a monetarist policy always maintains a **Constant Rate of Expansion of the Money** supply (henceforward referred to by the mnemonic CREM) of $\dot{P}_0$ per year and undertakes *no discretionary* changes in fiscal policy. Given a negative demand shock to the economic system, what are the macroeconomic effects and implications of such a monetarist non-interventionist CREM policy?

In Chart 14-3 we have replicated the negative demand shock which appeared in Chart 14-2. Given the new depressed IS_1 curve, the economy moves from position A to position B: income falls from Y^* to Y_1 and the inflation rate moderates along the *PEP* curve from $\dot{P}_0$ to $\dot{P}_1$. The economy is again thrust into a recession because of a negative demand shock. Rather than attempt to shift the IS_1 curve back to IS_0, the monetarist approach relies on the self-correcting adjustment forces implicit within a CREM policy to carry the economy back to Y^*. Throughout the monetarist adjustment process described below, *we continue to assume that inflation expectations are constant* and equal to the long-run equilibrium inflation rate $\dot{P}_0$, which the government is validating ($\dot{P}^e = \dot{P}_0 = \dot{\$}$). Even though the current *"shocked"* inflation rate $\dot{P}_1$ differs from the *equilibrium* inflation rate $\dot{P}_0$, we assume that people do *not* adjust their inflation expectations during the short-run adjustment period.[15] While inflation expectations are *incorrect* during the short-run *disequilibrium* adjustment period, inflation expectations are *correct* once the economy has returned to its long-run *equilibrium* position.

Returning to Chart 14-3, the negative demand shock has lowered the inflation rate to $\dot{P}_1$, below the Constant Rate of Expansion of the nominal Money supply ($\dot{\$} = \dot{P}_0$). Thus the *real* money supply $\$/P$ will automatically start to *increase* (because the numerator $\$$ is rising at a faster rate than the denominator P). This automatic increase in the *real* money supply during a negative demand shock under a monetarist CREM policy will push the LM_0 curve down to LM_1, which in turn will lower interest rates (to R_2 in Chart 14-3). Investment expenditures will increase in response to the new lower rate of interest and the level of income will begin to rise (to Y_2). But at Y_2, the inflation rate $\dot{P}_2$ is still *less* than the Constant

---

[13]See Case Study 9 in Chapter 20.

[14]Since most monetarists have very strong conservative leanings, the second plank in the monetarist platform is frequently stated in somewhat stronger terms—the government should always balance its budget. See Chapter 6 for a discussion of the multiplier effects of a balanced-budget policy.

[15]Chapter 17 provides a complete analysis of inflation expectations and of how inflation expectations might change when a demand shock occurs.

CHART 14-3 Monetarist policy for a negative demand shock

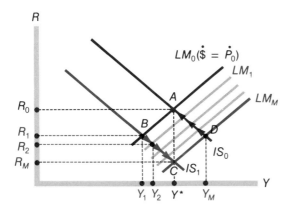

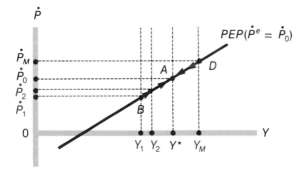

Rate of Expansion of the nominal Money supply. Again, the *real* money supply will automatically rise and the *LM* curve will shift down another notch (again lowering interest rates and raising investment spending, income levels and the inflation rate). This natural, self-correcting adjustment process under a monetarist CREM policy will continue to operate until the inflation rate has returned to $\dot{P}_0$, the rate at which the *nominal* money supply is being increased. At this point the *real* money supply is constant and the *LM* curve becomes stationary once again (at LM_M). As the arrows in the upper panel of Chart 14-3 reveal, a monetarist CREM policy will automatically move the economy from position *B* to position *C*. The economic system slides down the *"shocked"* IS_1 curve from Y_1 to Y^* as the inflation rate climbs back up the *PEP* curve from $\dot{P}_1$ to $\dot{P}_0$. Without any (Keynesian) help from the government, the natural adjustment forces inherent in a monetarist, non-interventionist CREM policy ensure that the economy will return to its equilibrium income level Y^* when a negative demand shock hits the economic system.

However, the monetarist story is not quite over. When the negative demand shock terminates, the economy will still be subject to the *new lower* LM_M curve.

Consequently, when the negative demand shock ends—say, when the U.S. comes out of its recession and Canadian exports return to their normal level—the economy will experience a higher income level Y_M, point D in Chart 14-3, where the *original IS*$_0$ curve intersects the *new lower LM*$_M$ curve. But at this higher income level Y_M, the rate of inflation $\dot{P}_M$ along the *PEP* curve will exceed the CREM. A monetarist policy maintains a *Constant* Rate of Expansion of the *nominal* Money supply ($\dot{\$} = \dot{P}_0$), which is now *lower* than the prevailing inflation rate $\dot{P}_M$. Consequently, the *real* money supply will begin to *decline* and the *LM*$_M$ curve will start to shift back up again. As the *LM* curve drifts upwards, interest rates will rise, investment expenditures will decline and output levels will decrease. The economy will continue to climb back up the original *IS*$_0$ curve and slide back down the *PEP* curve (see arrows in Chart 14-3) until the inflation rate has been brought back down to $\dot{P}_0$, the rate at which the *nominal* money supply is increasing. The economy will eventually return to its *original long-run equilibrium* position A, with an income level of Y^*, an interest rate of R_0 and an inflation rate of $\dot{P}_0$ once again equal to the CREM ($\dot{\$} = \dot{P}_0$).

In summary, a monetarist non-interventionist Constant Rate of Expansion of the Money supply (CREM) policy ensures that the economic system will return to its long-run equilibrium position when a demand shock occurs. The *IS-LM-PEP* macroeconomic model is stable about its long-run equilibrium position. As discussed in Chapter 16, the Governor of the Bank of Canada clearly recognized the inherent stabilizing features of "stable monetary expansion" in the context of aggregate demand instability. It is important to note, however, that under a monetarist CREM policy there are two distinct adjustment phases associated with each demand shock: one when the demand shock starts (the "shock on" phase) and another one when the shock terminates (the "shock off" phase). Just as the Keynesian fiscal policy offset must be removed when the demand shock is over, the self-adjustment forces implicit in a monetarist CREM policy must unwind after the demand shock terminates.

Positive Demand Shocks and The Implications of a "Flip-Flop" Stabilization Policy

We now turn to a brief examination of Keynesian and monetarist policy in the context of *positive* demand shocks and an analysis of the interesting possibility that a government might implement a "flip-flop" policy by using Keynesian policy for *negative* demand shocks and monetarist policy for *positive* demand shocks. Suppose that a positive demand shock, rather than a negative demand shock, hits the economic system. In Chart 14-4, the *IS*$_0$ curve shifts outwards to *IS*$_1$, say from an export boom, and the economy moves from position A to position B: income levels increase from Y^* to Y_1, accompanied by a modest amount of additional inflation ($\dot{P}_1$ compared to $\dot{P}_0 = \dot{\$}$). Following the same logic as above, Keynesian stabilization policy would counter this *positive* demand shock with a *negative restrictive* fiscal policy offset, say a tax increase. The *IS*$_1$ curve would be shifted back to *IS*$_0$, the economy returned to position A in Chart 14-3, and income levels would be

CHART 14-4 Stabilization policy for positive demand shocks

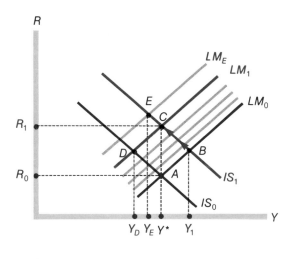

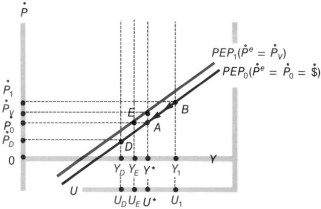

stabilized at Y^*, the long-run equilibrium level. When the positive demand shock is over, the negative restrictive fiscal policy would be removed.

While the economics of a *restrictive* Keynesian stabilization policy for *positive* demand shocks are straightforward, the politics may not be very compelling. Imagine that you are the Minister of Finance for an economy experiencing a positive demand shock: the unemployment rate has substantially declined (from U^* to U_1 in Chart 14-4) and the inflation rate is only modestly higher ($\dot{P}_1$). Your cabinet colleagues think that you are an economic genius for "creating" this welcomed prosperity and your political advisers are mapping out strategy for an upcoming leadership convention. However, your dour senior economic advisers in the Department of Finance, well-versed in the principles of Keynesian economics, are urging you to counteract this economic boom with a good dose of *restrictive* fiscal policy. The IS_1 curve must be shifted back to IS_0 and the unemployment rate must be forced back up to the natural rate. Several hundred thousand Canadians must lose their "new found" jobs in the interest of output stability! How would you respond as Minister of Finance to such Keynesian advice? For fairly obvious political reasons, most governments are very reluctant to implement restrictive demand-management policies to counteract positive demand shocks, preferring the *short-run* benefits of lower unemployment rates and only modest additional inflation.

Faced with such a positive demand shock, the government might well decide that Keynesian economics is "old-fashioned" and that now is the time to switch to monetarism. Rather than applying a restrictive fiscal policy, why not let the economic system look after itself (without any Keynesian help from the government). Having discovered monetarism, suppose that the government now decides to adopt a non-interventionist approach to stabilization policy and simply maintain a Constant Rate of Expansion of the Money supply ($\dot{\$} = \dot{P}_0$). The short-run economic benefits from a positive demand shock will be enjoyed, with CREM. As the arrows in Chart 14-4 illustrate, a monetarist non-interventionist CREM policy will automatically move the economy up the *shocked* IS_1 curve and back down the PEP_0 curve to its long-run *equilibrium* income level Y^*. The *positive* demand shock generates an inflation rate ($\dot{P}_1$ in period one) which exceeds the CREM ($\dot{\$} = \dot{P}_0$), thus eroding the *real* money supply and causing the LM curve to shift upwards. The LM curve will continue to drift upwards (to LM_1 in Chart 14-4) until the inflation rate has been brought back down to $\dot{P}_0$ and the real money supply is once again constant. While the economic system will eventually return to position C in the upper panel of Chart 14-4, with an income level of Y^*, during the entire short-run adjustment period the economy enjoys the benefits of an unemployment rate *below* the "natural" rate U^*, output levels in excess of the long-run equilibrium output level Y^*, and a declining inflation rate.

Unfortunately, a monetarist CREM policy will turn sour once the positive demand shock ends. The economic prosperity that accompanied the commencement of a positive demand shock under a monetarist non-interventionist policy will turn into an economic slump once the positive demand shock ends. When the *shocked* IS_1 curve returns to its original IS_0 position, the economy will still be subject to the high LM_1 curve (corresponding to a *lower real* money supply). Consequently, the termination of the positive demand shock will throw the economy into a serious recession with a low income level Y_D, a high unemployment rate U_D, and a low inflation rate $\dot{P}_D$ (position D in Chart 14-4). Even though the self-correcting adjustment forces implicit in a monetarist CREM policy (the *real* money supply will start to *increase* since $\dot{P}_D$ is now less than $\dot{\$}$) will carry the economy back down the IS_0 curve to Y^* (position A) via a reverse set of downward LM curve shifts, during the entire short-run adjustment phase following the *termination* of a *positive* demand shock the economy suffers from abnormally high unemployment and rising inflation. Under a monetarist CREM policy, the economic prosperity at the *beginning* of a positive demand shock will be matched by a painful recession at the *conclusion* of the positive demand shock.

Having adopted a monetarist non-interventionist CREM policy when the positive demand shock hit the economic system and now facing a painful recession when the positive demand shock ends, a "politically" motivated government might decide that Keynesian economics is really not that old-fashioned after all. When depressed, there's nothing like a good shot of Keynesian stimulation. Since the new monetarist LM_1 curve (in Chart 14-4) is functioning like a *negative* demand shock to the economic system (given the original IS_0 curve), a good dose of Keynesian stimulus is required to stabilize the level of output at Y^* and avoid a short-run bout of high unemployment (U_D in Chart 14-4). Either the nominal money supply must be increased (the LM_1 curve shifted down to LM_0) or an expansionary fiscal policy should be adopted (the IS_0 curve shifted up to IS_1).

In summary, there are undoubtedly strong political temptations to switch back and forth between Keynesian and monetarist policies (political "flip-flops"). When a *negative* demand shock hits the economic system, *Keynesian* stimulation is often regarded as a political necessity (to avoid a painful recession). On the other hand, when a *positive* demand shock hits the economic system, a non-interventionist *monetarist* policy may be very attractive (why counteract economic prosperity?). However, when the positive demand shock ends, the "down-side" of the monetarist non-interventionist policy may prompt a quick "flip-flop" back to Keynesian intervention (again to avoid a recession). In short, governments are prone to be *monetarist* for *positive* demand shocks and to be *Keynesian* for *negative* demand shocks. Unfortunately, such an inconsistent or "flip-flop" stabilization policy will likely have serious long-run, inflationary consequences.

Returning to Chart 14-4, suppose that a (politically motivated) government uses a *monetarist* CREM policy when a positive demand shock hits the economic system, but a *Keynesian fiscal* stimulation policy when the positive demand shock ends. By following a *monetarist* policy in the face of a *positive* demand shock (which shifts the IS_0 curve out to IS_1), the government allows the LM_0 curve to drift up to LM_1 and the economy to move from position B up to position C. When the positive demand shock is over and the IS_1 curve shifts back to IS_0, the higher LM_1 curve and a monetarist CREM policy would produce a recessionary short-run adjustment period. To avoid this monetarist recession at the end of a positive demand shock, the government *switches* to a Keynesian fiscal stimulation policy and shifts the IS_0 curve back up to IS_1 (to hold the economy at position C and maintain Y^*). Such a monetarist-Keynesian "flop-flop" policy will leave the economy with a higher monetarist LM_1 curve and a higher Keynesian IS_1 curve *after the demand shock is over*. While output and unemployment rates are back at their equilibrium or *natural* rates Y^* and U^*, the following economic variables will have changed:

1) The interest rate is permanently higher (R_1 versus R_0).
2) Consequently, investment will be permanently lower (the crowding out effect).
3) The government deficit will be higher (the additional Keynesian fiscal stimulation has not been reversed).
4) The real money supply will be lower.
5) The expected rate of inflation *may* rise.

Since these last two effects may not be as obvious, a brief explanation is in order. Under a monetarist-Keynesian "flip-flop" policy for a positive demand shock, the actual inflation rate will, on average, exceed $\dot{P}_0$. During the monetarist part of the policy, the inflation rate is above $\dot{P}_0$ as the economy slides down the PEP_0 curve (from position B to A in Chart 14-4). However, the Keynesian part of the policy *prevents* the inflation rate from falling below $\dot{P}_0$ (to $\dot{P}_D$, position D in Chart 14-4). On average, *the inflation rate must exceed $\dot{P}_0$* during this "flip-flop" policy. Since the nominal money supply is increasing at the constant rate $\dot{P}_0$, the real money supply must be lower at the end of the "flip-flop" policy (giving rise to a higher interest rate and the crowding out of investment noted above).

Throughout this analysis we have assumed that inflation expectations remain constant and equal to $\dot{P}_0$. However, since the average inflation rate during this "flip-flop" policy exceeds $\dot{P}_0$, people *might* adjust their inflation expectations upwards (say to $\dot{P}_V$, the average of $\dot{P}_0$ and $\dot{P}_1$ in Chart 14-4). If the government *continually* adopted "flip-flop" policies which perpetually had the economy to the right of Y^* with an average inflation rate above $\dot{P}_0$ (say at $\dot{P}_V$), sooner or later people *will revise upwards* their inflation expectations. As discussed in Chapter 12, once inflation expectations are adjusted upwards, the original PEP_0 curve will shift upwards (to PEP_1 in Chart 14-4), *and the government is trapped*. Given the IS_1, LM_1, and PEP_1 curves, the government must *either validate* this new higher inflation rate $\dot{P}_V$ with an *increase* in the Constant Rate of Expansion of the Money supply (to $\dot{\$} = \dot{P}_V$) *or* let the economy *slide into a recession*. If the government does *not* increase the CREM, an inflation rate of $\dot{P}_V$ at Y^* will erode the *real* money supply ($\dot{P}_V > \dot{\$} = \dot{P}_0$), causing the LM curve to shift upwards. The resulting higher interest rates will decrease investment, output and employment (carrying the economy back to postion E in Chart 14-4).[16] If the government has been consistently avoiding recessions (such as Y_E) by "flip-flopping" Keynesian and monetarist policies, it might seem quite natural at this point to switch to a third policy (the "flub") and *validate* this higher inflation rate $\dot{P}_V$ by increasing the rate of monetary expansion to $\dot{\$} = \dot{P}_V$. While such a "flip-flop-flub" policy consistently avoids unemployment rates above the natural rate (that is, it consistently avoids all recessions), it clearly will increase the inflation rate, the nominal interest rate[17] and the size of the government deficit.[18]

A former Deputy Governor of the Bank of Canada, G.E. Freeman, has argued that a basic reason for the phenomenon of "chronic accelerating inflation" during the 1960s and 1970s was the *inconsistent* or *biased* way in which monetary and fiscal policies were conducted. According to Freeman, governments *repeatedly* turned on expansionary monetary and fiscal policies to stimulate spending but only "fitfully and with great reluctance" *reversed* such expansionary policies when the "circumstances changed":

---

[16]The economy will remain at position E until inflation expectations (of $\dot{P}_V$) are lowered.

[17]As the expected inflation rate rises, the real rate of interest will decline, investment expenditures will rise and the IS curve will shift further upwards (leading to higher nominal interest rates and *another round* of "flip-flop-flub" policies).

[18]Since Keynesian fiscal stimulation is turned on but not off in this "flip-flop" policy, the size of the government deficit must be permanently larger.

The basic reason for this phenomenon...lies in the way that fiscal and monetary policies have tended to be conducted in countries like Canada since it became widely known how these policies could be used to help bring a country out of a severe depression such as that of the 1930s. In order to stimulate spending and economic activity in circumstances of this kind, the policy combination recommended by Lord Keynes and his followers envisaged temporary resort to deficit spending by the government together with central bank action to keep interest rates from rising in consequence—action that would temporarily involve a rapid increase in the quantity of money. This important and useful discovery implied that in extreme circumstances it was quite justifiable for governments to incur large deficits and for central banks to permit more rapid monetary expansion—provided that these policies were promptly and fully reversed as and when these circumstances changed.

The first and more popular part of this policy prescription has been invoked repeatedly in Canada in recent decades, for a time with remarkable success, as a means of stimulating the pace of economic activity whenever it has shown signs of faltering. The second and less popular part of the prescription has been invoked only fitfully and with great reluctance, so that the necessary shift towards greater moderation in the degree of fiscal and monetary stimulus as renewed expansion turned into impending boom has generally been a case of too little and too late. When undertaken at last, on most occasions the effort to moderate the degree of stimulus to spending has soon been abandoned in the face of slowing growth and rising unemployment—before it could have much lasting effect in moderating the size of price and cost increases. Thus we have had repeated inflationary over-heating of the economy interspersed with relatively brief and mild recessions....

If the worsening trend of inflation is to be halted (let alone reversed), it seems to me absolutely essential that this bias in the way monetary and fiscal policies have been conducted in the past must change.[19]

The moral of the above analysis is clear. If the government wants to avoid "the worsening trend of inflation," it must *consistently* run *either* a Keynesian *or* a monetarist stabilization policy. If the government "chooses" to be Keynesian, it must remove its fiscal offsets when the demand shock is over and it must offset *both* positive and negative demand shocks. Similarly, if the government "chooses" to be monetarist, it must *maintain* a non-interventionist CREM policy during and after the demand shock, for *both* positive and negative demand shocks. In either case, it must take the good with the bad. "Flip-flopping" back and forth between Keynesian and monetarist policies (trying to avoid the "down-side" of each) will only lead to an *over*-stimulated economy and an accelerating inflation rate.

A true monetarist would set the money supply growing at a *constant* rate and would avoid discretionary fiscal intervention at all times. The economic system

[19]G.E. Freeman, "Inflation and Canada's Monetary Policy," *Bank of Canada Review*, November 1980, pp. 22-23.

would correct for *both* positive and negative demand shocks, and society would live with the prosperity and slumps which accompany the short-run adjustment periods. A monetarist, when faced with the hangover from a positive demand shock, would take his stabilization coffee with CREM but no fiscal sugar.[20] Similarly a true Keynesian would offset "politically attractive" positive demand shocks as well as painful negative demand shocks. Counter-cyclical policy would be applied to both sides of the business cycle. In explaining his *General Theory* to the lay public, Keynes was very precise about countering positive demand shocks (booms) as well as negative demand shocks. We quote from a section of this interesting pre-World War II article entitled "Boom Control":

> Just as it was advisable for the Government to incur debt during the slump, so for the same reasons it is now advisable that they should incline to the opposite policy. . . . In view of the high cost of armaments, which we cannot postpone, it would put too much strain on our fiscal system actually to discharge debt, but the Chancellor of the Exchequer should, I suggest, meet the main part of the cost of armaments out of taxation, raising taxes and withholding all reliefs for the present as something in hand for 1938 or 1939, or whenever there are signs of recession. The boom, not the slump, is the right time for austerity at the Treasury.
>
> Just as it as advisable for local authorities to press on with capital expenditure during the slump, so it is now advisable that they should postpone whatever new enterprises can reasonably be held back. I do not mean that they should abandon their plans of improvement. On the contrary, they should have them fully matured, available for quick release at the right moment. But the boom, not the slump, is the right time for procrastination at the Ministry of Health.[21]

Parenthetically, we note that the 1937 "boom" that Keynes wanted to control had an unemployment rate of 12 per cent!

Keynesian Versus Monetarist Stabilization Policy

Faced with a choice of being either consistently Keynesian or consistently monetarist, which stabilization approach should the government choose? This is perhaps *the* key policy question in macroeconomics and is the subject of intense debate between economists of a Keynesian persuasion and more conservative monetarist (and new classical) economists. In this section of the chapter we review the major issues in this important debate over the choice of an appropriate stabilization policy.

---

[20]Since most monetarists are passionately opposed to inflation and believe that inflation is "always and everywhere a monetary phenomenon," most monetarists would probably take their stabilization coffee black without any CREM (that is, the money supply growth rate would be controlled to prevent inflation in the long run).

[21]*The Times of London*, 13 January 1937.

The Monetarist Approach

A monetarist non-interventionist stabilization policy relies on the automatic adjustment forces within a market economy to correct for any demand shocks. If the government maintains a *Constant* Rate of Expansion of the Money supply (the CREM), the economic system will automatically return to its long-run equilibrium position, both when the demand shock hits the economic system and when it ends (see Chart 14-3). Without any Keynesian fiscal help from the government, the free enterprise system *with* CREM will automatically correct for any and all demand shocks. Thus, the two major advantages of a monetarist CREM stabilization policy for demand shocks are (1) it always works and (2) there is no chance for any policy implementation errors. Since there are no discretionary elements in a monetarist non-interventionist policy, the government cannot destabilize the economic system.

While a monetarist CREM stabilization policy will automatically correct for demand shocks to the economic system, this automatic correction mechanism is not instantaneous. Under a monetarist CREM policy a short-run adjustment period is required to move the economy back to its long-run equilibrium position, both at the beginning and again at the conclusion of the demand shock. In terms of Chart 14-3, *a succession of LM curve shifts* restores Y^* as the intersection point of the (shocked) *IS* curve and a new *LM* curve. The effects of each successive *LM* curve shift, triggered by a *new* inflation rate which is different from the Constant Rate of Expansion of the Money supply (the CREM), will take time to work its way throughout the economic system and bring about the next *LM* curve shift.[22]

The major Keynesian argument *against* a monetarist non-interventionist CREM policy is the economic dislocation and hardship which occurs during this short-run adjustment period. Under a monetarist CREM policy, a *negative* demand shock will be accompanied by a *short-run period of increased unemployment* (an unemployment rate above the long-run equilibrium unemployment rate). As discussed at length in Chapter 3, the economic costs of increased unemployment are very substantial. Additional output and income are foregone for all time. Increased unemployment creates no winners, only income losers. Much of this lost income from increased unemployment would have been widely dispersed throughout the economic system (fewer hours worked by the employed, less overtime pay, fewer bonuses, less corporate profits, and so on). However, the *relative* burden of increased unemployment falls most heavily on small well-defined segments of the labour force who lose their jobs while the monetarist CREM policy is slowly bringing the economic system back to its long-run equilibrium position. In addition to the economic costs of increased unemployment, an *unexpected* change in the rate of inflation accompanying a demand shock will redistribute wealth and purchasing power between debtors and creditors. For example, an unexpectedly *low* inflation rate accompanying a *negative* demand shock will transfer purchasing power from debtors (such as mortgaged-home owners) to creditors. Thus, a

[22]See Case Study in Chapter 12.

monetarist stabilization policy approach for negative demand shocks will impose serious economic hardships on the unemployed (who lose their jobs), the employed (who are working fewer overtime hours and earning less income), and people with debts.

The extent of these economic losses under a non-interventionist monetarist policy depends crucially on the length of the short-run adjustment period. Not surprisingly, monetarists regard the short run as being very short, whereas Keynesians think that the short-run adjustment period is very long. As discussed in Chapter 10 (and again in Chapter 13), the length of the short-run adjustment period depends primarily on the nature of the underlying *PEP* curve. If the Phillips curve is very flat, then the short-run adjustment period will be prolonged. The higher unemployment rate associated with a negative demand shock will have relatively little effect on moderating the rate of wage and price inflation. Consequently, there will be only *slight* increases in the *real* money supply and very modest downward shifts in the *LM* curve. For a very flat Phillips curve, it will take a long time for the economy to crawl back up the *PEP* curve (from position *B* to *A* in Chart 14-3).[23] Given the inflation psychology of the 1970s and early 1980s, it is unlikely that the (*slight*) moderation of the inflation rate associated with a negative demand shock would prompt individuals to lower their inflation expectations (which would shift the *PEP* curve down and speed up the short-run adjustment). In an economy subject to long-term wage contracts, a relatively flat underlying Phillips curve and downward rigidity in inflation expectations, the short-run adjustment period accompanying a negative demand shock will be prolonged and a monetarist non-interventionist CREM policy will inflict serious economic hardships on society.[24]

The Keynesian Approach

A Keynesian interventionist stabilization policy is premised on a belief that the short-run adjustment period for a non-interventionist policy is apt to be very long—so long that "in the long run we're all dead"! Rather than wait for the *slow-working* automatic adjustment forces of the free enterprise system to bring the economy back to its long-run equilibrium position, a *Keynesian* would actively intervene to *speed* the economy back to its long-run equilibrium position. To the extent that the government could *successfully* offset demand shocks (both positive and negative) and stabilize the *IS* and *LM* curves, the economic system would remain at its long-run equilibrium position. By applying counter-cyclical stabilization policies, aggregate demand would be managed and the business cycle would be smoothed out. The economic hardships associated with serious recessions and runaway booms would be alleviated by appropriate Keynesian policy intervention.

---

[23]See also Chapter 10, pp. 272–73.

[24]To the extent that wage rates and inflation expectations may adjust faster on the up-side than on the down-side, the short-run adjustment period for a *positive* demand shock may be shorter than for a *negative* demand shock. Such an economic asymmetry in the Phillips "curve" may lead to biased or inconsistent ("flip-flop") stabilization policies.

While monetarists have numerous theoretical objections to Keynesian stabilization policy,[25] much of the monetarist criticism of Keynesian stabilization policy focuses on the *presumption* that a government *can* implement a *consistent successful* demand-management policy. Monetarists contend that *discretionary* stabilization policy changes will likely end up doing more harm than good. Rather than run the risk that the government's choice of discretionary demand-management policy might be wrong (and therefore might further destabilize the economic system), society would be better off to let the automatic adjustment forces implicit in a non-interventionist monetarist CREM policy stabilize the economy. Even though these automatic self-correcting adjustment forces may not be as swift as one might wish, they are at least always working in the right direction.

There are three different, but interrelated, sets of factors that tend to militate against a successful (textbook) Keynesian stabilization policy: (1) lags, (2) uncertainty, and (3) political economy considerations. Each of these three sets of factors will be briefly discussed.

1) Lags in the Economic System

As discussed on many occasions throughout this textbook, there are very long lags associated with government policy. First, a government must *recognize* that there is indeed a stabilization problem that requires government action. The government must sift through a myriad of current economic statistics, which frequently conflict with each other and are often revised at a later date, to ascertain the present state of the economy and to decide whether a discretionary stabilization policy is required. Second, the government must then formulate its policy response and prepare the necessary stabilization program and/or legislation (perhaps prepare a new budget to be introduced in Parliament). As discussed in Chapter 6, there are an infinite number of Keynesian policy options available to manage aggregate demand and the Cabinet must decide which tax rates to change or which expenditure program to alter. Even after the government has decided to act and has passed a new bill or budget through Parliament (all of which might have taken six to twelve months), a considerable length of time will be required for the multiplier effects of this new policy to work their way throughout the economic system. A study using the Bank of Canada econometric model[26] found that an increase in government expenditures has a maximum effect on output *two and one-half years after* the policy is implemented (a multiplier effect of 1.5). *Ten years later*, this increase in government expenditures still has a modest effect on output (a multiplier effect of 0.4).[27]

---

[25]See, for example, the discussion of the permanent income hypothesis of consumption in Chapter 19, and the discussion of rational expectations in Chapter 17.

[26]L. De Bever and T. Maxwell, "An Analysis of Some of the Dynamic Properties of RDX2," *Canadian Journal of Economics*, May 1979, pp. 162-70.

[27]Our analysis of Chapter 10 predicted that the *long-run* multiplier effects from a change in government expenditures would be zero. The Bank of Canada's econometric macroeconomic model would suggest that the Canadian *short run* is at least ten years long; that is, the Keynesian multiplier still has not reached zero after ten years.

2) Uncertainty

Given the long lags between the implementation of policy and its economic effects, a government must be able to make extremely accurate forecasts of future economic events (such as a U.S. recession) in order to start the slow-working policy antidote so that it may come "on line" when it is needed. The Keynesian offset must be implemented well before it is needed, at a time when forecasts of a future recession are most uncertain. Keynesian policy is not for the faint of heart! If one waits until the economy is in the middle of a recession to apply the fiscal stimulus (when it is obvious that there is a recession), by the time the fiscal stimulus reaches its peak effect (two or three years later) the economy may have recovered on its own. Under such circumstances, the *ill-timed* Keynesian stabilization policy would no longer be an offset, but rather would function as an additional stimulant leading to the inflationary consequences of an over-heated economy. Demand-management policies which are not synchronized with changes in exogenous variables may end up destabilizing the economy rather than stabilizing output levels.[28] Accurate forecasting and precise timing are crucial for a successful Keynesian stabilization policy. Unfortunately, accurate forecasting has never been known as one of economics' strong suits. While economists may be quite good at predicting economic trends, the implementation of Keynesian *counter-cyclical* policy requires accurate prediction of future *turning points* in economy activity. Under the present state of economic technology (which is vastly superior to that of twenty years ago), accurate forecasts of the size and timing of shocks are more often a product of good luck than good economic measure.

There are many additional elements of uncertainty in policy formulation. To determine *exact* Keynesian stabilization policy instrument settings requires a substantial amount of *accurate quantitative* information concerning basic structural relationships within the economy, the current status of all economic variables, as well as forecasts of future values of key exogenous variables. But different econometricians have produced different statistical estimates for the underlying behavioural parameters within the macroeconomic model. For example, the Bank of Canada's econometric macroeconomic model predicted that the government expenditure multiplier effect on GNP would be 0.96 in the first year and 1.41 in the third year whereas the Economic Council of Canada's econometric macroeconomic model predicted that the first and third year multiplier effects would be 1.70 and 1.65 respectively.[29] Which, if either, of these *multiplier estimates* should the government adopt in its determination of the *exact* amount of Keynesian fiscal policy required for stabilization purposes? In addition, various participants in the economy (consumers, unions, investors, firms) might change their underlying behaviour or expectations in response to a change in government policy. For example, if the marginal propensity to consume or if inflation expectations were to change because of the implementation of Keynesian stabilization policy, then the stabilization policy predictions from our *IS-LM-PEP*

---

[28]See Case Study 9 in Chapter 20.

[29]T. Maxwell and H.E.L. Waslander, "Comparing the Dynamics of Canadian Macro Models," *Canadian Journal of Economics*, May 1979, pp. 181-94.

macroeconomic model would be incorrect (see Chapter 17). Again, the government would be uncertain of the likely macroeconomic effects from its stabilization policy.

In short, there are very serious technical problems to the *successful* implementation of Keynesian stabilization policy. Unfortunately the world that the policy maker lives in is not nearly as clean, clear and certain as the textbook world. While a professor can glibly shift a blackboard *IS* (or *LM*) curve to stabilize output at the long-run equilibrium level Y^*, the policy maker is never really sure (1) what level of output corresponds to Y^*, (2) where the real world *IS* and *LM* curves are located, and (3) how much and when the *IS* and *LM* curves will shift for a given dose of Keynesian stabilization policy. Knowing *when* and by *how much* to turn the real world monetary and fiscal policy levers is no easy task. If the policy maker misreads the current status of the economy or does *not* accurately forecast the future or has adopted an incorrect set of estimates for the multiplier effects, then the Keynesian stabilization policy implemented will be incorrect. Rather than manage aggregate demand by offsetting a predicted demand shock, the *incorrect* Keynesian stabilization policy could act as an additional new demand shock to the economic system. Even though well-intentioned, *incorrect* Keynesian policy could end up *destabilizing* rather than stabilizing the economy.

3) Political Economy Considerations

As discussed above, there are undoubtedly strong political temptations *not* to offset positive demand shocks with restrictive Keynesian policy, or *not* to reverse a stimulative Keynesian fiscal policy once the negative demand shock terminates. The fiscal tap is much easier to turn on than off. Government expenditures and transfer programs typically have very vocal political constituencies to defend their continued existence, and no one likes a tax increase. Since politicians presumably are trying to maximize the probability of getting re-elected next time, they are unlikely to adopt *restrictive* Keynesian policies that inflict short-run economic hardships on the electorate.[30] Monetarists have grave doubts that governments will ever have the political courage to implement a *consistent* Keynesian stabilization policy, with "unpopular" *restrictive* fiscal policy to counteract *positive* demand shocks as well as "popular" expansionary fiscal policy to counteract recessions. The implementation of a Keynesian stabilization policy most likely means short-run fiscal stimulation, without any restrictive policies when positive demand shocks occur. As the former Deputy Governor of the Bank of Canada has acknowledged, the *inconsistent* use of Canadian monetary and fiscal policy (to stimulate but not to restrict) during the 1960s and 1970s led to a "chronic, accelerating inflation rate."

In summary, many of the key economic issues in the stabilization policy debate between Keynesian and monetarist economists tend to be empirical: (1) *how long* does it take for the monetarist non-interventionist CREM policy to work, and (2) in

---

[30]Again imagine yourself as Minister of Finance trying to explain to the electorate why you must raise taxes to counteract the current economic prosperity and "unemploy" several hundred thousand Canadians.

an uncertain, unpredictable world, *how accurate* (and well-timed) is the Keynesian policy prescription likely to be? These are fundamental questions, and reasonable men and women can disagree on the answers to these key questions. Without wishing to endorse the monetarist position, there are indeed serious economic and political limitations to the implementation of a successful, *consistent* Keynesian stabilization policy and Keynesian fiscal activists of the 1960s undoubtedly overstated the ability of economists and policy makers to "fine tune" the economy. As the OECD, an organization *not* noted for monetarist leanings, has concluded:

> The authorities should bear in mind the difficulties inherent in carrying out discretionary demand management policies, which are better understood now than they were ten years ago. The lag before new trends are recognized, the fallibility of forecasts, the delay before action is taken, and uncertainty about the timing and magnitude of the responses in the economy to the action taken, all conspire to render the task extremely difficult. For these reasons we believe that demand management policies should also be *cautious* in the sense that when there is an apparent need to change course, there should be a presumption against taking all the expansionary or restrictive action apparently required in one go.[31]

On the other hand, if a *large* demand shock is *predictable* (such as the Great Depression in 1930-31, or an investment boom associated with a huge Tar Sands project), then Keynesian aggregate demand offsets *which are reversed when the demand shock ceases* will stabilize output levels and avoid the short-run adjustment costs implicit in non-interventionist policy.

Key Concepts

demand shock
supply-price shock
Keynesian demand-management policy
monetarist Constant Rate of Expansion
  of Money (CREM) policy

---

[31]P. McCracken et al., *Towards Full Employment and Price Stability,* Report to the OECD (Paris: OECD, 1977), pp. 190-91.

Review Questions

1. How do shocks to the economic system arise? Distinguish between demand and supply-price shocks (and provide illustrations of each).
2. Given a *negative* demand shock, analyze the various Keynesian policy options that might be implemented to stabilize income and employment levels. What would happen if the government fails to remove its Keynesian stabilization policy after the demand shock is over? Explain.
3. Given a *negative* demand shock, analyze a monetarist non-interventionist CREM policy.
4. Compare the short-run effects of Keynesian and monetarist stabilization policies for a *positive* demand shock to the Canadian economic system. (Do not forget to analyze the "shock-off " effects of both policies.)
5. "There are strong political temptations to switch back and forth between Keynesian and monetarist stabilization policies." Do you agree? Discuss. Why are such "flip-flop" stabilization policies likely to lead to rising interest rates, inflation, and government deficits? Explain.
6. Given a choice between implementing a consistent Keynesian or consistent monetarist policy for a negative demand shock, which would you choose? Fully discuss the advantages and disadvantages of both Keynesian and monetarist stabilization policy approaches and indicate the reasons for your choice of stabilization policy.

Stabilization Policy: Supply-Price Shocks

15

Life is much less amusing since I became Minister of Finance. . . .

John Crosbie, former Minister of Finance

In the previous chapter we analyzed the macroeconomic implications of demand shocks to the economic system, shocks or disturbances which originate within the *IS-LM* quadrant of our macroeconomic model. As demonstrated in Chapter 14, both Keynesian and monetarist stabilization policy options can be theoretically defended in the context of demand shocks. The choice between these two radically different policy approaches depends on a number of empirical and practical issues, which are fully discussed at the end of Chapter 14.

In this chapter we analyze shocks or disturbances that originate within the Phillips curve quadrant of our model. While the quadrupling of international oil prices in early 1974 was the most visible and dramatic supply-price shock of the last several decades, a number of other supply-price shocks hit the Canadian economic system in the early 1970s. Collectively this set of supply-price shocks caused the price expectations Phillips curve to shift upwards, imposing an unambiguous economic cost on society. Unfortunately, there are few available macroeconomic policies that can be implemented to offset supply-price shocks. Both Keynesian demand-management and monetarist (CREM) policies operate in the upper *IS-LM* quadrant of our model, and are *not* appropriate for supply-price shocks that originate in the lower Phillips curve quadrant of the model. What's good medicine for a demand shock (or an ear infection) will not necessarily cure a supply-shock (or a broken ankle). As Professor Robert Gordon has noted, "the advent of supply shocks as a major destabilizing force has caused the monetarist tide to ebb"[1] and a new set of policy antidotes (such as "cost-oriented changes in taxes and subsidies") must be found to counteract the effect of supply-price shocks, the economic disease of the 1970s.

Illustrations of Supply-Price Shocks

Shocks or disturbances that enter our model via the Phillips curve quadrant have been classified as supply-price shocks. In general, such shocks originate in the supply sector of the economy and are reflected in the pricing decisions of firms

---

[1]Robert J. Gordon, "Postwar Macroeconomics: The Evolution of Events and Ideas," in M. Feldstein, ed., *The American Economy in Transition* (Chicago: University of Chicago Press for the National Bureau of Economic Research, 1980).

and labour market participants. The key exogenous variable within the Phillips curve quadrant of our model is the relative inflation rate of internationally traded goods, commodities and raw materials. If the relative price of internationally traded goods changes, then the short-run *PEP* curve will shift, inflicting a supply-price shock on the macroeconomic system.

As discussed in Chapter 9, price changes for internationally traded goods and raw materials have had a major impact on the Canadian inflation rate and have been a persistent source of short-run instability during the 1970s (see Table 9-1). While Canadian food prices fluctuated within a fairly narrow interval (around 3 per cent) during the 1960s, food price increases rapidly accelerated during the 1970s, exceeding 12 per cent in five different years. The rapid escalation and volatility of food price increases during the early 1970s was but one example of a general commodity price boom, as raw material and commodity price increases during 1973 and 1974 were simply astounding. For example, the British *Economist* index of world commodity prices more than doubled during these two years (again, see Table 9-1). Table 15-1 presents annual price increases for 15 selected commodities for the years 1972, 1973 and 1974. Considering only the year 1973, the prices of wheat, rice, cocoa and zinc all doubled, while cotton, rubber, logs and copper chalked up price increases in the 65 to 95 per cent range. This unprecedented explosion of raw material and commodity prices on world markets was reflected in higher material input prices in Canada and the wholesale price index of manufactured products increased by almost 33 per cent during 1973-74. (Average weekly wages within the manufacturing industry rose by only 19 per cent during these two years.)

Then there was OPEC. Perhaps no event since the Great Depression has caused such consternation for government policy makers and economists as the dramatic increase in oil prices during the 1970s. In late 1973, the OPEC cartel flexed its

TABLE 15-1 Annual Percentage Increases for Selected Commodity Prices

	1972	1973	1974
Wheat	11.5	106.5	41.6
Rice	15.1	132.9	54.8
Sugar	25.0	15.5	187.1
Coffee	9.6	24.6	6.4
Cocoa	20.3	100.0	51.7
Beef	9.9	35.3	−21.1
Cotton	5.9	65.6	6.3
Rubber	1.2	95.2	9.9
Logs	24.8	94.4	−9.0
Copper	0.0	65.5	15.8
Iron Ore	−4.7	33.4	14.7
Tin	7.6	28.1	70.6
Lead	19.0	42.9	37.6
Zinc	22.1	126.1	45.2
Aluminum	−8.9	−4.9	36.1

Source: Department of Finance, *Canada's Recent Inflation Experience*, November 1978, p. 12.

monopoly muscles and quadrupled the price of oil. The posted price of Venezuelan crude oil sold to Canadian refineries jumped from $3.10 per barrel in January 1973 to $14.85 in January 1974, a staggering 379 per cent price increase. Since crude oil represented 1.7 per cent of Canadian GNP in 1973, this 379 per cent increase in the price for OPEC oil would have raised the average price level of all goods by at least 6.4 per cent (.017 × 379%)[2] if Canadian domestic oil prices had increased to OPEC levels.

Faced with the prospects of a wrenching inflation, the minority Liberal government decided to *phase in* the 1973-74 oil price shock. Rather than allow the domestic oil price to jump to $14 per barrel, the federal government reached an agreement with the provinces in March 1974 to *fix* the price of domestic oil at $6.50 and to review this *government-controlled* price in June 1975. In the words of Energy Minister Donald Macdonald, such a policy "could even out somewhat the rate of price increase and allow a better adjustment period for the Canadian consumer."[3] During each of the next four years, oil prices were increased by one or two dollars per barrel and by the end of 1978 the *government-controlled* domestic oil price had been raised to $13.50 per barrel, compared with the 1978 OPEC price of approximately $17.

Unfortunately, as Canadian domestic oil prices were catching up to international oil prices, OPEC again flexed its monopoly muscles in 1979-80 and doubled the cartel oil price to $32 U.S. or about $38.00 Canadian. While everyone agreed that Canadian domestic oil prices would have to increase substantially, the federal and Alberta governments became involved in a bitter dispute over how the huge additional oil revenues would be shared. The 1980 federal budget imposed a new, higher domestic oil price schedule (that would have raised the price of oil to $38.75 by 1986), additional federal taxes, controls on the petroleum industry, and a new financial split of energy revenues. In response to the federal government's unilateral actions, Alberta retaliated by imposing a series of oil production cutbacks. After a year of intense bargaining, in September 1981 Alberta and the federal government signed a five-year energy agreement that instituted a *two-tier* pricing system for oil, *accelerated* increases in oil prices, and a new split in petroleum revenues. Under the terms of this complex agreement, *old* oil (conventional oil pools discovered before 1981) would *triple* in price between 1981 and 1986, rising to a ceiling of 75 per cent of the international price, and *new* oil would be priced at world levels. According to this agreement, the "blended" domestic price of oil was slated to rise by almost 25 per cent *per year* during the 1981-86 period.

The world-wide recession in the early 1980s produced a surplus of oil on world markets, however, and OPEC could not maintain its cartel price. Given the declining international price for oil, the federal and Alberta governments had to amend the 1981 (five-year) agreement in June 1983, freezing the price of oil at $29.75 per barrel. With world oil prices still depressed in March 1985 (about

---

[2]This calculation includes the direct effect at the gas pump and the indirect effects as higher oil prices are transmitted through each stage of industrial activity, but it does *not* allow for any increase in wages which labour might obtain to offset rising price levels (which would further increase price levels).

[3]Donald Macdonald, Address to the Canadian-American Committee, Ottawa, 28 September 1973.

$27.00 U.S.), the newly-elected federal Conservative government signed a new agreement with the western producing provinces to *deregulate* the Canadian petroleum industry. On June 1, 1985 Canadian oil prices were *decontrolled* and allowed to respond to international market conditions. After more than a decade of *controlled* domestic oil prices, Canadian consumers began to pay world (OPEC) prices for gasoline and petroleum products.

In summary, the rapid escalation in prices for internationally traded commodities during the 1970s was unprecedented. Nearly all major industrial countries were simultaneously pursuing expansionary policies during the early 1970s, and supplies of raw materials could not be increased quickly enough to satisfy world-wide demands. In addition, there are a host of interesting "micro" stories which can be told concerning "special" circumstances which accounted for particular commodity price movements during the 1970s: poor agricultural crops around the world, problems with the catch of Peruvian anchovies, and political unrest in countries that were important producers of raw materials. Whatever the reason, the price of internationally traded commodities rose dramatically in the early 1970s and represented a very serious external supply-price shock to the Canadian economic system. While the Canadian government decided to *phase in* the quadrupling of OPEC oil prices in 1973-74 and the subsequent doubling of OPEC oil prices in 1978-79, Canadian oil prices still increased fivefold during the 1970s. Rather than absorbing two massive oil price shocks (in 1974 and 1979), the Canadian government chose to spread these two large oil price increases into a series of smaller price shocks over *many* years. Consequently, the Canadian economy continued to experience the oil price shock well into the mid-1980s. While the rest of the world enjoyed declining oil prices in 1983-85, the Canadian government was still *phasing* in the 1970s OPEC oil price increases. Canadians had to wait until 1986, when the international price of oil plunged to $12 U.S. per barrel, to enjoy lower domestic gasoline prices.

Macroeconomic Analysis of a Supply-Price Shock

We now turn to an analysis of the macroeconomic implications of supply-price shocks, the economic disease of the 1970s. In Chart 15-1 we have reproduced our standard *IS-LM-PEP* depiction of the macroeconomic system. Initially we assume that our hypothetical economy is resting in long-run equilibrium at point A along the PEP_0 curve. The economy is at the *natural* rate of unemployment U^* with an inflation rate of $\dot{P}_0$, which is fully validated ($\dot{\$} = \dot{P}_0$) and fully expected ($\dot{P}^e = \dot{P}_0$). Now assume that a severe external price shock hits this economy, such as the commodity price boom of the early 1970s.

In terms of our underlying *PEP* curve, this external supply-price shock will translate into a large increase in the annual percentage change of the relative price of internationally traded commodities ($f\dot{F}P$ in the *PEP* equation 9-5, see Chapter 9). For example, if the price of internationally traded goods (relative to domestic unit labour costs) jumps by 50 per cent over a *two-year period* (the commodity price boom), then on an *annual* basis there will be *two successive* increases in $\dot{F}P$ of

CHART 15-1 A supply-price shock under a Monetarist policy

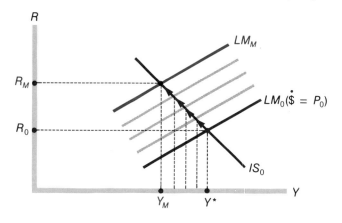

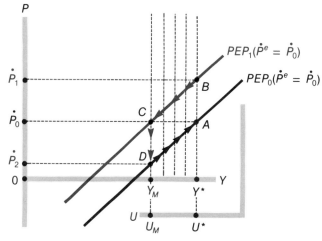

approximately 25 per cent in the *PEP* equation. If the structural parameter *f* in the *PEP* equation has an estimated value of say, .20, then the *PEP* curve will shift upwards by 5 per cent (.20 × 25%) and will retain this higher position for *two* successive years. If the commodity price boom ends after two years, in the third year the *PEP* curve will shift back down to its *original* position (because $\dot{F P}$ is no longer +25 per cent). The external supply-price shock has caused a temporary (two-year) upward shift in the underlying *PEP* curve. In terms of Chart 15-1, the original PEP_0 curve will temporarily shift upwards to PEP_1, because $f\dot{F P}$ has temporarily increased.

Returning to Chart 15-1, the *initial* impact of this external supply-price shock will be to shift the economy from point *A* on the PEP_0 curve to point *B* on the PEP_1 curve, raising the inflation rate from $\dot{P}_0$ to $\dot{P}_1$. The increase in the price of internationally traded goods has a direct, immediate impact on the domestic rate of price inflation. However, since this new *higher* "shocked" inflation rate $\dot{P}_1$

exceeds the constant growth rate of the *nominal* money supply ($\dot{\$} = \dot{P}_0$), the *real* money supply will start to decline and the *LM* curve will begin to drift upwards (see red *LM* curves in Chart 15-1). Rising interest rates will choke off new investment expenditures, causing output to fall below Y^* and the unemployment rate to rise above the *natural* rate U^*. The supply-price shock has not only raised the inflation rate, it has also pushed the economy into a recession! A supply-price shock produces the worst possible result—abnormally high inflation, rising interest rates and rising unemployment levels (in other words, *stagflation*).

Stabilization Policy Options for a Supply-Price Shock

Given the economic hardships that accompany a supply-price shock, what, if anything, can the government do? We begin our analysis by tracing through the macroeconomic implications of a "grin and bear it" monetarist non-interventionist approach to supply-price shocks. Next we examine various government interventionist approaches that might be implemented in an attempt to counteract supply-price shocks. While *demand*-management policies are shown to be *in*appropriate for *supply-price* shocks, fiscal *price* management policies ("cost-oriented tax changes") should *theoretically* work. Unfortunately such *theoretical* fiscal price management stabilization policies are very difficult to implement in practice. We postpone until Chapter 16 a review of the Canadian government's policy response to the large external price shock that hit the Canadian economy in the early 1970s—the "validation" road to wage and price controls.

Monetarist Non-Intervention: A "Grin and Bear It" Policy

Under a monetarist stabilization policy, the government would undertake *no* new fiscal initiatives and would simply continue to increase the *nominal* money supply by the same *constant* amount ($\dot{\$} = \dot{P}_0$, the CREM). As indicated above, such a non-interventionist monetarist policy approach would produce a supply-price-shock-induced recession. The new higher inflation rate $\dot{P}_1$ will erode the *real* money supply ($\dot{P}_1$ exceeds $\dot{P}_0 = \dot{\$}$ in Chart 15-1), causing the *LM* curve to drift upwards. Higher interest rates will choke off new investment spending, which will lower output and raise unemployment. The economic system will climb up the IS_0 curve via a sequence of *LM* curve shifts and will slide down the *higher PEP₁* curve.[4] This *contractionary* process (see arrows in Chart 15-1) will continue until the level of output has sufficiently fallen (to Y_M) to lower the inflation rate along the *new higher PEP₁* curve back down to $\dot{P}_0$, the Constant Rate of Expansion of the nominal Money supply (the CREM). At this *lower* income level Y_M (position C in Chart 15-1) the inflation rate $\dot{P}_0$ along the higher *PEP₁* curve is once again fully validated and fully expected. Thus, a monetarist approach to supply-price shocks has "coun-

---

[4]We assume that inflation expectations are *not* revised upwards, even though the actual inflation rate has been (temporarily) shocked upwards. If inflation expectations are revised upwards, the *PEP₁* curve would shift further upwards and the *LM* curve would shift upwards at an accelerated rate (that is, the economy would move into a recession at a faster pace!).

tered" the supply-price shock by throwing the economy into a serious recession (low income, high unemployment, and high interest rates).

It is very important to note that the economy will stay in this recession (position C in Chart 15-1) under a monetarist non-interventionist policy as long as the supply-price shock remains in force (as long as $\dot{FP}$ remains at 25 per cent). Unlike the monetarist CREM policy for demand shocks, the economy does *not* gravitate back to its long-run equilibrium position Y^* under a monetarist non-interventionist policy throughout the duration of the supply-price shock. As long as the supply-price shock is in force, a monetarist non-interventionist policy ensures that the economy will remain stuck in a recession.

However, once the supply-price shock terminates ($\dot{FP}$ declines to its original value), a monetarist CREM policy will bring the economy back to its long-run equilibrium position Y^*. Suppose that the supply-price shock was in force a sufficient length of time so that the monetarist CREM policy moved the economy all the way over to Y_M (position C in Chart 15-1). When the supply-price shock terminates and the PEP_1 curve shifts back down to PEP_0, the economic system will experience a *new*, *lower* inflation rate $\dot{P}_2$ at Y_M (position D in Chart 15-1). Given a *Constant* Rate of Expansion of the nominal Money supply equal to $\dot{P}_0$, this *new*, *lower* inflation rate $\dot{P}_2$ will lead to an *increase* in the *real* money supply. As the real money supply increases, the LM curve will start to drift back downwards to the right, interest rates will decline, investment expenditures will pick up, and the level of output will begin to increase. In the "shock off" phase of a monetarist CREM policy, the economy will climb back up the original PEP_0 curve (see arrows in Chart 15-1) and will slide back down the IS_0 curve. Under a monetarist policy, the adjustment process triggered by the *termination* of the supply-price shock will return the economy to its long-run equilibrium position (point A in Chart 15-1), with an inflation rate $\dot{P}_0$, which is fully validated and expected. The supply-price "shock off" adjustment phase under a monetarist policy simply unwinds the "shock on" adjustment phase, as the LM_M curve returns to its *original* position LM_0.

In summary, a monetarist non-interventionist policy ensures that the economy will return to its long-run equilibrium position, *but only after the supply-price shock has terminated*. Throughout the duration of the supply-price shock a monetarist non-interventionist policy will keep the economy in a recessionary state. Society is clearly worse off during the *entire* supply-price shock period since it must endure higher inflation rates, higher interest rates and higher unemployment rates.[5] For supply-price shocks, a monetarist policy is very much a "grin and bear it" approach. Only when the supply-price shock ends will economic conditions improve. Faced with such grim consequences, government policy makers are prone to try some form of intervention to combat the recessionary tendencies of a supply-price shock.

---

[5] For a *negative* supply-price shock which shifts the PEP curve *downwards*, a monetarist policy bestows an unexpected *bonus* on society (lower inflation, lower interest rates and lower unemployment rates). It is unfortunate that all of the supply-price shocks that have hit the Canadian economic system during the 1970s went the "wrong way." Perhaps we will get lucky again in the late 1980s and early 1990s (as we were in the 1960s).

A "Traditional" Keynesian Fiscal Demand-Management Policy

Rather than allow an *eroding real* money supply to push the economy into a serious recession when a supply-price shock hits the economic system, the government might try to stabilize output levels by implementing an *expansionary* fiscal policy. Each upward shift in the *LM* curve triggered by the price shock (see Chart 15-1) would be *matched* by a government-induced upward shift in the *IS* curve. The contractionary effects of the eroding real money supply during a supply-price shock would be offset by the stimulative effects from *repeated* doses of expansionary fiscal policy. The economy would be stabilized at an income level of *Y** during the entire supply-price shock, and no recession would occur.

While a stimulative fiscal policy during a supply-price shock can prevent the economy from sliding into a recession, such a stimulative Keynesian demand-management policy will have very serious inflationary side effects in the context of supply-price shocks. To illustrate the detrimental effects of using Keynesian fiscal *demand* offsets for *supply*-price shocks, in Chart 15-2 we have replicated our hypothetical *IS-LM-PEP* economy with a supply-price shock (PEP_0 shifts up to PEP_1). Assuming that the government maintains a *constant* rate of expansion of the nominal money supply ($\dot{\$} = \dot{P}_0$), this new higher "shocked" $\dot{P}_1$ inflation rate will erode the *real* money supply causing the LM_0 curve to shift up to LM_1. To prevent the economy from sliding into a recession (the IS_0-LM_1 intersection point), the government decides to implement a stimulative fiscal policy to shift the IS_0 curve up to IS_1. The economy is prevented from sliding down the "shocked" PEP_1 curve and is stabilized at $Y*$, *but with a $\dot{P}_1$ inflation rate*.

Unfortunately, as long as the supply-price shock remains in force, the *LM* curve will *continually shift upwards* (because $\dot{P}_1 > \dot{\$} = \dot{P}_0$) and the government must implement *further and further increases* in its expansionary fiscal policy. During the life of the supply-price shock, a succession of *LM* curve shifts (LM_1, LM_2, and LM_3 in Chart 15-2) must be countered by a succession of *IS* curve shifts (IS_1, IS_2 and IS_3). To hold income at $Y*$ in the face of a continuing supply-price shock, the government must continually *expand* its fiscal policy stimulus. Once the supply-price shock ends and the PEP_1 curve shifts back down to PEP_0, the inflation rate will return to $\dot{P}_0$, the *real* money supply will again be constant, the *LM* curve will be stationary, and *no further increases* in fiscal stimulation will be required. However, after the conclusion of the supply-price shock, the economy will remain subject to the *higher LM_3* curve (from the erosion of *real* money during the supply-price shock) and the higher IS_3 curve (from the past increases in fiscal stimulus during the supply-price shock). If the government were to terminate all of its past stimulative fiscal policies when the supply-price shock ended, a major recession would occur (the LM_3-IS_0 intersection point in Chart 15-2).

The detrimental side effects of using fiscal *demand*-management policies to fight *supply*-price shocks are obvious. During the life of the supply-price shock, interest rates and the government deficit are continually rising, and both will remain *permanently* higher once the supply-price shock ends. During the life of the supply-price shock, the inflation rate is persistently higher than it was ($\dot{P}_1$

CHART 15-2 A price shock under a Keynesian fiscal demand management policy

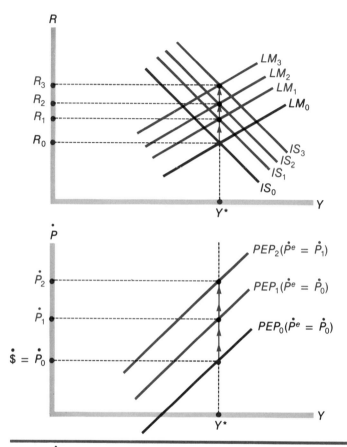

versus $\dot{P}_0$). If this supply-price shock lasts for several years, labour market participants will likely revise upwards their inflation expectations (from $\dot{P}_0$ to $\dot{P}_1$, the *new* inflation rate at which the government is stabilizing the economic system). *Once inflation expectations are adjusted upwards, the supply-price shock PEP$_1$ ($\dot{P}^e = \dot{P}_0$) curve will shift further upwards to PEP$_2$ ($\dot{P}^e = \dot{P}_1$) bringing about an even higher inflation rate ($\dot{P}_2$ in Chart 15-2) and even larger upward LM curve shifts.* If the government continues its fiscal intervention policy, *larger and larger* doses of stimulative fiscal policy will be required, leading to even higher interest rates, larger government deficits and further upward revisions of inflation expectations. The government is caught in the wage-price spiral discussed in Chapter 12. If the government tries to hold the economy at Y^* during a *persistent supply-price* shock with expansionary *demand*-management policies, interest rates, the government deficit, inflation, and inflation expectations will continually rise (probably at accelerating rates). While the recessionary effects of the supply-price shock have been (temporarily) avoided, the legacy of such a policy is a *perma-*

nently higher interest rate, a *permanently higher* government deficit, a *permanently higher* inflation rate and a *permanent increase* in inflation expectations. While governments are undoubtedly tempted to use fiscal demand-management policies to prevent the recessionary effects of persistent supply-price shocks, such "buy now, pay later" policies must be resisted if the future inflation rate is to be kept under control.

A Monetary Validation Policy

A monetary validation policy for a supply-price shock has the same long-run inflation consequences as a fiscal demand-management policy, but avoids the effects of a rising government (structural) deficit. Rather than offset the supply-price-shock-induced *LM* curve shift with a fiscal-policy-induced *IS* curve shift, the government could increase the rate of expansion of the nominal money supply to prevent the *LM* curve from drifting upwards. By *validating* the new higher shocked inflation rate ($\dot{\$} = \dot{P}_1$), the *LM* curve would remain stationary and the economy would stay at the Y^* and R_0 position during the supply-price shock, *but with a higher $\dot{P}_1$ inflation rate* (see Chart 15-2).

As discussed in Chapter 12, this *validation* policy will only work as long as people are "fooled" about the inflation rate—they expect $\dot{P}_0$ but $\dot{P}_1$ materializes. Once people realize that the government is deliberately validating the higher inflation rate $\dot{P}_1$ (with $\dot{\$} = \dot{P}_1$), they will revise upwards their inflation expectations (to $\dot{P}_1$) and the PEP_1 ($\dot{P}^e = \dot{P}_0$) curve will jump upwards to PEP_2 ($\dot{P}^e = \dot{P}_1$) in Chart 15-2. The government would be then forced to either *further* increase its rate of monetary expansion (to $\dot{\$} = \dot{P}_2$) or let the economy slide into a recession from an eroding *real* money supply (because $\dot{P}_2 > \dot{\$} = \dot{P}_1$). To keep the economy at Y^* during a persistent supply-price shock, the government's monetary validation policy must run faster and faster (with escalating inflation rates). Again the government is trapped in the treadmill of a wage-price spiral. Avoiding the recessionary effects of a persistent supply-price shock by validating a higher (and potentially escalating) inflation rate only postpones the day of reckoning. When the supply-price shock terminates, the economy will be left with a *permanently* higher inflation rate (and interest rate[6]), which can only be lowered by tolerating a future recession or possibly imposing wage and price controls (see Chapter 13).

An Interventionist Fiscal Price-Management or "Supply-Side" Policy

The basic tenet of Keynesian economics is that the government should intervene within the economic system for stabilization purposes. For demand shocks to the economic system, the Keynesian policy approach is straight-forward. The government would attempt to counteract a demand shock to the *IS* curve with a fiscal policy offset. By using appropriate demand-management policies, the govern-

---

[6]Since the upward revision in inflation expectations will also cause the *IS* curve to shift upwards (the real interest rate effect on investment spending), the nominal interest rate will rise in tandem with the inflation rate.

ment would attempt to shift the "demand-shocked" *IS* curve back to its original position, thereby restoring the equilibrium values for output, unemployment and inflation. When the demand shock terminated, the fiscal policy offsets would be removed and the economic system would remain at its equilibrium position.

While the basic tenet of Keynesian economics remains valid for supply-price shocks, it is much more difficult for the government to implement fiscal *price* offsets for supply-*price* shocks. *In principle*, if a supply-price shock shifts the *PEP* curve upwards, then the government might attempt to shift the *PEP* curve back down to its original position, thereby stabilizing output and inflation rates at their original equilibrium values. Unfortunately most policy instruments, such as government expenditures, operate on the *IS* curve, *not* the *PEP* curve. The entire orientation of Keynesian economics is towards the *IS-LM* quadrant of our model, not towards the Phillips curve quadrant where supply-price shocks originate. As discussed above, demand-management (*IS-LM*) policies are not appropriate in the context of supply-price shocks to the *PEP* curve. To effectively counter *PEP* curve instability, a *Keynesian-oriented* government requires policy levers that will directly shift the *PEP* curve to offset supply-price shocks.

In recent years economists have questioned the traditional Keynesian proposition that tax rate changes affect only the *IS* curve and aggregate demand. Besides the aggregate demand effects associated with tax changes, one must also consider the direct effects of tax rate changes on pricing (and supply) decisions throughout the economy. In the parlance of the microeconomist, a change in tax rates may be shifted forward into price levels, which would lead to a shift in the Phillips curve. Tax rate changes can have both aggregate demand (*IS* curve) effects as well as aggregate supply (*PEP* curve) effects. To the extent that taxes are forward shifted into price levels, the government has a policy instrument available to shift the *PEP* curve and potentially stabilize the economy when supply-price shocks occur.

To explore further the possibility of a tax-induced shift in the *PEP* curve, we briefly consider the role of various sales taxes in the determination of prices. Included in the final price of consumer goods are not only the costs (and profits) associated with producing these goods, but also a number of indirect taxes such as provincial sales tax, manufacturing sales tax and excise taxes. The imposition of these sales taxes drives a wedge between the price that the consumer must pay for the product and the price that the firm receives for producing the product. As noted in Chapter 3, Statistics Canada includes provincial sales tax rates directly in the Consumer Price Index. By Statistics Canada decree, each and every change in the rate of provincial sales tax is fully and automatically incorporated into the CPI. Clearly an increase in provincial sales tax, federal manufacturing sales tax or various special excise taxes (applied to gasoline, beer and cigarettes) directly affects the final price that the consumer has to pay. Collectively all indirect taxes in Canada amounted to over $50 billion in 1983, which represents 31 per cent of all government tax revenues and 13 per cent of GNP.

Thus the price markup model developed in Chapter 9 should be enlarged to include the government's *tax markup* factor. Denoting sales and indirect tax rates by the symbol t_s, our enlarged price markup model can be written in the following manner (where UC represents unit costs and λ represents the firm's markup factor):

(15-1) $P = (1 + t_s) \, \lambda \, (UC)$

If, for example, there is a 5 per cent sales tax on all goods, then our original price level equation must be multiplied by 1.05 to reflect the government tax markup. This government markup factor $(1 + t_s)$ represents the sales tax wedge between the firm's supply price and final price the consumer must pay. In percentage change form, our enlarged price markup equation can be approximated by the following equation, assuming λ is constant:[7]

(15-2) $\dot{P} = \dot{W} - PR\dot{O}DAV + f\dot{F}P + \left(\dfrac{t_s}{1 + t_s} \right) \dot{t}_s$

If sales tax rates rise from 5 per cent to 6 per cent (which is a 20 per cent increase), then the rate of price inflation will increase by almost a full percentage point [$(0.05 / 1.05) \times 20\% = 0.95\%$ to be exact] *during the year in which sales tax rates are increased*. If there is *no change* in the rate of sales tax ($\dot{t}_s$ is zero), then there will be *no* government tax effect on the *inflation rate*. Sales and indirect taxes only spur inflation when tax rates are increasing ($\dot{t}_s$ is positive).

Substituting our wage adjustment equation (9-3) into this new enlarged price inflation equation (15-2) produces the following enlarged *PEP* curve equation, which includes the forward shifting effects of tax rate changes:

(9-3) $\dot{P} = \left[f\dot{F}P + \dot{P}^x + \left(\dfrac{t_s}{1 + t_s} \right) \dot{t}_s \right] + j \, (U^* - U)$

Any increase in sales tax rates is assumed to be passed on to consumers in the form of higher prices. Thus, in the year in which sales tax rates are increased, the annual inflation rate will be higher, because $\dot{t}_s$ is positive in the *PEP* equation. Similarly, if the government were to lower the rate of sales tax (make $\dot{t}_s$ negative), the inflation rate should moderate during the year in which the tax rate is lowered and the *PEP* curve should temporarily shift downward. As John Turner, then Minister of Finance, noted in his 1974 budget: "I believe that tax cuts can help to reduce prices and costs directly or indirectly and thus slow down the upward momentum of inflation."[8]

Consequently, if a supply-price shock temporarily shifts the *PEP* curve upwards (say from a temporary increase in $f\dot{F}P$ in the *PEP* equation), the government might be able to counteract this upward shift in the *PEP* curve by cutting tax rates (making $\dot{t}_s$ negative in the *PEP* equation). Under such circumstances, the supply-price shock would be offset, the *PEP* curve would remain in its original position (the *negative* $\dot{t}_s$ policy cancels the *positive* $f\dot{F}P$ shock to the *PEP* curve), and the economy would stay at its equilibrium income level Y^* *with an inflation rate of* $\dot{P}_0$ (see Chart 15-1 or 15-2). Society would be spared the short-run stagflation of a

---

[7] Ignoring subscripts, the percentage change in $(1 + t)$ is computed in the following manner:

$$\frac{\Delta(1 + t)}{1 + t} = \frac{\Delta t}{1 + t} = \left(\frac{t}{1 + t} \right) \left(\frac{\Delta t}{t} \right) = \left(\frac{t}{1 + t} \right) \dot{t}$$

[8] *Hansard*, 18 November 1974, p. 1422.

"grin and bear it" monetarist policy for a supply-price shock, as well as the long-run inflation consequences of a stimulative *demand*-management policy. *Theoretically*, the government could implement "cost-oriented changes in taxes to counteract the effect of supply shocks on the overall price level."[9]

Assuming that tax rate changes are shifted forward into wage and price levels, there are a number of severe *practical* problems associated with the implementation of tax rate changes to stabilize the *PEP* curve. First, for each year in which the supply-price shock remains in force, there must be an *additional* tax cut. At the conclusion of a two or three year supply-price shock, the *cumulative offsetting* tax cuts (and government deficit) may be very large. Unfortunately for the government, this new *lower* tax rate must remain a *permanent* part of the economic system after the supply-price shock is over. If the government raises tax rates back to their original levels after the supply-price shock has terminated, the act of raising tax rates would generate a *new* supply-price shock to the economic system, shifting the *PEP* curve upwards once again. The government would simply have *delayed* the original supply-price shock, *not offset it*.

Second, when the government cuts tax rates to offset a supply-price shock to the *PEP* curve, *the IS curve will also shift*. As discussed in Chapter 6, lower tax rates will stimulate consumer spending and either shift or rotate the *IS* curve outwards to the right. To prevent a *positive demand shock to the economic system* when the government cuts tax rates to stabilize the *PEP* curve, the government must implement an *additional restrictive demand-management policy* to *offset* the stimulative effects from the tax-cut-induced shift in the *IS* curve. For example, the government could couple tax cuts with *reductions* in government expenditures to maintain the *IS* curve in its original position. Alternatively, the government could reduce the *nominal* money supply, thereby shifting the *LM* curve to the left to counteract the tax cut rightward shift in the *IS* curve (and maintaining Y* as the intersection point for the new *higher IS* and *LM* curves). Without such an *additional, restrictive* demand-management policy, the government would end up creating an inflationary demand shock to the economic system as it attempts to offset an inflationary supply-price shock. If the supply-price shock is large or persistent, the government may decide that it *cannot* afford the required *permanent* tax cuts and *permanent* reductions in government expenditures (or money supply). In fact, if the government were to offset all supply-price shocks with a combined tax rate change–government expenditure change policy (for both *PEP* and *IS* curve stability), the *long-run* relative size of the government would be fortuitously determined by the cumulative history of past positive and negative supply-price shocks. For example, a string of strong positive supply-price shocks might require cumulative tax and government expenditure cuts which would eliminate the federal government![10]

---

[9]Gordon, *Postwar Macroeconomics*, p. 103.

[10]Alternatively, if the government offset all supply-price shocks with a combined tax rate change–nominal money supply change policy (for total aggregate demand stability), the level of the interest rate and the size of the government deficit would be fortuitously determined by the cumulative history of past supply-price shocks.

Finally, there are the usual Keynesian problems of incomplete information, uncertainty, and lags in the economic system. The odds of getting the *analytically correct* stabilization policy working at the *right time* are at best an even-money proposition. Trying to implement a complicated *permanent* tax-cut-reduced government expenditure policy to offset a *temporary* supply-price shock (to simultaneously stabilize both the *PEP* curve and aggregate demand) may be beyond the reach of a 1980s vintage economist.

In conclusion, supply-price shocks have the unfortunate properties of being both very painful for society and very difficult for governments to offset. A monetarist, non-interventionist, "grin and bear it" approach solves the problem by waiting for the supply-price shock to go away! *Demand*-management policies are analytically *in*appropriate for *supply*-price shocks, and will typically convert a *temporary* supply-price shock into a *permanently* higher inflation rate. Unlike fiscal stabilization policies for demand shocks (which are reversed when the demand shock ends), fiscal tax rate changes to offset supply-price shocks become a *permanent* feature of the economic system. Price stabilization–tax rate change policies are notoriously difficult to implement and may cast a very long shadow. More often than not, government fiscal price stabilization policies (such as the "phasing-in" of the OPEC oil price shock) simply *delay* the impact and unfortunate consequences of a supply-price shock, rather than offset the supply-price shock. Such "buy now, pay later" policies are obviously open to political manipulation, and the application of such so-called stabilization policies may have much more to do with the election cycle than the economic or business cycle.

Review Questions

1. How does a supply-price shock to the economic system arise? Provide several illustrations of supply-price shocks.
2. Explain why a supply-price shock will lead to rising unemployment, rising interest rates and higher inflation rates.
3. Analyze a monetarist non-interventionist CREM policy for an economy that suffers from recurring supply-price shocks (both positive and negative).
4. Given a *persistent* supply-price shock to the economic system, analyze the macroeconomic effects of the following two policies:
   a) monetary validation of the supply-price shock
   b) an expansionary fiscal *demand*-management policy designed to stabilize income levels.
5. Analyze the merits of a fiscal interventionist tax/subsidy policy to stabilize an economy which experiences recurring supply-price shocks.
6. Evaluate the macroeconomic effects of the Canadian government's decision to phase in the 1973-74 oil price shock.

The 1970s and the 1980s: The Rise of Monetarism

16

In thought and word, the Bank of Canada probably qualifies for the designation of the world's most monetarist central bank. The Saskatoon monetary manifesto and the 1975 Annual Report *embody an articulation of the monetarist approach that is second to none. Even Milton Friedman has conceded as much. Referring to the Governor's Saskatoon speech, he asserted: "It is a marvellous speech. It is the best speech I have ever heard a central banker give.... I could have written it myself." Hence, 1975 will go down in the annals of Canadian central banking as a most significant year—the year in which the Bank of Canada...embraced a monetarist philosophy.*

Thomas J. Courchene[1]

In previous chapters we have developed a small theoretical macroeconomic model, the *IS-LM-PEP* model, to explain the interrelated problems of unemployment, inflation and interest rates. Each component and major conclusion of this theoretical model has been checked for empirical accuracy, typically using "scatter diagrams". In this chapter we examine the empirical reliability of the model as a *whole*. Can this theoretical model "explain" the unprecedented macroeconomic problems of the 1970s and 1980s? In particular, what circumstances led to the emergence of double-digit inflation during the 1970s? Why did the Bank of Canada switch to a monetarist policy in 1975? Given a monetarist policy, why did double-digit inflation continue until 1982? What caused the unemployment rate to jump to 11 per cent in 1982? How did the federal government end up with annual deficits of $30 billion in the mid-1980s? These key policy questions form the agenda for this policy overview chapter.

We begin this chapter with a brief review of the 1960s, a decade of unprecedented economic prosperity and tranquillity. Against this buoyant economic backdrop of the 1960s, we analyze events and government policy decisions of the 1970s and early 1980s. In picking our way through the 1970-85 period, we have identified four separate subperiods characterized by very different policy approaches:

1. the 1969-71 recession, engineered by restrictive monetary and fiscal policy;

---

[1]T.J. Courchene, *Monetarism and Controls: The Inflation Fighters* (Montreal: C. D. Howe Research Institute, 1976), p. 111.

2. the 1972-74 inflationary expansion, fuelled by very expansionary monetary policy;
3. the 1975-81 period of stagflation, which included the use of a *gradualist* monetarist policy and *temporary* wage and price controls; and
4. the 1982-85 period of high unemployment and very large government deficits, which featured a very restrictive monetary policy and the rejection of Keynesian fiscal policies.

The 1960s

During the eight years from 1962 through 1969, the Canadian economy maintained an unprecedented average growth rate of almost 6 per cent per year. A number of positive demand shocks contributed to this eight years of rapid economic growth:

1. Over this eight-year period exports increased by almost 10 per cent every year (see Chart 14-1), due in large part to the boom induced by the Vietnam War in the U.S. and a devalued Canadian dollar.
2. A strong investment boom took place in Canada during the mid-1960s (see Chart 14-1).
3. Monetary policy was expansionary (see Chart 14-1), and fiscal policy did not attempt to offset the positive demand shocks arising from increased exports and investment.

Given the combined effects of strong export demand, a domestic investment boom and an expansionary monetary policy, both the *IS* and *LM* curves continually shifted to the right during the 1960s. In Chart 16-1 we present initial (1961) and final (1969) *IS* and *LM* curves, suppressing the *IS* and *LM* curves for the intervening years.[2] The large rightward shifts in both the *IS* and *LM* curves generated substantial increases in real output, and the unemployment rate was driven down to 4.4 per cent by 1969.

As the unemployment rate began to decline during the 1960s, however, the inflation rate gradually started to increase. In the lower quadrant of Chart 16-1 we have drawn a 1961-vintage *PEP* curve assuming an expected inflation rate of 1 per cent (the average inflation rate from 1958 to 1961) and have also included a vertical line depicting the natural rate of unemployment (assumed to be approximately 6 per cent in the early 1960s). To simplify the diagrammatic analysis in this chapter, we focus our attention on the inflation-unemployment axis in the *PEP* diagram.[3] As the unemployment rate declined during the 1960s, the economy was

---

[2]We continue to ignore the *BP* (balance of payments) curve and leave it to a senior course to complete the macroeconomic story with a shifting *BP* curve and a floating exchange rate (which in turn will cause the *BP*, *PEP* and *IS* curves to shift).

[3]As discussed in Chapter 10, the growth of the labour force will cause the equilibrium output level to increase and the inflation-output *PEP* curve to shift downwards to the right. If we focused on the inflation-output axis in the *PEP* diagram, we would have to draw a new set of downward-shifting *PEP* curves to represent a growing economy. It would then be difficult to distinguish diagrammatically the *net* effects of rising inflation expectations (*upward* shifts in the *PEP* curve) in an economy with a growing labour force. Using the inflation-unemployment axis in the *PEP* quadrant allows us to focus directly on rising inflation expectations without the complications of a growing labour force.

CHART 16-1 The buoyant 1960s

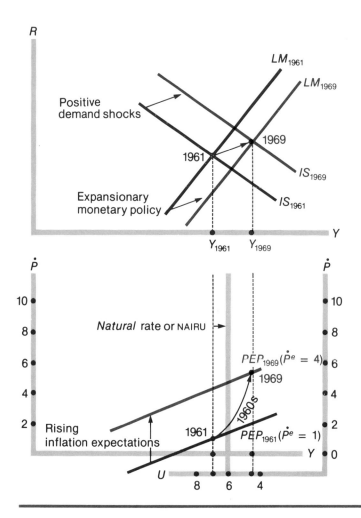

pushed up the *PEP* curve to higher rates of inflation, and gradually this escalating inflation rate began to translate into rising inflation expectations. By the end of the decade, the 1961-vintage *PEP* curve (with $\dot{P}^e$ = 1 per cent) likely shifted upwards by about 3 per cent (to *PEP* 1969 with $\dot{P}^e$ = 4 per cent).[4] The combination of positive demand shocks, expansionary monetary policy and rising inflation expectations drove the inflation rate up to 4.5 per cent in 1969, and positioned the economy on a much higher *PEP* curve (see Chart 16-1). As noted by the Anti-Inflation Board,

[4]As discussed in Chapter 12, rising inflation expectations will also cause a further upward shift in the *IS* curve and lead to a higher nominal interest rate. We assume that our higher 1969 *IS* curve in Chart 16-1 also captures the effect of rising inflation expectations on investment spending.

In retrospect, the experience of the 1960s was a preview of the more substantial problems to follow in the 1970s. It was demonstrated that aggressive demand management policies could lead, for a time, to impressive output increases and a significant decline in unemployment rates: price and wage effects were manifested only after significant lag; and there was a continual underestimation of the momentum of accelerating inflation once it had started. Throughout the 1960s governments and the public were attempting to achieve high employment and output goals without taking account of the inflationary consequences that would follow. Only when inflation reached unprecedented heights in 1969 was there support for more restrictive policies.[5]

The 1969-1971 Mini-Recession

In reaction to the gradually rising inflation rate of the late 1960s the government fundamentally altered its policy approach. In 1969 *both* monetary and fiscal policy were abruptly reversed from an expansionary stance to a tightly restrictive position. In the words of Prime Minister Trudeau, inflation would be "wrestled to the ground."

Compared with an average annual increase in the Canadian money supply of 7 per cent during the 1965-68 period, from May 1969 to May 1970 the nominal money supply remained virtually constant. In real terms the Canadian money supply actually declined, pushing the *LM* curve back to the left (see Chart 16-2). The Governor of the Bank of Canada explained his new, restrictive ("stringent") monetary policy in the following words:

> The need for stringent monetary policies to help contain and combat the erosion in the purchasing power of money has been widely accepted in Canada. . . . Some slowing down of the economy was indeed, in the circumstances, a necessary prelude to a reduction of price and cost pressures. . . . Policy will not achieve its objective if it is abandoned at the first sign of success, namely as soon as the growth of the economy shows signs of deceleration. This is particularly the case if there are widely held inflationary expectations.[6]

Along with a "stringent" monetary policy, the government abruptly applied the brakes to fiscal policy. In both the June 1969 and March 1970 federal budgets, "the number one priority" of the government was to "squeeze inflation out of the economy". We briefly quote from Finance Minister Benson's March 1970 budget speech:

> Mr. Speaker, in presenting the budget to the House last June, I expressed the government's view that a strong fiscal position was essential to check the rise in prices and smooth the way toward more balanced and sustained economic growth. . . . This year by a national effort we must

[5]Anti-Inflation Board, *Inflation and Public Policy* (Ottawa, 1979), pp. 24-26.
[6]Bank of Canada, *Annual Report*, 1969, pp. 6-8.

CHART 16-2 Trudeau's 1969-71 mini-recession

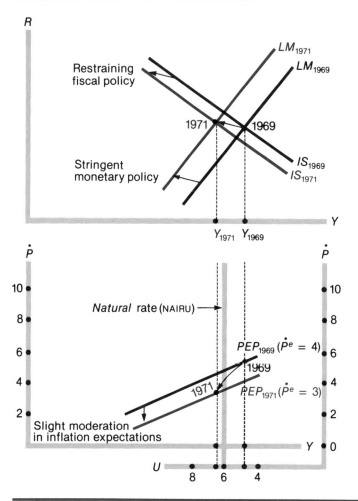

reduce the rate at which prices are increasing. . . . It is the policy of the government to restrain the growth of total spending in the economy, for that is a necessary condition for achieving our primary economic objective.[7]

The result of the government's surtaxes and other restrictive fiscal policies was an *increase* of over $1 billion in the federal government's net budgetary position (revenues minus expenditures), leaving the federal government with a record-high $1 billion *surplus* in 1969.

The government's abrupt switch to a very restrictive monetary and fiscal policy clearly did slow down the growth of the Canadian economy. With a decline in the

---

[7]*Hansard*, 12 March 1970, p. 4740.

real money supply and a record high government surplus, the government restrained aggregate demand by shifting both the *IS* and *LM* curves backwards to the left (see Chart 16-2).[8] The real growth rate of the economy was cut in half and the unemployment rate began to climb (5.7 per cent in 1970 and 6.2 per cent in 1971). This government-engineered recession at least partially achieved the government's anti-inflation objective. By restraining aggregate demand, the government pushed the economy back down the *PEP* curve to a lower inflation rate. As this "stringent restraint" policy began to bite, inflation expectations may have modestly declined (say to 3 per cent) and the *PEP* curve may have shifted downwards (say, to *PEP* 1971 with $\dot{P}^e$ = 3 per cent in Chart 16.2).[9] The combination of rising unemployment and moderating inflation expectations lowered the inflation rate from 4.5 per cent in 1969 to 2.8 per cent in 1971.

The 1972-74 Expansion and the Emergence of Double-Digit Inflation

Faced with the recessionary effects of its highly restrictive, almost Draconian, monetary and fiscal policies of 1969 and 1970, the Trudeau government abruptly switched to a very expansionary policy in 1971 (perhaps in anticipation of the 1972 federal election). Fighting unemployment rather than inflation became the number one priority. The fiscal brakes were released, the heavy "Keynesian" foot of the government stomped on the monetary accelerator, and the Canadian economy sped away to double-digit inflation. Before analyzing the Canadian government's expansionary policies in the 1972-74 period, we first review the nongovernmental shocks to the Canadian system during this period. As we shall see, the government responded to these shocks by flooding the economy with dollar bills.

During the 1971-73 period, the Canadian economy experienced a sustained positive demand shock: real investment rose by 29 per cent and exports rose by 23 per cent, easily outstripping the growth of potential output, and the *IS* curve shifted to the right (see Chart 16-3). Combined with a very expansionary monetary policy (see below), the Canadian economy received strong demand stimulus during the early 1970s.

In addition to these positive demand shocks, two important supply-price shocks affected the Canadian economy during the early 1970s. As discussed in Chapters 9 and 15, large price increases for internationally traded goods and raw materials had a major impact on the rate of Canadian inflation between 1972 and 1974. During this three-year period, world commodity prices increased by 159 per cent and world food prices increased by 183 per cent! This unprecedented explosion of raw material and commodity prices on world markets was undoubtedly reflected in higher material input prices in Canada, which were passed on to consumers in

---

[8]While the underlying growth factors in the economy (such as export growth) would be constantly pushing the *IS* curve to the right, to keep our diagram as simple as possible we have ignored all growth factors. In reality, the government's restrictive fiscal policy would have *reduced* the rightward (growth) shift in the *IS* curve, leading to a slower growth in real output.

[9]Such a moderation in inflation expectations would also decrease investment expenditures and push the *IS* curve back to the left.

CHART 16-3 The 1972-74 inflationary expansion

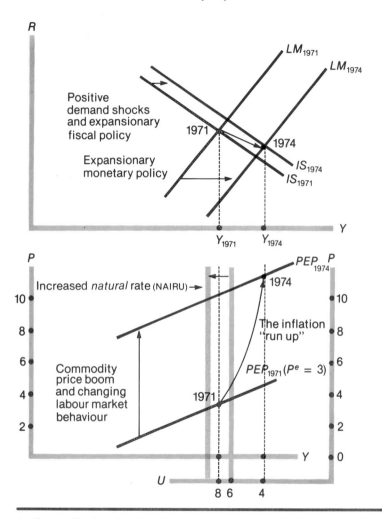

the form of higher final product prices. In terms of Chart 16-3, this unprecedented (external) commodity price boom of 1972-74 pushed the *PEP* curve substantially upwards, exerting a strong, positive supply-price shock on the Canadian economic system.

As discussed in Case Study 6 in Chapter 12, fundamental structural changes were also occurring in the Canadian labour market during the early 1970s. The demographic composition of the labour force shifted to younger, less experienced, secondary workers and the traditional stereotype of the unemployed worker as a prime-age male with a family to support became less and less true during the 1970s. In addition, the government substantially liberalized the unemployment insurance program in 1971, which significantly altered the incentive structure within the labour market (particularly for secondary workers). As a consequence of this enriched unemployment insurance program, the more heavily subsidized unemployed exercised more discretion over the choice of jobs they would accept (longer job search) and employers were forced to offer higher wages to fill vacant jobs. The combination of demographic shifts and an enriched unemployment insurance program increased the equilibrium, or natural rate of unemployment, producing a further upward shift in the *PEP* curve (see Chart 16-3).

In the face of these strong positive demand and supply-price shocks, the Canadian government decided to reverse its "stringent" policies of 1969-70 and again implement a very expansionary monetary and fiscal policy. Such a policy decision is neither Keynesian nor monetarist. The government deliberately intervened within the economic system to *reinforce* and *validate* the inflationary shocks that were occurring. Before examining why the government chose such an inflation-prone policy, we briefly review the government's fiscal and monetary policy during the 1971-74 period.

In his June 1971 budget, Finance Minister Benson dramatically changed his macroeconomic strategy. The policy of the government abruptly switched from fighting inflation and restraining aggregate demand to fighting unemployment and expanding aggregate demand. In the following two budgets of Finance Minister John Turner, the opening lines of each clearly identify reducing the unemployment rate as the number one priority of the government:

May 1972 budget: "Mr. Speaker, my first words to this House as Minister of Finance last February were that the most urgent priority was jobs. This remains my first priority."[10]

February 1973 budget: "Mr. Speaker, the purpose of this budget is—first and foremost—to bring about a substantial reduction in unemployment. . . . This budget is aimed at faster growth."[11]

In a deliberate attempt to stimulate consumer and investment spending, a wide variety of tax reductions and incentives were introduced into these three successive federal budgets, including the *inflation indexation of the income tax system* (see Case Study 1 in Chapter 3). The federal government surpluses of 1969 and 1970 were deliberately converted into deficits in 1971 and 1972 (see Table 16-2 later in this chapter). At minimum, the government's fiscal policy was mildly expansionary during the 1971-73 period and further nudged the *IS* curve in Chart 16-3 upwards to the right (reinforcing the nongovernmental positive demand shocks that were occurring).

Monetary policy was unambiguously *expansionary* during the early 1970s. Forgetting its own advice (that a "stringent" monetary policy "will not achieve its objective if it is abandoned at the first signs of success"), the Bank of Canada reversed its stringent policy of 1969-70, and in 1971 the Canadian money supply began to grow at a record rate. Compared with a 2.5 per cent increase in the money supply in 1970, the *average annual* increase in the money supply over the next three years was an incredible 13.9 per cent (which compounds to a 48 per

---

[10]*Hansard*, 8 May 1972, p. 1998.
[11]*Hansard*, 19 February 1973, p. 1428.

cent increase over this three-year period)! In terms of our *IS-LM-PEP* model, the Bank of Canada's flood of new dollar bills pushed the *LM* curve far to the right-hand side of the page.

Chart 16-3 summarizes the major shocks and policy changes that occurred during the 1972-74 period. Rapidly expanding export sales, an investment boom, and expansionary fiscal policy pushed the *IS* curve to the right. A very expansionary monetary policy shifted the *LM* curve far to the right. The commodity price boom pushed the *PEP* curve substantially higher. Finally, a structural shift in labour market behaviour increased the natural rate of unemployment and reinforced the upward shift in the PEP curve.

Given this set of demand and supply-price shocks (including government policy changes), our *IS-LM-PEP* model in Chart 16-3 predicts that (1) real output will substantially increase, (2) unemployment will fall, (3) the inflation rate will dramatically rise, and (4) the interest rate may (initially) decline. Each of these predictions turns out to be surprisingly accurate. From 1970 to 1973, real GNP increased by an average annual rate of 6.9 per cent. The unemployment rate declined from 6.2 per cent in 1971 to 5.3 per cent in 1974. The Canadian inflation rate was accelerating at a rapid pace: 2.8 per cent in 1971, 4.8 per cent in 1972, 7.6 per cent in 1973 and 10.9 per cent in 1974. Finally, interest rates were moderately lower in 1972-3 than they were in 1970 (see Chart 1-2).

Monetary and Fiscal Policies of the 1971-74 Period Reconsidered

Although our *IS-LM-PEP* model can explain the macroeconomic track record of the early 1970s, it does *not* explain *why* the government pursued such an expansionary set of policies in the context of the positive demand and supply-price shocks that were occurring. Five years later, the Department of Finance admitted that its expansionary policies were wrong: "in retrospect it is clear that the aggregate demand policy in the period 1971-73 was excessively expansionary."[12]

In implementing such an "excessively expansionary" policy during the early 1970s, the government seriously underestimated the inflationary consequences of its policies. Most economists and policy makers of the early 1970s still subscribed to an *incorrect* inflation-unemployment *trade-off* view of macroeconomic policy; that is, expansionary aggregate demand policies could permanently lower the unemployment rate with only modest increases in the inflation rate. Friedman's *natural* rate of unemployment hypothesis, advanced in 1967, was not well understood and the possibility that the inflation rate might continually accelerate if the unemployment rate was pushed below the *natural* rate was dismissed as theoretical speculation. In addition, economists and policy makers of the 1960s and early 1970s had considerably overstated their own ability to "fine tune" or manage the economy. Having driven the economy into a recession in 1970 by braking fiscal and monetary policy, the government assumed that it could pull the

---

[12]Department of Finance, *Canada's Recent Inflation Experience* (Ottawa, November 1978), p. 14.

economy out of its recessionary state by simply accelerating on the money supply and fiscal gas pedals.

Mistaking the relatively flat *short-run* Phillips curve for a *long-run* inflation-unemployment *trade-off* curve, the Canadian government proceeded to expand aggregate demand rapidly in an attempt to lower the 6 per cent unemployment rate, incorrectly presuming that only a modest increase in the inflation rate would materialize. Unfortunately, fundamental structural changes in the labour market, at least partially attributable to another government policy (the 1971 liberalization of unemployment insurance), had caused an increase in the natural rate of unemployment. The government was driving the economy to an unemployment rate well below the new natural rate. While government policy makers may or may not have understood the implications of Friedman's natural rate concept,[13] they certainly would have rejected the notion that the Canadian natural rate of unemployment was in excess of 6 per cent, the prevailing Canadian unemployment rate in 1971-72. In effect, macroeconomic monetary and fiscal policies of the early 1970s were trying to reduce the amount of unemployment while microeconomic labour market policies (unemployment insurance) were encouraging unemployment. This clash of macro-micro policies produced only minor reductions in the unemployment rate but considerable inflationary pressures. Even without the commodity price shocks (which the government chose to validate—another policy error), such an "excessively expansionary" monetary and fiscal policy during the early 1970s sowed the seeds for almost a decade of double-digit inflation.

Part of this "excessive expansion" of the money supply can also be attributed to the government's unwillingness to let the Canadian dollar appreciate on foreign exchange markets. As Finance Minister Benson stated in his June 18, 1971 budget,

> I have said on many occasions that the government did not wish to see the Canadian dollar appreciate. A higher dollar works with increasing effect against our exporters and against domestic producers who must try to meet foreign competition. Since the appreciation affects the economy in this way, it works against our policy of trying to expand employment opportunities in Canada.[14]

As discussed in Chapter 7, the Bank of Canada can prevent the Canadian dollar from appreciating by demanding foreign currencies (in exchange for Canadian money) and maintaining a low interest rate (to discourage capital inflows). As Courchene has noted:

> The policy error over this period [the early 1970s] arose from the authorities' belief that Canada could simultaneously achieve a less-than-world inflation rate and an unchanged exchange rate.... The policy error during this period is obvious—the money supply was allowed to grow far too rapidly. In turn the principal reason why this rate of

---

[13]The statement from the 1969 *Annual Report* of the Bank of Canada (supra footnote 6) suggests that the Bank of Canada understood the inflationary implications of an expansionary monetary policy.

[14]*Hansard*, 18 June 1971, p. 6904.

monetary expansion occurred was that the Bank and the government attempted to stabilize the exchange rate at or near parity with the U.S. dollar.[15]

While rapid monetary expansion prevented the Canadian dollar from appreciating and thereby (temporarily) assisted Canadian exporters, such rapid monetary growth eventually led to an accelerating domestic inflation rate, a subsequent deterioration in Canada's international export competitiveness, and a dramatic decline in the value of the Canadian dollar during the late 1970s and early 1980s.

In retrospect, the government and the Bank of Canada committed a series of grave macroeconomic policy errors in the 1971-73 period. A partial list of policy mistakes would include the following:

1) Attempting to run the economic system with an unemployment rate below the natural rate.
2) Reinforcing rather than offsetting positive demand shocks.
3) Validating supply-price shocks.
4) Simultaneously trying
    a) to subsidize unemployment through an enriched UI program, and
    b) to lower the unemployment rate by expansionary monetary and fiscal policies.
5) Trying to prevent the Canadian dollar from appreciating.

In concert, these policy errors manifested themselves in an "excessively expansionary" monetary and fiscal policy, which in turn led to "chronic accelerating inflation".

In fairness to the government of the day, however, academic economists of the early 1970s were *not* criticizing the government's "excessively expansionary" policies, as most economists still clung to a belief in a *long-run* inflation-unemployment *trade-off* curve and the desirability of a 3-4 per cent unemployment rate. Opposition critics in Parliament were demanding even more expansionary policies. In criticizing the February 1973 Liberal budget, Progressive Conservative Finance Critic James Gillies stated:

> The really fundamental question one has to ask in considering this budget and its effect on employment in the economy is: is the deficit large enough?... I would argue, that it is not.... If a Progressive Conservative government had been in power...[the] budget would have been substantially more expansionary....[16]

The NDP, which held the balance of power in Parliament throughout most of the 1972-74 period, was just as vocal in demanding a more expansionary policy: "We have reservations about the size of the deficit. We think it should have been larger...."[17] In terms of academic and political commentary of the day, it would

---

[15]T.J. Courchene, *Money, Inflation, and the Bank of Canada* (Montreal: C.D. Howe Research Institute, 1976), pp. 13-14.

[16]*Hansard*, 22 February 1973, pp. 1559-60.

[17]Max Saltsman, NDP finance critic, in *Hansard*, 21 February 1973, p. 1527.

not have been obvious to the 1971-73 Canadian government that its macroeconomic policies were "excessively expansionary" or incorrect.

Double-Digit Inflation and the Bank of Canada's Conversion to Monetarism

Echoing the words of the Governor of the Bank of Canada, "there is no great mystery about the nature and origins" of the emergence of double-digit inflation in Canada in 1974. Positive demand shocks and supply-price shocks that are reinforced and validated by a rapid expansion of the money supply will lead to short-run output gains but at the expense of a rapidly accelerating inflation rate. Any government that chooses to expand the money supply by 13.9 per cent per year for three successive years (1971-73) ought not to be surprised by the emergence of (persistent) double-digit inflation in the fourth and fifth years (1974-75). Unfortunately, once double-digit inflation has existed for several years, fuelled by excessively expansionary monetary policy, people will come to expect it to continue. Canadian inflation expectations of 3-4 per cent in the early 1970s were undoubtedly revised upwards to 10 per cent in the mid-1970s. Even though the commodity price shock ended in 1974, the Canadian *PEP* curve did *not* shift back down. Higher inflation expectations held the *PEP* curve of Chart 16-3 in its new higher position and inflation began to feed on itself. The inappropriate *short-run* stabilization policy of the early 1970s produced higher *long-run* inflation and interest rates,[18] which persisted well into the 1980s. As discussed at length in Chapter 13, once the inflation genie is let out of the bottle, it is very difficult to get it back into the bottle. Double-digit inflation became the major preoccupation of the government for almost a decade, and the government's various battles against inflation created a whole new set of macroeconomic problems for the 1980s (notably, high interest rates, high unemployment rates, and high government deficits).

Having spent most of the previous decade stimulating the economy with an "excessively expansionary" monetary policy, the Bank of Canada abruptly switched to a *restrictive , long-term* monetary policy in 1975 and embraced the tenets of monetarism. The Bank of Canada's conversion to monetarism was based on four key interrelated propositions. The first two of these were set out in a 1975 speech given in Saskatoon by the Governor of the Bank of Canada when he clearly identified *inflation* as the number one priority of the government and a restrictive monetary policy as the major weapon in the battle against inflation:

> The first proposition is that it is very much in the public interest that the drift into deepening inflation in Canada be halted and reversed. . . . The second proposition is that, whatever else may need to be done to bring inflation under control, it is absolutely essential to keep the rate of monetary expansion within reasonable limits. Any programme that did

---

[18]As discussed in Chapter 12, this higher expected inflation rate also caused the *IS* curve to shift upwards, eventually leading to a higher nominal interest rate (reflecting a higher inflation premium).

not include this policy would be doomed to failure. There is no way of preserving its value if money is created on an excessive scale.[19]

Coming from the Governor of the Bank of Canada who had allowed the Canadian money supply to increase by an average rate of 13 per cent for the previous five years (1971 through 1975), this is indeed a remarkable admission that the Bank of Canada's monetary policies during the early 1970s were "doomed to failure".

Third, while the Bank of Canada was firmly committed to restricting the long-run growth rate of the money supply, it thought this objective could best be attained by gradually reducing the rate of monetary expansion and by supplementing a restrictive monetary policy with wage-price controls. Going "cold turkey" from a 15 per cent to a 5 per cent rate of monetary expansion was considered to be "too disruptive in economic and social terms to be sensible or tolerable."[20] By imposing a *gradually* restrictive monetary policy coupled with wage and price controls, the central bank hoped that the inflation rate could be lowered without Canadians having to endure a painful recession (see Chapter 13).

The fourth and final proposition of the Bank of Canada's new monetarist position was a rejection of Keynesian counter-cyclical changes in monetary policy:

> In the past, the approach followed by most central bankers was to try to offset undesired variations in national expenditures that were believed likely to occur in the immediate future by action which often involved wide swings in the rate of monetary expansion from one period to the next. Although intended to be stabilizing, this approach often had a de-stabilizing influence on the trend of expenditure growth in the economy. The reasons for this include the difficulty of making reliable short-term forecasts, the long and variable time lags involved in monetary policy, and the difficulty of making judgements about appropriate interest rate levels in periods when future inflation is expected. A further difficulty with this approach and one that limits the scope for using it as a stabilizing device is that any escalation of the rate of monetary growth must be fully reversed in due course if the longer run trend of monetary expansion is not to accelerate over time.[21]

The Governor of the Bank of Canada recognized that a steady (or constant) rate of monetary expansion would not only control inflation in the long-run but would also act as a *short-run stabilizing* policy in the context of demand shocks to the economic system (see Chapter 14).

The Canadian Economy Under a Decade of Monetarism

Before analyzing the Canadian government's monetary and fiscal policies from 1975 to 1984, we briefly recap the major events and shocks of this period. A review of Canadian inflation and unemployment rates suggests that this decade of

---

[19]Reprinted in *Bank of Canada Review*, October 1975, pp. 23-24.
[20]Bank of Canada, *Annual Report*, 1975, p. 10.
[21]*Ibid.*, p. 11.

monetarism can be subdivided into two distinct periods. During the first seven years (1975-81), the Canadian inflation rate averaged 9.6 per cent (reaching 12.5 per cent in 1981), while the unemployment rate averaged 7.5 per cent (ranging between 6.9 per cent in 1975 and 8.3 per cent in 1978). In 1982, however, the unemployment rate jumped to 11.0 per cent and remained in excess of 11 per cent for the next two years. With (post-Depression) record high unemployment rates, the Canadian inflation rate fell to 5.8 per cent in 1983 and 4.4 per cent in 1984. The first seven years of monetarism featured double-digit inflation, followed by a period of double-digit unemployment.

During the first seven years of monetarism, the Canadian economy grew at an average annual real rate of 2.9 per cent. The only major demand shock that occurred during this period was a strong export boom in 1976-78 (when real exports increased by almost 10 per cent per year for three successive years), which drove the unemployment rate down to 7.4 per cent in 1979. Perhaps more important, the Canadian economy was subject to another strong set of supply-price shocks between 1976 and 1981. During these five years, world commodity prices and world food prices increased by average annual rates of 16.7 per cent and 18.7 per cent respectively (see Chapter 9). In addition, the Canadian government was phasing in world oil price increases and the price of gasoline jumped by 19 per cent in 1980, 36 per cent in 1981, and 21 per cent in 1982 (a cumulative increase of 96 per cent)! Not surprisingly, these large supply-price shocks pushed the Canadian inflation rate up to 10.1 per cent in 1980 and 12.5 per cent in 1981.

The other major event of this initial period of monetarism was the imposition of wage and price controls for the 1975-78 period. As discussed at length in Chapter 13, while the Anti-Inflation Board substantially reduced wage increases and lowered price increases for *controlled* goods, the aforementioned supply-price shocks prevented the *overall* inflation rate from declining. With inflation still running at 8-9 per cent when controls were lifted in mid-1978, inflation expectations never moderated and the double-digit Canadian *PEP* curve did not shift down.[22] Notwithstanding the government's restrictive monetary policy (discussed below), the supply-price shocks in the post-AIB period continued to push the inflation rate upwards.

As indicated above, the Canadian economy went into a tailspin in 1982. The unemployment rate increased from 7.5 per cent in 1981 to 11 per cent in 1982 and real GNP *declined* by 4.4 per cent in 1982. A number of factors were responsible for this major recession. The U.S. economy was in a high interest rate, recessionary state, which it "exported" to Canada (Canadian exports declined by 1.6 per cent in 1982). Perhaps more important, the Canadian government's restrictive monetary policy was finally starting to bite. As discussed below, substantial reductions in the real money supply in 1980-82 (in conjunction with high U.S. interest rates) led to record high Canadian interest rates (peaking at over 20 per cent in 1981) and a consequent reduction in investment and aggregate demand. The government was finally able to purge inflation out of the system, with a good "old fashioned" recession.

---

[22]For a complete analysis of the Canadian government's 1975-78 experiment with temporary wage and price controls, see Case Study 8 in Chapter 13.

Monetary Policy During the 1975-84 Period

Following four years of economic expansion and accelerating inflation, Canada's major economic policy objectives in 1975 were to reduce inflation (which had reached double-digit levels in both 1974 and 1975), lower Canada's high interest rates, and foster continued economic expansion. To achieve these ultimate economic objectives, the Bank of Canada switched to a monetarist policy approach. The theoretical arguments that had been put forward by monetarists throughout the 1960s and early 1970s had gradually gained wide acceptance within the community of economists and policy makers. Canada's conversion to monetarism was announced by the Governor of the Bank of Canada in his Saskatchewan address and was fully endorsed by the leading proponent of monetarism, Professor Milton Friedman (see the quotation at the beginning of this chapter).

Canada's version of a monetarist policy involved three intermediate objectives through which the ultimate economic goals were to be achieved. As has already been discussed, the first and foremost was the decision to permanently reduce the growth rate of the money supply. This, of course, recognizes the link between monetary growth and price inflation—a link that had been demonstrated beyond question by 1975. But to minimize the recessionary effects of a tight monetary policy, the Bank of Canada opted for gradualism. That is, the growth rate of the money supply was to be reduced gradually over a period of many years, rather than suddenly lowered to a rate which is consistent with zero inflation.

The second aspect of the new policy framework was the annual announcement of monetary growth *targets*. By committing itself to monetary growth targets the Bank of Canada removed the possibility of *discretionary* monetary actions. Moreover, by announcing its objectives, the Bank of Canada exposed itself to more thorough criticism than ever before. The public could not only dispute the appropriateness of the declared targets but could also evaluate the Bank of Canada's performance in meeting its own stated objectives. What benefits did the Bank of Canada expect to reap by publicly announcing the monetary growth targets, benefits over and above those that would follow from simply adopting without fanfare a monetarist approach to policy? By mid-1975 the rate of inflation had been rising for several years, and undoubtedly, inflation expectations had been adjusting upwards. The government hoped that wage and price controls coupled with the announcement of a dramatic shift in monetary policy would have an immediate effect on reducing inflationary expectations. The resulting downward shift in the *PEP* curve would mean that the government's anti-inflation policies would not increase unemployment as much as if inflation expectations had remained high.

The third component of monetary policy was to reduce the *variability* of the growth in the stock of money. Monetarists firmly believe that changes in the stock of money have strong *real* effects in the short run, but only *price* effects in the long run. Consequently, sharp changes in the money supply will lead to wide fluctuations in employment and output. In addition, the central bank recognized that to make the new monetary policy credible to the public at large, it would be necessary to reduce the rate of growth of the money supply smoothly. This would clearly demonstrate the Bank of Canada's commitment to the new policy regime and thereby help to reduce inflation expectations. On the other hand, erratic money supply behaviour would create grave doubts in the minds of the public that the Bank of Canada was capable of achieving its own targets. Clearly, it is very difficult for the public to confirm a declining trend in monetary growth if monetary growth is highly erratic.

To implement this new monetary policy, the Bank of Canada faced a substantial practical difficulty. As discussed in Chapter 18, given the vast array of deposits (demand deposits, daily interest chequable deposits, notice deposits and term deposits), there is no single measure of the money supply. Yet, the setting of monetary growth targets required the Bank of Canada to declare precisely which measure of the stock of money it intended to control. In 1975 the two major candidates were M1 and M2. The first, M1, is a *narrow* definition that measures immediately spendable money (often referred to as transactions balances); M1 consists of the public's cash and demand deposits. M2 is a much *broader* definition that includes savings accounts and term deposits. In deciding which definition of money to use as a monetary target, the Governor of the Bank of Canada made the following observations:

> To be useful in setting targets for monetary policy a money supply aggregate should satisfy two principal requirements. First, there should be a sufficiently well-established link between the growth in the aggregate and the growth of total spending in the economy to permit the monetary authority to decide with reasonable confidence what growth path for the aggregate is consistent with a desired growth path for total spending. The second requirement is that the growth of the money supply aggregate should be sufficiently exposed to the influence of the monetary authority to give that authority a reasonable chance of attaining its monetary target over a reasonable period of time without generating great instability and uncertainty in financial and foreign exchange markets.[23]

Based on these considerations, the Bank of Canada decided to control M1 rather than a broader measure of the money supply, because it is more directly related to total spending (and nominal income) and because it is more easily controlled.

Table 16-1 and Chart 16-4 summarize Canada's six-year experiment with monetary growth targets, spanning the years 1975-81. At the end of 1982, when the seventh target range was due to be announced, the policy was abruptly cancelled.

The first target range for the growth of M1 was announced in November 1975. The first year's objective was to keep the growth of M1 within the range of 10 to 15 per cent. Interestingly, the period over which this target was to be achieved did not begin on the November announcement date but back in May of 1975. Consequently, when the Bank of Canada set the first annual growth target, almost half of the year had elapsed and the Governor knew what the actual path of M1 had been over that period. This practice of announcing the base period well after the

[23]Bank of Canada, *Annual Report*, 1978, p. 15.

TABLE 16-1   Canada's Monetary Targets

Base Date*	Announcement Date	Target Range M1	Actual Growth in Year Following Base Date	
			M1	M2
May 1975	November 1975	10 – 15%	9.7%	12.6%
March 1976	August 1976	8 – 12	6.9	15.5
June 1977	October 1977	7 – 11	9.0	10.1
June 1978	October 1978	6 – 10	9.0	15.7
May 1979	October 1979	5 – 9	3.4	19.5
Sep 1980	January 1981	4 – 8	−0.3	16.3

*The base money stock is calculated as a three-month average around the month indicated.

CHART 16-4 The era of monetary targets in Canada, 1975– 1982

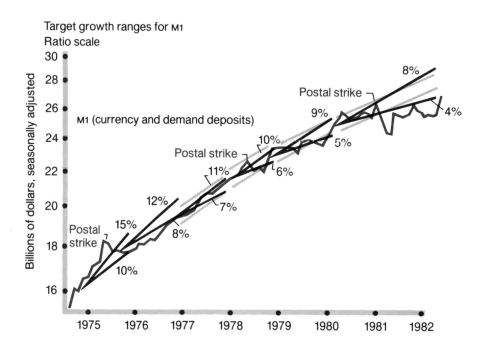

event continued throughout the six years of monetary targetting and clearly made it easier for the Bank of Canada to achieve its announced targets. Nevertheless, the Bank of Canada did gradually lower the target ranges as it had promised in 1975, until the range fell to 4-8 per cent in the 1980-81 period.

The fourth column of Table 16-1 lists the actual growth rates of M1 during the twelve months following the base dates. These figures indicate that three of the first four years of targetting were successful in the sense that the *actual* growth of M1 fell within the *target* range (in 1976 M1 growth fell below the target range). But, in the next two years, 1979 and 1980, the growth of M1 fell well below the bottom of the target range. This is illustrated very clearly in Chart 16-4, which also shows that throughout 1982 M1 continued to be well *below* the target range. In terms of the Bank of Canada's chosen monetary indicator M1, monetary policy was much tighter over the 1979-81 period than the Bank of Canada's openly declared policy. The view that monetary policy was very restrictive in this period is also supported by data on the *real* stock of M1. As early as 1979, the real stock of M1 fell 2 per cent, then in 1980 it fell a further 3.5 per cent, followed by a 7.6 per cent decline in 1981 and a whopping 9.2 per cent drop in 1982.

One explanation for this overly restrictive (below target) monetary growth during the early 1980s concerns the influence of record high U.S. interest rates. As discussed in Chapter 11, if the Bank of Canada responds to high U.S. interest rates by allowing the Canadian foreign exchange rate to float downwards, a short-run period of excess demand, output growth, and increased inflation will occur. Since the Bank of Canada was (desperately) trying to control inflation during this period, it was most reluctant to let the value of the Canadian dollar decline, with its accompanying inflationary pressures. Consequently, the Bank of Canada responded to high U.S. interest rates by attempting to moderate the decline in the Canadian exchange rate. As discussed in Chapter 11, to prevent the Canadian dollar from declining in value (given an increase in U.S. interest rates), the Bank of Canada had to demand Canadian dollars in foreign exchange markets, thereby reducing the domestic money supply and forcing Canadian interest rates up in tandem with U.S. interest rates. In effect, high U.S. interest rates were exported to Canada, as the Bank of Canada restricted the Canadian money supply to prevent a major decline in the value of the Canadian dollar which would have triggered additional inflationary pressures.

Unfortunately, during the late 1970s and early 1980s the usefulness of M1 as a measure of monetary policy was steadily being eroded by institutional changes in the financial system. Part of the reason M1 was growing so slowly was because the *demand* for M1 was declining. In his 1982 annual report, the Governor of the Bank of Canada stated:

> Over the past two years the relationship between M1 and economic developments has become so distorted that M1 can no longer be taken at its face value; it requires so much interpretation that it is, for the time being at any rate, no longer suitable for use as a monetary target. The combination of inflation, high interest rates, computer-based technology and competition among financial institutions has resulted in innovations in financial services that have permitted Canadians both to reduce appreciably the average size of balances they hold for making payments and to hold more of those balances in interest-bearing forms that are not included in M1.[24]

[24]Bank of Canada, *Annual Report*, 1982, p. 27.

In short, Canadians were switching away from M1 and into other kinds of deposits, such as daily interest chequable deposits and chequable deposits at trust companies, none of which are included in M1 (note the much more rapid growth of the broader definition of money, M2, presented in the last column of Table 16-1). Canada's experiment with monetary targets was over because the centrepiece of this policy framework, M1, was no longer a meaningful quantity.

Now let us consider the primary objective of Canada's experiment with monetary targets, which was to reduce the inflation rate that had accelerated to double-digit levels in 1974 and 1975. Success on this front was long in coming. After a substantial but temporary dip in the inflation rate in 1976, inflation rose steadily in the second half of the 1970s to reach a new peak of 12.5 per cent in 1981. After five years of monetary targetting, inflation was actually 1.7 percentage points higher than it had been in 1975! We have already pointed out that supply-price shocks played their part in this, but monetary policy itself needs to be examined.

As early as 1980, Governor Bouey began to express doubts about the merits of *gradualism*:

> The battle against inflation is never easy. It has not been easy over the past five years during which we have been pursuing monetary targets, and I confess that I am disappointed by the results to date.... In retrospect, given some of the largely unpredictable economic and financial developments that occurred over that period, it might have been better if the moderation of excessively rapid growth since 1975 had been less gradual so that the moderating effect on inflation would have been greater.[25]

The Governor is not questioning the overall strategy of monetarism but rather the tactics of implementation. Perhaps a *cold shower* approach (in which the growth of M1 would have been immediately reduced to lower levels) would have had a greater impact on inflationary expectations and the rate of inflation than did gradualism. Another factor that worked against the downward revision of inflation expectations was the erratic behaviour of the growth of M1. Contrary to the Bank of Canada's stated goals in 1975, the growth of M1 actually became more variable after 1975 than before.

In summary, the Bank of Canada's experiment with explicit monetarist policies has not been a happy one. Inflation failed to respond to the gradually reduced rates of growth of M1 until the deep recession of 1982. Meanwhile, continuous changes in the financial system eroded the foundations of M1, which can no longer serve as an indicator of the impact that monetary policy has on the economy. Only for a short time did it appear that the stance of monetary policy could be measured by a single monetary aggregate. In his annual report of 1984, the Governor of the Bank of Canada recognized the complexity of evaluating monetary policy:

> One technical difficulty that arises in implementing monetary policy, as I have explained in previous Reports, is that there are no aggregate

---

[25]Remarks by G.K. Bouey to The Empire Club of Canada, Toronto, 13 November 1980, reprinted in *Bank of Canada Review*, November 1980, pp. 3-11.

measures or indicators of the rate of monetary expansion in Canada that are sufficiently reliable at present to be used as targets for policy, or that are uniquely helpful in the task of explaining the impact of monetary policy. However, in deciding monetary policy the Bank of Canada has always attached great importance to evidence in the economic and financial scene that goes beyond the performance of particular aggregates. In current circumstances it relies on its analysis of a broad range of financial and economic variables, including the trend of total spending in the economy and exchange rate developments, as well as the various monetary and credit aggregates, to come to judgements regarding monetary policy.[26]

An Assessment of Fiscal Policy: Some Preliminary Comments

The key indicator of fiscal policy is the size (and changes in the size) of the government deficit. In 1973 and 1974, the federal government had a budgetary *surplus* totalling $1.5 billion (see Table 16-2). Four years later, the federal government ran a deficit of over $10 billion, and in 1984 the federal deficit reached almost $30 billion. This string of unprecedented, large federal deficits over the 1975-84 period increased the federal debt level from approximately $21 billion in 1974 to $200 billion in 1985! Perhaps no other statistic has galvanized public opinion as much as the size of recent government deficits (and the matching increases in government debt). To most citizens, $20 billion–$30 billion deficits are considered to be an obvious manifestation of government mismanagement and a major cause of inflation or unemployment or both.

Do Large Government Deficits Cause Inflation?

From our previous analysis it is clear that persistent government deficits that are financed by printing dollar bills will lead to sustained inflation. On the other hand, if government deficits are financed by borrowing funds in the bond market, then sustained inflation need not occur. As demonstrated in Chapter 12, it is the continual expansion of the money supply that fuels, validates and sustains inflation. To argue that government deficits cause sustained inflation one must demonstrate that there is a close link between the size of the government deficit and the expansion of the money supply. While some government deficits are undoubtedly financed by printing dollar bills (for example, during wars), there is no reason to believe that *all* government deficits necessarily lead to monetary expansion. Nor is there any reason to believe that rapid monetary expansion occurs because of government deficits. For example, the record-high 14.5 per cent increase in the Canadian money supply in 1973 occurred while the federal government enjoyed a surplus budgetary position.

[26]Bank of Canada, *Annual Report*, 1984, p. 8.

TABLE 16-2 Federal Deficit

	Actual Deficit	Cyclical Component	Cyclically Adjusted Deficit	Inflation Component	Structural Deficit	% of GNP	
						Actual Deficit	Structural Deficit
1971	−0.1	−0.1	0.0	−0.4	+0.4	−0.2	+0.4
1972	−0.6	+0.1	−0.7	−0.5	−0.2	−0.5	−0.2
1973	+0.4	+1.0	−0.6	−1.2	+0.6	+0.3	+0.5
1974	+1.1	+1.3	−0.2	−1.3	+1.1	+0.8	+0.7
1975	−3.8	0.0	−3.8	−0.9	−2.9	−2.3	−1.8
1976	−3.4	+0.7	−4.1	−1.0	−3.1	−1.8	−1.6
1977	−7.3	−0.5	−6.8	−1.1	−5.7	−3.5	−2.7
1978	−10.6	−0.6	−10.0	−1.7	−8.3	−4.6	−3.6
1979	−9.1	−0.3	−8.8	−4.3	−4.5	−3.5	−1.7
1980	−10.4	−1.8	−8.6	−5.0	−3.6	−3.5	−1.2
1981	−7.4	−1.6	−5.8	−6.1	+0.3	−2.2	+0.1
1982	−18.9	−9.5	−9.4	−5.5	−3.9	−5.3	−1.1
1983	−24.1	−11.1	−13.0	−2.8	−10.2	−6.2	−2.6
1984	−29.6	−9.0	−20.6	−3.2	−17.4	−7.0	−4.1

Perhaps the easiest way to refute the proposition that inflation is caused by government deficits is to look at the Canadian record. From 1971 to 1974 the Canadian inflation rate jumped from 2.8 to 10.9 per cent. During these three years of rapidly escalating inflation, however, the federal government ran up a total budgetary *surplus* of almost $1 billion! It was not until 1975 that the federal government had a substantial *deficit* ($3.4 billion), two years *after* the emergence of double-digit inflation. Turning to the *dis*inflation of the 1980s, the Canadian inflation rate *fell* from 12.5 per cent in 1981 to 4.4 per cent in 1984 as the federal government deficit *increased* from $7 billion to $30 billion. Recent Canadian evidence clearly contradicts the hypothesis that large or growing government deficits cause inflation. Any empirical relationship appears to suggest that sustained double-digit inflation may lead to government deficits.

In fact there is a direct link between inflation and the size of the government deficit. Recall from Chapters 3 and 12 that the expected inflation rate will be reflected in nominal interest rates (the higher the expected inflation rate, the higher the nominal interest rate). Consequently, in inflationary periods the government will have to pay higher interest charges on the public debt and the size of the government deficit will increase accordingly.[27] In a non-inflationary world the government would only have to pay the real interest rate (perhaps 4-5

---

[27]Except for interest charges on the public debt, inflation should have little effect on the (real) size of the government deficit. Both government spending (on goods, services, and transfer payments) and government revenues (income and sales taxes) should be rising at roughly the inflation rate, assuming no new government programs or tax rate changes. Thus if the government budget is initially in balance, then inflation should not throw the government budget out of balance as both sides of the budget should be increasing at roughly the same rate. Interest charges on the public debt (which increase in a disproportionate manner with increases in the inflation rate) are the major exception to the argument that inflation has a neutral effect on the size of the real government deficit.

per cent) to service the public debt, and thus the government deficit would be considerably less in the absence of inflation. As discussed below, the size of the government deficit should be adjusted for the effects of *inflation*.

Do Large Government Deficits Cause Unemployment?

As discussed in earlier chapters, Keynesian economic theory predicts that an *increase* in the size of the government deficit (either from an increase in government spending or a decrease in taxes) will have a positive (multiplier) effect on output and employment levels, which in turn will lead to a *decrease* in the unemployment rate. Monetarists do not deny that an increase in the size of the government deficit will have a *short-run* effect on the unemployment rate, but argue that Keynesian policy will have no *long-run* effects on the unemployment rate—the natural rate of unemployment is independent of fiscal policy. A casual look at data from the 1980s, however, suggests that very large government deficits are associated with high unemployment rates. When the Canadian unemployment rate increased from 7.5 per cent in 1981 to 11.0 per cent in 1982, the federal government deficit increased from $7 billion to almost $20 billion.

There is, in fact, a *positive* relationship between the size of the deficit and the unemployment rate, but the lines of causality run from high unemployment to large government deficits. When the economy falls into a recession (or a cyclical downturn), the government budgetary position will automatically be pushed towards a deficit position as tax revenues decline and government transfer payments for unemployment insurance and welfare rise. Given various automatic stabilizers within the fiscal system, the government deficit will *automatically* rise when the economy is in recession and fall when the economy is in a buoyant state. The existence of such automatic fiscal stabilizers (such as income tax and unemployment insurance) limit the size of the short-run multiplier effects associated with negative (positive) demand shocks by automatically moving the government budget towards a deficit (surplus) position.[28]

Given the presence of such automatic stabilizers, it is very important to distinguish between (1) changes in the deficit which are *caused* by a change in aggregate demand, and (2) changes in the deficit which *cause* a change in aggregate demand. As discussed below, to correct for such *automatic cyclical* movements in the government budgetary position, the Department of Finance *cyclically adjusts* government expenditures and revenues data to correct for cyclical variation.

Measuring the Government Deficit

The discussion in the previous section suggests that both inflation and unemployment will lead to a larger government deficit. To assess the current fiscal position, it is useful to measure what the size of the government deficit would be if there

---

[28]As discussed in Chapter 6, if the government deliberately balanced its budget each year, then the multiplier effects would be larger and the economy would be much less stable.

were no cyclical unemployment nor any inflation. How large would the current government deficit be if the economy were at the *natural* rate of unemployment with a *zero* inflation rate? Alternatively, how much of the current deficit is simply the result of *cyclical* unemployment and inflation? In April 1983 the federal government released a special study entitled "The Federal Deficit in Perspective," which provides estimates of the size of the cyclical unemployment and inflation components of the federal deficit.

The cyclical component of the deficit provides an estimate of lost tax revenues and additional government expenses that are directly attributable to the economy experiencing *above-average* unemployment rates. The second column of Table 16-2 presents the Department of Finance's *estimate* for the cyclical component of the federal deficit. A *positive* value (such as in years 1972-76) indicates that the economy experienced *below-average* unemployment rates, and thus the actual deficit was lower than it would have been under average unemployment conditions (because of extra tax revenues and lower unemployment insurance payments associated with a below-average unemployment rate). By subtracting this cyclical adjustment factor (column 2 of Table 16-2) from the actual deficit, the effects of the business cycle are removed and we obtain the *cyclically adjusted* government deficit (column 3 of Table 16-2). "The cyclically-adjusted balance...represents the balance that would prevail under the existing revenue and expenditure structure if the economy were operating in any given year at an average level of activity."[29] Clearly a substantial portion (approximately $10 billion) of the large government deficits in 1982-84 can be attributed simply to the depressed state of the Canadian economy. If the large amount of cyclical unemployment in the early 1980s could have been eliminated, the government deficit would have been substantially lower.

Since nominal interest rates reflect the expected inflation rate, interest charges on the public debt will increase as inflation increases (even if the existing public debt remains constant). To correct for this inflation distortion of the government deficit, the Department of Finance computes an inflation adjustment (see column 4 of Table 16-2) by multiplying net government liabilities by the annual inflation rate. The rationale for adjusting the government deficit for the effects of inflation can best be explained by considering the key characteristic of the *inflation-adjusted* deficit. If the government chooses to balance the inflation-adjusted budget, the national debt will remain *constant* in real (purchasing power) terms, regardless of the inflation rate. On the other hand, balancing the *actual* government budget that is not adjusted for the effects of inflation will result in a *decline* in the real debt at a rate equal to the prevailing inflation rate. Since a neutral fiscal policy maintains a constant real national debt, the inflation-adjusted government deficit provides an appropriate indicator of the government's fiscal position.

Government deficits will arise as a natural by-product of inflation for all economies that choose to maintain a constant real public debt. If society chooses to pass on to the next generation the same real public debt that was inherited from

[29]Department of Finance, *The Federal Deficit in Perspective* (Ottawa, April 1983), p. 57.

the previous generation, in an inflationary world the nominal value of the public debt must rise by an amount equal to the inflation rate. A *balanced-budget* policy maintains the size of the public debt in *nominal* terms. In an inflationary world, a policy of balancing the actual government budget is effectively a policy that retires part of the existing real public debt. Eventually inflation will erode away the constant nominal value of the public debt (under balanced-budget conditions) to a real value that approaches zero. The inflation correction of the government deficit approximates the decline in value of the real public debt which is attributable to inflation.

If we subtract the *inflation adjustment* from the *cyclically adjusted* government deficit we obtain the so-called *structural* government deficit (column 5 of Table 16-2). The structural deficit describes the current budgetary position of the government after correcting for the effects of cyclical unemployment and inflation. In theoretical terms, the structural deficit provides an estimate of the budgetary position for the government, assuming a *constant real* public debt and *no cyclical unemployment* (that is, assuming the economy to be hypothetically at the *natural* rate of unemployment and output). In general, a structural deficit signifies that the government has adopted a stimulative fiscal policy that would increase the real public debt even if the economy were at its long-run equilibrium output and employment level.[30]

A Keynesian would be willing to run structural deficits during recessionary years (to speed the economy back to its long-run equilibrium position), offset by structural surpluses in boom years (see Chapter 14). On the other hand, a monetarist would advocate a *zero* structural deficit each year; that is, no discretionary fiscal policies to help the economy get back to its equilibrium position. Given the automatic fiscal stabilizers that exist, a monetarist policy would not eliminate the actual government deficit each year, as the *cyclical* component of the deficit would still be operative.

After correcting the actual government deficit for its cyclical unemployment and inflation components, a somewhat different picture emerges. For example, the $7.4 billion federal deficit in 1981 can be entirely explained in terms of cyclical unemployment and inflation. Unlike a rose, a deficit is not always a deficit. With respect to the $20 billion-$30 billion deficits of the 1982-84 period, more than half of these record-high deficits are accounted for by the severe recession and the continuing presence of inflation. Finally, since it is easy to be shocked by *nominal* dollar figures (for example during the 1970-84 period, nominal GNP increased by 591 per cent!), we have scaled both the actual and structural deficits

[30]As Bruce and Purvis point out:

> Changes in the structural deficit can come about from autonomous changes other than discretionary policy changes. For example, changes in the interest rates or the world price of oil would affect the structural deficit in Canada without any government policy changes. Nevertheless, changes in the structural deficit are a useful indicator of the discretionary fiscal stance.

See Neil Bruce and Douglas D. Purvis, "Consequences of Government Budget Deficits," in John Sargent, Research Co-ordinator, *Fiscal and Monetary Policy*, Royal Commission on the Economic Union and Development Prospects for Canada, Volume 21 (Toronto: University of Toronto Press, 1985).

by nominal GNP (columns 6 and 7 of Table 16-2). In relative terms, the deficit, no matter how it is measured, is substantially larger in 1984. The actual 1984 deficit reached $29.6 billion, while the structural deficit exceeded 4 per cent of nominal GNP.

The Long-run Implications of Government Deficits

Most of the concern about government deficits arises from the cumulative effects that persistent deficits have on the size of the public debt. Each year the nominal public debt rises by the size of the actual government deficit. In the 1982-84 period, the record-high government deficits translated into an increase in the federal debt of over $70 billion, bringing the federal debt to more than $200 billion in 1985. As journalists and editorial writers are fond of reminding us, this translates into a substantial debt for each Canadian citizen (approximately $8,000 per capita in 1985). Is this escalating public debt a major economic problem in Canada?

Before discussing the *long-term* implications of a rising government debt, several popular misconceptions about the public debt should be addressed. First, by historical standards the *relative* size of the federal debt in the 1980s is not excessively large. As displayed in Chart 16-5, while the ratio of federal debt to GNP reached 40 per cent in 1984 (up dramatically from under 15 per cent in 1974), the 1984 ratio is certainly not a record. The federal debt to GNP ratio was roughly at a similar level during the 1957-63 period, and exceeded this level prior to 1953. Going back to World War II, the debt to GNP ratio actually exceeded 100 per cent and was well above 50 per cent during the Great Depression. At various times, Canada has had a relatively larger federal debt (compared to GNP) than existed in the 1980s.

Second, while the federal debt is substantial, the government also *owns* many assets (highways, airports, countless government buildings and real estate holdings, airplanes, trains, trucks and other capital equipment). A complete government balance sheet in which the government's assets were carefully evaluated would undoubtedly reveal a positive net asset to debt position for the government. It is not obvious why one generation should feel compelled to reduce the size of the public debt if public assets are going to benefit future generations. Unfortunately, the large increases in the public debt during the 1980s were not matched by increases in capital assets that will benefit future generations.

Finally, analogies between *government* deficits/debt and *private sector* deficits/debt can be misleading. While households or firms which continually borrow to finance current (not capital) expenditures in excess of revenues will eventually go bankrupt, the federal government will never go bankrupt. Unlike firms and households, the government can service its debt by taxing the private sector (which would involve a transfer of money from one set of Canadians—taxpayers— to another set of Canadians—government bond holders) or by printing money (an inflation tax). The economic consequences of a mounting government debt are not the ultimate bankruptcy of the country but rather the potential negative effects that this growing government debt may have on the performance of the economy.

There are two potential sets of long-run costs associated with persistent govern-

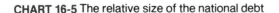

CHART 16-5 The relative size of the national debt

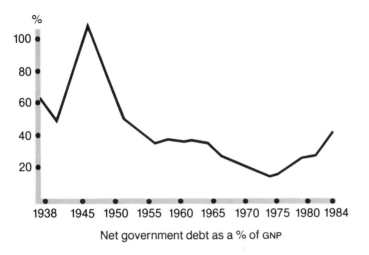

Net government debt as a % of GNP

ment deficits. First, a rising *real* government debt may have a negative effect on future economic growth. As discussed in Chapter 18, an increase in wealth will lead to an increase in consumption expenditures and a reduction in savings. Assuming that government debt (bonds) is perceived as wealth by individuals,[31] consumption will increase at the expense of saving. With less saving available to society, the nation's capital stock will grow at a slower rate, which will lead to less economic growth in the future.[32] To the extent that rising government debt lowers aggregate saving, crowds out private sector borrowing, and reduces capital formation, economic growth will be diminished and future generations will bear the cost of current government deficits. For an open economy, such as Canada, large government deficits will also lead to a trade account deficit and an increasing level of foreign indebtedness.

In addition, persistent government deficits and rising public debt levels may lead to less than optimal future policy decisions by the government. For example, large structural deficits push up real interest rates which may pressure the Bank of Canada to monetize the rising debt level, a policy response that would eventually lead to greater inflation.[33] Alternatively, if the government raises tax rates to reduce the size of the deficit, inefficiencies and tax distortions will arise (for

[31]Robert Barro, a leading exponent of the new classical economics, has argued that individuals will *not* consider government debt as part of their wealth. Associated with each government bond is a matching *future* tax liability (when the government must pay off the bond holder by raising tax revenues). This future tax liability cancels the asset value of the government bond, leaving the government bond holder with *no* increase in *net* wealth.

[32]Alternatively, if individuals desire to hold a fixed amount of wealth (relative to income), increasing government debt will *crowd out* private sector debt that would have been used to finance private sector capital formation.

[33]The threat of the government monetizing the public debt may lead to higher inflation expectations and consequently higher interest rates.

example, rising income tax rates encourage nonmarket and leisure activities). Finally, a large public debt places a straight-jacket on stabilization policy as little room is left for the government to introduce discretionary counter-cyclical expenditure increases or tax reductions. As Bruce and Purvis point out, "there is little doubt that the large prevailing federal deficit and outstanding stock of debt severely reduced the 'politically acceptable' scope for fiscal expansion in the April 1983 budget to combat the 'great recession.' "[34] Indeed, reducing the size of the federal government deficit became the number one priority of the newly elected Conservative government (in 1984), despite the existence of double-digit unemployment rates.

Fiscal Policy During the 1975-84 Period

During the late 1970s the government conducted a somewhat expansionary fiscal policy. While federal government spending (including transfer payments) rose by 48.7 per cent from 1975 to 1979 (compared to an increase in nominal GNP of 58.2 per cent), federal government revenues rose by only 37.3 per cent during this period. Even though government spending was being restrained during the late 1970s, government revenues were growing at an even slower pace. Much of this slow growth in government revenues during the late 1970s can be explained by a series of discretionary tax reductions. Perhaps the most important tax reductions during this period were the following measures:

1. An increase in the minimum *personal income tax credit* in October 1977 (from $200 to $300 per year).
2. The introduction of the *child tax credit* in August 1978.
3. A reduction of the *federal manufacturers' sales tax rate* from 12 to 9 per cent on all products with the exception of tobacco and alcohol in November 1978.
4. A federal government funded reduction in *provincial retail sales taxes* of 3 per cent for six months in 1978.

The net effect of these tax cuts was a substantial increase in the size of the federal government deficit. As shown in Table 16-2, the actual federal deficit increased from $3.4 billion in 1976 to $10.6 billion in 1978 (the year in which most of the tax cuts were implemented). In *cyclically adjusted* and *structural* terms, the federal government deficit increased by over $5 billion during this two-year period (perhaps in anticipation of the 1979 election). While the Bank of Canada preached a monetarist sermon, between 1976 and 1978 the Liberal government practised a stimulative Keynesian fiscal policy.

With the quick defeat of Prime Minister Clark's minority Conservative government and the re-election of a majority Liberal government in 1980, fiscal policy tightened up (in an attempt to get the deficit under control) and the government reverted to a more monetarist fiscal stance. Consider, for example, the October 1980 budget of the newly elected Liberal government (which introduced the controversial National Energy Program). When this budget was introduced in

[34]Bruce and Purvis, supra footnote 30, p. 29.

Parliament, the growth rate in real output was *negative* (–1.7 per cent for the first six months of 1980), interest rates were at record-high levels, and the United States was heading into a recession. Rather than adopting an expansionary Keynesian fiscal policy to offset the predicted decline in export sales to the U.S., the Canadian government tightened its monetary and fiscal screws. The 1980 federal budget of Finance Minister MacEachen further restrained government expenditures and offered no new tax cuts, in an attempt to reduce the size of the federal government deficit and lower the inflation rate:

> The long-heralded recession in the United States has become a reality with a sharp drop in real output.... In this environment the tasks of economic policy obviously present a great challenge. Within industrial countries, we have all learned that we cannot achieve full employment, stable prices and other economic goals simply by influencing the demands for goods and services by cutting taxes or by increasing government expenditure.... The problems are obviously deeper and more complex... there are no quick solutions, so we will need to be patient and plan in a longer-term framework.... One of my main tasks as Minister of Finance will be to reduce the very large deficits in the government's accounts to more manageable proportions.... Otherwise we will run the risk of a new outbreak of inflationary pressure.... In order to achieve the essential reduction in the deficit, great restraint over expenditures has, therefore, been required... the Bank of Canada will have my continuing support in holding down the rate of monetary expansion... we will not accommodate double-digit rates of inflation.[35]

As is obvious from the above quotation, in 1980 the Canadian government rejected short-run ("quick solution") Keynesian policies in favour of a monetarist "long-term framework" to deal with the "deep-seated" problems of chronic inflation and large government deficits. By its own medium-term budget projections, the government was prepared to adopt restrictive policies that would drive the unemployment rate to 8.7 per cent in 1981 and 8.4 per cent in 1982 in the hope that inflation could be lowered to 8.8 per cent in 1983. With a restrictive fiscal policy firmly in place during the early 1980s, the *structural* deficit declined in 1980 and 1981, reaching a small surplus position in 1981 (see Table 16-2). However, the combined fiscal and monetary restraint of the 1980-81 period was a major factor in producing the severe recession in 1982, with an unemployment rate of 11 per cent (not 8.4 per cent as predicted in the 1980 budget) and an escalating actual federal deficit.

With the Canadian economy slowly beginning to emerge from the longest and deepest recession since the 1930s, Finance Minister Lalonde's April 1983 budget attempted to generate a limited amount of Keynesian *short-run* fiscal stimulus (in 1983-84), while at the same time reducing the structural deficit in the *medium term*:

> My dominant concern in preparing this budget has been to help the more than one and a half million Canadians who want to work but cannot find

[35]*Hansard*, 28 October 1980, pp. 4184-85.

jobs. Economic recovery is under way in Canada.... Yet the pace, scope, stability and duration of the recovery remain highly uncertain. Employment has started to grow again, but unemployment remains very high and will decline only gradually....

This recovery budget, therefore, has two central and inseparable goals. The first is to make sure that recent stirrings of growth pervade the whole economy as quickly as possible. The second is to make the recovery a durable one by beginning immediately to create the conditions required for sustained growth and development during the rest of the eighties. Underlying these goals is the government's determination to ensure that Canadians are provided with the jobs they need.... The pursuit of these twin goals calls for actions that take hold immediately but that are also geared to the medium term. The first goal demands additional stimulus this year. But the second goal would be unattainable without decisive action now to reduce the deficit in future years. Expenditure restraint will therefore continue, and measures will be introduced to raise more revenue as the recovery buoys up income and employment.

Strong, lasting recovery and the significant reduction of unemployment we need will come primarily through the private sector: the economy's main engine of growth. I shall accordingly introduce measures to strengthen the financial position of Canadian businesses, farmers and fishermen.... I have concluded that the recovery must be given an additional boost in its early stages. Federal capital projects planned for later in this decade will therefore be speeded up.... The direct impact of all the measures I have announced tonight will be to increase the deficit by $1.9 billion in the current fiscal year and by $650 million next year. In the following fiscal years, as the economy improves, these measures will reduce the deficit by $1.8 billion and $2.6 billion, respectively.[36]

By providing modest tax reductions and implementing a (four-year) $4.6 billion "Special Recovery Program" consisting of "speeded up" public sector capital projects and "Special Recovery Incentives" for private sector investment (such as a more generous investment tax credit), Finance Minister Lalonde hoped to "boost" aggregate demand in 1983-84. In the following years, this additional fiscal stimulus would be gradually withdrawn through substantial increases in personal income taxes, a one percentage point increase in the general federal sales tax rate effective October 1984 (euphemistically referred to as a "Special Recovery Tax"), and the phasing out of the "Special Recovery Capital Projects" expenditure program. While a Keynesian might quibble about the amount of fiscal stimulus or with the choice of fiscal instruments, the philosophical foundation of the April 1983 budget was clearly Keynesian.[37] The actual federal deficit would increase to

[36]*Hansard*, 19 April 1983, pp. 24658-70.

[37]The cynic might, again, argue that the timing of the government's fiscal actions had more to do with the election cycle than the business cycle.

$28.2 billion during the initial year of the budget, but was then projected to decline steadily in the next three years as the recovery gathered strength (to a $17.2 billion projected deficit in fiscal 1986-87).

From a macroeconomic perspective, the February 1984 federal budget was a non-event:

> Unlike last year, there are few major changes in the current [fiscal] plan. This reflects the fact that economic developments since the April 1983 budget have been largely as anticipated in early 1983, and as a result there is at the present time no need for large adjustments to the planning framework in 1984.[38]

Despite the fact that the January 1984 (seasonally adjusted) unemployment rate stood at 11.2 per cent (and was projected by the government to average 10.9 per cent for the year 1984), only $150 million was added to job creation programs (targetted on youth unemployment). All the future tax increases included in the previous April 1983 budget were allowed to take effect, and the federal deficit was expected to be $25 billion for the 1984-85 fiscal year.

With the election of a Conservative government in September 1984, the fiscal game plan again changed. Facing much larger deficits than projected in previous budgets, the government made reducing the size of the deficit its number one priority:

> The growing public debt and the prospect of a rising trend in the ratio of debt to national output pose a serious obstacle to the prospects for economic renewal and sustained non-inflationary growth over the remainder of the decade. . . . If the past pattern of large federal deficits and growing debt were allowed to continue, upward pressure would be maintained on interest rates, the government's control over fiscal policy would be jeopardized, private sector investment would be reduced and ultimately growth and employment prospects for the economy would be seriously endangered. . . . This budget represents a major step towards controlling the growth of the federal public debt. . . . By the end of the decade, the measures introduced in this budget together with the actions taken last November will directly reduce the deficit by about $20 billion and the stock of debt by about $75 billion from what it would otherwise have been.[39]

In its first year in office, the Conservative government reduced total government expenditures by $4 billion (to $99.6 billion), offered the business community various investment incentives and implemented an assortment of tax increases (most of which did not take full effect until 1986). With respect to personal income taxation, inflation indexation was limited to inflation in excess of 3 per cent (see Chapter 3), the federal tax reduction was eliminated, and a surtax on incomes in excess of $40,000 was introduced. In addition, the federal sales tax was again increased, the sales tax base was broadened (to include, among other

[38]Department of Finance, *The Fiscal Plan* (Ottawa, February 15, 1984), p. 1.
[39]Department of Finance, *The Fiscal Plan* (Ottawa, May 1985), pp. 1-3.

things, candy, soft drinks, and health products) and the taxes on gasoline, alcohol and tobacco were also raised. Income and sales tax increases combined to produce a $0.5 billion tax increase for individuals in fiscal 1985-86 and a $3.0 billion tax increase in fiscal 1986-87. On the other side of the ledger, a $500,000 lifetime capital gains tax exemption was granted, and the petroleum and natural gas revenue tax was phased out (resulting in a $1.5 billion loss in revenues in fiscal 1986-87).

The *net* result of these various fiscal actions was a projected $4.4 billion reduction in the federal deficit in fiscal 1985-86 and a $12.7 billion reduction in the deficit in fiscal 1986-87. Despite an 11 per cent unemployment rate, the Conservative government deliberately restrained its own spending in an attempt to get the deficit and federal debt under control, while offering Canadians various incentives "to invest in small and large businesses." Based on this new budget, the Department of Finance projected that the unemployment rate would decline to 10.3 per cent by the end of 1986, with a real growth rate of 2.4 per cent in 1986 (compared with 4.7 per cent in 1984).[40]

A Summary of the 1975-84 Period

As discussed above, the late 1970s were generally characterized by high inflation, stable unemployment and moderate economic growth. The major nongovernmental shocks to the Canadian economy during this period were an export demand shock in 1976-78 and persistent supply-price shocks during the 1977-81 period. Government policy during this period was generally expansionary. Although the Bank of Canada implemented a *gradualist* monetarist policy in 1975, the real money supply *increased* by 2.5 per cent during the 1975-79 period. In addition, considerable *fiscal* stimulus was injected into the economy during the 1977-78 period. Given an expansionary fiscal policy, export growth, and at minimum a neutral monetary policy, the Canadian unemployment rate stabilized at 7.5 per cent in 1979 and 1980. Even though the government's use of temporary wage and price controls during the 1975-78 period reduced the rate of wage inflation, the *positive* demand and supply-price shocks (including the government's decision to exempt oil price increases from the price controls program) kept the rate of price inflation high (reaching 12.5 per cent in 1981).

In 1982 economic conditions abruptly changed. Real output in Canada fell by 4.4 per cent and the unemployment rate jumped to 11 per cent. A number of factors caused this deepest recession since the 1930s. First, a major recession developed throughout the world in 1981 and Canadian exports fell by 1.6 per cent in 1982. However, this rather modest decline in exports cannot account for why the Canadian recession was, in the words of the Department of Finance, "particularly severe in terms of both its depth and its duration."[41] As discussed above, in late 1980 both Canadian monetary and fiscal policy turned very restrictive. The

---

[40]*Ibid*, p. 23.

[41]Department of Finance, *Canada's Economic Prospects, 1985-1990: The Challenge of Economic Renewal* (Ottawa, May 1985), p. 6.

federal government began taking steps to reduce the size of the government deficit, and the growth rate of the money supply was below the target ranges (in large part due to the Bank of Canada's attempts to prevent the Canadian exchange rate from rapidly declining in the face of record-high U.S. interest rates). While the nominal money supply increased by 3.9 and 0.6 per cent in 1981 and 1982, in real terms the money supply *declined* by almost 20 per cent over this two-year period. In short, the policy actions of the government during the 1981-82 period were exerting a severe negative demand shock on the Canadian economy, mostly through a reduction in the real money supply.

The cumulative effects of the government's restrictive monetary and fiscal policies, the decline in exports, and the aftermath of the supply-price shocks in the 1970s was a "particularly severe" recession. With unemployment rates of 11-12 per cent for three successive years (1982-84), inflation plunged to 5.8 per cent in 1983 and 4.4 per cent in 1984. There is nothing like an old-fashioned recession to purge inflation and high inflationary expectations out of the economic system!

The 1983-84 Canadian recovery was led by a strong surge in exports (totalling 36.8 per cent over two years) as the U.S. economy resumed very rapid economic growth. The more relaxed fiscal and monetary policies during 1983-84 perhaps played a minor role in the Canadian recovery. Holding back the recovery was a decline in business investment expenditures, which were down 8.6 per cent in real terms over the 1983-84 period. As the Department of Finance noted,

> The exceptional weakness of investment in Canada, both during the recession and over 1983 and 1984, was due to a number of factors. Principal among these were: large amounts of excess capacity, the weak financial position of Canadian corporations, high levels of real interest rates, the fall-off in energy investment, and weak primary product prices in many resource sectors.[42]

The 1983 and 1985 federal budgets offered a variety of measures directly aimed at revitalizing investment in the private sector. Only time will tell whether these medium-term measures were successful.

In conclusion, it can be argued that the Bank of Canada and the federal government's policies during 1975-84 were monetarist in name only. While the expansion of the nominal money supply was controlled to a greater extent than in the early 1970s, the growth rate of the money supply was clearly not steady nor constant (for example, M1 increased by 0.7 per cent, 10.2 per cent, and 2.3 per cent during 1982, 1983, and 1984 respectively). More important, on numerous occasions the government undertook *discretionary* fiscal and monetary policies to influence the course of the economy (for example, the expansionary fiscal policies of 1977-78 and 1983-84, and a more restrictive monetary policy in 1980-82 in an attempt to stabilize the foreign exchange rate). On the other hand, it would be difficult to describe the discretionary use of monetary and fiscal policy during this period as consistently Keynesian. In particular, the government's macroeconomic strategy in the 1980s has been largely directed towards the elimination of inflation and the reduction of the government deficit, targets which are more in keeping with a monetarist approach than a Keynesian approach.

[42]*Ibid.*, p. 9.

Inflation Expectations and the *New* Classical Macroeconomics

17

To see a World in a Grain of Sand
And a Heaven in a Wild Flower,
Hold Infinity in the palm of your hand
And Eternity in an hour.

William Blake

Throughout the last eight chapters, inflation expectations have played a prominent role in our macroeconomic analysis. As discussed in Chapter 9, nominal wage changes will reflect current labour market conditions as well as the expected inflation rate. Given that investment decisions depend on the *real* interest rate (see Chapters 12 and 20), an important link exists between investment expenditures, nominal interest rates, and the expected inflation rate. An increase in the expected inflation rate will shift both the price-expectations-augmented Phillips (*PEP*) curve and the *IS* curve upwards, with the vertical shift in both curves corresponding to the exact increase in inflation expectations.

Although the expected inflation rate is a key variable within our *IS-LM-PEP* model, we have not yet provided an explanation of the process by which individuals forecast future inflation rates. Our macroeconomic model lacks a relationship (or equation) to describe the formation of inflation expectations. In Chapters 10, 11, 14 and 15 we simply assumed inflation expectations would remain constant, irrespective of various shocks or disturbances that might impinge on the economic system. In Chapters 12 and 13 we assumed inflation expectations would reflect the *validated* inflation rate, but the precise manner in which inflation expectations change was not spelled out. It was simply assumed that at some point, after the actual inflation rate reached the new rate of monetary expansion, people would adjust their inflation expectations (in a *single-step* adjustment) to reflect this new validated inflation rate.

The major objectives of this chapter are (1) to analyze the process by which individuals form their expectations of the future inflation rate, and (2) to examine the macroeconomic implications of different assumptions concerning the formation of inflation expectations. Clearly, inflation expectations cannot be regarded as constant or exogenously determined in a complete macroeconomic model. Expectations about future inflation rates are not independent of recent inflation experience, nor are they independent of government policy. While all macroeconomists would agree that inflation expectations must be considered as *endogenous* within a macroeconomic model, there is considerable controversy over exactly how individuals form their expectations of the future inflation rate. It is not an issue that can be easily settled by examining the facts, because inflation expectations, by their very nature, are highly subjective and very difficult to quantify. Lacking reliable data about the expected inflation rate, much of the macroeconomic debate about inflation expectations has been conducted on a highly abstract, theoretical level.

Two different inflation expectations models have been hypothesized by macroeconomists: the *adaptive* expectations model and the *rational* expectations model (both of which are discussed in this chapter). This adaptive inflation expectations model was first introduced into macroeconomics by Cagan in the mid-1950s and became part of the monetarists' arsenal in their early attack on Keynesian economics (under adaptive inflation expectations, prices become more flexible thus reducing the length of the short run). While the assumption of rational expectations can be traced back to a 1961 paper by Muth, it did not infiltrate macroeconomics until the 1970s. Once the striking macroeconomic implications of assuming rational inflation expectations were fully appreciated, however, a whole new school of macroeconomic thought emerged, the *new* classical macroeconomics. The latter part of this chapter is devoted to an analysis of the key assumptions (including rational expectations) of the new classical macroeconomics and an evaluation of its striking policy conclusion that *anticipated* government policy will have absolutely *no* effect on output or employment levels (the *policy ineffectiveness proposition*).

Adaptive Inflation Expectations

Under an **adaptive expectations** (or forecasting) model, individuals are assumed to adjust their expectations by taking into account past forecasting errors. Adaptive models typically assume that individuals revise their forecasts of the future by incorporating a portion of their past forecasting error. In other words, individuals learn (or adapt) as a result of past mistakes.

To illustrate the essential characteristics of an adaptive model, consider the problem of forecasting tomorrow's weather temperature. Suppose that we predict tomorrow's (Monday's) temperature to be 30°, but the actual temperature turns out to be 32°. The forecast error for Monday is 2°. In order to improve our temperature forecast for Tuesday, suppose that we revise our Monday forecast by one-half of Monday's forecast error: we adaptively forecast Tuesday's temperature to be 31° (30 + 0.5 × 2). Now if the actual temperature on Tuesday is also 32°, our forecast error for Tuesday is 1° and our adaptive forecasting model would lead us to predict Wednesday's temperature to be 31.5°; (31 + 0.5 × 1). As long as the actual temperature remains *constant* at 32°, our adaptive forecasting model would lead us to predict Thursday's temperature to be 31.75° and Friday's temperature to be 31.875°. Future temperature forecasts converge fairly rapidly on the constant value of 32°[1] with the speed of convergence depending on the weight applied to the past forecast error (0.5 in the above illustration).

---

[1]Even if our Monday forecast had been very bad, say 20° rather than 30°, our adaptive forecasting model would still produce a Friday forecast of 31.25°, quite close to the actual value of 32°.

Applying a similar adaptive forecasting model to inflation expectations, suppose that the expected inflation rate today $\dot{P}^e_t$ is forecast by adapting yesterday's expected inflation rate forecast $\dot{P}^e_{t-1}$ by a fraction δ of yesterday's inflation forecast error $\dot{P}^a_{t-1} - \dot{P}^e_{t-1}$, where $\dot{P}^a_{t-1}$ is yesterday's actual inflation rate.

(1) $\qquad \dot{P}^e_t = \dot{P}^e_{t-1} + \delta(\dot{P}^a_{t-1} - \dot{P}^e_{t-1})$

$\qquad\qquad = \delta\dot{P}^a_{t-1} + (1-\delta)\dot{P}^e_{t-1}$

Similarly, we can express inflation expectations for *previous* forecast periods in a comparable manner:

(2) $\qquad \dot{P}^e_{t-1} = \dot{P}^e_{t-2} + \delta(\dot{P}^a_{t-2} - \dot{P}^e_{t-2})$

$\qquad\qquad = \delta\dot{P}^a_{t-2} + (1-\delta)\dot{P}^e_{t-2}$

(3) $\qquad \dot{P}^e_{t-2} = \dot{P}^e_{t\ 3} + \delta(\dot{P}^a_{t-3} - \dot{P}^e_{t-3})$

$\qquad\qquad = \delta\dot{P}^a_{t-3} + (1-\delta)\dot{P}^e_{t-3}$

Now if we sequentially substitute equations (2) and (3) into equation (1), we can express *today's expected* inflation rate $\dot{P}^e_t$ in terms of *past actual* inflation rates $\dot{P}^a_{t-1}$, $\dot{P}^a_{t-2}$, and $\dot{P}^a_{t-3}$:

(17-1) $\qquad \dot{P}^e_t = \delta\dot{P}^a_{t-1} + (1-\delta)[\delta\dot{P}^a_{t-2} + (1-\delta)\dot{P}^e_{t-2}]$

$\qquad\qquad = \delta\dot{P}^a_{t-1} + \delta(1-\delta)\dot{P}^a_{t-2} + (1-\delta)^2[\delta\dot{P}^a_{t-3} + (1-\delta)\dot{P}^e_{t-3}]$

By a similar set of substitutions for $\dot{P}^e_{t-3}$, $\dot{P}^e_{t-4}$, and so on, all past $\dot{P}^e$ variables can be replaced by past $\dot{P}^a$ variables. Under an adaptive inflation expectations formation model, *future inflation expectations are simply a weighted average of past actual inflation rates*.[2] By adapting future forecasts on the basis of past forecast errors, individuals implicitly form their inflation expectations solely on the basis of past actual inflation rates. An adaptive inflation expectations model assumes that future inflation rates are predictable from past, or historical, inflation rates.

An Anti-Inflationary, Restrictive Monetary Policy Under the Assumption of Adaptive Inflation Expectations

To illustrate the macroeconomic implications of *adaptive* inflation expectations, we return to our *IS-LM-PEP* analysis of a restrictive monetary policy (see Chapter 13). Again we assume that a hypothetical economy is in long-run equilibrium at Y^* with a fully anticipated and validated inflation rate of 10 per cent (position A in Chart 17-1). Now suppose that the government decides to lower this 10 per cent inflation rate to 5 per cent and therefore reduces the rate of *nominal* monetary

---

[2]Since the weight δ attached to the past forecast error is assumed to be less than one, the weights attached to past inflation rates geometrically decline over time. The larger the weight δ attached to the forecast error, the less important distant past values are in the geometrically declining weighted moving average. If the weight on the forecast error is set at unity, then $\dot{P}^e_t$ is simply equal to $\dot{P}^a_{t-1}$. (In terms of our temperature illustration, today's forecast temperature is yesterday's thermometer reading.)

CHART 17-1 Effects of an anti-inflationary, restrictive monetary policy under adaptive inflation expectations

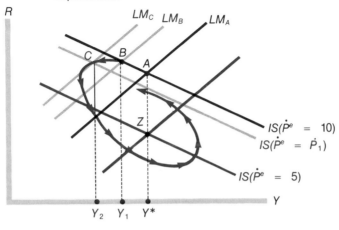

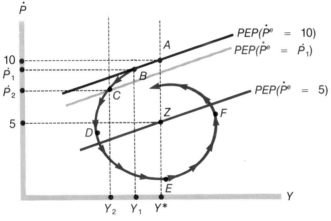

expansion to 5 per cent. What short-run adjustment path will our hypothetical economy follow if inflation expectations are formed in an adaptive manner?

Before we can analyze this short-run adjustment path, we must first identify the precise form of the adaptive inflation expectations model. To keep our analysis as simple as possible, we assume that the error correction coefficient in the adaptive expectations model (δ, in equation 17-1) is *unity*. With a weight of unity applied to the past forecast error, the expected inflation rate in the *current* period is simply the actual inflation rate in the *previous* period. Thus if the actual inflation rate increases by 1 per cent in period 1, then in period 2 the expected inflation rate will increase by 1 per cent and both the *IS* and *PEP* curves will shift upwards by 1 per cent. Our simplifying assumption that δ is unity implies a rapid adjustment of inflation expectations.

In the initial period when the growth rate of the nominal money supply is reduced from 10 to 5 per cent, individuals will still base their inflation expectations on last period's inflation rate of 10 per cent. Consequently, inflation expectations will remain at 10 per cent for this initial period and the original (solid black line) *IS* and *PEP* curves corresponding to 10 per cent inflation expectations will remain in force. However, with the new 5 per cent growth rate of the *nominal* money supply and an initial inflation rate of 10 per cent, the *real* money supply will decline (by 5 per cent) causing a substantial upward shift in the *LM* curve (to LM_B in Chart 17-1). During period 1 of the short-run adjustment phase, the economy will move from position *A* to position *B* in Chart 17-1, as higher real interest rates *crowd out* investment expenditures and lower output levels (from Y^* to Y_1). Down in the *PEP* curve panel, this lower output level (and associated higher unemployment rate) begins to moderate the inflation rate, from 10 per cent down to $\dot{P}_1$.

In the second period of the adjustment phase, the real money supply will again decline as the new inflation rate ($\dot{P}_1$) still exceeds the 5 per cent growth rate of the nominal money supply. The *LM* curve will again shift upwards (to LM_C), although by a smaller amount than in the initial period (because the inflation rate has declined and is now closer to the 5 per cent growth rate of the nominal money supply). Given our assumption of adaptive expectations, in the second period inflation expectations will be lowered from 10 per cent to the inflation rate that prevailed in the first period ($\dot{P}_1$). Thus in period two, both the *PEP* curve and the *IS* curve will shift downwards, reflecting this lower expected inflation rate. At the end of period two, the economy will be at position *C* in the upper panel of Chart 17-1 with a much lower income level Y_2, because both the *LM* curve and the *IS* curve have shifted to the left. The combination of this lower income level Y_2 and lower *PEP* curve (based on lower inflation expectations of $\dot{P}_1$) will substantially reduce the rate of price inflation in period 2, down to $\dot{P}_2$ in the lower panel of Chart 17-1. The assumption of adaptive inflation expectations accelerates the downward adjustment of the inflation rate for two reasons. First, the lowering of inflation expectations raises real interest rates, which reduce investment expenditures and output levels, thus pushing the economy further down the *PEP* curve. Second, the lowering of inflation expectations produces lower wage settlements throughout the economy, which shifts the *PEP* curve downwards.

As long as the *declining* inflation rate remains above 5 per cent, both the *IS* and *LM* curves will continue to shift leftwards, propelling the economy further into a recession. Furthermore, the declining inflation rate will lead to further *reductions* in inflation expectations and further *downward* shifts in the *PEP* curve. With falling output levels and declining inflation expectations, the actual inflation rate will rapidly decline. However, once the inflation rate falls below 5 per cent the recession will begin to "bottom out". With an inflation rate less than the 5 per cent growth rate of the nominal money supply, the real money supply will begin to increase and the *LM* curve will start to shift downwards to the right (not shown in Chart 17-1). At some point the *rightward* shift in the *LM* curve (because of an increasing real money supply associated with inflation rates less than 5 per cent) will dominate the *leftward* shift of the *IS* curve (inflation expectations continue to decline, albeit at a slower pace). Once this happens, say at point D in Chart 17-1, real interest rates will begin to decline and investment expenditures and income levels will start to increase. The economy will begin to recover and rebound back towards its equilibrium income level Y^*.

The pace of the recovery will accelerate as the inflation rate declines further below 5 per cent (the lower the inflation rate, the greater the increase in the real money supply and the larger the rightward shift in the LM curve). As income levels increase and the unemployment rate decreases, however, the economy will be moving upwards on a *PEP* curve. This *upward* movement along the *PEP* curve will tend to offset the *decrease* in inflation expectations (and downward shifts in the *PEP* curve). At some point, such as E in Chart 17-1, the *positive* inflation effects associated with the increase in income generated by the large rightward shifts in the LM curve will outweigh the *negative* inflation effects from the slight declines in inflation expectations, producing a *net increase* in the inflation rate. In the labour market, wage settlements will begin to rise as the positive effects from a large decline in the unemployment rate outweigh the negative effects from a small decline in inflation expectations. Note that at point E in Chart 17-1, the level of income has passed the equilibrium income level Y^*.

Once the inflation rate begins to *rise*, the increases in output will become smaller and smaller. As the inflation rate rises towards 5 per cent, the real increases in the money supply and the associated rightward shifts in the LM curve become progressively smaller and smaller. In addition, as the inflation rate rises individuals adaptively increase their inflation expectations, which shifts both the IS and *PEP* curves upwards and accelerates the increase in the inflation rate. In short, the inflation rate is rising at a faster and faster pace while the increases in output are becoming smaller and smaller. Once the inflation rate *exceeds* 5 per cent, the real money supply will once again begin to decline and the LM curve will start to shift upwards to the left. At some point, such as F in Chart 17-1, the *leftward* shift in the LM curve (because the real money supply is falling) will dominate the *rightward* shift in the IS curve (because inflation expectations are still rising) and the level of income will begin to fall. As the inflation rate rises further and further above 5 per cent, the decreases in the real money supply will become larger and larger, and the LM curve will shift upwards to the left by greater and greater amounts. Income levels will continue to decrease as rising real interest rates lower investment expenditures and the economy will accelerate back towards its equilibrium income level Y^*, with a moderating inflation rate.

Having traced through one complete output-inflation cycle under the assumption of adaptive expectations, we end our analysis of Chart 17-1 at this point. Assuming that the economy is stable in a dynamic sense, this cyclical adjustment path will continually repeat itself until the economy finally spirals into its new equilibrium position, labelled as point Z in Chart 17-1.

If we compare the adjustment path for an anti-inflationary, restrictive monetary policy under the assumption of *adaptive* expectations with that described in Chapter 13 (where inflation expectations adjusted in *one single* step after the inflation rate was driven down to the new lower rate of monetary expansion), two interesting points emerge. First, under adaptive inflation expectations the recession that accompanies a restrictive monetary policy is not as deep. The downward adjustments in inflation expectations repeatedly shift the *PEP* curve down, accelerating the decline in the inflation rate. Unlike our earlier analysis in Chapter 13, which required massive amounts of unemployment to lower the inflation rate down to the new lower rate of monetary expansion, the assumption of adaptive inflation expectations reinforces the decline in inflation associated with rising unemployment rates, thus requiring much less unemployment to drive wage and price inflation down. Similarly under the assumption of adaptive expectations, increases in nominal interest rates are not as large (because declining inflation expectations shift the *IS* curve downwards).

Second, while the economy does not undergo as deep a recession following the implementation of a restrictive monetary policy under the assumption of adaptive expectations, the adaptive expectations adjustment path will over-shoot its equilibrium position and oscillate around this equilibrium position. Instead of the rather simple parallelogram path analyzed in Chart 13-1, the adjustment path under adaptive inflation expectations will consist of a rather complicated set of dynamic inward spirals. The assumption of adaptive inflation expectations reduces the magnitude of the income effect from a shock or disturbance to the economic system, but creates a recurring set of oscillations as the economic system continually over-shoots its equilibrium position. The presence of adaptive inflation expectations is, in fact, one explanation for the existence of the business cycle.

A Critique of the Adaptive Inflation Expectations Model

Throughout the 1960s and 1970s the adaptive expectations model was the most commonly used expectations model in macroeconomics. The popularity of the adaptive expectations model was largely due to its intuitive plausibility (that is, individuals learn from their forecasting errors), its conceptual simplicity, and the ease with which it could be implemented empirically. There are, however, a number of serious problems with the adaptive expectations model, which eventually led many macroeconomists to switch to an alternative expectations model.

1. The adaptive expectations model fails to take into account any other variables (other than the past inflation rate) that might determine the current inflation rate. For example, our analysis in Chapters 12 and 13 points to the importance of current and past rates of monetary expansion as determinants of the inflation rate. If you accept the monetarist proposition that *inflation is a monetary phenomenon*, then you would want to examine current and past rates of monetary expansion before forecasting the inflation rate. More generally speaking, you would want to take into account all possible variables that might influence the inflation rate (such as monetary and fiscal policy, as well as other possible demand and supply-price shocks) before committing yourself to an inflation expectations forecast, and not simply limiting yourself to past movements in the actual inflation rate.

2. The adaptive expectations model is entirely *backward-looking*. Under the assumption of adaptive expectations, the expected inflation rate depends solely

on *past* inflation rates. Future events that might affect the inflation rate (such as an announced future increase in the rate of sales tax) are totally ignored in the adaptive expectations model. The adjustment of inflation expectations to such events occurs only after the inflation rate has actually changed, and then in a sluggish fashion as individuals are unlikely to correct for 100 per cent of their forecast error under the adaptive expectations model.

3. Under the adaptive expectations model it is likely that you are making systematic forecasting errors for many periods in a row. For example, in the simple temperature-forecasting illustration at the beginning of this chapter, we systematically under-predict the actual temperature of 32 degrees each and every day. If you are truly learning from your past mistakes, surely at some point you would discover this systematic tendency to under-predict and would modify the adaptive expectations model so that you did not make such systematic forecasting errors.

Rational Inflation Expectations

Given the problems outlined above, many macroeconomists abandoned the ad hoc and mechanical adaptive expectations forecasting model and turned to the **rational expectations** model, first suggested by Muth in 1961. The two key components of the rational expectations hypothesis are that (1) individuals use all the information that is available to them, subject to its cost, to formulate their expectations, and (2) individuals do not make any systematic forecasting errors. Equations 17-2 formalizes the rational expectations hypothesis, where the symbol $E[\ ]$ represents the expected value, Z represents the information available to the individual and v represents a random error term.

(17-2) $E[P_t/Z_{t-1}] = P_t + v_t$

In words, equation 17-2 states that under *rational* expectations, the expected value of the variable P in period t will be based on the information Z available in period $t - 1$, and this *expected* value of the variable P will be equal to the *actual* value of the variable P in period t plus a *random* error term.

The key point of departure for the rational expectations model is the assumption that all forecast errors will be random with a zero expected value. This does not imply that under rational expectations individuals will correctly forecast the inflation rate on each occasion. Individuals make forecast errors, but over the long haul these forecast errors average out to zero (that is, there will be as many positive errors as negative errors in repeated forecasting exercises). *On average* the individual *correctly* forecasts the value of the variable, but each particular forecast will be subject to a *random, nonsystematic* error.[3] Muth, the first economist to advocate rational expectations, argued that utility-maximizing individuals will use all of the information available to them (subject to its cost) to form their expectations. Part of the information available to individuals is the history of past

---

[3] In statistical terms, rational inflation expectations provide an unbiased forecast of the inflation rate.

forecast errors. Thus if in the past a person made systematic forecast errors (such as always underpredicting the variable), sooner or later he or she would infer that the forecasting model was incorrect and would use this information about systematic past forecast errors to improve future forecasts. One would extract all of the systematic information out of past forecast errors until one's forecast errors were random.

The rational expectations hypothesis, however, goes one step further. Part of the information available to individuals concerns the *structure* of the economy. Muth argued that rational individuals would use their knowledge of the structure of the economic system in forming their expectations. In Muth's words, "I would like to suggest that expectations, since they are informed predictions of future events, are essentially the same as the predictions of the relevant economic theory."[4] In other words, the rational expectations hypothesis assumes that individuals form their expectations by using the quantitative predictions of economic theory. For example, if inflation is theoretically determined by the rate of monetary expansion, then under rational expectations individuals will form their expectations of the inflation rate by taking into account the growth rate of the nominal money supply. As McCallum has noted,

> After a slow start, the rational expectations hypothesis moved forward strongly during the 1970s into its current position as the dominant hypothesis concerning expectation formulation. One reason for its success, I believe, was the dawning realization that it is the "natural" hypothesis to use in neoclassical economic analysis. More specifically, the basic idea of the hypothesis is simply that economic agents behave purposefully in collecting and using information, just as they do in other activities, an idea that it is hard for an economist to reject without considerable embarrassment. But in practice, of course, this compelling idea usually gets translated into the requirement that expectations are, in the model at hand, formed in a way that is stochastically consistent with the behaviour of the realized values of the variables in question. This is clearly a much stronger hypothesis, one that an economist can reasonably dispute.[5]

The New Classical Macroeconomic Model

To illustrate the macroeconomic implications of assuming *rational* inflation expectations, we present the basic model associated with the new classical school of macroeconomics. This group of economists, led by Lucas, Sargent, Wallace, McCallum, Parkin and Barro, have radically changed the policy implications of macroeconomics. The major conclusion of the new classical macroeconomic model is that *anticipated* government policy will have absolutely *no* effect on

---

[4]J. Muth, "Rational Expectations and the Theory of Price Movements," *Econometrica*, July 1961, p. 316.

[5]B. T. McCallum, "Rational Expectations and Macroeconomic Policy," *Journal of Money, Credit and Banking*, November 1980 (Part 2), p. 717.

output or employment levels, even in the immediate short-run. As we shall see, the assumption of rational expectations plays a prominent role in the new classical model and in the assertion that anticipated government policy will have no output or employment effects. Before we derive this radical new policy conclusion, we will outline the major ingredients in the new classical model.

The Conventional *IS* and *LM* curves

The new classical model incorporates conventional *IS* and *LM* curves as the first two equations in the model. To simplify the subsequent algebra, we have rewritten these two equations in a new, more compact, notation.

(17-3) $Y = aA - bR + u$ *IS* equation

(17-4) $M - P = cY - dR + v$ *LM* equation

The symbol A represents all of the exogenous components contained within the *IS* curve intercept, such as exports and government spending. To avoid the nonlinear problems associated with dividing the nominal money supply M (formerly represented by $\$$) by the price level P, these equations are written with all variables expressed in logarithmic form (the *real* money supply simply becomes $M - P$ in logarithmic form). Finally, random error terms (u and v) are included in both equations. The expected value of each of these random error terms is zero.

The Price Surprise Supply Function (*PSSF*)

Rather than using a price expectations Phillips curve to describe the price-supply side of the model, the new classical model includes the following aggregate supply function:

(17-5) $Y = Y^* + e(P - P^e) + w$ *PSSF* equation

In this equation Y^* represents the natural rate of output, P^e is the expected value of the price level (P) and w is another random error (again all variables are written in logarithmic form).

As discussed in Chapter 8, the three key assumptions implicit in the **price surprise supply function**, or *PSSF*, are that (1) economic agents optimize, (2) all markets always clear, and (3) individuals do not have perfect information. With respect to this third assumption, it is assumed that each agent has very good information about movements in the price of the product which he or she is producing or selling but has very limited information about movements in the prices of other goods, most of which are bought or sold only infrequently. As Lucas and Sargent point out, this key limited-information assumption leads to the assertion that output levels will exceed the natural rate of output when price levels are higher than expected (*PSSF* equation 17-5). In their words:

> The new classical models continue to assume that markets always clear and that agents optimize. The postulate that agents optimize means that their supply and demand decisions must be functions of real variables,

including perceived relative prices. Each agent is assumed to have limited information and to receive information about some prices more often than other prices. On the basis of their limited information... agents are assumed to make the best possible estimate of all of the relative prices that influence their supply and demand decisions. Because they do not have all of the information that would enable them to compute perfectly the relative prices they care about, agents make errors in estimating the pertinent relative prices, errors that are unavoidable given their limited information. In particular, under certain conditions, agents will tend temporarily to mistake a general increase in all absolute prices as an increase in the relative price of the good that they are selling, leading them to increase their supply of that good over what they had previously planned. Since everyone is, on average, making the same mistake, aggregate output will rise above what it would have been.... This increase of output above what it would have been will occur whenever this period's average economy-wide price level is above what agents had expected this period's average economy-wide price level to be.[6]

To give a simple illustration of the economic rationale behind the price surprise supply function, consider the case of a cobbler. If a cobbler observes that the price of shoes has unexpectedly risen but does not realize that all other prices have also unexpectedly risen, he will mistakenly assume that the relative price of shoes has increased. As a good optimizer, he will increase his production of shoes, based on his mistaken belief that the relative price of shoes has unexpectedly increased.[7] If all cobblers, butchers, bakers and candlestick makers behave in a similar fashion, aggregate output will increase (beyond its natural rate level) whenever the price level is higher than it was expected to be. Again the key assumptions are limited information and mistaking a general price increase for a relative price increase. Once our cobbler discovers that all other prices have risen and that there was in fact no increase in the relative price of shoes, he will cut back his production of shoes to the original (natural rate) production level. The extra production of shoes is temporary, and only lasts as long as our cobbler is mistaken about general price movements (that is, until he has the correct price information). However, it is important to point out that during the period of time when the output of shoes exceeded the natural rate of production, our cobbler continued to act in an optimizing manner and the market for shoes continued to clear.

One last comment about the price surprise supply function. As you may have noticed, equation 17-5 bears a striking resemblance to our *PEP* curve. If we rewrite the logarithmic *PSSF* equation with P on the left-hand side and Y on the right-hand side (and substract P_{t-1} from both sides of the equation), it is very similar to the inflation-output *PEP* curve presented in Chapter 10 (with a new set

---

[6]R. E. Lucas, Jr. and T. J. Sargent, "After Keynesian Economics," in *After the Phillips Curve: Persistence of High Inflation and High Unemployment*, Federal Reserve Bank of Boston, Conference Series No. 19, 1978, p. 60.
[7]We assume that the substitution effect dominates the *income* effect.

of parameters). While the equation for the *PEP* curve is very similar to an inverted *PSSF* equation, the economic theory (and lines of causality) behind the *PEP* curve and the *PSSF* are very different. As discussed above, the *PSSF* assumes that markets always clear and that the price level moves instantaneously to its new market-clearing level. On the other hand, the *PEP* curve is premised on a disequilibrium model in which markets do not always clear and prices do not instantaneously move to their new equilibrium level. In the *IS-LM-PEP* macroeconomic model, deviations of output from the natural rate represent nonmarket clearing and cause price adjustments. In the new classical *PSSF* macroeconomic model, markets always clear and deviations of output from the natural rate are caused by unexpected price changes (assuming limited information about general price movements).

The Assumption of Rational Expectations

The final ingredient in the new classical model is the assumption that individuals form their expectations of the inflation rate or price level in a *rational* manner. Under rational expectations, individuals are assumed to base their expectations of the price level on the predictions of economic theory. Thus to obtain the *rational* expectations forecast of the price level, we must first solve our macroeconomic model (equations 17-3, 17-4 and 17-5) to determine the *equilibrium* price level.

First we rewrite the *IS* equation (17-3) with R on the lefthand side,

$$R = \frac{aA - Y + u}{b}$$

Next, we substitute this equation into the *LM* equation (17-4).

$$P = M - cY - v + \frac{d(aA - Y + u)}{b}$$

(17-4a) $P = M - v + \dfrac{adA}{b} + \dfrac{du}{b} - \left(c + \dfrac{d}{b}\right)Y$

Finally we substitute the *PSSF* equation (17-5) for Y in the above equation.

(17-6) $P = M - v + \dfrac{adA}{b} + \dfrac{du}{b} - \left(c + \dfrac{d}{b}\right)(Y^* + eP - eP^e + w)$

Equation 17-6 describes the equilibrium price level in the new classical model.

Under the assumption of rational expectations, individuals' predictions of the price level will be identical to the predictions of equation 17-6. The rational expectations forecast of the price level (P^e) is obtained by taking the expected value of equation 17-6. Since the expected values of the random error terms (u, v, w) are zero, the rational expectation of the price level is the following equation,

$$P^e = M^e + \frac{adA^e}{b} - \left(c + \frac{d}{b}\right)(Y^* + eP^e - eP^e)$$

where P^e, M^e and A^e represent the expected values of the variables P, M and A. (Note that the expected valued of Y^* is Y^*, as the natural rate of output Y^* is assumed to be fixed, and that the expectation of the expected price level, P^e, remains the expected price level.) The last two P^e terms in the above equation cancel each other out and we are left with the following equation for the expected value of the price level.

$$(17\text{-}7) \quad P^e = M^e + \frac{adA^e}{b} - \left(c + \frac{d}{b} \right) Y^*$$

Under the assumption of rational expectations, the expected price level depends on the expected money supply (M^e) and on the expected level of the exogenous components of the *IS* curve (A^e), such as government spending and exports. A change in either M^e or A^e will directly affect the expected price level in the new classical model. Since we assume that the natural rate of output is constant, we ignore the effect of Y^* on P^e.

The Policy Ineffectiveness Proposition (*PIP*)

The new classical macroeconomic model consists of an *IS* curve (equation 17-3), and *LM* curve (equation 17-4), a *PSSF* (equation 17-5) and the assumption of rational price expectations (equation 17-7). To examine the macroeconomic implications of the new classical model, we first must obtain the reduced form equation for output. Substituting equations 17-4a and 17-7 into the *PSSF* equation 17-5 produces the following reduced form output equation for the new classical macroeconomic model.

$$Y = Y^* + e(M - M^e) - ev + \frac{ead}{b}(A - A^e) - \left(ec + \frac{ed}{b} \right)(Y - Y^*) + \frac{edu}{b} + w$$

Collecting the common Y terms and the common Y^* terms produces the final version of our reduced form output equation, where

$$k = \frac{1}{\dfrac{1}{e} + c + \dfrac{d}{b}}$$

$$(17\text{-}8) \quad Y = Y^* + k\left[(M - M^e) - v + \frac{ad}{b}(A - A^e) + \frac{du}{b} + \frac{w}{e} \right]$$

The following important new classical conclusions can be derived from this reduced form output equation:

1) If monetary policy is correctly anticipated—that is, $M = M^e$—then the level of output will not be affected by monetary policy (the **policy ineffectiveness proposition**). In equation 17-8, when the level of the money supply is correctly anticipated, the M and M^e terms cancel each other out and the reduced form output equation does not contain any monetary policy variables. To repeat, a *correctly anticipated* monetary policy will have absolutely *no* effect on output or employment levels in the new classical macroeconomic model. Thus if the government announces a new anti-inflationary restrictive monetary policy, as soon as people hear this policy

announcement (and assuming that they believe the government), they will immediately revise their price expectations downwards (according to equation 17-7), and the economy will move immediately to a lower inflation rate without any short-run reduction in the level of output. The new classical macroeconomics predicts that an anti-inflationary monetary policy will be completely painless; that is, there will be no short-run recession with high interest rates.

2) Similarly, if the level of A (which incorporates government spending, tax rates, exports, etc.) is correctly anticipated, output levels will be unaffected by any changes in A. Again the A and A^e terms will cancel each other out in equation 17-8. A *correctly anticipated* fiscal policy (or change in exports) will also have absolutely *no* effects on output or employment levels. In the new classical macroeconomic model one's expectations of monetary and fiscal policy are formed in a *rational* manner, using all available information. Thus any systematic *Keynesian* stabilization policy could easily be forecast and consequently would have no effect on output levels when it was implemented (again the policy ineffectiveness proposition). There is no role for traditional Keynesian policies in the new classical macroeconomics; since systematic demand management policies would be fully anticipated, they can have no effect on output levels.

3) Unanticipated monetary or fiscal policy, or an unanticipated change in exports, however, will affect output levels. Whenever the actual money supply M does not equal the expected money supply M^e, output levels will change by the factor k. Similarly, whenever the actual value of A does not equal the expected value of A (that is, A^e), output levels will change by the factor $k(ad/b)$. Only *unexpected* events or *surprise* government policies affect output and employment levels. As discussed above, systematic Keynesian stabilization policy could not be unexpected under the assumption of rational expectations.

4) Finally, if both A and M are correctly anticipated and if the random errors have their zero expected values, the level of output will simply be equal to the natural rate Y^*. It is unexpected changes in M or A and random error disturbances that cause the level of output to deviate from its natural rate Y^*. The new classical macroeconomic model, as presented above, predicts that output levels will be *randomly* distributed about the natural rate Y^* and denies the existence of systematic output and unemployment movements through time (the phenomenon of the business cycle).

Necessary and Sufficient Conditions for the Policy Ineffectiveness Proposition

Given the very strong *policy ineffectiveness* conclusions of the new classical macroeconomics, it is important to identify the key assumptions that generate these striking conclusions. The policy ineffectiveness proposition of the new classical macroeconomics is not only diametrically opposed to the *policy effectiveness* conclusions of Keynesian economics, on a *theoretical* level new classical macroeconomists part company with monetarists (even though they obviously share some common views on the inappropriateness of Keynesian policy). Unlike Milton Friedman, who believes that monetary policy has long and variable lags, new classical economists predict absolutely no lag for anticipated monetary policy. While Keynesians and monetarists debate whether the short-run adjustment period following a policy change or demand shock is long or short, new classical economists contend that the economy adjusts *instantaneously* (that is, the short-run adjustment period collapses to zero).

Since the new classical macroeconomic model also contains conventional *IS* and *LM* equations, these striking policy ineffectiveness results must emanate from the two new hypotheses in the new classical model: the assumption of *rational* expectations and the *price surprise supply function*. Suppose a macroeconomic model consists of an *IS* curve, an *LM* curve and a *PSSF*. In place of *rational* expectations, however, let us assume that individuals form their inflation expectations in an adaptive manner. In other words, our model now consists of equations 17-3, 17-4, 17-5 and a price-level version of equation 17-1, the *adaptive* expectations assumption. To simplify the algebra, let us rewrite our adaptive expectations assumption in the following form:

(17-1a) $P^e = P_{lag}$

where P_{lag} represents all of the lagged actual price terms that are present in the original adaptive expectations formulation. Now if we substitute our equations for P and P^e into the price surprise supply function, we obtain the following *new* reduced form output equation under the assumption of *adaptive* expectations:

$$Y = Y^* + e\left[M - v + \frac{adA}{b} + \frac{du}{b} - \left(c + \frac{d}{b}\right)Y\right] - eP_{lag} + w$$

Collecting the Y terms together produces the following result, where k is again equal to $1/(1/e + c + d/b)$:

(17-9) $Y = k\left(\frac{Y^*}{e} + M - v + \frac{adA}{b} + \frac{du}{b} - P_{lag} + \frac{w}{e}\right)$

From equation 17-9 it is clear that under the assumption of *adaptive* expectations, a change in monetary policy, be it correctly anticipated or not, will have an impact on output levels. A one-unit increase in M will increase Y by k units in the initial time period (before price expectations begin to adjust). Similarly, a change in fiscal policy or exports (the variable A) will have an initial impact effect on output levels. There are systematic output effects following a change in monetary (or fiscal) policy when economic agents form their price expectations in an adaptive manner, effects not unlike those described earlier in this chapter using the *IS-LM-PEP* model. The strong policy ineffectiveness proposition of the new classical macroeconomic model requires the assumption of *rational* expectations. Under the assumption of adaptive expectations, the *IS-LM-PSSF* model generates conclusions very similar to those obtained by Keynesians and monetarists using an *IS-LM-PEP* model.

While the assumption of rational expectations is a *necessary* assumption to obtain the policy ineffectiveness proposition, it is not a sufficient condition. In addition to the assumption of rational expectations, the policy ineffectiveness proposition requires that markets always clear. Even if agents form their expectations in a rational manner, if markets do not clear (because prices do not instantaneously adjust to their new equilibrium values), then there will be systematic output effects associated with a change in anticipated monetary or fiscal policy. During the period of time in which wages or prices are adjusting to their new equilibrium values (following a demand shock or policy change), output levels will deviate from their equilibrium or natural rate levels. As demonstrated in an appendix to this chapter, the necessary and sufficient conditions for the policy ineffectiveness proposition are that individuals form their expectations in a rational manner and that markets instantaneously clear. The new classical economics requires the joint assumptions of rational expectations and continual market equilibrium.

A Critique of the New Classical Macroeconomic Model

Given the striking policy ineffectiveness conclusions of the new classical macroeconomics, it should come as no surprise that the assumptions, predictions and conclusions of the new classical model have been strongly challenged. Like the *General Theory* of Keynes some forty years earlier, the new classical view of macroeconomics has sparked a lively and heated debate among economists. In the following analysis of the new classical macroeconomics, we have organized our review of the arguments against the policy ineffectiveness proposition around the major assumptions within the new classical model: *rational expectations, market-clearing* and the *price surprise supply function.*

The Validity of the Assumption of Rational Expectations

As demonstrated above, a *necessary* condition for the *policy ineffectiveness proposition* is the assumption of *rational* expectations. Individuals' expectations are assumed to be the same as the predictions of economic theory. The assumption of rational expectations implies that individuals know what the true economic model is and know the values of all of the structural parameters within this model. But what is the *true* economic model? While it is convenient (but intellectually arrogant) to assume that the new classical model is the true model, economists have been known to show undue confidence in the reliability of their current set of theories, which are often scrapped or revised in later years—as are theories in physics, psychology and other disciplines. Since economists with advanced degrees have great difficulty in understanding and predicting economic events, how can one assume that individuals without any training in economics and statistics know the true economic model and formulate their expectations in such a "rational" manner. In short, the amount of information that individuals are assumed to command under rational expectations appears to be excessive and unreasonable.

Proponents of the new classical macroeconomics have responded to this criticism in two ways. First, there are many private firms and agencies engaged in economic analysis and forecasting. For a relatively small price (such as the cost of a newspaper) one has access to these widely disseminated forecasts and analyses of economic events. Even if one ignores the availability of public forecasts and economic commentary, one need not assume that the entire population have degrees in economics. Just because an expert billiard player can make very difficult shots (which can be represented by complex mathematical formulas), one should not assume that he or she has degrees in mathematics and physics. Similarly, firms manage to maximize profits without actually evaluating (and drawing) their marginal cost and revenue curves, and most individuals would have no idea what their utility function (or indifference curves) actually look like but seem to make reasonably good economic decisions concerning what goods to buy. New classical and monetarist economists argue that one should judge a theory on the accuracy of its predictions, not on the literal accuracy of its assumptions. In constructing an economic model, one simply proceeds "as if" individuals possessed this economic knowledge.

Under the rational expectations assumption, individuals are not only assumed to possess (or act "as if" they possessed) an amazing amount of economic and statistical information, they are also assumed to know what government policy is likely to be. This raises an important question concerning the credibility of government policy announcements. For example, if the Prime Minister goes on national TV to announce a new anti-inflationary policy of monetary restraint, do individuals believe that the government will actually implement and stick with this policy even if the unemployment rate increases by three or four percentage points? If individuals believe that the government will likely abandon its policy when the going gets tough, they will tend to dismiss this policy announcement and not revise their inflation expectations. In these circumstances, any new policy that individuals have dismissed as not being credible will have short-run output and employment effects.

Not to belabour the point, the stagflation of the 1970s and the high unemployment of the early 1980s have dealt a serious blow to the credibility of economists and their theories. In addition, governments have been known to change their policies abruptly, as Prime Minister Trudeau's reversal on wage and price controls in 1975 clearly demonstrates. It is conceivable that individuals might formulate their expectations of future inflation by observing and adapting to actual past inflation rates, rather than by believing the predictions of economists and the assurances of politicians.

Ideally one would like to test empirically the assumption of rational inflation expectations (the methodological objections of new classical economists notwithstanding), but unfortunately we have no continuous data on inflation expectations in Canada. There are, however, surveys of reported inflation expectations available in other countries and numerous statistical studies have been conducted to determine if inflation expectations are formed in a rational manner. Perhaps the most widely used expectations data are those collected by a U.S. journalist, Joseph Livingston, who has surveyed American economists in business, government and academia every six months since 1947 for their forecasts on a wide variety of economic variables. While there are a number of studies investigating the Livingston data on inflation expectations, the empirical results are mixed, and different researchers have interpreted their evidence as either supporting or contradicting the assumption of rational expectations. After surveying this literature, Carter and Maddock conclude, "Taken as a whole, the literature which attempts to test the rationality of reported expectations cannot be regarded as favourable to the rational expectations hypothesis."[8] For example, a recent econometric study of this Livingston data, by Figlewski and Wachtel, concluded that "the data indicated that inflation expectations in the post-war period were formed in a manner that is inconsistent with rational expectations. . . . The adaptive expectations model is the one which best describes inflation expectations."[9] At minimum, the assumption of rational inflation expectations should be viewed with a certain degree of empirical skepticism, no matter how theoretically appealing this assumption might be.

Do Markets Always Clear?

As demonstrated in the appendix to this chapter, the policy ineffectiveness proposition requires that markets always clear in addition to the assumption of rational expectations. If prices do not instantaneously adjust to clear the market, then a change in policy will affect output levels. The most damaging criticism levelled against the new classical macroeconomic model concerns the assumption of perfectly flexible prices and continuous market clearing. Even the most casual observations about the real world, with unemployment rates above 11 per cent in the 1982-84, are clearly at variance with the assumption that markets are *always* in equilibrium. Fifty years ago, the Great Depression prompted John Maynard Keynes to write a rather influential book about the macroeconomic implications of nonmarket clearing. Today, critics of the new classical macroeconomics argue that the widespread use of contracts (both explicit and implicit), among other things, impedes the adjustment of wages and prices. Because of such contracts, prices are inflexible in the short run and the economic system can be characterized by quantity adjustments, not price adjustments.

First let us consider the labour market. Approximately 40 per cent of the Canadian labour force is unionized and signs wage contracts that typically run for two or three years. During the life of this multi-year contract, the wage schedule for the firm and worker is fixed; any adjustments to this wage schedule to reflect an unexpected change in the labour market cannot be made until this long-term contract expires. Workers who are not unionized are usually paid the same wage rate for a year, with an annual performance review triggering an annual wage adjustment. In short, the labour market is not an auction market, where wages are

[8]M. Carter and R. Maddock, *Rational Expectations, Macroeconomics for the 1980's*, Macmillan Publishers Ltd., (London: 1984), p. 126.

[9]S. Figlewski and P. Wachtel, "The Formation of Inflationary Expectations", *The Review of Economics and Statistics*, February 1981, p. 1.

renegotiated every day. For most workers, wage rates are fixed for at least one year. Given such contractual wage rigidities, a change in government policy can affect output and employment levels.[10]

Turning to the product market,[11] there are a number of commodities (such as copper, lumber, wheat and pork-bellies) that are bought and sold in auction markets where prices adjust almost instantaneously. However, many other goods are sold at a given price in markets where the price (tag) does not change on an hourly or daily basis. Unlike auction markets where commodities tend to be standardized and homogeneous, price-tag markets typically consist of very heterogeneous and nonstandardized commodities (such as cars, appliances, and houses). In price-tag markets customers usually shop around before they purchase the commodity, comparing heterogeneous products in different stores. Firms who are interested in maintaining a continuing relationship with their customers do not wish to alienate regular customers by continually changing the price tags, nor do they wish to incur the substantial cost of changing all of their price tags and catalogues. To promote recurrent sales, most stores offer customers an implicit contract that they will sell their merchandise at stable prices. In such *customer-oriented price-tag* markets, prices will likely adjust quite slowly and it is not uncommon to observe dramatic shortages or huge surpluses of price-tag commodities. If wages and/or prices do *not* instantaneously adjust, then government policy, even if it is correctly anticipated, will affect output and employment levels.

The Price Surprise Supply Function

In addition to the market-clearing assumption, the *price surprise supply function* of the new classical model has also been criticized. For example, Okun questions the nature of the missing information and misperceptions about relative prices that are crucial to the *PSSF*, and chides new classical macroeconomists for not giving these important relative-price misperceptions more operational content. In the words of Okun,

> I wish to be told what the decision makers don't know, for how long they don't know it, and why they don't find out. Is there any direct empirical evidence that sellers lack timely information about other prices?...By reading newspapers, market participants obtain a virtually costless flow of information from the reporting on the monthly indices of consumer and producer prices.[12]

Again focusing on the nature of the missing information, Benjamin Friedman has raised an interesting counter-example to the *PSSF* presented by new classical

---

[10]The first formal analysis of the macroeconomic implications of overlapping long-term wage contracts in a rational expectations framework was a paper by S. Fischer, "Long-term Contracts, Rational Expectations and the Optimal Money Supply," *Journal of Political Economy*, February 1977, pp. 191-205.

[11]The classic analysis of implicit contracts in customer "price tag" markets is contained in the book by A. M. Okun entitled *Prices and Quantities*, (Washington, D.C.: Brookings Institution, 1981).

[12]A. M. Okun, "Rational Expectations-with-Misperceptions As a Theory of the Business Cycle," *Journal of Money, Credit and Banking*, November 1980.

macroeconomists. Recall our story about the cobbler observing an unexpected increase in the price of shoes, but not observing that all other prices in the economy were also rising. Mistaking a general price increase for a relative increase in the price of shoes, our profit-maximizing cobbler increases his production of shoes. What would happen, however, if our cobbler observed that the price of leather and other inputs to shoe production unexpectedly rose but did *not* realize that the shoe market will pay a higher price for his shoes (that is, he remains unaware of the increase in the price of shoes at other cobblers or of the general price increase for all other goods)? Being a good profit-maximizer, he will *reduce* his production of shoes because he will mistakenly perceive a relative increase in the cost of producing shoes.

> The point of this illustration is that the crucial aggregate supply function is valid if, and only if, agents learn the prices of goods they are *selling* before learning the prices of goods they are *buying*. If instead a producer typically learns the price he has to pay for his *inputs* before learning the price at which he can market his *output*, this aggregate supply function implies results exactly opposite to those which it is assumed to produce...as described by Professors Lucas and Sargent.[13]

If our cobbler read his newspaper he would know the current price of shoes and the inflation rate for all goods, and there would be no effect on shoe production (because there would be no perceived change in the relative price or costs of shoes). In other words, the effect of a price increase on aggregate output can be positive, negative or zero, depending upon the informational assumptions and asymmetries assumed within the model. Okun is clearly right. Before proceeding too far with the *PSSF*, new classical macroeconomists should demonstrate empirically exactly what price information the profit-maximizing firm has available to it. Without this information, any theoretical result is possible.

One final criticism has been levelled against the *PSSF*. The new classical model, as outlined above, implies that output will always be equal to the natural rate of output Y^*, plus or minus a *random* error. In equation 17-8, a difference between Y and Y^* arises when any of the following occurs: (1) M does not equal M^e, or (2) A does not equal A^e, or (3) the random errors, u, v, and w have values other than zero. Under the assumption of rational expectations, M will equal M^e subject to a random error and A will equal A^e subject to a *random* error. Thus, any differences between Y and Y^* will be completely *random*. Since successive random disturbances are, by definition, *not* correlated with each other, successive values for output (and unemployment) will also not be correlated with each other. The new classical macroeconomic model predicts that the unemployment rate will randomly fluctuate around the natural rate.

This prediction of the new classical model is obviously at variance with the facts. The Canadian unemployment rates for 1982, 1983 and 1984 were 11.0, 11.9, and

[13]B. M. Friedman, "Comment" on paper by R. E. Lucas, Jr. and T. J. Sargent entitled "After Keynesian Economics," in *After the Phillips Curve; Persistence of High Inflation and High Unemployment*, Federal Reserve Bank of Boston, Conference Series No. 19, 1978.

11.3 per cent respectively. Unless one believes that the Canadian natural rate of unemployment was around 11.5 per cent, these three successive years were characterized by *persistent cyclical* unemployment (unemployment persistently above the natural rate). Any empirical study of output levels, employment levels, or the unemployment rate reveals systematic movements through time, not random fluctuation. Until new classical macroeconomists can provide a convincing explanation for persistent cyclical unemployment (such as was experienced in the 1930s or early 1980s), their strong policy-ineffectiveness conclusions remain open to question.[14]

In conclusion, critics of the new classical macroeconomics argue that the policy ineffectiveness proposition has been repudiated by recent Canadian empirical evidence. Beginning in 1975 the Bank of Canada announced and carried out a policy of monetary restraint designed to lower the inflation rate. While the growth rate of the nominal money supply declined during the 1976-82 period (more or less as had been announced), the inflation rate did not appreciably decline *until 1983*, when the unemployment rate had peaked at over 12 per cent (5 percentage points higher than the unemployment rate was when the monetary restraint policy was announced and implemented in 1975). In short, the inflation rate did not immediately adjust to the new monetary restraint policy, and a substantial persistent increase in unemployment accompanied this policy of monetary restraint. The new classical macroeconomic model's prediction that an anti-inflationary restrictive monetary policy will quickly and painlessly lower the inflation rate is refuted by Canadian evidence from the late 1970s and early 1980s.

Summary

In this chapter we have examined two different models of inflation expectations and their macroeconomic implications. The *adaptive* expectations model assumes that individuals adjust their inflation forecasts by taking into account past forecasting errors: individuals learn from their past mistakes. Implicitly the adaptive expectations model assumes that inflation rates are predictable from past inflation rates. To illustrate the macroeconomic implications of assuming adaptive inflation expectations, we re-examined an anti-inflationary restrictive monetary policy. Assuming that current inflation expectations are based on the inflation rate of the last period, our *IS-LM-PEP* analysis suggests that the recession accompanying a restrictive monetary policy will be less severe and the economy will rebound more quickly back towards its equilibrium output level. This faster rebound will, however, cause the economy to overshoot its equilibrium income level and then oscillate back and forth around this equilibrium income level. Under the assumption of adaptive expectations, shocks or disturbances to the economic system give rise to business cycles.

[14]To overcome this persistence problem, new classical macroeconomists often include a lagged output term in the *PSSF*, which they (loosely) rationalize in terms of adjustment costs in changing output and employment levels. Nevertheless, new classical economists are still forced to argue that the severe persistent unemployment of the 1930s and early 1980s represented the voluntary intertemporal substitution of leisure for work (because of misperceptions about the real wage rate).

In recent years the assumption of adaptive inflation expectations has been criticized on the grounds that it ignores other economic variables that influence the inflation rate, that it is entirely backward-looking and that it is subject to systematic forecasting errors. The rational expectations model has been proposed to overcome these inherent problems in the adaptive expectations model. Under the assumption of rational expectations, individuals are assumed to use all information available to forecast future inflation rates (including the economic model that explains how inflation rates are determined) and are assumed to make no systematic forecast errors. Rational expectations are characterized by random forecasts errors.

The leading proponents of rational expectations are economists associated with the new classical school of macroeconomics. A new classical macroeconomic model consists of conventional *IS* and *LM* equations, the assumption of rational expectations and a price surprise supply function (*PSSF*). The *PSSF* asserts that output will deviate from its natural rate whenever price levels are different from what was expected, with price level expectations being formed in a rational manner. This new classical macroeconomic model produces the striking conclusion that anticipated government policy will have absolutely no effect on output levels, the policy ineffectiveness proposition. Only unexpected policy decisions will affect output and employment levels. New classical economists argue that governments cannot systematically affect output levels and consequently there can be no role for Keynesian policy.

The necessary and sufficient conditions for the policy ineffectiveness proposition are that individuals form their expectations in a rational manner and that all markets continually clear. Both of these assumptions have been strongly challenged. The amount of information that individuals are assumed to possess under the assumption of rational expectations is regarded as excessive and unacceptable by many economists. Although the empirical evidence available is mixed, it cannot be regarded as favourable to the rational expectations hypothesis.

The strongest criticism of the new classical model has been directed at the key assumption of continual market clearing. If prices do not instantaneously adjust to clear the market, then the policy ineffectiveness proposition no longer holds. The existence of explicit wage contracts in the labour market and implicit customer contracts in "price tag" goods markets impedes the flexibility of wages and prices. Given sluggish wage and price adjustments, output and employment levels can systematically deviate from their equilibrium levels, and (Keynesian) government policy may still be able to offset demand shocks to the economic system. Finally, the price surprise supply function has been criticized for its informational assumptions and for its assertion that output will be equal to the natural rate of output subject to a random error process. The new classical macroeconomic model has yet to provide a convincing explanation of persistent systematic deviations in the unemployment rate from the natural rate of unemployment.

Appendix: Necessary and Sufficient Conditions for the New Classical Policy Ineffectiveness Proposition

This appendix demonstrates that the *necessary* and *sufficient* conditions for the new classical policy ineffectiveness proposition are continual market-clearing (with perfectly flexible price levels) and rational expectations.[1] If prices do not instantly adjust to their new equilibrium levels, then anticipated monetary and/or fiscal policy will affect output levels, *even if price expectations are formed in a rational manner*. Throughout this appendix we assume economic agents form their expectations in a rational manner and investigate the implications of nonmarket-clearing (because of sluggish price adjustment).

An expression for the market-clearing price level($\overline{P}$) in the new classical model can be obtained from the price surprise supply function (equation 17-5):

$$(17A\text{-}1) \qquad \overline{P} = \frac{1}{e}(Y - Y^*) + P^e$$

This market-clearing price level ($\overline{P}$) need not equal the expected price level (P^e) in the new classical model. Market equilibrium will occur whether price expectations turn out to be correct or incorrect.

Now suppose that the price level does not instantaneously adjust to this market-clearing level. Equation 17A-2 describes a partial price adjustment model in which the change in price levels ($P_t - P_{t-1}$) is only a fraction λ of the gap between the current market-clearing price level ($\overline{P}_t$) and the previous actual price level (P_{t-1}).

$$(17A\text{-}2) \qquad P_t - P_{t-1} = \lambda(\overline{P}_t - P_{t-1})$$

We assume that equation 17A-2 exactly represents actual price movements. Note that if λ equals 1.0, then prices instantly adjust to the market-clearing price level ($P_t = \overline{P}_t$) and we have a market-clearing model. The new classical school of macroeconomics implicitly assumes that λ is unity. A value for λ less than unity implies that "markets are not clearing" since prices would not be at their equilibrium level.

We now derive the *rational* expected price level assuming that the movement of actual prices is correctly represented by equation 17A-2. Substituting equation 17A-1 into 17A-2 produces the following price level equation:

$$P_t - P_{t-1} = \frac{\lambda}{e}(Y_t - Y^*) + \lambda P_t^e - \lambda P_{t-1}$$

$$(17A\text{-}3) \qquad P_t = (1 - \lambda)P_{t-1} + \lambda P_t^e + \frac{\lambda}{e}Y_t - \frac{\lambda}{e}Y^*$$

The income variable (Y_t) can be eliminated from equation 17A-3 by combining the *LM* equation (17-4) with the *IS* equation (17-3).

---

[1] The proof presented in this appendix is based on a paper by W. H. Buiter, "The Macroeconomics of Dr. Pangloss: A Critical Survey of the New Classical Macroeconomics," *Economic Journal*, 1980, Volume 90, pp. 39-50.

$$Y_t = aA_t - \frac{b}{d}(cY_t - M_t + P_t + v_t) + u_t$$

(17A-4) or $$Y_t = \left[\frac{1}{1 + \dfrac{bc}{d}}\right]\left(aA_t + \frac{b}{d}M_t - \frac{b}{d}P_t - \frac{b}{d}v_t + u_t\right)$$

To simplify the subsequent algebra, we rewrite equation 17A-4 with $\pi = \dfrac{a}{1 + bc/d}$ and $\theta = \dfrac{b/d}{1 + bc/d}$:

(17A-4a) $$Y_t = \pi A_t + \theta M_t - \theta P_t - \theta v_t + (\pi/a)u_t$$

Equation 17A-4a is substituted into equation 17A-3:

(17A-5) $$P_t = (1 - \lambda)P_{t-1} + \lambda P_t^e - \frac{\lambda}{e}Y^* + \frac{\lambda}{e}\left[\pi A_t + \theta M_t - \theta P_t - \theta v_t + \frac{\pi}{a}u_t\right]$$

Since we assume that price expectations are formed in a rational manner, economic agents use equation 17A-5 to form their expectations of the price level. Note that our price level equation (17A-5) is a function of the still unknown price expectation, P_t^e. Equation 17A-6 presents the "rational" expected price level.

$$P_t^e = (1 - \lambda)P_{t-1} + \lambda P_t^e - \frac{\lambda}{e}Y^* + \frac{\lambda}{e}(\pi A_t^e + \theta M_t^e - \theta P_t^e)$$

(17A-6) or $$P_t^e = \frac{(1 - \lambda)P_{t-1} - \dfrac{\lambda}{e}Y^* + \dfrac{\lambda}{e}\pi A_t^e + \dfrac{\lambda}{e}\theta M_t^e}{1 - \lambda + \dfrac{\lambda\theta}{e}}$$

In calculating this "rational" expected price level, the expected values of the two error terms (u_t and v_t) are zero, and the expected value of the natural rate of output (Y^*) is assumed to be constant. We can now eliminate the P_t^e term in our price level equation (17A-5) by substituting equation 17A-6:

(17A-7) $$\left(1 + \frac{\theta\lambda}{e}\right)P_t = (1 - \lambda)P_{t-1} - \frac{\lambda}{e}Y^* + \frac{\lambda}{e}\left(\pi A_t + \theta M_t - \theta v_t + \frac{\pi}{a}u_t\right)$$

$$+ \left(\frac{\lambda}{1 - \lambda + \dfrac{\lambda\theta}{e}}\right)\left[(1 - \lambda)P_{t-1} - \frac{\lambda}{e}Y^* + \frac{\lambda\pi}{e}A_t^e + \frac{\lambda\theta}{e}M_t^e\right]$$

Finally, equation 17A-7 can be substituted into the income level equation (17A-4a). Rather than writing out this extremely long final equation in its full algebraic glory, we focus our attention on the algebraic coefficients for the key M_t and M_t^e variables.[2]

(17A-8) $$Y_t = \left(\frac{\theta}{1 + \dfrac{\lambda\theta}{e}}\right)M_t - \left[\frac{\lambda^2\theta^2/e}{\left(1 + \dfrac{\lambda\theta}{e}\right)\left(1 - \lambda + \dfrac{\lambda\theta}{e}\right)}\right]M_t^e + f(A_t, A_t^e, Y^*, P_{t-1}, u_t, v_t)$$

What will be the effect on income levels for a change in monetary policy which is fully anticipated? Setting $M_t = M_t^e$ in equation 17A-8 produces the following result:

$$Y_t = \left[\left(\frac{\theta}{1 + \dfrac{\lambda\theta}{e}} \right) - \frac{\lambda^2\theta^2/e}{\left(1 + \dfrac{\lambda\theta}{e}\right)\left(1 - \lambda + \dfrac{\lambda\theta}{e}\right)} \right] M_t^e + f(A_t, A_t^e, Y^*, P_{t-1}, u_t, v_t)$$

(17A-9)

$$Y_t = \left[\frac{\theta(1 - \lambda)\left(1 + \dfrac{\lambda\theta}{e}\right)}{\left(1 + \dfrac{\lambda\theta}{e}\right)\left(1 - \lambda + \dfrac{\lambda\theta}{e}\right)} \right] M_t^e + f(A_t, A_t^e, Y^*, P_{t-1}, u_t, v_t)$$

Now if $\lambda = 1.0$, then the numerator for the M_t^e coefficient will be zero. If one assumes that the economy is always in equilibrium, with prices instantly adjusting to their (new) market-clearing levels, then correctly anticipated monetary policy will have absolutely no effect on the level of income. Equation 17A-9 provides a restatement of the new classical policy ineffectiveness proposition when $\lambda = 1.0$; that is, when prices instantly adjust to maintain market equilibrium.

However, if λ is less than unity, then the coefficient for the M_t^e variable is unambiguously positive. Therefore, even when price expectations are formed in a rational manner, correctly anticipated monetary policy will have a positive (short run) effect on output levels when price levels do not instantly adjust to their market-clearing levels. While rational expectations is a *necessary* condition for the new classical policy ineffectiveness proposition, it clearly is *not a sufficient* condition. *We also require that markets continually clear*. The necessary and sufficient conditions for the policy ineffectiveness proposition are *rational expectations* and *market clearing*. If markets are *not* continually in equilibrium, then anticipated monetary and/or fiscal policy *will* affect employment and output levels.

---

[2]It can easily be demonstrated that when $\lambda = 1.0$, the coefficients in equation 17A-8 are identical to those presented in the main body of the chapter. Substituting the underlying structural parameters for θ, the coefficient for M_t in equation (17A-8) is in fact k (as given in equation 17-9):

$$\frac{\theta}{1 + \dfrac{\theta}{e}} = \frac{\dfrac{b/d}{1 + bc/d}}{1 + \dfrac{b/d}{(1 + bc/d)e}} = \frac{eb/d}{e(1 + \dfrac{bc}{d}) + b/d} = \frac{1}{\dfrac{d}{b} + c + \dfrac{1}{e}} = k$$

Key Concepts

adaptive expectations
rational expectations
the price surprise supply function (*PSSF*)
the policy ineffectiveness proposition

Review Questions

1. What is meant by *adaptive* inflation expectations? Carefully explain (or demonstrate) why an *adaptive* inflation forecast depends exclusively on *actual past* inflation rates. Provide an illustration of an *adaptive* forecasting exercise in which the forecast errors are systematically negative.
2. Analyze the macroeconomic implications of an increase in the growth rate of the *nominal* money supply from 3 per cent to 10 per cent assuming that inflation expectations are formed in an *adaptive* manner.
3. Assuming a constant growth rate in the *nominal* money supply, analyze the macroeconomic implications of a *negative demand* shock under the assumption of *adaptive* inflation expectations.
4. Explain the concept of *rational* expectations. Why are the forecast errors *random* under the assumption of *rational* expectations?
5. Outline the necessary assumptions for the price surprise supply function. Carefully explain why an unexpected price decline will lead to a *temporary* decrease in production. Why is the decrease in production only *temporary*?
6. Demonstrate that the *PSSF* equation is an *inverted PEP* equation. Contrast the theory behind the *PSSF* with the theory behind the *PEP* curve.
7. Assuming *rational* expectations and a price surprise supply function, demonstrate the following new classical macroeconomic propositions:
   a) *Anticipated* monetary policy will have no effect on the level of output.
   b) *Anticipated* fiscal policy will have no effect on the level of output.
   c) *Un*anticipated monetary or fiscal policy will affect the level of output.
   d) The actual level of output will deviate from the *natural* rate of output by a *random* (nonsystematic) error.
8. Demonstrate that *rational* price expectations are a *necessary* condition for the new classical policy ineffectiveness proposition.
9. Evaluate the relative merits of the assumption of *rational* inflation expectations versus *adaptive* inflation expectations.
10. Evaluate the new classical policy ineffectiveness proposition.

Part5

The Supply and Demand for Money Balances

18

I find that the high prices we see today are due to some four or five causes. The principal and almost the only one (which no one has referred to until now) is the abundance of gold and silver which is today much greater in this Kingdom than it was four hundred years ago.

Jean Bodin (1568)[1]

In this chapter we will be concerned exclusively with the money market, where the supply and demand for money balances determine the rate of interest. There are three parts to this chapter. The first is concerned with the nature of money itself and the way in which the stock of money is measured in Canada. A discussion of the nature and functions of money leads naturally to the development of theories that can explain what quantity of money balances the public wants to hold, that is, the demand for money balances. This is taken up in the second part. Finally, we turn to the supply side of the money market. Here we will be concerned with how the Bank of Canada exercises its influence over the Canadian money market.

The Functions and Definitions of Money

Perhaps the best way to think about the role that money plays in our modern economy is to imagine what it would be like if money did not exist. An important feature of any economy, other than the most primitive subsistence economies, is that people trade with each other—labour services are supplied to firms so that in return people can obtain the goods and services that are produced by firms. If there were no money, payments would have to be made in kind. For example, farm workers would be paid in agricultural products. This would clearly be very inefficient: imagine being paid in peaches, which are bulky and perishable. How would you arrange to buy a car if all your income came in the form of fresh peaches? You would have to find a car salesman who needs a truckload of fresh peaches! Money solves these awkward trading problems, since it is neither bulky nor perishable and can be used in any exchange. This is the first and single most important function of money: it serves as a **medium of exchange**. Money balances

[1]Jean Bodin, "The Dearness of Things," in A.E. Monroe, ed., *Early Economic Thought* (Cambridge Mass.: Harvard University Press, 1924), p. 127.

that are kept for the purpose of making payments are often referred to as *transactions balances*.

A closely related issue is that of pricing and accounting. Suppose that our imaginary, moneyless economy produces only four different items (*A, B, C, D*). There are six different pairs of items that can be traded in a four-item economy (*AB, AC, AD, BC, BD, CD*). This means there would be six rates of exchange between pairs of goods, or six "prices". In a fifteen-item economy, the number of two-item exchanges exceeds 100 (105 to be exact), and in a one-hundred-item economy the number of two-item exchanges that are possible rises to 4950. Obviously, keeping track of all the "prices" in a moneyless economy would be exceedingly difficult. In a monetary economy, each product and service has just one dollar price, so that it is possible to add up the value of a number of different items by expressing their value in terms of the unique monetary unit. This in turn greatly simplifies accounting procedures and points to the second function of money, which is to provide a **unit of account**.

Another feature of modern economies is the phenomenon of borrowing and lending. For example, a mortgage contract requires the borrower to pay specific sums of money on specific dates, say, $500 on the first of each month for fifteen years. In this instance, money acts as a **means of deferred payment**.

The fourth function of money is related to its durable nature. Money is a **store of value**, or wealth. There are many kinds of assets that people can own; stocks, bonds and real estate being just three examples. Money is another kind of asset that can be part of an overall portfolio of wealth. An interesting question to ask is: what are the factors that determine the share of total wealth that people should keep in the form of money? Obviously, if stock prices are about to fall it is better to hold money than stocks. But this question brings us to the demand for money balances itself, which will be discussed more fully later. Let us first look at how the stock of money is measured in Canada.

Four definitions of money that are regularly reported by the Bank of Canada are presented in Table 18-1. Two of the functions of money we have just described motivate these definitions. First, money's major function is to serve as a *medium of exchange*. With this as a guide, everything that can be used to make payments (transactions balances) should be included in a definition of money. The most narrowly defined concept of money, labelled M1, is an attempt to conform to this criterion. M1 includes the currency in circulation and chequable demand deposits held at chartered banks, both of which can be used directly to make payments. However, there are other types of deposits that can be used to make payments. In recent years daily interest chequing accounts have become increasingly popular. These accounts, together with nonpersonal notice deposits, are added to M1 to produce M1A. But even this wider definition of money does not include all chequable deposits held at chartered banks.

Possibly an even more important difficulty in measuring spendable deposits is the exclusion of chequable deposits held at financial institutions other than banks. The importance of this omission is illustrated by a comparison of the growth rates of M1 and chequable deposits held at trust and mortgage loan companies; call this latter quantity MTM for short (money at trust and mortgage companies). Over the

TABLE 18-1 Measures of the Stock of Money, December 1986
(Millions of Dollars)

Currency	Currency + Demand Deposits	Currency + All Chequable Deposits	Currency + All Chequable Notice and Personal Term Deposits	Currency + Privately Held Bank Deposits
	M1	M1A	M2	M3
14,804	32,637	72,834	175,836	216,124

five-year period from the end of 1979 to the end of 1984, M1 grew 23 per cent while MTM grew a huge 412 per cent. At the beginning of this five-year period MTM was only 4 per cent of the size of M1, but five years later MTM had grown to 18 per cent of the size of M1. Clearly, the growth of M1 has understated the growth of "spendable deposits" in recent years for two separate reasons. First, chartered banks have created new kinds of chequable deposits that pay interest, and these are not included in M1. Second, institutions other than banks have been increasingly successful at competing for the public's chequable deposits, and these are not included in M1. The continuously changing financial system has made it impossible to define a single measure of the stock of money that accurately reflects total spendable deposits over a lengthy period of time and the Bank of Canada has had to modify its monetary definitions as circumstances have changed.

The wider definitions of the stock of money, M2 and M3, go beyond the concept of transactions balances (immediately spendable deposits). For example, M2 includes personal term deposits—that is, deposits that are left with a bank for a specific term and that can be liquidated only at some cost. These deposits are *stores of wealth* that are considered closer to money than to other kinds of financial assets such as long-term bonds or stocks, both of which have the potential for large capital gains or losses. A still more comprehensive monetary aggregate is M3, which includes nonpersonal term deposits and foreign currency deposits of Canadian residents booked in Canada. These wider definitions, nevertheless, do not include the term deposits and guaranteed investment certificates offered by trust companies, which serve essentially the same purpose as term deposits at chartered banks. In recent years the Bank of Canada has recognized the growing importance of trust and other financial companies and now refers to a quantity called M3+ which includes all of M3 as well as the deposits held at financial institutions other than banks.

In summary, defining the stock of money is not a simple task. The difficulty is not merely an abstract one. As we discussed in Chapter 16, M1 was the centrepiece of monetary policy over the period 1975 to 1982. At the time, the Governor of the Bank of Canada clearly believed that M1 was the most appropriate concept of money on which to base Canada's monetary policy:

> This aggregate [M1]... moves with the trend of aggregate spending in the economy in a fairly predictable manner and is susceptible to control by the central bank through the adjustment of short-term interest rates without causing great instability in financial markets. Our experience to date in using M1 has confirmed in my mind its usefulness as a proximate

target in the conduct of monetary policy.

Those money supply aggregates that are appreciably broader in their coverage than M1 do not appear in Canada's present circumstances to meet the requirements noted above as well as M1.[2]

But in 1984 the Governor was considerably less enthusiastic:

One technical difficulty that arises in implementing monetary policy... is that there are no aggregate measures or indicators of the rate of monetary expansion in Canada that are sufficiently reliable at present to be used as targets for policy, or that are uniquely helpful in the task of explaining the impact of monetary policy.[3]

With these practical difficulties in mind, we turn now to the theories of the demand for money balances.

Demand for Money Theories

The alternative theories of the demand for money focus on the most important functions of money. As discussed earlier, the usefulness of money as a medium of exchange creates a *transactions demand* for money. We will examine below the variables that are important determinants of the transactions demand for money. A somewhat broader view of money is that it provides one form in which wealth can be held. The distinguishing feature of money in this context is that it is liquid; its money value is certain (unlike bonds, stocks and real estate) and it can be exchanged for other assets, goods or services with little or no transactions cost. We begin our discussion of the demand for money with the transactions approach, which focuses on the medium of exchange function of money.

The Transactions Demand for Money

The **transactions demand** for money arises because the receipt of income by individuals and firms is not perfectly synchronized with the payments that they have to make. If, in fact, all household payments could be made on the *same* day that the monthly paycheque is paid into the bank, there would be no need to keep either cash or chequable deposits. All bills could be settled on payday and the surplus (savings) could be invested in some interest-bearing asset. In practice, of course, individuals do need to make payments between paycheques and they hold money for this purpose.

To illustrate the costs and benefits of holding money, consider two extreme strategies. The first is to exchange the monthly paycheque for an interest-bearing asset (for example, a savings account or a bond) as soon as the paycheque is received. Appropriate amounts are then cashed in whenever a payment has to be made. This approach will maximize the individual's interest income, but substantial transactions costs will be incurred (such as repeated trips to the bank to

---

[2]Bank of Canada, *Annual Report*, 1978, p. 15.
[3]Bank of Canada, *Annual Report*, 1984, p. 8.

transfer funds, or commission charges that would have to be paid if bonds were sold). These transactions costs are often simply referred to as brokerage costs. The other extreme strategy is to avoid brokerage costs altogether by keeping the entire month's cash requirements in the form of cash at all times. The cost of this strategy is the interest that could have been earned on the idle cash. The optimal strategy is to hold a level of money balances that minimizes the sum of brokerage costs and foregone interest.[4]

Suppose, for example, that the total value of transactions a household makes in a month is T and that these payments are spread evenly throughout the month. The decision that has to be made is the following: how many times per month should transfers be made between interest-earning assets (say bonds) and money? Chart 18-1 illustrates two possibilities. The first involves two transfers. On payday half of the month's cash requirements is kept as cash and the other half is invested in a bond, at a cost of b (the brokerage fee). During the first half of the month cash balances are gradually run down to zero, and on the middle day of the month the bond is cashed in, again at a cost of b. The red line in Chart 18-1 represents the *average* level of cash held during the entire month, which is $(T/2) \div 2 = T/4$. Notice that for half the month (the first and third quarters) cash balances are above $T/4$ and during the other half of the month cash balances are below $T/4$. The loss of interest income can be represented by R times $T/4$, where R is the monthly interest rate. The total cost of holding this particular level of average cash balances is therefore the sum of the two brokerage charges and the foregone interest, $2b + RT/4$.

The right-hand panel of Chart 18-1 shows the household's cash position throughout the month when three financial transactions are made between bonds and cash. The day the paycheque is received, two-thirds are put into bonds. Cash balances steadily run down to zero by the tenth day of the thirty-day month. Bonds are then cashed (again at a cost b) to provide enough money to last another one-third of a month, at which point the remainder of the bonds are cashed. Three financial transactions between money and bonds have been made at a cost of $3b$. Average cash balances are only $(T/3) \div 2 = T/6$, implying foregone interest of only $RT/6$. The total cost of this strategy is $3b + RT/6$. In general, if the individual makes n financial transactions the brokerage and lost-interest costs amount to

$$nb + \frac{RT}{2n}$$

The astute individual will be concerned with the value of n that minimizes this total cost. If n is treated as a continuous variable rather than as a whole number, then it can be shown that the optimal level of average money balances is[5]

$$(18\text{-}1) \qquad \$^D = \sqrt{\frac{bT}{2R}}$$

[4]This approach to the transactions demand for money was first developed by W. Baumol in "The Transactions Demand for Cash: An Inventory Theoretic Approach," *Quarterly Journal of Economics*, November 1952, pp. 545-56.

[5]Students familiar with the calculus can demonstrate this by differentiating the total cost expression with respect to n. Setting the first derivative to zero (the first order condition for total cost minimization) and substituting the optimal value of n in the expression $\$^D = T/2n$ gives equation 18-1.

CHART 18-1 The average level of cash balances depends on the frequency of transfers between bonds and cash

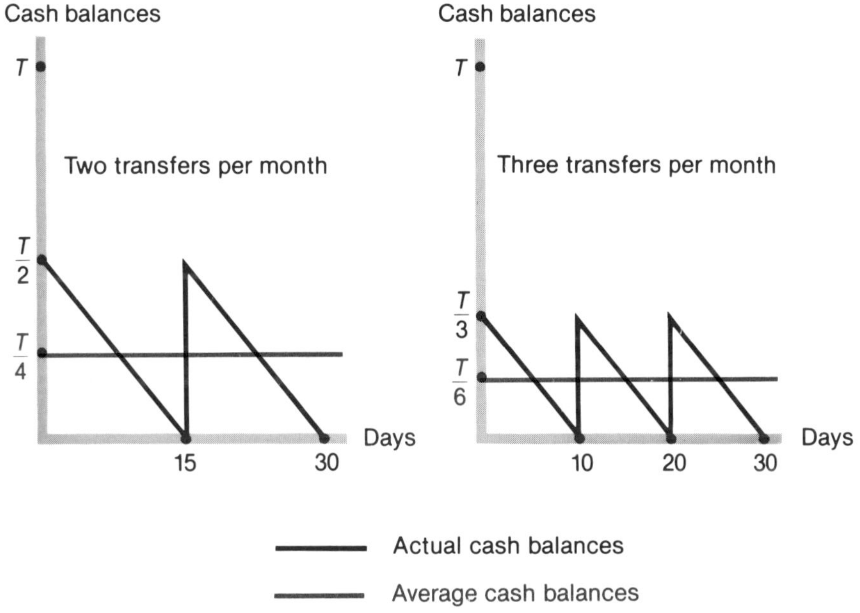

Actual cash balances

Average cash balances

It is interesting to compare this demand function with equation 5-3 of Chapter 5, which we reproduce here for convenience.

(5-3) $\qquad \$^D = kY - \ell R$

In Chapter 5 it was argued (with empirical support) that the demand for real money balances depends directly on the level of real income Y and inversely on the interest rate R. The linear specification 5-3 proved to be a convenient form for our algebraic manipulations and is broadly consistent with the theoretically based equation 18-1. For example, when the price level is *fixed*, equation 18-1 can be interpreted as the demand for *real* money balances. In this case T varies with the *volume* of transactions and is therefore likely to be highly correlated with the level of real income. Equation 18-1 is therefore consistent with the view that the demand for real money balances varies directly with the level of real income. Second, in both equations 5-3 and 18-1, an increase in the rate of interest R leads to a reduction in the demand for real money balances.

When the price level is *flexible*, the $\$^D$ of equation 18-1 must be interpreted as the demand for *nominal* money balances and T is the *value* of transactions. How does the demand for nominal money balances vary with the price level? Suppose the price level doubles but all real magnitudes remain unchanged. Since both the *value* of transactions T and the price of brokerage fees b will double, the product

bT quadruples. However, $\$^D$ depends on the square root of bT so that the quadrupling of this product leads to only a doubling of the demand for nominal money balances. This argument shows that Baumol's transactions demand for money approach predicts that a doubling of the price level will lead, *ceteris paribus*, to a doubling of the demand for nominal money balances.

Keynesian Liquidity Preference

Keynes recognized the transactions motive behind the demand for money and, in fact, broke it down into two components: the demand due to regular, planned transactions (which Baumol considered in detail) and a demand for precautionary purposes. The precautionary demand accounts for the money balances that are held in order that unforeseen transactions can be made. But more important than this distinction is Keynes' recognition that money also serves as a store of liquid wealth. Money is an asset just as real estate, stocks and bonds are assets. But because the prices of most assets vary considerably and/or substantial transactions costs are incurred when they are bought and sold, it is sometimes advantageous to hold money rather than income-earning assets. In particular, just before bond and stock prices fall, it would be convenient to hold money rather than bonds and stocks. Financial analysts are certainly aware of this role of money: "Investors should keep a substantial part of their portfolio in short-term debt or cash to be able to move in and out of the stock market, a report from McLeod Young Weir Ltd. of Toronto says."[6]

To capture the essence of the problem Keynes confined his analysis to a situation in which wealth can be held in two forms: money and long bonds. The choice between these alternatives depends on their relative rates of return. Of course in nominal terms, money pays no return at all. Long bonds, on the other hand, can give either positive or negative returns over a period of, say, one year. Bonds pay a fixed annual interest payment, usually referred to as the coupon. But the market price of a bond can change dramatically from one year to the next. The bond-holder therefore stands to lose or gain (in any given year) depending on how bond prices move. In general the price of an asset, such as a bond, depends on the flow of income that it generates and the market interest rate. Let us consider in more detail the determination of bond prices.

When the government (or a corporation) issues a bond it undertakes to pay the bondholder an annual interest payment C—the coupon—and to redeem the face value F of the bond on the maturity date. For example, Table 18-2 gives some information on an $11\frac{3}{4}$ per cent Government of Canada bond that will mature in February 2003. The $11\frac{3}{4}$ per cent refers to the size of the annual coupon payment. If the face value of the bond is $100, the annual coupon payment is $11.75. The table also shows that the market price of the bond in July 1981 was $67.88. In other words, at that time investors were prepared to pay $67.88 for the right to receive $11.75 every year up to the year 2003 (the coupon payment) and an additional $100 in the year 2003 (the face value of the bond). The price that

---

[6]*Globe and Mail*, 6 October 1980.

TABLE 18-2 Bond Yields and Bond Prices

	Long Bond		Short Bond	
	($11\frac{3}{4}\%$, due February 2003)		(10.5%, due October 1984)	
Date	Price	Yield	Price	Yield
July 1981	67.88	17.5%	82.0	18.2%
July 1983	96.73	12.2%	99.6	10.1%

individuals (or pension funds) are prepared to pay for the bond is often referred to as the bond's present value.

To see what determines the present value or price of this bond let us consider the general case in which the annual coupon C is to be paid for N years. In the Nth year the bond matures and the bondholder receives the face value F. The present value of the bond is the value of this stream of income. We will consider the problem in several stages. Suppose the present value of the first coupon payment (which will be received in one year's time) is PV_1. That is, an individual is prepared to pay PV_1 now in order to receive C in one year's time. What alternatives does the individual have? If the annual rate of interest is currently R, then the individual could invest the sum PV_1, say in a savings account, and receive $PV_1 (1 + R)$ in one year's time. The individual will be indifferent between these two alternatives only when the sum accumulated in the savings account is equal to the coupon C, that is, when $PV_1 (1 + R) = C$. This can be rearranged to give

$$PV_1 = \frac{C}{1 + R}$$

This equation says that at the annual interest rate R, the present value of C (to be paid in one year) is $C/(1 + R)$. To illustrate this formula consider the present value of $10 (to be paid in one year) when the annual interest rate is 8 per cent ($R = 0.08$). The formula indicates that it is $10/(1 + 0.08) or $9.26. Note that if $9.26 is placed in a savings account that pays 8 per cent per annum the accumulated sum after one year will be $9.26 (1 + 0.08) or $10. Paying $9.26 for the right to receive C ($10) is just as profitable as placing these funds in a savings account. No one would pay more than $9.26 now for $10 next year because even $9.27 will accumulate to more than $10 in one year at 8 per cent interest. If the annual interest rate were 12 per cent rather than 8 per cent, the present value of next year's $10 would be $10/(1.12) or $8.93. No one would pay more than $8.93 to receive $10 next year because at 12 per cent per annum a greater sum could be accumulated by putting the funds into a savings account. This example illustrates the inverse relationship between the present value of an asset and the rate of interest. We will say more on this later.

Now let us turn to the present value of the coupon payment that will be received in two years' time, PV_2. The alternative to receiving the coupon is to place the funds in a savings account that pays an annual interest rate R. The accumulated value in the account after one year would be $PV_2 (1 + R)$. If this is left in the account for a second year it becomes

$$[PV_2(1 + R)](1 + R) = PV_2(1 + R)^2$$

The individual will be indifferent between paying PV_2 for the coupon C (to be paid in two years) and putting PV_2 into the savings account if $PV_2 (1 + R)^2 = C$. This can be rearranged to give the present value in terms of the coupon and the interest rate:

$$PV_2 = \frac{C}{(1 + R)^2}$$

Again, suppose C is $10 and the interest rate is 8 per cent ($R = 0.08$). At this interest rate, the present value of $10 (which will be paid in two years' time) is $10/(1 + 0.08)^2$ or $8.57. This is less than the present value of the first coupon payment ($9.26) and in general the further into the future is the date that the $10 will be paid, the less will be its present value. In fact, similar calculations to those above show that the present value of the coupon to be received n years from now is:

$$PV_n = \frac{C}{(1 + R)^n}$$

Consider again the bond that pays C in each of N years and F in the Nth year. This bond has a present value equal to the sum of the present values of all the coupon payments as well as face value F.

$$(18\text{-}2) \qquad PV_N = \frac{C}{(1 + R)} + \frac{C}{(1 + R)^2} + \ldots + \frac{C}{(1 + R)^N} + \frac{F}{(1 + R)^N}$$

Equation 18-2 shows that the present value of a bond depends on the size of the stream of payments and the interest rate. As the interest rate R rises the present value of the bond falls. The sensitivity of the present value to changes in the interest rate depends on the term to maturity N. When N is large, a small change in R can cause a large change in $(1 + R)^N$ and therefore a large change in the present value. This is well illustrated in Table 18-2. The 11¾ per cent bond that sold for $67.88 in July 1981 had a market value of $96.73 two years later, an increase of $28.85 or 43 per cent. Over this period the long-term interest rate (measured by the yield on long bonds held to maturity) fell from 17.5 to 12.2 per cent, a decline of 5.3 percentage points. If you had bought one of these bonds in July 1981, by July 1983 you would have received two coupon payments worth $11.75 each and seen the price of your bond rise in value by $28.85, giving a total return of $52.35. This works out to a 77 per cent return on an initial outlay of $67.88. Of course, these spectacular gains are far from assured. It is equally possible to suffer large capital losses by investing in long-term bonds. This happened between March 1979 and March 1980, when long-term bond prices fell 25 per cent during the rapid run-up in long-term interest rates.

   In 1981, the long-term bond illustrated in Table 18-2 had 22 years to go before its maturity date. In contrast, the short bond illustrated in the same table was to mature in 1984. As of July 1981, it had a much shorter life of just over three years.

Over the next two years, short-term interest rates fell sharply from 18.2 to 10.1 per cent, a drop of 8.1 percentage points. Although short rates fell more than long rates, the capital gain on the short bond was much less—just $17.60 on an initial outlay of $82. Had you bought one of these bonds in July 1981, your total yield over the next two years would have included two coupon payments of $10.50 each and a capital gain of $17.60, giving a total return of $38.60; that is, an overall yield of 47 per cent on an outlay of $82.

These examples illustrate that during periods of falling interest rates, bond prices rise, and the longer the term to maturity the more sensitive bond prices are to changes in the rate of interest. This works the other way. When interest rates rise, bond prices fall. Huge capital losses can be suffered on long bonds when long-term rates rise.

Keynes' theory of **liquidity preference** stresses the role of potential capital gains or losses in the individual's portfolio decision. If long-term interest rates are expected to fall, then the individual expects to earn capital gains by holding bonds. In these circumstances the demand for money will be low (there is little preference for liquidity). However, if long-term interest rates are expected to rise sufficiently far, then capital losses will wipe out the interest income and the individual will be better off if he holds cash rather than bonds (there is a great preference for liquidity). Keynes argued that long-term interest rates follow a cyclical pattern around a "normal" interest rate. The higher are long-term interest rates, the greater will be the number of people who anticipate that interest rates will fall and therefore that bond prices will rise. Most people will prefer to hold bonds rather than money when interest rates are high. On the other hand, the lower are interest rates, the greater will be the number of people who expect rates to rise and bond prices to fall. Therefore, the lower are interest rates, the greater will be the demand for money. Thus, Keynes argued that the demand for speculative money balances varies inversely with the current rate of interest.

Tobin's Analysis of Liquidity Preference

A much more persuasive and influential approach to the analysis of how individuals decide how to allocate their wealth between alternative financial assets was pioneered by Professor James Tobin.[7] Tobin's approach can be applied to the general problem of determining the optimal combination of assets in a portfolio, as well as providing a rationale for the inverse relationship between the demand for money and the rate of interest. Here we want to focus on the latter, so our discussion will again be confined to the choice between two assets: money and bonds. Tobin assumes that the owners of wealth want to increase the value of their wealth by investing in assets that have a high expected yield. However, such assets are often risky in that while the expected yield is high there is also a high probability that the actual yield will differ considerably from the expected yield. The second assumption is that individuals prefer to avoid risk rather than take risk.

[7]J. Tobin, "Liquidity Preference as a Behaviour Towards Risk," *Review of Economic Studies*, February 1958, pp. 65-86.

Thus, of two equally risky assets, individuals typically prefer the one with the higher expected yield, and of two assets with the same expected yield, individuals typically prefer the less risky of the two.

Money has an expected yield of zero, but is also riskless. Bonds on the other hand usually have a positive expected yield, although there is some risk because future bond prices are unknown and there is a possibility that a large capital loss will be incurred. The individual's problem is how to allocate his or her total wealth (which is given) between the two alternative forms. A portfolio of money is riskless, but yields no return. A portfolio made up entirely of bonds, on the other hand, has both a maximum expected yield and maximum risk because of potentially large capital losses. The riskiness of the overall portfolio can be reduced by replacing bonds with money, but the cost of reducing risk is the loss in expected yield. The optimal portfolio is one in which any further reductions in risk are simply not worth the cost in terms of lower expected yield. Tobin showed that under reasonable assumptions the optimal portfolio will include both money and bonds. Thus, some liquidity (money) is preferred to none because individuals generally seek to avoid risk. Moreover, if the expected yield on bonds rises without any change in their riskiness, then the individual has an incentive to increase the proportion of bonds in the portfolio and reduce the size of money holdings. Consequently, an increase in expected bond yields (without any change in risk) leads to a reduction in the demand for money. To the extent that an increase in the actual interest rate leads to an increase in the expected yield on bonds but no change in their riskiness, the demand for money is a decreasing function of the interest rate on bonds.

Tobin's approach demonstrates that there will be a portfolio demand for money balances despite the fact that money pays no interest precisely because money is riskless whereas all other assets are risky. However, in practice, savings accounts can be thought of as riskless assets and they do pay interest. This poses a problem: if money is held only because it is riskless, but some kinds of riskless money pay interest and others don't, Tobin's theory predicts that no one will hold the non-interest-bearing money. Tobin's theory can therefore explain why interest-bearing deposits are held, but not cash and demand deposits. The theories of Baumol and Tobin are complementary rather than alternatives. Baumol's transactions demand model is intended to explain the holding of M1, which corresponds to transactions balances. Tobin's theory is able to explain the holding of those components of M2 which are not included in M1.

The Quantity Theory of Money, Old and New

The origins of the traditional **quantity theory of money** go back to the the beginnings of economics as a discipline. The fundamental identity that underpins this approach to the demand for money is Irving Fisher's "equation of exchange."[8]

$$\$^S V = PY$$

---

[8] I. Fisher, *The Purchasing Power of Money* (New York: Macmillan Co., 1911).

The "equation of exchange" is in fact an identity which defines the velocity of money V: $V = (PY)/\$^S$. In this expression P is the aggregate price level, Y is the level of real annual income (GNP) so that PY is the value of nominal GNP. As we learned in Chapter 2, this is simply the annual value of all transactions involving the exchange of final goods and services. By dividing this total volume of transactions by the stock of money $\$^S$, we find how many times the typical dollar changes hands during the year (the velocity of money).[9]

Quantity theorists argue that both the velocity of money and real income are, in the long run, determined by factors other than the stock of money. Velocity, the rate at which money changes hands, is in large part determined by institutional and technological factors such as the frequency with which paycheques are issued and the speed with which financial institutions settle accounts. Thus, while velocity may change slowly over the long run, these changes are unrelated to changes in the stock of money. Similarly the level of real income is determined by the supplies of the factors of production, land, labour and capital and the state of technology (see Chapter 8). Changes in the supply of money have no bearing on the capacity of the economy to produce real goods and services.

Having assumed that both the velocity of money and the level of real income are independent of the stock of money, the quantity theorist is now able to demonstrate that a given percentage change in the stock of money will, of itself, ultimately cause an equal percentage change in the aggregate price level. This is shown by rearranging the equation of exchange to read

$$P = \left(\frac{V}{Y}\right) \$^S$$

Given that the ratio V/Y does not depend on the stock of money, a doubling of $\$^S$ will lead, *ceteris paribus*, to a doubling of the aggregate price level. Second, because velocity is slow to change, the level of nominal income PY will bear a stable relationship with the quantity of money. This is shown by the equation of exchange itself.

$$PY = V\$^S$$

The modern quantity theory developed by Professor Milton Friedman embraces both of these conclusions, and has become the cornerstone of the monetarist approach to macroeconomics.

Friedman's view of money is similar to Tobin's in that money is seen as an asset. But rather than treating money simply as a riskless financial asset, Friedman regards money as a durable good that "yields its return solely in kind, in the usual form of convenience, security, etc."[10] From the point of view of firms, money is a factor of production, or capital good. Friedman has analyzed the key variables that

---

[9]Fisher's original "equation of exchange" defined the transactions velocity of money; that is, all transactions were included, not just those involving final goods and services. Modern economists have found the income velocity concept more useful because it relates the stock of money to the level of nominal GNP rather than to the total volume of transactions.

[10]Milton Friedman, "The Quantity Theory of Money, A Restatement," in Milton Friedman, ed., *Studies in the Quantity Theory of Money* (Chicago: University of Chicago Press, 1956), pp. 3-21.

determine households' and firms' demand for money balances and concludes that these are sufficiently similar that no distinction needs to be made between them. Consequently, the total demand for money balances can be written as

(18-3) $$\frac{\$^D}{P} = f(\dot{P}, r_b, r_e, Y, w)$$

First, note that Friedman defines the demand for money in terms of the demand for real money balances, $\$^D/P$, because it is through its purchasing power that money yields its benefit. As in Tobin's analysis, the arguments of the demand function include the rates of return that can be earned on alternative assets. Friedman classifies these alternatives into three types. The first category is physical goods. The relevant rate of return is the rate of price inflation, $\dot{P}$. Thus, the higher is the rate of inflation, the greater is the incentive to buy physical goods and reduce one's holdings of real money balances. The second and third alternatives are bonds and equities, which have rates of return r_b and r_e respectively. The greater are the rates of return on bonds and equities, the lower is the demand for real money balances. The fourth variable, Y, represents permanent income.[11] This is a proxy for Friedman's all-encompassing return on wealth. Friedman's concept of wealth includes both financial wealth (stocks, bonds, and physical assets such as land, houses and consumer durables) and human wealth. The latter concept recognizes that, for example, just before Wayne Gretzky started his professional hockey career he may not have been financially wealthy. However, his personal skills amounted to wealth in that they were about to earn him a high income and are expected to do so for many years to come. Compared with an individual who has considerable financial wealth or capital, an individual with an equal amount of wealth, but most of it in the form of human capital, will tend to hold a smaller proportion of his wealth as money. Consequently, it is not only total wealth that determines the demand for money, but also the form that the wealth takes. Accordingly, Friedman includes w, the ratio of human to nonhuman wealth, in his demand for money function.

The key distinguishing feature of Friedman's demand for money function lies in the presence of the rate of return on physical assets in the demand function. Unlike Keynesians who emphasize the substitutability of money for financial assets such as bonds and stocks, monetarists argue that physical assets are also direct substitutes for money. This has important implications for the transmission mechanism of monetary policy. The traditional Keynesian view is that an open market purchase of treasury bills, for example, will bid up the price of treasury bills (and depress interest rates). Firms now find that the funds they might need for expansion purposes are now less costly to obtain and as a result, firms have an additional incentive to undertake investment projects, so aggregate demand increases.

Monetarists accept this traditional Keynesian chain reaction from declining interest rates to increasing investment expenditures, but argue that it is not the only route through which monetary policy affects aggregate demand. The open market purchase of treasury bills by the Bank of Canada will increase the supply of

[11]See Chapter 19 for a more extensive discussion of permanent income.

money. The public's portfolios will be out of balance; these portfolios will include too much money in relation to other assets, including physical goods. The public will not only purchase financial assets as their portfolios are put in order, but will also purchase physical goods such as cars and television sets. Hence, there is a *direct* link between changes in the stock of money and aggregate spending. By emphasizing this direct link, monetarists are able to argue that changes in the nominal stock of money have a strong influence on aggregate demand. Indeed, monetarists believe that the impact of changes in the stock of money on nominal aggregate demand is much greater than the effect of fiscal measures such as a change in income taxes or government spending.

At the foundation of these views is the belief that velocity is stable over the long term. This can be interpreted to mean that the demand for money is a **stable** function. From Fisher's equation of exchange we have

$$\frac{\$^S}{P} = \frac{Y}{V}$$

Setting the left-hand side equal to the demand for real money balances, we have

$$f(\dot{P}, r_b, r_e, Y, w) = \frac{Y}{V}$$

or

$$V = \frac{Y}{f(\dot{P}, r_b, r_e, Y, w)}$$

The velocity of money is simply the ratio of real income to the demand for real money balances. Monetarists argue that over the long term central banks cannot influence the level of *real* income, nor the *real* return on bonds and equities. As long as the demand for money is a stable function of these variables, the velocity of money will be stable and there will be a direct link between the stock of money and both the price level P and the level of nominal income PY. In the next section we will look at some of the empirical evidence on the properties of the demand for money function.

Empirical Evidence on the Demand for Money

The theories of the demand for money that were discussed in the previous section suggest several hypotheses that can and have been tested empirically. A fairly general specification of the demand for money which allows these hypotheses to be tested is the following:

(18-4) $$\$^D = A P^{a_1} Y^{a_2} R^{a_3}$$

In this equation $\$^D$ represents the demand for nominal money balances, P is the aggregate price level, Y is the level of real income and R is an interest rate which measures the opportunity cost of holding money. The symbols A, a_1, a_2 and a_3 are parameters that are estimated by fitting the function 18-4 to actual data. This is a particularly useful functional form since the parameters a_1, a_2 and a_3 can be interpreted directly as elasticities. That is to say, a_3, for example, is the interest elasticity of demand for money.

All of the theories of the demand for money that we discussed earlier are consistent with the hypothesis that the demand for nominal money balances is proportional to the aggregate price level or, in other words, that the demand for money should be expressed in real terms. In terms of equation 18-4, this amounts to saying that a_1 is unity, in which case both sides of the expression can be divided by P to give

$$(18\text{-}5) \qquad \frac{\$^D}{P} = AY^{a_2} R^{a_3}$$

While many empirical studies have taken an equation such as 18-5 as the starting point for the analysis, there is strong empirical support for the hypothesis that the demand for money balances is proportional to the price level. For example, White[12] estimated equations very similar to 18-4 and found that the Canadian data are consistent with the hypothesis that a_1 is unity. Other important issues raised by the theoretical literature which have been tested empirically include the following:

1) Does the rate of interest influence the demand for money?
2) Are there economies of scale in holding money; that is, is the income elasticity of demand less than unity?
3) Is current income or wealth the appropriate variable to include in the demand for money function?
4) Should money be defined in a narrow (M1) or a wide sense (M2)?
5) Is the demand for money a stable function of a few variables?

The most important question that concerned the early literature is that of the role of the interest rate in the demand for money function. As we saw in Chapter 5, the initial debate between Keynesians and monetarists concerned the slopes of the *IS* and *LM* schedules. Monetarists argued that the demand for money is not influenced greatly by the rate of interest. Although Friedman's theoretical reformulation of the quantity theory allows for interest rate effects, as an empirical matter, Friedman found that permanent income alone determines the demand for money over the long term and that even during business cycles when current income deviates from permanent income, movements in interest rates do not affect the demand for money.[13] Consequently, monetarists such as Friedman believe that the *LM* curve is very steep, if not vertical, and that fiscal policy is ineffective because increases in government spending inevitably raise interest rates and crowd out private spending.

However, Friedman's empirical work on the role of interest rates stands alone as the evidence is now overwhelming that interest rates do indeed affect the demand for money. While the size of the interest rate elasticity does depend on the precise specifications of the model, the literature has come to a broad consensus. In studies that have used a narrow definition of money, the interest elasticity is found

[12]W.R. White, *The Demand for Money in Canada and the Control of Monetary Aggregates: Evidence from the Monthly Data*, Bank of Canada Research Study, 12 (Ottawa: 1976).

[13]Milton Friedman, "The Demand for Money: Some Theoretical and Empirical Results," *Journal of Political Economy*, August 1959, pp. 327-51.

to be in the range of −0.1 to −0.2.[14] Investigators who have used a wider definition of the stock of money such as M2, which includes interest-bearing deposits, have found somewhat weaker interest rate effects on the demand for money. Goldfeld[15] claims that it is not sensible to specify the demand for money in terms of M2. The holding of non-interest-bearing deposits satisfies the transactions motive and the two key variables are income and the opportunity cost of holding money, say the rate paid on savings accounts. A rise in the savings account interest rate will reduce the demand for cash and demand deposits, and raise the demand for savings deposits. Consequently, M1 will show a negative relationship with the rate of interest paid on savings accounts, but the relationship between M2 and this rate of interest is ambiguous; one component rises (savings deposits) and one component falls (M1) as interest rates rise. Consequently, one would expect to find clearer and larger effects of changes in short-term interest on the demand for M1 than on the demand for M2. This is exactly what the data show.

As we have seen, the transactions motive for holding money suggests that the level of current income is an important determinant of the demand for money because the total volume of transactions is likely to be related to the level of income. Studies that have found the current level of income to be a significant determinant of the demand for money have confirmed the prediction of Baumol's theoretical approach that there are economies of scale in holding money balances. That is to say, as real income rises, the demand for real transactions balances also rises but by a smaller proportion. While both White and Goldfeld were concerned with the total demand for real money balances, their studies confirm this prediction since income elasticities were found to be between 0.6 and 1.0.

We turn now to the issues of the stability of the demand for money function. If the demand for money can be shown empirically to be a function of only a few variables and if the effect of each of these variables on the demand for money does not change over time, then we can say that the demand for money is stable. The stability of the demand for money has assumed some importance for monetarist policy prescriptions. As we saw in the last section, the monetarist position has been that the velocity of money is stable. This is critical to the proposition that the stock of money bears a stable relationship to nominal income and to the price level and, therefore, that by controlling the rate of growth of the money supply, central banks can ultimately control the rate of inflation. But we also saw in the last section that the velocity of money is simply the ratio of real income to the demand for money. The argument that, over the long term, velocity is stable boils down to the argument that, over the long term, the demand for money is stable. The large amount of empirical evidence that had been accumulated by the 1970s confirmed the existence of stable demand for money functions in many countries. Goldfeld found that the demand for M1 was more stable than the demand for M2. White, in his 1976 study, also determined that in Canada the demand for M1 was stable. The

[14]Both White, in "Demand for Money," and Goldfeld (see note 15 below) found the short-term interest rate elasticity to be close to −0.15. In both cases a narrow definition of money was used.

[15]M. Goldfeld, "The Demand for Money Revisited," *Brookings Papers on Economic Activity*, vol. 3, 1973, pp. 577-638.

Canadian results provided a foundation for the use of M1 as the central indicator of monetary policy over the period from 1975 to 1982, when growth targets for this narrow measure of the stock of money were set annually.

In the mid-1970s, however, Goldfeld detected a sudden downward shift in the demand for M1 in the United States.[16] The U.S. economy appeared to be functioning with far less money than the estimated demand curves predicted, given the existing levels of output and interest rates. Only a part of this shift could be attributed to changes in banking legislation. What had earlier seemed to be a solid and well understood relationship between the demand for narrowly defined money and its determinants turned into a controversial area once again as researchers sought to solve the puzzle of what Goldfeld called the case of the missing money.

Subsequently, in Canada, similar difficulties were experienced with the use of M1 as the principal measure of monetary policy. From mid-1981 to the end of 1982, M1 grew so slowly that it fell well below the *lower* limit of the Bank of Canada's target range. The shifts in the demand for money were so substantial that at the end of 1982 the Bank of Canada abandoned its seven-year experiment with monetary targets.[17] The demand function for money seems to have been a casualty of the turbulent 1970s and has presented researchers with a new set of challenges in an area that was previously thought to be well understood.

The Money Supply Process

To complete our discussion of the money market we turn now to the supply side of the market. We will focus on the two major institutions that are involved in the money supply process, namely the Bank of Canada and the chartered banks.

The Role of the Chartered Banks

The greater part of the money supply, M1, is made up of demand deposits held at chartered banks. In this section we examine the role of chartered banks in the money creation process. The chartered banks in Canada are privately owned, profit-making institutions which are in the business of financial intermediation. That is to say, banks (and other financial institutions such as trust companies and caisses populaires) act as intermediaries between those who want to lend funds and those who want to borrow funds (the ultimate lenders and borrowers). For this to be a profitable enterprise the banks must offer services to the borrowers and lenders that they bring together. Let us examine some of the more important services.

An important role of financial intermediaries, such as banks, is that of reducing risk in financial markets. Take, for example, the case of an individual who is considering holding (investing in) a mortgage. If the going mortgage rate is 11 per

---

[16]M. Goldfeld, "The Case of the Missing Money," *Brookings Papers on Economic Activity*, vol. 3, 1976, pp. 683-730.

[17]A detailed discussion of Canada's recent monetary policy is given in Chapter 16.

cent, the lender has a chance of either earning 11 per cent on his investment or something far worse; the borrower may default and the lender may not even recover the principal of the loan. Holding a mortgage is clearly much more risky than leaving the money in a savings account where the chance of not being able to withdraw the funds due to bank failure is so remote as to make the investment essentially riskless. Unlike the individual lender, a bank is able to hold thousands of mortgages simultaneously. Even if each of these mortgages is as risky as the one we discussed above, the portfolio of mortgages as a whole is far less risky. The bank can be almost certain that some mortgages will be defaulted, but it can be equally certain that the vast majority will be repaid in full with interest. Unlike the individual mortgage holder, the bank does not care *which* of the mortgages goes into default as long as it can predict roughly what proportion of the total will be defaulted. This is because the losses can be spread over the whole portfolio. If 2 per cent of the portfolio yields a return of zero but 98 per cent of the portfolio yields 11 per cent, then the portfolio as a whole will yield (0.98×11) or 10.8 per cent. Because the bank can be quite sure that the actual return on the portfolio will be close to this figure, the bank can guarantee to its deposit holders that they will be paid, say, 7 per cent on their savings account. The margin of 3.8 per cent covers the expenses of the bank as well as the return to the owners of the bank, its stockholders.

The purpose of this example has been to illustrate how financial institutions can reduce the risks associated with lending by pooling together the relatively small savings of individuals. This pooling of loanable funds has other important advantages. First, the pooling together of small amounts of savings allows huge projects to be financed more easily than if the ultimate borrower had to deal directly with hundreds of small investors. Second, because of the vast size of their lending operations, financial institutions are able to accumulate the information and expertise necessary for the proper evaluation of the credit-worthiness of borrowers, be they individuals or firms. Third, financial intermediation offers ultimate borrowers and lenders a greater flexibility in choosing the term of the debt or the loan than would be possible if ultimate borrowers and lenders had to deal directly. Let us develop this last point in more detail.

Table 18-3 shows the assets and liabilities of the chartered banks at the end of March 1985. Note that loans and mortgages make up a large proportion of total Canadian dollar assets. On the other side of the ledger, deposits are the most important component of Canadian dollar liabilities. The banks are channelling the "liquid" funds that firms and individuals have placed in savings and notice accounts into longer-term assets, for example, loans and mortgages that fall into the "less liquid" category. The term *liquid* has a specific meaning in this context. Assets whose prices show little fluctuation and which can be readily (without significant transactions costs) exchanged for money (M1) are described as liquid. Oil stocks and gold can be readily converted into money but their prices show considerable variability over time and for this reason these assets are not described as liquid. The variability of price means that at any particular time the price of the asset may or may not be favourable for cashing in. Consequently, such assets are unlikely to be desirable forms for holding wealth if there is a high probability they may have to be cashed in at a moment's notice. Government bonds are more or less liquid depending on the term to maturity. As we have seen, the price of a financial asset is inversely related to its rate of return. Moreover, the asset price is more sensitive to changes in the rate of return the longer-lived is the asset. The prices of bonds and securities with very long terms to maturity show considerable variability, and are certainly less liquid than treasury bills, which mature in a matter of months and do not have wildly fluctuating prices.

The data of Table 18-3 show clearly that banks tend to borrow "short" and lend "long." In this way, the funds that individuals or firms wish to lend for only a short period of time are in fact loaned out for longer periods than suit the original lender. Suppose, for example, that you deposit $1,000 in a savings account. The bank may lend it to someone who wants to buy a car and the car loan may extend over a period of four years. If you turn up a month later and ask for your $1,000, is the bank going to be able to pay you? One possibility is that another individual (or individuals) will deposit $1,000 at the bank, allowing the bank to pay you. In this way the bank can finance the car loan by a sequence of deposits. It does not matter to the bank who owns these deposits; what is important is that there are sufficient deposits at all times to cover the loans that the bank has made. Of course, in practice no bank will invest all its liabilities (deposits) in long-term assets such as bank loans because if the total value of deposits were to fall the bank would have to call in loans to pay its depositors. Consequently, banks keep a sufficiently large share of their assets in the form of cash reserves to ensure that such temporary reductions in deposits can be accommodated.

The cash reserves of the chartered banks are made up of Bank of Canada notes held in the vaults of chartered banks plus the deposits that chartered banks hold at the Bank of Canada. Table 18-3 shows that at the end of March 1985 all chartered banks together held cash reserves of $4,760 million. Neither vault cash nor

TABLE 18-3 Chartered Bank Assets and Liabilities, March 1985
(Millions of Dollars)

Assets		Liabilities	
Liquid Assets		Deposits	
Bank of Canada Deposits		Demand Deposits	16,333
and Notes	4,760	Government of Canada	4,424
Other Liquid Assets	3,811	Personal Savings	112,635
Treasury Bills	12,338	Notice Deposits	44,355
Less-Liquid Assets		Other Liabilities	
General Loans	122,653	Bank of Canada Advances	259
Mortgages	35,888	Other Liabilities	25,765
Canadian Securities	12,062		
Other Assets	35,540		
Total Canadian Dollar Assets	227,052	Foreign Currency Liabilities	200,950
Total Foreign Currency Assets	194,829	Shareholders Equity	17,160
Total Assets	421,881	Total Liabilities	421,881

deposits at the Bank of Canada earn interest, and it is a matter of convenience how individual chartered banks decide to hold their cash reserves. Some must be kept in vaults to allow the public to withdraw cash. The deposits at the Bank of Canada are used to settle accounts between the chartered banks. For example, when an individual writes a cheque on his demand account held at bank A, his account will be reduced by $100. The person who receives the cheque may deposit it at bank B, where his account will be credited with $100. However, bank B must somehow obtain the funds from bank A. This can be done simply by reducing bank A's deposits at the Bank of Canada by $100, and crediting bank B's account at the Bank of Canada by $100 (the Bank of Canada is the chartered banks' bank). In this example the total volume of cash reserves is unchanged, but the effect of the transaction is that bank B gains cash reserves at the expense of bank A.

What volume of cash reserves should a prudent bank hold? This depends on the size of its deposits and the variability of these deposits. In fact, federal legislation dictates the minimum *cash reserves* that chartered banks must hold. This minimum level of cash reserves not only protects the public but also provides the means for the Bank of Canada to manipulate the size of the stock of money. We will examine this latter point in more detail below. Under the present Bank Act, for every dollar of demand deposits banks must hold 10 cents in the form of cash reserves and for every dollar of savings or notice deposits banks must hold 3 cents in the form of cash reserves. The value of savings and notice deposits is much greater than the value of demand deposits (see Table 18-3) so the required reserve ratio, averaged over all deposits, is usually close to 0.04. In order to be sure of meeting the **reserve requirements**, banks tend to keep reserves in excess of the minimum. These excess reserves do not earn interest for the bank and are usually very small (typically less than one-tenth of one per cent of total deposits).

Should a bank have difficulty in meeting the reserve requirements, perhaps because of a large unexpected cash drain, the bank can obtain a cash loan from the Bank of Canada. Such loans are short-term. They are shown in Table 18-3 under the heading Bank of Canada Advances.

A Simple Model of the Money Supply

The basic objective of the chartered banks is to generate profits by using depositors' funds to make loans and to buy corporate or government securities and other interest-bearing assets. The major constraint that banks face is that the public may wish to withdraw funds that have been tied up in the form of less liquid assets (loans and securities). Consequently, banks keep, and are required by law to keep, cash reserves that can be used when deposits decline. In this section we develop a model of the supply of money for a simplified financial system. We begin with an equation that defines the supply of money $\$^S$, which is the sum of deposits D and cash held by the public Cp:

$$(18\text{-}6) \qquad \$^S = D + Cp$$

The Bank Act specifies the minimum level of the ratio of reserves to deposits, which we call rr (the reserve ratio). The quantity of required reserves RR depends on the reserve ratio and the volume of banks' deposit liabilities,[18]

(18-7) $RR = rr \cdot D$

Since banks earn no interest on cash reserves there is an incentive for banks to keep reserves as low as possible. As we saw above, it is not much of a distortion to assume that banks keep no excess reserves at all, so that the actual level of reserve holdings is equal to required reserves. In addition, we assume that banks hold just two kinds of assets: reserves RR and loans L, and only one kind of liability: deposits D. For each bank, and therefore all banks together, total assets must equal total liabilities,

(18-8) $D = RR + L$

Reserves can be thought of as cash held in chartered bank vaults, although in practice some reserves are held as deposits at the Bank of Canada. The remainder of the Bank of Canada's notes circulate throughout the economy as cash held by the public, Cp. The total amount of cash issued by the Bank of Canada is called **high powered money**, and we will use the symbol H to represent this quantity. Since the quantity of cash issued by the Bank of Canada, H, must either be held by the banks as required reserves RR or by the nonbank public as currency Cp, it follows that:

(18-9) $H = Cp + RR$

The four equations we have just discussed make up our model of the money supply. The four endogenous variables are D, L, RR, and $\$^S$. The variable that we are most interested in is $\$^S$, the money supply. Of secondary interest is L, the value of loans, since this is a more direct measure of the volume of credit within the economy. The exogenous variables in our model are H and Cp. Cash is just one way for the nonbank public to hold its wealth and this model does not attempt to explain the level of cash holdings; we simply take Cp as given.[19] The quantity of high powered money H is controlled by the Bank of Canada. We leave to the next section a discussion of the mechanisms available to the Bank of Canada for controlling this quantity. Our immediate task is to establish the reduced-form equation for $\$^S$.

First, substitute equation 18-7 for D in equation 18-6

$$\$^S = \frac{RR}{rr} + Cp$$

Using equation 18-9, we can substitute for RR. This gives us the reduced-form equation for $\$^S$.

$$\$^S = \frac{H - Cp}{rr} + Cp$$

---

[18]The reader will be aware that RR has been used in other chapters to represent the real rate of interest. In this chapter alone, RR represents the quantity of required reserves.

[19]One way to convert Cp into an endogenous variable is to assume that cash balances are a constant proportion of deposits ($Cp = cD$), where c is the ratio of cash to deposits. This implies that when the money stock doubles, so too does the level of deposits and the level of cash holdings.

(18-10)   or $\$^S = \dfrac{H}{rr} + Cp - \dfrac{Cp}{rr}$

We have noted in earlier chapters that the coefficients of reduced-form equations can be interpreted as multipliers. Accordingly we have

$$\frac{\triangle \$^S}{\triangle H} = \frac{1}{rr}$$

This multiplier indicates that a one-dollar increase in high powered money leads to an increase in the money supply of $(1/rr)$ dollars. Before looking at a numerical example, let us discuss the reduced-form equation for bank loans. First, rearrange equation 18-8 and then substitute for RR using equation 18-7.

$$L = D - RR$$
$$ = D(1 - rr)$$

To eliminate D, note that equation 18-6 implies $D = \$^S - Cp$, and using the reduced-form equation 18-10 we have

$$L = \frac{(H - Cp)}{rr} (1 - rr)$$

The multiplier effect on loans of a change in the quantity of high-powered money is therefore

$$\frac{\triangle L}{\triangle H} = \frac{(1 - rr)}{rr}$$

The numerical example shown in Table 18-4 illustrates how this expansion of loans and deposits comes about after an increase in high powered money. In the initial situation the total level of deposits is 100. Assuming that the required reserve ratio is 0.1 (to keep the arithmetic simple) and that banks keep no excess reserves, the level of reserves will be 10. The volume of loans is initially at 90. Now suppose that two units of cash are injected into the system and that these are deposited at a chartered bank (the public's cash holdings remain unchanged throughout the exercise). Table 18-4 shows that deposits rise to 102. Total reserves have risen by the same amount, to 12, but required reserves rise only to $(0.1 \times 102) = 10.2$. This means the bank has vault cash of 1.80 that is earning no interest and is not needed as a reserve to back up deposits. The chartered bank is likely to loan out these excess reserves in order to increase profits. Step 2 of the table shows the effect of this is to increase loans by 1.80 to 91.80. How does a bank extend loans? The bank simply credits the borrower's account with an amount equal to the size of the loan. In this case, deposits rise by the "stroke of a pen" to 103.80 from 102.00. The borrower will typically spend the money he has just borrowed, but as he does so the account of some other individual will be credited with 1.80 (recall that the nonbank public's cash holdings are assumed to be constant). Since deposits of 103.80 require reserve holdings of only 10.38, banks will again want to increase loans. The excess reserves (1.62) will be loaned out and both loans and deposits expand together dollar-for-dollar. This process will come

---

TABLE 18-4   Effect of an Increase in High-Powered Money on
Chartered Bank Assets and Liabilities

		Assets		Liabilities
Initial Situation	Reserves:		Deposits	100
	Required	10		
	Excess	0		
	Total	10		
	Loans	90		
		100		100
Injection of Cash	Reserves:		Deposits	102.00
	Required	10.20		
Step 1	Excess	1.80		
	Total	12.00		
	Loans	90.00		
		102.00		100.00
	Reserves:		Deposits	103.80
	Required	10.38		
Step 2	Excess	1.62		
	Total	12.00		
	Loans	91.80		
		103.80		103.80
Final Position	Reserves:		Deposits	120.00
	Required	12.00		
	Excess	0.00		
	Total	12.00		
	Loans	108.00		
		120.00		120.00

to a stop only when excess reserves are back to zero. Since vault cash is 12, deposits have to be 120 before excess reserves are driven to zero. Thus, comparing the final position with the initial situation we find deposits have risen by 20. Two units of these extra deposits come from the injection of cash and the remaining 18 are created as excess reserves are put to work in the form of loans. In this numerical example it is assumed that the required reserve ratio is 0.1, implying a monetary multiplier of $1/rr = 10$ and a loan multiplier of $(1 - rr)/rr = 9$. Note that the increase in reserves of two units leads to a monetary expansion of 20 and an increase in loans of 18, confirming the multipliers we derived algebraically.

The **money multiplier** process we have described does not require that banks extend loans at each stage. In practice banks may purchase income-earning assets such as government bonds. However, this will also cause deposits to rise in exactly the same way because banks will credit the bond seller's chequing account with the value of the bonds. No other deposits are reduced so the net effect is for each bank's deposits to rise by an amount equal to the increase in its bond holdings.

Equation 18-7 above reminds us that the total of bank assets always equals total liabilities. An increase in reserves will result in an equal expansion of both liabilities (chiefly deposits) and bank assets (reserves, loans, securities).

The Role of the Bank of Canada

The model of the money supply that we have just developed indicates how the stock of high powered money, required reserve ratios, and the behaviour of the banks and the public interact to determine the supply of money and bank credit. In this section we discuss the means used by the Bank of Canada to control the supply of money. In the words of the Governor of the Bank of Canada, "I should point out that the technical means available to the Bank of Canada for slowing down the growth of the money supply is to restrict the quantity of cash reserves it makes available to the banking system."[20] In order to see how the Bank of Canada changes the quantity of reserves let us first examine the balance sheet of the Bank of Canada as it stood at the end of March 1985. This is shown in Table 18-5.

The first item on the liabilities side is notes in circulation. These are the Canadian dollar bills that are either held by chartered banks (part of their reserves) or by the nonbank public (part of M1). The second item is Canadian dollar deposits, the most important component of which is the deposits of chartered banks (the remaining part of banks' cash reserves). As we mentioned above, these deposits are used to settle transactions between individual chartered banks. The Government of Canada also keeps deposits at the Bank of Canada, although these are small and are not the government's working balances. Generally, the Government of Canada uses its deposits at chartered banks for its transactions with the private sector.

1) Open Market Operations

The assets of the Bank of Canada largely consist of government securities such as treasury bills and longer-term bonds. It is through the purchase and sale of treasury bills and other government securities on the open market that the Bank of

TABLE 18-5 Bank of Canada, Assets and Liabilities, March 1985
(Millions of Dollars)

Assets		Liabilities	
Government of Canada securities:		Notes in circulation	13,727
Treasury Bills	2,993	Canadian dollar deposits:	
Other maturities	13,574	Government of Canada	438
Advances to chartered banks	259	Chartered Banks	2,856
Foreign currency deposits	282	Foreign Currency liabilities	110
All other assets	4,293	All Other liabilities	4,270
Total assets	21,401	Total liabilities	21,401

[20]Comments made by the Governor of the Bank of Canada to the Fredericton Chamber of Commerce, June 1976.

Canada controls the quantity of high powered money. These financial transactions are called **open market operations**. Suppose, for example, that the Bank of Canada sells treasury bills valued at $100 in the open market. If the purchaser is a corporation, then the firm will pay for the treasury bills by writing a cheque on its account at a chartered bank. The Bank of Canada will present this cheque to the chartered bank for payment. Payment can be made by simply reducing the chartered bank's deposits at the Bank of Canada by $100 (the Bank of Canada now owes the chartered bank $100 less than before). The net result of these transactions is that the corporation now has treasury bills worth $100 and a reduced bank account while the Bank of Canada has reduced both its assets (treasury bills) and its liabilities (chartered bank deposits). The chartered banks collectively have also reduced equally their assets (reserves in the form of deposits at the Bank of Canada) and their liabilites (deposits held by corporations). However, a $100 reduction in both reserves and deposit liabilities leaves the chartered banks with insufficient reserves. Banks are not likely to call in loans to get the extra cash they need to meet the required reserve ratio. Rather, chartered banks will typically sell liquid assets such as treasury bills in an attempt to obtain cash reserves. The increased supply of treasury bills will put downward pressure on their price and therefore upward pressure on interest rates. As the nonbank public purchases the treasury bills, they do so with cheques drawn on demand deposits and consequently the volume of deposits falls. The process will come to an end when deposits have fallen sufficiently to bring reserve ratios into line with the legal requirements.

The impact of open market sales of treasury bills by the Bank of Canada is to raise short-term interest rates and reduce banks' holdings of liquid assets as well as the stock of money. Ultimately the effect of the policy will be felt in the market for loans since banks will want to restore their liquidity position. As bank loans are paid off, banks will acquire more liquid assets rather than extend new loans, resulting in higher interest rates on bank loans. Open market purchases of securities by the Bank of Canada have the reverse effects. Chartered bank reserves are increased and an expansion of chartered bank assets and liabilities ensues. The pressure on interest rates is in the downward direction.

2) Transfers of Government Deposits

As we mentioned earlier, the Government of Canada keeps deposits at both the chartered banks and the Bank of Canada. A transfer of deposits from the Bank of Canada to the chartered banks has the effect of increasing the quantity of cash reserves. A transfer in the opposite direction leads to a reduction in cash reserves. Suppose, for example, that the federal government moves $100 from the Bank of Canada to the chartered banks. One way to visualize how this process works is to assume the government withdraws cash from its Bank of Canada account and deposits this cash with the chartered banks. The federal government has exchanged one asset for another: deposits at chartered banks for deposits at the Bank of Canada. The Bank of Canada has exchanged one liability for another (government deposits are down $100 and notes outstanding are up $100). The chartered banks find both assets (cash reserves) and liabilities (government deposits) are up $100. Since the reserves required to back the $100 of government deposits amount to just $12, the chartered banks have excess reserves that will be put to work. The result will be a multiple expansion of bank assets and liabilities.

The procedure that we have just described is the second stage of a process that is sometimes referred to as the "monetization of government debt." In Chapter 6 we discussed the alternative ways that the government can finance its spending on goods and services and on transfer payments. The first is through tax revenue. The difference between total government spending and total tax receipts is called the government deficit (if tax revenues exceed government spending the difference is referred to as a budget surplus). The government has two choices in its decision on how to finance a deficit. The first is to sell bonds to the public. But, to persuade the public to buy bonds, a sufficiently high rate of return has to be offered. Sales of large volumes of government bonds will cause market interest rates to rise because the government has to compete for funds along with the private sector (corporations and individuals). The second method of financing the deficit avoids the competition for private sector funds. In this case the government sells its bonds to the Bank of Canada and receives in return bank deposits at the Bank of Canada. In order to spend these deposits they are transferred to the chartered banks. In effect the government has "monetized" the debt (bonds) by selling the bonds to the Bank of Canada and receiving cash in return. Put differently, the government has simply printed money to pay for its spending. The relationship between the government's budget deficit, DF, and the two methods of financing can be represented algebraically:

$$DF = \triangle B + \triangle H$$

This identity says that a government deficit must be reflected in either an increase in government bonds $\triangle B$ or an increase in high powered money $\triangle H$. Since a deficit requires the government to sell bonds to the public or to the Bank of Canada, a deficit must increase the total indebtedness of the government; that is, it increases the size of the national debt. The national debt is simply the accumulation of all previous government deficits. In order to reduce the size of the national debt the government must run a budget surplus;[21] if taxes exceed government spending, the difference can be used to retire (buy back) part of the national debt.

One further point can be made from the deficit equation. Note that if the government's budget is balanced the deficit will be zero and

$$\triangle B = - \triangle H$$

In this case the equation describes the result of open market operations. As the Bank of Canada, acting on behalf of the government, sells government bonds ($\triangle B$ is positive but not because of a government deficit) the quantity of high powered money falls by the same amount. Open market operations simply change the

---

[21]The reader is reminded that all the quantities in this discussion are in nominal terms. The real value of the national debt will fall as long as the rate of inflation exceeds the growth rate of the nominal national debt.

composition of the national debt—more bonds for less high powered money or vice versa—but not the size of the national debt. The shuffling of the composition of the national debt can also take the the form of changing the types of bonds that are issued (long or short bonds, for example). This shuffling is referred to as debt management.

3) Other Bank of Canada Activities

The Bank of Canada is not only charged with the responsibility of maintaining orderly domestic financial markets, but also has the responsibility of carrying out government policy in the foreign exchange market. As we saw in Chapter 7, it is in this market that the value of the Canadian dollar in terms of other currencies is determined. From time to time the Bank of Canada intervenes in the foreign exchange market, either buying or selling foreign exchange. The Canadian dollar funds that the Bank uses are federal government deposits at the Bank of Canada. As these are spent (when foreign exchange is purchased) cash is injected into the banking system, and the stock of high powered money increases. Unless the Bank of Canada takes offsetting action, a purchase of foreign exchange by the Bank of Canada leads to an increase in the stock of high powered money and a sale of foreign exchange leads to a reduction in the size of this stock. In Chapter 7 we discussed more fully the foreign exchange rate, the balance of payments adjustment mechanism, and monetary and fiscal policy in an open economy.

Our discussion in this section has focused entirely on the ways in which Bank of Canada actions influence the size of cash reserves. As our earlier quote of the Governor of the Bank of Canada indicates, this is the principal channel of Canadian monetary policy. However, there are other discretionary instruments available to the Bank of Canada that we do not explore further. These include the bank rate, secondary reserve requirements and moral suasion. The student is referred to other sources for an analysis of these monetary policy instruments.[22]

The Supply and Demand for Money: A Summing Up

In the first part of this chapter we discussed the four functions of money: medium of exchange, unit of account, means of deferred payment and store of wealth. We also looked at the way in which the Bank of Canada actually measures the stock of money. The narrow definitions are motivated by the *medium of exchange* function of money; that is, bank balances that are immediately spendable (transactions balances). The wider definitions take into account the *store of value* function of money. From this point of view, savings deposits, for example, which are not immediately spendable, are considered to be money. Two practical problems in defining money are: repeated changes in the type of bank deposits made available by banks and the growing importance of nonbank financial institutions in providing "banking" services.

---

[22]*Money, Financial Markets and Economic Activity* by Norman E. Cameron (Don Mills, Ontario: Addison-Wesley, 1984) gives a full description of the instruments of monetary policy in Canada.

In the second section, we considered several theories of the demand for money balances. These theories imply hypotheses about the nature of the demand for money which have been tested empirically. Briefly put, these studies have confirmed that the demand for nominal money balances is inversely related to the rate of interest, directly related to the level of real income, and proportional to the price level.

In the final section, we turned to the supply side of the money market. In the most general models of the money supply process, the stock of money is determined by the behaviour of the chartered banks, the nonbank public and the Bank of Canada. In the simple model developed in this chapter, the key factors are the stock of high powered money and the required reserve ratios that are prescribed by the Bank Act. An implication of this model is that the supply of money does not depend on the rate of interest; it is interest-inelastic. This is precisely the assumption that was made in Chapter 5 where the *LM* curve was first introduced. There the supply curve for money was shown in Chart 5-7 as a vertical line. Because the Bank of Canada ultimately controls the quantity of high powered money, the Bank of Canada can control the stock of money. The major instrument of control is the open market operations of the Bank.

Key Concepts

the four functions of money:

1) medium of exchange
2) unit of account
3) means of deferred payment
4) store of value

definitions of the stock of money: M1, M1A, M2, M3
the transactions demand for money
liquidity preference
bond prices and bond yields
the quantity theory of money
the stability of the demand for money
required reserves
high powered money
the money multiplier
open market operations

Review Questions

1. Why are there so many definitions of the stock of money?
2. Are Baumol's transactions demand for money and Tobin's theory of liquidity preference substitutes or complements?
3. Why are long-term bond prices more sensitive to changes in long-term interest rates than are short-term bond prices to short-term interest rates?

4. What is meant by the "transmission mechanism" of monetary policy?
5. How have Keynesian and monetarist views differed on this transmission mechanism?
6. Chartered banks make profits by lending individual A's money to individual B. Why do A and B not get together, split the bank's profit and eliminate the need for the bank?
7. Use the money supply model that is developed in this chapter to answer the following.
   a) State all the assumptions required to derive the money and loan multipliers that are given in the text under the heading *A Simple Model of the Money Supply*.
   b) If the required reserve ratio is 0.2, what will be the size of the money and loan multipliers?
8. How does the Bank of Canada influence the money supply through its open market operations?
9. State all the assumptions underlying the money supply model that is developed in the text and use this model to analyze the effects of the following events. In each case state the effect on the money supply and show the final balance sheets. Begin each part with the following initial balance sheets:

Nonbank Public

ASSETS			LIABILITIES
Treasury bills	50	58	Loans
Demand deposits	100		
Cash	10		
	160	58	

Chartered Banks

ASSETS			LIABILITIES
Reserves	12	100	Demand deposits
Treasury bills	50	20	Government deposits
Loans	58		
	120	120	

Bank of Canada

ASSETS			LIABILITIES
Treasury bills	42	22	Notes outstanding
		20	Government deposits
	42	42	

a) What is the initial money supply?
b) The government transfers 2 units from its deposits at the Bank of Canada to the chartered banks.
c) The government spends 2 units of its (i) chartered bank deposits, (ii) Bank of Canada deposits. Why are the government's working balances kept at the chartered banks?
d) The Bank of Canada buys 2 units of treasury bills from (i) the nonbank public, (ii) the chartered banks. When the Bank of Canada undertakes

open market operations to influence the money supply, does it matter
who the other participant in the open market transaction is?

e) The nonbank public withdraws 2 units of its demand deposits to hold as
extra cash. How can the Bank of Canada offset the effects of this event on
the money supply?

The Theory of Consumption

19

The study of the consumption function has undoubtedly yielded some of the highest correlations as well as some of the most embarrassing forecasts in the history of economics.

Franco Modigliani and Richard Brumberg[1]

The consumption function is the centrepiece of Keynes' *General Theory*. It formed the basis of Keynes' analysis of the reasons why unemployment is likely to be a characteristic of capitalist economies and it also played the key role in the theory of the multiplier process. The simplicity and importance of the aggregate consumption function was so compelling that it soon became the focal point of a vast amount of statistical and theoretical research. In the 1940s and early 1950s a large body of data on consumption patterns was collected and the theory of the aggregate consumption function was pushed forward to meet the challenge of the new observations. In this chapter we will discuss these theoretical developments as well as more recent issues such as the implications of rational expectations for the theory of consumption. In addition, we will consider the effects of fiscal policy measures that are designed to work through the consumption sector.

Facts About Consumption

When researchers first investigated the consumption function, a curious paradox was noticed. This paradox is illustrated in Chart 19-1. First, time series data collected over a relatively short period of time, say twenty years, result in consumption functions that are relatively flat. In other words, the short-run marginal propensity to consume is relatively low and by implication the short-run marginal propensity to save is high. This is illustrated by the line labelled with the consumption function $C = a_0 + bY_d$ in Chart 19-1. Short-run variations in income during the ebb and flow of the business cycle are associated with movements up and down this flat consumption function. As the economy moves up the short-run consumption function, the ratio of consumption to disposable income, C/Y_d, rises. The consumption ratio is equal to the tangent of the angle between the dotted line

[1]F. Modigliani and R. Brumberg, "Utility Analysis and the Consumption Function: An Interpretation of Cross-Section Data," in *Post-Keynesian Economics*, ed. K. Kurihara (New Brunswick, N.J.: Rutgers University Press, 1954), p. 388.

CHART 19-1 Short-run and long-run consumption functions

Consumption (C)

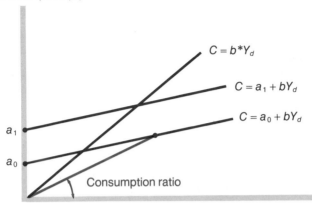

Disposable income (Y_d)

and the Y_d axis. As income rises during a short-run economic expansion, the angle narrows and the consumption ratio declines.

This behaviour is usually discussed in terms of the **savings ratio**, which is the ratio of savings to disposable income. Since disposable income is the sum of consumption and savings, the consumption and savings ratios always add up to unity. Consequently, when the economy expands and the consumption ratio falls, the savings ratio must be rising. Conversely, during an economic downturn the savings ratio falls. Keynes, who was the first to write about the consumption function, explained the short-run procyclical behaviour of the savings ratio in terms of people's consumption habits, which he argued are fixed in the short run. Because people are creatures of habit, they will not immediately increase their consumption when income rises. Rather, the extra income will be saved, at least initially. The relatively flat consumption function is consistent with Keynes' view of consumer behaviour.

The second empirical fact associated with consumption is that the short-run consumption function drifts upwards over time; that is, the intercept parameter a gets larger as the block of (twenty) observations moves forward in time. In Chart 19-1, the line $C = a_1 + bY_d$ represents a more recent set of data than the parallel but lower line.

The third empirical fact is that if all available data over a very long period of time are considered together, the fitted consumption function is (1) steeper than the short-run functions and (2) passes through the origin. In Chart 19-1 the long-run consumption function is labelled $C = b^*Y_d$. It passes through the origin and has a slope, b^*, which is steeper than the short-run consumption functions. Because the long-run consumption function passes through the origin, the consumption ratio, C/Y_d, *does not* vary with income. It is always equal to b^*. Over the long run, the proportions of income that are consumed and saved are essentially constant, despite short-run cyclical variations.

The conflict between **long-run and short-run** estimates of the **consumption function** is illustrated in Table 19-1. These Canadian results are broadly consistent with Chart 19-1. The first estimate is based on a fairly long time series covering the years from 1926 to 1984. It has a small intercept and a large slope coefficient; that is, it passes close to the origin and is fairly steep. On the other hand, the two short-run consumption functions that are based on just a few years of data have smaller slope coefficients and larger intercepts. Moreover, the estimates demonstrate clearly that the short-run consumption function has shifted upwards through time.

In addition to the **time series** results that we discussed above, other data selected at a particular time, referred to as **cross-section data**, have shown that high income families save a higher proportion of their income than low income families; that is, the savings ratio rises with individual income levels. But how can these cross-section findings be reconciled with the long-run time-series results which show that as real incomes rise over time, the average savings ratio remains essentially stable? Answers were provided in the mid-1950s by two influential theoretical developments.[2] The first is the life-cycle theory proposed by Franco Modigliani and his associates. The second is the famous permanent income hypothesis developed by Milton Friedman. Both approaches are able to account for the apparent contradictions in the cross-section and the short- versus long-run time-series findings. In addition, both approaches have significant policy implications that will be taken up in a later section. Our first task, however, is to deal with some preliminaries concerning the definition of consumption which we have already alluded to in Chapter 2.

The Measurement of Consumption

As we discussed in Chapter 2, the National Income Accounts record the total value of goods and services that consumers purchase each year. These data form the basis of time-series studies of the aggregate consumption function. Unfortunately, the data in their raw form do not correspond to the economist's concept of

---

TABLE 19-1   Least Squares Estimates of the Consumption
Function

$$C = a + b\,Y_d$$

Data Period	Number of Years	Coefficients Intercept (a)	Marginal Propensity to Consume (b)
1926-84	59	1,122	0.87
1926-39	14	2,857	0.72
1967-84	15	7,680	0.79

---

[2]A third theory that we do not discuss here is J.D. Duesenberry's relative income hypothesis.

personal consumption. The difficulty lies in the fact that the amount *spent* by an individual in a given period does not necessarily coincide with his *consumption* of goods and services. Take, for example, the case of an automobile that sells for $10,000. Obviously the automobile yields a flow of services to the owner during the whole life of the automobile. For simplicity we may assume that the car lasts for five years and that each year the consumer receives services from the car which are valued at $2,000. After five years the car is rusted out and is worth nothing. The purchaser has consumed all the services that were initially embodied in the car at the rate of $2,000 per year.

While the National Income Accounts record the spending of $10,000 on the car in the year when the purchase is made under the heading of personal expenditure on durable goods, this figure greatly overestimates the individual's actual consumption of car services during the first year. In fact, we have argued that actual consumption is valued at only $2,000. It is true that the individual spent $10,000 of his income on the car, but $8,000 of this is actually savings that will be tied up in the form of the car at the end of the first year.[3] In the second year of car ownership, the individual makes no outlays under the heading of car purchases, but consumption is again valued at $2,000 per year. At the end of the second year the wealth that the individual has in the car has declined to $6,000.

An implication of this argument is that the flow of consumption services derived from a car is much smoother than the individual's flow of spending on new cars. Spending takes place in discrete lumps while consumption is maintained at a more or less even level. While this argument becomes much weaker when we aggregate over a number of individuals, because not all individuals replace their durable goods at the same point in time, the replacement of durable goods nevertheless tends to coincide with the expansion phase of the business cycle. A large part of this spending on durable goods is not consumption but it is in fact saving.

In their studies of the determinants of consumption, economists often attempt to adjust the personal expenditure figures that are recorded in the National Income Accounts. The simplest method is to omit the expenditures on durable goods and to focus only on non-durable consumption. The second approach is to reconstruct the data so that they more nearly correspond to personal consumption. This is done by subtracting actual expenditure on consumer durables and adding back an estimate of the flow of consumption services that is derived from the current stock of durable goods.

The Life-Cycle Hypothesis

The life-cycle theory of consumption was first proposed by Modigliani and Brumberg in 1955.[4] The central feature of this theory is that the individual's current consumption and savings decisions are part of a lifetime plan that recognizes that the typical individual does not have a constant flow of income throughout his lifetime. How much is consumed and how much is saved out of current income does not depend only, or even chiefly, on the level of *current income*. In

---

[3] Note that consumption is equal to the depreciation that takes place each year. In practice, depreciation is likely to be greater in the earlier years than in later years but this refinement does not change the essentials of the argument.

[4] Modigliani and Brumberg, "Utility Analysis and the Consumption Function."

retirement, for example, income usually falls well below the pre-retirement level. Yet few individuals would plan their affairs so that their level of consumption would fall dramatically as soon as they retire. It is much more likely that an individual would prefer to maintain a fairly constant level of consumption. This can be achieved by saving during the high-income years and dissaving during the low-income years.

Chart 19-2 illustrates a typical lifetime profile of income and consumption. The income profile is shown in red and the consumption profile is shown in black. Throughout his *working* life the individual consumes less than his income. Savings accumulate steadily up until retirement in year N. At this point the individual's wealth, which is at its lifetime peak, is represented by the red area. As soon as he retires his income likely falls sharply, but consumption is maintained at a steady level as the individual's wealth is gradually reduced during retirement. By the end of his life in period L, the total amount of dissaving during retirement is equal to the grey area.[5]

Central to the life-cycle hypothesis is the argument that the level of consumption in any particular period depends much more on an individual's expected lifetime resources than on his current income, which for one reason or another may be unusually low or unusually high in relation to average lifetime income. This proposition clearly contradicts the hypothesis that underlies the simple conventional Keynesian consumption function, namely that *current* consumption is a function of *current* disposable income. As we shall see, Modigliani and Brumberg's theoretical analysis leads them to include two more variables, other than current income, in the aggregate consumption function. The analysis begins, however, at the level of the individual.

The Individual Consumption Function

Consider an individual who expects to retire after N years of working. He plans to accumulate sufficient wealth during his working life so that his consumption will remain constant throughout his working and retirement years. Suppose he expects to live until the year L so that the total number of retirement years is $(L - N)$. Given that he expects no income during retirement,[6] and that he plans to maintain a constant level of consumption c, the amount of wealth he must accumulate by the end of his working life W_N is the product of the number of retirement years $(L - N)$ and the annual consumption c:

$$(19\text{-}1) \quad W_N = (L - N)c$$

Suppose we observe this individual at the beginning of year t, sometime during his working life. The amount of wealth that he has already accumulated by the end

---

[5]Depending on how accurately the individual forecasts L and the individual's desire to "bequeath a fortune" (Keynes, *General Theory*, p. 108), the grey area may be smaller than the red area.

[6]We make the same simplifying assumption as Modigliani and Brumberg, which is that the interest rate is zero. This means that wealth earns no return and we can add up money values from different time periods without compounding past values and discounting future values. The relaxation of this assumption does not change any significant conclusions.

CHART 19-2 Lifetime consumption and income profiles
for the typical individual

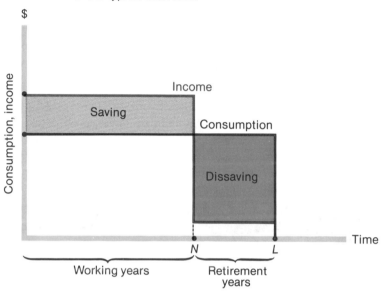

of period $(t - 1)$ is W_{t-1} and his current income is y_t. During the rest of his working life, which amounts to $(N - t)$ years after the current year, his real income can be represented by the symbols $y_{t+1}, y_{t+2}, \ldots, y_N$. The individual himself may think of this possibly irregular stream of income in terms of an average annual income that he expects to earn over the remaining $(N - t)$ years of his working life. We will use the symbol y_t^e to represent this expected average income:

$$y_t^e = \frac{(y_{t+1} + y_{t+2} + \ldots + y_N)}{(N - t)}$$

At the beginning of year t, the total lifetime resources of this individual consist of his accumulated wealth W_{t-1}, his current income y_t and the average annual income y_t^e he expects to earn in each of the next $(N - t)$ years. His total lifetime resources, as they appear at the beginning of year t, amount to

$$W_{t-1} + y_1 + (N - t)y_t^e$$

To compute the annual consumption level that can be maintained throughout his working and retirement years he must divide his total lifetime resources by the number of years he expects to live. Since he expects to die at the end of year L and it is now at the beginning of year t, he expects to live another $(L - t + 1)$ years. The life-cycle hypothesis leads to the following individual consumption function:

$$(19\text{-}2) \quad c_t = \frac{1}{(L - t + 1)}[W_{t-1} + y_t + (N - t)y_t^e]$$

The first point to note is that the quantity of wealth appears in the consumption function. From equation 19-2, the marginal propensity to consume out of wealth is $1/(L - t + 1)$, which clearly depends on the age of the individual. As the individual gets older, $(L - t + 1)$ becomes smaller, so that the change in consumption becomes larger for any given change in wealth. For example, when $t = L$ the individual is at the beginning of the last year of his life. In this case the marginal propensity to consume out of wealth is unity; any increase in wealth is consumed entirely. However, when $t = L - 1$ the individual is at the beginning of his penultimate year. The marginal propensity to consume out of wealth is 0.5, which means that one-half of any windfall increase in wealth at this point in time will be consumed in each of the two remaining years. At the other extreme, an individual who is just starting to work and who expects to live another 50 years will have a marginal propensity to consume out of wealth of only 0.02.

The marginal propensity to consume out of income MPC_y cannot be determined uniquely from equation 19-2 because a change in current income y_t may induce the individual to change his expectations concerning his future average income. The sensitivity of expectations about future income to changes in current income influence the size of the MPC. In general, we have

$$\Delta c_t = \frac{1}{(L - t + 1)}[\Delta y_t + (N - t)\Delta y_t^e]$$

For purposes of illustration, suppose that the change in current income is assumed by the individual to be a permanent change in his income so that $\Delta y_t^e = \Delta y_t$. In this case, the marginal propensity to consume out of income is

$$\text{MPC}_y = \frac{\Delta c_t}{\Delta y_t} = \frac{1 + (N - t)}{(L - t + 1)}$$

As age increases, MPC_y declines. To illustrate, suppose that the typical working life is 40 years $(N = 40)$ and that the retirement period lasts for 10 years $(L = 50)$. At the beginning of the tenth year of work $(t = 10)$, MPC_y is $(40 - 10 + 1)/(50 - 10 + 1)$, which is approximately 0.75. By the beginning of the thirtieth year of work, MPC_y has fallen to $(40 - 30 + 1)/(50 - 30 + 1)$, which is approximately 0.5. The common sense of this arithmetic is that a young person who receives a permanent increase in income has many years over which to accumulate savings for his retirement. He can therefore afford to consume a large proportion of any increase in income. An older person has fewer years left to save for his retirement and must therefore consume less of any increase in his income if he is to maintain a higher level of consumption throughout his working and retirement life. Modigliani and Brumberg cite cross-section statistical evidence that shows the marginal propensity to consume does indeed decline with age.

Cross-Section Studies

By the mid-1950s a large body of information had been collected on consumption behaviour. Cross-sections of the general population, for example, showed that the personal savings ratio tends to rise with the level of income. As we have seen, this

CHART 19-3 Cross-section consumption functions

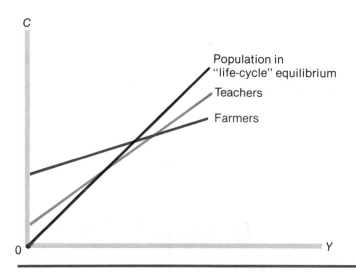

means that an aggregate consumption function that is estimated from cross-section data has a positive intercept on the vertical axis. More careful analysis of different sub-groups within society revealed some interesting differences in behaviour. For example, cross-section analysis of groups whose individual members have highly unstable incomes, such as farmers, showed that the savings ratio has a great deal of variation within the cross-section compared to the general population; the aggregate consumption function for a group with unstable incomes is relatively flat and has a positive vertical intercept. This is illustrated in Chart 19-3. In contrast, for groups that have very stable incomes over time, such as teachers and college professors, the savings ratio was found to be essentially constant and independent of the level of income—that is, the intercept of the aggregate consumption function is close to zero. This case is also illustrated in Chart 19-3.

In order to demonstrate how the life-cycle hypothesis can account for these apparently puzzling cross-section findings, it is useful to introduce the notion of "life-cycle" equilibrium for the individual. There are two aspects to this concept. The first condition that must be satisfied is that the individual's current income must be identical to his future expected income,

$$(19\text{-}3) \quad y_t = y_{t+1}^e$$

The second condition concerns the individual's stock of wealth. As we have seen, the individual plans to accumulate sufficient wealth after working for N years so that his current level of consumption c_t can be maintained throughout his working and retirement years. Equation 19-1 shows that the required amount of wealth that must be accumulated by the end of his working life is $W_N = (L - N)c$, where c is the constant level of consumption. At the beginning of year t, the individual has already worked for $(t - 1)$ of his total N working years. If the savings plan is on schedule, his wealth at the end of year $t - 1$ (or the beginning of year t) must be a fraction $(t - 1)/N$ of the final objective W_N.

$$(19\text{-}4) \quad W_{t-1} = \frac{(t - 1)}{N} W_N = \frac{(t - 1)}{N}(L - N)c_t$$

If equations 19-3 and 19-4 are both satisfied, the individual can be said to be in "life-cycle" equilibrium. His current income is no different from his expected future income and his stock of wealth is precisely where it ought to be at this point in his life if he is to achieve his long-term goals. The substitution of these two conditions into the consumption function, equation 19-2, gives the following result:[7]

$$(19\text{-}5) \quad c_t = \frac{N}{L} y_t$$

The individual who is in life-cycle equilibrium has a remarkably simple consumption function. Regardless of his age, he consumes a constant proportion of his income throughout his working life. His marginal and average propensities to consume out of income are both equal to N/L. Using the figures we suggested earlier, this ratio will be approximately 40/50 or 0.8. This in turn implies a savings ratio $(L - N)/L$ of 0.2.

Now consider what we would find if we interviewed a cross-section of individuals, *all of whom are in life-cycle equilibrium*. To the extent that every person has approximately the same values for N and L, their savings ratios will all be approximately the same and equal to $(L - N)/L$ *regardless* of age and income level. The aggregate consumption function for such a group would be identical to equation 19-5. It would pass through the origin and have a slope equal to N/L (see Chart 19-3). In practice no social group consists of individuals who are all in equilibrium. However, such groups as teachers and professors have very modest fluctuations in their annual incomes compared to the population as a whole. The current income of a teacher is very likely to be close to his expected income. In addition, the stability of his income makes it more likely that his actual wealth will be close to the desired level, given the individual's lifetime goals. Consequently, individuals with stable incomes likely come close to satisfying the two equilibrium conditions described by equations 19-2 and 19-3. The prediction of the life-cycle hypothesis that the aggregate cross-section consumption function for a group with stable incomes will pass through the origin is confirmed by the facts.

---

[7]Multiply equation 19-2 throughout by $(L - t + 1)$ and then substitute equations 19-3 and 19-4. This gives:

$$(L - t + 1)c_t = \frac{(t - 1)(L - N)}{N}c_t + y_t + (N - t)y_t$$

Multiply throughout by N and collect terms in c_t and y_t.

$$[N(L - t + 1) - (t - 1)(L - N)]c_t = N(1 + N - t)y_t$$

$$L(1 + N - t)c_t = N(1 + N - t)y_t,$$

or
which reduces to
$$c_t = \frac{N}{L} y_t$$

Let us turn now to consider the savings behaviour of an individual whose income differs from his expected lifetime average. Suppose that he is initially in equilibrium, but suddenly experiences an unexpected increase in his current income. This raises his lifetime resources and therefore his lifetime consumption.[8] Since retirement consumption will also be increased, the amount of wealth that must be accumulated by the retirement age W_N is correspondingly increased. The current level of wealth is now too low given the upward revision in W_N, so the individual must raise his savings ratio to build up his wealth to the appropriate level. Once this is done, and if there are no further changes in income, the individual will be back in equilibrium and the savings ratio will be reduced once more to $(L - N)/N$. The conclusion of the analysis is that an individual whose current annual income is above his expected annual income will save a higher proportion of his current income than others who are in equilibrium, regardless of their age or income level. Conversely, an individual with a current income that is below his expected lifetime average will save a smaller share of his current income than those who are in equilibrium.

As we have seen, cross-section analysis of the farming population reveals a positive correlation between the level of income and the savings ratio. The aggregate consumption function is relatively flat and has a positive vertical intercept rather than passing through the origin. According to the life-cycle hypothesis, the reason for this is that at any given time, most individuals are not in equilibrium. Because incomes fluctuate from year to year, the high-income group within the cross-section will have a relatively large share of individuals whose incomes are above their lifetime average. Conversely, the low-income group within the cross-section will have a relatively large share of individuals whose incomes are below their lifetime average. As a result, the high-income group will consist of a relatively large share of individuals whose savings ratios are above the equilibrium value of $(L - N)/N$. Similarly, the low-income group in the cross-section will have a relatively large share of individuals whose savings ratios are below the equilibrium value of $(L - N)/N$. It is not surprising that in cross-section studies of farming communities, investigators have found a positive correlation between the level of income and the savings ratio, and determined that the aggregate consumption function has a positive intercept and is relatively flat.

Within the population as a whole, most individuals experience considerable fluctuations in their annual incomes, perhaps on a smaller scale than farmers or salesmen but more than teachers and college professors. According to the life-cycle hypothesis, it is the variability in income *over time* that gives rise to the positive relationship between income and the savings ratio *within a cross-section*. If each individual's income were always equal to his expected lifetime average, everyone would save the same proportion of his income, regardless of age and income. For such a group, the aggregate cross-section consumption function would pass through the origin.

---

[8]We continue to make the key assumption that consumption will be maintained at a constant level until death.

Time-Series Studies

The major difficulty with the simple Keynesian consumption function is that the intercept a must be positive to account for the short-run pro-cyclical behaviour of the savings ratio but must be zero to explain the tendency of the savings ratio to be constant in the long run. To resolve the paradox note that equation 19-2 suggests that the *aggregate* consumption can be represented by

$$(19\text{-}6) \qquad C_t = \alpha W_{t-1} + \beta_1 Y_t + \beta_2 Y_t^e$$

where C_t and Y_t are total consumption and total disposable income respectively in period t. Y_t^e is total average annual expected future income as perceived in period t and W_{t-1} is the value of real wealth that is carried over from the previous period.

A major difficulty in using aggregate time-series data to estimate the unknown parameters α, β_1, and β_2 in equation 19-6 is that there are no published data for the variable Y_t^e, since this variable exists only in the minds of consumers. In practice it is necessary to measure *expected* future income indirectly. Ando and Modigliani consider a number of possibilities;[9] the simplest is to assume that expected future income is proportional to current income,[10]

$$Y_t^e = \gamma Y_t$$

The substitution of Y_t^e in equation 19-6 gives the following consumption function:

$$C_t = \alpha W_{t-1} + (\beta_1 + \gamma \beta_2) Y_t$$
$$(19\text{-}7) \quad \text{or} \quad C_t = \alpha W_{t-1} + \beta Y_t, \text{ where } \beta = \beta_1 + \gamma \beta_2.$$

Note that as far as the current period is concerned, the quantity of real wealth that is left over from the previous period is given. Equation 19-7 shows that the product of the wealth parameter α and the lagged value of wealth W_{t-1} serves as a positive intercept in the short-run consumption function.

First, consider the consumption function in period one, which is labelled C_1 in Chart 19-4. Total consumption can be broken down into two components. The first of these depends on the lagged value of real wealth αW_0, which is fixed in period one. The second component depends on the level of income in period one, Y_1. Total consumption in period one can take any number of potential values depending on the level of current income. These possible values all lie on the short-run consumption function. For example, if income in period one is relatively low due to a cyclical downturn, say Y_1', the ratio of consumption to income will be relatively high and the savings ratio will be relatively low. Conversely, if income in period one is at a cyclical peak, say Y_1'', the savings ratio will be relatively high. As we saw earlier in this chapter, it is the positive intercept in the short-run

---

[9]A. Ando and F. Modigliani, "The 'Life-Cycle' Hypothesis of Saving: Aggregate Implications and Tests," *American Economic Review*, March 1963, pp. 55-84.

[10]Alternatively, expected income may be a weighted average of current and past levels of income. See the permanent income hypothesis which is discussed below.

CHART 19-4 Short-run and long-run consumption functions —
the Life-Cycle hypothesis

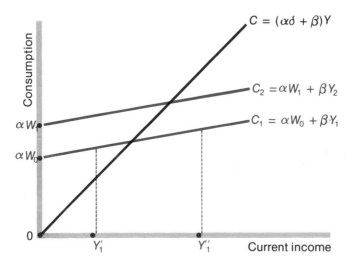

consumption function that guarantees that the savings ratio follows a pro-cyclical path. In the life-cycle hypothesis it is the presence of real wealth in the aggregate consumption function that serves as the positive intercept.

Over time, however, the level of real wealth increases and the vertical intercept αW_{t-1} shifts upwards. In Chart 19-4 the short-run consumption function for period two is above and parallel to the short-run consumption function of period one. While the level of real wealth is taken as given in the short run, in the long run real wealth grows steadily. In fact, over the long term real wealth and real incomes have grown at approximately the same rates, which means that over the long term these two variables are roughly proportional to each other,

$$W_{t-1} = \delta Y_t.$$

The substitution of W_{t-1} in equation 19-7 gives the following long-run consumption function:

(19-8) $C_t = (\alpha\delta + \beta)Y_t$

In the long run, consumption is proportional to income and the savings ratio is constant at all levels of income. Note that the long-run marginal propensity to consume is $\alpha\delta + \beta$, which exceeds the short-run marginal propensity to consume by the positive quantity $\alpha\delta$. The empirical evidence presented by Ando and Modigliani suggests that the short-run marginal propensity to consume β is approximately 0.7. The short-run marginal propensity to consume out of wealth α is approximately 0.04. Finally, the ratio of wealth to income δ over the long term is approximately 5. These rough figures suggest a long-run marginal propensity to consume out of income of about 0.9.

The Permanent Income Hypothesis

The permanent income hypothesis, which was proposed by Professor Milton Friedman[11] in 1957, is also capable of explaining the cross-section and time-series findings on the behaviour of aggregate consumption. The permanent income hypothesis differs only in its details from the life-cycle hypothesis that we have already discussed. Both hypotheses share the important point that current consumption depends not on current income but rather on a longer-run concept of income which Friedman termed permanent income. Although Modigliani and Brumberg also wrote of the permanent component of income, this term is now almost exclusively associated with the name of Friedman. In developing this concept, Friedman began with a definition of income that was first proposed by Sir John Hicks.[12]

According to Hicks, an individual's real annual income is the maximum amount that he could consume while maintaining intact his stock of real wealth. Suppose, for example, that an individual's wealth amounts to $100,000. If this wealth is invested in a variety of assets that yield an average real rate of return of 5 per cent per annum, this individual could consume $5,000 per annum in real terms without eroding the real stock of wealth, which will remain at $100,000 in real terms. Accordingly, this individual's real income is defined to be $5,000 per year.

Friedman pointed out that there are two distinct types of wealth, human and non-human. Human wealth reflects the individual's capacity to earn income. Suppose that an individual's current and future annual earned incomes are y_0, y_1, y_2, ..., y_N. The present value of this stream of future incomes constitutes his or her human wealth W_H:

$$W_H = y_0 + \frac{y_1}{(1 + RR)} + \frac{y_2}{(1 + RR)^2} + \cdots + \frac{y_N}{(1 + RR)^N}$$

In addition to human wealth, an individual may own some non-human wealth W_{NH}, such as stocks, bonds and durable goods. The individual's total wealth W would be the sum of his or her human and non-human wealth:

$$W = W_H + W_{NH}$$

Friedman defines the individual's real permanent income to be

$$y^p = RR \cdot W$$

where RR is the representative real rate of return earned on all forms of wealth.

In any given year, an individual's actual income is likely to be different from his permanent income. There are many possible reasons for this. It may be that a worker has been temporarily laid off so that his current income y is below his permanent income y^p. The difference between the two is called transitory income, $y^t = y - y^p$, which in this case is negative. Throughout an individual's lifetime there will be periods when transitory income is positive and periods when it is negative.

---

[11]M. Friedman, *A Theory of the Consumption Function* (Princeton, N.J.: Princeton University Press, 1957).

[12]J.R. Hicks, *Value and Capital* (Oxford: Oxford University Press, 1939).

However, the central assumption of the permanent income hypothesis is that consumption is proportional to permanent income and is quite unrelated to transitory income. This means that the worker who has just been temporarily laid off will not reduce his consumption unless being laid off causes him to change his views about his permanent income. Similarly, a temporary income tax cut will lead to a temporary increase in disposable income; since permanent income will be essentially unchanged, Friedman would argue that a temporary tax cut will do nothing to stimulate consumption. A temporary tax cut, according to the permanent income hypothesis, will lead to a temporary increase in the savings ratio.

The permanent income hypothesis that the individual's consumption is proportional to his permanent income can be written in the form of an equation,

$$(19\text{-}9) \quad c = k \cdot y^P$$

Since y^P is not directly observable, empirical research requires an additional assumption about the way in which individuals form expectations of their future incomes. The two distinct alternatives are rational and adaptive expectations, which were discussed in Chapter 17. The implications of rational expectations for the theory of consumption were first recognized by Robert Hall.[13] These are taken up in the next section. We will then turn to the more traditional adaptive expectations approach.

Rational Expectations and Permanent Income

The most important feature of expectations that are formed rationally is that they cannot consistently over- (or under-) forecast the target variable. Forecast errors made under rational expectations must be purely random and therefore cannot contain any predictable component. For example, if an individual were to consistently over-forecast the hours he would be able to work in the upcoming week, the rational thing to do would be to modify the forecast rule to correct this systematic error. As soon as the systematic errors are eliminated, the forecast errors would then be truly random.

In order to estimate the value of human wealth, it is necessary to forecast the flow of future labour income. In making the rational forecast, all available relevant information must be taken into account. From one period of time to another, events may occur that will require the forecasts to be modified. The essence of the rational expectations assumption is that only unpredictable, or random, events will cause a change in the forecasts of future labour income and hence in the estimate of human wealth. All other events that are anticipated with certainty— for example, graduation, job promotion or marriage—will already enter into the calculations before they actually occur. Given that these events are anticipated with certainty, their actual occurrence at some later date will not result in changes in expectations about the future nor in the estimate of human wealth. In short, if life's plan unfolds according to previously held expectations, then there will be no

---

[13]Robert E. Hall, "Stochastic Implications of the Lifecycle–Permanent Income Hypothesis: Theory and Evidence," *Journal of Political Economy* (1976) 86, pp. 971-88.

need to modify the plan. Only *unforecastable, random* events, such as an unexpected long-term illness or disability, will lead to revisions in the estimate of human wealth. This in turn means that any subsequent changes in the estimate of human wealth must themselves be random and unforecastable. This proposition can be expressed simply in mathematical terms. Using subscripts to denote the time period and assuming the real interest rate is constant, we can write income in periods t and $t + 1$ as

$$y_t^P = RR \cdot W_t$$

and

$$y_{t+1}^P = RR \cdot W_{t+1}$$

Subtracting values in period t from those in period $t + 1$ gives

$$y_{t+1}^P - y_t^P = RR(W_{t+1} - W_t)$$
$$= RR \cdot u$$

where u represents the random, unforecastable change in total wealth between periods t and $t + 1$. The implication is that permanent income also changes in a random and unforecastable manner through time. In the special case in which no random events occur to disturb previously held expectations, then u would be zero and permanent income would remain constant through time.

The importance of this argument for consumption is revealed by equation 19-9, which implies

$$c_{t+1} - c_t = k(y_{t+1}^P - y_t^P)$$
(19-10) $$c_{t+1} - c_t = k \cdot RR \cdot u$$

or, taking c_t to the right-hand side

(19-11) $$c_{t+1} = c_t + k \cdot RR \cdot u$$

The interpretation of equation 19-10 is that changes in consumption from period t to $t + 1$ are random because u is random. This proposition is usually expressed by the statement that consumption follows a *random walk*. Equation 19-11 illustrates a second point: namely, that the best and rational forecast for consumption in period $t + 1$ is simply the observed level of consumption in period t, since the other component on the right-hand side is random and unforecastable. This is bad news indeed for those who make their living by selling "sophisticated" economic forecasts!

The rational expectations model of consumption therefore has two related implications that are testable. The first is that consumption follows a *random walk* and the second is that the only relevant information for forecasting *next period's* level of consumption is the *current* level of consumption. If the rational expectations model is correct, then it should be impossible to find additional information that will improve this simple forecast. Hall has presented statistical evidence that actually does give some support to the rational expectations version of the permanent income hypothesis. Nevertheless, in many large-scale econometric models, the equations of the consumption sector are based on the more traditional adaptive expectations model, which will be discussed in the next section.

Adaptive Expectations and Permanent Income

In many empirical applications of the permanent income hypothesis, the adaptive expectations formulation of permanent income has been used. The principal feature of the adaptive expectations approach is that expectations about the future are assumed to be modified in the light of recent experience. It seems perfectly plausible that if current events are at variance with previously held expectations, then expectations are likely to be changed. For example, if current income is repeatedly below permanent income, then it is very likely that permanent income will be revised downwards. A simple equation illustrates the adaptive expectations interpretation of permanent income where $0 < a < 1$:

$$(19\text{-}12) \quad y_t^P = (1 - a)y_{t-1}^P + ay_t$$

The first point to notice about equation 19-12 is that permanent income remains unaltered as long as actual income continues to equal permanent income. This can be demonstrated by setting current income, y_t, equal to the previous level of permanent income, y_{t-1}^P. However, if current income differs from the previous value of permanent income, then permanent income will change. The parameter a represents the speed with which permanent income is altered when actual and permanent income are different. In the extreme case that a equals zero, permanent income never changes; that is, expectations never adjust. In the other extreme case, $a = 1$, permanent income instantly adjusts to equal the current level of actual income. For values of a between zero and unity, permanent income is a weighted average of its previous value and the current value of actual income, with high values of a corresponding to rapid adjustment in expectations.

The adaptive expectations assumption plays a vital role in empirical studies of the consumption function because it allows us to express *unobservable permanent income* in terms of *directly observable actual income*. This can be demonstrated by noting that equation 19-12 holds at all points in time. In period $t - 1$, for example,

$$y_{t-1}^P = (1 - a)y_{t-2}^P + ay_{t-1}$$

By substituting y_{t-1}^P into equation 19-12, we obtain

$$y_t^P = ay_t + (1 - a)ay_{t-1} + (1 - a)^2 y_{t-2}^P$$

Now eliminate y_{t-2}^P by a similar procedure:

$$y_t^P = a[y_t + (1 - a)y_{t-1} + (1 - a)^2 y_{t-2}] + (1 - a)^3 y_{t-3}^P$$

Repeating this process a total of n times allows us to express the current level of *permanent income* in terms of previous levels of *actual income*.

$$(19\text{-}13) \quad y_t^P = a[y_t + (1 - a)y_{t-1} + (1 - a)^2 y_{t-2} + \ldots + (1 - a)^n y_{t-n}] + (1 - a)^{n+1} y_{t-n-1}^P$$

Notice that because a and $(1 - a)$ are fractions, the coefficients on distant income levels are small. In particular, the process of repeatedly substituting for permanent income on the right-hand side steadily reduces its coefficient towards zero; that is, $(1 - a)^{n+1}$ tends to zero as n gets larger. It is also interesting to note that when a is close to unity, the coefficient on current income, y_t, is large and the coefficients on the lagged levels of income decline very rapidly because $(1 - a)$ is close to zero. Thus, when a is large and expectations adjust very quickly, permanent income is primarily determined by current and very recent levels of actual income. On the other hand, when a is small and expectations adjust slowly, permanent income depends less on current income and more on the long history of actual income levels.

As mentioned above, the significance of the adaptive expectations assumption is that it makes the permanent income hypothesis operational by allowing the parameters of the consumption function to be estimated using data on consumption and actual income. Equations 19-9 and 19-13 can be combined to give the following consumption function for the individual:

$$(19\text{-}14) \qquad c_t = b_0 y_t + b_1 y_{t-1} + b_2 y_{t-2} + \ldots$$

where the parameters b_0, b_1, etc. depend on k and a. Theoretically, there are an infinite number of terms on the right-hand side, but because the coefficients b_0, b_1, b_2, etc. decline towards zero, only the first few need be considered in empirical work. In Milton Friedman's original analysis of the aggregate consumption function, 17 terms were included on the right-hand side, but the first four coefficients accounted for 80 per cent of the total (the sum of all 17 coefficients). In the next section, we will illustrate how the adaptive expectations version of the permanent income hypothesis is able to explain time-series data.[14]

Time Series Studies

Our starting point is equation 19-14. But to simplify the analysis, consider an example in which only three terms appear on the right-hand side. Specifically, suppose that aggregate permanent income is estimated by a weighted average of current income and income during the last two years (with weights of $1/2$, $1/3$, and $1/6$).

$$(19\text{-}15) \qquad Y_t^p = \frac{1}{2} Y_t + \frac{1}{3} Y_{t-1} + \frac{1}{6} Y_{t-2}$$

Note that the weights sum to unity. This ensures that if actual income remains constant for an indefinite period, permanent income will be equal to actual income. However, an increase in current income of \$1 raises permanent income in our example by only 50¢ in the current period. This is because the individual is not sure that the increase in Y is indeed permanent. If the increase in income persists for another period, permanent income is raised by another 1/3 of \$1 or 33¢.

[14]The manner in which the permanent income hypothesis accounts for the positive relationship between the level of income and the savings ratio which is found in cross-section studies is similar to the explanation offered by Modigliani and Brumberg. Essentially, the high savings ratio of the high-income group within a cross-section reflects the large number of individuals within this group who have positive transitory incomes. Since transitory income is saved, the high-income group has a high savings ratio. Similarly, the low-income group has a large number of individuals who have negative transitory income and who therefore have low savings ratios.

Finally, if the increase in current income is maintained into the third period, permanent income will be adjusted by another 1/6 of $1 or 17¢. In our simple illustration it takes three periods for a change in current income to be fully reflected in an equal change in permanent income. The substitution of Y_t^p into the long-run aggregate consumption function, equation 19-9, gives the following short-run consumption function:

$$(19\text{-}16) \quad C_t = k\left(\frac{1}{3} Y_{t-1} + \frac{1}{6} Y_{t-2}\right) + \frac{k}{2} Y_t$$

From the point of view of the current period, the income levels Y_{t-1} and Y_{t-2} are given. The relationship between current income and current consumption is therefore linear. The term $k(Y_{t-1}/3 + Y_{t-2}/6)$ is the intercept and the term $k/2$ is the short-run marginal propensity to consume out of current income. The intercept of the short-run consumption function is determined, in part, by the levels of income in the two previous periods. Since the marginal propensity to consume out of current income is just $k/2$, the short-run consumption function is relatively flat. The fundamental reason for this, as we have seen, is that increases in current income are not considered to be permanent. Individuals therefore consume only a small fraction of any increase in current income. The following numerical example illustrates the relationship between the short-run and long-run consumption functions.

Friedman estimates that the long-run marginal propensity to consume out of permanent income k is about 0.9 and this is the figure we will use in our example. Suppose that the level of income is 100 in periods one, two and three; $Y_1 = Y_2 = Y_3 = 100$. Because income has been equal to 100 for three periods, permanent income in period three is also 100. Using equation 19-15, we have

$$Y_3^p = \frac{1}{2} 100 + \frac{1}{3} 100 + \frac{1}{6} 100 = 100$$

Chart 19-5 shows that consumption in period three (point C_3) lies on both the short-run and the long-run consumption functions. For example, the long-run consumption function, equation 19-9, gives

$$C_3 = (0.9)(100) = 90$$

Similarly, the short-run consumption function, equation 19-16, gives

$$C_3 = 0.9\left(\frac{1}{3} Y_2 + \frac{1}{6} Y_1\right) + 0.45 \, Y_3$$

$$= 0.9\left(\frac{1}{3} 100 + \frac{1}{6} 100\right) + (0.45)(100)$$

$$= 45 + 45 = 90$$

Now suppose that in period four income rises to 110. The short-run consumption function shows the effect on current consumption:

$$C_4 = 0.9\left(\frac{1}{3} Y_3 + \frac{1}{6} Y_2\right) + 0.45 \, Y_4$$

$$= 0.9 \left(\frac{1}{3} \, 100 + \frac{1}{6} \, 100 \right) + (0.45)(110)$$

$$= 45 + 49.5 = 94.5$$

The increase in income of 10 leads to an increase in consumption of 4.5, which confirms that the short-run marginal propensity to consume is 0.45. If the higher income level is maintained through period four to period six, permanent income will gradually be adjusted upwards until it too is equal to 110. Meanwhile consumption will also be adjusted upwards as the short-run consumption function shifts vertically. By period six, the short-run consumption function will have an intercept of 49.5:

$$C_6 = 0.9 \left(\frac{1}{3} \, Y_5 + \frac{1}{6} \, Y_4 \right) + 0.45 \, Y_6$$

$$= 0.9 \left(\frac{1}{3} \, 110 + \frac{1}{6} \, 110 \right) + 0.45 \, Y_6$$

$$= 49.5 + 0.45 \, Y_6$$

By period six, actual consumption C_6 lies on both the short-run and the long-run consumption functions, as shown in Chart 19-5. According to the short-run function,

$$C_6 = 49.5 + 0.45(110) = 99$$

Similarly, given that permanent income in period six is 110, the long-run consumption function gives the same value:

$$C_6 = 0.9(110) = 99$$

The permanent income hypothesis is therefore able to explain both the short-run and the long-run reactions of consumption to a change in income. According to the permanent income hypothesis the intercept of the consumption function depends on lagged values of income, whereas under the life-cycle hypothesis the intercept depends on the quantity of real wealth. In both cases, however, the short-run MPC out of current income is considerably lower than the long-run MPC.

Theoretical Implications

Real Wealth and Consumption

Both the permanent income and life-cycle theories of consumption emphasize the role of wealth in the consumption decision. In the permanent income hypothesis it is the flow of income from total wealth (human and non-human) that determines the level of consumption. Changes in the quantity of real wealth will cause changes in permanent income and therefore in consumption. The life-cycle theory gives an even more prominent role to wealth since the quantity of real wealth appears explicitly in the consumption function itself. From a practical point of view, the life-cycle formulation would seem to have a key advantage. For example, both approaches predict that an increase in the real value of stocks or

CHART 19-5 Short-run and long-run consumption functions —
the Permanent Income hypothesis

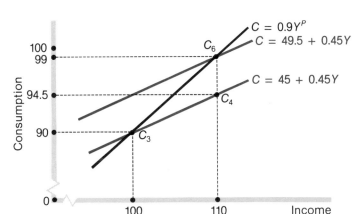

bonds will ultimately lead to an increase in consumption. In the life-cycle theory this effect is realized through an upward shift of the short-run consumption function, since the quantity of real wealth determines the size of the vertical intercept. However, in *applications* of the permanent income hypothesis, permanent income is proxied by a weighted average of current and past values of actual income. Since an increase in real wealth in the current period in no way affects current and past income levels, the measure of permanent income that is most frequently used in macroeconomic analysis cannot capture this change in real wealth. For this reason Modigliani's approach is more useful for empirical studies into the quantitative effects of changes in wealth on consumer spending.

The life-cycle and permanent income theories both give rigorous theoretical explanations for the role of wealth in the consumption function. But the idea that the quantity of real wealth influences consumption was proposed long before these theories were developed. In fact, it was the cornerstone of the classical economists' counterattack on Keynes' *General Theory*. Professor A. Pigou, also of Cambridge University, led the charge against Keynes in 1936 by arguing in support of the classical proposition that full employment is the normal state of affairs and that there are natural forces which push an under-employed economy towards full employment. Pigou reasoned that since the object of saving is the accumulation of real wealth, any event that increases real wealth will cause a reduction in savings and an increase in consumption. Before the era of chronic inflation, recessions were accompanied by a falling aggregate price level which, given a fixed *nominal* stock of money, raised the quantity of *real* money balances. Pigou argued that this increase in real wealth would ultimately create a sufficiently large increase in consumption to restore full employment. This effect has come to be known as the *Pigou effect* or the **real balance effect**.

The real balance effect adds stability to the economic system and was presented as an argument against the logical necessity of government intervention for the restoration of full employment.[15] Chart 19-6 illustrates how the real balance effect helps the economy to return to the equilibrium level of output. In the upper panel, the initial position is labelled A, the point where the curves LM_0 and IS_0 intersect. Note that the position of the IS curve depends on the size of real money balances $\$^S/P$. A decline in the price level will increase the real stock of money and make consumers wealthier. Through the real balance effect on consumption, the IS curve will shift to the right when the price level declines. In the initial position, the level of output is Y_0, which corresponds to a zero rate of price inflation (see the lower panel). As long as the Bank of Canada maintains a constant money supply, both the IS and LM curves will remain stationary at IS_0 and LM_0 respectively. Now suppose that there is a drop in autonomous demand, which shifts the IS curve downwards to IS_1. Through the multiplier effect, the level of output will decline to Y_1. The lower panel shows that at this level of output the price level will be falling at the rate $\dot{P}_1$. While the economy is at point B in the upper panel, the real stock of money will be rising at the rate $\dot{P}_1$. Not only will the LM curve shift downwards to LM_1, but the IS curve will shift upwards to IS_2 as the increase in real money balances stimulates expenditures on goods and services. The final equilibrium position is labelled C, the point where the level of output is once more Y^* and the rate of inflation is again zero.

In the absence of the real balance effect the IS curve would remain stationary at IS_1 during the adjustment period; the new equilibrium position would be at point D, which is below point C; and the LM curve would need to drop further. The level of output would have been below Y^* for a longer period of time. The real balance effect helps to shorten the period of unemployment following the decline in autonomous demand.

The theoretical validity of the real balance effect has not been denied, but its quantitative significance has been seriously questioned. It is important to note that the real balance effect refers specifically to the effect of price changes on the real value of wealth and in turn on consumer spending. However, there are many other ways in which real wealth can change.

An important determinant of the quantity of wealth is the rate of interest. As we have seen, wealth is the present value of a stream of future income which is discounted by the appropriate interest rate. The higher the rate of interest, the lower will be the present value of any given stream of income. In Chapter 18 we saw that bond prices are very sensitive to changes in the rate of interest. A sudden upward movement in long-term interest rates will wipe out billions of dollars of private wealth as bond prices fall. In addition, since stocks and bonds are substitutes within financial portfolios, a fall in bond prices will, *ceteris paribus*, have a depressing effect on stock values. Yet the very increase in interest rates that

---

[15]Not surprisingly, this argument was adopted and developed by monetarist economists (the new classical economists) at the University of Chicago under the leadership of Milton Friedman. As we saw in Chapter 18, monetarists used portfolio theory to link changes in real money balances to changes in spending on durable goods. When real balances rise, consumer spending increases not only because people are wealthier, but because their portfolios are out of kilter. To restore balance, money is exchanged for other assets including durable goods.

CHART 19-6 An illustration of the real balance effect

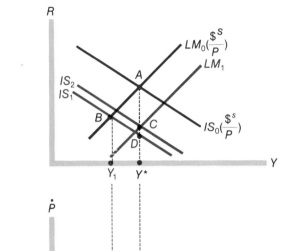

caused bond prices to collapse also makes bonds attractive because they offer a higher yield. Portfolio managers have an incentive to buy bonds and to sell stocks. This in turn depresses stock prices and thereby raises the yield on stocks. Ultimately, the equilibrium relationship between bond and stock yields is restored.

This argument suggests an important channel through which monetary policy can influence consumer spending. For example, a tight monetary policy that causes interest rates to rise will depress the value of both bonds and stocks. Modigliani's life-cycle theory predicts that the short-run consumption function will shift downwards as private sector wealth declines, causing consumption spending to fall. This channel of monetary policy, however, is of course supplementary to the familiar linkage between interest rates and the rate of investment.

Fiscal Policy and the Consumption Function

There are two channels through which fiscal policy can influence the level of consumption and therefore the level of aggregate demand. First, the government can cut or raise income taxes, thereby increasing or decreasing disposable income.

This type of fiscal experiment was tried on two occasions in the United States during the 1960s.[16] The indexation of the income tax system in Canada in 1974 could also be described as a tax cut since that legislation raised the disposable income of Canadians from that time on. Second, the government can cut sales taxes. This became an increasingly popular fiscal tool in Canada in the 1970s, particularly at the provincial level. The objective of sales tax cuts is to reduce the price of consumer goods, thereby raising real disposable income and stimulating consumption.

Case 1: A Temporary Income Tax Cut

Modern theories of consumption predict that current consumption depends on lifetime or permanent income rather than on current income. Consequently, the effect of a cut in the rate of income tax will have an impact on consumption only to the extent that permanent income is increased. Clearly, if the tax cut is known or believed to be temporary, the effect on permanent income will be negligible and consumption will be largely unaffected. The additional income resulting from a **temporary tax cut** will probably be saved, wealth will be increased, and to the extent that this raises permanent income, consumption will also rise. However, the stimulus that this will give to aggregate demand is not likely to be particularly large. In short, temporary changes in the tax system are not likely to provide an effective means of influencing the level of aggregate demand.

In econometric models that use the adaptive expectations interpretation of the permanent income hypothesis, permanent income is defined as a weighted average of previous levels of actual income. This has the effect of spreading the impact of a one-period rise in actual income over several future periods. Equation 19-15 illustrates a case in which permanent income is a three-period weighted average of actual income. In this illustration a one-period cut in taxes that increases actual income by, say, $1 million for just one period will increase permanent income in each of the next three periods by approximately $0.5 million, $0.3 million, and $0.2 million respectively. However, the effect on permanent income and current consumption in any one of these periods is relatively small compared to the one-period change in actual income.

The length of time over which the effects of the one-period tax cut is spread depends on the length of the lag in the permanent income specification. In actual econometric models this lag is typically very long so that the impact in any particular year will be very slight. In contrast, in the simple Keynesian model *all* of the impact on consumption would be felt in the period when the tax cut took effect. The adaptive expectations version of the permanent income theory implies that instead of getting one large stimulus right away, the economy will receive a *very modest* increase in aggregate demand over a fairly long period of time.

---

[16]In 1964 the U.S. government passed legislation that permanently cut individual and corporation tax rates. Then, in 1968, a temporary tax surcharge was imposed on individuals and corporations in an attempt to reduce inflationary pressure.

Case 2: A Permanent Tax Cut

We turn now to the case in which the government announces a **permanent income tax cut**. Provided the public trusts its government and believes that the tax cut will not be reversed at some later date, there will be an upward revision in the estimate of both *present* and *future* disposable income; that is, permanent income will rise. This in turn will result in an increase in consumption both in the present and in the future. Consequently, a permanent income tax cut has a much greater effect than a temporary income tax cut on consumption and aggregate demand. It is important to note, however, that if the government tries to gain greater fiscal leverage by repeatedly announcing permanent tax cuts that turn out to be temporary, the government will soon lose credibility and any future announcements of further permanent tax cuts will have little impact on consumption.

The adaptive expectations version of the permanent income hypothesis that appears in many econometric models has the effect of imposing a long period of adjustment following a permanent income tax cut. Actual income must be higher for as many periods as there are in the definition of permanent income before permanent income itself reaches its new and higher level.

Again, we should point out that the longer the lag in the permanent income specification, the longer will be the time interval over which the full adjustment following a permanent change takes place. As we mentioned earlier, in practical applications of the permanent income hypothesis the lag structures are typically very long, implying long adjustment periods.

Not surprisingly, the permanent income hypothesis fits neatly into the monetarist arsenal: the economy is essentially stable. Even large demand shocks cause only small ripples and the government's counter-cyclical policies have small effects. What is not so widely recognized is that Keynes himself would have found no argument with the proposition that income tax policies aimed at stimulating consumption spending are likely to be ineffectual. As we pointed out earlier, Keynes believed that through firmly held *habits* consumption patterns are very stable. There is no doubt that Keynes, the discoverer of the consumption function, anticipated the permanent income theory of consumption. We leave the last word to him:

> I doubt if it is wise to put too much stress on devices for causing the volume of consumption to fluctuate in preference for devices for varying the volume of investment.... People have established standards of life.... A remission of taxation on which people could only rely for an indefinitely short period might have very limited effects in stimulating their consumption.[17]

---

[17]J.M. Keynes, "Activities, 1943-46: Shaping the Postwar World: Employment and Commodities," in *The Collected Writings*, vol. 27, ed. D. Moggridge (Cambridge and New York: Cambridge University Press, 1980), pp. 319-20.

Sales Tax Cuts

The stimulation of aggregate demand through temporary **cuts in sales taxes** has become an increasingly popular fiscal tool in Canada. In 1975 the Ontario government reduced the provincial sales tax from 7 per cent to 5 per cent between April and December. In addition, the provincial sales tax on new cars was removed entirely between July and December of the same year. More recently, in 1978 the federal government encouraged the provinces to temporarily reduce their sales taxes when it offered to compensate the provinces for the lost tax revenue by transferring federal government income tax revenues to the provinces. The federal offer allowed those provinces that levy sales taxes (only Alberta does not) to reduce their tax rates by either 3 percentage points for 6 months or 2 percentage points for 9 months. Finally, in November 1980, the Ontario government, encouraged either by the success of its earlier program or by the upcoming election, removed the sales tax from a wide selection of durable goods until June 1981.

There are two channels through which cuts in sales taxes stimulate consumer spending and aggregate demand. First, by directly reducing the market prices of consumer goods, real disposable income is increased. According to the modern theories of consumption we would not expect this to provide much stimulus to consumer spending because the modest increase in real disposable income is temporary and contributes very little to lifetime or permanent income. The second effect of a temporary sales tax cut is to change the intertemporal relative price of a product. This intertemporal relative price effect provides a strong incentive to buy now what might otherwise be bought in the near future. This is particularly true of durable goods. The very fact that the sales tax cut is temporary gives it a powerful influence over current spending. Consumers can take advantage of the tax cut only if they spend during the tenure of the program. While a *permanent* sales tax cut will raise lifetime real income, and therefore lifetime consumption, there is no intertemporal price effect. The real income effect of a permanent sales tax cut will be spread out over all future years and the immediate impact may be very small indeed.

Peter Gusen has undertaken a study of the Ontario government's auto sales tax rebate in 1975.[18] Gusen estimates that the dropping of the 5 per cent retail sales tax during the second half of 1975 stimulated additional car sales to the tune of 46,000 in 1975. However, most of these sales were borrowed from 1976. Gusen estimates that car sales in 1976 were lower by 41,000 than they would otherwise have been in the absence of a sales tax rebate in 1975. Although the program is estimated to have raised car sales over both years by a mere 5,000 units (just over 1 per cent of annual sales), Gusen argues that the sales tax rebate proved to be a successful counter-cyclical policy:

> It can be argued that even a pure shifting forward of demand might in itself have been desirable. The year 1975 was one of decline for the

---

[18]P. Gusen, *The Role of Provincial Governments in Economic Stabilization: The Case of Ontario's Auto Sales Rebates*, Canadian Studies: No. 53 (Ottawa: The Conference Board of Canada, 1978), p. 115.

Ontario economy, with real Gross Domestic Product falling by 0.6%, whereas in 1976 a short-lived economic recovery took place as evidenced by the 4.9% growth in output.[19]

The attractive feature of a temporary sales tax cut is its ability to influence the *timing* of spending decisions by changing intertemporal relative prices. Unlike the temporary income tax cut, it can be expected to provide a substantial stimulus in the current period. It is therefore a potentially useful counter-cyclical device.

Key Concepts

the savings ratio
long-run and short-run consumption functions
time-series and cross-section data
the life-cycle hypothesis
the permanent income hypothesis
the real balance effect
income tax changes, temporary and permanent
sales tax cuts

Review Questions

1. Discuss the distinction between personal consumption and personal spending.
2. In the life-cycle theory the individual consumption function (equation 19-2) shows that the marginal propensities to consume out of wealth and income depend on age.
   a) Explain why the marginal propensity to consume out of wealth rises with age.
   b) Derive the marginal propensities to consume out of current income under the alternative assumptions that a change in current income results in (i) no change in expected future income y^e and (ii) an equal change in expected future income. Explain why in one case the marginal propensity to consume declines with age and in the other it rises with age.
3. How does the life-cycle theory account for the fact that the short-run consumption function shifts upwards through time?
4. The following questions may be answered either qualitatively or quantitatively. In the latter case, assume the working and retirement periods last 40 and 10 years respectively.
   a) Under the life-cycle hypothesis, what would you expect the aggregate savings ratio to be in a stable population, that is, one in which every age group remains a constant size through time? (Assume there is no real income growth.)

[19]*Ibid.*

  b) How does your answer change when the real income *per capita* of
      successive generations in a stable population rises by, say, 2 per cent per
      year when (i) there are no income transfers between people of different
      age groups and (ii) income transfers equalize *per capita* incomes across
      all age groups?

  c) What do you expect the savings ratio to be in a population that is
      growing at, say, 1 per cent per year? (Assume there is no *per capita* real
      income growth.)

  d) What would be the effect on the Canadian savings ratio of a decline in
      the rates of growth of both real income and the total population?

5. How do temporary and permanent income tax changes affect aggregate
   consumption?

6. In what sense does the permanent income hypothesis lend stability to a
   macro model?

The Theory of Investment

The instability of private investment is, of course, at the heart of the problem of the business cycle.

R.A. Gordon[1]

We have seen in earlier chapters that investment expenditures are the most volatile of all the components of aggregate demand. For example, in Chapter 14, Table 14-1 presented some statistical information on the year-to-year changes in the major expenditure components over the period 1960-84. The table clearly indicates that over this period investment expenditures on plant and equipment (business investment) and residential construction were a major source of instability in the Canadian economy. The year-to-year changes in investment expenditures were clearly very erratic. For example, the annual growth of residential construction varied between a low of minus 21.0 per cent and a high of 29.5 per cent. The significance of this for the rest of the economy would not be great if investment expenditures were only a small part of total demand. But in fact, as we saw in Chapter 2, total private investment expenditures have accounted for approximately 20 per cent of GNE since 1950. Consequently, the fluctuations in such an important component have had a significant impact on the total demand in the Canadian economy.

The instability of investment spending has led economists to study the determinants of investment expenditures in order to better understand the role of this variable in the generation of business cycles. An understanding of what factors influence investment spending is important if successful stabilization policies are to be adopted. Both monetary and fiscal policies have impacts on the amount of investment that businesses undertake. Tax rates, for example, influence the net return that an investment project will yield and therefore tax rates enter into the calculations of an investment project's profitability. The effect of interest rates on the profitability of investment projects is an important channel of monetary policy. As we saw in Chapter 5, investment spending is inversely related to the level of interest rates. Residential construction in particular has been shown to be very sensitive to the level of interest rates.

---

[1]R.A. Gordon, "The Stability of the U.S. Economy," in *Is the Business Cycle Obsolete?*, ed. M. Bronfenbrenner (New York: John Wiley, 1969), p. 13.

Investment spending is of interest not only because of its key role in business cycles but also because today's investment determines in part the economy's potential output tomorrow. It is through net investment that the total stock of capital goods is increased. In the minds of policy makers, more net investment means more jobs both to produce the capital equipment and to work with it once the new equipment is in place. Further, improvements in technology are usually embodied in new capital goods, so that it is often through net investment that long-term improvements in productivity are achieved.

The relationship between investment and the capital stock is best shown in the form of an equation:

(20-1) $K_t = K_{t-1} + I_t - \delta K_{t-1}$

In this equation K_{t-1} represents the size of the capital stock at the end of period $t-1$. During period t, gross investment I_t takes place. Recall from Chapter 2 that the national accounts record the total value and volume of gross investment rather than net investment. During the unit time period (say one year) a part of the capital stock is used up through wear, tear, and obsolescence. This quantity we can take to be a constant proportion of the capital stock. We will use the symbol δ to represent the rate of depreciation so that δK_{t-1} represents the quantity of capital that is used up during period t. The net addition to the capital stock (net investment, I_t^N) is therefore:

(20-2) $I_t^N = I_t - \delta K_{t-1}$

The quantity of net investment is added to K_{t-1} to obtain the size of the capital stock at the end of period t (K_t). By substituting I_t^N into equation 20-1 and rearranging it we obtain the following expression for net investment:

(20-3) $I_t^N = K_t - K_{t-1}$

Equation 20-3 says that **net investment** is simply the change in the capital stock.

This observation suggests an important point: it is discrepancies between the desired capital stock (we will use the symbol K for this concept) and the actual capital stock that give rise to net investment. Indeed, the theory of investment has two distinct components. The first is a theory of capital which tells us what determines the size of the desired capital stock. The second is a theory of how the economy adjusts the actual capital stock so that it is equal to the desired capital stock. This adjustment may take more than one time period to complete. Having recognized that its current stock of capital is smaller than the optimal level, a firm first has to order the capital equipment. Depending on the type of equipment, delivery may take only a matter of days (typewriters and automobiles) or a matter of years (oil tankers and pipelines). Consequently, the period between the time when the desired capital stock changes and the time when the equipment is in place may be considerably longer than the unit time period of the analysis. Net investment during the interim will be only a fraction of the difference between the current capital stock and the desired capital stock. However, once the actual capital stock is equal to the desired capital stock there is no incentive for firms to make net additions to the stock of capital: net investment will be zero. This does not mean there will be no investment whatsoever, because the capital stock will continue to wear out as it is used. To maintain the stock of capital there will be **replacement investment**. Only if the desired stock of capital falls below the current stock can gross investment be zero. This would occur if all firms were so overcapitalized that none needed to replace even worn-out equipment. In these very depressed circumstances, gross investment would be zero (the capital goods industry would be completely shut down), and net investment would be negative and equal to the quantity of capital that is worn out each period. This can be seen from equation 20-2, which reduces to:

$$I_t^N = -\delta K_{t-1}$$

once gross investment I_t is set to zero.

To summarize these introductory comments, the theory of investment is a derivative of the theory of capital. The essential ingredient in the theory of capital concerns the determinants of the desired capital stock. Once this desired capital stock is determined, it is clear what net investment is required in order to move the current stock of capital to the desired stock of capital. This second step may well not be completed in one period. A theory of investment must specify the factors that determine the speed of adjustment from the current stock of capital to the desired stock of capital.

The Accelerator Theory of Investment

Accelerator theories of investment emphasize that the *level* of investment spending is determined not by the level of income but by the *change* in income. As we will see below, this dynamic investment function can create considerable instability in the economy. Any change in output that results from an exogenous shock, such as a rise in exports or an increase in government spending, will generate an investment boom, because investment depends on the *change* in output. The investment boom itself reinforces the original disturbance and will create further increases in output and therefore further increases in the level of investment spending. The accelerator theory of investment injects a dynamic element into macro models. Disturbances in the current period feed through the **accelerator** mechanism and have repercussions in future time periods. As we shall see, accelerator models of investment can account for the cyclical behaviour that free enterprise economies exhibit.

We begin with a theory of what determines the size of the desired capital stock. In the simple accelerator theory this is very straightforward: the desired stock of capital K^* is assumed to depend upon the current level of income Y_t,

(20-4) $K_t^* = kY_t$

The rationale for this simple formulation is the following: to produce a given level of output, certain quantities of inputs (labour, land, capital and materials) are required. If the level of output increases, then the inputs required to produce this output will also increase. This is to say, the quantity of inputs will be approximately proportional to the level of output. In particular, as equation 20-4 states, the desired capital stock will be proportional to the level of output. While a number of criticisms can be levelled against the simplicity of the specification in equation 20-4, we will defer our discussion of these criticisms until later.

The next step in the analysis is to formulate the method of adjustment to changes in the desired capital stock. The simplest assumption is to suppose that any discrepancy between the size of the capital stock that was left at the end of the last period and the desired capital stock of this period will be removed entirely in the current period. In other words, net investment in the current period will be exactly equal to the difference between the last period's capital stock K_{t-1} and this period's desired capital stock K_t^*:

$$(20\text{-}5) \qquad I_t^N = K_t^* - K_{t-1}$$

This implies that the capital stock at the end of a period will always be equal to its desired level. Last period's net investment, for example, was exactly equal to whatever was required to make last period's capital stock K_{t-1} equal to its desired level K_{t-1}^*. We can therefore substitute K_{t-1}^* for K_{t-1} in equation 20-5:

$$I_t^N = K_t^* - K_{t-1}^*$$

Now, substituting from equation 20-4, we have the accelerator theory of investment, which relates the level of investment to changes in the level of output:

$$I_t^N = k(Y_t - Y_{t-1})$$
$$(20\text{-}6) \quad \text{or} \quad I_t^N = k\Delta Y_t$$

A famous model constructed by Professor Samuelson[2] well illustrates the power of the accelerator model of investment to affect the dynamic properties of a macro model. It is discussed in the next section.

Samuelson's Accelerator–Multiplier Model

Samuelson's model consists of three equations:

$$(20\text{-}7) \qquad Y_t = G_t + I_t + C_t$$

$$(20\text{-}8) \qquad C_t = bY_{t-1}$$

$$(20\text{-}9) \qquad I_t = \bar{I} + k(C_t - C_{t-1}) = \bar{I} + k\Delta C_t$$

The first equation is the familiar equilibrium condition. The second equation represents a simple consumption function: consumption is proportional to the last period's income. The third and final equation is Samuelson's version of the accelerator model of investment. The first component of gross investment, $\bar{I}$, is constant and can be interpreted as replacement investment. Since additions to the

---

[2]P.A. Samuelson, "Interactions Between the Multiplier Analysis and the Principle of Acceleration," *Review of Economics and Statistics*, May 1939, pp. 75-78.

capital stock are small in relation to the existing capital stock it is not unreasonable to assume that replacement investment is constant. The second component of total investment is net investment, which Samuelson assumes is proportional to the change in consumption. The change in consumption is in turn proportional to the lagged change in income, which can be demonstrated by substituting equation 20-8 into equation 20-9. The three equations 20-7 to 20-9 can be used to obtain an equation that describes the dynamic path of income. The substitution of equations 20-8 and 20-9 into equation 20-7 gives:

$$(20\text{-}10) \quad Y_t = \bar{I} + G_t + b(1 + k)Y_{t-1} - kbY_{t-2}$$

Equation 20-10 describes the path of income through time once the values of replacement investment $\bar{I}$, government spending G_t, the parameters b and k, and the initial levels of income are specified.

Before we examine the nature of the possible dynamic paths of income, let us first consider the long-run equilibrium properties of the model. Suppose that government spending remains at the level $\bar{G}$ indefinitely. What is the level of income (say $\bar{Y}$) that will persist indefinitely given that $G_t = \bar{G}$ for all time? Since income will be equal to $\bar{Y}$ indefinitely, it follows that:

$$\bar{Y} = Y_t = Y_{t-1} = Y_{t-2} = \ldots$$

Substituting $\bar{Y}$ and $\bar{G}$ into 20-10 gives

$$\bar{Y} = \bar{I} + \bar{G} + b(1 + k)\,\bar{Y} - bk\bar{Y}$$

or
$$\bar{Y} = \bar{I} + \bar{G} + b\bar{Y}$$

Solving for $\bar{Y}$ gives

$$(20\text{-}11) \quad \bar{Y} = \frac{\bar{I} + \bar{G}}{1 - b}$$

Note that equation 20-11 is precisely the solution we would get if we solved the following simple two-equation static model:

$$Y = \bar{G} + \bar{I} + C$$

and
$$C = bY$$

The accelerator plays no role whatsoever in determining the long-run solution to the dynamic model described by equations 20-7 through 20-9. Note that the accelerator coefficient k does not appear in equation 20-11. This is because the long-run equilibrium solution is characterized by constant values for all variables. When the levels of income and consumption are constant, investment spending is restricted to replacement investment $\bar{I}$ as no new capital equipment is required.

However, the accelerator does play a vital role in the adjustment process that takes the economy from one long-run equilibrium to another. Chart 20-1 illustrates several possibilities. Suppose that the marginal propensity to consume b has the value 0.6, that the level of replacement investment $\bar{I}$ is 10 and that, initially, the level of government spending $\bar{G}$ is 10. Using equation 20-11, the long-run income level is:

$$\bar{Y} = \frac{10 + 10}{1 - 0.6} = 50$$

That this income level actually is the equilibrium value can be demonstrated easily. Using the consumption function (equation 20-8), the level of consumption is $0.6 \times 50 = 30$. The sum of replacement investment $\bar{I}$ and government spending $\bar{G}$ is $10 + 10 = 20$. Consequently, the sum of consumption, replacement investment and government spending is 50, exactly what the equilibrium condition (equation 20-7) requires. Net investment is zero in equilibrium.

Now suppose that the level of government spending rises from 10 to 12. The new long-run equilibrium level of income will be:

$$\bar{Y} = \frac{10 + 12}{1 - 0.6} = 55$$

The 2-unit increase in government spending, magnified by a multiplier of $1/(1 - 0.6) = 2.5$, leads to a rise in income of 5.

The path that the economy follows as it moves from one long-run equilibrium position to another depends crucially on the size of the accelerator coefficient k. Three different types of response are illustrated in Chart 20-1. If the accelerator coefficient k is relatively small, such as 0.1, the level of income gradually adjusts upwards as the full multiplier effect works its way through the economy. In this particular case the effect of the accelerator is to speed up the multiplier process. In the first time period following the increase in government spending, the level of income rises by 2 units, exactly the same as the increase in government spending. In the second time period income rises again as part of the extra income of 2 units is spent on consumption goods. This is the familiar multiplier process. However, as consumption rises, the accelerator theory of investment (equation 20-9) dictates that net investment will also increase because the desired capital stock is higher. This extra boost to total demand from an increase in net investment pushes the economy towards the new equilibrium at a faster pace than if the accelerator were not in operation ($k = 0.0$). However, the accelerator does not change the nature of the new equilibrium because the successive rounds of the multiplier effect result in ever smaller increases in income and consumption. Since the level of net investment depends on the *change* in consumption spending, net investment declines as the changes in consumption move towards zero. In the new equilibrium the levels of income and consumption are both constant. The desired capital stock remains unchanged and so the level of net investment is zero.

In the second example (shown in Chart 20-1), the accelerator coefficient has a value of 1.5, making net investment much more sensitive to changes in consumption than in the previous case. This creates a cyclical effect in the economy's

CHART 20·1 The response of income to a change in government spending

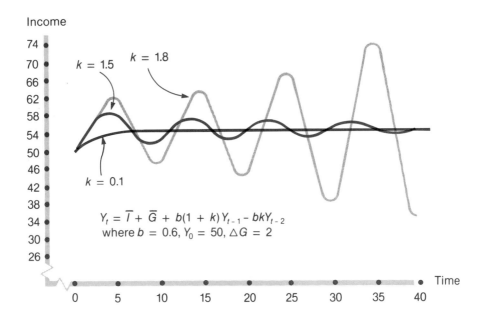

Income

$$Y_t = \overline{I} + \overline{G} + b(1 + k)Y_{t-1} - bkY_{t-2}$$
$$\text{where } b = 0.6, \, Y_0 = 50, \, \Delta G = 2$$

adjustment to an exogenous shock. As before, the increase in government expenditure raises income and then consumption, but investment responds more sharply than before to the *change* in consumption. As a result, the path of income rises much more steeply than in the previous case and even overshoots the long-run equilibrium value of 55. However, the economy soon runs out of steam and income begins to fall, because investment depends on the *change* in consumption, i.e., the growth of consumption. Only a decline in the *rate of growth* of consumption is required to cause a drop in the production *level* of investment goods. Consequently, even while the consumption sector of the economy is still growing (but at a slower pace), the investment-goods sector suffers an absolute decline in its level of production. This weakens demand further until ultimately the level of total income declines, falling into a trough that lies below the long-run equilibrium value of income.

A similar mechanism turns the economy around at the bottom of the cycle: only a slowing down of the *rate of fall* of income and consumption is required to increase the *level* of investment-goods production. When this happens, the free fall ends and the increasing output of investment goods gradually outweighs the slowing decline of consumption. Eventually the bottom of the trough is reached and total output begins to rise once again.

The economy continues to cycle in this fashion, but the amplitude of the cycles diminishes and the level of income gradually approaches its long-run equilibrium value of 55. This example of the interaction of the accelerator and the multiplier mechanisms illustrates how important the capital goods sector is in generating business cycles. The model suggests that any slowing down in the growth of the economy will ultimately cause a recession during which total income will fall. This is because the *level* of investment declines as the growth of the economy slackens off.

For larger values of the accelerator coefficient, net investment may be so sensitive to changes in consumption (or income, depending on the specific formulation of the accelerator equation) that a demand shock creates an unstable sequence of recessions and expansions. This is illustrated in Chart 20-1 in the case where k is 1.8. While the new equilibrium level of income is still 55 following the increase in government spending, the economy will never come to rest at this level of income. The accelerator is so powerful that an **explosive cycle** follows the increase in government spending. An income roller coaster races along a cyclical path of ever increasing amplitude.

A fourth mathematical possibility, which we have not illustrated, occurs if the accelerator coefficient is very large. In this case the economy does not follow a cyclical pattern at all in the wake of an exogenous shock. It simply races off to infinity (if the demand shock is positive). Such an economy can also be described as unstable in that once it is disturbed it can never settle down to its new equilibrium position.

While the two unstable cases are of mathematical interest, they have no relevance for the behaviour of actual economies. However, the second example that we looked at does illustrate how the instability of investment can result in damped boom and bust oscillations of declining amplitude as the economy lurches towards its new elusive equilibrium position. In reality the economy never reaches its long-run equilibrium position. New shocks continually impinge on the economy and the actual behaviour we observe is the amalgamation of the effects of a sequence of shocks: some small, some large, some recent and some of the distant past. The shock waves of all these events combine to produce the actual cyclical path that the economy follows. It is this complex dynamic world that faces government policy makers. The cyclical instability that the investment sector imparts to the economy as a whole strongly suggests the need for counter-cyclical government policies. However, given the lags in the policy process itself—lags in recognition of the problem, implementation of policy and the lagged response of the economy to the policy measures—there is considerable danger that counter-cyclical policies will actually be pro-cyclical, exacerbating the unavoidable shocks that disturb the economy in the ordinary course of events.

In the following case study we simulate the effects of fiscal policy in a dynamic macroeconomic model. A version of Samuelson's accelerator–multiplier model is used to illustrate how a lack of synchronization between an exogenous shock and the intended countervailing policy response can lead to destabilizing effects.

Case Study 9:   Can Fiscal Policy Be Destabilizing?

Chart 20-2 illustrates how the lags involved in implementing fiscal policy can actually result in fiscal policy having a **destabilizing** rather than a stabilizing influence. Suppose that the structure of the economy is described by Samuelson's accelerator–multiplier model (equations 20-7 to 20-9) and that the marginal propensity to consume b and the accelerator coefficient k are 0.6 and 1.5 respectively. As we saw earlier, this particular model exhibits damped oscillations following a disturbance; that is, the level of income follows a cyclical path as it moves from one equilibrium position to another. Initially, the levels of exogenous investment $\bar{I}$ and government spending $\bar{G}$ are both equal to 10. Using equation 20-11, the long-run income level is

$$\bar{Y} = \frac{10 + 10}{1 - 0.6} = 50$$

In Chart 20-2 the level of income is shown to be initially equal to 50. Then, in period one the economy is subject to a *temporary* shock: exogenous investment declines to 6 from 10 *for one period* and then returns permanently to 10 in period two. The black line in Chart 20-2 shows the path of income following this temporary negative demand shock given that the level of government spending remains at 10 (there is no fiscal response to the demand shock). In period one, income immediately falls by exactly the same amount as the decline in investment, to 46 from 50. The interaction of the multiplier and accelerator then projects the economy along a cyclical trajectory that oscillates around, and gradually converges towards, the long-run equilibrium income level of 50. Note that the long-run equilibrium position is not affected by temporary disturbances.

The ideal fiscal response to this demand shock would be for the government to raise its level of spending in period one by exactly the same amount as the decline in investment. Essentially, the economy would be hit by two offsetting demand shocks in period one. The level of income would remain at 50. In period two, when exogenous investment returns to its earlier level of 10, the government would reduce its spending back to 10. In all periods the sum of $\bar{I}$ and $\bar{G}$ would be 20 so that the level of aggregate demand would remain constant and income would never deviate from its long-run value of 50.

This perfect counter-cyclical policy is unlikely to be realized in practice. Since government spending levels must be planned, in order to synchronize the increase in government spending with the drop in investment the government must be able to forecast both the exact amount by which investment will decline and the exact time when this decline in spending will take place. Forecasting techniques are simply not good enough for the government to be able to accurately predict either of these two critical factors—the size of the shock and exact time when it will hit. Indeed, it may be argued that by their very nature some shocks are impossible to forecast. It is much more likely that the government will simply react to today's crisis. In addition, the impact of the policy may lag behind the implementation of the policy. We will refer to the time between the exogenous shock and the impact of the fiscal response as the **fiscal lag**.

CHART 20-2 The path of income following a temporary demand shock under alternative fiscal policy responses

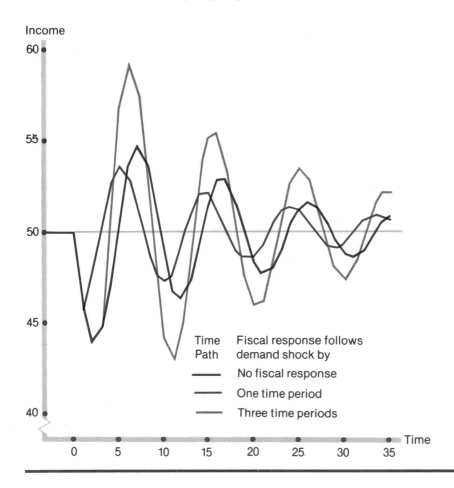

Chart 20-2 illustrates the paths that the level of income follow if the fiscal response takes effect one or three periods after the temporary decline in investment spending. In both cases, the fiscal response is a one-period increase in government spending which is *the same size* as the one-period decline in investment spending; that is, government spending is raised to 14 from 10 for one period. Consider first the case where the fiscal lag is just one period. As shown in Chart 20-2, the effect of the fiscal stimulus in period two is to halt the continued decline in the level of income. In the absence of a fiscal response, the level of income falls to 44 in period two. With the fiscal stimulus of 4 units of additional government spending in period two, the level of income is 48. Even though the fiscal stimulus is one period late, it does reduce the depth of the first recession. Indeed, in all subsequent periods it is clear from Chart 20-2 that a fiscal response with a one-period lag leads to a less volatile cyclical path than what would exist if there were no fiscal response whatsoever.

However, in this particular model, if the fiscal lag exceeds one period, then the fiscal policy actually causes the cycle to be more volatile. Chart 20-2 also illustrates the case where the fiscal lag is three periods. In this case the fiscal stimulus actually takes effect when the level of income is *below* the level of income in period one. The economy is still in a very depressed state. But at this point the natural forces within the economy are pushing the level of income upwards, albeit from a very low level. The fiscal stimulus augments the natural multiplier and accelerator forces and sends the level of income surging upwards well beyond the long-run equilibrium level. Despite the fact that the fiscal stimulus takes effect near the trough of the first cycle, the resulting income cycle is very much more volatile than if *no* fiscal policy measures at all had been taken. The situation is even worse if the fiscal lag is five rather than three periods (this case is not illustrated).[3] In this case the fiscal stimulus takes effect just before the first cyclical peak is reached. Just as the level of income is about to peak and turn down towards the long-run equilibrium level, the fiscal stimulus pushes the level of income even higher and further away from the long-run equilibrium income level. The economy then embarks on a very volatile, cyclical path that gradually converges to the long-run equilibrium income level of 50.

These examples have illustrated the difficulties that fiscal lags pose for policy makers. The fiscal lag comprises the *recognition lag*, the *policy implementation lag* and the *effectiveness lag*. The existence of these lags, together with the shortcomings of forecasting techniques, means that it is virtually impossible to guarantee the exact synchronization of the fiscal response and the exogenous shock that it is supposed to offset. As we have seen, this does not rule out the possibility that fiscal policy can be counter-cyclical, but it does raise the distinct possibility that a fiscal stimulus that takes effect even near the trough of a business cycle will be destabilizing. Monetarists have made much of our ignorance of the lag structures within free enterprise economies, claiming that this ignorance together with unavoidable fiscal lags makes counter-cyclical fiscal policy a dangerous experiment that is more likely to do harm than good. Keynesians have come to accept the limitations of fine-tuning but do not believe that the best policy in the face of all conceivable exogenous shocks is to do absolutely nothing.

Extensions to the Simple Accelerator

While the simple accelerator model of the economy is suggestive of how the instability of the investment sector can lead to fluctuations in economic activity, it has several limitations. One limitation is that for a large range of seemingly reasonable values of the two important parameters—the marginal propensity to consume b and the accelerator coefficient k—the model characterizes an unstable economy, an economy that can never attain equilibrium once it is disturbed by an

---

[3]Such a case may arise if the government takes action in period three, but there is a two-period lag before the policy takes effect.

exogenous shock. Such a model can hardly purport to represent actual economies. For example, a reasonable estimate of the capital/output ratio, which is the accelerator coefficient k, is 3. That is to say, the ratio of the value of Canada's capital stock to the value of annual output is approximately 3. In our illustrations of Samuelson's accelerator–multiplier model we saw that a marginal propensity to consume of 0.6 coupled with a capital/output ratio of only 1.8 results in unstable behaviour. With a capital/output ratio of 3, the marginal propensity to consume would have to be less than 0.33 in order for the model to be stable. But no one would suggest that the marginal propensity to consume out of income is as low as, say, 0.3.

There are a number of factors that are ignored in the Samuelson accelerator–multiplier model that serve to make actual economies more stable than this particular version of the accelerator model suggests. In the case of an unstable economy, a positive demand shock would cause the level of income either to race off towards infinity or to follow a cyclical path of ever increasing amplitude. In both cases supply constraints are likely to prevent the level of income from growing at a rapid rate for anything more than just a few periods. For example, the capital goods industry is of limited size in the short run and it is likely that the increases in the output of capital goods which are called for by the accelerator equation (20-9) simply could not be produced. Since it is the rapid expansion of the investment goods sector that fuels demand, this supply constraint will act as a governor on the growth of demand. Similarly, in the recession phase of the unstable cycle the decline in the total spending on capital goods cannot push total investment spending below zero; gross investment cannot be negative. The worst that can happen is that the whole capital goods industry closes down. Yet equation 20-9, which determines the volume of gross investment, will generate negative figures for gross investment if the decline in consumption from one period to another is sufficiently large, as it will be for an economy which oscillates on a wild cyclical path. If realistic bounds were placed on the range over which gross investment can vary, then the model would be much less unstable.

A second stabilizing influence is that the desired capital stock K^* is more likely to depend on permanent income Y than on current income.[4] Since capital goods have the potential to produce output for many years, firms are unlikely to react instantly to a rise in demand by building additional productive capacity. A sudden increase in demand (which may turn out to be short-lived) is more likely to be met by having employees work overtime and by the use of backup equipment. Only if the increase in demand is believed to be permanent will the desired capital stock rise. To illustrate how this creates a stabilizing influence, suppose that in the view of firms, permanent income is estimated by taking the simple average of actual income during the current period and the previous three periods,

$$Y_t^p = 0.25 \; (Y_t + Y_{t-1} + Y_{t-2} + Y_{t-3})$$

[4]This theory was proposed in R. Eisner, "A Permanent Income Theory for Investment: Some Empirical Explanations," *American Economic Review*, June 1967, pp. 363-90.

In addition, the desired capital stock is proportional to permanent income,

$$K_t^* = kY_t^p$$
or $$K_t^* = 0.25k(Y_t + Y_{t-1} + Y_{t-2} + Y_{t-3})$$

For the moment we continue to assume that the volume of net investment in any given period is equal to the change in the desired capital stock during that period, or that any difference between the actual capital stock and the desired capital stock is removed during the current period. Net investment is therefore

$$I_t^N = K_t^* - K_{t-1}^*$$
$$= 0.25k(Y_t + Y_{t-1} + Y_{t-2} + Y_{t-3}) - 0.25k(Y_{t-1} + Y_{t-2} + Y_{t-3} + Y_{t-4})$$
(20-12) $$I_t^N = 0.25k(\Delta Y_t + \Delta Y_{t-1} + \Delta Y_{t-2} + \Delta Y_{t-3})$$

An implication of the permanent income theory of investment is that the current level of net investment depends on both current and past changes in the level of income.

Consider now the effect on net investment of a once-and-for-all increase in income that takes place in period t following several periods of stable income.[5] Since income is constant up to period t, it follows that

$$\Delta Y_{t-1} = \Delta Y_{t-2} = \Delta Y_{t-3}$$

so that net investment during period t is, according to equation 20-12,

$$I_t^N = 0.25k\Delta Y_t$$

In the next time period $(t + 1)$ there is no further change in demand $(\Delta Y_{t+1} = 0)$ so that net investment in period $(t + 1)$ will be

$$I_{t+1}^N = 0.25k(\Delta Y_{t+1} + \Delta Y_t + \Delta Y_{t-1} + \Delta Y_{t-2})$$
or $$I_{t+1}^N = 0.25k\Delta Y_t$$

Similar arguments show that

$$I_{t+2}^N = 0.25k\Delta Y_t$$
and $$I_{t+3}^N = 0.25k\Delta Y_t$$

But net investment in period $(t + 4)$ and all later periods will be zero since there is no further change in output after period t:

$$I_{t+4}^N = 0.25k(\Delta Y_{t+4} + \Delta Y_{t+3} + \Delta Y_{t+2} + \Delta Y_{t+1}) = 0$$

Consequently, in this permanent income model, net investment is positive for four periods following a once-and-for-all increase in output. In each of these four time periods, net investment is $0.25k\Delta Y_t$ so that the *total* increase in the capital stock after four periods of positive net investment is $k\Delta Y_t$. This turns out to be exactly the increase in the capital stock that would take place in the current

---

[5]In a complete dynamic model it is not possible to experience a once-and-for-all increase in income that takes place in a single period. Repercussions in future periods are bound to follow. However, the present illustration is used simply to demonstrate some of the implications of the permanent income specification.

income version of the accelerator. Equation 20-6 shows the response of net investment to a change in output in the current income accelerator model:

(20-6) $I_t^N = k\triangle Y_t$

All of the adjustment to the higher level of output is achieved in period t. In period $(t + 1)$ and all subsequent time periods the change in output is zero. Consequently, net investment returns to zero in period $(t + 1)$ and remains at zero indefinitely.

The permanent income and current income versions of the accelerator model of investment *do not* differ in the total response of the capital stock to a *permanent* change in output. In both cases the capital stock rises by the amount $k\triangle Y_t$. However, the manner in which the capital stock is adjusted does differ between the two models. In the current income version it takes just a single period of net investment to achieve the desired change in the capital stock. In the permanent income version the same amount of net investment is spread out over several time periods. Consequently, the permanent income model does not generate the massive swings in net investment that occur when the desired capital stock depends on current income. In the context of accelerator-multiplier models such as the one we discussed earlier, the effect of the permanent income accelerator is to increase the stability of the model given the values of the key parameters—the marginal propensity to consume b and the capital output ratio k.

Finally, accelerator models that recognize the production lags in the investment process tend to be less prone to instability than models of the sort we examined earlier. To this point we have continued to assume that any difference between the actual stock of capital and the desired stock of capital will be made up in the current period. As we mentioned earlier, this is probably a reasonable assumption for certain types of capital goods such as office equipment (desks, chairs and typewriters). But for heavy machinery, office buildings, power stations, oil tankers and pipelines, the time taken for an increase in the desired stock of capital to be reflected in the actual capital stock may be several years. Given construction and delivery lags, only a proportion of the difference between the actual capital stock that was left at the end of the previous period and the desired capital stock will be closed by net investment in the current period. Suppose this proportion is λ. An equation that represents a gradual capital **stock-adjustment** process is the following:

(20-13) $I_t^N = \lambda(K_t^* - K_{t-1})$

If the value of the adjustment coefficient λ is 0.5, then 50 per cent of the discrepancy between the actual capital stock left at the end of the last period and the desired capital stock for this period will be removed by current net investment. It will take 4 periods before 90 per cent of the gap is removed. For example, suppose that in the initial period the capital stock is 100 units and that suddenly the desired capital stock rises to 110 units. The difference between the desired and actual capital stocks is initially 10 units. According to equation 20-13, with $\lambda = 0.5$, one-half of this difference of ten units will be removed in the first period, and net investment will be 5 units. The actual capital stock rises from 100 to 105. In the second period the gap between the desired and actual capital stocks is 5 units (110 − 105 units). Net investment in the second period will be one-half of this gap, or 2½ units. At the end of the second period the actual capital stock will rise from 105 by the amount of net investment (2½ units) to 107½ units. Consequently, after just two periods 75 per cent of the initial gap has been removed. The process of adjustment will continue indefinitely as the actual capital stock gradually approaches the desired capital stock.

The size of the adjustment coefficient λ determines the speed with which the gap between the actual and desired capital stocks is closed. For example, in the extreme case in which λ is unity, the gap is closed entirely within the current period. This is the assumption that we have maintained up until the present discussion. The greater the production and construction lags in getting net investment in place, the smaller will be the coefficient λ and the slower will be the adjustment towards the net desired capital stock. As equation 20-13 makes clear, the smaller is λ, the less responsive is net investment to changes in the desired capital stock and implicitly to changes in output. Consequently, the incorporation of a stock adjustment process, such as the one described in equation 20-13, into the accelerator model of investment will tend to reduce the range of instability in macro models.

In this section we have discussed three modifications to the simple accelerator model of investment. First, supply constraints in the capital goods industries will limit the growth of demand during expansion phases of business cycles and will therefore tend to reduce the chance of the macro model being unstable.[6] Second, lags in the investment process can result from the slowness in adjusting the desired capital stock to changes in output. We saw that if the desired capital stock depends on permanent output rather than the current level of output, net investment will be less sensitive to short-run changes in output. Third, lags in the investment process can arise from production and construction lags. The fact that it takes several periods for some kinds of capital goods to be put in place following an increase in the desired capital stock means that the effect of an increase in the desired capital stock on the level of net investment will be spread out over many periods.

However, we have continued to rely on the assumption that the desired capital stock essentially depends on output alone (either current or permanent). This has allowed us to highlight the role of the accelerator model of investment as a source of instability. But there are a number of other important variables that determine the desired stock of capital and the speed of adjustment towards equilibrium. For example, the rate of interest is likely to influence the size of the desired capital stock and the speed of the adjustment parameter λ. Consequently, the rate of interest in part determines the level of net investment. Recall that Chart 5-1 in Chapter 5 shows statistical evidence which suggests that investment expenditures

---

[6]Recall that in this context, an unstable economy is one that cannot move from one equilibrium position to another, but will either race off directly to infinity or embark on a path of explosive cycles once its initial equilibrium position is disturbed.

tend to be inversely related to the nominal interest rate. In the next two sections we will examine in more detail the variables that determine the desired stock of capital. Since the desired stock of capital will be shown to be the outcome of a rational decision-making process within the firm, we will from now on refer to this concept as the **optimal capital stock**.

The Optimal Capital Stock

Firms make profits by combining factors of production such as labour, materials and capital to produce output. Unlike labour and materials, which are purchased each period, capital equipment lasts for many periods. Consequently, the calcula-tions that have to be made in order to judge the profitability of a piece of capital equipment involve an assessment of all the profits or losses that can be expected during the whole life of the equipment. This is a complex calculation because it requires an evaluation of a stream of profits that will be spread out over several years. In Chapter 18 we discussed in some detail the concept of present value, which can be thought of as the price one would be prepared to pay *today* in order to receive a stream of payments over a period of several future years. The concept of present value is an important one for the rational investment decision.

Consider the case of a project that involves the purchase of a piece of capital equipment today at a cost of C. The capital equipment will be combined with labour L to produce real output Y for N periods into the future. At that time the capital will be scrapped and, for simplicity of exposition, we will assume that this scrap value will be zero. In the first period of operation (indicated by the subscript 1) the net profit will be $P_1Y_1 - W_1L_1$, where P_1 and W_1 are the prices of output Y_1 and labour L_1 respectively. Note that we are assuming the production process involves just two factor inputs—capital and labour. As we showed in Chapter 18, the present value of this profit which will be earned one period from the present is

$$\frac{P_1Y_1 - W_1L_1}{(1 + R)}$$

where R is the rate of interest. The rate of interest is expressed in decimal form; for example, 0.05 represents a rate of interest of 5 per cent. The factor $1/(1 + R)$ is used to *discount* next year's net profit $(P_1Y_1 - W_1L_1)$ in order to evaluate it in terms of today's money. The present value of the entire stream of profits that will accrue over the N periods *less* the initial costs C of the capital equipment is

(20-14) $$PV = -C + \frac{P_1Y_1 - W_1L_1}{(1 + R)} + \frac{P_2Y_2 - W_2L_2}{(1 + R)^2} + \ldots + \frac{P_NY_N - W_NL_N}{(1 + R)^N}$$

The cost of the capital equipment is not discounted because it is paid out in the present period. Because this outlay is a cost it has a negative sign, just as the outlays on labour have a negative sign in equation 20-14. In order to compute the present value of the project, the firm must make some estimate of the output that will be produced from this project, the market price that this output will be sold for as well as all future labour requirements and wage rates. While the firm knows the cost of the equipment and the current market interest rate, all of the other elements in the present value calculation have to be estimated. Clearly, expectations about the future are of paramount importance in the investment decision.

Having made its estimates of the future net returns, the firm can calculate the present value of the project. But what decision rule should the firm use in order to judge rationally the viability of the project? The following example illustrates that the optimal strategy for the firm is to undertake an investment project if the present value calculation yields a positive number. If the present value turns out to be negative, the project should be rejected, since the funds that would be needed to purchase the capital equipment could be put to better use by simply loaning them out at the current rate of interest R.

Suppose, for example, that the cost of the machine C is 100 and that it will produce output for just one period in the future. Suppose further that the value of this output PY is estimated to be 210 and that the labour costs WL are estimated to be 100. Using equation 20-14, the present value of the investment project is

$$PV = -100 + \frac{210 - 100}{(1 + R)}$$

We will evaluate this present value at three different interest rates. First, consider 8 per cent, or $R = 0.08$. In this case the present value is

$$PV = -100 + \frac{(210 - 100)}{(1 + .08)}$$
$$= -100 + 101.9$$
$$= 1.9$$

The present value is positive, which indicates that it is better to invest in this new capital project than to lend the funds at 8 per cent. Note that if the funds that are needed to purchase the equipment are in fact loaned out at 8 per cent, the firm would give up 100 in the present in order to have 100 $(1 + .08) = 108$ at the end of the next period. The purchase of the equipment would also cost 100 in the current period, but net returns at the end of the next period would be $(210 - 100) = 110$. This is an alternative way of demonstrating the superiority of the investment project over loaning funds at the prevailing interest rate of 8 per cent.

If the rate of interest were 10 per cent rather than 8 per cent, the present value calculation would yield

$$PV = -100 + \frac{(210 - 100)}{(1 + .10)}$$
$$= -100 + 100$$
$$= 0$$

At this rate of interest the firm would be indifferent between the investment project and loaning out the funds. Either way, the firm invests 100 in the present period and receives 110 (net) one period later.

At a higher rate of interest the investment project is no longer worthwhile and the present value calculation will yield a negative number. For example, at a rate of interest of 12 per cent the present value is

$$PV = -100 + \frac{(210 - 100)}{(1 + .12)}$$
$$= -100 + 98.2$$
$$= -1.8$$

The firm would be better off if it loaned out its funds at the current interest rate of 12 per cent rather than investing in the project. At 12 per cent, a loan of 100 pays 120 in the next period, but the project yields a net return of only 110 in the next period.

These three calculations demonstrate that the higher the rate of interest, the lower the present value of an investment project. In our example, as the rate of interest rises from 8 per cent through 10 per cent to 12 per cent, the present value of the project falls from 1.9 through 0 to −1.8. The present value of any particular project is *inversely* related to the rate of interest. This can be seen from equation 20-14 directly. As the interest rate R increases, each term on the right-hand side that involves R declines. Consequently, the present value PV is a declining function of the interest rate R.

In order to calculate the size of the optimal capital stock it is necessary to consider all potential investment projects. Given all the factors that affect the present values of these potential projects, it is possible in principle to add up the value of all projects that have a positive present value. The total value of these profitable investment projects (which have yet to be undertaken) together with the value of the capital stock currently in use gives the current optimal capital stock. How does the rate of interest affect the size of the optimal capital stock? We have already seen that an increase in the rate of interest reduces the present value of all investment projects. In some cases, a rise in the rate of interest will be sufficient to push the present value of the projects from a positive number to a negative number. At a higher interest rate, some investment projects will no longer be profitable and the optimal capital stock will be smaller. In other words, the optimal stock is inversely related to the interest rate R.

The conclusion that the optimal capital stock and the *nominal* interest rate R are inversely related is based on the fact that the present value of potential investment projects declines as the nominal interest rate rises. This conclusion is correct as long as expected inflation is zero. However, as we argued in Chapter 12, when expected inflation is not zero, the investment decision depends upon the *real* interest rate rather than the *nominal* interest rate. This can be demonstrated here by examining the role of prices in the present value calculation. To keep the analysis simple we will assume that the volume of output and labour inputs remain constant at the levels Y and L respectively throughout the life of the new capital equipment. In this case equation 20-14 becomes

$$(20\text{-}15) \qquad PV = -C + \frac{P_1 Y - W_1 L}{(1 + R)} + \frac{P_2 Y - W_2 L}{(1 + R)^2} + \ldots + \frac{P_N Y - W_N L}{(1 + R)^N}$$

In order to illustrate the role of prices in the present value calculation, suppose that prices and wages are both expected to rise at a constant and identical rate, $\dot{P}^e$.[7] Let P and W be the level of prices and wages respectively at the time when the capital equipment is purchased. One period later, when the first output is produced, prices and wages will be

$$P_1 = P(1 + \dot{P}^e)$$
$$W_1 = W(1 + \dot{P}^e)$$

The level of profits in this period will be

$$PY(1 + \dot{P}^e) - WL(1 + \dot{P}^e) = (PY - WL)(1 + \dot{P}^e)$$

Similarly, in the next time period the level of profits will be

$$(PY - WL)(1 + \dot{P}^e)^2$$

By making the appropriate substitutions in equation 20-15 we have

$$PV = -C + \frac{(PY - WL)(1 + \dot{P}^e)}{(1 + R)} + \frac{(PY - WL)(1 + \dot{P}^e)^2}{(1 + R)^2} + \ldots + \frac{(PY - WL)(1 + \dot{P}^e)^N}{(1 + R)^N}$$

(20-16)

$$PV = -C + (PY - WL)\left(\frac{1 + \dot{P}^e}{1 + R}\right) + (PY - WL)\left(\frac{1 + \dot{P}^e}{1 + R}\right)^2 + \ldots + (PY - WL)\left(\frac{1 + \dot{P}^e}{1 + R}\right)^N$$

Note that if $\dot{P}^e = 0$, then equation 20-16 is equivalent to equation 20-14, which was derived on the assumption that the expected rate of inflation is zero. Equation 20-16 shows clearly that the expected rate of inflation has a positive influence on the present value of the investment project. *Given* the level of the nominal interest rate R and the levels of output Y and labour input L, the higher the rate of price inflation, the greater will be the future net profit flow and the number of profitable investment projects, and the larger will be the optimal capital stock.

As we argued in Chapter 12, given the *nominal* interest rate R, the higher the expected rate of inflation, the lower is the real interest rate ($RR = R - \dot{P}^e$). It is the *real* interest rate that is important for investment decisions. This can be demonstrated as follows. The ratio $(1 + \dot{P}^e)/(1 + R)$ can be approximated by the following expression: $1/(1 + R - \dot{P}^e)$.[8] Consequently, the formula that gives the present value

[7]Historically, wages have risen at a faster pace than the price of output, i.e., the real wage has risen. This has been possible because of gains in productivity. Here we are assuming that labour productivity associated with a particular piece of capital does not change during the life of the equipment. The conclusions of the analysis in the text do not change if we allow for productivity improvements with a given piece of equipment, but the mathematical argument is slightly more complicated.

[8]For example, if the expected rate of inflation is 5 per cent and the rate of interest is 8 per cent the first ratio is:

$$(1 + \dot{P}^e)/(1 + R) = 1.05/1.08$$
$$= 0.972$$

For the same interest rate and expected rate of inflation we have

$$1/(1 + R - \dot{P}^e) = 1/(1 + .08 - .05)$$
$$= 0.971$$

of the investment project can be written as:

$$(20\text{-}17) \quad PV = -C + \frac{(PY - WL)}{(1 + R - \dot{P^e})} + \frac{(PY - WL)}{(1 + R - \dot{P^e})^2} + \ldots + \frac{(PY - WL)}{(1 + R - \dot{P^e})^N}$$

where $R - \dot{P^e}$ is the *real* rate of interest. An increase in the real rate of interest will reduce the present value of all potential investment projects and lower the optimal capital stock. An increase in the real rate of interest will occur if, for example, the nominal interest rate rises for a given expected rate of inflation or if the expected rate of inflation declines given the nominal interest rate.

While the nominal rate of interest and the expected rate of inflation both have an effect on the present value of an investment project, the effects of these two factors are subsumed under the effect of the *real* interest rate on the present value of the project. Since the present value of any particular project decreases as the real interest rate rises, the higher the real rate of interest, the fewer will be the number of projects which have a positive present value and the smaller will be the size of the optimal capital stock.

Finally, equation 20-17 can be used to show that an increase in future output will lead to an increase in the size of the optimal capital stock. Suppose, for example, that the firm doubles its estimate of the quantity of output Y that can be placed on the market without altering the price of the product. This will require additional inputs. Let us assume that a doubling of output requires a doubling of both labour and capital inputs; consequently, that both L and C in equation 20-17 increase by a factor of two. It is clear from this equation that the present value also doubles, so that

$$2PV = -2C + \frac{2(PY - WL)}{(1 + R - \dot{P^e})} + \frac{2(PY - WL)}{(1 + R - \dot{P^e})^2} + \ldots + \frac{2(PY - WL)}{(1 + R - \dot{P^e})^N}$$

Given that the original investment project is worthwhile (its present value is positive), an increase in the level of expected future output will lead to an increase in the optimal stock of capital. As we assumed in the case of the simple accelerator, the optimal capital stock depends positively on the level of expected output. However, we have also shown that the size of the optimal capital stock depends inversely on the real rate of interest. In symbols, this relationship can be expressed as follows:

$$K^* = K^*(Y, RR)$$

where Y is the level of output and RR is the real rate of interest.

In this section we have considered in some detail the key factors that influence the profitability of potential investment projects. By summing the values of all profitable investment projects (those with positive present values) and adding this total to the capital stock that is currently in use, we obtain the optimal capital stock.

It is important to stress the distinction that we have made before between the theory of capital and the theory of investment. The latter is concerned with the volume of net investment that occurs in a particular time period. Generally, this will not be equal to the gap between the optimal capital stock and the actual capital stock because of, for example, the long production and construction lags involved in some types of projects and the uncertainty of future sales. However, to the extent that the level of net investment does depend on the size of the gap between the actual and optimal capital stocks, the level of net investment will be a function of both real output and the real rate of interest.

The Neoclassical Theory of Capital and Investment

The neoclassical theory of the optimal capital stock is based on the profit-maximizing behaviour of firms. Unlike the discussion in the previous section, the production function and the choice of factor inputs play central roles. A production function describes in a formal way the relationship between the factors of production (capital and labour) and the quantity of output that these factors produce. Specifically, a production function describes the various combinations of capital and labour that can be used to produce a given level of output. A certain quantity of, say, shirts, can be produced in a variety of ways—some relatively labour-intensive and some relatively capital-intensive. The actual technique that is used to produce a given quantity of shirts depends on the relative prices of labour and capital. The lower the price of capital relative to the price of labour, the more capital-intensive will be the technology that is used to produce shirts. The differences in the techniques used to produce shirts in different countries can be explained largely by differences in the relative prices of capital and labour.

The price of labour is usually expressed in terms of an hourly wage rate, or the cost of hiring one unit of labour for one hour. Similarly, the cost of using capital equipment for, say, one hour is referred to as the **user-cost** of capital. Firms generally own the capital goods that they use, but the user-cost of capital can be thought of as the rental cost of using a piece of capital equipment for a certain period of time. For example, there are rental markets for office equipment and trucks. In equilibrium, the cost of renting office equipment for, say, one week will be the same as the implicit user-cost that is incurred each week by firms that own their own office equipment. Consider a situation in which the firm intends to produce a certain quantity of output indefinitely. Given this level of output and the relative prices of the two factors of production (labour and capital), the firm will decide on the levels of these inputs that minimize the costs of production. Since the level of output is to be maintained at a constant level indefinitely, the quantities of inputs will also remain constant indefinitely (as long as their relative price remains unchanged).

The first cost associated with capital equipment is due to the fact that funds are tied up in the equipment itself; the funds used to purchase the equipment could have been used to purchase some other income-earning asset, such as a bond. The return that can be earned on the bond is the real rate of interest RR, which is the nominal rate of interest that is paid out by the issuer of the bond less the rate of price inflation that cuts into the purchasing power of the income generated by the bond. Again, the initial cost of the capital equipment will be represented by the symbol C. Funds equal to C will be tied up in the form of capital equipment indefinitely. *Each period*, a real interest return of $C \cdot RR$ will be forgone by the owner of the capital equipment. This is the interest rate component of the user-cost of capital.

The second component of the user-cost of capital is due to the wear and tear that inevitably takes place as the capital equipment is used. Since the firm is assumed to produce a given level of output indefinitely, the firm's capital requirements remain constant (again assuming there is no change in the relative price of inputs). Consequently, *each period* the firm will need to replace that part of the capital stock which is eroded away through wear and tear. Suppose that a certain proportion d of the capital stock is worn out each period. The cost of replacement investment will be Cd, where the proportion d is expressed in the form of a decimal. For example, if replacement investment per period is 10 per cent of the capital stock, then d will be 0.10.

The interest and replacement costs of capital must be added together to give the total user-cost of capital. In terms of the symbols we have used, the user-cost of capital can be expressed as $C(RR + d)$, where C is the cost of the capital equipment, RR is the real interest rate and d is the rate of replacement investment. To illustrate the calculation of the interest and replacement components of the user-cost of capital, suppose that the cost of the equipment is $100. If the real rate of interest is 5 per cent per annum and replacement investment is 10 per cent per annum, then the user-cost per $100 of capital is $100 (.05 + .10) = $15 per annum. The user-cost of capital, just like the real interest rate, can be expressed in decimal form. In this example, the user-cost of capital is 0.15. Alternatively, if the firm were to rent the equipment that is worth $100, then the annual rental cost would be $15. Of this, $5 would be compensation for the interest cost incurred by the firm that owns the equipment and $10 would be compensation for the annual wear and tear, known as depreciation.

Once the firm has determined the user-cost of capital, the price of labour, and the appropriate level of output, the firm will be able to choose that particular production technique which minimizes total cost. One result of this optimizing behaviour is a determination of the optimal size of the capital stock, or the firm's demand for capital. The optimal size of the capital stock is an increasing function of output and a decreasing function of the user-cost of capital. As the user-cost of capital rises relative to a given wage rate, the firm will find that by using less capital and more labour the same output can be produced at a lower total cost.

Our discussion so far has focused entirely on the determinants of the optimal capital stock. Nothing has been said about the determinants of net investment—that is, the factors that determine the rate of net investment given that the optimal capital stock differs from the actual capital stock. In this regard the neoclassical theory is not at all special. Typically, in empirical studies of investment, a stock adjustment process of the type we discussed earlier is specified.[9] This specification recognizes that changes in the desired capital stock are not necessarily immediately translated into net investment. Once firms have recognized that the

---

[9]See, for example, R.E. Hall and D.W. Jorgenson, "Tax Policy and Investment Behaviour," *American Economic Review*, June 1967, pp. 391-414.

optimal capital stock has increased, it takes time for specific plans to be finalized, orders to be placed, equipment to be delivered, and finally, to put the capital equipment in place. The effects of an increase in the optimal capital stock on net investment are therefore distributed over many periods.

The neoclassical theory of capital is a useful framework for analyzing theoretically and estimating empirically the effects of monetary and fiscal policies on net investment. There are two distinct ways in which monetary and fiscal policies can influence the volume of investment. The first is through their effects on the size of the optimal capital stock. Any measure that increases the size of the capital stock will result in additional net investment which is equal to the gap between the original optimal capital stock and the new value. Of course, this investment may take place over a period of many years. The second way in which monetary and fiscal policies influence the volume of investment spending is through their effects on the timing of investment. The government may introduce temporary measures which encourage firms to make investment outlays in the present that would otherwise have been made sometime in the future.

It is through their effects on the user-cost of capital that monetary and fiscal policies have a *direct* influence on the optimal capital stock and therefore on net investment.[10] An expansionary monetary policy, for example, which reduces nominal and real interest rates, will also reduce the user-cost of capital. This encourages firms to adopt more capital-intensive techniques than they otherwise would. Net investment spending is correspondingly increased as firms move towards more capital-intensive production methods. However, if the decline in the real rate of interest and the user-cost of capital turn out to be temporary, then the optimal capital stock will return to its earlier level. The net investment that earlier increased the size of the actual capital stock will be offset by a decline in replacement investment that will continue until the capital stock is restored to the original optimal size.

An alternative route through which monetary policy may affect the volume of investment that is currently being undertaken is through the influence of monetary policy on the *timing* of investment outlays. Net investment may be given a boost when long-term financing is available at below-average interest rates. On the other hand, net investment may slacken off despite the existence of a gap between the optimal and actual capital stocks when the real cost of borrowing is at a cyclical peak. The effect of monetary policies on the timing of investment spending is muted, however, by the fact that the borrowing and spending decisions do not necessarily have to be taken at the same time. A firm that intends to build a new plant next year may well borrow the funds now to take advantage of low interest rates; this does not mean that the firm has to begin building the plant ahead of schedule.

Fiscal Policy and Investment

There are a number of ways in which fiscal policy can be used to influence the size of the optimal capital stock and the timing of investment spending. Investment tax

[10]Monetary and fiscal policies have an indirect effect on net investment via their influence on the level of output.

credits and the tax treatment of capital cost allowances both have their influence on the optimal capital stock through their effect on the user-cost of capital. Changes in the corporate income tax rate affect the after-tax profitability of investment projects and can therefore influence the number of projects that firms are willing to undertake.

Let us first consider **investment tax credits**. This type of fiscal stimulus was first introduced in 1975, at which time firms investing in new buildings or machinery and equipment in manufacturing and processing industries were entitled to tax credits equal to 5 per cent of the value of the investment. Since that time the credits have become more generous. As of 1985, the general tax credit rate was 7 per cent but higher rates (up to 50 per cent) applied in certain regions. Small businesses were also favoured under the program by being entitled to an investment tax credit rate of 35 per cent. To illustrate how the program works, consider a firm that spends $100,000 on an investment project. At the general tax credit rate of 7 per cent, the firm is able to reduce its federal tax bill by $7,000.[11] This is equivalent to reducing the cost of capital equipment by 7 per cent and clearly reduces the user-cost of capital, thereby encouraging the use of more capital-intensive techniques. Permanent tax credit programs permanently increase the size of the optimal capital stock.

The additional net investment required to raise the size of the capital stock may be spread out over several years. Consequently, while a permanent investment tax credit will increase net investment, there is unlikely to be a surge in investment spending. A temporary tax credit, on the other hand, can be an advantage to firms only if they make investment outlays during the tenure of the program. A temporary investment tax credit is therefore likely to lead to a bunching of investment as firms bring forward their investment programs. A temporary investment tax credit is a potentially useful fiscal tool for influencing the timing of investment spending.

An alternative way to reduce the user-cost of capital is to increase the rate at which firms are allowed to depreciate their capital equipment for tax purposes. When a firm spends $100,000 on a machine, this is clearly a business expense that must be deducted from gross income in order to arrive at a net income figure. However, since the machine will not be used up entirely during its first year of operation, it is reasonable to allow only part of the initial cost of the machine to be deducted from the first year's gross income. For illustration purposes, suppose the machine will last five years and the firm spreads the total cost of $100,000 equally over the five years. The annual capital cost allowance or depreciation cost in this case would be $20,000. It is in a firm's interest to depreciate its plant and equipment as quickly as possible, but firms are limited by what the tax laws allow. For example, consider the firm that invests in a machine which costs $100,000. If all of this expenditure could be deducted from gross income in the first year of operation, the firm would reduce its taxes by, say, $50,000 (we are assuming that

---

[11]Special provisions exist for firms that do not happen to have federal tax liabilities in the year that the investment expenses are incurred, for example, partial refunds of investment expenses and the option to carry forward unused tax credits into other tax years.

the corporate tax rate is 50 per cent). Under these circumstances, the firm spends $100,000 on the machine and saves $50,000 in taxes. On the other hand, if the firm deducts the cost of the machine over a five-year period ($20,000 per year), the firm will reduce its tax bill by $10,000 per year for five years. To compare this situation with the first, we need to calculate the present value of five payments of $10,000 each. This calculation requires information on the rate of interest. Assuming that the real rate of interest is 5 per cent, the present value of $10,000 per year for five years is $45,459. Consequently, the firm would be $4,541 better off ($50,000 − $45,459) if it could deduct the whole cost of the machine from current income compared with deducting one-fifth of the cost in each of five years. This represents just over 4.5 per cent of the cost of the machine itself. If the firm were to benefit from such a fast write-off, or **accelerated depreciation**, of its equipment, it would be equivalent to reducing the cost of capital equipment by approximately 4.5 per cent (compared to a five-year write-off period). The user-cost of capital would be similarly reduced.

Again, a distinction can be made between temporary and permanent programs. A temporary program will encourage firms to bring forward their planned investment outlays. It would require a permanent program to change the optimal stock of capital permanently. As a case in point, in 1972, machinery and equipment used in manufacturing and processing industries became eligible for a two-year write-off. This was initially intended to be a short-term measure to stimulate investment spending. However, in 1974 the two-year write-off was extended indefinitely and in 1976 certain energy-efficient equipment was added to the list of eligible items. The purpose of these measures has been to strengthen Canada's manufacturing and processing sectors by encouraging new investment. New investment is associated with improvements in productivity, which in turn reduce unit costs and thereby help to maintain Canada's international competitive position.

The third major fiscal instrument that has been used to stimulate investment spending is the tax rate applied to corporate income. Corporate tax rates differ according to the type of business, the size of the business and the type of ownership. Generally, the tax structure has been designed to favour manufacturing and processing firms, and particularly small Canadian businesses. The rate of corporate income tax influences the after-tax profitability of investment projects. By lowering income tax rates, projects that would otherwise be unprofitable may become profitable. In this way, corporate income taxes do influence the size of the optimal capital stock and therefore the rate of net investment.

Summary

Economists have long thought of investment spending as one of the major sources of instability in free enterprise economies. The simple accelerator models of investment, which relate investment expenditures to *changes* in the level of output, provide a powerful insight into the origins of business cycles. In addition, we have used a simple dynamic model to illustrate how fiscal lag can make an intended counter-cyclical fiscal policy actually pro-cyclical. The model showed that, contrary to expectations, even a fiscal stimulus that takes effect near the trough of a business cycle can have a destabilizing effect.

Several extensions to the simple accelerator model have been suggested. First, the optimal capital stock is likely to depend on *expected* output rather than current output. Because expectations are slow to adjust, a sudden change in current output will not be expected to persist indefinitely. It will take several periods at the new level of output for the change to be fully incorporated into expectations about future output. This implies that the relationship between the optimal capital stock and the level of output will involve long lags. This in turn means that the ratio of the capital stock to the current level of output will not be constant. Eisner's permanent income theory of investment recognizes the importance of expectations in the theory of capital and investment.

Second, simple accelerator models assume that discrepancies between the optimal stock of capital and the current stock of capital will be removed (through net investment) within the current period. Even if the time period of the analysis is one year, this is an unreasonable assumption to make about many kinds of investment projects. The time interval between the point when it is recognized that the optimal capital stock has changed and the point when the capital is in place may be several years. We have seen how the stock adjustment model allows for these delays and how this adds a further complication to the lag structure of investment spending.

Third, the simple accelerator theories of investment do not recognize the role of the real rate of interest in determining the size of the optimal stock of capital. As we have seen, a rise in the real rate of interest will reduce the present value of potential investment projects and will consequently reduce the size of the optimal capital stock. Once this point is recognized, we can see how monetary policy directly influences investment spending through the effect of changes in the money supply on the real rate of interest. However, the Bank of Canada's control of interest rates is largely effected through its influence on the treasury bill rate, which, of course, is a *nominal* interest rate. The Bank of Canada's control of *real* interest rates is indirect in that it comes through the control of nominal interest rates.

For the neoclassical theory of investment, the instability of investment expenditures is not the focal point of the analysis. Rather, the neoclassical theory provides a rigorous treatment of optimal capital accumulation for the profit-maximizing firm. Given the level of output, firms will choose more or less capital-intensive production techniques depending on the relative prices of the inputs into the production process (capital and labour). Thus, in this theory, the price of capital services, the user-cost of capital, plays a major role. A reduction in the user-cost of capital, given the wage rate, will favour more capital-intensive techniques; the demand for capital will rise and therefore the flow of investment will increase.

A great advantage of the neoclassical approach is that it provides a framework for systematically analyzing the channels through which monetary and fiscal policies influence investment spending. Both monetary and fiscal policies affect the user-cost of capital and therefore the relative prices of capital and labour. A reduction in the real rate of interest (monetary policy) reduces the user-cost of capital and encourages the use of more capital-intensive techniques. Investment tax credits and accelerated depreciation (fast write-off) schemes are two examples of fiscal policies that subsidize capital inputs and directly affect the user-cost of capital. In addition, corporate income tax rates influence the overall profitability of investment projects and therefore affect the investment decision.

Key Concepts

net and replacement investment
the accelerator
damped and explosive cycles
fiscal lag and destabilizing fiscal policy
the optimal capital stock
the stock adjustment model
the user-cost of capital
investment tax credits
accelerated depreciation

Review Questions

1. Which of the following investment projects are likely to be most affected by interest rate considerations: the Bay of Fundy hydro-electric scheme, the purchase of railway rolling stock, the construction of a large office tower, or the purchase of a mini-computer? Explain your answer.
2. Explain the role of expectations in the investment decision.
3. Explain the channels through which monetary policy influences investment spending.
4. Discuss two fiscal measures that are aimed at increasing investment spending.
5. What is the motivation for the stock adjustment model of investment?
6. Explain why it is the real rate of interest rather than the nominal rate of interest that determines the profitability of an investment project.

Index

W